T0214868

Communications in Computer and Information Science   1031

Commenced Publication in 2007
Founding and Former Series Editors:
Phoebe Chen, Alfredo Cuzzocrea, Xiaoyong Du, Orhun Kara, Ting Liu,
Krishna M. Sivalingam, Dominik Ślęzak, Takashi Washio, and Xiaokang Yang

More information about this series at http://www.springer.com/series/7899

Jyotsna Kumar Mandal ·
Somnath Mukhopadhyay ·
Paramartha Dutta · Kousik Dasgupta (Eds.)

Computational Intelligence, Communications, and Business Analytics

Second International Conference, CICBA 2018
Kalyani, India, July 27–28, 2018
Revised Selected Papers, Part II

Springer

Editors
Jyotsna Kumar Mandal
Department of Computer Science
and Engineering
University of Kalyani
Kalyani, West Bengal, India

Somnath Mukhopadhyay
Department of Computer Science
and Engineering
Assam University
Silchar, Assam, India

Paramartha Dutta
Department of Computer and Systems
Sciences
Visva Bharati University
Santiniketan, West Bengal, India

Kousik Dasgupta
Department of Computer Science
and Engineering
Kalyani Government Engineering College
Kalyani, West Bengal, India

ISSN 1865-0929   ISSN 1865-0937 (electronic)
Communications in Computer and Information Science
ISBN 978-981-13-8580-3   ISBN 978-981-13-8581-0 (eBook)
https://doi.org/10.1007/978-981-13-8581-0

This Springer imprint is published by the registered company Springer Nature Singapore Pte Ltd.
The registered company address is: 152 Beach Road, #21-01/04 Gateway East, Singapore 189721, Singapore

Foreword

Writing a foreword for the proceeding of an international conference, in the form of an edited volume, cannot but be an intellectual pleasure, which I can ill afford to desist from. But, I would like to avail the opportunity to write a few words for the foreword of the recently concluded Second International Conference on Computational Intelligence, Business Analytics, and Communication (CICBA-2018). The conference was organized by the Kalyani Government Engineering College in association with the Computer Society of India, during July 27–28, 2018, on the Kalyani Government Engineering College campus. The conference was technically co-sponsored by the CSI Kolkata Chapter, IEEE Kolkata chapter, IEEE Young Professionals, Kolkata, as well as the IEEE Computational Intelligence Society, Kolkata chapter. The proceeding of the conference are published by Springer in their CCIS series.

The conference included distinguished general chairs such as Prof. Carlos A. Coello Coello, Investigador Cinvestav, CINVESTAV-IPN, México, and Prof. Xin Yao, Southern University of Science and Technology (SUSTech), China. Prof. Kalyanmoy Deb, Michigan State University, USA, Prof. Hisaob Ishibuchi, Southern University of Science and Technology (SUSTech), China, Prof. Mike Hinchey, University of Limerick, Ireland, Prof. Ashok Deshpande, University of California, Berkeley, USA, were the keynote speakers, and there were luminaries from leading industries and research/academic institutes as invited speakers. The event could attain the true international standard that it intended to achieve.

There were 240 papers submitted from across the globe including countries like Australia, Bangladesh, Indonesia, Lithuania, Nigeria, Portugal, South Korea, USA, and Vietnam – out of which 76 papers were accepted and presented. Three special sessions of the conference were titled Computational Intelligence, Data Communications, and Data Mining and Advanced Data Analytics. The sub-tracks of the conference were Signal Processing, Computational Forensics (Privacy and Security), Microelectronics, Sensors, and Intelligent Networks.

Last but not the least, from my experience, I strongly believe that the conference was undoubtedly commendable, thanks to the organizers, who made it a grand success. CICBA 2019, which will be the third event in the CICBA series, will be organized by, and held at, Jadavpur University Kolkata during December 13–14, 2019, and I am sure that the event will be able to prove its standing as a successful series among the research community in the days ahead.

May 2019 Oscar Castillo

Preface

Kalyani Government Engineering College, in collaboration with the Computer Society of India, organized the Second International Conference on Computational Intelligence, Communication, and Business Analytics (CICBA 2018), during July 27–28, 2018, on the Kalyani Government Engineering College Campus. This was the second activity of the Computer Society of India in an Eastern region with Springer as the publication partner. This conference was organized in technical collaboration with the Computer Society of India Kolkata Chapter, IEEE Kolkata section, IEEE Young Professionals, and IEEE CIS Kolkata. This mega event covered all aspects of computational intelligence, communications, and business analytics where the scope was not limited only to various engineering disciplines such as computer science, electronics, and biomedical engineering researchers but also included researchers from allied communities like data analytics and management science etc.

The volume is a collection of high-quality peer-reviewed research papers received from all over the world. CICBA 2018 attracted a good number of submissions from the different areas spanning over three tracks in various cutting-edge technologies of specialized focus, which were organized and chaired by eminent professors. These three special sessions were: Computational Intelligence, Data Communications, and Data Mining and Advanced Data Analytics. The sub-tracks of the conference were Signal Processing, Computational Forensics (Privacy and Security), Microelectronics, Sensors, and Intelligent Networks. Based on a rigorous peer-review process by the Technical Program Committee members along with external experts as reviewers (national as well as international), the best quality papers were identified for presentation and publication. The review process was extremely stringent with a minimum of three reviews for each submission and occasionally up to six reviews. Checking of similarities and overlaps was also done based on the international norms and standards. Submitted papers came from countries like Australia, Bangladesh, Indonesia, Lithuania, Nigeria, Portugal, South Korea, the USA, and Vietnam. Out of the submission pool of received papers, only 30% were accepted for these proceedings.

The Organizing Committee of CICBA 2018 was made up of strong international academic and industrial luminaries and the Technical Program Committee comprised more than 200 domain experts. The proceedings of the conference are published as one volume in *Communications in Computer and Information Science* (CCIS), Springer, indexed by ISI Proceedings, DBLP, Ulrich's, EI-Compendex, SCOPUS, Zentralblatt Math, MetaPress, Springerlink and will be available at http://www.springer.com/series/7899. We, in our capacity as volume editors, convey our sincere gratitude to Springer for providing the opportunity to publish the proceedings of CICBA 2018 in their CCIS series.

The conference included distinguished general chairs and speakers such as Prof. Carlos A. Coello Coello, Investigador Cinvestav 3F, CINVESTAV-IPN, México, Prof. Xin Yao, Southern University of Science and Technology (SUSTech), China, Prof. Kalyanmoy Deb, Michigan State University, USA, Prof. Hisaob Ishibuchi, Southern University of Science and Technology (SUSTech), China, Prof. Mike Hinchey, University of Limerick, Ireland, Prof. Ashok Deshpande, University of California, Berkeley, USA, Prof. Pabitra Mitra, IIT Kharagpur, India, and Prof. Atal Chaudhuri, Vice-Chancellor, Veer Surendra Sai University of Technology (VSSUT), Burla, Odisha, India.

The editors express their sincere gratitude to Prof. Kalyanmoy Deb, Michigan State University, and Prof. Mike Hinchey, University of Limerick, Ireland, for offering their time to provide valuable guidance and inspiration to overcome various difficulties in the process of organizing the conference. We would like to take this opportunity to extend our heartfelt thanks to the honorary chair of this conference, Prof. Sankar Kumar Ghosh, Vice-Chancellor, University of Kalyani, India, for his active involvement from the very beginning until the end of the conference; without his support, this conference could never have assumed such a successful shape. Sincerest thanks are due to Prof. Bijay Baran Pal, University of Kalyani, and Prof. P. K. Roy, APIIT, India, for their valuable suggestions regarding the editorial review process. We express our sincere thanks to Prof. Samiran Chattopadhyay, Jadavpur University, for supporting us as in an important role in the Springer award committee. The editors also thank the other members of the award committee of CICBA 2018 for their efforts in selecting the best papers from of pool so many formidable accepted submissions.

Special words of appreciation are due to the Kalyani Government Engineering College, for coming forward to host to the conference, which incidentally was the second in the series. It was indeed heartening to note the enthusiasm of all the faculty, staff, and students of Kalyani Government Engineering College who organized the conference in a professional manner. The involvement of faculty coordinators and student volunteers is particularly praiseworthy in this regard. The editors leave no stone unturned and we the thank technical partners and sponsors for providing all the support and financial assistance.

It is needless to mention the role of the contributors. But for their active support and participation the question of organizing a conference is bound to fall through. The editors take this opportunity to thank the authors of all the papers submitted for their hard work, more so because all of them considered the conference as a viable platform to showcase some of their latest findings, not to mention their adherence to the deadlines and patience with the tedious review process. The quality of a refereed volume primarily depends on the expertise and dedication of the reviewers who volunteer with a smiling face. The editors are further indebted to the Technical Program Committee members and external reviewers who not only produced excellent reviews but also did these in short time frames, in spite of their very busy schedule. Because of their quality work, it has been possible to maintain the high academic standard of the proceedings.

The editors would like to thank the participants of the conference, who have considered the conference a befitting one in spite of all the hardships they had to undergo.

Last but not the least, the editors acknowledge all the volunteers for their tireless efforts in meeting the deadlines and arranging every minute detail meticulously to ensure that the conference achieved its goal, academic or otherwise. Happy Reading!

May 2019

J. K. Mandal
Somnath Mukhopadhyay
Paramartha Dutta
Kousik Dasgupta

Organization

Conference Tracks (Not Limited to)

Sushmitra Mitra	Indian Statistical Institute Kolkata, India
Shaikh Anowarul Fattah	BUET, Bangladesh
Biplab Sikdar	National University of Singapore, Singapore
Basabi Chakraborty	Iwate Prefectural University, Japan

General Chair

Xin Yao	Southern Univeristy of Science and Technology, Shenzhen, China
Carlos A. Coello Coello	Investigador Cinvestav 3F, CINVESTAV-IPN, México

Technical Program Committee Chairs

J. K. Mandal	University of Kalyani, India
Paramartha Dutta	Visva Bharati University, India
Somnath Mukhopadhyay	Assam University Silchar, India
Kousik Dasgupta	Kalyani Government Engineering College, India

Patron

Sourabh Kumar Das	Kalyani Government Engineering College, India

Conveners

Malay Kumar Pakhira	Kalyani Government Engineering College, India
Kousik Dasgupta	Kalyani Government Engineering College, India

Co-conveners

Swapan Kumar Mondal	Kalyani Government Engineering College, India
Shib Shankar Saha	Kalyani Government Engineering College, India

International Advisory Board

A. Damodaram	Jawaharlal Nehru Technological University, India
A. K. Nayak	Computer Society of India, India
A. Kaykobad	Bangladesh University of Engineering and Technology, Bangladesh
Amiya Nayak	Ottawa University, Canada

Anirban Basu   Computer Society of India, India
Arun Baran Samaddar   National Institute of Technology, Sikkim, India
Atal Chowdhury   Jadavpur University, India
Atulya Nagar   Liverpool Hope University, UK
Aynur Unal   Stanford University, USA
B. K. Panigrahi   Indian Institute of Technology Delhi, India
Barin Kumar De   Tripura University, India
Bidyut Baran Chaudhuri   Indian Statistical Institute Kolkata, India
Girijasankar Mallik   University of Western Sydney, Australia
Hyeona Lim   Mississippi State University, USA
K. V. Arya   Indian Institute of Information Technology
                                 and Management Gwalior, India
Millie Pant   Indian Institute of Technology Roorkee, India
Mrinal Kanti Naskar   Jadavpur University, India
Nandini Mukhopadhyay   Jadavpur University, India
Prith Banerjee   Schneider Electric, USA
Rahul Kala   Indian Institute of Information Technology Allahabad,
                                 India
Rajkumar Buyya   University of Melbourne, Australia
Sajal Das   University Texas at Arlington, USA
Santosh Mohanty   TCS Mumbai India
Shikharesh Majumdar   Carleton University, Canada
Somnath Mukhopadhay   Texas University, USA
Subarna Shakya   Tribhuvan University, Nepal
Subhansu Bandyopadhyay   Calcutta University, India
Vadim L. Stefanuk   Institute of Transmission Problems, Russia

Technical Program Committee

Arindam Pal   TCS Innovation Lab, India
A. C. Mondal   University of Burdwan, India
A. Chattopadhyay   Siliguri Institute of Technology, India
A. M. Sudhakara   University of Mysore, India
Abhishek Bhattacharya   Institute of Engineering and Management, India
Ajay K. Khan   Assam University Silchar, India
Alok Kumar Rastogi   Institute for Excellence in Higher Education Bhopal,
                                 India
Amiya Kumar Rath   Veer Surendra Sai University of Technology, India
Amlan Chakrabarti   Calcutta University, India
Andrew M. Lynn   Jawaharlal Nehru Technological University, India
Angshuman Bhttacharyya   National Institute of Technology Durgapur, India
Angsuman Sarkar   Kalyani Government Engineering College, India
Anindita Roy   BP Poddar Institute of Management and Technology,
                                 India
Anirban Guha   Jadavpur University, India
Anuradha Banerjee   Kalyani Government Engineering College, India

Arnab K. Laha	Indian Institute of Management Ahmedabad, India
Arpita Chakraborty	Techno India Salt Lake, India
Arundhati Bagchi Misra	Saginaw Valley State University, USA
Ashok Deshpande	University of California, USA
Ashok Kumar Rai	Gujarat University, India
Asif Ekbal	Indian Institute of Technology Patna, India
Asok Kumar	MCKV Institute of Engineering, India
Atanu Kundu	Heritage institute of Technology, India
Atta Ur Rehman Khan	COMSATS Institute of Information Technology Abbottabad, Iraq
Ayan Datta	IACS Kolkata, India
B. B. Pal	University of Kalyani, India
Balakrushna Tripathy	Vellore Institute of Technology, India
Bandana Barman	Kalyani Government Engineering College, India
Banshidhar Majhi	National Institute of Technology Rourkela, India
Bhaba R. Sarker	Louisiana State University, USA
Bhabani P. Sinha	Indian Statistical Institute Kolkata, India
Bhagvati Chakravarthy	University of Hyderabad, India
Bhaskar Sardar	Jadavpur University, India
Bibhas Chandra Dhara	Jadavpur University, India
Bijan Tadayon	Z Advanced Computing, Inc. (ZAC TM), USA
Bikash Patel	Kalyani Government Engineering College, India
Biplab K. Sikdar	Indian Institute of Engineering Science and Technology Shibpur, India
Brojo Kishore Mishra	C. V. Raman College of Engineering, India
Buddhadeb Manna	University of Calcutta, India
C. K. Chanda	Indian Institute of Engineering Science and Technology, India
C. Srinivas	Kakatiya Institute of Technology and Science, India
Carlos A. Bana e Costa	Universidade de Lisboa, Portugal
Celia Shahnaz	Bangladesh University of Engineering and Technology Dhaka, Bangladesh
Chandan Bhar	Indian School of Mines, India
Chandreyee Chowdhury	Jadavpur University, India
Chilukuri K. Mohan	Syracuse University, USA
Chintan Bhatt	Charotar University of Science and Technology Gujarat, India
Chintan Mandal	Jadavpur University, India
D. D. Sinha	Calcutta University, India
Dac-Nhuong Le	Haiphong University Haiphong, Vietnam
Dakshina Ranjan Kisku	National Institute of Technology Durgapur, India
Debashis De	Maulana Abul Kalam Azad University of Technology, India
Debasish Nandi	National Institute of Technology Durgapur, India
Debdatta Kandar	North East Hill University, India
Debesh Das	Jadavpur University, India

Debidas Ghosh	National Institute of Technology Durgapur, India
Debotosh Bhattacharjee	Jadavpur University, India
Deepak Khemani	Indian Institute of Technology Madras, India
Deepak Kumar	Amity University, India
Dhananjay Bhattacharyya	Saha Institute of Nuclear Physics Kolkata, India
Dhananjay Kumar Singh	Global ICT Standardization Forum for India (GISFI), India
Dharampal Singh	Namibia University, Namibia
Diganta Goswami	Indian Institute of Technology Guwahati, India
Dilip Kumar Pratihar	Indian Institute of Technology Kharagpur, India
Dipanwita Roychowdhury	Indian Institute of Technology Kharagpur, India
Dulal Acharjee	Purushottam Institute of Engineering and Technology, India
Durgesh Kumar Mishra	Computer Society of India, India
Esteban Alfaro Cortés	University of Castilla-La Mancha, Spain
Ganapati Panda	Indian Institute of Technology Bhubaneswar, India
Goutam Sanyal	National Institute of Technology Durgapur, India
Goutam Sarker	National Institute of Technology Durgapur, India
Govinda K.	Vellore Institute of Technology, India
Gunamani Jena	Roland Institute of Technology, India
H. S. Lalliel	University of Derby, UK
Hirak Maity	College of Engineering and Management Kolaghat, India
Indrajit Saha	National Institute of Tech. Teachers' Training and Research Kolkata, India
Irina Perfilieva	University of Ostrava, Czech Republic
J. V. R. Murthy	Jawaharlal Nehru Technological University Kakinada, India
Jimson Mathew	University of Bristol, UK
Jyoti Prakash Singh	National Institute of Technology Patna, India
K. Kannan	Nagaland University, India
K. Srujan Raju	CMR Group of Institutions, India
K. Suresh Basu	Jawaharlal Nehru Technological University, India
Kameswari Chebrolu	Indian Institute of Technology Bombay, India
Kamrul Alam Khan	Jagannath University, Bangladesh
Kandarpa Kumar Sarma	Gauhati University, India
Kartick Chandra Mandal	Jadavpur University, India
Kathleen Kramer	University of San Diego, USA
Kazumi Nakamatsu	University of Hyogo, Japan
Koushik Majumder	Maulana Abul Kalam Azad University of Technology, India
Krishnendu Chakraborty	Government College of Engineering and Ceramic Technology, India
Kui Yu	University of South Australia, Australia
Kunal Das	Narula Institute of Technology, India
Le Hoang Son	Vietnam National University, Vietnam

Lothar Thiele	Swiss Federal Institute of Technology Zurich, Switzerland
M. Ali Akber Dewan	Athabasca University, Canada
M. S. Prasad Babu	Andhra University, India
M. Sandirigama	University of Peradenia, Sri Lanka
Malay Bhattacharyya	Indian Institute of Engineering Science and Technology, India
Manas Kumar Bera	Haldia Institute of Technology, India
Manas Ranjan Senapati	Centurion University of Technology and Management, India
Manish Kumar Kakhani	Mody University, India
Massimo Pollifroni	University of Turin, Italy
M. Marjit Singh	North Eastern Regional Institute of Science & Technology, India
Md. Iftekhar Hussain	North East Hill University, India
Mohammad Ubadullah Bokhari	Aligarh Muslim University, India
Mohd Nazri Ismail	National Defence University of Malaysia (NDUM), Malaysia
N. V. Ramana Rao	Jawaharlal Nehru Technological University, India
Nabendu Chaki	Calcutta University, India
Nhu Nguyen	Duy Tan University, Vietnam
Nibaran Das	Jadavpur University Kolkata, India
Nilanjan Dey	Techno India College of Technology, India
Olema Vincent	University of Pretoria, South Africa
P. Premchand	Osmania University Hyderabad, India
P. S. Neelakanta	Florida Atlantic University, India
Parama Bhaumik	Jadavpur University, India
Partha Pratim Sahu	Tezpur University, India
Pawan Kumar Jha	Purbanchal University, Nepal
Pradosh K. Roy	Asia Pacific Institute of Information Technology, India
Pramod Kumar Meher	Nanyang Technological University, Singapore
Pranab K. Dan	Indian Institute of Technology Kharagpur, India
Prasanta K. Jana	Indian School of Mines Dhanbad, India
Prashant R. Nair	Computer Society of India, India
Pratyay Kuila	National Institute of Technology Sikkim, India
R. K. Jana	Indian Institute of Social Welfare and Business Management, India
R. Sankararama Krishnan	Indian Institute of Technology Kanpur, India
Rajeeb Dey	National Institute of Technology Silchar, India
Ram Sarkar	Jadavpur University, India
Rameshwar Dubey	Montpellier Business School, France
Ranjan Kumar Gupta	West Bengal State University, India
Ray Zhong	University of Auckland, New Zealand
Rober Hans	Tshwane University of Technology, South Africa
S. V. K. Bharathi	Symbiosis International University, India

S. A. Fattah	Bangladesh University of Engineering and Technology Dhaka, Bangladesh
S. D. Dewasurendra	University of Peradenia, Sri Lanka
S. K. Behera	National Institute of Technology Rourkela, India
S. P. Bhattacharyya	Texas A&M University, USA
S. G. Deshmukh	Indian Institute of Technology Mumbai, India
Saikat Chakrabarti	CSIR-IICB Kolkata, India
Samar Sen Sarma	University of Calcutta, India
Samiran Chattopadhyay	Jadavpur University, India
Sanchayan Mukherjee	Kalyani Government Engineering College, India
Sandip Rakshit	Kaziranga University, India
Sanjib K. Panda	Berkeley Education Alliance for Research in Singapore Ltd., Singapore
Sankar Chakraborty	Jadavpur University, India
Sankar Duraikannan	Asia Pacific University of Technology and Innovation, Malaysia
Santi P. Maity	Indian Institute of Engineering Science and Technology Shibpur, India
Sarbani Roy	Jadavpur University, India
Satish Narayana Srirama	University of Tartu, Estonia
Seba Maity	College of Engineering and Management Kolaghat, India
Shangping Ren	Illinois Institute of Technology Chicago, USA
Sheng-Lung Peng	National Dong Hwa University, Taiwan
Soma Barman	University of Calcutta, India
Soumya Pandit	University of Calcutta, India
Sripati Mukhopadhyay	Burdwan University, India
Sruti Gan Chaudhuri	Jadavpur University, India
Subhadip Basu	Jadavpur University, India
Subhranil Som	Amity University Noida, India
Subrata Banerjee	National Institute of Technology Durgapur, India
Sudhakar Sahoo	Institute of Mathematics and Applications, India
Sudhakar Tripathi	National Institute of Technology Patna, India
Sudip Kumar Adhikari	Cooch Behar Government Engineering College, India
Sudip Kumar Das	Calcutta University, India
Sudip Kundu	Calcutta University, India
Sudipta Roy	Assam University, India
Sukumar Nandi	Indian Institute of Technology Guwahati, India
Sumit Kundu	National Institute of Technology Durgapur, India
Sunita Sarkar	Assam University Silchar, India
Supratim Sengupta	Indian Institute of Engineering Science and Technology Shibpur, India
Sushmita Mitra	Indian Statistical Institute Kolkata, India
Swapan Kumar Mandal	Kalyani Government Engineering College, India
Syed Samsul Alam	Aliah University, India
T. K. Kaul	Sikkim University, India

Contents – Part II

Intelligent Data Mining and Data Warehousing

Computational Forensics (Privacy and Security)

Contents – Part I

Data Science and Advanced Data Analytics

Enhancing Interaction with Social Networking Sites for Visually Impaired People by Using Textual and Visual Question Answering

Akshit Pradhan(✉), Pragya Shukla, Pallavi Patra, Rohit Pathak,
and Ajay Kumar Jena

School of Computer Engineering, Kalinga Institute of Industrial Technology,
Deemed to be University, Bhubaneswar, India
akshitpradhan22@gmail.com, topragyashukla@gmail.com,
pallavijsrl9@gmail.com, rohitpathaknk@gmail.com,
ajay.bbs.in@gmail.com

Abstract. Question Answering (QA) is an all-around inquired issue in Natural Language Processing (NLP). This paper expands the boundaries of Question Answering by including textual and visual aspects, then further combining it with the SNS for enhancing its interaction with visually impaired people. In our proposed work, a text supported with an image is fed into the hybrid model which is a combination of CNN and LSTM, producing the most accurate result with the highest probability. Both questions and answers are open ended visual and textual queries in specifically targeted diverse regions of a picture including the subtle elements of a text. Subsequently, we created a framework that required a point by point comprehension of the picture which is more complex than the framework delivering just pictorial inscriptions. The model achieved better results than other models. By using this model, we enhanced interaction with the SNS with greater efficiency.

Keywords: Question answering · Natural language processing ·
Social network sites · Convolutional neural network ·
Long short term memory networks

1 Introduction

Question Answering is a way of representing information consisting of a series of questions followed by their answers. Queries are raised by users in a natural language. Initially, the QA used the Natural Language Processing (NLP) technique to extract answers from a collection of unstructured natural language documents. NLP is a technique by which computers break down and comprehend human language in a smart way [2]. A question-answering system includes extraction of facts, understanding of questions and generation of answers, which are further integrated onto Social Networking Sites (SNS). Social Networking Sites are defined as an online platform where people build their social networks with each other and share their common interests, day to day activities etc. Social Networking Sites mainly include pictures and few textual data which cannot be generally comprehended by visually challenged people.

© Springer Nature Singapore Pte Ltd. 2019
J. K. Mandal et al. (Eds.): CICBA 2018, CCIS 1031, pp. 3–14, 2019.
https://doi.org/10.1007/978-981-13-8581-0_1

Neural network based strategies have made colossal advancement in picture and content-grouping [1, 9, 13]. Further advancements have been made on more unpredictable errands that require legitimate thinking. This achievement is situated to some degree on the expansion of consideration segments within complex neural networks and memory related to it. In this paper, we aim to combine and compare the models proposed earlier in order to enable the new system to answer a combination of both visual and textual data given as the input. Outputs are generated for respective inputs, in the form of confidence scores that are given by our model. Finally, the answer with the highest score is outputted. Here, we tried to implement question answering for visual and textual elements focusing on implementing hybrid models consisting of Convolutional neural network (CNN) [11] and Long short-term memory networks [5] along with modified Dynamic memory networks [13] by tuning the regularization constant (l2) 0.001 for reducing over-fitting so that the variance of our estimated regression parameters could be reduced.

Question Answering is a topic which has been well researched in the past and a lot of advancements have been made in the field [1, 2]. However, very less work has been witnessed in terms of its application for the benefit for the visually impaired people in the society. Hence this paper will be helpful for the community of the visually challenged people. With this intent, we were motivated to propose a novel approach in order to combine various machine learning algorithms and implement it in a way such that it is useful in handling both textual and visual aspects of the queries.

The remaining work is organized as follows. The groundwork and the basic concepts are discussed in Sect. 2. Reviews of the related work are presented in Sect. 3. Our proposed approach is described in Sect. 4. In Sect. 5, we described the working principle of the proposed model. The detailed implementation and results are discussed in Sect. 6. Section 7 concludes the work with future direction.

2 Basic Concepts

In the following section, we provide a brief review of the basic concepts and literature that form an integral part of our work.

Long Short Term Memory (LSTM) - Traditionally the neural networks had a major shortcoming that is of understanding every word it encountered from scratch. Recurrent Neural Networks (RNN) [6] addresses this issue as they are networks with loops which allow information to persist. LSTM is a special kind of RNN which works much better than the standard version of the aforementioned model. LSTM also contains a structure which represents that of a chain. But, the module which is repeating has a contrasting structural form altogether. There are four layers interacting amongst each other for a single neural network layer s in a very particular way.

Convolutional Neural Networks (CNN) - The above technologies are used in combination with the CNN, a type of Feed Forward Neural Network. CNN's are used in multiple fields comprising of patterns, images, speech recognition, video analysis, and natural language processing. Functions like pattern recognition and feature extractors in traditional models were hand crafted. The fully connected layer used for classification and the weights included in the convolutional layer used for feature extraction are determined during the training process. Various features of the input are extracted during the convolution operation. The low-level features like corners, edges and lines are extracted in the very first layer. The following layers extract the higher level features.

Text Detection is done by breaking down the question into its relevant word vectors using Glove [7] and implementing it with popular Word2Vec model [8]. Then the image is passed into CNN. Later the aforementioned models were used and the respective accuracies of the answers were calculated. The model figures out how to choose the important actualities from a bigger set. We demonstrated how the adjustments in the memory module, causes a notable enhancement in the visual question replying.

Recurrent Neural Networks (RNN) - is an artificial neural network class containing a directed cycle is formed between its corresponding units. It differs with the Feed Forward Neural Network (FFNN) in the way that its internal memory functions. The internal memory in RNN, used to capture information preconceived by it so far, helps to process random sequences of inputs. This behavior of the neural network is caused due to the RNN's capability of looking back to a few steps executed earlier.

Google's Word2Vec - represents the words into their vector spaces containing several hundred dimensions. The continuous bag-of-words (CBOW) or continuous skip-gram are distributed representation of words produced by the two model architectures incorporated by Word2Vec. We applied the CBOW model because it is faster than the continuous skip-gram model along with Word2Vec in order to produce word embeddings. In this paper, we have incorporated the Google cloud speech to text API in order to input the questions in the form of speech. We have further converted it in the form of text so as to feed it into the model.

3 Related Work

Recently there have been various parallel endeavors on both making datasets and proposing new models [4, 17, 18]. Gao et al. [18] utilized MS-COCO [15] pictures and furthermore made a publicly available dataset through human created inquiries and their solutions. A few inquiries required consistent thinking with a specific end goal in order to answer accurately. Malinowski et al. [17], as well as Gao et al. [18] implemented recurrent networks to encode the sentences, which in turn yielded the appropriate response. While Malinowski et al. used a distinct network to deal with both encoding and translating, Gao et al. used two different networks, an encoder along with a decoder. Ultimately, bilingual adaptations (here, Chinese and English) of the QA dataset were accessible in the work of Gao et al. Ma et al. [4] used CNN's to concentrate on both picture highlights and sentence highlights. The highlights were then circuited together with another multi-modular CNN.

Xiong et al. [13] proposed an architecture with memory attention mechanisms for exhibiting certain reasoning capabilities and one such architecture is the dynamic memory networks. The architecture included memory attention mechanisms that exhibited reasoning capabilities. They also incorporated a new technique. However, they failed to achieve reliable results for the question and answer in the absence of supporting facts.

Agrawal et al. [10] presented a model in Visual Question Answering(VQA) that considered image along with a natural question about that image and the model hence produces natural language as its answer. They experimented with two image embedding namely I and norm I. Bag-of-Words Question (BoW Q) was used for the question channel in which top 1000 words in the questions were picked to create a bag of words. They first used LSTM Q with only one hidden layer and later a deeper LSTM Q with two hidden layers was also implemented along with it. The two LSTM(s) were combined to get a single embedding which was further passed into a Multi Layer Perceptron(MLP). They then compared the obtained results with that of other models.

Yang et al. [3] proposed a model, which used multilayer stacked attention networks (SANs) to enable multiple step reasoning for image QA. The SAN consisted of a CNN, an LSTM and a stacked attention model. SAN extracted one vector from each image region-wise along with the semantic vector of the question. It then searched for the related regions in the image that were close to the actual answer. This model outperformed the previous approaches. However, a minor portion of the outcomes witnessed wrong predictions and ambiguous answers.

Ren et al. [12] presented a model which used visual denotation embedding to merge a CNN and an RNN for generic end-to-end image based QA. A question generating algorithm was also proposed which converted image descriptions into QA form. A new dataset called the COCO-QA was generated using this algorithm. This model worked on a restricted zone of questions and provided only single word answers. A few baselines were designed to monitor the effectiveness of the proposed model. These baselines can be further used to develop a more complex and sophisticated end to end image QA system. To start the work with the following motives, for VQA we gathered the dataset from MS COCO [15] and for textual question answering we gathered data from the bAbI dataset [16]. The MS COCO dataset is a large-scale object detection, segmentation and captioning dataset. It contains 330,000 images containing 80 object categories, having 5 captions per image and around 1.5 million object instances. While the bAbI dataset have 1000 questions for training and 1000 questions for testing in English as well as in Hindi.

4 Proposed Model

In this section, we proposed our work to generate optimized question answers from the questions asked by the user in the social media sites. This model uses the questions asked by the user is either text or speech form. With the help of the Google cloud speech API, this converts the query into a textual form and passes it on to the model. Figure 1 shows a pictorial representation of our proposed work. The model we are proposing will perform as per the following steps.

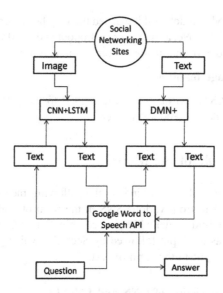

Fig. 1. Architecture of the proposed model for question and answering

A. Accept a question from the user in text/speech

As shown in Fig. 1, there are three inputs required to our proposed model, i.e. Image, Text, and Question. The respective image and text are taken directly from social networking sites using web scraping tools and for the questions that are taken from the users as speech voices or in the text as per user's convenience.

B. Conversion of speech to text

After accepting the question in its audio form, we have used the open source Google cloud speech API to convert the respective speech voice into its textual form and the output is forwarded in the text format to our model.

C. Convert sentence into their respective word embeddings

The text is further converted into its respective word vectors using Word2Vec from Stanford known as GloVe. GloVe reduces the word vector into a 300-dimensional representation, which is then forwarded to our LSTM(s) input.

D. Feeding the word vectors into LSTM

The hybrid model of CNN and LSTM runs a 3 layered LSTM on the word embeddings, it was sufficient enough to feed the word embeddings directly into the merge layer and the results achieved were close to the state of art results.

E. Extracting the image features

We used VGG Net for extracting image features from CNN, as VGG Net is a very simple and versatile pretrained model. It is relatively smaller than other models and most importantly it is very portable. We acquired the raw image by scraping from the SNS and passed it into our CNN model until it reached the very last layer. We avoided the use of the last two layers of VGG Net as they were a dropout and 1000 way softmax, thus we extracted 4096 dimensions of the image features of image from VGG-16.

F. Extracting the image features

Finally, all of the LSTM(s) outputs are provided to the softmax layer in its last phase as the input in order to produce answers.

5   Working Principle of the Model

The model we proposed will be working on the following mentioned principle. The input to our model is taken from various SNS in the form of both image and text. In Sect. 5.1 we defined a hybrid model which is a combination of CNN along with LSTM which takes the image as the input followed by Sect. 5.2 which gives an overview of the model which takes input in the form of text.

5.1   Hybrid Model Consisting of CNN and LSTM

In our approach we considered the state of art model without using any attention models and memory networks that were previously used by [12]. We used a classical model which consisted of CNN and LSTM as represented in Fig. 1 and then combined them together. Softmax was then trained on the combined features. Here we used the pre-trained model of VGGnet. VGG 16 relu features were used for image embeddings. While VGGnet is not the best CNN model for image features unlike GoogleNet/ ResNet, but it is very versatile, simple and relatively small.

The image features were extracted by taking a raw image and running it through the model until we reached the last layer. We intentionally dropped out the last two layers of VGGnet because the last layer of VGGnet is 1000 way softmax and the second last layer is the dropout. Thus we extracted 4096 dimensions' image features from VGG-16. For using text and question, we need to convert the words into some sort of word embeddings. A Word2Vec model from Stanford called GloVe was used to reduce our question and text into a 300-dimension vector.

The combined model for visual and textual question answering was then made to run on a Softmax as shown in Fig. 2. We settled on running a 3 layered LSTM on the word embeddings. This model's results outperformed the results obtained by using only a few layers.

The parameters of LSTM are weight matrix and the bias which are learned on training data as

$$I_t = \sigma[b_i + W_{hi}W_{ht} - 1 + W_{xi}W_{ti}] \tag{1}$$

$$f_t = \sigma\left[b_f + W_{xf}W_t + W_{hf}h_{t-1} - 1\right] \tag{2}$$

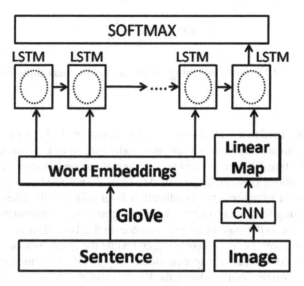

Fig. 2. Hybrid model of CNN and LSTM

$$o_t = \sigma[b_0 + W_{xo}W_t + W_{io}h_{t-1} - 1] \tag{3}$$

Coordinate-wise max operation is used over these vectors for max pooling. For convolutional feature maps of different sizes and then we concatenated them to form the feature representation vector of the whole question sentence, where $Q = [Q_1 \dots Q_p]$.

$$c_t = t_t c_{t-1} + i_t \tanh(W_{xc}x_t + W_{hc}h_{t-1} + b_c) \tag{4}$$

$$h_t = o_t \tanh(c_t) \tag{5}$$

Here i, f, o, c refers to the input gate, forget gate, output gate, and memory cell respectively.

For combining prior knowledge and for better understanding we resort to an example. Suppose we ask the color of a white fish swimming in blue water The output may be white because the previous obtained probability is less. We denoted S as color, O as the object of interest and I as the image taking O and I to be conditionally independent.

$$P(S|O,I) = \frac{P(S|O,I)}{\sum_{s \in S} P(S|O,I)} = \frac{P(O|S)P(S|I)}{\sum_{s \in S} P(O|S)P(S|I)} \tag{6}$$

So, $P(C|X)$ is output is given to CNN features as input and then we estimated $P(O|S)$ and

$$\widehat{P}(O|S) = \frac{count(O,S)}{count(S)} \qquad (7)$$

We, further used Laplace smoothing on our model for smoothing of the results.

5.2   DMN+

In this section, we tried to use DMN+ proposed by Xiong et al. [13] for textual question answering. The primary segment is a sentence reader used to just encode the words into a sentence implanting. The second part is the information combination layer taking into account collaborations between sentences. As slopes do not need to engender through the words between sentences, the combination layer additionally takes into account removed supporting sentences to have a more straightforward cooperation. This model reached quite close to the state of art performance on the 10 K dataset of bAbI dataset with weak supervision (i.e. no supporting facts) while the regularization rate was same as previous (l2 = 0.001). As the paper previously suggested, 10 training runs were used for tasks and the weights that produced the lowest validation loss were used in testing. The l2 optimization parameter was not given in the paper, so fully optimizing the l2 regularization would close the final significant performance.

6   Implementation and Results

As shown in Fig. 1, there are three inputs required for our proposed model. The inputs are Image, Text, and Question. The respective image and text are taken directly from social networking sites using web scraping tools. The questions that are fed into the model are taken in two formats i.e. either in the form of speech which is converted into their respective text by the Google cloud speech API or directly by text.

Figure 2 depicts the model that we have created for processing the images and Fig. 3 is for processing the text. Furthermore, Fig. 2 shows how we separated words from sentences. The input image is passed through the convolutional neural network after which they are linearly mapped. The output of the previous step is then passed through the dropout layer of LSTM which is also described in exploring model and data from Image Question Answering by Ren et al. but the regularization rate (l2) here is taken to be 0.001. Here as the LSTM(s) are not bidirectional which in turn increases our model accuracy. The input is fed into the LSTM and then a dense layer. The DMN+ module replaced single GRU with different components and is further described in Fig. 3. The fusion layer represented in Fig. 3 where the sentence reader encodes the sentence and GRU(s) are connected bi-directionally, which allows the flow of information.

The hybrid model consisting of CNN and LSTM model was trained on the batch size of 100 and on 10 epochs. Hence by increasing the batch size and epochs the accuracy of the model can be further increased. The DMN+ model was trained separately and 10 training runs were used for several bAbI tasks. The weights which produced the lowest validation loss were used for testing.

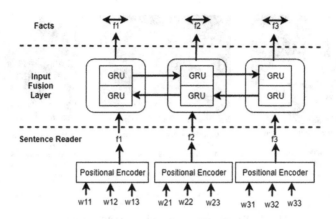

Fig. 3. DMN+ model proposed by Xiong et al.

The Image features were extracted by taking the raw image and running it through the model until we reached the last layer. In our case the model was not exactly the same, so we extracted the 4096 dimensions of image features from VGG and the image was transformed and re-sized into 224 × 224 as VGG was trained as the image of 224 × 224 and then transformed into its respected RGB. Finally, all combined modules were tested by inputting a picture and asking a question. The following tables show the results of our model after its implementation.

Table 1 presents some statistics about the new dataset used. This dataset contains 117684 images out of which, 78736 were used for training our model and 38948 images were used for the purpose of testing. The statistics mentioned in Table 1 were automatically generated from image captions, ranging from 4 types of questions i.e. object, color, number, and location. Both the training as well as the testing accuracies are shown in Table 1 accordingly.

Table 1. COCO-QA question type break-down

Category	Train	Accuracy %	Test	Accuracy %
Object	54992	71.23%	27206	70.89%
Number	5885	8.13%	2755	7.92%
Color	13059	21.29%	6509	21.75%
Location	4800	8.10%	2478	8.34%
Object	54992	71.23%	27206	70.89%
Number	5885	8.13%	2755	7.92%
Total	78736	100%	38948	100.00%

For better understanding, a sample question and its respective accuracy has been mentioned in Fig. 4, which shows that the output produced by our model matches with the ground truth.

Q. How many dogs are there in this mage?

A. 2	63%
1	27%
0	7%
3	2%

Ground Truth : 2

Q. Which animal is there in this picture?

A. Giraffe	95.21%
Tiger	2.12%
Monkey	1.54%
Lion	0.02%

Ground Truth : Giraffe

Q. Which vehicle is there in this picture?

A. Motorcycle	51.21%
Cycle	48.12%
Car	1.23%
Train	0.04%

Ground Truth : Motorcycle

Fig. 4. Sample questions with respective results

Table 2 depicts the test error rates of two architectures on bAbI English 10k dataset. DMN+ shows the result of the model that was implemented by Xiong et al. [13] and DMN shows the result of our model that was modified after tuning the hyper-parameters.

Table 2. Test error rates of our model and DMN+ on bAbI

bAbI task ID [16]	DMN test error rate	DMN+ test error rate
2: 2 supporting facts	0.8	0.3
5: 3 argument relations	0.5	0.5
7: counting	2.7	2.4
9: simple negation	0.1	0.0
14: time reasoning	0.0	0.2
18: size reasoning	2.1	2.1
Mean error	1.03	0.92

The end goal of our paper is to implement Visual Question answering in aiding the visually impaired who can interact with the system while using various Social Networking Sites (SNS). The model enables live interaction by allowing the users to ask the queries verbally and get the answers back in a reasonable amount of time in form of speech or voice.

7 Conclusion

By using combined models namely LSTM and CNN along with DMN+, we have achieved more accurate result as compared to the previously implemented models in certain tasks. According to the discussion provided in our paper, we have posited that by taking the regularization rate (l2) as 0.001 and by incorporating LSTM(s) as non-bidirectional, a significant change in the performance of the model is achieved. The performance of our model architecture was further enhanced by the use of DMN+, which comprises of two segments namely input representation and attention mechanisms. By implementing this model, we tried to help the visually challenged individuals in using SNS with much more ease. Our model provides them with a live and open ended interaction with the SNS, where they can ask questions verbally and get the required responses in the form of speech. In the future, training with larger data sets and tuning the hyper parameters might have the potential to further improve the model accuracy.

References

1. Mishra, A., Jain, S.K.: A survey on question answering systems with classification. J. King Saud Univ.-Comput. Inf. Sci. **28**(3), 345–361 (2016)
2. Nadkarni, P.M., Ohno-Machado, L., Chapman, W.W.: Natural language processing: an introduction. J. Am. Med. Inform. Assoc. **18**(5), 544–551 (2011)
3. Yang, Z., He, X., Gao, J., Deng, L., Smola, A.: Stacked attention networks for image question answering. In: Proceedings of the IEEE Conference on Computer Vision and Pattern Recognition, pp. 21–29 (2016)
4. Ma, L., Lu, Z., Li, H.: Learning to answer questions from image using convolutional neural network. In: AAAI, vol. 3, no. 7, p. 16, February 2016
5. Hochreiter, S., Schmidhuber, J.: Long short-term memory. Neural Comput. **9**(8), 1735–1780 (1997)
6. Mao, J., Xu, W., Yang, Y., Wang, J., Huang, Z., Yuille, A.: Deep captioning with multimodal recurrent neural networks (M-RNN). arXiv preprint arXiv:1412.6632 (2014)
7. Pennington, J., Socher, R., Manning, C.: Glove: global vectors for word representation. In: Proceedings of the 2014 Conference on Empirical Methods in Natural Language Processing (EMNLP), pp. 1532–1543 (2014)
8. Mikolov, T., Sutskever, I., Chen, K., Corrado, G.S., Dean, J.: Distributed representations of words and phrases and their compositionality. In: Advances in Neural Information Processing Systems, pp. 3111–3119 (2013)
9. Kumar, A., et al.: Ask me anything: dynamic memory networks for natural language processing. In: International Conference on Machine Learning, pp. 1378–1387, June 2016
10. Agrawal, A., et al.: VQA: visual question answering. Int. J. Comput. Vis. **123**(1), 4–31 (2017)
11. Simonyan, K., Zisserman, A.: Very deep convolutional networks for large-scale image recognition. arXiv preprint arXiv:1409.1556 (2014)
12. Ren, M., Kiros, R., Zemel, R.: Exploring models and data for image question answering. In: Advances in Neural Information Processing Systems, pp. 2953–2961 (2015)
13. Xiong, C., Merity, S., Socher, R.: Dynamic memory networks for visual and textual question answering. In: International Conference on Machine Learning, pp. 2397–2406, June 2016
14. He, K., Zhang, X., Ren, S., Sun, J.: Deep residual learning for image recognition. In: Proceedings of the IEEE Conference on Computer Vision and Pattern Recognition, pp. 770–778 (2016)
15. MSCOCO Dataset. http://cocodataset.org
16. The bAbI Dataset. https://research.fb.com/downloads/babi

17. Malinowski, M., Rohrbach, M., Fritz, M.: Ask your neurons: a neural-based approach to answering questions about images. In: Proceedings of the 2015 IEEE International Conference on Computer Vision (ICCV), pp. 1–9. IEEE Computer Society, December 2015
18. Gao, H., Mao, J., Zhou, J., Huang, Z., Wang, L., Xu, W.: Are you talking to a mach? Dataset and methods for multilingual image question. In: Advances in Neural Information Processing Systems, pp. 2296–2304 (2015)

Design and Implementation of a Mobile-Based Personal Digital Assistant (MPDA)

Oluranti Jonathan[1], Charles Ogbunude[1], Sanjay Misra[1(✉)],
Robertas Damaševičius[2], Rytis Maskeliunas[2], and Ravin Ahuja[3]

[1] Covenant University, Ota, Ogun State, Nigeria
{jonathan.oluranti,
sanjay.misra}@covenantuniversity.edu.ng
[2] Kaunas University of Technology, Kaunas, Lithuania
{robertas.damasevicius,rytis.maskeliunas}@ktu.lt
[3] University of Delhi, Delhi, India
ravinahujadce@gmail.com

Abstract. In this work we present a mobile-based personal digital assistance for students of higher institutions of learning. These days, the need for a To-Do list or a daily plan cannot be over-emphasized. This is because so many things compete for our valuable. It appears that the 24 h of a day are no longer sufficient for our daily activities. Although this appears true, however, prioritizing our activities generally may go a long way in helping to manage our time. Several platforms and media that existed some years ago were based on the use of pen and paper to organize activities for the day. These can no longer match up recent advances in technology and information flow which are at a very great speed. This work leverages on the current proliferation of mobile devices where each student now has a mobile device for personal use. In this work a mobile-based personal digital assistant is developed specifically on the Android platform. The system adopts Google's material guidelines for the design of its user interface. Android Java was used for the implementation of the core aspects of the system while SQLite was used for the database. The application will help students in prioritizing and organizing their daily activities thereby making them more responsible.

Keywords: Android · Information processing · Mobile ·
Personal digital assistant

1 Introduction

In today's busy world, everyone needs a personal assistant which in most cases is not usually or readily available. Human-based personal assistant is prone to mistakes, tiredness or fatigue, and may likely forget important events or make decisions based on emotions. To prevent this from happening, there is need for technology and this has resulted in what we know today as personal digital assistants (PDAs). In this work, we focus on students who, these days are encumbered with so many tasks and activities

© Springer Nature Singapore Pte Ltd. 2019
J. K. Mandal et al. (Eds.): CICBA 2018, CCIS 1031, pp. 15–28, 2019.
https://doi.org/10.1007/978-981-13-8581-0_2

than was the case some years back. Students have to keep track of assignments, deadlines, projects, personal pursuits and all these on the long run can weigh down the students.

Decades ago, personal digital assistants were not available; unlike what is available today; all things had to be put down on paper. People still have diaries and books where they did their major planning, but with the advent of mobile computing, applications and artificial intelligence, those methods are being replaced. Mobile electronic products are now common because of the convenient and versatile function the provide [1]. One of such devices is the personal digital assistant (PDA) which can help students to organize their time and programs thereby focusing on very important activities. A PDA is a multi-functional information and communication tool that can help students properly prioritize their activities [2]. With the growth in sales of mobile devices, there is a great opportunity to help students through the mobile platform.

According to Google, over 50 billion apps have been downloaded of Google play, that figure alone shows that a lot of people do download and use applications. The implication is that a lot of people can be influenced through mobile applications. According to Google, there are over one billion active Android users and 1.5 million devices are activated daily [3]. Android platform and devices therefore constitute a good choice on which to deploy a mobile application for students.

Although there are personal digital assistants already existing on Google play store, our own application is uniquely geared towards students with their unique features and activities. The traditional method of using pen and paper to document tasks though still very good, cannot keep up with the increasing rate of information flow. The aim of this study is to design and implement a mobile-based personal digital assistant for use by students of higher institutions. This is to be achieved by the implementation of an Android application with user interface designed using Google's creative vision design principles. The system is intended to run on Android-based devices only. The development tool used is Android studio, which is the most popular integrated development environment for developing android applications. Android studio is more preferred than Eclipse as it is more robust and support is readily available. The main programming language used is Java, XML (extensible markup language) was used for the design while SQLite was used for the database, SQLite is portable and fast. The application will help students in prioritizing and organizing their daily activities thereby making them generally more productive and responsible.

2 Related Works

Students these days have more things to learn and deal with than in the past. They are bombarded daily with distractions and alternatives, for which without proper planning and adequate help a student can stray away. With a PDA, students need not bother about some tasks. Remembering when to submit assignments or keeping track of a project can be done better with the help of the digital assistant.

Before the term personal digital assistant came to be, there were personal planners, which were in paper format already existing. As people were more engaged and nations grew, things needed to be organized. PDAs gradually became popular, but were not as powerful as what we have today. Actually, the term PDA referred to a device, which was sold to assist people and help them organize and plan their schedule. Today PDA's are not just devices but can also be software, which run on different devices. Also the PDA's are intelligent and can make use of the available hardware power in today's computer [4].

Several works have been carried out with respect to the adoption, acceptance, use and applications that run on PDAs. PDAs have been used in a number of medical and educational environments to enhance learning and data collection. The work of [5] focused on the use of PDAs as tools for learning in clinical internships while the work of [6] evaluated the usage of PDAs among undergraduate medical students. They studied the trends, barriers and the advantages of mobile devices to students. Other works which are include the one by [7–9, 14]. The work in [7] focused on using PDAs for collecting data on HIV/AIDS in an African country while [8, 9] considered the experience of Nursing students with respect to the use of PDAs. The work in [14] is also related to collection of data on infectious diseases in South American country of Peru. The work in [10, 11] though similar in part, to the one intended in this study like organizing assignments, is focused on adolescents with Asperger Syndrome and other developmental disabilities. The study in [12] assessed the practical performance of using PDAs. A general history of PDAs was provided in [13] but for the period covering 1980–2000. In [15–17], PDAs applications were developed to help students in health-related fields to effectively collect data and carry out their activities.

Today personal digital assistants go from the simple to the complex where artificial intelligence is involved. Also, each new Microsoft Windows system comes with a popular system known as Cortana, an intelligent personal assistant that uses voice commands to execute tasks on Windows operating system. There are also the less intelligent versions, which can be on a smart phone as an application. Assistant, which is also an intelligent personal assistant, is a mobile application unlike Cortana, which has a desktop version. It does tasks like telling you the nearest location to get a drink or buy some clothes [12]. There are other personal assistants such as My Study Life [13], which do not make use of artificial intelligence. Not every PDA needs artificial intelligence; in fact, some PDAs are better off without the complexities of implementing artificial intelligence.

There are existing personal digital assistants available on Google's play store, an online application store where developers can upload their applications and user can download any application of their choice. Some are free while others involve some payment before or after download. Effectiveness is a personal digital assistant carefully designed with excellent features. Accomplish [13] is another mobile-based PDA with which you can easily recognize with a reddish logo. It helps you graphically plan your time, which is a lot easier and actually, more fun that using a pen and paper. It uses a simple and conventional to-do list. MSL or My study Life is another successful digital assistant on play store with success in the likes of My Effectiveness. My study life has 1,000,000 to 5,000,000 downloads on play store with over 23,000 5-star ratings.

One great feature about MSL application is the face that it was designed for students, teachers and lecturers. It is to make ones study life easier to manage. It has functionalities to store assignments and exams, which use the cloud to make it available on any device. It even has features to show home works due for submission, classes that conflict with exams and even that ability to add a revision task for a specific exam. Like others, Roubit [13] is another good digital assistant, though not with as many features as the others offer. It is an application that specializes in routine work that someone does every day. Roubit has a simple but well-designed interface. Roubit has an authentic blue colour, which is the default theme of the application. It has days of the week from Monday to Sunday and you can add tasks on those days using the floating button. The application makes use of material design animation such as circular reveal animation and custom check boxes.

It is certain that PDAs applications have been developed and used in a number of fields and for specific needs, our study concerns only students of higher institutions in Nigeria. This is on the premise that our educational system presently makes it necessary for students to seek assistance in the aspect of organizing their daily activities because they usually overwhelming many times.

2.1 Features of a Student Personal Digital Assistant

There are some common features of mobile-based student personal digital assistants, these features should be present in all others, and they are discussed below. These features may not be available in every single student PDA but they are feature of a modern standard PDA for students.

Android Creative Vision: The Android creative vision and design principles were created to keep user's best interest in mind. Most modern applications are designed using android creative vision. Google even says they will soon only allow applications that use material design to feature on Play Store. Apps that work in expected ways are instantly familiar to Android users, gain their trust, and ensure they engage with the app's consent, functionality, and features.

Ease of Use: The users of these applications are students so therefore, the user interface should not be complex and as much as possible the learning curve should not be steep. Addition of task and deletion should not take time or involve a long process and the app should contain short cuts of operations to enable students easily accomplish what they want with a few clicks.

Notification: With the old method of using papers, there was no notification, but with digital power, there is a lot that can be done, one of which is notification. A notification can be a simple pop up and beep that notifies the user of when a task is due, this helps the user remember because he is prone to even forgetting what he has planned. A notification runs on a service that is available even when the student is not using the application.

Planning and Scheduling: With digital assistants, students can make plans and not just for the day but for future days, they can look at their schedule for the day and make changes where necessary. With the old method of documenting on paper, planning was possible but not as convenient as planning with a digital assistant because you can edit with a digital assistant and delete peradventure the user's schedule changes. When using digital assistants you can see a whole month at a glance and see what and when you have appointments. Some PDAs even have the functionality of informing you when you have clashing tasks, which is priceless information.

Information: If a student was to plan his year with the traditional method of writing it down, he may not be able to give account of how many goals he has per month, how many are due, or how many he has accomplished. He may have little information about all this, but a digital assistant can give real time information about all things that pertains the students life, his assignments, projects and to-do list. A PDA can give the student a summarized view of all he has documented down so that he can use that information to plan further.

3   Issues with Existing Personal Digital Assistants

As with most technologies, existing personal digital assistants have some issues requiring attention. Some of the issues are highlighted below.

3.1   Lack of Features

A common reason for low star rating of applications on play store is lack of features, the issue is that an application may not be able to have all the feature desired by a particular student. A good application should be one that each student feels the application was specially designed for him or her. Some students want all in one package, while some other students love simplicity; they want the application to include just what the need and not every possible functionality. This does not make it easy for developers because they have to include the right amount to functionality to satisfy the majority of users.

3.2   Privacy and Security

Personal information is stored such as personal tasks or goals. Unauthorized persons could have access to those personal information and cause havoc. Personal things should remain personal and when designing applications that keep personal information, they should be designed to be reliable and dependable.

3.3   Learning Curve

The learning curve of some applications is actually steep though they may be great applications, and example is My Effectiveness. Learning curve indicates how hard it is to learn software or in other words how fast a user can understand and get used to software. A steep learning curve is one that is not so easy to understand and can get complex quite quickly. My Effectiveness is a great application, one of the great names but it is complex, it has everything and some students may not like the complexity, but there are simple apps such as Roubit or the most successful of the listed, which is My Study Life, has a very simple self-explanatory interface.

3.4 Internet Access

There are parts of the world where Internet access is not readily available, and there are student digital assistants that work with the Internet. A lot of the great PDAs synchronize and this involves the use of Internet connection. Google advises developers not to develop applications that are data intensive or need constant connection. This is so that users in developing countries can use all the functionalities of these applications; updates should be less frequent also.

4 Requirements Analysis

Software system requirements are classified into functional and non-functional requirements; these will be discussed with respect to the mobile-based personal assistant system [18].

4.1 Functional Requirements of Application

Functional requirements represent what the system should do, the behaviour of the system in relation to the system's functionality. Below are the functional requirements for the mobile-based personal assistant.

- The user shall be able to add a new task for the day.
- The user shall be able to edit and delete added tasks.
- The user shall be able to view the list of all saved task.
- The system shall be able to notify the user of a task using notification manager.
- An ID shall uniquely identify each notification in the system.
- The user shall be able to view the classes he has in a day.
- The user shall be able to add new classes to any day he wishes.
- The user shall be able to edit and delete his classes.
- The system shall show the user pending tasks for a day.
- The system shall be allowing the user view the number of classes he has per day.
- The user shall be able to add, edit and delete new assignments.
- The user shall be able to add, edit and delete new projects.
- The system shall inform the user of pending assignments and projects.

4.2 Non-functional Requirements

Requirements that are not directly concerned with the specific services derived by the system to the users are referred to as non-functional requirements. Non-functional requirements, include security, reliability, availability or performance usually specify or constrain characteristic of the system as a whole [19].

5   System Design and Modeling

The system is designed based on the requirements documented. It is in three specifications, which are physical design, the logical design and conceptual design [20, 21].

5.1   Logical Design

Logical design describes processes, and this is without suggesting how they are conducted. It involves defining business entities and relationships. Physical details are defined during the design phase when these logical models are refined into physical models. All these provide information needed to build the system.

Class Diagram: Class Diagram provides an overview of the target system by describing the objects and classes inside the system and the relationships between them [22, 23]. Figure 1 below shows the various classes of the system, from the task list also called to-do list to the Lectures which is also called classes, to the project, contacts and assignment.

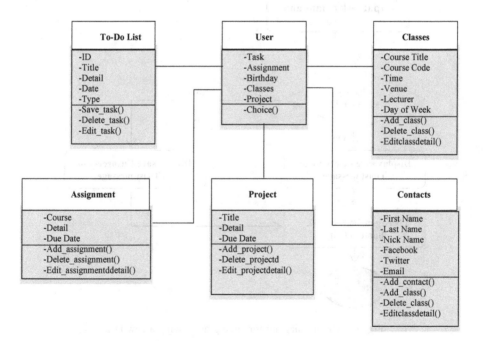

Fig. 1. Class diagram representing a mobile-based student PDA

Activity Diagram: Activity diagrams are graphical representations of workflows; they are representations of stepwise activities and actions, which include support for choice, iteration and concurrency (Fig. 2).

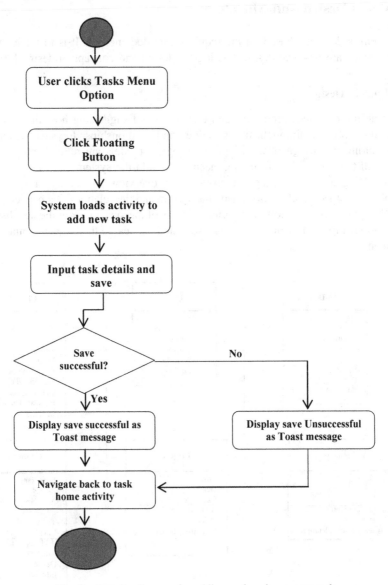

Fig. 2. Activity diagram for adding and saving a new task

Sequence Diagram: The sequence diagram is used primarily to show the interactions between objects in the sequential order that those interactions occur [24]. Figure 3 shows the sequence diagram for a user saving a task and deleting a task respectively.

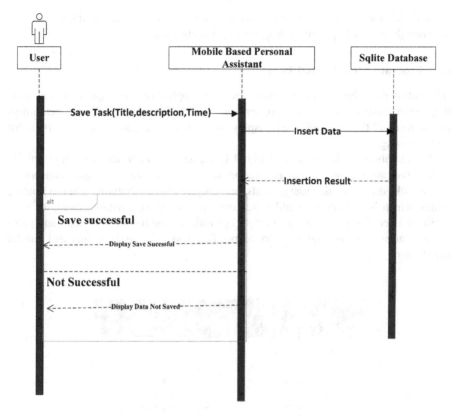

Fig. 3. Sequence diagram for user saving a task

6   System Implementation

The student personal digital assistant has been designed with material design guidelines which one of its sayings is "having a simple interface is important". According to Google, elegant, usable, highly rated apps also have simple user interfaces.

6.1   Implementation Tools Used

Android studio is the tool used for the development and deployment of the application. Android java and XML (extensible markup language) being the main programming languages used. Android java, which is object oriented, is for the functionalities and logic while XML was used for the design and presentation of the application.

SQLite [10, 11] is a portable version of the popular SQL database, unlike the server-client nature of the typical SQL database SQLite is used when a local, portable, lightweight database is needed. Therefore, it should be no surprise that a lot of android application use SQLite.

Android studio is free and very powerful, with its own device emulator, which is fast enough for development, debugging and testing purposes.

6.2 Program Modules and Interfaces

This section describes the various modules of the application. The application is made of different modules, which are independent of each other; the dashboard gets information from all these modules and displays it to the user in a summarized version for quick viewing.

The Dashboard: The diagram in Fig. 4 is the dashboard, which is the first activity the user sees after launching the application. It displays the status of things concerning the user, like due tasks, due assignments, and projects. On the bottom-right is a floating button, which is a shortcut to add task, assignment or project without using the navigation drawer. The dashboard is what sort of links all the modules together and gives the student summarized information of pending tasks due assignments and similar information.

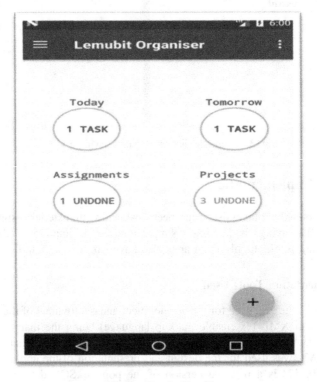

Fig. 4. The dashboard

The Navigation Drawer: Figure 5 which is the navigation drawer is the part of the user interface that displays available modules or functions of the application, the user just has to swipe right on the screen to open the navigation drawer and swipe left to close it, this enables and organised navigation with delightful motion.

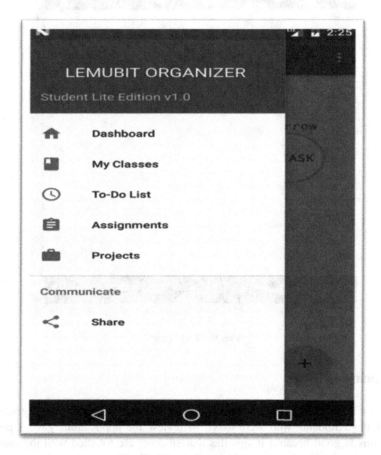

Fig. 5. The navigation drawer

To-Do List Module: This is where the student inputs their task for the day or future days. The student can go back to check saved tasks, the system notifies the student through a notification service when time is due for a particular task (Fig. 6).

Fig. 6. Task view

7 Conclusion

The student mobile personal assistant will aid the students in their day-to-day activities and planning. Students who were asked to review the applications gave a positive review; this is good because it signifies that students are satisfied with the functionalities and user interface. The material design guideline was used to give a nice look and feel to the application. More and even better improvements will be made to the application's future releases to include or remove features desired by students. Any student using such an application will be more productive than his or her peers, will have less things to think about and will be more organized.

In order for the system to be used effectively, students need to be adequately educated about the system and how to use it. Students should also be encouraged to use the application because a user cannot know how good a product is neither can he benefit from it if he has not used it. For best experience, students should use android marshmallow for the performance and beautiful aesthetics.

Acknowledgement. We acknowledge the support and sponsorship provided by Covenant University through the Centre for Research, Innovation and Discovery (CUCRID).

References

1. Chen, M., Lin, M., Wang, C., Chang, A.C.: Use HCA and TOPSIS approaches in PDA memo-icon interface design. Int. J. Ind. Ergon. **39**, 689–702 (2009)
2. Pauline, E.J., Goran, I.P., Gunilla, C.N.: Nursing students' experience of using a personal digital assistant (PDA) in clinical practice – an intervention study. Nursing Educ. Today **33**, 1246–1251 (2013)
3. McCarthy, M.: The Daily American Planner (2013). https://www.bostonglobe.com/ideas/2013/06/01/the-daily-planner-american-history/WncDRG5hq7B9m0w3cE5jkM/story.html. Accessed 20 Nov 2017
4. Ray, B., McFadden, A., Patterson, S., Wright, V.: Personal digital assistants in the middle school classroom: lessons in hand. Meridian – Middle Sch. Comput. Technol. J. (2010). http://www.ncsu.edu/meridian/sum2001/palm/index.html. Accessed 22 Nov 2017
5. Ikegune, D.O., Abiola, A.O.: Computer self-efficacy and perceived ease-of-use of personal digital assistants for academic activities by undergraduates in University of Ibadan. Libr. Philos. Pract. (e-journal) 1457 (2016)
6. Sanne, A., Renee, F.: The use of personal digital assistants as tools for work-based learning in clinical internships. J. Res. Technol. Educ. **43**(4), 325–341 (2011)
7. Trish, C., Dagmara, C.: Personal digital assistants usage among undergraduates medical students: exploring trends, barriers and the advent of smartphones. J. Med. Libr. Assoc. JMLA **98**(2), 157–160 (2010)
8. Karen, G.C., Francisco, E., Ricardo, E.V., Khai, N.T.: Barriers to acceptance of personal digital assistants for HIV/AIDS data collection in Angola. Int. J. Med. Inf. **80**, 579–585 (2011)
9. Pauline, E.J., Goran, I.P., Gunilla, C.N.: Personal digital assistant with a barcode reader – a medical decision support system for nurses in home care. Int. J. Med. Inf. **79**, 232–242 (2010)
10. Logan, P., Collins, S.: PDA survey of medical residents: ebooks before e-mail. J. Can. Health Libr. Assoc. **30**(1), 3–10 (2009)
11. Myles, B.S., Ferguson, H., Hagiwara, T.: Using a personal digital assistant to improve the recording of homework assignments by an adolescent with Asperger syndrome. Focus Autism Dev. Disabil. **22**, 96–99 (2007)
12. Treadwell, I.: The usability of personal digital assistants (PDAs) for assessment of practical performance. Med. Educ. **40**, 855–861 (2006)
13. Viken, A.: The History of Personal Digital Assistants 1980–2000. Agile Mobility (2009). Accessed 18 July 2015
14. Joaquin, A.B., Cohen, T., Rodriguez, P., Kim, J., Fraser, H.S.: Personal digital assistant (PDA) to collect tuberculosis bacteriology data in Peru. Int. J. Infect. Dis. **13**(2009), 410–418 (2009)
15. Campbell, J.K., Ortiz, M.V., Ottalini, M.C., Birch, S., Agrawal, D.: Personal digital assistant (PDA)-based self-work sampling study of pediatric interns quantifies workday and educational value. Res. Pediatr. Educ. **17**(3), 289–295 (2017)
16. Elsayed, T.M., Jamshed, S.Q., Elkalimi, R.M.: The use of medical and drug information software programs for personal digital assistant among pharmacy students in a Malaysian Pharmacy School. Curr. Pharm. Teach. Learn. **7**(2015), 484–491 (2015)
17. Chen, Y., Chiu, H., Tsai, M., Chang, H., Chong, C.: Development of a personal digital assistant-based wireless application in clinical practice. Comput. Methods Programs Biomed. **85**(2007), 181–184 (2007)
18. Sommerville, I.: Software Engineering, 9th edn, p. 82 (2011)

19. Post, A.: System Analysis and Design. Lecture, University of Kentucky (2015)
20. UML Structural Models. http://www.sparxsystems.com/enterprise_architecture_user_guide/9.3/standard_uml_models/structuraldiagrams.html. Accessed 21 Nov 2017
21. SQLite Database. https://www.sqlite.org/about.html. Accessed 21 Nov 2017
22. Vetter, D.J., Kumar, P.D.: Overview of System Analysis & Design (2011). http://download.nos.org/cca/ccal.pdf. Accessed 02 Dec 2017
23. Roth, R.M., Dennis, A., Wixom, B.H.: System Analysis and Design, 5th edn, p. 13 (2012)
24. The sequence diagram. http://www.ibm.com/developerworks/rational/library/3101.html. Accessed 21 Nov 2017

Multilayer Based Improved Priority Scheduling Algorithm in Cloud Environment

Soumen Swarnakar[✉], Chandan Banerjee, Kaushal Kishor Bharti,
and Aditya Prabhakar

Department of Information Technology, Netaji Subhash Engineering College,
Kolkata, India
soumen_swarnakar@yahoo.co.in,
chandanbanerjee1@gmail.com, iamkaushal70@gmail.com,
haditya57@gmail.com

Abstract. Load balancing is one of the big challenges nowadays in cloud computing environment. End users requests distribute the load dynamically across multiple nodes. Load balancing among different virtual machines of different distributed system is very much important to improve efficiency in resource utilization. In this paper a Multi layer based load balancing approach has been proposed where traffic of incoming requests is managed using improved priority scheduling algorithm in multiple level of controlling while balancing the loads of different virtual machines in different clusters or data centers. Expected response time finding of each job to virtual machine and comparing the average response time with the existing algorithms of cloud load balancing has been discussed in this paper. The process of multilayer based approach for balancing load among all the virtual machines starting from dynamic load balancer and managed by Local cluster Scheduler (LCS), is better than existing load balancing algorithms has been shown in this paper.

Keywords: Cloud computing · Load balancing ·
Multilayer based cloud computing · Round robin

1 Introduction

In cloud computing environment, network based distributed computing happens providing three types of services like Infrastructure as a Service (IaaS), Platform as a Service (PaaS) and Software as a Service (SaaS). In cloud computing two things can be considered, one is client and second is service provider. Client send request to a cluster of distributed system which is a service provider and which can compute the request of client and replied back to client. Different user requested jobs need different execution time, so different virtual machines will not execute the requested job in same time. As a result, balancing the load among different virtual machines of different clusters of service providers for the coming requests is a challenging issue in cloud computing. By means of load balancing utilization of resources of different clusters of service providers, the requests can get response in less time, so throughput is also improved.

J. K. Mandal et al. (Eds.): CICBA 2018, CCIS 1031, pp. 29–39, 2019.
https://doi.org/10.1007/978-981-13-8581-0_3

As internet users are increasing day by day, so to respond the users request either the capacity of the servers should be increased or efficient load balancing among the servers are required, which can reduce response time, completion time of the incoming requests or jobs.

In cloud computing large scale of users are involved to get processed their requests through the available resources or virtual machines. Load balancing among different virtual machines can be done in two ways: first one is to distribute the tasks among different virtual machines at a time and the other one is to distribute the tasks among different virtual machines by monitoring their load and capacity. So, dynamically balancing load among virtual machines is a challenging issue now days. Therefore, it is the important task to design a dynamic load balancer architecture to send the user requests to available virtual machines in efficient way, so that no virtual machine is overloaded or under loaded condition.

In this paper, multilayer based improved priority scheduling has been used where priority of users requests are considered as well as the load of the virtual machines are also considered to improve the efficiency of the cloud system through the use of various data structure in multiple levels. The main objective of the proposed algorithm is to balance the load among different clusters' virtual machines. Here, dynamic load balancer takes the decision to send incoming requests or jobs to a particular LCS according to the load of the all LCS. On the other hand, the LCS sends the requests to an idle virtual machine in that cluster according to the priority of the job.

This paper is divided into 5 sections. Second and third section covers the related work and proposed multilayer based improved priority scheduling algorithm for load balancing in cloud computing respectively, whereas forth section covers experimental results with analysis and at last Conclusion and future scope has been discussed.

2 Related Works

In this section the related work has been discussed based on priority based load balancing technique.

Jain et al. [1] proposed a multi stage load balancing technique (MSLBT) by combining join idle queue and join shortest queue approach. Here, a two level scheduler for load balancing in cloud environment has been proposed by integrating Join Shortest Queue approach and Join Idle Queue approach. Here, no priority of jobs has been considered. Alworafi et al. [2] described an improved SJF scheduling algorithm (ISS) in cloud computing environment. In this paper, the main idea of the modified Shortest Job First is to sort the tasks in an ascending order based on the task length and calculate the average of all the tasks length. Then for all tasks the algorithm checks each task length, if it is less than the average of tasks length and number of tasks in VM1 less than the number of tasks in VM2, then the task will be sent to VM1, else to VM2. Wang and Casale [3] proposed an algorithm for evaluating Weighted Round Robin Load Balancing for Cloud Web Services, where focus was given in particular on algorithms based on closed queuing networks for multi-class workloads, which can be used to describe application with service level agreements differentiated across users. Shaw and Singh [4] have done a survey on scheduling and load balancing techniques in cloud computing environment. Here, discussion on different algorithms on load balancing in cloud environment has been proposed to resolve the issue of load balancing and task scheduling. Here, some of the shortcomings for further development have been proposed. VM migration issues involved in load balancing are also described briefly. James et al. [5] proposed an efficient VM load balancing algorithm for a cloud computing environment, where firstly analysis of different Virtual Machine (VM) load balancing algorithms is done. Secondly, a new VM load balancing algorithm has been proposed and implemented for an IaaS framework in simulated cloud computing environment using CloudSim tools for load balancing among the available virtual machines in different data centers to achieve better performance parameters such as response time and Data processing time. Bryhni et al. [6] showed the comparison and evaluation of different load balancing algorithms for scalable Web servers. Here, various queuing models were introduced to address this problem based on waiting queues models for each broker in the cloud system which can increase performance of system, reducing the average queue length and waiting time than the traditional approach of having only one server. Domanal et al. [7] presented a novel VM-assign load balancing algorithm which allocates the incoming requests to the all available virtual machines in an efficient manner and the performance is analyzed using Cloudsim simulator and compared with existing Active-VM load balance algorithm. Dam et al. [8] proposed an ant colony based load balancing algorithm to balance load by searching under loaded cloud nodes using imitating behavior of ant colonies. Shen [9] described a Resource Intensity Aware Load balancing method to reduce significantly the time and cost to achieve load balance and also the method was proposed in a cloud that migrates Virtual machines from overloaded physical machines to lightly loaded Physical machines. Milani et al. [10] presents a literature review of existing load balancing techniques proposed and depending on different criteria analysis of the existing techniques have been done. Also, some important challenges have been discussed for developing more efficient load balancing techniques. Dhinesh et al. [11] proposed an algorithm based on honey bee behavior which also balances the priorities of tasks on the machines where total waiting time of the tasks in the queue is minimal. In our proposed algorithm, a comparison has been done with existing load balancing and scheduling algorithms, which shows dropping of waiting time of tasks in queue.

3 Proposed Algorithm

Jain et al. [1] considered queue length of each local cluster, where as a job execution time of a task cluster centers is higher in a queue, then it would have not given a productive result. To overcome this problem, we have introduced that the job burst time has been considered in the queues of different cluster LCS (Local Cluster

Scheduler). Alworafi et al. [2] have considered the burst time of the jobs but priorities of jobs have not been considered. In this paper, LCS has been considered as cloud centers of each cluster. So when the jobs have been arrived to the dynamic load balancer then the jobs are stored in the priority queue of dynamic load balancer. Dam et al. [8] used random searching algorithm, which has been obtain more time to search Idle virtual machines in a LCS.

We have introduced dynamic load balancer with two data structure, one is priority queue and another is an array LS [1…n] containing the load status of every LCS. Here, load status means total burst time requirement of all the job requests coming to each LCS in a particular time. Subsequent to that in consultation with the array holding the load status of each LCS in dynamic load balancer, the decision would be taken by the dynamic load balancer to allocate the incoming jobs to a specific cluster LCS which has shortest total burst time of all the jobs which are already allotted in different virtual machines.

In LCS for a particular cluster, there is also a priority queue and an array AVM[1… m] for containing the list of allocated virtual machines with their burst time. It helps dynamic load balancer to show load status of that particular LCS which is executing number of jobs with specific burst time. Here, in LCS one queue named IVM[1..m] is considered to hold all idle virtual machines. It assists LCS to search the idle virtual machine very fast and allocation of a job to a specific virtual machine. The searching time of virtual machine is very less because of getting idle virtual machines from IVM [1..m]. So, when a virtual machine would be idle after completion of execution, it will be added from AVM[1..m] to array IVM[1..m] to give service to incoming requests. So, waiting time and response time of the incoming jobs would be lesser than the existing algorithms. The terms waiting time, response time and turnaround time and load balance percentage for the proposed algorithm have been discussed below:

Response Time: Response time is the time involved in getting first response from the virtual machine after arrival in dynamic load balancer, which will start execution of user requested job.

Response time of n tasks T_R can be described as follows:

$$T_R = \sum_{i=1}^{n}(R_i - A_i), \text{ here no of task i} = 1…n.$$

Now average response time for n tasks is as follows:

$T_{AR} = \frac{T_R}{n}$, Here T_{AR} is the average Response time of n tasks.
R_i is first response of a virtual machine to a task i.
A_i is arrival time in Dynamic load balancer of a task i.

Waiting Time: The time involved by a process in waiting state of the priority queues in dynamic load balancer and time involved in the priority queue of LCS after arrival In specific cluster.

Waiting time of n tasks T_{WT} can be described as follows:

$T_{WT} = \sum_{i=1}^{n}(PQ_i + LCS_i)$, here no of task i = 1...n.

Now average waiting time for n tasks is as follows:

$T_{AWT} = \frac{T_{WT}}{n}$, T_{AWT} is the average waiting time for n tasks.

PQ_i is waiting time of a task i in priority queue in dynamic load balancer until the task is allotted to specific LCS and LCS_i is the waiting time of that task i in a specific LCS for allocation in a virtual machine.

Here, $PQ_i = AL_i - A_i$, where AL_i is the allotment time in a specific LCS and A_i is the arrival time in dynamic load balancer of a particular task i.

$LCS_i = AV_i - ALCS_i$, where AV_i is the allotment time of a task i in a specific virtual machine and $ALCS_i$ is the arrival time of that task i in LCS of a particular cluster.

Turnaround Time: It is the time taken to complete execution of a job through specific virtual machine after arrival in dynamic load balancer.

Turn around time of n tasks T_{TA} can be described as follows:

$T_{TA} = \sum_{i=1}^{n}(C_i - A_i)$, here no of task i = 1...n.

Now average turn around time for n tasks is as follows:

$T_{ATA} = \frac{T_{TA}}{n}$, T_{ATA} is the average turn around time for n tasks.
C_i is completion time of a task i after execution of a virtual machine.
A_i is arrival time of a task i in Dynamic load balancer.

Load Balance Percentage: As the array AVM[m] is holding jobs with burst time in a specific LCS, it can help to calculate the load balance percentage.

Let, total burst time difference between each pair of LCS would be as follows:

$\sum_i^p L_i - \sum_j^q L_j$, where $\sum_i^p L_i$ and $\sum_j^p L_j$ are total burst times of LCS_i and LCS_j, if there are p and q number of tasks are currently running respectively.

So, average burst time length difference of possible n_{c_2} different pair of LCS would be as follows:

$S = \frac{\sum_i^p L_i - \sum_j^q L_j}{n}$, where n is total number of LCS in cloud.

Here load balance percentage would depend upon minimum value of S calculated among different cloud load balancing algorithms results best load balanced in different virtual machines of different LCS.

Load Balance percentage = (100-S)%.

The procedural flow of multilayer based improved priority scheduling algorithm for load balancing is shown in Fig. 1.

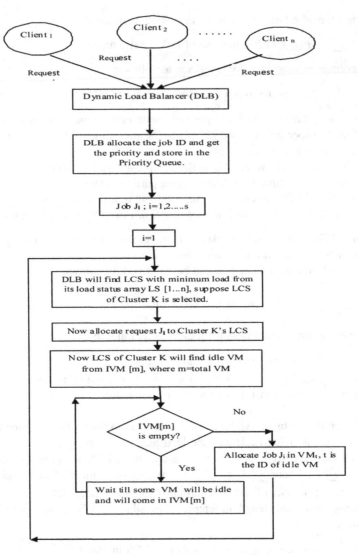

Fig. 1. The procedural flow of multilayer based improved priority scheduling algorithm for load balancing

4 The Proposed Methodology of Load Balancing

The proposed structure of load balancing is shown in Fig. 4. The methodology of balancing load among different virtual machines of different LCS is described below:

1. Here the dynamic load balancer has two data structure shown in Fig. 2, one is priority queue holding different jobs like J1, J2 etc. and another is an array LS [1...n] containing the load status of every LCS for n set of cloud clusters. Here load

status means total burst time requirement of all the job requests coming to each LCS. In Fig. 2, T1, T2…Tn are the total burst time of each LCS.

2. In each LCS, there is also a priority queue holding different jobs like J1, J2 etc. and two arrays, array of allocated virtual machines and array of idle virtual machines. Array of allocated virtual machines AVM[m] which basically holds the burst times of allotted jobs. On the other hand array of idle virtual machine IVM[m] which basically hold the IDs of idle virtual machines in a specific cluster as shown in Fig. 3.

3. When the request comes to Dynamic load balancer, it would have allocated an id of that request and verifying the priority of the request, it has been set a priority id for each request. It holds these requests in a priority queue until allocation into a virtual machine is done.

4. After that in consultation with the array holding the load status of each LCS of dynamic load balancer and priority of the incoming job, the dynamic load balancer have to take the decision to allocate the incoming jobs to a specific cluster LCS which has shortest total burst time of all the jobs already allotted from AVM[m] of that LCS, where AVM[m] is list of allocated virtual machine list. After allocation of job to a particular LCS, dynamic load balancer stops the access from priority queue of itself.

5. Now the specific LCS has been allocated the job to a specific Virtual machine according to the priority of jobs which are there in priority queue and availability of idle virtual machines hold in IVM[m] where m is total number of virtual machines. Suppose Job J_i is allocated in Virtual machine VM_t. Therefore, that virtual machine entry will be removed from the queue IVM[m] and listed in allocated virtual machine list AVM[m]. When a virtual machine will complete execution of a particular job, then the ID of that virtual machine would be enlisted in the array IVM [1..m].

6. After allocation of a request id to a particular virtual machine of a cluster, LCS would eliminates that request id or job id entry form the priority queue of itself.

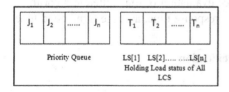

Fig. 2. Data structure of dynamic load balancer

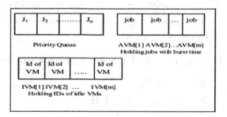

Fig. 3. Data structure of LCS

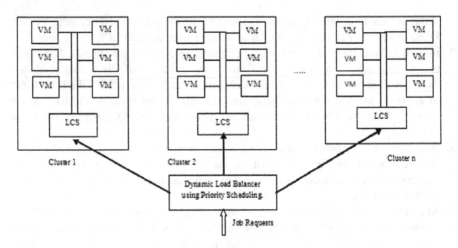

Fig. 4. Proposed structure of cloud load balancing

5   Experimental Results

CloudSim is an abstract cloud computing environment using java language used to experiment proposed algorithm. The experiments are implemented on the incoming requests to the dynamic load balancer with five datacenters with 50 VMs and 500 tasks of different burst time. Here, response time of a particular job has been calculated by the first response by a virtual machine in a cluster and turnaround time of a particular job has been calculated after completion of execution. Average response time, average turnaround time and average waiting time for all the incoming tasks are calculated and compared with existing load balancing algorithm described in the algorithm by Jain et al. [1] (MSLBT), algorithm by Alworafi et al. [2] (ISS), FCFS and RR algorithm. In this experiment it has been shown that the average response time for the incoming tasks and the average turnaround time for them showing better than other existing algorithms. Graphs are plotted for the performance evaluation of four different algorithms on the basis of experimental result for average response time, average turnaround time and average waiting time.

Data Center or LCS Virtual Machine Specification:

RAM = 1 GB
Storage quota = 5 GB
Architecture = x86
Operating system = Linux

The result of average response time, average waiting time, average turnaround time and load balance percentage using the existing algorithms MSLBT, ISS, FCFS, RR and with the algorithm proposed here have been shown in Table 1.

Table 1. Result of five algorithms on the basis of avg. response time, average waiting time and average turnaround time

Algorithm	Average response time (s)	Average turn around time(s)	Average waiting time (s)	Load balance percentage in all LCS
MSLBT	0.75	4.24	0.62	85.6
ISS	1.35	5.70	1.75	65.4
FCFS	2.13	7.22	2.14	57.8
RR	1.16	4.12	1.84	83.2
Proposed	0.45	3.47	0.54	96.7

The graphical representation of the above table is shown in Figs. 5, 6, 7 and 8. Average response time, average turnaround time, average waiting time for the tasks of the proposed algorithm showing better than all the algorithms compared with. It is also seen that load balancing percentage using proposed algorithm is also showing better than other existing algorithms used here. The experimental result of proposed algorithm is showing better result as multi layer approach has been considered for taking the decision for allocating requests or jobs to different idle virtual machines and as priority of the jobs have also been considered. So, all the jobs according to their priority are scheduled to idle virtual machines in a specific cluster.

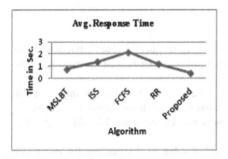

Fig. 5. Avg. response time of different algorithms

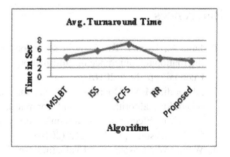

Fig. 6. Avg. turnaround time of different algorithms

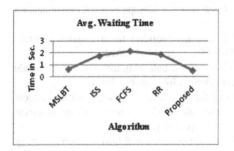

Fig. 7. Avg. waiting time of different algorithms

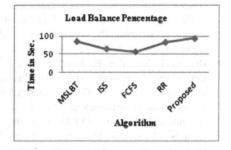

Fig. 8. Load balance percentage in all LCS using different algorithms

6 Conclusion

In this paper a multilayer based improved priority scheduling algorithm in cloud environment has been discussed for load balancing among the LCS or data centers. Objective of the proposed algorithm was to schedule the incoming jobs in a cloud environment in an efficient way to minimize expected average response time comparing with the existing cloud load balancing algorithms. As dynamic load balancer in first layer sends job requests to a LCS which has comparatively less load and as each LCS uses two different array consisting of a list of allocated virtual machines and a list of idle virtual machines, searching time for a idle virtual machine will take very less time in that LCS. Therefore, waiting time of jobs is showing less using this proposed approach, as shown in experimental result. As total burst time of the jobs are considered for load measuring of different LCS, it helps to dynamic load balancer to send the incoming requests to a particular cluster LCS or data centers with minimum load and as priority of tasks are considered, that's why the response time or waiting time become lesser for the priority jobs. So the average waiting time, average turnaround time, average response time for the incoming jobs are also becoming lesser. As scheduling in multilayer approach always considers load balancing started from dynamic load balancer through LCS of each cluster to all Virtual machines, the load balancing in this cloud environment system showing better results compared to existing cloud load balancing algorithms discussed here.

References

1. Jain, A., Kumar, R.: A multi stage load balancing technique for cloud environment. In: International Conference on Information Communication and Embedded Systems (ICICES), Chennai, pp. 1–7 (2016)
2. Alworafi, M.A., Dhari, A., Al-Hashmi, A.A., Darem, A.B., Suresha: An improved SJF scheduling algorithm in cloud computing environment. In: International Conference on Electrical, Electronics, Communication, Computer and Optimization Techniques (ICEEC-COT), Mysuru, pp. 208–212 (2016)
3. Wang, W., Casale, G.: Evaluating weighted round robin load balancing for cloud web services. In The 16th International Symposium on Symbolic and Numeric Algorithms for Scientific Computing, Timisoara, pp. 393–400 (2014)
4. Shaw, S.B., Singh, A.K.: A survey on scheduling and load balancing techniques in cloud computing environment. In: The International Conference on Computer and Communication Technology (ICCCT), Allahabad, pp. 87–95 (2014)
5. James, J., Bharma, B.: Efficient VM load balancing algorithm for a cloud computing environment. Int. J. Comput. Sci. Eng. (IJCSE) 4(9), 1658–1663 (2012)
6. Bryhni, H., Klovning, E., Kure, O.: A comparison of load balancing techniques for scalable web server. IEEE Netw.: Mag. Glob. Internetworking 14(4), 58–64 (2000)
7. Domanal, S.G., Reddy, G.R.M.: Optimal load balancing in cloud computing by efficient utilization of virtual machines. In: The Sixth International Conference on Communication Systems and Networks (COMSNETS), Bangalore, pp. 1–4 (2014)
8. Dam, S., Mondal, G., Dasgupta, K., Dutta, P.: An ant colony based load balancing strategy in cloud computing. Adv. Comput. Netw. Inf. 2, 403–413 (2014)

9. Shen, H., Chen, L., Sapra, K.: RIAL: resource intensity aware load balancing in clouds. In: The Proceedings of IEEE INFOCOM 2014 - IEEE Conference on Computer Communications, Toronto, pp. 1294–1302 (2014)
10. Milani, A.S., Navimipour, N.J.: Load balancing mechanisms and techniques in the cloud environments: systematic literature review and future trends. J. Netw. Comput. Appl. **71**, 86–98 (2016)
11. Dhinesh, B.L.D., Krishna, P.V.: Honey bee behavior inspired load balancing of tasks in cloud computing environments. Appl. Soft Comput. **13**(5), 2292–2303 (2013)

Geomorphological Changes in Sundarbans Delta Using GIS and Remote Sensing Data

Krishan Kundu[1(⊠)] and Prasun Halder[2]

[1] Department of Computer Science and Engineering, Govt. College
of Engineering & Textile Technology, Serampore, Hooghly, India
`krishan_cse@rediffmail.com`
[2] Department of Computer Science and Engineering, Purulia Government
Engineering College, Purulia, West Bengal, India
`prasunhalder@gmail.com`

Abstract. The present study focus on the detection of shoreline changes of various islands of Sundarban during last 43 years (1975–2018) using remote sensing data and geographic information system (GIS). Five multi-spectral satellite data have been used to extract the shoreline. The study area connected with nine islands which are located extremely periphery on southern surface of the Sundarban and each of them dynamically changes their shorelines due to rising sea level, strong waves and wind blow over the surface. The outcomes indicates that shoreline along the sea surface or riverbank area has been changes. The changes are classified as erosion, accretion and unchanged or stable area. From the study, it is reported that each island area has been decreased during the period 1975–2018, while it was not uniform over the period. In the study, it is seen that more erosion has been taken place in compared with the accretion along the surface of each island. The most eroded and vulnerable islands are Jambudwip, Haliday and Bhagaduni island where more than 40% area has been eroded of each island during the period. Moreover, it reveals that the overall 68.28 km^2 area was eroded and erosion rate is 1.59 km^2 per year.

Keywords: Remote sensing and GIS · Erosion · Accretion ·
Shoreline change · Sundarban

1 Introduction

Sundarbans (India and Bangladesh) is the biggest continuous tidal halophytic mangrove [1] forest delta in the world. Its net areas reside by around 10,000 km^2. Among these areas 40% areas are present in India [2] and residual area are belongs to the Bangladesh region. It is the largest complex intertidal region where the three major rivers (Ganges, Brahmaputra and Meghna) accumulate the Bay of Bengal. It is delimited by the Hooghly River on the west, on the east Ichamati-Kalindi-Raimangal, on the south Bay of Bengal, on the north Dampier Hodge line. Out of 102 islands in Sundarban [3] region, 48 islands are reserved for forest and remaining island for the human settlement. The region also name as the leading halophytic development beside the shoreline. It was declare as biosphere reserve [4] by United Nations Educational

© Springer Nature Singapore Pte Ltd. 2019
J. K. Mandal et al. (Eds.): CICBA 2018, CCIS 1031, pp. 40–53, 2019.
https://doi.org/10.1007/978-981-13-8581-0_4

and Scientific Co-operation (UNESCO) and world heritage site by International Union for Conservation of Nature (IUCN) in 1989 and 1987 respectively. The present study area consists of nine islands which are Jambudwip, Lothian, Dhanchi, Bulchery, Haliday, Mayadwip, Bhagaduni, Machua and Baghmara island and all the islands are positioned extremely rim on the southern region of the Sundarban.

The change in climate [5] outcomes influence [6] by variation of magnitude such as changes in arctic temperature and ice, salinity of ocean, structure of wind, extensive change in rainfall amounts, and aspects of tremendous weather includes dearth, heavy rainfall, warm waves and intensity of clammy cyclones, shoreline changes and deluge of low lying areas. During the last century it was reported that sea level [7] has been raised by 1.7–1.8 mm/year while there is an absence of more precise regional scenarios. Over the last 100–150 years the sea level raises perhaps causatives to coastal erosion in several places of the Earth. The industrial movement such as rate of CO_2 emission [8] acceleration is hampered by the hazard of worldwide climate change. The experimental results shows that rapid growth in the mixing ratio of CO_2 concentration in the environment increased from 315 ppm in 1960 to around 390 ppm in 2010. The swift raise in CO_2 emissions experimental throughout the last 250 years is unspecified to persevere for numerous forthcoming decades and expected to make several hard impacts in our livelihood system.

Shoreline change analysis means changes in shoreline by obtaining the measuring distinction in past and present shoreline position through processes of erosion and deposition/accretion and it can be investigated by the geographic information system (GIS). Shoreline changes primarily depend on the some factor such as rise in sea level, high tides, and strong waves [9]. The main key factor to disturbing the coaster erosion [10] is the strength of wave where the waves are breaks along the coastline. Wave fetches and wind speeds are two parameters directly controlled by the strength of the wave. Larger fetches and stronger winds create larger, more powerful waves that have more erosive power. Tides are generated by the gravitational effect of the sun and moon. Waves are produced by storms, wind, or fast moving motor craft, etc. As outcomes coastal erosion happen this may take the elongated losses of sediment and rocks, or simply the momentary relocation of coastal sediments. Erosion in one site may consequence in deposition or accretion in other places. Current and waves [11] influence this movement of sediment, but changes in sediment levels, in twist, affect the currents and waves. Erosion affects the surrounds such as the declined of trees, submerge of forests, destruction from wind erosion, etc. Coastal erosion which may drain a way of coastal land or beaches is primarily caused by the impact of waves beside the shoreline. It also creates negative effects such as structural damage, degraded water quality and losses of property and habitat. Coastal erosion [12] may be prevent such as mangrove forest and other coastal vegetation density can trim down wave height noticeably and guard the coast from erosion, as well as effectively protect coastal sand dune shifting during sturdy winds. A latest study, which map the overall human affect on the seas for the first time has exposed that the scenario is very worse than the researchers or scientist expected. In recent studies shows that 40% of the world oceans have been seriously affected by human dealings including fishing, coastal development and population growth from shipping.

The change in shoreline [13] is chiefly associated with waves, tides, winds, an episodic storm, sea level varying, geomorphic processes [14] of erosion and accretion or deposition and manmade activities. Shoreline also depicts the recent development and destructions that have happened along the shore. Waves can vary the coastline morphology [15] and shapes the distinctive coastal landforms. The movable coarse sediments constantly respond to the ever-changing waves and currents. The seaside profile is significant, in that it can be viewed as effective natural machinery, which causes waves to split and scatter their energy. When breakwaters are constructed, they upset the natural balance between the sources of beach sediment and the littoral drift pattern. In response, shoreline changes [16] its configuration in attempt to reach a new stability. Monitoring changes in shoreline helps to identify the nature and processes that caused these changes in any specific area, to assess the human impact and to plan management strategies. Remote sensing data could be used effectively to monitor the changes along the coastal zone including shoreline with reasonable accuracy. Remote sensing data support and/or replaces the normal survey by its repetitive and less cost effectiveness and less time consume. Hence, in order to study the coastal progression or erosion in Sundarban region, the shoreline change, were analyzed using Remote Sensing data and GIS techniques.

Due to coastal erosion, declined fresh water supply and increased level of salinity of the water is endangered by the mangrove forest [17]. Mangrove ecosystem is characterized by the usual deluge of tidal water. The creation and the dynamic of this busted ecosystem is generally depends on supply of fresh water from inland area and tidal wave from the sea. The mangrove forest plays a key role to alter the universal temperature and rising sea level. The protection of coastal erosion [18] and balancing the ecological system are controlled by the mangrove forest or any other vegetation. Presently sea level rise measured at 3.24 mm/year that can terrorize to unbalance the Sundarban mangrove forest water forces. Whereas the change in waterline is very tiny, but change in a dynamic energy system can be a rigorous threat, which already happen periodic catastrophes in the region. The main objective of this study is to enumerate the scenery [19] and pattern of coastal erosion in the various islands in the Sundarban region. The decision makers or planners have to take measurement to survive land resources as well as mangrove forest of the Sundarban Delta.

2   Study Area

Sundarban is located in the district of south 24 paragana at West Bengal state in India. It lies between 21°27′06″ N to 21°50′18″ N latitude and 88°14′26″ E to 88°53′05″ E longitude. The area enclosed by Bay of Bengal on the south, on the east border line of India and Bangladesh, on the west river Ganga and on the north Dampier Hodge line. The present study area consists of nine islands and marked by circle which is shown in Fig. 1. The nine islands are Jambudwip, Lothian, Dhanchi, Bulchery, Haliday, Mayadwip, Bhagaduni, Machua and Baghmara. All islands are situated on the edge of south surface of Sundarban region and its areas (nine islands) are covered by about 323.72 km^2. The area is bounded with the almost entire reserve forest of the Sundarban with various flora and fauna. It has exists more than 27 mangrove species, 35 species of reptiles, 40 species of mammals and 260 bird species. Wildlife species found in the area include the Indian python, man-eating Royal Bengal tiger, sharks, spotted deer, crocodiles, macaque monkey and wild boar. Forests area constructs mainly three tree species like Sundri, Goran and Gewa. Other species that build up the forest crowd includes Avicenia, Xylocarpus, Sonneratia, Bruguiera, Rhizophora and Nypa palm. The area experiences exceptional ecological processes such as monsoonal rains, flooding, delta creation, tidal influence and mangrove immigration. Rainfall in the area is as high as 2800 mm, mostly during the monsoon season lasting from June to October. Storms, cyclones and tidal surges are relatively familiar throughout the Sundarban. In recently survey that one meter raise of sea level is expected to influence about 1000 km^2 area of the Sundarban region imperil rare floral and faunal species of Sundarban.

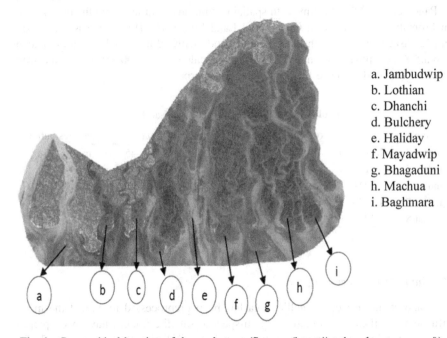

a. Jambudwip
b. Lothian
c. Dhanchi
d. Bulchery
e. Haliday
f. Mayadwip
g. Bhagaduni
h. Machua
i. Baghmara

Fig. 1. Geographical location of the study area (Source: (https://earthexplorer.usgs.gov/))

3 Material and Methodology

3.1 Data Source

In this article, five multi-temporal Landsat satellite image were collected from the earth explorer website (https://earthexplorer.usgs.gov/) which are freely available on the Internet. The details of Landsat satellite data information are presented in Table 1. From the table (Table 1), it is obviously observe that all the images were obtained more or less in the identical season. All the satellite data were cloud free and clear. Multispectral Scanner (MSS) sensor was get from Landsat 3 satellite and its four spectral bands includes green (0.5–0.6 μm), red (0.6–0.7 μm), near infrared (NIR) (0.7–0.8 μm) and near infrared (NIR) (0.8–1.1 μm) with spatial resolution is 60 m. Landsat Thematic Mapper (TM) sensor was obtained from Landsat 5 satellite and it consists of seven spectral bands namely blue (0.45–0.52 μm), green (0.52–0.60 μm), red (0.63–0.69 μm), near infrared (NIR) (0.76–0.90 μm), shortwave infrared 1 (SWIR1) (1.55–1.75 μm), thermal (10.40–12.50 μm) and shortwave infrared 2 (SWIR2) (2.08–2.35 μm) with spatial resolutions is 30 m excluding the thermal band. Landsat Enhanced Thematic Mapper plus (ETM+) sensor was carried on from Landsat 7 satellite and it exists of eight spectral bands such as blue (0.45–0.52 μm), green (0.52–0.60 μm), red (0.63–0.69 μm), near infrared (NIR) (0.77–0.90 μm), shortwave infrared 1 (SWIR1) (1.55–1.75 μm), thermal (10.40–12.50 μm), shortwave infrared 2 (SWIR2) (2.09–2.355 μm), and Panchromatic (.52–.90 μm) with spatial resolutions is 30 m except the thermal and panchromatic bands. Landsat Operational Land Imager (OLI) sensor was carried out from Landsat 8 satellite with nine spectral bands with 30 m spatial resolution except the band 8. A topographic map ((79 C/9) with scale of 1:50,000 were collected from survey of India which used for geo-referencing purpose.

Table 1. Details description of Landsat data

Satellite type	Sensor	No. of bands	Date of acquisition	Path and row	Spatial resolution
Landsat 3	MSS	4	05.12.1975	p-148, r-45	60 m
Landsat 5	TM	7	03.01.1990	p-138, r-45	30 m
Landsat 7	ETM+	8	17.11.2000	p-138, r-45	30 m
Landsat 7	ETM+	8	25.11.2010	p-137, r-45	30 m
Landsat 8	OLI	9	12.01.2018	p-138, r-45	30 m

3.2 Image Pre-processing

Five Landsat multispectral satellite data has been preprocessed to extract the meaningful and significant information. Multi-spectral satellite images have been preprocessed by the image processing software such as TNTmips Professional 2017. The images were geometrically corrected, radiometric calibration and drop lines or systematic striping or banding are removed from the collected images. Histogram equalization techniques are used for improving the quality of the image. The Discreet Fourier Transform (DFT) technique [20] was used to minimize the noise from 1978 image. If size of the image is M × N, the two-dimensional DFT is given by the following equation.

$$F(u, v) = \frac{1}{MN} \sum_{x=0}^{M-1} \sum_{y=0}^{N-1} f(x, y) e^{-j2\pi(ux/M + vy/N)} \tag{1}$$

where $u = 0, \ldots, M - 1, v = 0, \ldots, N - 1$ and f(x, y) is the image in the spatial domain and the exponential term indicates that basis function corresponding to each point F (u, v) in the Fourier domain. The noise was minimized at a level through Fourier analysis.

3.3 Methodology for the Present Work

Five multi-spectral satellite images have been collected from the earth explorer site for the year of 1975, 1990, 2000, 2010 and 2018. The images were geometrically corrected and radio-metric calibration operation performed by the TNTmips Professional 2017 software. Then, recognized the nine islands which are almost vulnerable, namely as Jambudwip, Lothian, Dhanchi, Bulchery, Haliday, Mayadwip, Bhagaduni, Machua and Baghmara island. A vector layer is created for each island and then digitized it. From every vector layer calculate the area of each island and compute the length of each island. For each island, two different vector layers (i.e. 1975–1990, 1990–2000, 2000–2010 and 2010–2018) are combined into a single vector layer. Each single vector layer contains two different year shoreline (i.e. 1975–1990) which are distinct by dissimilar color and produce the multiple polygons. Then, create a database and mark the status (increased or decreased area) of each island. Marking status (whether land covers areas has been increased or decreased) hold the database. Depending on the marking status (increased or decreased) select the appropriate polygon and mark it and assign the color for each status (increasing or decreasing) for each island. Erosion (mark by red color) and accretion (mark by green color) are represented which are shown from Figs. 3, 4, 5, 6, 7, 8, 9, 10 and 11. Figure 2 illustrates the methodology for the study area.

4 Results and Discussions

Digital shoreline of nine islands for five multi-spectral satellite images (1975, 1990, 2000, 2010, and 2018) is illustrates in this article. All islands are situated on the edge of southern surface of Sundarban region. Every island shoreline changes are not identical for various time intervals. From the Table 2, it is demonstrate that Jambudwip island land cover area has been declined during the period 1975–1990, while reverse trends was observed during 1990–2000, while declined trend seen since 2000. The net area is loss in this island from the year 1975 to 2018 is almost 39.66% and very tiny deposition or accretion is happen on the eastern surface of the island during the same period. Lothian island land cover area has been decreased during the era 1975–1990, whereas during the period 1990–2000 area has been increased and opposite trend is observed during the 2000–2018 episodes. The total area is lost by about 3.79% during the study period and most erosion is occurs on the southern surface of the island. The Dhanchi island is located on the edge of the Sundarban and its land cover area has been declined during the era 1975–1990, while land cover area are unchanged during the period 1990–2000, whereas area has been declined during the period 2000–2018. The net area is loss almost 3.85% during the era 1975–2018, but most of the erosion is happen on the southern surface of the island and deposition occur on the eastern surface of the island. Bulchery island is located on the extremely edge of the Sundarban region and its land cover area has been more eroded during the era 1975–1990, whereas its areas

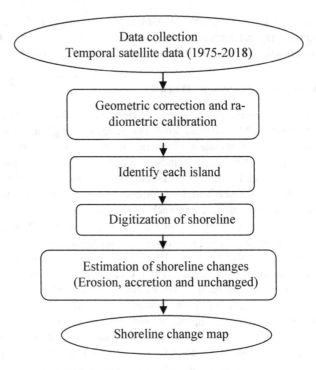

Fig. 2. Methodology for the study area

gradually declined from the year 1990 to 2018. It is also view that, some little deposition takes place during the period 1990–2000 on the surface of eastern, western and northern. The net area is loss 30.85% during the era 1975–2018 of this island.

Table 2. Different island area (km^2) of 1975, 1990, 2000, 2010 and 2018

Island	1975 Area (km^2)	1990 Area (km^2)	2000 Area (km^2)	2010 Area (km^2)	2018 Area (km^2)
a	7.01	5.87	6.37	4.39	4.23
b	35.89	33.80	37.32	35.90	34.53
c	37.88	35.49	35.29	33.95	36.42
d	30.30	26.58	25.44	22.36	20.96
e	3.18	2.28	1.72	0.58	0.19
f	79.89	71.90	68.17	62.04	60.16
g	42.83	37.38	31.04	25.30	22.88
h	19.58	19.16	18.88	17.74	17.58
i	67.17	63.31	62.09	59.86	58.50

The Haliday Island is situated alongside of the Bidyadhari River. It is a very little island in the Sundarban region. Its land cover area has been gradually decreased during the period 1975–2018. In this island, more erosion trend is seen during the period

1975–1990 and 2000–2010 on all around the surface. There is no deposition or accretion during the era 1990–2000 and 2000–2010. The net area is loss almost 94.03% during the period 1975–2018 and it is the most vulnerable island among them. The Mayadwip island is sited on the extremely edge of the southern surface of the Sundarban. Its land cover area has been more eroded during the period 1975–1990, while its land cover area gradually decreased during the period 1990–2018. The total land is loss almost 24.70% during the period 1975–2018, and more erosion is seen on the southern surface of this island and tiny deposition is happen during the same period on the eastern or western surface of the island. Bhangaduni island is situated on the extremely edge on the southern surface in the Sundarban. It is also the most vulnerable island and its land cover area has been declined during the period 1975–2018 on the southern surface, while small deposition take place during the period 1990–2000 and 2010–2018 on the north-east, north and north-west surface. The net erosion has been occurs about 46.58% during the period 1975–2018. Machua island is positioned on the edge of the southern surface in the Sundarban region and its land cover area almost equal during the 1975–1990 and 1990–2000, while more erosion has been observed during the period 2000–2010 and 2010–2018. More deposition has been seen during the period 1975–2000, but little accretion has been occurs during the period 2000–2018. The net area has been loss about 10.21% during the era 1975–2018. Baghmara island is situated extremely edge of the south surface of the Sundarban. Its land cover area has been more eroded during the period 1975–1990, but from the year 1990 to 2000 slightly decreased its land cover area. The tiny deposition is occurs during the period 1990–2000 on the eastern surface. The net area has been eroded about 12.91% during the period 1975–2018. Table 3 illustrates the erosion, accretion/deposition area for the period of 1975–1990, 1990–2000, 2000–2010, and 2010–2018. From Figs. 3, 4, 5, 6, 7, 8, 9, 10 and 11 illustrates that graphical representation of nine islands erosion area (red color), accretion area (green color) for the period of 1975–19990, 19990–2000, 2000–210, and 2010–2018. It is also clearly observe that (Fig. 12) Jambudwip (Fig. 12a), Bulchery Fig. 12d), Haliday (Fig. 12e), Bhagaduni (Fig. 12g) are the most eroded island and their erosion has been happen in the southern surface of each island.

Table 3. Erosion, accretion (km^2) of 1975–1990, 1990–2000, 2000–2010 and 2010–2018

Island	1975–1990 (km^2)		1990–2000 (km^2)		2000–2010 (km^2)		2010–2018 (km^2)	
	Erosion	Accretion	Erosion	Accretion	Erosion	Accretion	Erosion	Accretion
a	2.19	1.05	1.58	2.08	2.56	0.59	0.78	0.62
b	2.61	0.52	3.93	0.41	2.23	0.86	1.16	0.89
c	2.55	0.17	0.99	0.79	1.74	0.40	0.18	0.24
d	3.82	0.10	2.53	1.39	3.13	0.06	1.55	0.15
e	0.91	0.01	0.56	0	1.14	0	0.78	0.62
f	8.27	0.28	4.48	0.37	6.30	0.17	2.62	0.73
g	5.46	0.01	6.36	0.02	5.75	0.01	2.53	0.10
h	0.71	0.28	0.53	0.25	1.44	0.09	0.59	0.43
i	3.92	0.07	1.64	0.43	2.38	0.15	1.63	0.27

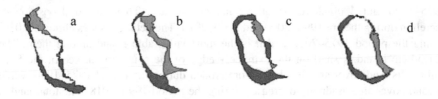

Fig. 3. Jambudwip island shoreline erosion and accretion of (a) 1975–1990 (b) 1990–2000 (c) 2000–2010 (d) 2010–2018 (Color figure online)

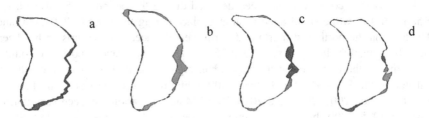

Fig. 4. Lothian island shoreline erosion and accretion of (a) 1975–1990 (b) 1990–2000 (c) 2000–2010 (d) 2010–2018 (Color figure online)

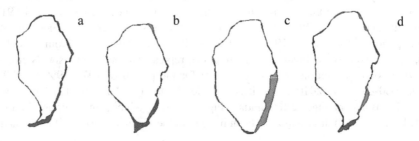

Fig. 5. Dhanchi island shoreline erosion and accretion of (a) 1975–1990 (b) 1990–2000 (c) 2000–2010 (d) 2010–2018 (Color figure online)

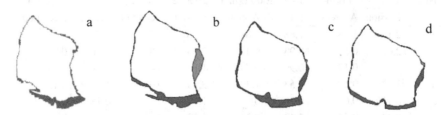

Fig. 6. Bulchery island shoreline erosion and accretion of (a) 1975–1990 (b) 1990–2000 (c) 2000–2010 (d) 2010–2018 (Color figure online)

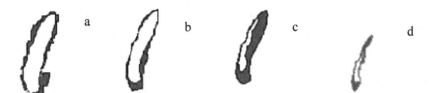

Fig. 7 Haliday island shoreline erosion and accretion of (a) 1975–1990 (b) 1990–2000 (c) 2000–2010 (d) 2010–2018 (Color figure online)

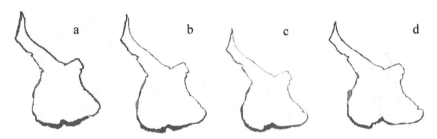

Fig. 8. Mayadwip island shoreline erosion and accretion of (a) 1975–1990 (b) 1990–2000 (c) 2000–2010 (d) 2010–2018 (Color figure online)

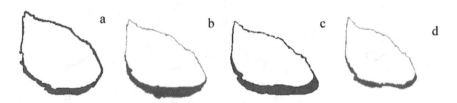

Fig. 9. Bhagaduni island shoreline erosion and accretion of (a) 1975–1990 (b) 1990–2000 (c) 2000–2010 (d) 2010–2018 (Color figure online)

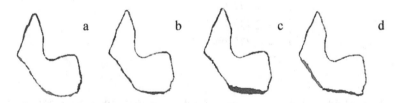

Fig. 10. Machua island shoreline erosion and accretion of (a) 1975–1990 (b) 1990–2000 (c) 2000–2010 (d) 2010–2018 (Color figure online)

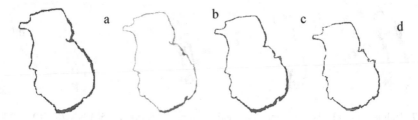

Fig. 11. Baghmara island shoreline erosion and accretion of (a) 1975–1990 (b) 1990–2000 (c) 2000–2010 (d) 2010–2018 (Color figure online)

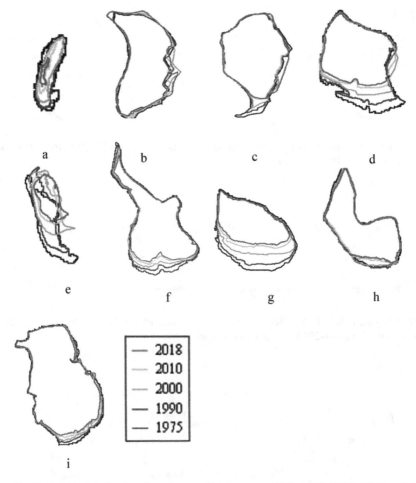

Fig. 12. Each island (a–i) shoreline changes for the year 1975, 1990, 2000, 2010 and 2018 (Color figure online)

Due to natural and human persuaded reason the pattern of the Sundarban islands has been changed constantly over the moment. The flat sandy coastal belts, deltaic estuarine low lying region in the Sundarban have been rigorously affected by natural processes includes lengthy shore current, macro tidal hurry, recurring cyclonic behavior, land subsidence, relative sea level rise etc. On the other side also affected by anthropogenic processes such as embankment formation, deforestation, unripe land renovation and bank dwellings etc. The both process have jointly prejudiced by the natural scenery of Sundarban region. The area chiefly its trivial parts have been strictly influence by the erosion process and salt water ingression. Coastal strap in the extreme southern parts, mainly low lying islands in the mouth reaches of the estuaries and exposed river banks of the Sundarban region have been severely eroded by the enormous tidal tires resulting regressive changes in the morphological outline and extent of the seashore pattern. During the period land loss becomes a significant natural crisis of this deltaic part of Sundarban region.

5   Conclusions

Remote sensing and GIS are efficient tools to control the dynamism of shoreline changes in the various islands in Sundarban region. Based on the investigation of multi-temporal satellite data over 43 years in the Sundarban deltas, it is examined that land cover area as well as mangrove forest area has been more eroded in compared with deposition of each island. From the study, it is seen that some island may be vanished after a long period. Jambudwip and Lothian island land cover areas has been declined during the era 1975–1990, whereas reverse trend is observed during the period 1990–2000, while it is also declined since 2000. Therefore, a few islands which has been almost vanished in the year of 1990, and it has been reappeared in the year of 2000. It indicates that at some places erosion happen, on the other side deposition or accretion is taken place. Jambudwip, Haliday and Bhagaduni are the most eroded islands due to their land cover area has been eroded more than 40% during the period 1975–2018 and those islands considered as vulnerable islands. The causes of erosion are high tidal tides, frequently occur storm, cyclones, longer strong waves, sea level rise, wind blow over the surface, etc. The medium vulnerable islands are Bulchery (30.83%), Mayadwip (24.70%), Machua (10.21%) and Baghmara (12.91%) because of their land cover areas has been eroded more than 10% during the era 1975–2018. The less eroded islands are Lothian (3.79%), Dhanchi (3.85%) and their land cover area has been decreased less than 10% during the study period. From the study it is shows that the southern region of the Sundarban delta has been more eroded radically as compared to the other side during the era 1975–2018. On the other hand, small deposition has been taken place in the eastern, western and northern region during the study period. Therefore, the decision makers or planners have to take measurement to survive the natural land cover resources as well as mangrove forest Delta in Sundarban region.

References

1. Danda, A.A., Sriskanthan, G., Ghosh, A., Bandyopadhyay, J., Hazra, S.: Indian Sundarbans delta: a vision, p. 40. World Wide Fund for Nature-India, New Delhi (2011)
2. Ghosh, A., Schmidt, S., Fickert, T., Nüsser, M.: The Indian Sundarban mangrove forests: history, utilization, conservation strategies and local perception. Diversity **7**(2), 149–169 (2015)
3. Gopal, B., Chauhan, M.: Biodiversity and its conservation in the Sundarban Mangrove Ecosystem. Aquat. Sci. **68**(3), 338–354 (2006)
4. Mukhopadhyay, S.K., Biswas, H., De, T.K., Sen, B.K., Sen, S., Jana, T.K.: Impact of Sundarban mangrove biosphere on the carbon dioxide and methane mixing ratios at the NE Coast of Bay of Bengal, India. Atmos. Environ. **36**(4), 629–638 (2002)
5. Raha, A., Das, S., Banerjee, K., Mitra, A.: Climate change impacts on Indian Sunderbans: a time series analysis (1924–2008). Biodivers. Conserv. **21**(5), 1289–1307 (2012)
6. Alongi, D.M.: The impact of climate change on mangrove forests. Curr. Clim. Change Rep. **1**(1), 30–39 (2015)
7. Michener, W.K., Blood, E.R., Bildstein, K.L., Brinson, M.M., Gardner, L.R.: Climate change, hurricanes and tropical storms, and rising sea level in coastal wetlands. Ecol. Appl. **7**(3), 770–801 (1997)
8. Ray, R., Jana, T.K.: Carbon sequestration by mangrove forest: one approach for managing carbon dioxide emission from coal-based power plant. Atmos. Environ. **171**, 149–154 (2017)
9. Purkait, B.: Coastal erosion in response to wave dynamics operative in Sagar Island, Sundarban delta, India. Front Earth Sci. China **3**(1), 21 (2009)
10. Bruun, P.: Sea-level rise as a cause of shore erosion. J. Waterways Harbors Div. **88**(1), 117–132 (1962)
11. Kaliraj, S., Chandrasekar, N., Magesh, N.S.: Impacts of wave energy and littoral currents on shoreline erosion/accretion along the south-west coast of Kanyakumari, Tamil Nadu using DSAS and geospatial technology. Environ. Earth Sci. **71**(10), 4523–4542 (2014)
12. Kaliraj, S., Chandrasekar, N., Magesh, N.S.: Evaluation of coastal erosion and accretion processes along the southwest coast of Kanyakumari, Tamil Nadu using geospatial techniques. Arab. J. Geosci. **8**(1), 239–253 (2015)
13. Mahapatra, M., Ratheesh, R., Rajawat, A.S.: Shoreline change analysis along the coast of South Gujarat, India, using digital shoreline analysis system. J. Indian Soc. Remote Sens. **42**(4), 869–876 (2014)
14. Bheeroo, R.A., Chandrasekar, N., Kaliraj, S., Magesh, N.S.: Shoreline change rate and erosion risk assessment along the Trou Aux Biches-Mont Choisy beach on the northwest coast of Mauritius using GIS-DSAS technique. Environ. Earth Sci. **75**(5), 444 (2016)
15. David, T.I., Mukesh, M.V., Kumaravel, S., Sabeen, H.M.: Long-and short-term variations in shore morphology of Van Island in gulf of Mannar using remote sensing images and DSAS analysis. Arab. J. Geosci. **9**(20), 756 (2016)
16. Misra, A., Balaji, R.: A study on the shoreline changes and LAND-use/Land-cover along the South Gujarat coastline. Procedia Eng. **116**, 381–389 (2015)
17. Hazra, S., Ghosh, T., DasGupta, R., Sen, G.: Sea level and associated changes in the Sundarbans. Sci. Cult. **68**(9/12), 309–321 (2002)
18. Maiti, S., Bhattacharya, A.K.: Shoreline change analysis and its application to prediction: a remote sensing and statistics based approach. Mar. Geol. **257**(1–4), 11–23 (2009)

19. Rahman, A.F., Dragoni, D., El-Masri, B.: Response of the Sundarbans coastline to sea level rise and decreased sediment flow: a remote sensing assessment. Remote Sens. Environ. **115** (12), 3121–3128 (2011)
20. Jain, A.K.: Advances in mathematical models for image processing. Proc. IEEE **69**(5), 502–528 (1981)

LDA Topic Modeling Based Dataset Dependency Matrix Prediction

Hindol Bhattacharya[1][✉], Arnab Bhattacharya[2], Samiran Chattopadhyay[1], and Matangini Chattopadhyay[1]

[1] Jadavpur University, Kolkata, India
hindolbhattacharjee12@gmail.com, samirancju@gmail.com, matanginic@gmail.com
[2] Indian Institute of Technology, Kanpur, India
arnabb@cse.iitk.ac.in

Abstract. Classification of text based datasets has many applications in the field of Computer Science. Some of the key application areas include scientific article recommendation, news article tagging, multimedia content search assistance, etc. We are interested in the problem of data placement of text based datasets in a distributed storage system. Distributed data placement entails placing related data together at a local site. Thus, classifying related data from the unrelated ones is a prerequisite for any such data placement system. Classification of datasets can be accomplished using information provided to the system about the relatedness of a pair of dataset. However, when such information are not available, the relatedness of pairs of dataset need to be inferred from content of the dataset itself. In literature, topic modeling has been used to find similarity between text documents and in classifying these documents according to the similarity between them. We intend to develop a novel classification system of text based datasets using topic modeling, as a precursor to a data placement scheme to be developed for distributed data storage system.

Keywords: Topic-modeling · Supervised learning · Dataset classification

1 Introduction

Intelligent placement of data in distributed storage system has direct impact on the performance of the task being run on such systems. An intelligent data placement scheme would ideally place all datasets required by a task at a local site. Such localized placement not only minimizes the execution stalls due to

Hindol Bhattacharya would like to thank the Department of Science and Technology, Ministry of Science and Technology, Govt of India for supporting this research work under DST-INSPIRE AORC fellowship scheme, vide number: DST/INSPIRE Fellowship/[160562] Dated: June 9, 2017.

© Springer Nature Singapore Pte Ltd. 2019
J. K. Mandal et al. (Eds.): CICBA 2018, CCIS 1031, pp. 54–69, 2019.
https://doi.org/10.1007/978-981-13-8581-0_5

non-availability of datasets, but also minimizes the latency and bandwidth consumption due to remote data migration. For such an intelligent data placement scheme to work, the system requires the following information:

- Task placement: Which tasks are being placed at which nodes.
- Dataset requirement per task: The list of datasets that are required by each task to complete its execution.
- Dependency of tasks on the output of another task: Sometimes one task may require the output dataset of another task as its input. A good task placement scheme would ensure that both the producer and consumer tasks are placed at the same site to prevent migration of the data. However, a discussion of task placement schemes is beyond the scope of this work.

Based on these information, the data placement system would calculate how each dataset is related to another dataset, which is measured by counting the number of tasks which require both the datasets. A data Dependency Matrix is calculated, which summarizes the relatedness between every pair of dataset in quantitative terms. The localized placement of datasets are based on how closely related the datasets are to each other. [13,16] are some of the influential works in literature which follow this data placement scheme.

Our work deals with cases where the above listed information may not be available; especially the information on the dataset requirement per task. Generally when no information is supplied to the system, the task-dataset requirements are learned by the system through the usage history of the dataset, available in system logs [13]. This approach works for datasets which has been used by tasks and hence has its usage history recorded in system logs. However, when a new dataset arrives or the system is in its initial state, no such information is available. It is in view of this scenario that we propose our topic modeling based intelligent classification system. Such a system would not require any externally supplied information for clustering the datasets; rather the content of the datasets themselves would be used for clustering and classification of such datasets.

Topic modeling (LDA) [3] using Latent Dirichlet Allocation has been used to extract latent topics from a corpus of documents. Such topic extraction has found applications in finding semantic similarity between documents; which in turn has been used to develop efficient recommender systems. Further, use of topic modeling based clustering of text documents has also been investigated in literature.

1.1 Motivation

In [13], the authors exploited the concept of interest locality to suggest that data are accessed as a group, with the all the data in the group being related to a common topic. If we introspect, we find that data accessed by a task indeed belong to a common topic. For example, consider a task launched by a high energy physicist, astrophysicist and micro-biologist each. In a broader context data accessed by high energy physicist and astronomer will have a common topic of physics; while data accessed by task launched by the microbiologist will concern biology related data. Again at a more granular level, data accessed by a task of high energy physicist and by astrophysicist will differ. This intuition suggests that datasets accessed by each task share a set of common topic. Hence, datasets could be classified by topic modeling and analysis.

Text based datasets allow them to be classified using topic modeling methods like Latent Dirichlet Allocation. Thus text based datasets could be classified using the topic modeling using the content itself without requiring additional task-dataset requirement information.

In this work we test whether we can use the topic modeling approach as the sole classification and clustering tool for text based datasets, without requiring any other information. We are given a group of datasets. Our proposed algorithm will aim to predict a Dependency Matrix based on the topic modeling based semantic analysis alone. We then proceed to test whether a Clustered Matrix, formed from the application of Bond Energy Algorithm to the Dependency Matrix, would cluster the datasets with reasonable accuracy. If topic based classification is able to categorize the datasets with acceptable accuracy; then such an approach could be used to propose a data placement algorithm, which would perform data placement in an information scarce system. Such data placement algorithm would not require any externally supplied information or access logs for it to work.

Our work is organized as follows. In section two, we briefly discuss the important works in literature related to the context. In section three, we discuss the important background concepts necessary to fully understand this work. This includes Latent Dirichlet Allocation (LDA), topic modeling using LDA, data placement, finding statistical distance between the two probability distributions and Bond Energy Algorithm. The dataset classification algorithm is discussed in section four. The performance of the developed system is discussed in section five. We conclude this work in section six with an outline on future research directions.

2   Related Works

The concept of Dependency Matrix based data placement has been explored in [16]. The data placement algorithm proposed in this work was aimed at scientific cloud workflows where tasks requiring datasets are executed in a cloud environment. Amongst the notable works in literature which further improved this work is by Wang et al. [13]. While Yuan et al. assumed that the relationship between tasks and their related dataset is provided by the user; Wang et al.'s work made no such assumption and inferred the relationship among datasets from the system logs. These two works are the basis of this work. Some other variations of this methods exists as in [15].

Data mining is an important technique for data and replica placement in grid based storage systems. Data mining approaches can be classified into three categories: 1. Association analysis, 2. Classification and regression and 3. Clustering analysis. Hamrouni et al. [7] and Slimani et al. [12] proposed a dataset (file in their terminology) correlation based technique which uses the file access history to mine for their maximal frequent correlated pattern. Association rule mining based approaches have been used for data placement in distributed systems. In the context of Map-Reduce based distributed system, ScadiBino [1] is a good example of the use of association rule mining based technique. Prediction and pre-fetching approaches are also very popular in the domain of data and replica placement. Algorithms such as the one proposed by Nagarajan et al. [9], PDDRA [11] are the key examples in this regard.

The concept of Latent Dirichlet Allocation has been proposed in [4]. The application of Latent Dirichlet Allocation for Topic Modeling has been proposed in [3]. The use of topic modeling and statistical distance for determining similarity among documents have been explored in [10]. [2] proposed a topic modeling based clustering of video courses by finding similarity of topics analyzed from the transcripts. Another interesting application is the use of topic models to recommend articles to users as proposed in [5].

3 Background Concepts

In order to fully appreciate this work, it is necessary to be familiar with the essential concepts that we have used in our work. In this section we discuss these important concepts.

3.1 Data Placement

The distributed storage system is made up of storage cum compute nodes distributed across a network. Each node of the system hosts a set of tasks; which executes certain analytics job on the dataset stored in the system to produce some insightful knowledge from the dataset. The nodes being storage nodes as well, stores datasets which are used by the tasks. Ideally nodes should store all the datasets that are required by the tasks placed on the same node. However, complete localization may not be possible due to practical reasons; resulting in some local datasets being placed remotely. A good data placement algorithm ensures maximum possible localization of datasets given the constraints.

Dependency Matrix Based Placement. The concept of Dependency Matrix based data placement was first introduced by Yuan et al. [16]. The concept due to its simplicity and effectiveness has since been widely adopted. Here we briefly explain the working principle of the data placement scheme.

Consider a system with five datasets (ds_1 to ds_5) and five tasks ($Task\_1$ to $Task\_5$). Each tasks are dependent on a collection of datasets for it's execution. Let the dependency profile be as follows:

- $Task_1 = \{ds_1, ds_3\}$
- $Task_2 = \{ds_1, ds_2, ds_3\}$
- $Task_3 = \{ds_2, ds_4\}$
- $Task_4 = \{ds_2, ds_4, ds_5\}$
- $Task_5 = \{ds_5\}$

Using this basic information, we can create a list of tasks which are dependent on each dataset as given below:

- $ds_1.T_1 = \{Task_1, Task_2\}$
- $ds_2.T_2 = \{Task_2, Task_3, Task_4\}$
- $ds_3.T_3 = \{Task_1, Task_2\}$
- $ds_4.T_4 = \{Task_3, Task_4\}$
- $ds_5.T_5 = \{Task_4, Task_5\}$

Once we have the list of dependent tasks for each dataset, we can proceed to find the dependency between a pair of dataset. The dependency between datasets ds_i and ds_j is calculated as:

$$dependency_{ij} = Count(ds_1.T_1 \cap ds_2.T_2) \tag{1}$$

Thus dependency between datasets ds_1 and ds_2 is calculated as $dependency_{12}$ = Count($ds_1.T_1 \cap ds_2.T_2$) = 1, since only one task $Task_2$ is common between them. Similarly we can compute the dependency between all pair of dataset. These values compose the Dependency Matrix as shown in Fig. 1 below.

	ds1	ds2	ds3	ds4	ds5
ds1	2	2	1	0	1
ds2	2	3	2	0	1
ds3	1	2	3	1	1
ds4	0	0	1	1	0
ds5	1	1	1	0	2

Fig. 1. Dependency matrix

With the Dependency Matrix available, the system has enough information as to which datasets are closely related to the other. An intelligent data placement algorithm needs to utilize this information from the matrix to place highly related datasets locally and unrelated datasets remotely. The data placement algorithm computes the ideal placement using this Dependency Matrix as its input. When task dataset dependencies are not available, such dependencies needs to be mined or in the scenario presented in this paper, computed through semantic analysis of the content of the dataset.

3.2 Topic Model

Topics form the basis for many important decisions that we make in our life everyday. It is highly likely that the reader must have been recommended this article while searching for the topic of data placement or topic modeling. While reading through this article, the reader would notice that it has been divided into many sections. The sectional divisions are not random; rather each division concerns a specific topic of interest. A reasonably literate reader would deduce that the each of the sectional headings of this article deals with the topic that is elaborated in the contents.

While such processing of natural languages is an easy task for humans; computers need to employ sophisticated machine learning tools to analyze a document semantically. Topic modeling is a statistical method for discovering abstract topics from a given document. Latent Dirichlet Allocation is one of the most popular topic modeling methods available.

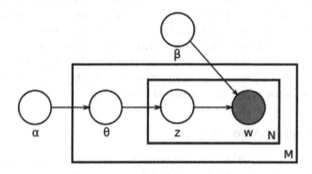

Fig. 2. Plate notation of Latent Dirichlet Allocation, from [14].

Latent Dirichlet Allocation. Latent Dirichlet Allocation is a generative statistical model of natural language processing used to find latent topics from a corpus of documents. It was first proposed by Blei et al. [4] Fig. 2 denotes the document generation model which shows how a words in a document are statistically generated from a known statistical distribution of topics. Each word is assumed to be generated as follows:

- Consider that there are K topics. β is the probability distribution for K topics.
- Find the probability of each topic. The proportion of topics in each document is given by parameter θ; which is derived in-turn from the parameter α.
- Using the above values find the probability of each word in the document using the parameter z, which denotes the per word topic assignment.

The process of computing the latent topics is just to backtrack the generative process. Here the words are already given to the system in the form of document corpus. The words are assumed to have been generated by the above generative model. The system backtracks the available words, and figures out which topics in what proportions could have led to the generation of the given words in the document. Thus, when a document is provided about animal care, the LDA system assumes that topics related to animals could statistically generate the given document.

3.3 Statistical Divergence and Distance

Latent Dirichlet Allocation is essentially a probability distribution of topics in a document corpus. In order to measure similarity of two document, we need to find how the two probability distributions are similar to each other. The similarity is indirectly measured from statistical divergence between the distributions. Statistical divergence is a measure of how two probability distributions are different from one another. A low value of statistical divergence means the probability distributions are similar, which in topic modeling context means that the two documents are similar in topic. A related concept of statistical distance is used when symmetric measure is needed; i.e in statistical distance difference between distributions q and p is same as difference between distributions p and q. We will use the Hellinger distance measure in this work as this has been shown to be appropriate measure for topic modeling purposes in [10]. Also, while discussing the algorithm, we will present our own argument for the utility of this measure rather than the non-symmetric statistical divergence.

3.4 Bond Energy Algorithm

Bond Energy Algorithm [8] has its roots in the concept of fragmentation in distributed database systems. In distributed database systems, the relation tables are fragmented vertically or horizontally, such that the fragments may be distributed across different sites in the distributed database system. An Attribute Affinity Matrix (AAM) is created which like the Dependency Matrix, explained above, represents the attribute affinity measure of two attributes. More the attribute affinity measure between a pair of dataset, it is more likely that these two attributes would be used in the query together. The AAM is given as an input to the Bond Energy Algorithm (BEA), which through repeated permutation of rows and columns of the matrix, attains a state such that the global affinity measure of the resulting matrix is maximized. The resulting matrix is known as the Clustered Affinity Matrix. The adjacent attributes in the resulting re-arranged rows or columns will be frequently used in the query.

In our work, the predicted Dependency Matrix will act as the Attribute Affinity Matrix. This Dependency Matrix will be given as input to the BEA to output a Clustered Matrix. The concept of attribute in distributed database system is replaced with the concept of dataset in our work, while the concept of query dependency is replaced with the concept of task dependency.

4   Algorithmic Solution

In this section we first discuss the problem that we intend to solve in this work. We follow up with the solution to the problem in the form of a prediction algorithm. To facilitate proper understanding of the algorithmic solution, an explanation of the working of the algorithm has been discussed as well.

4.1   Discussions of the Problem

Consider a distributed storage system, which stores a collection of text based dataset on which tasks would be executed. While the task is placed according to an appropriate task placement algorithm; the data placement is carried out using the Dependency Matrix based scheme, described in the section on background concepts above. However, when no information on the task-dataset requirement is available or when such relationship could not be determined from past access history; it becomes difficult to predict which type of tasks are likely to use the dataset. Intelligent data placement could not be made in such an information scarce situation. However, a random placement of the datasets is likely to incur performance penalties. It becomes necessary to predict a Dependency Matrix based on semantic analysis of the contents of the dataset alone.

4.2   Dependency Matrix Prediction Algorithm

Our problem requires us to predict the inter-dependency values between the new dataset and all pairs of datasets using semantic analysis. As we have discussed earlier, topic modeling could be used to classify and find similarity between text documents. Hence, the definition of inter-dependency between datasets needs to be re-defined. In our work we define inter-dependency between pair of dataset as follows:

Definition 1. *Inter-dependency between two datasets ds_i and ds_j is the probabilistic complement of the Hellinger distance between the topic distribution of the two datasets.*

Mathematically, for given Hellinger distance measure $stat\_dist_{ij}$ between datasets ds_i and ds_j, the inter-dependency between datasets ds_i and ds_j, $dependency_{ij}$ is given by the equation below:

$$dependency_{ij} = 1 - stat\_dist_{ij} \qquad (2)$$

The Hellinger distance between datasets ds_i and ds_j is calculated from the Eq. 3 as follows:

$$stat\_dist_{ij} = \frac{1}{\sqrt{2}} \sqrt{\sum_{i=1}^{T} \left(\sqrt{p_i} - \sqrt{q_i} \right)^2} \qquad (3)$$

where q and p are per topic probability for datasets i and j respectively.

With inter-dependency between all the dataset pairs have been computed we can represent them in terms of Dependency Matrix as described earlier. It should be noted here that in a Dependency Matrix, $dependency_{ij}$ should always be equal to $dependency_{ji}$. This would be only possible with the use of symmetrical statistical distance measure like Hellinger distance. Thus, we have used Hellinger distance rather than non-symmetric divergence measures like Kullback-Leibler divergence.

Training Phase. The proposed algorithm is given input of a set of training datasets. The training datasets comprises of individual text files which have been pre-processed to remove punctuations, infrequent words and short and long words. The preprocessing also involves converting all text to lower case and normalizing the words using Porter stemmer. It is to be noted that the pre-processing of the dataset is not part of the algorithm; rather it is used as a specification of the expected input to the algorithm. The algorithm creates a bag of words from the input training datasets and fits an LDA model on it. This comprises the training phase of our algorithm. The datasets used in this phase are the ones for which task-dataset relationships are available or could be inferred from the usage history. Thus, they are ideal for use as a labeled dataset for training part of the algorithm.

Prediction Phase. For prediction phase of our algorithm, a different set of processed datasets are input to the algorithm. From the trained LDA model, the topic distribution for each input test dataset is obtained. Datasets which are similar topically would have similar distribution of topics. Thus two datasets which deals with biology topic would exhibit high probability distribution for the topics related to biology, while having lower probability of topics related to astrophysics. The topic distribution for all the input datasets are measured and recorded in a distribution table. A Hellinger distance is calculated to record the statistical distance between every pair of dataset, according to Eq. 3. The topical similarity between the datasets is calculated by subtracting 1 from the statistical distance value; which according to our new definition is the inter-dependency between the datasets The algorithm in its final step summarizes the inter-dependency values between all pairs of datasets into a matrix called Dependency Matrix. The datasets used in the prediction phase are the new datasets for which no task-dataset relationship are available. These datasets are the ones which need to be placed using topic model based predictions.

Clustering. Once the Dependency Matrix is available, it needs to be re-arranged such that datasets with high dependency with each other are clustered together. We utilize the Bond Energy Algorithm, as suggested by [16], to achieve this objective. The resulting clustered dependency matrix can then be used for data placement according to the algorithms available in literature; as we envisage to do in our future work.

4.3   Algorithm Pseudocode

We present the algorithm pseudocode as Algorithm 1.

Algorithm 1. DependencyMatrixPrediction

1: **procedure** CALCULATEBEA
2:      $numTopics \leftarrow Number\ of\ topics$
3:      $trainSet \leftarrow Collection\ of\ text\ files\ for\ training$
4:      $testSet \leftarrow Collection\ of\ text\ files\ for\ prediction$
5:      $model \leftarrow TrainTopicModel(trainSet, numTopics)$
6:      $numTopicDistr[.] \leftarrow PredictTopicDistribution(model, testSet)$
7:      $stat\_dist_{ij}[.][.] \leftarrow CalculateStatDist(numTopicDistr[.])$
8:      $RearrangedMatrix \leftarrow BEA(stat\_dist_{ij}[.][.])$

9: **procedure** TRAINTOPICMODEL(trainSet,numTopics)
10:      $bagOfWords \leftarrow Extract\ each\ word\ from\ trainSet$
11:      $model \leftarrow LDA(bagOfWords, numTopics)$
12:      return model

13: **procedure** PREDICTTOPICDISTRIBUTION(model, testSet, numTopics)
14:      **while** $num(testSet) \neq 0$ **do**
15:          $numTopicDistr[.] \leftarrow Topic\ distribution\ for\ the\ test\ dataset$
16:          return numTopicDistr[.]

17: **procedure** CALCULATESTATDIST(numTopicDistr[.])
18:      **for** All elements in numTopicDistr[.] **do**
19:          $firstDistr \leftarrow each\ element\ of\ numTopicDistr[.]$
20:          **for** All elements in numTopicDistr[.] **do**
21:              $secondDistr \leftarrow each\ element\ of\ numTopicDistr[]$
22:              $stat\_dist_{ij}[.][.] \leftarrow Hellinger(firstDistr, secondDistr)$
23:              $dependency_{ij} = 1 - stat\_dist_{ij}[.][.]$
         return $dependency_{ij}$

24: **procedure** HELLINGER(firstDistr,secondDistr, numTopics)
25:      **for** every i in numTopics **do**
26:          $temp \leftarrow temp + \left(\sqrt{firstDistr_i} - \sqrt{secondDistr_i}\right)^2$
27:      $hellingerDist \leftarrow \frac{1}{\sqrt{2}}temp$
28:      $return\ hellingerDist$

Explanation of the Pseudocode. The algorithm consists of five procedures which performs five important tasks and subtasks of the algorithm as explained below:

- CalculateBEA: This is the main procedure from which other procedures are invoked as required. The algorithm's main purpose is to produce a clustered Dependency matrix such that it could be used by data placement algorithms.
- TrainTopicModel: The first procedure to be called by CalculateBEA. This procedure takes number of topics and collection of training data as inputs and is used to train a topic model using LDA.

- PredictTopicDistribution: The second procedure to be invoked by Calculate-BEA. This procedure takes the trained model, collection of new datasets and number of topics as input. The new datasets are the ones for which the inter-dependency values are to be computed. Probability distribution of all the topics as per the input number of topics is calculated for each dataset.
- CalculateStatDist: This procedure is used to invoke a procedure Hellinger, which calculates the Hellinger distance between all pair of dataset. This procedure accepts the result of the Hellinger distance and computes the inter-dependency between the datasets according to Eq. 2.
- Hellinger: Computes the Hellinger distance between two topic distribution. In our algorithm CalculateStatDist procedure invokes this procedure with two topic distribution, each corresponding to the topic distribution of a dataset. The Hellinger distance is calculated and returned to the invoking procedure.

5   Experimental Results

The proposed algorithm needs to be tested for its efficacy. Our algorithm serves to create a Dependency Matrix through topic modeling based predictions. A Bond Energy Algorithm (BEA) rearranges the Dependency matrix such that highly inter-dependent datasets are clustered together. In our proposed algorithm, the BEA clusters the algorithm both at the top level categories as well as the fine grained sub-categories. This experimental setup uses BBC news article dataset provided by [6]. It has five top-level category of Business, Entertainment, Sports, Technology and Politics. The Sports category is further fine grained sub-categorized into Athletics, Cricket, Football, Rugby and Tennis.

5.1   Setup

The given BBC news article datasets consist of text file of news clippings; which are considered as an individual text based dataset. The topic model has been computed using the Text Analysis Toolbox of MATLAB^{TM}, while the statistical distance and Bond Energy Algorithm based Dependency Matrix rearrangement has been calculated using Python. The essential setup parameters are given in Table 1. All other parameters which have not been mentioned takes default values.

Three of our experiments concern classification and clustering of high level datasets in which 10, 20 and 30 datasets are chosen from each high level categories for training as well as testing. The datasets used for training and testing are different from each other. These datasets are mixed together to ensure the algorithm can only determine their classification through topic modeling. A Bond Energy Algorithm is executed on the predicted Dependency Matrix. From the resulting rearranged Dependency matrix, now called clustered matrix, we extract ten elements (dataset ID) in every iteration. We measure what percentage of datasets in the clusters are actually from the same high level categories. For 100% accuracy, BEA is expected to cluster all datasets from a high-level

Table 1. Important setup parameters

Parameters	Values
Total number of datasets (per category)	Training: each top-level category 10, 20, 30 sports subcategory classification each sub-category: 10 Testing: each top-level category 10, 20, 30 sports subcategory classification each sub-category: 10
Number of categories	Top-level categories 5 sports subcategory classification 9 4 for high level category 5 for sports subcategory
Number of topics	50
Short words	≤ 2 characters
Long words	≥ 15 characters

category in their respective cluster. For example, if datasets 1 to 30 are from business category, then for 100% accuracy, we will be able to extract three groups of ten datasets from the BEA rearranged clustered matrix, which belongs exclusively to business category. We call this measure Correct Predictions. Further a confusion matrix has been presented to understand the prediction errors made by the developed system.

For experiment involving Sports category sub-categorization, apart from the above measure, we also measure whether the sub-categories have also been correctly clustered in addition to the high-level categories.

5.2 Results

The results of the experiments in the form of confusion matrix and the percentage of correct predictions as well as the layout of the dataset per cluster is shown in Tables 2, 3 and 4 below.

The interpretation of the results as follows:

- The correct prediction for high level classifications is 72%, 93% and 92% respectively for 10, 20 and 30 datasets per category. The high prediction accuracy validates the use of our algorithm for Dependency matrix prediction purposes.
- For fine grained sub-category classification, we find a correct prediction percentage of 88.89%; which is very high accuracy. Almost all predictions are at 90% accuracy. It also validates the fact that our algorithm can also make fine grained classification while predicting Dependency Matrix.

Table 2. Confusion matrix for 10 dataset sports subcategory classification

| | | Predicted | | | | | | | | |
		Athletics	Cricket	Football	Rugby	Tennis	Business	Entertainment	Politics	Tech
Actual	Athletics	9	1	0	0	0	0	0	0	0
	Cricket	0	9	1	0	0	0	0	0	0
	Football	0	0	9	1	0	0	0	0	0
	Rugby	0	0	0	9	1	0	0	0	0
	Tennis	0	0	0	0	9	1	0	0	0
	Business	0	0	0	0	0	9	1	0	0
	Entertainment	1	0	0	0	0	0	8	1	0
	Politics	0	0	0	0	0	0	0	9	1
	Tech	0	0	0	0	0	0	1	0	9

Table 3. Confusion matrix for 10, 20 and 30 dataset

10 dataset per category

| | | Predicted | | | | |
		Business	Entertainment	Politics	Sport	Tech
Actual	Business	7	0	0	1	2
	Entertainment	3	7	0	0	0
	Politics	0	2	7	1	0
	Sport	0	0	3	7	0
	Tech	0	1	0	1	8

20 dataset per category

| | | Predicted | | | | |
		Business	Entertainment	Politics	Sport	Tech
Actual	Business	19	1	0	0	0
	Entertainment	1	18	1	0	0
	Politics	0	0	19	1	0
	Sport	0	1	0	18	1
	Tech	0	0	0	1	19

30 dataset per category

| | | Predicted | | | | |
		Business	Entertainment	Politics	Sport	Tech
Actual	Business	25	0	0	1	4
	Entertainment	1	29	0	0	0
	Politics	0	1	29	0	0
	Sport	1	0	1	28	0
	Tech	3	0	0	1	26

- A careful observation also reveals that most of the mis-predictions are at the border of each cluster. This also reveals that a further sophisticated placement scheme would yield better results. Designing sophisticated cluster placement

Table 4. Cluster-wise dataset layout and prediction accuracy

10 dataset sports subcategory classification										
Cluster ID	Dataset ID									Correct predictions
Cluster 1	88	90	66	87	86	85	84	83	82	81	90.00%
Cluster 2	80	79	78	77	76	89	75	74	73	72	90.00%
Cluster 3	71	70	69	68	67	1	65	64	63	62	80.00%
Cluster 4	61	60	59	58	57	56	55	54	53	52	90.00%
Cluster 5	51	50	49	48	47	46	45	44	43	42	90.00%
Cluster 6	41	40	39	38	37	36	35	34	33	32	90.00%
Cluster 7	31	30	29	28	27	26	25	24	23	22	90.00%
Cluster 8	21	20	19	18	17	16	15	14	13	12	90.00%
Cluster 9	11	10	9	8	7	6	5	4	3	2	90.00%
Overall										88.89%

10 dataset										
Cluster ID	Dataset ID									Correct predictions
Cluster 1	47	20	48	46	45	44	43	42	41	40	80.00%
Cluster 2	37	36	34	38	35	33	31	30	29	28	70.00%
Cluster 3	27	26	25	24	23	22	21	19	39	15	70.00%
Cluster 4	18	17	16	3	14	13	11	10	9	12	70.00%
Cluster 5	50	8	49	32	7	6	5	4	1	2	70.00%
Overall										72.00%

20 dataset										
Cluster ID	Dataset ID									Correct predictions
Cluster 1	99	100	96	98	97	71	95	94	93	92	90%
Cluster 2	91	90	89	88	87	86	85	84	83	82	100%
Cluster 3	81	80	79	78	77	76	75	74	73	72	90.00%
Cluster 4	40	70	69	68	67	66	65	64	63	62	90%
Cluster 5	61	60	59	58	57	56	55	54	53	52	90%
Cluster 6	51	50	49	48	47	46	45	44	43	42	1000%
Cluster 7	41	18	39	38	37	36	35	34	33	32	80%
Cluster 8	31	30	29	28	27	26	25	24	23	22	100%
Cluster 9	21	20	19	1	17	16	15	14	13	12	90%
Cluster 10	11	10	9	8	7	6	5	4	3	2	100%
Overall										93.00%

30 dataset										
Cluster ID	Dataset ID									Correct predictions
Cluster 1	148	150	149	147	8	9	144	143	142	141	80.00%
Cluster 2	139	138	11	146	136	136	135	134	133	132	90.00%
Cluster 3	131	130	129	128	127	126	10	124	123	122	90.00%
Cluster 4	121	120	119	118	117	116	115	114	113	112	90.00%
Cluster 5	111	110	109	108	107	106	105	104	103	102	100.00%
Cluster 6	101	100	99	98	97	96	95	1	93	92	90.00%
Cluster 7	91	90	89	88	87	86	85	84	83	82	90.00%
Cluster 8	81	80	79	78	77	76	75	74	73	72	100.00%
Cluster 9	71	70	69	68	67	66	65	64	63	62	100.00%
Cluster 10	61	60	59	58	57	56	55	54	53	52	90.00%
Cluster 11	51	47	49	48	47	46	44	44	43	42	100.00%
Cluster 12	41	40	39	38	37	36	35	34	33	32	100.00%
Cluster 13	31	30	29	28	27	26	25	24	23	22	90.00%
Cluster 14	21	20	19	18	17	16	15	14	13	12	100.00%
Cluster 15	137	94	145	146	7	6	5	4	3	2	70.00%
Overall										92.00%

scheme is beyond the scope of this work, but would be considered in our future work.
– The confusion matrix also corroborates the above result by the fact that only a few mis-predictions can be seen in them.

6   Conclusion and Future Works

In this work, we have proposed an algorithm to predict a Dependency Matrix between text datasets, in an information scarce scenario. Dependency matrix computation is a pre-requisite for many data placement algorithms. Topic modeling based Dependency Matrix prediction requires analyzing the datasets themselves. As the experiments suggest, similarity in the topic distribution between two datasets gives a very good measure on the inter-dependency between the datasets. The experimental results also suggest that when a new dataset arrives without any dependency information available; our algorithm could be used to predict its dependency with other datasets with fair amount of accuracy. Some future directions of research could be given here. An obvious future work would be to propose a data placement algorithm based on the predicted Dependency Matrix. While Latent Dirichlet Allocation is found to be the obvious choice here, a comparative study with other statistical topic modeling tools such as Latent Semantic Allocation could be performed. Also, our work limits itself with text based datasets. This is an obvious limitation of topic modeling. A work around for multi-media based approaches should be sought.

References

1. Barkhordari, M., Niamanesh, M.: ScadiBino: an effective MapReduce-based association rule mining method. In: Proceedings of the Sixteenth International Conference on Electronic Commerce, p. 1. ACM (2014)
2. Basu, S., Yu, Y., Zimmermann, R.: Fuzzy clustering of lecture videos based on topic modeling. In: 2016 14th International Workshop on Content-Based Multimedia Indexing (CBMI), pp. 1–6. IEEE (2016)
3. Blei, D.M., Lafferty, J.D.: Topic models. Text Min.: Classif. Clustering Appl. 10(71), 34 (2009)
4. Blei, D.M., Ng, A.Y., Jordan, M.I.: Latent dirichlet allocation. J. Mach. Learn. Res. 3(Jan), 993–1022 (2003)
5. Gopalan, P.K., Charlin, L., Blei, D.: Content-based recommendations with poisson factorization. In: Advances in Neural Information Processing Systems, pp. 3176–3184 (2014)
6. Greene, D., Cunningham, P.: Practical solutions to the problem of diagonal dominance in kernel document clustering. In: Proceedings of 23rd International Conference on Machine learning (ICML 2006), pp. 377–384. ACM Press (2006)
7. Hamrouni, T., Slimani, S., Charrada, F.B.: A data mining correlated patterns-based periodic decentralized replication strategy for data grids. J. Syst. Softw. 110, 10–27 (2015)
8. McCormick Jr., W.T., Schweitzer, P.J., White, T.W.: Problem decomposition and data reorganization by a clustering technique. Oper. Res. 20(5), 993–1009 (1972)

9. Nagarajan, V., Mohamed, M.A.M.: A prediction-based dynamic replication strategy for data-intensive applications. Comput. Electr. Eng. **57**, 281–293 (2017)

10. Rus, V., Niraula, N., Banjade, R.: Similarity measures based on latent dirichlet allocation. In: Gelbukh, A. (ed.) CICLing 2013. LNCS, vol. 7816, pp. 459–470. Springer, Heidelberg (2013). https://doi.org/10.1007/978-3-642-37247-6_37

11. Saadat, N., Rahmani, A.M.: PDDRA: a new pre-fetching based dynamic data replication algorithm in data grids. Future Gener. Comput. Syst. **28**(4), 666–681 (2012)

12. Slimani, S., Hamrouni, T., Charrada, F.B.: New replication strategy based on maximal frequent correlated pattern mining for data grids. In: 2014 15th International Conference on Parallel and Distributed Computing, Applications and Technologies (PDCAT), pp. 144–151. IEEE (2014)

13. Wang, J., Shang, P., Yin, J.: DRAW: a new Data-gRouping-AWare data placement scheme for data intensive applications with interest locality. In: Li, X., Qiu, J. (eds.) Cloud Computing for Data-Intensive Applications, pp. 149–174. Springer, New York (2014). https://doi.org/10.1007/978-1-4939-1905-5_7

14. Wikipedia, the free encyclopedia. Latent dirichlet allocation (2018). Accessed 7 Apr 2018

15. Wu, J., Zhang, C., Zhang, B., Wang, P.: A new data-grouping-aware dynamic data placement method that take into account jobs execute frequency for Hadoop. Microprocess. Microsyst. **47**, 161–169 (2016)

16. Yuan, D., Yang, Y., Liu, X., Chen, J.: A data placement strategy in scientific cloud workflows. Future Gener. Comput. Syst. **26**(8), 1200–1214 (2010)

Adaptive Customer Profiling for Telecom Churn Prediction Using Computation Intelligence

Swarup Kumar Das, Soumen Kundu, Subrata Majee$^{(\boxtimes)}$,
Chandrika Sarkar, and Manju Biswas

Department of Computer Science and Engineering, Kalyani Government
Engineering College, Kalyani, India
swarupdas.cp.cst@gmail.com, soumenkundu272@gmail.com,
majeesubrta@gmail.com, chandrikasarkar12@gmail.com,
cse.majnubiswas@gmail.com

Abstract. Nowadays, the telecom industries are going through a big problem that is customer churn. Recently, the market for mobile telecom industry has to change very promptly and there is a ferocious competition between them. Most of the telecom companies always concentrate on to obtain a new customer, but they do not pay too much attention to their existing customer. That's why the company tries to find out that customers those have tendency to switch over in future. The information picked up from telecom industry to find out the logic of churning and try to solve those problems. The company targets those customers with a special program. The aim of this paper is to predict the customer churn for telecom industries using machine learning techniques namely Logistic Regression, Naïve Bayes and Decision Trees. In telecom industries, the principal objective of churning is to accurately calculate the customer survival and customer risk capabilities to gather the entire information of churn over the client residency. This paper summarizes the technique of predicting the churn so have a wide understanding of the customer churn. So that the telecom industries are aware in advance the big hazard customer and rectify their services to repeal the decision of churn. Customer profiling for predicting the customer who have churned in advance are also analyzed.

Keywords: Churn prediction · Feature selection · Logistic regression ·
Naive Bayes · Decision tree and customer profiling

1 Introduction

There are many telecom organizations available everywhere throughout the world. Telecommunication market is facing numerous loss of income because of expanding competition among from them and the loss of possible customers [9]. Many organizations are trying to find out the reasons for losing clients by estimating client faith to recover the customers who are lost. To stay with the competition and to own many subscribers, most administrators contribute an enormous measure of income to grow their business before all else. In this way, it has turned out to be important for any

© Springer Nature Singapore Pte Ltd. 2019
J. K. Mandal et al. (Eds.): CICBA 2018, CCIS 1031, pp. 70–83, 2019.
https://doi.org/10.1007/978-981-13-8581-0_6

telecom operators to bring back the amount they have invested along with minimum profit within a very short time.

When the clients leaving the present organization and moving to another telecom organization because of the disappointment [11] of the administrations and better offers which belongs from other telecom service providers within the affordable price range it is called "churn". Customer Churn [15] is going to become a major problem in any telecom industry in the world. It is more expensive to acquire a new customer. Therefore the companies always try to provide best in class services and very attractive offer to their existing customer as much as possible to keep their customer in a company [5]. When a customer leaves a service provider then it brings a huge loss in industry. So the industries always try to find out those customers whose have the tendency to churn and this is the very important task. The above-mentioned process is defined as customer churn prediction in telecom industry [9].

1.1 Types of Churns

There exist two types of churn in telecom industry. One is voluntary and other is involuntary. Involuntary churn [10] is quite bit easy to find. Involuntary churn is one where only the telecom industry has the power to eliminate the customer for non-payment, fraud and those customers who don't use the service. Then again, Voluntary churn [11] is very hard to figure out; here it is the choice of the customer to deactivate the service because the service provider didn't fulfill the demand of the customer. Most operators endeavoring to manage these kinds of churns mainly [14]. Churn rate strongly affects the lifetime estimation of the clients since it influences the length of administration and the future salary of the association. Telecom organizations invest the extensive amount of money to obtain a new customer and when that customer deactivate [4] the service, the organization not just loses the future income from that client yet, in addition, the assets spend to get that customer.

1.2 Churn Management

Churn management [11] is very important for decreasing churns as obtaining a new client is more cost-effective than holding the existing customer. Churn rate is the estimation of the number of clients go away and in amid a particular time period. On the off chance that the purpose behind churning is known, the suppliers would then be able to enhance their administrations to fulfill the necessities of the customers [7]. Churns can be lessened by breaking down the past history of the potential clients efficiently. An expansive measure of data is kept up by telecom companies for every one of their clients that continues changing quickly because of the focused environment. This data incorporates the insights about charging, calls and system information. The data available can be classified in different perspectives to give different approaches to the operators to presume and scale down churning. Only the suited details are used in the analysis which adds to the investigation of the data given.

1.3 Feature Selection

A feature is a piece of information that is potentially useful for prediction. "Feature Engineering" is not a formally defined term, just a vaguely agreed space of tasks related to designing feature sets for machine learning applications [13]. For churning, there exist 4 types of features:

Customer: State, Area Code, and Phone.
Plan: Intl_plan, Vmail_plan.
Behaviour: Vmail_Messages, Day_Mins, Day_Calls, Day_Charge, Eve_Mins, Eve_Calls, Eve_Charge, Night_Mins, Night_Calls, Night_Charge, Intl_Mins, Intl_Calls, and Intl_Charge.
Other: Account Length, Custserv_Calls, and Churn.

In Feature Engineering churn prediction changes from one business to the other. If it is not sure that whether a particular feature is useful or not, it will be easily discarded when creating the model [6]. To build a model in machine learning, feature selection is an important part.

Error Analysis
The final type of feature engineering is called error analysis. This is performed after training the first model. Error analysis is a broad term that refers to carefully studying the misclassified or high error observations from our model and deciding on our next step for improvement.

1.4 Key Contributions

In this paper, an approach for churn prediction is proposed and prospect the effectiveness of various predictive modeling technique for predicting the churn in the telecom industry.

The paper will illustrate the following contribution:

- Proposed a churn prediction approach using different classifier techniques.
- Performed experiments on a telecom dataset.
- Experimented performance of different classifier then calculates accuracy.

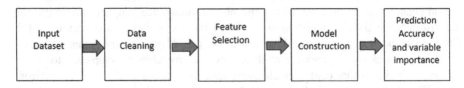

Fig. 1. Overview of the proposed churn prediction methodology

Figure 1 shows the outline of the suggested churn prediction technique, it consists of four steps (1) Data cleaning or preprocessing, (2) Feature selection, (3) Model construction using different classification algorithm and (4) Predict the approximate accuracy and the report of variable importance.

1.5 Customer Profiling

Customer profiling [21] is a way to retain the existing customer by offering them better services. Addition of new customer is a difficult task for companies having good market value. It is more expensive to add a new customer than retaining the existing customers. Clutching existing customers isn't an undemanding strategy; an organization must know its customers and their needs.

The rest portion of the paper is illustrated as follows. In Sect. 2, related works are presented. In Sect. 3, we present the experimental setup of proposed churn prediction in the telecom industry. The result and performance are presented in Sect. 4. In Sect. 5, conclusion and future work are illustrated.

2 Related Work

Authors of [14] have proposed a simple model for data mining to trace customers and their behavior in contrast to churn. In this approach, SVM (Support Vector Machine Algorithm) provides better outcomes to predict the customer churn in telecom industry. Comparison between decision tree and logistic regression technique have been shown by the author of [15]. Logistic regression approach provides 66% accuracy in the field of churn prediction where decision tree approach can provide 71.16% accuracy. To construct the churn prediction model, the authors of [16] have used two approaches namely decision trees and Neural Networks. In authors opinion, by selecting the proper sequence and adjusting the right threshold values can give more appropriate results. To find out the active customers and churners the author of [17] have used several machine learning algorithms like K-means clustering, linear and logistic regression, ANN (Artificial Neural Networks) and decision trees. The perfect results were obtained by decision tree algorithms. To present quality measures, the author of [18] used different prediction models such as naïve bayes, decision tree, regression analysis, and neural networks. According to the author, development of new prediction models are required. A particular training dataset was used by the author of [19] to make an experiment by using decision tree on customer churn factor. With the help of decision tree, rule information can easily be understood. Author of [20] has analyzed that commonly decision tree based techniques, regression technique, and neural network trees are applied in the prediction of churn. Decision tree technique provides the best results in terms of accuracy. From the above literature work, it can be concluded that in most of the cases, Decision trees gives better performance than other techniques for predicting churn in telecom industry.

3 Experimental Setup of Proposed Churn Prediction in the Telecom Industry

After selecting the needed features from the dataset the later step is model construction [6]. Here three classifiers are used like (1) Logistic Regression classifier (2) Decision Tree classifier and the last one is (3) Naive Bayes classifier to predict the probability of customer churn in the telecom industry.

3.1 Dataset Preparation

The dataset is downloaded from kaggle, which is publicly available. The dataset has 3333 rows and 21 columns. Fortunately, the dataset does not contain any missing values, null values. So further clean is not needed otherwise, to clean the dataset various data cleaning technique are required. Out of 21 predictor variables, the 'Phone', 'State', 'Area Code' attributes which are unnecessary for churn prediction and remaining variables are used as feature variables are removed.

3.2 Logistic Regression for Predict the Customer Churn in the Telecom Industry

Before entering into logistic regression [2], first of all, need to know about the background of the classification algorithm borrowed by the supervised machine learning from the glebe of statistics. As it is an adaptive conventional statistical method by which a dataset can analyze in which there are one or more independent variables and the outcomes are determined by that variables. This method is used to predict the binary outcomes It is used to say what take will place in the future a based on two outcomes which is YES/No or 1/0 or True/False given a group of independent variables able to be changed. Binary outcomes are represented by dummy variables. Logistic regression [8] is one type of algorithm which is coming up with a probability function that can give us 'the chance, for an input to belong to any one of the various classes' that have (classification). It is used to describe data and to give an account of the relation between one independent binary variable based on a one or more titular or interim independent variables.

Algorithm

I. A linear model has to fit the feature space determined by the training data. This is required for calculating the best parameters to fit the model (Fig. 2).

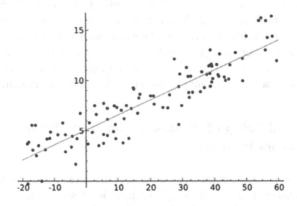

Fig. 2. An example of a linear model fit to the feature space

This model is an n-dimensional vector given by the equation below.

$$z = \emptyset_0 + \sum_{i=1}^{n} \emptyset_i X_i \tag{1}$$

II. Now the task is to determine the z value for a testing point using the parameters found in step 1.

III. Between the ranges 0 to 1 map the z value of testing point using the logistic function or sigmoid function. This is the way of determining the probability that these features are associated with customer churn (Fig. 3).

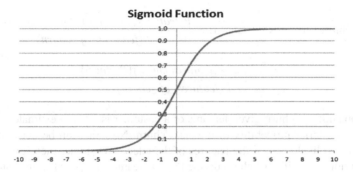

Fig. 3. Sigmoid function graph

$$p(churn|z) = \frac{1}{1+e^{-z}} \tag{2}$$

$$p(notchurn|z) = 1 - p(churn|z) = \frac{e^{-z}}{1+e^{-z}} \tag{3}$$

The S shape curve of sigmoid Function gives the output based on the probability function. The curve has a finite limit, $-\infty$ is used for 0 and ∞ is used for 1 respectively. The output of sigmoid function will 0.5 when a = 0. So in this strategy, if the output of the curve is more than 0.5 then the outcomes will classify as 1 or Yes otherwise 0 or no if the output is less than 0.5.

The sigmoid function helps us to translate a continuous input to discrete values (0 or 1 equivalently churn or not churn).

3.3 Naïve Bayes for Predict the Customer Churn in the Telecom Industry

A Naive Bayes classifier is a simple adaptive machine learning method that is based on Bayes theorem.

Bayes Theory:

$$P(X|Y) = \frac{P(Y|X)P(X)}{P(Y)} \tag{4}$$

Where,

P (X|Y) = Posterior Probability
P (Y|X) = Likelihood
P (X) = Class prior probability
P (Y) = Predictor prior probability

Bayes Theorem can be used in customer churn prediction in the telecom industry like:

$$P\,(churn \mid features\_of\_churn) = \frac{P(features\_of\_churn|churn)P(churn)}{P(features\_of\_churn)} \tag{5}$$

$$= \frac{\left[\pi_{features}P(features|churn)\right]P(churn)}{P(features\_of\_churn)} \tag{6}$$

So the probability of churn given features of a customer is what to estimate and this is actually the posterior probability of the class churn. Now this can be decomposed by base rule as the likelihood of the features of the telecom customer then it was a churn times the prior probability of churn divided by the features of the telecom customer, all right probability of the features of the telecom customer, and divide by Naive Bayes [8] condition it can assume that the different features of the customer are conditionally independent given that the class is already known to be churn.

The task is to determine the probability that a customer is churn or not, given the evidence of features (F1, F2…..Fn). Then compare P(churn | F1, F2, …..Fn) to P(not churn| F1, F2, …..Fn) and determine which is more likely. Churn and not churn are represented as "C " in the equation which is described below.

$$p(C|F_1,.....,F_n) = \frac{p(c)p(F_1,.....,F_n)}{p(F_1,.....,F_n)} \tag{7}$$

When comparison takes place P(churn| F1, F2 …Fn) to P(not churn| F1, F2, …..Fn), the denominators are the same. Thus it can easily compare by the following equation:

$$p(C|F_1,.....,F_n) \propto p(C)p(F_1,.....,F_n|C) \tag{8}$$

Now, to determine the probability whether the customer is churned or not just select the class (C = churn or C = not churn) that maximizes the following equation.

$$arg_c\, max\, p(C = c) \prod_{i=1}^{n} p(F_i = f_i|C = c) \tag{9}$$

3.4   Decision Tree for Predict the Customer Churn in the Telecom Industry

A decision tree [8] uses a tree structure to specify sequences of decisions and consequences. Decision tree algorithm can be used for both classification problem as well as a regression problem [3]. Representation and estimation of decision tree approach are done in top-down way. Any decision tree can be created with the help of two stages, first one is tree building and another one is tree pruning [8]. The decision tree is build up from the primary root node by defining a classified feature. Selecting a component might be possible by evaluating its information gain ratio. With the help of divide and conquer strategy the child nodes are constructed in the same way related to root node. ID3 (Iterative Dichotomiser 3) C4.5 (successor of ID3), CART (Classification and Regression Tree) and CHAID (CHi-squared Automatic Interaction Detector) [1] are the example of different types of decision tree algorithms. The well-known Iterative Dichotomiser 3(ID3) is used to generate the decision tree. This algorithm constructed the decision tree depending on gini index. The formulas are given below.

$$Gini(D) = 1 - \sum_{i=1}^{m} p_i^2 \tag{10}$$

$$Gini_A(D) = \frac{|D_1|}{|D|} Gini(D_1) + \frac{|D_1|}{|D|} Gini(D_2) \tag{11}$$

$$\Delta Gini(A) = Gini(D) - Gini_A(D) \tag{12}$$

Algorithm

   I. Find the impurity of D using Eq. (10).
  II. Find the impurity of each resulting partition using Eq. (11).
 III. Find reduction in impurity using Eq. (12).
  IV. Now select the best attribute which gives the minimum gini index overall.

After using the above algorithm and using the raphviz function and pydotplus python packages are used to construct the tree structure of customer churn prediction analysis. As decision tree approach is adaptive so it is working for our dataset.

4   Result and Performance

In this section, the experimental result and performance for predicting the customer churn in the telecom industry for a telecom dataset are illustrated. To implement the churn prediction model all the required steps are needed in python programming language. Python has a lot of fixed libraries such as scikit-learn, pandas, numpy etc. The total workflow is done in Jupyter notebook which opens in a web browser for quick co-operation.

4.1   Performance Metrics

The performance metrics [6] are illustrated as follows:

(a) *Confusion Matrix:* It is represented by a tabular form which is consist of two rows and two columns respectively which contains the number of false positive (FP), false negative (FN), true positive (TP), true negative (TN). To predict the customer churn in terms of false, the performance of a classification model is described for figure out the accuracy [12].

(b) *Accuracy:* It is characterized as following
$$ACC = (TP + TN)/(TP + TN + FP + FN)$$

(c) *Precision and Recall:* It is characterized as following
$$Precision = TP/(TP + FP)$$
$$Recall = TP/(TP + FN)$$

(d) *F1-Score:* It is characterized as following
$$F1 = 2 \times (precision \times recall)/(precision + recall)$$

4.2   Experiment Result

In this part, the results of the experiment are described by confusion matrix and classification report which are calculated by the Logistic Regression, Naïve Bayes and Decision Tree classifiers.

Confusion Matrix

Table 1. Confusion matrix of logistic regression

Predicted churn Actual churn	Predicted: No	Predicted: Yes
Actual: No	682	15
Actual: Yes	112	24

In Table 1 shows that the Logistic Regression algorithm made a total of 833 predictions. Out of those 833 customers, the classifier predicted "yes" 39 times and "no" 794 times. In reality, 136 customers are churned and 697 customers are not churned. So the accuracy will be (682 + 24)/833 i.e. 0.8475.

Table 2. Confusion matrix of Naïve Bayes

Predicted churn Actual churn	Predicted: No	Predicted: Yes
Actual: No	644	53
Actual: Yes	61	75

In Table 2 shows that the Naïve Bayes classifier made a total of 833 predictions. Out of those 833 customers, the classifier predicted "yes" 128 times and "no" 705 times. In reality, 136 customers are churned and 697 customers are not churned. So the accuracy will be (644 + 75)/833 i.e. 0.8631.

Table 3. Confusion matrix of decision tree

Predicted churn Actual churn	Predicted: No	Predicted: Yes
Actual: No	665	32
Actual: Yes	39	97

In Table 3 shows that the Decision Tree classifier made a total of 833 predictions. Out of those 833 customers, the classifier predicted "yes" 129 times and "no" 704 times. In reality, 136 customers are churned and 697 customers are not churned. So the accuracy will be (665 + 97)/833 i.e. 0.9147.

Classification Report

The classification report displays the precision, recall and F1 scores for the model.

Table 4. Classification report of logistic regression

	Precision	Recall	f1-score	Support
0	0.87	0.98	0.92	857
1	0.51	0.15	0.24	143
Avg/total	0.82	0.86	0.82	1000

In Table 4 shows that the precision, recall, f1-score result of Logistic Regression classifier. Precision is the ratio of correctly predicted positive observations to the total predicted positive observations. Recall is the ratio of correctly predicted positive observations to all observations in actual class - yes. The weighted average of Precision and Recall is nothing but F1-score. The results of logistics regression algorithm achieved 0.82 precision, 0.86 recall, and 0.82 f1-score.

Table 5. Classification report of Naïve Bayes

	Precision	Recall	f1-score	Support
0	0.91	0.91	0.91	857
1	0.47	0.46	0.47	143
Avg/total	0.85	0.85	0.85	1000

Similarly in Table 5 shows that the precision, recall, f1-score result of Naïve Bayes classifier. The results of naïve bayes algorithm achieved 0.85 precision, 0.85 recall, and 0.85 f1-score.

Table 6. Classification report of decision tree

	Precision	Recall	f1-score	Support
0	0.95	0.95	0.95	857
1	0.69	0.73	0.71	143
Avg/total	0.92	0.91	0.91	1000

Similarly in Table 6 shows that the precision, recall, f1-score result of Decision Tree Classifier. The results of decision tree algorithm achieved 0.92 precision, 0.91 recall, and 0.91 f1-score.

ROC Curve

A receiver operating characteristics curve i.e. ROC curve is one where a binary classifier system is represented graphically that illustrate the diagnostics ability of that classifier system. The true positive rate against the false positive rate is plotted in the graph for creating the ROC curve.

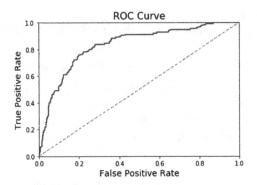

Fig. 4. ROC curve of logistic regression

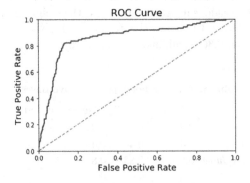

Fig. 5. ROC curve of Naïve Bayes

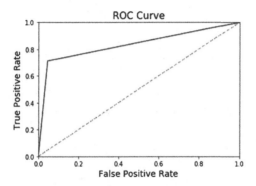

Fig. 6. ROC curve of decision tree

Figures 4, 5 and 6 represents the receiver operating curve of Logistic Regression, Naïve Bayes, and Decision Tree classifier respectively.

Accuracy Comparison
Here the comparison between the accuracy of three classifier technique i.e. Logistic Regression, Naïve Bayes and Decision Tree classifier using a bar graph which is plotted in below.

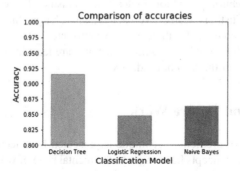

Fig. 7. Accuracy comparison graph

```
Accuracy of Naive Bayes Classification: 85.0
Accuracy of Logistic Regression: 85.8
Accuracy of Decision Tree: 91.4
```

Fig. 8. Accuracy of different classification

From the comparison graph in Fig. 7 and the accuracy of three classifiers from Fig. 8, it is clear that the decision tree classifier gives us the highest accuracy to predict the customer churn analysis in the telecom industry which is denoted by the longest bar on the above Fig. 7.

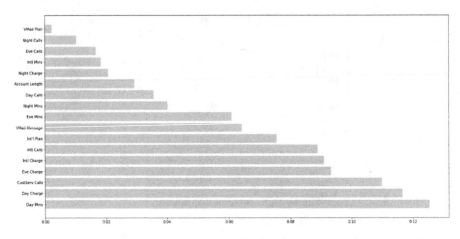

Fig. 9. Feature importance graph

Feature Importance

From Fig. 9, it is clear that the highest probability of customer churn in the telecom industry depends on 'Day Mins'. The variable importance plot in Fig. 9 shows that among from all attribute only seven variables have importance more than 50% regarding customer churn prediction in telecom industry. These variables are Day Mins, Day Charge, CustServ Calls, Eve Charge, Intl Charge, Intl Calls and Intl Plan respectively. Apart from this, also there exist five attributes which have less importance which is more than 20% and the remaining attributes are least important for predicting the churned customer in the telecom industry.

5 Conclusion and Future Work

In this paper, the churn prediction technique is presented for telecom industry. A certain accurate and clear concepts have made to the mental state of what will take place in the future of churners and not - churners and further help to effectively control and maintain customer churn in order to keep existing customer. Telecommunication industry should maintain a certain level of their service to predict the customer churn and monitor each and every customer about their rate of usage. Each customer attribute is monitored in terms of importance and concluded that only seven variables have importance more than 50% regarding customer churn prediction in telecom industry.

The future direction of this work may comprise conducting considerable experiments for respective category of customer churn attributes. In this work, we observed that the customer switched their service from one service provider to another based on some particular attributes. In future, we will try to solve those problems, analyze those attributes for which the customer have tendency for churning and try to retain those churned customers by providing special incentives if possible. And we want to develop another model for customer profiling so that the probability of churned customer may be predicted in advance.

References

1. Saini, M.N.: Churn prediction in telecommunication industry using decision tree. Streamed Info-Ocean **1**(1) (2016)
2. Olle, G.D.O., Cai, S.: A hybrid churn prediction model in mobile telecommunication industry. Int. J. e-Educ. e-Bus. e-Manag. and e-Learn. **4**(1), 55 (2014)
3. Dahiya, K., Bhatia, S.: Customer churn analysis in telecom industry. In: 4th International Conference on Reliability, ICRITO (2015)
4. Sindhu, M.E., Vijaya, M.S.: Predicting churners in telecommunication using variants of support vector machine. Am. J. Eng. Res. (AJER) **4**(3), 11–18 (2015). e-ISSN 2320-0847, p-ISSN 2320-0936
5. Brandusoiu, I., Toderean, G.: Churn prediction in the telecommunications sector using support vector machines. Annals of the Oradea University Fascicle of Management and Technological Engineering ISSUE#1, May 2013
6. Umayaparvathi, V., Iyakutti, K.: Attribute selection and customer churn prediction in telecom industry. In: International Conference on Data Mining and Advanced Computing (SAPIENCE) (2016)
7. Yabas, U., Ince, T., Cankaya, H.C.: Customer churn prediction for telecom services. In: 2012 IEEE 36th International Conference on Computer Software and Applications (2012)
8. Last updated: 20 March 2018. https://ese.wustl.edu/ContentFiles/Research/Undergraduate Research/CompletedProjects/WebPages/sp14/SongSteimle/WebPage/classifiers.html
9. Last updated: 23 March 2018. https://aws.amazon.com/blogs/machine-learning/predicting-customer-churn-with-amazon-machine-learning/
10. Last updated: 27 March 2018. https://www.datascience.com/blog/what-is-a-churn-analysis-and-why-is-it-valuable-for-business
11. Last updated: 27 March 2018. http://www.computerscijournal.org/vol10no1/churn-analysis-in-telecommunication-using-logistic-regression/
12. Last updated: 29 March 2018. http://www.dataschool.io/simple-guide-to-confusion-matrix-terminology/
13. Last updated: 30 March 2018. http://blog.keyrus.co.uk/a_simple_approach_to_predicting_customer_churn.html
14. Shaaaban, E., Khedr, A., Nasr, M., Helmy, Y.: A proposed churn prediction model. IJERA **2**(4), 693–697 (2012). ISSN 2248-9622
15. Gürsoy, U.T.Ş.: Customer churn analysis in telecommunication sector. Istanbul Univ. J. Sch. Bus. Adm. **39**(1), 35–49 (2010). ISSN 1303-1732
16. Umayaparvathi, V., Lyakutti, K.: Applications of data mining in telecom churn prediction. Int. J. Comput. Appl. **42**(20), 5–9 (2012). ISSN 0975-8887
17. Qureshi, S.A., Qamar, A.M., Kamal, A., Rehman, A.S.: Telecommunication subscribers' churn prediction model using machine learning, pp. 131–136. IEEE (2013)
18. Lazarov, V., Capota, M.: Churn prediction. Technische Universität München (2007)
19. Oseman, K.B., Binti, S., Shukor, M., Haris, N.A.: Data mining in churn analysis model for telecommunication industry. J. Stat. Model. Anal. **1**(19–27), 19–27 (2010). ISSN 2180-3102
20. Almana, A.M., Alzaharni, R., Aksoy, M.S.: A survey on data mining techniques in customer churn analysis for telecom industry. IJERA **4**(5), 165–171 (2014). ISSN 2248-9622
21. Tiwari, A., Hadden, J., Turner, C.: A new neural network based customer profiling methodology for churn prediction. In: ICCSA, Computational Science and Its Applications – ICCSA 2010, pp. 358–369 (2010)

Survey of Textbased Chatbot in Perspective of Recent Technologies

Bhriguraj Borah[✉], Dhrubajyoti Pathak, Priyankoo Sarmah,
Bidisha Som, and Sukumar Nandi

Centre for Linguistic Science and Technology,
Indian Institute of Technology Guwahati, Guwahati 781039, Assam, India
{bhriguraj,drbjl53,priyankoo,bidisha,
sukumar}@iitg.ac.in

Abstract. Chatbots are computer programs capable to carry a conversation with human. They can be seen as an artificial agent designed to serve the purpose of conversation with the end user. Chatbots are gaining popularity especially in business and health sector as they have the potential to automate service and reduce human efforts. Widespread use of Apps, maturation of Artificial Intelligence (AI) technologies and integration of Natural Language Processing (NLP) fuels up the growth of chatbot. In this paper, we present different models of chatbots along with an architectural overview of computationally intelligent chatbot in context of recent technologies. In the three layer architecture, we have given insights of how the NLP, Natural Language Understanding (NLU) and Decision engine work together with Knowledge Base to achieve AI using Recurrent Neural Network (RNN) and Long Short Term Memory (LSTM). In addition, we also discuss different chatbot platforms and development frameworks of recent times. Our core emphasis is on analysis of recent development approaches of textbased conversational systems. We identify few challenges in intelligent chatbot development that may be helpful for future research works.

Keywords: Intelligent chatbot · Artificial intelligence · Machine learning · Natural language processing · Chatbot framework

1 Introduction

The most natural form of communication of human being is natural language. This motivates the idea of developing chatbots based on natural language. People write to communicate with others. When people write digitally their texts are processed using NLP techniques and responses are provided through chatbot. Since the starting of AI and Computational Linguistics, designing a human like chatbot is an emerging area in academia as well as in industry. The evolution of chatbot from the birth of ELIZA to the advance intelligence system like ALEXA [1] is really a promising area for researchers. The process of chatbot development is believed to have started as early as 1950 with Alan Turing's intelligent machine [2]. In 1966 another intelligent agent named ELIZA [3] came as a physiotherapist that could conduct human like

© Springer Nature Singapore Pte Ltd. 2019
J. K. Mandal et al. (Eds.): CICBA 2018, CCIS 1031, pp. 84–96, 2019.
https://doi.org/10.1007/978-981-13-8581-0_7

conversations. The terminology "chatbot" originated from the system CHATTERBOT, which was invented as a game character for the 1989 multiuser dungeon game "TinyMUD". Perez-Marin in [4] summarized the following processing steps of a chatbot: preprocessing, pattern-matching, generating response based on template. The pattern matching method selects predefined responses from existing collection. Predefined responses create constraint on the conversational agent. Perez-Marin in his work [5] explains keeping up the context of the conversation is also important for understanding the human inputs and the giving proper responses. The another category of conversational systems is "dialog system". McTear [6] differences between dialog systems and chatbots on the basis of domain. Dialog systems are closed domain whereas chatbots are capable of keeping open domain conversation. A dialog system typically requires four components: a preprocessing component, a natural language understanding component, a dialog manager and a response generation component [7].

Artificial Intelligence Markup Language (AIML) and NLP with Natural Language Understanding (NLU) are widely used to build conversational agent. Artificial Intelligence Markup Language (AIML) [8, 9] is an XML dialect aimed at creating conversational flows for the bot. It is completely based on pattern-recognition and pattern-matching methods. Natural Language Processing (NLP) and Natural Language Understanding (NLU) attempt to solve the problem of chatbot development by parsing input message into entities, intents and a few other categories [10]. Intents basically correspond to what actions are to be invoked or triggered as a response to a user input. Actions correspond to the steps the chatbot will take when specific intents are triggered by user inputs. Contexts are strings that store context of the object the user is taking about. Deep learning is a deeper level and subset of machine learning. It uses mass amounts of data and highly complex algorithms to learn and to simulate human-like decision making [11]. Neural probabilistic language model [12] and Neural machine translation [13] can be applied to generate responses from the input messages. RNN Encoder Decoder model [14] is widely used in generative model chatbots to frame responses of user messages through NLG [15] process.

In this paper, we present different models of chatbots along with an architectural overview of intelligent chatbot in context of recent technologies. It consists of three main layer: presentation layer, machine learning layer and data layer. In the three layer architecture, we have given insights of how the NLP, NLU and Decision engine work together with Knowledge Base to achieve AI using RNN and LSTM. Rest of the paper discusses about recent chatbot platform and development frameworks with their advantages and limitations. Lastly, we discuss about the challenges in development of intelligent chatbot.

2 Different Models of Chatbot

The process of response creation is different for different chatbots. Likewise, the domain and duration of conversation is not same for all chatbots. All these features make distinctions among them [1, 16, 17]. Chatbots are often associated with artificial intelligence. However, the large majority of chatbots are not artificially intelligent self-learning programs. They do, however, utilise natural language processing capabilities to extract user's intent from linguistic input to give proper response. Generally speaking, chatbots can be distinguished in following ways:

2.1   Retrieval-Based

Retrieval-based models use a repository of predefined responses and pick an appropriate response based on the input and context. These systems don't generate any new text. Features:

1. End users follow through the scripted interaction flow. The large majority of chatbots are scripted. Unable to handle unseen cases.
2. Generally, deals with one domain with less flexibility. Do not make grammatical mistakes.

2.2   Generative-Based

Generative models are based on Machine Translation techniques, but instead of translating from one language to another, translations are made from an input to an output response. It is also referred as Artificial Intelligence Chatbot. Main features are:

1. Successful implementation will make chatbot like a human being. Very flexible and can handle multiple domain.
2. It learns itself from large amount of interaction data. It is highly complex and very costly.

2.3   Long and Short Conversation

Depending upon the length of the conversations it can be divided as long and short conversation chatbots. Longer the conversation the more difficult to automate it as it is necessary to keep track of what has been said. In short conversation it is easy to track.

2.4   Open and Close Domain

In an open domain environment, the user can take the conversation anywhere. There is no well-defined goal or intention. A large amount of world knowledge about infinite number of topic are required to create reasonable response in open domain. In a closed domain, possible inputs and outputs are somewhat limited because the system is designed to achieve a very specific goal. So most of chatbots are closed domain in nature.

3   Conversation Capabilities of Chatbot

Chatbot conversation capabilities are different with respect to different domain. Some domain requires remembering all the conversation right from the initial point of time to the end. Only then we can make inference on the basis of all sequence of conversation. Where as in some discussion it is possible to infer on the basis of early few sequence of discussions. The different types of conversational capabilities [17] of chatbots can have divided in three state:

1. **Stateless**: It is also described as "memory less" chatbot. The chatbot handles each message in isolation, without taking previous messages into account.
2. **Semi Stateful**: These type of chatbots have limited ability to remember previous user input. The Chabot's memory capabilities are often confined to the current conversation.
3. **Stateful**: Stateful chatbots can remember context and previous conversations, and is able to generate responses based on this knowledge.

4 Architecture of Intelligent Chatbot

All intelligent chat systems have several major components, all are equally important and together they form a robust system to deliver a successful chatbot [18, 19]. Figure 1 portray an architectural view of a computationally intelligent chatbot. End users interact with the presentation layer, which encapsulate the various user interface components of the system. Messaging backend is responsible for receive and delivery of the message to the presentation layer. Machine learning layer is the backbone of intelligent chatbot which creates responses with the help of Knowledge Base. Final response is delivered to the user through Natural Language Generation process.

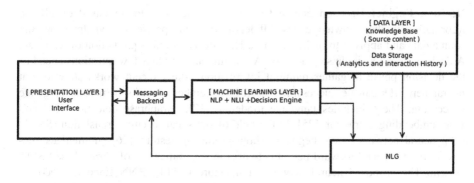

Fig. 1. Overall architecture of intelligent chatbot.

4.1 Presentation Layer

All components of user interface represent the presentation layer. This layer seamlessly caters the user interface to end users irrespective of device and platform. Multi-channel and multi-platform support facilitation is the core responsibility of the presentation layer.

4.2 Machine Learning Layer

Machine learning layer consist of three important components: Natural Language Processing (NLP), Natural Language Understanding (NLU) and decision engine. Combination of three components add Artificial Intelligent(AI) to the chatbot to process message intelligently.

Natural Language Processing: Most chatbot systems process the user's input before it is forwarded to the Natural Language Understanding component. The tasks of preprocessing are performed in various segments. Berger [20] summarized the preprocessing tasks of dialog systems in followings phases: sentence detection, co-resolution, tokenization, lemmatization, POS-tagging, dependency parsing, named entity recognition, semantic role labeling. There are terms like Intents, Actions, and Entities which are basically prepared from the user inputs with the help of natural language processing techniques.

Natural Language Understanding: Natural language understanding maps an input message text into semantic slots. The slots are pre-defined according to different scenarios. Typically, there are two types of representations [15]. One is the utterance level category, such as the user's intent category. The other is the word-level information extraction such as named entity recognition and slot filling. An intent detection is performed to detect the intent of a user. It classifies the utterance into one of the predefined intents. Deep learning techniques have been successively applied in intent detection [21–23].

Decision Engine: Decision engine task is to decide what to do based on all the information in the knowledge base. It learns domain specific knowledge from the source data and apply it to make decision. Here decision refers prediction of response. A decision is not a single step activity. An intelligent bot plans few questions ahead of the decision phase to gather required information. Many recent works showed that neural networks can be successfully used in a number of tasks in natural language processing. These includes language modeling [12], paraphrase detection [24] and word embedding extraction [25]. In the field of statistical machine translation (SMT), deep neural networks have begun to show promising results. [26] summarizes successful usage of feed forward neural networks in the framework of phrase-based SMT system. The proposed neural network architecture in [14], RNN Encoder Decoder, consists of two recurrent neural networks (RNN) that act as an encoder and a decoder pair. The encoder maps a variable length source sequence to a fixed-length vector, and the decoder maps the vector representation back to a variable length target sequence. The two networks are trained jointly to maximize the conditional probability of the target sequence given a source sequence.

1. Recurrent Neural Network: Human thoughts have persistence. Lack of persistence is one of the major drawback of traditional neural network. Recurrent neural networks [27] are a variety of neural network that makes it possible to model these long-distance dependencies. They are networks with loop in them allowing persistence in information (Fig. 2).

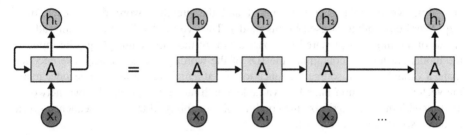

Fig. 2. Recurrent Neural Network (RNN) [28].

In the above diagram, a chunk of neural network, A, looks at some input X_t and outputs a value h_t. A loop allows information to be passed from one step of the network to the next. A recurrent neural network can be thought of as multiple copies of the same network, each passing a message to a successor. RNN have the problem of vanishing gradient and exploding gradient. This leads to a new design of neural network architecture named long short-term memory [29] neural network architecture. It is a very successful design and gaining popularity in a wide variety of sequential processing tasks.

2. Long Short Term Memory Network: Long Short Term Memory networks (LSTM) are special kind of Recurrent Neural Network. LSTM are designed to learn long term dependencies. In standard RNNs, this repeating module will have a very simple structure, such as a single tanh layer. LSTMs also have this chain like structure, but the repeating module has a different structure. Instead of having a single neural network layer, there are four, interacting in a very special way [31] as shown in the Fig. 3.

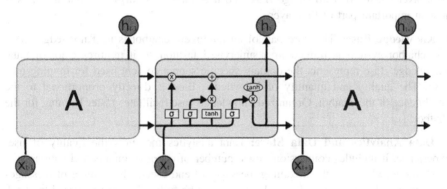

Fig. 3. Long Short Term Memory networks (LSTM) [30].

3. Neural Encoder and Decoder: The Sequence to Sequence model (seq2seq) consists of two RNNs - an encoder and a decoder. The encoder reads the input sequence, word by word and emits a context, which captures the semantic summary of the input sequence. Based on this context, the decoder generates the output sequence, one word at a time while looking at the context and the previous word during each time step. Word embedding is used in this model. The "vocabulary" list containing all the words of the model is prepared for construction of the word embedding. The input to the model are tensors containing the IDs of the words in the sequence. The encoder maps a variable length source sequence to a fixed length vector and the decoder maps the vector representation back to a variable length target sequence. The two networks are trained jointly to maximize the conditional probability of the target sequence given a source sequence [14] (Fig. 4).

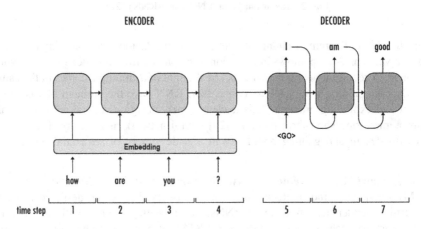

Fig. 4. Seq2Seq model: neural encoder and decoder [32].

4.3   Data Layer

Data layer consist of Knowledge Base and user interaction history. Data analytics is also an important part of this layer.

1. Knowledge Base: The core part of an intelligent chatbot is its Knowledge Base. The chatbot system is trained in a supervised fashion so it requires a lot of data. Knowledge Base represents the domain specific source content used for training purpose. The quality and quantity of Knowledge Base is directly proportional to the intelligence of the chatbot. Organized knowledge base facilitates faster learning for the chatbot.

2. Data Analytics and Data Store: Data analytics measures the quality of user experience. It includes conversion flows, number of count of intents and entities successfully decoded over the incoming messages of end users. The number of messages that a user had to type in order for his request to be fulfilled is also recorded to check and improve the effectiveness of chatbot. Chatbot interaction history is stored for future reference. The analyses of all the conversations between users and bots can give us the expectations and suggestion for optimization of the process in a convenient and clean graphical interface.

4.4   Natural Language Generation

The natural language generation component converts an abstract statement into natural language surface utterances. An encoder-decoder LSTM-based structure is adopted in [33] to incorporate the question information, semantic slot values, and dialogue act type to generate correct answers. In similar way, [34] also presented a natural language generator based on the sequence-to-sequence approach that can be trained to produce natural language strings as well as deep syntax dependency trees from input dialogue acts. It was further extended in [35] for preceding user utterance and responses.

5   Chatbot Platforms

These are simplest platform one can use to build a chatbot. It does not need any programming background. Without knowing NLP and Machine Learning one can build a chatbot. These type of platforms are mostly simple task oriented. Chatfuel, ManyChat, Motion.ai and MobileMonkey are widely used chatbot platforms [36]. We observe all of these platforms have some advantages as well as limitations.

Advantages:

1. Require less time to develop chatbot.
2. Visual development environment is available for developers.
3. Ideal for simple bot.

Limitations:

1. Functions are in prebuild format. Cannot build anything beyond simple, not appropriate for complex conversation bots.
2. Very less NLP and ML specific components.

6   Chatbot Development Frameworks

Chatbot development frameworks provides a lot more flexibility with deeper level of analytics. AI is also incorporated in this framework for Developers. Facebook Bot Engine, Dialogflow developed by Google, Microsoft Bot Framework, IBM Watson and Amazon Lex are the most famous and modern chatbot development frameworks, which allow developers to create own bots.

6.1   Facebook Bot Engine

The cloud based Facebook Bot Engine Wit.ai allows developing bot applications for Facebook Messenger platform. Stories are used as the main source for building the behavior of chatbot with Wit.ai. Stories are always full of examples of different real life scenarios and these examples provide the platform for Wit.ai to learn. The basic idea is that when user write similar examples, the Wit.ai process it, extracts entities and apply logic as per already learnt from story based examples [37].

A story consists of many user intents. These intents can be represented in graph format to represent the flow of conversation. Wit.ai lets developers define and use the predefined entities. Wit.ai facilitates webhook integration for developers [19].

Advantages:

1. Since it is based on concept of story so it is more powerful than isolated segment of conversation.
2. Wit.ai allows controlling the conversation flow using branches and also conditions on actions.

Limitations:

1. Even if stories are powerful concept, there are cases where it is difficult to control the flow of the conversation and the bot tends to misunderstand the user requests.

6.2   Dialogflow

Dialogflow provides a platform that allows developers to design and implement conversation interfaces which can be embedded in external applications like chatbots. Intents and Contexts are the key concepts to model the behavior of a chatbot with Dialogflow. Intents creates links between what a user says and what action should be taken by the chatbot. Contexts are string values, useful for differentiating requests which might have different meaning depending on context [38]. It has webhook integration for developers to customize the chatbot behavior. Dialogflow supports different platforms including Skype, Telegram, Slack, Cortana, Alexa and Facebook Messenger [37].

Advantages:

1. Dialogflow proposes a powerful way of modeling large and complex conversation flows using Intents and Contexts.
2. A section "Training" is available to train the chatbot with examples.

Limitations:

1. The handling of context and intent at the same time is very difficult task.

6.3   Microsoft Bot Framework

Microsoft bot framework is one of the best chatbot frameworks with machine learning. Microsoft Language Understanding Intelligent Service is very similar to Dialogflow. The user input is semantically checked with the prior knowledge to trigger corresponding intent. It also has the concept of entities to learn about the conversation. It provides facilities to create intents, entities, and agents but does not provide a visual representation of the conversation flows as Wit.ai does. The intelligence and assistant services based on this framework are far better than all of the other present days' solutions [37, 38].

Advantages:

1. Smarter and can learn alternative phrases which can trigger intents and alternative entities.
2. Language Understanding Intelligent Service also supports composite entities. None of the other AI frameworks support composite entities.

Limitations:

1. Does not allow developers to manage context parameters.
2. Does not include a rich set of domains for building chatbots like Dialogflow.

7 Challenges in Computationally Intelligent Chatbot Development

Eliminating Ambiguity in Conversation: Natural language is very much ambiguous in nature. Due to ambiguity a simple meaning can be represented through different set of words. So it is very difficult to model human conversation through chatbot. Though we are able to design chatbot with the application of deep learning to provide meaningful experiences in conversation but still a long way to go to achieve human like conversations.

Keeping Context of the Conversation: Context of the conversation is necessary to decide the flow of conversation. The biggest challenge of chatbot development is to keep track the context of the current conversation. Only proper context can lead us to achieve the desired goal of the conversation.

Incorporation of Loops, Splits and Recursion in Conversation: Most of the chatbots are atomic in nature and serve single purpose. Implementation of open domain chatbot includes different challenges like incorporation of loop, diversion on splits and recursion. In some conversation loop back into a previous specific conversation is necessary but through chatbots it is very difficult to incorporate.

Consistency in Natural Language Interpretation: Inconsistency in interpretation is one main issue of chatbot. This leads to incorrect and inappropriate answers. Microsoft Tay chatbot is also a victim of miss interpretation of natural language. Microsoft finally decided to close down the chatbot due to inconsistency in interpretation.

Building Character and Persona: One of the core challenges of building a productive chatbot is to add character and persona to the chatbot. These are some characteristics which will make the chatbot a human being in true sense. Only then we can achieve the saturation point of chatbot development.

Emotional Support Capability: Emotional support ability is not currently incorporated in chatbot. Building a chatbot intelligent enough to converse about subjective needs like emotional support, reducing anxiety and responding in a relevant way is still a major challenge.

8 Conclusion

In this paper, we discussed overall architecture of computationally intelligent chatbot and functionalities of different layers along with their constituents. Incorporation of intelligence to the chatbot by supervised learning through data and machine learning layer is explored thoroughly. We have also given an overview of RNN, LSTM, seq2seq model and NLG in context of intelligent response generation. The recent development in the field of NLP, NLU and machine learning enables developers to build computationally intelligent chatbot. Widespread Apps and maturation of AI fuels up the growth of intelligent chatbot. But challenges like ambiguity, inconsistency, coherent response, statefulness, context sensitivity, building character and persona are to be addressed properly to gain the real advantage of intelligent chatbot.

References

1. Ramesh, K., Ravishankaran, S., Joshi, A., Chandrasekaran, K.: A survey of design techniques for conversational agents. In: Kaushik, S., Gupta, D., Kharb, L., Chahal, D. (eds.) ICICCT 2017. CCIS, vol. 750, pp. 336–350. Springer, Singapore (2017). https://doi.org/10.1007/978-981-10-6544-6_31
2. Machinery, C.: Computing machinery and intelligence-AM turing. Mind **59**(236), 433 (1950)
3. Weizenbaum, J.: Elizaa computer program for the study of natural language communication between man and machine. Commun. ACM **9**(1), 36–45 (1966)
4. Perez-Marin, D.: Conversational Agents and Natural Language Interaction: Techniques and Effective Practices: Techniques and Effective Practices. IGI Global (2011)
5. Mauldin, M.L.: Chatterbots, tinymuds, and the turing test: entering the loebner prize competition. In: AAAI, vol. 94, pp. 16–21 (1994)
6. McTear, M.F.: Spoken Dialogue Technology: Toward the Conversational User Interface. Springer, London (2004). https://doi.org/10.1007/978-0-85729-414-2
7. Lester, J., Branting, K., Mott, B.: Conversational agents. In: The Practical Handbook of Internet Computing, pp. 220–240 (2004)
8. Wallace, R.: The elements of AIML style. Alice AI Foundation (2003)
9. Marietto, M.D.G.B., et al.: Artificial Intelligence Markup Language: A Brief Tutorial. CoRR abs/1307.3091 (2013)
10. Chowdhury, G.G.: Natural language processing. Ann. Rev. Inf. Sci. Technol. **37**(1), 51–89 (2003)
11. Sutskever, I., Vinyals, O., Le, Q.V.: Sequence to sequence learning with neural networks. In: Advances in Neural Information Processing Systems, pp. 3104–3112 (2014)
12. Bengio, Y., Ducharme, R., Vincent, P., Jauvin, C.: A neural probabilistic language model. J. Mach. Learn. Res. **3**(Feb), 1137–1155 (2003)
13. Bahdanau, D., Cho, K., Bengio, Y.: Neural machine translation by jointly learning to align and translate. arXiv preprint arXiv:1409.0473 (2014)

14. Cho, K., et al.: Learning phrase representations using RNN encoder-decoder for statistical machine translation. arXiv preprint arXiv:1406.1078 (2014)
15. Chen, H., Liu, X., Yin, D., Tang, J.: A survey on dialogue systems: Recent advances and new frontiers. arXiv preprint arXiv:1711.01731 (2017)
16. Deshpande, A., Shahane, A., Gadre, D., Deshpande, M., Joshi, P.M.: A survey of various chatbot implementation techniques. Int. J. Comput. Eng. Appl. **11** (2017). ISSN 2321-3469
17. Mobgea: The Power of Chatbots: The art of Conversation. White Paper (2017)
18. Shah, V.: Autopsy of a Chatbot: The 7 core components needed for a successful implementation (2017). https://medium.com/@vihangshah/the-magnificent-7-core-components-needed-for-a-successful-implementation-7b4e0d723e33
19. Kang, A.: Understanding the Differences Between Alexa, Api.ai, Wit.ai, and LUIS (2017). https://medium.com/@abraham.kang/understanding-the-differences-between-alexa-api-ai-wit-ai-and-luis-cortana-2404ece0977c
20. Berg, M.M.: Modelling of natural dialogues in the context of speech-based information and control systems (2014)
21. Bruni, E., Fernandez, R.: Adversarial evaluation for open-domain dialogue generation. In: Proceedings of the 18th Annual SIGdial Meeting on Discourse and Dialogue, pp. 284–288 (2017)
22. Shen, X., et al.: A conditional variational framework for dialog generation. arXiv preprint arXiv:1705.00316 (2017)
23. Williams, J., Raux, A., Ramachandran, D., Black, A.: The dialog state tracking challenge. In: Proceedings of the SIGDIAL 2013 Conference, pp. 404–413 (2013)
24. Socher, R., Huang, E.H., Pennin, J., Manning, C.D., Ng, A.Y.: Dynamic pooling and unfolding recursive autoencoders for paraphrase detection. In: Advances in Neural Information Processing Systems, pp. 801–809 (2011)
25. Mikolov, T., Sutskever, I., Chen, K., Corrado, G.S., Dean, J.: Distributed representations of words and phrases and their compositionality. In: Advances in Neural Information Processing Systems, pp. 3111–3119 (2013)
26. Schwenk, H.: Continuous space translation models for phrase-based statistical machine translation. In: Proceedings of COLING 2012: Posters, pp. 1071–1080 (2012)
27. Elman, J.L.: Finding structure in time. Cogn. Sci. **14**(2), 179–211 (1990)
28. Abolafia, D.: A Recurrent Neural Network Music Generation Tutorial (2017). https://magenta.tensorflow.org
29. Hochreiter, S., Schmidhuber, J.: Long short-term memory. Neural Comput. **9**(8), 1735–1780 (1997)
30. Srivastava, P.: Essentials of Deep Learning: Introduction to Long Short Term Memory (2017). https://www.analyticsvidhya.com/
31. Neubig, G.: Neural machine translation and sequence-to-sequence models: a tutorial. arXiv preprint arXiv:1703.01619 (2017)
32. Chablani, M.: Sequence to sequence model: Introduction and concepts (2017). https://towardsdatascience.com
33. Zhou, H., Huang, M., et al.: Context-aware natural language generation for spoken dialogue systems. In: Proceedings of COLING 2016, the 26th International Conference on Computational Linguistics: Technical Papers, pp. 2032–2041 (2016)
34. Dušek, O., Jurčíček, F.: Sequence-to-sequence generation for spoken dialogue via deep syntax trees and strings. arXiv preprint arXiv:1606.05491 (2016)
35. Dušek, O., Jurčíček, F.: A context-aware natural language generator for dialogue systems. arXiv preprint arXiv:1608.07076 (2016)

36. Zamanirad, S., Benatallah, B., Chai Barukh, M., Casati, F., Rodriguez, C.: Programming bots by synthesizing natural language expressions into API invocations. In: Proceedings of the 32nd IEEE/ACM International Conference on Automated Software Engineering, pp. 832–837. IEEE Press (2017)
37. Rahman, A., Al Mamun, A., Islam, A.: Programming challenges of chatbot: current and future prospective. In: 2017 IEEE Region 10 Humanitarian Technology Conference (R10-HTC), pp. 75–78. IEEE (2017)
38. Couto, J.: Building a Chatbot: Analysis and limitations of modern platforms (2017). https://tryolabs.com/blog/2017/01/25/building-a-chatbot-analysis–limitations-of-modern-platforms

DRSQ - A Dynamic Resource Service Quality Based Load Balancing Algorithm

Anindita Sarkar[1]([⊠]), Kshitij Pant[2], and Samiran Chattopadhyay[2]

[1] School of Mobile Computing and Communication, Jadavpur University,
Kolkata, India
sarkar.anindita5@gmail.com
[2] Department of Information Technology, Jadavpur University, Kolkata, India
kshitijjpant@gmail.com, samirancju@gmail.com

Abstract. In cloud computing domain, the main problem faced by cloud manager is to handle the huge amount of clients request at a single amount. For this reason, there have different types of load balancing algorithms, some are static algorithm and some are dynamic algorithm. But till, when the question is arrived to maintain service quality with the handling of work load balance than the shortage is occurred. In this paper, we proposed a novel dynamic load balancing algorithm named as Dynamic Resource Service Quality Based Load Balancing Algorithm (DRSQ). Besides supporting the load balance, it's main aim is to continue with a good performance rate by utilizing resources in proper way. To reach the goal, back-end resource selection is done based on the provided service quality by the resources. The service quality is measured by considering the request type (e.g., READ, WRITE) and the value set of resource metrics. To prove the usefulness, it goes through some experiments using some real temperature sensor generated datasets in private cloud environment. The most famous load balancing algorithm Round-Robin is considered for comparative analysis.

Keywords: Dynamic load balancing algorithm ·
Resource service quality · Private cloud · Resource monitoring ·
Resource metrics

1 Introduction

Cloud computing has recently emerged as a new pattern of hosting and delivering services over the Internet. It works as distributed computing pattern. Now-a-days, cloud computing becomes so popular that applications of different domains (e.g., health, industry, city, home etc.) desire to take facility of it, pointed in Fig. 1. According to Fig. 1, there have two zones. Data zone holds different application domains which are responsible to generate dataset and cloud zone holds resource pool which consists of resources. Here, each application of a single domain produces a large amount of dataset with a varied frequency rate

© Springer Nature Singapore Pte Ltd. 2019
J. K. Mandal et al. (Eds.): CICBA 2018, CCIS 1031, pp. 97–108, 2019.
https://doi.org/10.1007/978-981-13-8581-0_8

in concurrent manner. It creates a huge challenge to the cloud developer for handling such a vast data traffic. To solve this matter, load balancer [11] acts in between the applications and cloud resource pool [3].

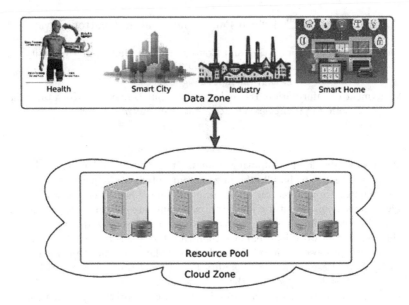

Health   Smart City   Industry   Smart Home

Fig. 1. Overview of cloud utilization by applications

Load balancer manipulates the feature of cloud computing and distributes the data traffics in between the resources of resource pool. The main task of the Load balancer is to ensure that all the resources of the resource pool never be overloaded and supports three factors of cloud computing: availability, reliability and flexibility [4,12]. Here, the question is how load balancer achieve this goal without any data loss. Therefore, load balancer primarily focus upon the resource scheduling tasks, done by load balancing algorithms [7].

There have two types of load balancing algorithm: static load balancing algorithm [2,19] and dynamic load balancing algorithm [20]. The difference between static and dynamic load balancing algorithm is at the time resource scheduling static load balancing algorithm does not consider present status of resources for resource selection but dynamic load balancing algorithm considers it. [18] This resource selection approach makes dynamic load balancing algorithm better by increasing decision accuracy rate higher. [21] Static load balancing algorithm are more stable than dynamic load balancing algorithm The example of the dynamic load balancing algorithms are ant colony [15], honey bee [10] etc. Round robin [9], Random [1,17], Threshold [16] are the example of static load balancing algorithm.

In this paper, we propose a novel dynamic load balancing algorithm named as dynamic resource service quality based load balancing algorithm. It helps load balancer to support the diverse frequency rate of application's requests at database level. To achieve this goal, load balancer selects the proper resource from resource pool based on the provided data service quality. To judge the service quality, we consider present status of certain resource metrics. They are CPU CLOCK SPEED, LOAD in last 15 min, number of processes, number of running processes, Number of CPU CORES, free RAM size, free SWAP memory size, free DISK size, BYTES IN and BYTES OUT. The contributions of this paper are,

- Without considering a single one, a set of resource metrics are assessed to understand the machine capability against of work load handling. In such way a proper resource is selected for a particular task. This concept helps to utilize resources in better way.
- This algorithm avoids the usage of back-end resources which are in dead state or in bottleneck situation.

The rest of the paper is organized in such way. The background study of different load balancing algorithm in cloud domain is explained in Sect. 2. Section 3 represents the structure of DRSQ algorithm in brief way with resource metrics. The comparative study between Round-Robin algorithm and DRSQ is described in Sect. 4 with experimental setup. Section 5 concludes this paper with mentioning the extension of this work in near future.

2   Related Work

Load balancing is a load allocation strategy which distributes the incoming load to the back-end servers equally, and eliminates any load imbalance problems, thus optimizes the overall performance of the system. There are two type of Load balancing algorithms [3]: static load balancing [19] and dynamic load balancing [1].

Static load balancing [12,16] is also called state independent balancing. It select a back-end server before the incoming request arrives, i.e. the algorithm does not consider the real time load status of the back-end server while assign the request, but instead makes the decisions and assign the request to the back-end server on the basis of known system static information. The advantages of static load balancing are that the simple to implement, incoming request can be quickly allocated to the back-end server. But the main disadvantage of static load balancing algorithm is that it does not consider the real time load of the back-end server, due to which the load allocation to the back-end server would be uneven distributed [18].

Dynamic load balancing [18] select a back-end server, by evaluating the real time load of each back-end server, the incoming request are allocated to the back-end server dynamically.

Active monitoring load balancer algorithm [13] proposed by Hemant S. Mahalle, Parag R. Kaveri and Vinay Chavan, distributes the incoming request between the back-end servers or virtual machines. When ever the load balancer gets an incoming request, it forwards the request to the least loaded Virtual Machine.

Modified throttled algorithm [6] was proposed by Shridhar G. Domanal and G. Ram Mohana Reddy is a dynamic algorithm, which distributes the incoming request between the back-end servers or virtual machines. Cloud Analyst simulator was used to check the result of the algorithm.

The main advantages of dynamic load balancing is that it can select the back-end server on the basis of real time load of the back-end server. Thus the back-end server selection can readjust its selection on the basis of load in the back-end server. The disadvantage of Dynamic load balancing algorithm is that the algorithm frequently collect the status of back-end server to select a back-end server to handle the incoming request which accounts to network overhead, which result in wastage of network bandwidth [18].

3   Overview of Workload Balance

3.1   Resource Performance Metric

In heterogeneous paradigm, each and every resources have different service quality. We use this knowledge in the dynamic resource service quality based load balancing algorithm to design it. A set of metrics are used to measure the performance of each resource in resource pool. The values of these metrics are changed frequently. On the basis of a single parameter at a unit time, not will be a good decision to judge a resource service quality.

We divide the set of resource performance metrics into four dimensions mentioned in Fig. 2: Memory, Processor, Load and Input/Output. A subset of metrics which are in memory dimensions represents the information about cache memory, swap memory, disk and memory itself. Processor dimensions represents the information about CPU and running processor number. Input/output and Load dimensions informed about direct impact with outsider. Therefore, each and every dimension have an role at the selection of best resource at a particular time.

In DRSQ, we use this concept by considering free RAM size, free SWAP memory size, free DISK size from memory dimension, number of processes, number of running processes, Number of CPU CORES, CPU CLOCK SPEED from Processor dimension, LOAD in last 15 min from Load dimension and BYTES IN and BYTES OUT from Input/Output dimension. These metrics act as a group and eligible to find out a proper resource at that time. This resource comparatively served better performance than others at that time.

3.2   Load Balancing Algorithm

The load balancer run the load balancing algorithm to reduce the gap between application generated concurrent dataset and the limited number of resources of resource pool by distributing the workload in between the resources. Performance of the load balancing algorithm is somehow depends upon the proper resource selection. Based on this concept we implement dynamic resource service quality

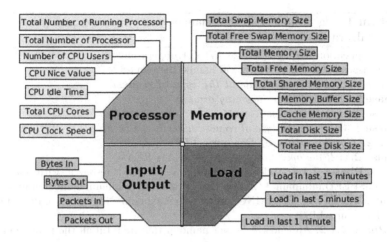

Fig. 2. Dimensions of resource performance metrics

based load balancing algorithm where resource is selected using performance metrics value-set.

DRSQ works under three phases: (a) Decision Making about the type of application requests (b) Configuration of resource list and (c) calculate the ultimate resource. The detailed algorithmic view of the phases are mentioned in algorithm 1. The working procedure of each phase is given in below.

– In first phase, Our algorithm will wait for the incoming request from the client. Once the request arrive at the load balancer, it will register the request. After the request is register, it will check the type of operation which need to be perform i.e. it is a WRITE query or a READ query. The main objective of this module is to check the type of query which is required to select the parameters on the basis of which we will select a back-end server.
– After knowing the type of operation in the Decision Making module, we will fetch the information of the back-end server depending on the type of operation in second phase. If incoming request will perform a WRITE operation, the algorithm will take into consideration the free primary memory, free swap memory, free secondary memory, bandwidth utilization and load in last fifteen minutes each active back-end server. Otherwise the incoming request will perform READ operation in which we will consider the CPU clock speed, Total processes in the server, Total number of running processes in the server, CPU cores, bandwidth utilization and load on the server in last fifteen minutes of each active back-end server. The algorithm will fetch these values and store it in system informations LIST for each back-end server. We have used Ganglia Monitoring Tool to fetch the system information from the back-end servers. This system informations LIST for each back-end server is forwarded to the Computing related jobs based on LIST components module for further processing.

Algorithm 1. Algorithmic view of dynamic resource service quality based load balancing algorithm

---

Input: Application Request (READ/WRITE) operation
Output: Backend resource which will handle the request
  Phase 1: Decision making about the type of request
    Phase 1.1: *Wait for the incoming request*
    Phase 1.2: *Register New Request*
    Phase 1.3: *Decide the type of request either it can be READ or WRITE*
  Phase 2: Configuration of Resource LIST
    Phase 2.1: *If the operation to be performed is READ*
        Phase 2.1.1: Select and store a back-end resource with maximum CLOCK_SPEED,minimum LOAD in last 15 minutes, minimum number of processes, minimum number of RUNNING processes, maximum Number of CPU CORES respectively in a LIST
      Phase 2.1.2: Append the Server name in the LIST till all the parameters are checked
    Phase 2.2: *If the operation to be performed is WRITE*
      Phase 2.2.1: Select and store a back-end resource with maximum FREE RAM, maximum FREE SWAP, maximum FREE DISK, minimum LOAD in last 15 minutes respectively in a LIST
      Phase 2.2.2: Append the resource in the LIST till all the parameters are checked.
  Phase 3: Computing ultimate resource based on LIST components
    Phase 3.1: *Select the resource which has maximum occurrence in LIST*
    Phase 3.2: *Forward the request to the selected resource*

- In third phase, we will compare each field of the system informations LIST which is created in the previous module (containing system informations) of each back-end server. The most suitable value of each field is taken into consideration and the name of that server is stored in a newly created resource LIST. After we have compared all the fields of the system informations LIST, we will check which server has dominated the resource LIST. After getting the name of that server, We will forward the registered incoming request to the selected server.

4   Experiment

4.1   Setup

The main aim of the load balancing algorithm is to control the network traffic. We also try to achieve this goal by using proposed Dynamic Resource Service Quality based Load Balancing Algorithm. Figure 3 describes the experimental system setup. This setup is divided into two parts, *Data Zone* responsible to client request and *Cloud Zone* presents the information about resources and load balancer. Here, four application domain is placed, each of them consists of temperature sensors. *Load Balancer* runs the DRSQ to select the resource for handling network traffic generated by the clients requests. According to this setup client's request is based on database related like read or write.

The efficiency of DRSQ is measured by the varied incoming data frequency rate means increasing and decreasing the network data traffic. We use real temperature sensor data to do the experiment. Here, total 6 temperature sensor is used, the data generation frequency rate of each sensor is varied. According to the setup in Fig. 3, at minimum range each application domain consists of a single temperature sensor and at maximum range each application domain holds two temperature sensors.

To do the experiment, five virtual machines and one load balancer machine are considered. MongoDB [8], Apache Tomcat [5] and Ganglia [14] are used to configure the machines according to their needs presented in Fig. 3. Ubuntu 14.04 is used as operating system of these machines. To collect the resource metrics value set corresponding of each machine, Ganglia plug-ins are used like, Gmetad 3.6.0 in Load balancer and Gmond 3.6.0 in resource part. MongoDB 3.6.19 is used as back-end database to put the incoming dataset. The used java based web applications are run on tomcat server 8.5.28.

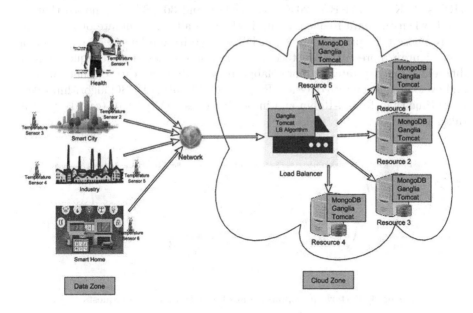

Fig. 3. Visualization of experimental system setup .

4.2   Illustration

We choose Round-Robin load balancing algorithm for doing the comparative study because it is considered as standard load balancing algorithm by the load

Table 1. Performance result-set of Dynamic resource service quality and Round-Robin load balancing algorithm

Algorithm	Execution time	CPU utilization	Memory utilization
Dynamic resource service quality based load balancing algorithm	1.98 s	0.451%	6 MB
Round-Robin load balancing algorithm	0.401 s	0.028%	5 MB

balancer designer in each and every application domain. If we compare the overall performance (i.e., CPU Utilization, Memory Utilization and Execution Time) between Round-Robin and DRSQ than we find out Round-Robin algorithm perform in all aspects, shown in Table 1.

To analyze the performance behavior in streaming data, we consider 5 data request from each sensor of applications (Fig. 3) which sends data request in 5 KB/s, 10 KB/s, 15 KB/s, 20 KB/s, 25 KB/s and 30 KB/s. We notice that in Fig. 4, when the data frequency rate is changed after few minute or hour than the response time pick is changed in DRSQ algorithm otherwise it maintains a line. Figure 5 represent characteristics of response times of each request under different frequency rates in more elaborate way. Here, we can see that, in each and every frequency rate only for 'Request 1' (Fig. 5(a)) DRSQ algorithm takes more time than Round-Robin and in other requests (Fig. 5[(b), (c), (d), (e)]) it takes less time.

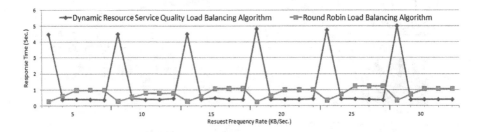

Fig. 4. Pattern of response times for streaming data requests

Dynamic Resource Service Quality algorithm selects the resource based on the system monitoring status value collected from ganglia generated log files. Initially the algorithm invests time to trigger the ganglia monitoring daemons to monitor the resources, connect with the back-end servers, fetch the log files generated by ganglia daemons and finally parse the desired values from the log files. When the next request is received by load balancer after few micro or nano second, it just modify the generated log file contents, analyzed the new value and send the incoming request to the selected resource. Hence reducing the ganglia triggering up time which diminishes the response time.

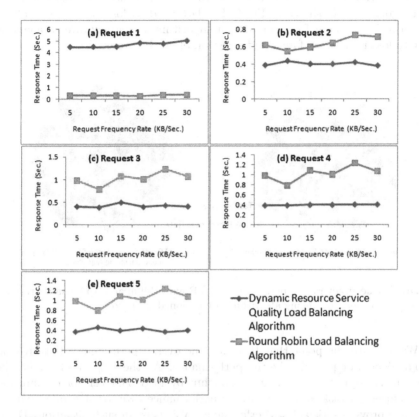

Fig. 5. Characteristics of each requests under different frequency rates

On the other end, Round-Robin algorithm selects the resources in circular way, one after another. In such situation, there are large chances that a crashed server or a heavily loaded server is selected as there will be many requests pending with it all the requests may cause a bottleneck situation at the back-end server which upsurge the response time. Therefore, some times response time is very low and some times it is very high. For the DRSQ, there is no chance to select a resource which is in bottleneck condition. For this reason, except first stage, the generated response times show the more or less similar value.

Also we consider 'Task Accuracy Rate' to justify the usefulness of DRSQ Load Balancing algorithm. For doing this experiment, we changed our setup as shown in Fig. 3 little bit where Resource 5 is in dead condition. Here, we made 10,000 'Write' requests continuously with a data bundle consists of 1000 data records in each request. According to the working principle of Round-Robin algorithm, Resource 5 was requested 2,000 times and every times it failed to store the data.

Whereas DRSQ does not select Resource 5 at a single time because before making request it checks the resource is in workable state or not. If we assume 1% packet loss is occurred by network issues than the computed accuracy percentage for both algorithms are shown in Fig. 6. For DRSQ, data loss is occurred only by the network issues but for Round-Robin algorithm inaccuracy rate is calculated by data loss in network faults and selection of crashed resources.

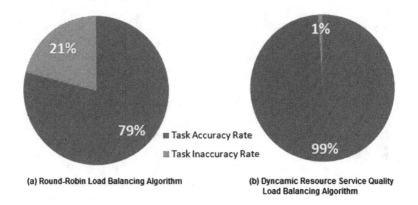

(a) Round-Robin Load Balancing Algorithm   **(b) Dyncamic Resource Service Quality Load Balancing Algorithm**

Fig. 6. Task accuracy rate in percentile for (a) Round-Robin and (b) Dynamic resource service quality load balancing algorithm in mentioned scenario

We come to the point that If we see the overall performance than Round-Robin algorithm provides better performance. At the respect of application domain, usage as load balancing algorithm by load balancer some confusions are occurred In task accuracy rate or performance rate for streaming data, it does not provide satisfactory performance. Whereas, in such situations DRSQ provides good performance.

5   Conclusions and Future Work

In this paper, we present a novel dynamic load balancing algorithm DRSQ which not only balance the work load and also provides an efficient application services. This algorithm makes the resource selection based on the system monitoring status. So, it omits the possibility to select a resource which is in dead state or in bottleneck situation.

In our future work, we will extend our algorithm with further optimization features. Firstly, it is important that we reduce the decision making time to select the back-end resource as it is a dynamic algorithm. To achieve this feature we need to integrate some optimization algorithms with our existing algorithm. Secondly, we wish to segregate the incoming request on the type of information rather than type of operation to be performed. To achieve this feature, we need to analyze the incoming data packet and check the type of data it is carrying.

References

1. Alakeel, A.M.: A guide to dynamic load balancing in distributed computer systems. Int. J. Comput. Sci. Netw. Secur. (IJCSNS) **10**, 153–160 (2010)
2. Belkar, S.P., Handur, V.: Comparative study of static load balancing algorithms in distributed system using cloudsim. Int. J. Adv. Res. Basic Eng. Sci. Technol. (IJARBEST) **5**, 26–30 (2017)
3. Casavant, T.L., Kuhl, J.G.: A taxonomy of scheduling in general-purpose distributed computing systems. IEEE Transact. Softw. Eng. **14**, 141–154 (1988)
4. Chang, H., Tang, X.: A load-balance based resource-scheduling algorithm under cloud computing environment. In: Luo, X., Cao, Y., Yang, B., Liu, J., Ye, F. (eds.) ICWL 2010. LNCS, vol. 6537, pp. 85–90. Springer, Heidelberg (2011). https://doi.org/10.1007/978-3-642-20539-2_10
5. Chopra, V., Li, S., Genender, J.: Professional Apache Tomcat 6. Wiley, Hoboken (2007)
6. Domanal, S.G., Reddy, G.R.M.: Load balancing in cloud computingusing modified throttled algorithm. In: 2013 IEEE International Conference on Cloud Computing in Emerging Markets (CCEM), October 2013
7. Fang, Y., Wang, F., Ge, J.: A task scheduling algorithm based on load balancing in cloud computing. In: Wang, F.L., Gong, Z., Luo, X., Lei, J. (eds.) WISM 2010. LNCS, vol. 6318, pp. 271–277. Springer, Heidelberg (2010). https://doi.org/10.1007/978-3-642-16515-3_34
8. Hows, D., Membrey, P., Plugge, E.: MongoDB Basics. Apress, New York (2014)
9. Jain, S., Saxena, A.K.: A survey of load balancing challenges in cloud environment. In: 2016 International Conference System Modeling Advancement in Research Trends (SMART), pp. 291–293 (2016)
10. Kaur, A., Kaur, B.: Load balancing in tasks using honey bee behavior algorithm in cloud computing. In: 2016 5th International Conference on Wireless Networks and Embedded Systems (WECON), pp. 1–5. IEEE (2016)
11. Khan, R.Z., Ahmad, M.O.: Load balancing challenges in cloud computing: a survey. In: Lobiyal, D.K., Mohapatra, D.P., Nagar, A., Sahoo, M.N. (eds.) Proceedings of the International Conference on Signal, Networks, Computing, and Systems. LNEE, vol. 396, pp. 25–32. Springer, New Delhi (2016). https://doi.org/10.1007/978-81-322-3589-7_3
12. Kunz, T.: The influence of different workload descriptions on a heuristic load balancing scheme. IEEE Transact. Softw. Eng. **17**, 725–730 (1991)
13. Mahalle, H.S., Kaveri, P.R., Chavan, V.: Load balancing on cloud data centers. Int. J. Adv. Res. Comput. Sci. Softw. Eng. **3**(1), 1–4 (2013)
14. Massie, M.L., Chun, B.N., Culler, D.E.: The ganglia distributed monitoringsystem: design, implementation, and experience. Parallel Comput. **30**, 817–840 (2004)
15. Nishant, K., Sharma, P., Krishna, V., Gupta, C., Singh, K.P., Nitin, Rastogi, R.: Load balancing of nodes in cloud using ant colony optimization. In: 2012 UKSim 14th International Conference on Computer Modelling and Simulation, pp. 3–8 (2012)
16. Rahmawan, H., Gondokaryono, Y.S.: The simulation of static load balancing algorithms. In: 2009 International Conference on Electrical Engineering and Informatics, pp. 640–645 (2009)
17. Rathore, N.: Dynamic threshold based load balancing algorithms. Wireless Pers. Commun. **91**, 151–185 (2016)

18. Sharma, S., Singh, S., Sharma, M.: Performance analysis of load balancing algorithms. World Acad. Sci. Eng. Technol. **38**, 269–272 (2008)
19. Tantawi, A.N., Towsley, D.: Optimal static load balancing in distributed computer systems. J. ACM **32**, 445–465 (1985)
20. Wang, M., Guan, J.: An adaptive dynamic feedback load balancing algorithm based on QoS in distributed file system. J. Commun. Inf. Netw. **2**, 30–40 (2017)
21. Zhou, L., Wang, Y.C., Zhang, J.L., Wan, J., Ren, Y.J.: Optimize block-level cloud storage system with load-balance strategy. In: 2012 IEEE 26th International Parallel and Distributed Processing Symposium Workshops & PhD Forum (IPDPSW), pp. 2162–2167. IEEE (2012)

Handwritten Indic Script Identification – A Multi-level Approach

Subhasmita Ghosh[1]([⊠]), Ashif Sheikh[1], Sk. Golam Sarowar Hossain[1],
Sk. Md. Obaidullah[1], K. C. Santosh[2], Nibaran Das[3],
and Kaushik Roy[4]

[1] Department of Computer Science and Engineering,
Aliah University, Kolkata, India
subhasmitaghosh@gmail.com, ashifsheikh.cse@gmail.com,
sarowar25@gmail.com, sk.obaidullah@gmail.com
[2] Department of Computer Science, The University of South Dakota,
Vermillion, SD, USA
santosh.kc@usd.edu
[3] Department of Computer Science and Engineering,
Jadavpur University, Kolkata, India
nibaranju@gmail.com
[4] Department of Computer Science, West Bengal State University, Barasat, India
kaushik.mrg@gmail.com

Abstract. Script identification is an emerging document analysis problem where we identify scripts type from multilingual documents. It is well known that there are 22 official languages in India and 11 scripts are used to write them. Traditional approaches for script identification consider all the scripts together and perform a classification at single level in brute force manner. In this paper, we propose a novel multi-level approach that separate 11 different scripts (Bangla, Devanagari, Gujarati, Gurumukhi, Kannada, Malayalam, Oriya, Roman, Tamil, Telugu & Urdu) from multi-script documents. A three-level hierarchy is followed during the grouping of different Indic scripts based on their structural similarities. The proposed approach not only performs well in terms of classification accuracy but also it shows more realistic way to separate multiple numbers of Indic scripts. We obtain an average script identification accuracy of 94.43% at individual script-level which is the encouraging observation of the current inherent complex problem.

Keywords: Script identification · Multi-script documents ·
Multi-level approach · Classification

1 Introduction

Modern technology mainly deals with paperless document, so handwritten script document have to be digitized for additional scopes. Here, OCR (Optical Character Recognizer) left an important footstep in the field of pattern reorganization and hand written script identification. OCR converts the hand written texts into machine readable one. But as OCR is script dependent, already used OCR for one script can't be used

© Springer Nature Singapore Pte Ltd. 2019
J. K. Mandal et al. (Eds.): CICBA 2018, CCIS 1031, pp. 109–123, 2019.
https://doi.org/10.1007/978-981-13-8581-0_9

further and this is the big issue. To handle this, a common approach is to design a preprocessor which will identify the scripts first before sending the document to the script specific OCR. An inclusive study on script identification was reported in [1, 2]. Page level identification using some structural features is reported by Obaidullah et al. [3]. Another page level script identification technique using textual features is proposed by Hochberg et al. [4]. Some of Indic and non-Indic script identification using a shape code-block based procedure is proposed by Zhu et al. [5]. Bangla, Devanagari, Roman, Urdu document is separated by texture based Gabor filter by Obaidullah et al. [6]. Six Indic scripts including Roman, Devanagari, Kannada, Tamil, Telugu, Malayalam classification is reported by Hangarge et al. [7]. To separate Bangla, Roman, Devanagari, Oriya Scripts at page level Obaidullah et al. [8] proposed a technique. A technique to separate Roman, Devanagari, Bangla, Urdu scripts using some digit pattern in block level is proposed by Basu et al. [9]. The Script identification of Bangla, Devanagari, Kannada, Malayalam, Oriya, Roman, Telugu, and Urdu in line level by using shape based feature is focused by Obaidullah et al. [10]. A methodology proposed by Sing et al. [11] using some 39 idiosyncratic features to Bangla, Devanagari, Malayalam, Telugu, Roman Scripts in word level. Pardeshi et al. [12] proposed work to identify 11 major scripts using multidimensional feature combining Radon transform, discrete wavelet transform, DCT and statistical filter. Four numeral scripts Bangla, Devanagari, Roman, Urdu identification technique in word level is proposed by Obaidullah et al. [13]. Obaidullah et al. [14] proposed a two stage approach for multi script handwritten document to compare their performance by using different classifier. From the state of art it is clearly seen that researcher give so many efforts to identify scripts by introducing different shades/sets of features considering a set of scripts at a single level. But for a multilingual country like India it is rigorous to discern where 11 official scripts are present. In this paper, our contribution is to propose a novel multi-level frame work to classify of 11 Indic scripts.

2   Contribution

This paper deals with the issues of handwritten Indic scripts at word level and established a hierarchal based model. In this paper word level technique is adopted because the complexity of feature extraction is less enhanced and spiny than page level and block level. At the initial stage of this paper Matra and non-Matra based script are pooled together in two separate classes. After this, different kinds of features are applied on those classes to get ultimate three level hierarchal structures. The aim of this paper is to facilitate the structural scenario as well as the characteristics of 11 Indic scripts.

3   Overview of Indic Scripts

3.1   Genesis of Indic Script

Spoken languages in India are mainly from three major language families – Indo-Aryan, Dravidian, Austro-Asiatic families. According to 8th schedule 22 languages are considered as official language but as per Indian Constitution no languages have the status of National language. There are 11 official scripts to represent these 22 languages namely Bangla, Devanagari, Gujarati, Gurumukhi, Kannada, Malayalam, Oriya, Roman, Tamil, Telugu, Urdu. 29 states and 7 territories of India vividly use these scripts (Table. 1).

Table 1. Different states and territories with their scripts

Script	Language that are represent by script
Bangla	Bangla, Assamese, Manipuri etc.
Devanagari	Hindi, Nepali, Marathi, Konkani, Sindhi etc.
Gujarati	Gujarati, Sanskrit, Kiutchi, Avestanetc.
Gurumukhi	Panjabi, Sanskrit, Sindhi, Brajbhasha, Kharibolietc.
Kannada	Kannada, Konkani, Tulu etc.
Malayalam	Malayalam
Oriya	Oriya, Sanskrit etc.
Roman	German, English, Spanish, Italian, Indonesian etc.
Tamil	Tamil, Sanskrit, Saurashtra, Baraga, Irula, Paniyaetc
Telugu	Telugu
Urdu	Urdu, Burushaski, Bati

3.2 Characteristics of Indic Scripts

One Script is different from another script based on their natures or their attributes. But sometime the writing style may overlap their characteristics. The primary attributes of scripts are briefly defined.

Some scripts that have a horizontal line on the upper part of a word which connected more than one letter is called 'matra' or 'shirorekha'. Bangla, Devanagari, Gurumukhi have matra.

Some South Indic scripts are quite similar in nature but some key features separate them. Telugu and Kannada script are quite similar but Telugu have a 'Tick' known as 'Telekattu' which separate Telugu from Kannada. Most irregular shaped script is Urdu and there exists '.' dot.

Most popular key feature that can identify scripts is orientation. Strokes of different scripts like Devanagari have $0°$, $90°$ Bangla have $0°$, $45°$, $135°$, Urdu have $60°$, $90°$ orientations. Telugu, Tamil have almost same orientation.

4 Proposed Work

One script that is quite different from other one and it is manifested by the script's own letters or attributes which have their particular aspects. By emphasizing this point 112 dimension of features are established that consider letters as well as words of the script and break down 11 Indic scripts in hierarchal fashion. Following diagram briefly described the process of the current work (Fig. 1).

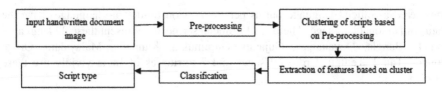

Fig. 1. Work methodology

Analogous features classify the script does not mean a particular feature may fruitful to other script. So some expedient feature set is built for constructive classification of scripts. Two type of feature set one is Structural (SF) and other is Textual (TF) set is involved.

- Structural Features (SF) based on the visual appearance, contour, formation, shape of the characters of the scripts. SF is local to script or script specific.56 dimension features is casting here.
- 56 dimensions of Textual features are essential to emphasize some deviation of texture patterns of some Indic scripts.

4.1 Structural Feature (SF)

- Fractal based 2d features (SF_{FD})
  The Fractal Theory [15] was introduced by Mandelbrot and Van Ness and it is the extension work of Hausdor-Besikvoich. It is a Geometric object that is non-uniform in nature. And these features stand on the idea of non-Euclidean geometry. The fractal dimension (D) is the ratio of the no of indistinguishable pieces (n) and a factor (1/r) into which an image may split.

$$D = \ln n / \ln(1/r) \tag{1}$$

This feature directly slog at pixel level and low dimensions in nature. As the handwritten documents are twisted, angled or sometimes continuous thus this feature is chosen. This two dimensional feature deals with upper part of the contour of an object that the longer connected component 'Matra' or 'Shirorekha' is extracted and lower part of contour the base pixel of the component is also extracted For example Bangla, Devanagari, Gurumukhi there exists matra and for the script Roman, Urdu there is no matra. So the pixel density of the upper and lower part of the component is different for different script.
This $2DSF_{FD}$ firstly apply on 11 Indic scripts that the matra and non matra scripts are separated into two different clusters which form the first order tree structure as show in Fig. 2.

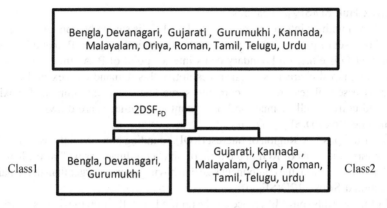

Fig. 2. 1st order tree structure (H$_1$)

- Chain Code 16 Dimensions Features (SF$_{CC}$)

  Chain code is the satisfactory algorithm for monochromic image. The region as well as the segment of the image can be estimated as the external as well as the internal characteristics and can be epitomized either in border or in the pixel of the region. The chain code captures the perimeter of a connected region. There are several directional chain codes, Freeman chain code of 8 directors, 3 orthogonal chain code, unsigned Manhatten chain code etc. In the scripts there are several directional strokes are present for example Matra for Bengla, Devanagari, Telekatu for Telugu and Kannada scripts. So Freeman chain code of 8 directions is chosen for this paper. After draw the component of the image chain code is putting on the inner and outer contour. Thus the component may vary for different scripts. The histogram is used as a feature (Fig. 3).

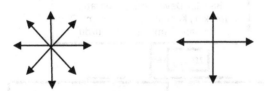

Fig. 3. 8 and 4 directional chain code example

- Circularity 10D Features (SF$_C$)

  Among the 11 Indic Scripts some scripts like Oriya, Malayalam are circular in nature, thus circularity is one of the most formidable feature. At first a circle that surround the component minimally is drawn this is called minimal circle and the radius is memorized. After this another circle that surround the contour of the component is drawn and radius is stored also, called fitted circle. If the difference of the radius of minimal circle and fitted circle is zero, it is considered that the component is perfect circular.

- Convex Hull 8D(SF_{CH}) Features
  A polygon with its interior angles is less than $180°$ is said to be convex polygon [16, 17]. For a set of points Q the convex hull is the tiniest polygon P, that all the points in the set Q is either on boundary or its interior point of P. As the scripts so many different shaped characters or attributes notify this demand convex hull is considered as essential features. To compute some statistical minimum and maximum covered convex hull of inner and outer contour of images are drawn.
- Bounding Box 8D(SF_{BB}) Features
  To measure possible Region of Interest (ROI) bounding box is vividly used. Bounding box returns the value of ROI in the form of pixel coordinates as well as the height and width. In Indic script, the component size that having matra is larger than the remaining.
- Directional Stroke 12D(SF_{DS})
  In 11 Indic scripts some difference can be notified visually. Previously it is clearly seen that some scripts like Bangla, Devanagari etc. Having matra that means they have larger continuous horizontal stroke, but the scripts that don't have matra have some vertical stroke like Gujarati, Oriya and Urdu etc. with the orientation like $60°, 90°, 45°$ mainly. Urdu scripts have also a right diagonal stroke that may horizontal rather than vertical. At this point 12 dimensional directional stroke based feature is introduced.
- Structural features' (SF) summery and applications
  56 dimensional Structural features as well as script independent features are used to approach next level of tree structure. As it is previously seen 2D Fractal based feature (SF_{FD}) is used to classify the scripts has matra and non matra. The rest of 54D feature including 16D SF_{CC}, 10D SF_C, 8D SF_{BB}, 8D SF_{CH}, 12D SF_{DS} are applied for further classification of class 1, that the cluster having matra (Fig. 4).

$$56D\ SF = SF_{FD}(2D) + SF_{CC}(16D) + SF_C(10D) + SF_{CH}(8D) + SF_{BB}(8D) + SF_{DS}(12D)$$

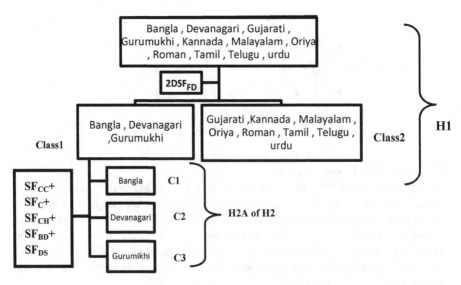

Fig. 4. 2nd order tree Structure (H2)

4.2 Textual Feature (TF)

- Wavelet Radon Transformation (TF$_{WR}$)
  Wavelet is used to compress an image by analyzing that image as well as converting that image into a set of mathematical expression. Mainly wavelet is an extent way to represent multi resolution analysis. Once the coefficient is applied, some wavelet depending upon how much decomposition is used for each image is found. From the decomposition horizontal, vertical, diagonal details of coefficient is recognized. Here Ingrid Daubechies's orthogonal wavelets for discrete wavelet transform is selected, where db1, db2, db3 represent the constant, linear and quadratic coefficient of image component respectively. From the image at db1, db2, db3 generates 12 wavelets. A collection of projections along various direction of image is represented by Represented Radon Transform. RT deals with different directional strokes. RT spectrum at $\theta = 0°$, $30°$, $60°$, $90°$, $120°$, $150°$, $180°$ are projected by combining wavelet with radon transform. The performance of wavelet 54 dimensional feature can be further reformed.
- Spatial Energy Distribution (TF$_{SED}$)
  As the spatial distribution of energy depends on the position of the particles in the medium and wavelet of excitation of light, thus it deviates according to the textual information. Notify this point SED is considered as one of the features. The distribution for spastic grey level the entropy is high but normally is complement of energy represent the entropy. It is also need to evaluate how much dispersion exists from the average of the pixel of binary image thus slandered deviation of binary image is need to measure. This is represented by the following equation.

$$f(x,y) = \sqrt{1/(mn-1) \sum\nolimits_{(r,c)\in w} (n(r,c) - 1/(mn-1) \sum\nolimits_{(r,c)\in w} n(r,c))2} \quad (2)$$

The operation takes place where 'r' and 'c' are row and column with in a window 'w' of size m × n and 'n' is noisy image.4 dimensional spatial energy distribution features is used.
- Textural features' (SF) summery and applications
  54 dimensional wavelets with radon transform (TF$_{WR}$) as well as 2 dimensional special energy distributions (TF$_{SED}$) are considered as script independent feature or textual feature.

$$TF(56D) = TF_{WR}(54D) + TF_{SED}(2D)$$

56 dimensional textual as well as 54 dimensional structural features excluding fractal based 2 dimensional features are applied over those scripts that have no matra i.e. the scripts of class 2 in first order hierarchy and divided class 2into next cluster C1 and C2. The class C1 consists of the scripts Kannada, Malayalam, Oriya, Tamil, Telugu and the other one C2 contains Gujarati, Urdu, and Roman (Fig. 5).

After this total feature set i.e.112 dimensional including 56D TF and 56D SF are applied over C1 as well as C2 of H2B to get further processing result (Fig. 6).

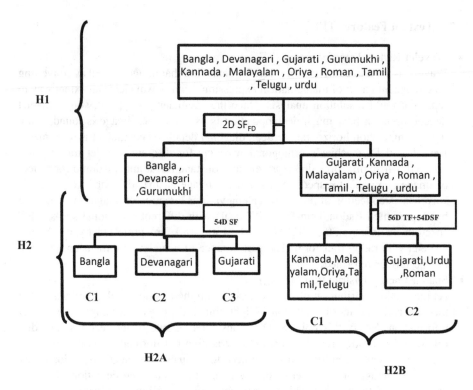

Fig. 5. 2nd order hierarchal structure after applying TF

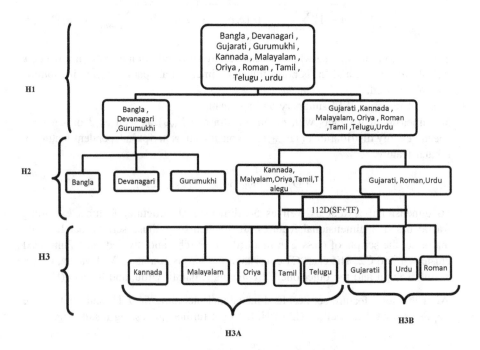

Fig. 6. 3rd order hierarchal structure

5   Classification

Classification is the way associated with categorization in which objects are recognized and differentiated. The goal is to classify 11 Indic Script in tree based approach in word level by assigning the value of input to a given set of class. Three most popular classifier Multilayer perceptron (MLP), Random forest (RF), Simple Logistic (SL) are chosen. And a comparative result of accuracy of three different classifiers at different hierarchal level is produced.

- Multilayer perceptron (MLP)
  An artificial neural network(ANN)is an information processing prototype that is motivated by the biological nervous system with the tasks classification, discrimination, estimation. MLP is a simple neuron called perceptron that represent interconnected Feed forward network where the information flow unidirectional and the relationship between nodes. MLP has more than two layers except input layer. The basic idea of perceptron was established by Rosenblatt in 1958 in which the input including bias have weight that attached to the input line to modify the input value and the weight is just multiplied with the input. The equation is as follows.

$$y = \varphi\left(\sum\nolimits_{i=1}^{n} w_i x_i + b\right) = \varphi(W^T X + b) \tag{3}$$

For the input i = 1, 2, 3,.... n the inputs x_i is multiplied with the weight vector w and add it with the bias b. The activation function φ is the sigmoid activation function.

$$\varphi = 1/(1 + e^{-x}) \tag{4}$$

To improve ANN's performance a mathematical logic is introduced called 'learning' with three categories supervised, unsupervised and reinforcement learning. Here supervised learning is selected where the training data consisting of the pairs of input and output are provided. The problem in MLP in supervised learning can be solved by the Back Propagation algorithm. The main motive of BPP algorithm is the output of ANN is evaluated against desire one. After random chose of network weight this algorithm decomposed into four steps – Feed Forward Computation, BP to output layer, BP to hidden layer, Weight update. This algorithm stopped when the value of error function has become sufficiently small.

- Random Forest (RF)
  To give an gentle introduction it must be said that Random Forest (Breman 2001) is an ensemble presentation that is as the form of neighbor predictor both in classification and regression task. An ensemble is dividing and conquers approach that is used to modify the performance of network. The key idea behind ensemble is that a group of 'weak learner' can come together to build a 'strong learner'. This RF is based on 'bagging method' most of the time. This classifier will handle the missing values. If there exist more trees in forest RF classifier won't over fit the model.

RF Algorithm.

1. Randomly select 'J' features from total 'F' features where F ≫ J.
2. Among the 'J' features, calculate the node 'd'using best split point.
3. Split the node into the child node.
4. Repeat steps 1 to 3 until reached leaf end node.

   Build the forest by traversing the step 1 to 4 to create 'n' number of trees.

- Simple Logistic (SL)
  The main area to use SL when there are nominal variable with two values and one measurement variable, where nominal dependent and measurement variable is independent variable. This SL regression is based on the idea of Logit Boost algorithm. The main advantage of SL is it has built in attribute section, when the cross validation classification error not decrease, it stops adding simple linear regression models.

6   Results and Analysis

In this work the justification is served regarding the grouping of the 11 Indic scripts for the tree based classification. This experiment is done over 6598 number of instants. For the initial stage two dimensional fractal based feature (SF_{FD}) is applied to group 11 Indic scripts based on the presence or absence of 'matra'. MLP classifier has the highest accuracy 77.20% in the first order hierarchy(H1). Where the Random Forest (RF) occupies second position with 76.78% and Simple Logistics (SL) occupy the third position with 72.734% accuracy. It can be notify in Fig. 7 that the accuracy between MLP and RF is slight but the difference percentage of accuracy is noticeable.

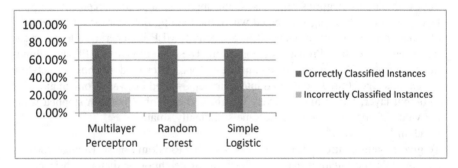

Fig. 7. Results of different classifier in 1st order hierarchy (H1)

The next hierarchy H2, there is 2 sub group H2A and H2B. After getting two cluster class1 consisting Bangla (1), Devanagari (2), Gurumukhi (3) and class 2 consisting of remains at H1. The further progress is done by applying 54D structural features on Class1 of H1and produced the sub group of 2nd order hierarchy (H2) i.e. H2A and classify the instance by MLP, RF and SL. It is noticed that the accuracy of all three classifier is increased as compared to previous level that means the percentage of correctly classified instance in H2A for all three classifier. But the random forest gives the best result with 87% accuracy. In Fig. 8 the performance chart of three classifiers is given bellow.

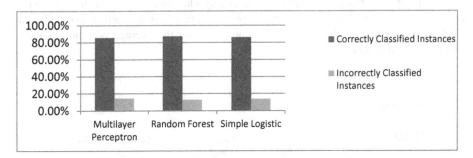

Fig. 8. Performance of three classifier in H2A

Excluding 2D fractral based feature (SF_{FD}) 54D structural as well as 56 D textual features are applied on the Class 2 of H1 and decomposed into two class C1 (Kannada, Malayalam, Oriya, Tamil, Telugu) and C2 (Gujarati, Urdu, Roman) that is the sub-group of H2 named H2B. As per the results it is seen that MLP has the highest 97.60% accuracy shown in Fig. 9.

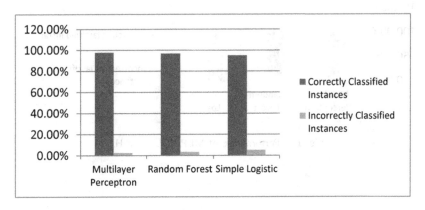

Fig. 9. Accuracy of MLP, RF, SL at the sub group H2B

The last hirarcal level that is H3vboth the 56D SF and 56D TF is applied over both in class1 and class2 to decompose into different sub group H3A ana H3B respectively. For the C1 (Kannada, Malayalam, Oriya, Tamil, Telugu) of H2B 112 dimenssional feature set ia applied and classify this class and create subgroup H3A. It is observed that the performance of all three classifier is increased and give satisfactory results. And for the another subgroup of H3 i.e. H3B the class C2 consisting of Gujarati, Urdu, Roman is decomposed by 112D features. It is visible that for this level of hirarkey i.e. H3B, it produced highest percentage of correctly classified instance compaired with previous one. Table 2 shows as the components are classified further into different clasters the accuracy is become more competent with the average accuracy 94.43% (Figs. 10, 11 and 12).

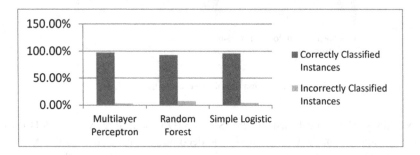

Fig. 10. Performace of MLP, RF, SL at H3A

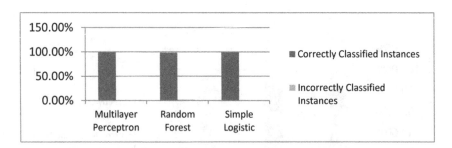

Fig. 11. Performance of MLP, RF, SL at H3

Table 2. Performance of all classifier at different levels of hierarchy

Hierarchy	Sub-hierarchy	Classifier	Correctly classified instances
H1	NA	MLP	77.20%
		RF	76.78%
		SL	72.7%
H2	**H2A** (Individual level of classification)	MLP	85.38%
		RF	**87.11%**
		SL	86.11%
	H2B	MLP	97.60%
		RF	96.66%
		SL	94.83%
H3	**H3A** (Individual level of classification)	MLP	**96.96%**
		RF	92.62%
		SL	95.76%
	H3B (Individual level of classification)	MLP	**99.22%**
		RF	98.27%
		SL	99%
Average accuracy			(87.11 + 96.96 + 99.22)/ 3 = **94.43%**

Hierarchy	classifier	True Positive Rate (TP)	False Positive Rate (FP)
H2A	Multilayer Perceptron	0.854	0.073
	Random Forest	0.871	0.064
	Simple Logistic	0.861	0.069
H3A	Multilayer Perceptron	0.970	0.008
	Random Forest	0.926	0.018
	Simple Logistic	0.958	0.011
H3B	Multilayer Perceptron	0.992	0.004
	Random Forest	0.983	0.009
	Simple Logistic	0.990	0.005

Fig. 12. TP and FP Rate for MLP, RF, SL classifiers

7 Conclusion

The paper presents a novel multi-level framework to separate 11 Indic scripts. Based on visual appearance the scripts are grouped into different clusters and appropriate features are computed for each category. Performance of three different classifiers namely multilayer perceptron, random forest and simple logistic are compared and we found that multilayer perceptron is the best performer in most of the scenarios followed by random forest. We obtained an average individual script-level accuracy of 94.43% which is quite encouraging to observe the inherent complexities of Indic scripts. In future we want to explore script dependent features to address few of the misclassification issues. Integrating classifiers and performing the statistical significance test over multiple datasets is also in our plan.

References

1. Ghosh, D., Dube, T., Shivprasad, S.P.: Script recognition—a review. IEEE Trans. Pattern Anal. Mach. Intell. **32**(12), 2142–2161 (2010)
2. Singh, P.K., Sarkar, R., Nasipuri, M.: Offline script identification from multilingual indic-script documents: a state-of-the-art. Comput. Sci. Rev. **15–16**, 1–28 (2015)
3. Obaidullah, S.M., Das, S.K., Roy, K.: A system for handwritten script identification from Indian document. J. Pattern Recogn. Res. **8**, 1–12 (2013)
4. Hochberg, J., Bowers, K., Cannon, M., Kelly, P.: Script and language identication for handwritten document images. J. Doc. Anal. Recogn. **2**(2/3), 45–52 (1999)
5. Zhu, X., Li, Y.Y., Doermann, D.: Language identication for handwritten document images using a shape codebook. Pattern Recogn. **42**, 3184–3191 (2009)
6. Obaidullah S.M., Das, N., Roy, K.: Gabor filter based technique for offline indic script identification from handwritten document images. In: International Conference on Devices, Circuits and Communications, ICDCCom 2014, pp 1–6 (2014)
7. Hangarge, M., Santosh, K.C., Pardeshi, R.: Directional discrete cosine transform for handwritten script identification. In: Proceedings of the International Conference on Document Analysis and Recognition, ICDAR, pp 344–348 (2013)
8. Obaidullah, S.M., Karim, R., Shaikh, S., Halder, C., Das, N., Roy, K.: Transform based approach for Indic script identification from handwritten document images. In: 3rd International Conference on Signal Processing, Communications and Networking, pp 1–7 (2015)
9. Basu, S., Das, N., Sarkar, R., Kundu, M., Nasipuri, M., Basu, D.K.: A novel framework for automatic sorting of postal documents with multi-script address blocks. Pattern Recogn. **43**(10), 3507–3521 (2010)
10. Obaidullah, S.M., Halder, C., Das, N., Roy, K.: An approach for automatic Indic script identification from handwritten document images. In: 2nd Doctoral Symposium on Applied Computation and Security Systems, pp 37–51 (2015)
11. Singh, P.K., Mondal, A., Bhowmik, S., Sarkar, R., Nasipuri, M.: Word-Level Script Identification from Handwritten Multi-script Documents. In: Satapathy, S.C., Biswal, B.N., Udgata, Siba K., Mandal, J.K. (eds.) Proceedings of the 3rd International Conference on Frontiers of Intelligent Computing: Theory and Applications (FICTA) 2014. AISC, vol. 327, pp. 551–558. Springer, Cham (2015). https://doi.org/10.1007/978-3-319-11933-5_62

12. Pardeshi, R., Chaudhuri, B.B., Hangarge, M., Santosh, K.C.: Automatic handwritten Indian scripts identification. In: 14th International Conference on Frontiers in Handwriting Recognition, pp 375–380 (2014)
13. Obaidullah, S.M., Halder, C., Das, N., Roy, K.: Numeral script identification from handwritten document images. Proc. Comput. Sci. J. **54C**, 585–594 (2015)
14. Obaidullah, S.M., Roy, K., Das, N.: Comparison of different classifiers for script identification from handwritten document. In: IEEE International Conference on Signal Processing, Computing and Control, pp. 019–024 (2013)
15. Mandelbrot, B.B.: The Fractal Geometry of Nature. Freeman, NY (1982)
16. Jayara, M.A., Fleyeh, H.: Convex hulls in image processing: a scoping review. Sci. Acad. Publ. **6**(2), 48–58 (2016)
17. Avis, D., Bremner, D., Seidel, R.: How good are convex hull algorithms? Comput. Geom. **7**, 265–301 (1997)

A Lemmatizer Tool for Assamese Language

Arindam Roy, Sunita Sarkar$^{(\boxtimes)}$, and Hsubhas Borkakoty

Assam University, Silchar, India
arindam_roy74@rediffmail.com,
sarkarsunita260l@gmail.com

Abstract. Word Sense Disambiguation (WSD) requires sense tagged corpora. Words in a corpus appear in inflected or morphed forms. Sense tagging can only be done with words in their root or lemmatized forms. Similarly for Part of Speech Tagging (POS), the words in a corpus are required to be available in their root forms. A WordNet, which is a lexical knowledge base, consists of words in their lemmatized forms. In this paper we present a scheme whereby a trie is constructed from words in the Assamese WordNet. An input word, which maybe in inflected form, is compared against an entry in the trie by searching the trie with the input word as key and following the principle of longest prefix match, the root form of an inflected word may be obtained. When there is a mismatch between an input word and an entry in the trie, a rule based morphological analyzer provides the lemmatized form of the inflected word.

Keywords: WSD · Corpus · Trie · WordNet

1 Introduction

In Natural Language Processing (NLP), Sense marked corpora or Sense annotated corpora is of utmost importance. It is used in Supervised WSD which generates the correct sense of a word in a given context. But a corpora is always available in inflected forms. The words in the corpora need to be converted to their root forms through Lemmatization. Similarly POS tagging of any corpora would require that the inflected words in the corpora are first rendered in their root forms and only then any POS tagging algorithm may be applied on the corpus containing words in their root forms. Lemmatization is also used in Information Retrieval to expedite the retrieval time and improve the relevance of retrieved documents [1].

Stemming is different from Lemmatization in the sense that stemming aims to convert a word into its base form which may or may not be a dictionary word. For example, a stemmer can produce "parti" from the word "parties" whereas a Lemmatizer has to produce the root word "party". A lemmatizer does not simply remove inflections but relies on WordNet to produce the correct root form of an inflected word. There are broadly three different approaches to Lemmatization. These are, namely, rule based, statistical and hybrid (both rule based and statistical).

In this paper we have also used a hybrid method which is different from the standard one. Here the longest prefix match has been used to generate the root word

© Springer Nature Singapore Pte Ltd. 2019
J. K. Mandal et al. (Eds.): CICBA 2018, CCIS 1031, pp. 124–133, 2019.
https://doi.org/10.1007/978-981-13-8581-0_10

from the trie. In cases where longest prefix match has been found to be deficient, morphological rule based method has been used.

2 Assamese Language

Assamese is a diverse and morphologically rich language. The language has its own script and literary texts since the ancient times (from 14th century). It belongs to eastern sub group of Indo Aryan languages which falls under Indo European languages. Currently it has around 15 million native speakers (Census 2010) [2]. It is the lingua franca of the Indian state of Assam. It is also partly spoken in some areas of Indian state of Arunachal Pradesh. An Assamese based Creole Language called Nagamese is widely used in the Indian state of Nagaland. Magadhi Prakrit, a middle Indo Aryan language, is believed to be the source of Assamese language [14]. Eastern Magadhi Prakrit and Magadhi Apabhramsa can be divided into four dialect groups: (1) Rādha dialects which represent standard Bengali colloquial in Western Bengal and Oriya in the south west (2) Varendra dialects of North Central Bengal (3) Kāmarūpa dialects which represent Assamese and some dialects of North Bengal and (4) Vanga dialects which represent the dialects of East Bengal [16].

Assamese WordNet is part of IndoWordNet which is a linked lexical knowledge base of major Indian languages belonging to Indo-Aryan, Dravidian and Sino Tibetan families. English WordNet was the first WordNet [17] to be built. Hindi WordNet [18] was the first of its kind in India and it followed the principle of expansion from English WordNet. The nationwide project of building Indian language WordNets followed suit and it also follows the expansion approach from Hindi WordNet. The Assamese WordNet consists of 14,958 synsets. The Part of Speech (POS) subdivision is as follows - (i) Noun-9065, (ii) Verb-1676, (iii) Adjective-3805, (iv) Adverb-412.

The rest of the paper is as follows: Sect. 3 is on literature survey. Section 4 and its subsections provide a description of Word formation in Assamese, Sect. 5 and its subsections presents the framework and methodology for a lemmatizer in Assamese, Sect. 6 describes experimental results while Sect. 7 winds up the discussion by presenting the conclusions and future work.

3 Literature Review

Lovins was the first to develop a stemmer [3], which was meant for IR/NLP applications. His methodology consisted of the use of a manually developed list of 294 suffixes, each linked to 29 conditions, plus 35 transformation rules. Given an input word, the suffix with an appropriate condition is checked and removed. Porter developed the Porter stemming algorithm [4] which became the most widely used stemming algorithm for English language. It was described in a very high level language known as Snowball. Statistical approaches have been significantly used for stemming. Significant works are Goldsmith's unsupervised algorithm for learning morphology of a language based on the Minimum Description Length (MDL) framework [5, 6], Creutz's unsupervised morpheme segmentation [7, 8] which uses probabilistic maximum a posteriori (MAP) formulation. Hidden Markov models have also been used in stemming [9]. In this approach each word is considered to be composed of two parts "prefix" and "suffix". HMM states are composed of two disjoint sets: Prefix state which generates the first part of the word and Suffix state which generates the last part of the word, if at all the word has a suffix. A complete and trained HMM can then perform stemming directly. A two level morphological analyser containing a large set of morphophonemic rules was developed by Karttunen et al., [10]. The work started in 1980 and the first implementation was available in 1983. An Arabic lemmatizer was proposed by El-Shishtawy [11]. Different Arabic language knowledge resources were used to generate accurate lemma form and its relevant features that support IR purposes and a maximum accuracy of 94.8% was achieved. A Turkish Morphological Analyzer called OMA gives all possible analyses for a given word with the help of finite state technology. As far as Indian languages are concerned, Ramanathan and Rao was the earliest work which performed longest match stripping on manually sorted suffix list to produce a Hindi stemmer [12]. Mazumder et al. [13] proposed a clustering based approach for discovering equivalence classes of root words and their morphological inflections. The equivalence classes are underpinned by a set of string distance measures to cluster the lexicon for a given text.

4 Word Formation in Assamese

The primary words or the Lemmas in Assamese have both Aryan and non Aryan origin. The secondary word formation of Assamese language is realized through two different approaches [14]. The approaches are affixation: addition of prefixes and suffixes and Compounding: addition of certain words to form a new word.

4.1 Affixation

Affixes are added before or after the word to create a new inflected form of the word with respect to number, person, tense, aspect and mood. There are 20 prefixes of Assamese words that can be added before the word to form a new word, such as

- প্ৰ: প্ৰমাণ (proof)
- পৰা : পৰাজয় (defeat)
- বি : বিপদ (danger)
- নি: নিহিত (contain)
- সু: সুকৃতি (good deedInitial Population)

4.2 Compounding

The Assamese compound words are formed in three different forms, viz. closed Form, Open form and Hyphenated form. Apart from these three forms, there also exist a set of compounds in which one word is of native origin and the other is of foreign origin. For example, the word বংঘৰ (palace) is compounded from the word বং which is a Thai word meaning palace and ঘৰ, which is an Assamese word meaning house.

Closed Form. In this formation, the words are formed by adding more than one word joined together to form a new word with new meaning. Some examples are given below:

- হিমালয় : হিম (ice) + আলয় (home)
- আগদিনা: আগ(before) + দিনা (day)
- চন্দ্রোদয়: চন্দ্র(moon) + উদয় (rise)
- যথোপযুক্ত: যথা(As) + উপযুক্ত(appropriate)
- শুক্রেশ্বৰ: শুক্র (name of a yogi) + ইশ্বৰ (god)

Open Form. In this form, two different words are added to form a new word. Here, combination of more than one word that work as a unit in order to convey different meaning. Examples include:

- কাঠৰ পুতলা (noun + noun): one who is entirely led by others
- মাটিৰ মানুহ (noun + noun): one who is humble,
- নপতা ফুকন (Adjective + Noun): A false leader
- হাত দীঘল (Noun+ adjective): Influential person
- গেলা গপ (Adjective + noun): vain boasting
- হাত টান (Noun + Adjective): one who is miser
- কপাল ফুটা (Noun + Adjective): one who is unlucky

Hyphenated Form: In this form, the words are joined together by a hyphen. Some of the examples are given below:

- হকা-বাধা (act of preventing something)
- মৰম-চেনেহ (act of love)
- মাত-বোল (act of calling someone)
- আলি-পদূলি (road)
- অহা-যোৱা (coming and going)
- উঠা-বহা (act of sitting and standing up)
- ঘৰ-বাৰী (Home)
- টকা-সিকা (money)
- মাৰ-পিট (to hit someone)
- হৰণ-ভগন (to lose something) etc

The noticeable thing about the words formed via this formation is that the parts of each word has similar meaning. For example, for the word মৰম-চেনেহ, both parts of the word (মৰম and চেনেহ) convey the same meaning, i.e. love.

4.3 Types of Suffixes in Assamese Language

Suffixes are added at the end of the words to form a new word. The suffixes are also termed as "প্রত্যয়" [12]. There exists four different types of suffixes in Assamese language. They are:

- বিভক্তি (suffix marker)
- স্ত্রীপ্রত্যয় (feminine suffixes)
- তদ্ধিত প্রত্যয় (derivational suffixes)
- কৃৎ প্রত্যয় (verbal suffixes)

বিভক্তি **(Word Suffix markers).** There exist seven different suffix markers for Assamese language. These are:

- Nominative: এ,ই :আখৰে (আখৰ+এ)) (of the letters, সামৰি (সামৰ+ই)) (finishing up)
- Accusative: অক: আখৰক (আখৰ+অক) (to the letters), মানুহক (মানুহ+অক) (to people)
- Dative: বে, দি, দ্বাৰা: পানীবে (পানী+বে)) (with water) , চক্কুবেদি(চক্কু+দি) (with eyes), মানুহৰদ্বাৰা (মানুহ+অৰ+দ্বাৰা)) (by people)
- Genitive : লৈ: মানুহলৈ (মানুহ+লৈ)) (to people)
- Ablative:পৰা: মানুহৰপৰা(মানুহ+ৰ+পৰা))(from people)
- Instrumental: অৰ: পানীৰ (পানী+অৰ) (of water)
- Locative: অত: পানীত (পানী+ত) (in water)

স্ত্রী-প্রত্যয় (Feminine Suffixes). The feminine suffixes in Assamese consists of two different suffixes: ঈ and অনী. Some of the examples depicting its use are given as follows:

ঈ: কলা (Deaf)+ঈ=কলী,
বুঢ়া (Old) + ই=বুঢ়ী
পেটুলা (Fat) + ঈ=পেটুলী
অনী:কুকুৰ (Dog) + অনী=কুকুৰনী,
হস্তী (Elephant) + নী=হস্তিনী, নাতি (Grandchild) + নী=নাতিনী

তদ্ধিত প্ৰত্যয় **(Derivational Suffix).** The derivational suffixes are added after the word in order to form a complete new word. The formation of derivational suffixed words can be achieved using proper suffixes with the given word. Examples:

Sanskrit Derivational Suffixes: ফি: দশৰথ+ফি: দাশৰথি (son of King Dasarath), বন্ধু+ষ=বান্ধৱ(friend) etc.

Assamese Derivational Suffixes: ঈ: তাম+ঈ:তামী (of brass), লুণীয়া (লোণ+ঈয়া) (salty), থঙাল(থং+আল) (angry) etc.

কৃৎ প্ৰত্যয় **(verbal suffixes).** The suffixes that are added to the root of the verb (ধাতু) are called কৃৎ প্ৰত্যয়. The suffixes are added to the respective verbs to convey a new meaning for the verb. It is not necessary that the root word be verb, these suffixes can also be added to, for example, adjectives. But these work better in case of verbal roots.
    Examples are: কৰা(কৰ+আ) (Do), শোৱন(শো+অন) (the act of sleeping), জিৰণি(জিৰ+অণি) (the act of taking rest), শিকাৰু(শিক+আৰু) (learner) etc.

5   Methodology

The approach that we have followed creates a trie data structure by inserting words into it from the Assamese WordNet. The words in a WordNet are in their root forms. It checks if a given word from the WordNet is in the trie or not. If not, then it is inserted in the trie. Whenever a word is given as input, the trie is searched using input word as key and longest prefix match is used to compare the input word with the corresponding entry in the trie. The corresponding branch of the trie which has the longest prefix match with the input word is considered as the root of the input word. If there is a mismatch between the input word and the corresponding entry in the trie, a morpho-logical rule based analyzer is called which provides the lemmatized form of the inflected word.
    For example let us take the word ৰাজ্যক. The root of the inflected word ৰাজ্যক is ৰাজ্য which is present in Assamese WordNet. So the word ৰাজ্য would be inserted in the trie. When the trie is searched with the inflected word ৰাজ্যক as key, by the principle of longest prefix match, the word ৰাজ্য would be output which is the root. Similar argument holds good for commonly occurring words in a corpus like প্ৰসঙ্গত, সম্প্ৰদায়ৰ,

শব্দৰ, অসমৰ, সংস্কৃতৰ, ভাষাত, পদাৰ্থৰ, মুখত, ভাষাতকৈ, মানচিত্ৰথন, অৱচেতনত,
, সপ্তাংশতকৈ, পুৰাণত, অলোচনাৰ etc.

5.1   Deviation from Trie Based Approach

Assamese language has a large number of verbs. There exist several irregularities in verbs in Assamese language also, like all other languages. In case of lemmatization, the problem arises when the structure of the verb changes with change in tense [15]. Some examples are mentioned below.

যা: গৈছিলো,গলোহেতেন, গলিহেতেন, গলাহেতেন ,গেছে, গল, গৈছ, গৈছা, গলো etc. (various forms of go)

অহা: আহা, আহক, আহিছা, আহিছিলা, আহিছিলি, আহিছিলে, আহিছিল, আহিছিলো etc. (various forms of come)

ৰোয়া :   ৰুইছিল, ৰুইছা (to sow)

Apart from the verbs, there are derivational suffixes which don't easily lend themselves to straightforward derivation from trie structure mentioned above. A few examples, which are representative in nature, will be in order:

কাৰুণ্য = কৰুণা + ষ্য (কৰুণা is the root)
সামীপ্য = সমীপ + ষ্য (সমীপ is the root)
গম্ভীযর্য = গম্ভীৰ + ষ্য (গম্ভীৰ is the root)
পনীয়া   = পানী   + ঈয়া (পানী is the root)
এটীয়া   = এটা   + ঈয়া (এটা is the root)
ভদীয়া = ভাদ   + ঈয়া(ভাদ is the root)
নুমলীয়া = নোমল + ঈয়া (নোমল is the root)
কপহৰা = কপাহ + উৰা (কপাহ is the root)

From these examples we can see that derivationally inflected words need to be split into its root form and suffix following the rules of the language. A morphological analyzer conforming to rules of suffix splitting for derivationally inflected words in Assamese language has been encoded in our system.

6 Experimental Results

The Assamese corpus was mainly taken from Assamese Corpora provided by TDIL (Technology Development for Indian Languages) under Ministry of Electronics and Information Technology, Government of India. The corpora consists of texts of Assamese history, Assamese society and community tourism, health etc.

A few snapshots of the output is shown below in Figs. 1, 2 and 3.

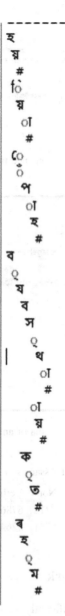

Fig. 1. Trie structure of a few words of Assamese Language

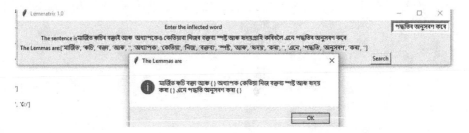

Fig. 2. Lemmatization of a sentence from Assamese corpus.

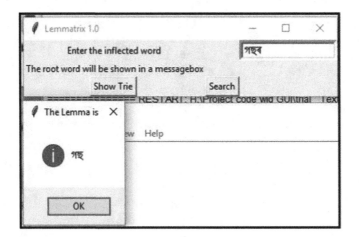

Fig. 3. A GUI depicting the lemma of an inflected Assamese word

Table 1. Result of Assamese Lemmatizer tool

	Noun	Verb	Adjective	Adverb
Total words in corpus	7312	6786	2134	517
Correctly analyzed words	5841	5264	1557	343

7   Conclusion and Future Work

We have tested our approach on significantly varied categories of text as mentioned above. Our method envisage obtaining the root of a word through prefix matching and suffix stripping with the aid of a trie data structure and rule based morphology. The results validate the efficiency of the proposed system. It has been noticed that, at times, Assamese WordNet does not contain the root form of inflected words in the corpus, specially, in the case of nouns and adjectives. Commonly used words in a corpus like

প্রতিবেদন, সামগ্রিক, ক্ষেত্র, প্রণালী, পোহ, সোমা, পিৰালি, প্রবর্তন, সাম্য

etc. are not present, till date, in Assamese WordNet. There are significant inflectional variations in case of verbs when there is a change of tense, all of which have not been addressed in the present system. As part of future work an exhaustive rule based morphological analyzer may be built to address the irregularities of verbs in Assamese language.

References

1. Christopher, M., Prabhakar, R.D., Hinrich, S.: Introduction to Information Retrieval. Cambridge University Press, Cambridge (2008)
2. https://www.ne.se/språk/världens-100-största-språk-2010
3. Lovins, J.B.: Development of a stemming algorithm. Mech. Transl. Comput. Linguist. 11(1-2), 22–31 (1968)
4. Porter, M.F.: An algorithm for suffix stripping. Program 14, 130–137 (1980)
5. Goldsmith, J.A.: Unsupervised learning of the morphology of a natural language. Comput. Linguist. 27(2), 153–198 (2001)
6. Goldsmith, J.A.: An algorithm for the unsupervised learning of morphology. Nat. Lang. Eng. 12(4), 353–371 (2006)
7. Creutz, M., Lagus, K.: Unsupervised morpheme segmentation and morphology induction from text corpora using Morfessor 1.0. Technical report A81, Publications in Computer and Information Science, Helsinki University of Technology (2005)
8. Creutz, M., Lagus, K.: Unsupervised models for morpheme segmentation and morphology learning. ACM Trans. Speech Lang. Process. 4(1), 1–34 (2007)
9. Massimo, M., Orio, N.: A novel method of stemmer generation based on hidden Markov models. In: CIKM 2003, New Orleans, Louisiana, USA (2003)
10. Karttunen, L.: KIMMO: a general morphological processor. In: Texas Linguistic Forum, vol. 22, pp. 163–186 (1983)
11. El-Shishtawy, T., El-Ghannam, F.: An accurate arabic root-based lemmatizer for information retrieval purposes. IJCSI Int. J. Comput. Sci. Issues 9(1, 3) (2012). ISSN 1694-0814
12. Ramanathan, A., Rao, D.D.: A lightweight stemmer for Hindi. In: Workshop on Computational Linguistics for South-Asian Languages, EACL (2003)
13. Majumder, P., Mitra, M., Parui, S.K., Kole, G., Mitra, P., Datta, K.: YASS: yet another suffix stripper. ACM Trans. Inf. Syst. 25(4), 18–38 (2007)
14. Kakati, B.: Assamese-its formation and development. Govt of Assam, Department of Historical and Antiquarian Studies, Narayani Handiqui Historical Institute, Guwahati, Assam (1941)
15. Bora, S.: Bahal Byakaran, Smt S Dey, College Hostel Road, Panbazar, Guwahati (2012)
16. Chatterjee, S.K.: Origin and Development of Bengali Language (ODBL), Rupa and Co. (2002)
17. Miller, G.A., Beckwith, R., Fellbaum, C., Gross, D., Miller, K.: Introduction to WordNet: An On-line Lexical Database. Princeton University, Cognitive Science Laboratory, Technical report (1993)
18. Narayan, D., Chakrabarty, D., Pande, P., Bhattacharyya, P.: An experience in building the indo WordNet-a WordNet for Hindi. In: 1st International Conference on Global WordNet (GWC 2002), Mysore, India (2002)

Portfolio Management by Time Series Clustering Using Correlation for Stocks

Arup Mitra[1(✉)], Abhra Das[2(✉)], Saptarsi Goswami[3(✉)],
Joy Mustafi[4(✉)], and A. K. Jalan[1(✉)]

[1] Mathematics Department, MCKV Institute of Engineering,
Liluah, Howrah 711204, India
arupmitra010@gmail.com, arun_k_Jalan@yahoo.com
[2] Calcutta University Data Science Group, Kolkata 700106, India
abhradas@gmail.com
[3] A.K. Choudhury School of Information Technology,
University of Calcutta, Kolkata 700106, India
saptarsi007@gmail.com
[4] MUST Research Club, Hyderabad 500107, India
mustafi.joy@live.com

Abstract. Investment diversification and portfolio building has been a great interest for share market investors, so as to minimize risk and maximize profit in a sensitive stock market. This paper gives an inside view of application of clustering for grouping 79 stocks (NSE), which can be used to build a diversified portfolio. Manually trying out different groupings to diversify portfolio is a computationally expensive task. In this paper, the closing price, time series of the stocks have been considered. Common effect due to market has been discounted using partial correlation, and a correlation based dissimilarity measure has been used for clustering. An equal investment strategy has been adopted to compare the portfolio's performance with SENSEX. The empirical results of the portfolios have been studied and presented in details.

Keywords: Time series · Clustering · Correlation analysis

1 Introduction

Prediction of stock market is very difficult due to high volatile nature of market conditions, various internal and external factors that influence the stock market sentiments. There are two types of analysis that investors perform in the securities market. First is fundamental analysis, it involves intrinsic value of securities performance of industry, economy, political, and social, etc., which may decide to participate in the market or not. On the other hand is Technical analysis which does not involve with intrinsic value of securities, it mainly participates in statistics generated market

---

https://www.r-project.org/
http://must.co.in/.

J. K. Mandal et al. (Eds.): CICBA 2018, CCIS 1031, pp. 134–144, 2019.
https://doi.org/10.1007/978-981-13-8581-0_11

activities, with various indicators, oscillators, price, volume, and pattern formation to predict any pictorial representation.

One of the major problems in financial market is portfolio selection. Under the mixed business environment, investors are investing in equity market mainly for two primary objectives, one is hedging against the risk over the period of time, and secondly mix investment basket that diversifies the risk to reduce the overall volatility of the portfolio. Burton Malkiel (Malkiel, 1973) stated that the "Past movement or direction of the price of the stock, or overall market can not be used to predict its future movement". Efficient market hypothesis by Malkiel and Fama (1970) states that prices of stock are information ally efficient, which means that it is possible to predict stock price based on the trading data.

Clustering is defined by Driver and Kroeber (1932) clustering is the process of organizing objects into a group and those groups are similar, and data point or group belonging to the different clusters are dissimilar. Hierarchical trees have been applied to stock market data by Mantegna [15] and exchange rate data by Naylor et al. [12]. Method of partial correlation network and partial correlation graphs has been applied to stock market data by Kenett et al. [5].

In this paper we focus on clustering by using correlation techniques. We also implement partial correlation to measure relationship with sensex in Indian stock market. The visual representation helps to understand similarity of stocks within the market, which is an effective method for portfolio management with low risk. An outlier analysis performed which can be useful for investor to make the right decision over a period of time.

Brief structure of these articles: Sect. 2 Literature review work in the area, Sect. 3 clustering and stock selection, Sect. 4 present different parameters and configuration and measures for experiment. Section 5 Experiments and results, Sect. 6 Conclusion of the work.

2 Related work

Nanda et al. [14] used clustering for building an optimal portfolio, different clustering techniques have been used namely K- mean, Fuzzy C means, and SOM. Among this K-mean shows better performance, finally Markowitze model is used for building a portfolio selection. The time period considered was 2007–2008. Goswami et al. [16] used a simple clustering technique for investigating the price and trend movement after the budget announcement 2017. Bini et al. [3] has used regression analysis for predicting stock price and applied various clustering techniques to find out the similarity between the stocks, a 6 months period has been considered. Partial correlation analysis is used for understanding external and internal market influence in Chinese stock market by Li et al. [19]. Jung and Chang [17]. They have used partial correlation to understand the strength of stock price, without index performance in Korean stock market. Gong and Son [9] used logistic regression and other methods like RBF-ANN model for stock prediction. They have considered index variable as well. Thakur et al.

[7] used Dampster Shafer theory for portfolio selection, they considered four fundamental metrics for stocks selection, where semi variance to return ratio measures individual stocks performance. And Finally Ant Colony Optimization (ACO) is used for portfolio building.

(A) Portfolio:
Portfolio is a mix investment basket or grouping of financial assets, which diversify the risk, it helps to reduce the overall volatility of the market over a period of time. Diversification of investment is a process of hedging risk.

(B) Clustering
Clustering is the grouping among the objects in to the high- interclass similarity and low- interclass similarity. It's a process of distance measurement according to nature and behaviors of the different objects, and robust against noise. Clustering is the process of finding the responsibility of homogeneous group for useful data class and also described unknown properties of outlier's determination.

3 Proposed Method

The proposed algorithm, compares the closing price of selected stocks for a given time period. Based on their similarity, the stocks are grouped into different clusters.

Algorithm: PMTSCCS (Portfolio Management by Time Series Clustering using Correlation for Stocks)
Input: Closing prices for 79 MSCI stocks and Sensex data with dates. There have been 3 separate spread sheets prepared with 3 months, 6 months and 9 months data.

3 Months data Date range: 1st October 2017–31st December 2017
6 Months data Date range: 1st July 2017–31st December 2017
9 Months data Date range: 1st April 2017–31st December 2017

Output: Portfolios that that would have given profitable return during the period of these tenures described above also with optimized reward to risk. The benchmark for this has been taken as standard share index.

BEGIN:

Step 1 Smoothing the Time Series
//The closing price/value time series of each stock and indices is taken 1st by using QUANDL package in python.
//The same are used to create a correlation matrix among the stocks and SENSEX during the tenures.

Step 2 Correlation Matrix
//A similarity matrix is constructed using the Pearson's product moment correlation matrix. If it is being done for 3 months, then:
    corr_stocks = months3.corr()

Step 3 Partial Correlation Matrix

If one truly wants to understand the correlation between 2 individual scrip values, then one must get rid of the influence of the movement of SENSEX. 2 different stocks can go up on a day when SENSEX is highly bullish. So we must remove the influence of SENSEX to get the correct correlation between these 2 stocks. Therefore, the concept of partial correlation is introduced.

The below formula is applied:

$$\rho XY \cdot Z = \frac{\rho XY - \rho XZ \rho ZY}{\sqrt{1 - \rho_{XY}^2}\sqrt{1 - \rho_{ZY}^2}}.$$

Where X and Y are individual stocks and Z is SENSEX data. ρXY denotes correlation between stocks X and Y. $\rho XY \cdot Z$ denotes correlation between X and Y after removing influence of SENSEX data Z. This is partial correlation. We implement the same in Python as:

```
for i in range (array_dim-1):
  for j in range(array_dim - 1):
    partial_corr[i, j] = (corr_as_array[i, j] - corr_as_array[i, array_dim - 1] *
corr_as_array[
      j, array_dim - 1]) / (math.sqrt(1 - corr_as_array[i, array_dim - 1] ** 2) *
math.sqrt(
      1 - corr_as_array[j, array_dim - 1] ** 2))
```

Here, array_dim denotes the number of rows(or columns) of the symmetric correlation matrix already developed in step 1 - corr_stocks. The target is to develop the partial correlation matrix - partial_corr.

Step 4 Dissimilarity Matrix

We ultimately endeavour to achieve the individual clusters of stocks to choose an optimum portfolio. To achieve this, and to apply PAM based clustering we next prepare a dissimilarity matrix:

```
for i in range (array_dim1):
  for j in range(array_dim1):
    dissimilarity_partial_corr[i, j] = (1 - partial_corr[i, j])
```

dissimilarity_partial_corr denotes the array of dissimilarity matrix.

Step 5 Searching for Optimum Number of Stocks in a Cluster

library("factoextra") is used to understand optimum number of clusters for a given tenure (i.e., 3 months or 6 months or 9 months)

Dissimilarity_Partial_Correlation_9mnths <-
read.csv('Dissimilarity_Partial_Correlation_only_Header_9months.csv')
# Now check the optimum number of clusters
fviz_nbclust(Dissimilarity_Partial_Correlation_9mnths, pam, method =
"silhouette") + theme_classic()

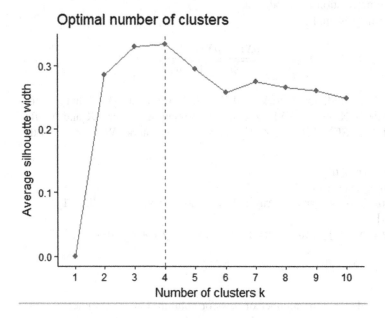

Now, for 9 months data we know that optimum cluster number is 4. So, next, we create 3 clusters with 9 months data:

1. One with 4 − 1 = 3 stocks in a cluster
2. Second one with optimum 4 stocks in a cluster
3. Third with 4 + 1 = 5 shares in a cluster

Step 6 Use PAM to Construct Portfolio

In this step, clustering is done using PAM and the cluster centers are used to construct portfolios.

As depicted in Point 5, we build 3 clusters. 1st with 3 shares, next with 4 shares and the last with 5 shares.

4 Materials and methods

1. NSE listed popular 79 MSCI (Morgan Stanley Capital International) approved stocks from 15 industry sectors, namely Automobile, Agriculture, Banking, Cement, Consumer Goods, Construction, Energy, Financial Service, IT, Lifestyle, Metals, Media & Entertainments, Pharma, Service, Telecom, is collected from Meta Stock and Advance GET.

The different stocks are followed sector-wise.

a. Automobile: - Ashok Leyland, Bajaj Auto Ltd, Bosch Ltd., Eicher Motors Ltd, Hero MotoCorp Ltd, MothersonSumi, Mahindra & Mahindra Ltd Maruti Suzuki India Ltd, Tata Motors Ltd DVR, Tata Motors Ltd.

b. Agriculture: - UPL Ltd, Grashim Industries.

c. Banking: - Axis Bank, IDFC Bank, State Bank of India, ICICI Bank, Yes bank.

d. Cement & Cement Products: - ACC Ltd, Ambuja Cements Ltd, and Shree Cement, UltraTech Cement Ltd.

e. Consumer Goods: - Asian Paints Ltd, Hindustan Unilever Ltd, I T C Ltd, Dabur India, Nestle India, Britannia Industries, Godrej Consumer, Marico Ltd, United Sprits.

f. Construction: - Larsen & Toubro Ltd.

g. Energy: - Bharat Petroleum Corporation Ltd, Bharat pertoleum Ltd, Hindusthan Petrochemical Ltd, Indian Oil Corporation Ltd, NTPC Ltd, Oil & Natural Gas Corporation Ltd (ONGC), Petronet LNG, Reliance Industries Ltd, Tata Power Co. Ltd, Rural Electrification, Bharat Heavy Electric, GAIL Ltd, Havells Industries.

h. Financial Services: - Housing Development Finance Corporation Ltd (HDFC), Indiabulls Housing Finance Ltd, Power Finance Corporation, Shriram Transport Finance Corporation, LIC Housing Finance, Bajaj Finance, Biaja Fin Service, Mahindra& Mahindra Finance.

i. IT: - Wipro Ltd, HCL Technologies Ltd, Siemens Ltd, Infosys Ltd, Tata Consultancy Services Ltd (TCS), Tech Mahindra Ltd.

j. Life style: - Titan Company.

k. Metals: - JSW Steel, Coal India Ltd, Hindalco Industries Ltd, Tata Steel Ltd, Vedanta Ltd, Bharat Forge.

l. Media & entertainment: - Zee Entertainment Enterprises Ltd.

m. Pharma: - AurobindoPharma Ltd, LupinPharma, GlenmarkPharma, Cipla Ltd, Dr. Reddy's Laboratories Ltd., Lupin Ltd, Sun Pharmaceutical Industries, Piramal Enterprises, Cadila Health Care.

n. Services: - Adani Ports and Special Economic Zone Ltd, Vakrangee Ltd, Container Corporation.

o. Telecom: - Idea Cellular, Bharti Airtel Ltd, Bharti Infratel Ltd,

2. In this experiment, the daily closing price data is considered for the period of one year, i.e. 1st April 2017 to 31st December 2017.

3. The closing price data has been classified into 1 month, 3 months, 6 months, 9 months and 12 months in this experiment.

4. PAM (Partitioning around medoid) is used as the clustering algorithm

5. All computational and statistical analysis has been done by R [17], and Python.

6. For finding optimal number of clusters (k) elbow method is used and in the current experiment, clustering has been performed with $k - 1$, k and $k + 1$ cluster choices. If $k - 1$ is 1, then that portfolio is ignored.

7. Finally we have compared the return of the portfolios with Benchmark, i.e. Sensex.

5   Results

In this section, we have presented and critically discussed about the results obtained from applying time series clustering on 79 MSCI approve NSE listed stocks. Results have been subdivided into three sections, in the first subsection we have enlisted the different portfolios that are obtained, in the second subsection, the return of those portfolios are analyzed and in the third section, these portfolios have been compared with sensex in terms of returns.

(A)   **Constituents of the Portfolio**

In this section, all the portfolios that have been obtained are enlisted (Table 1)

Table 1. Constitute of the portfolio

Portfolio	Name of the stock
3 Month K	(VEDL, MCDOWELL.N)
3 Month K + 1	(VEDL, MARUTI, BRITANNIA)
6 Month K	(TATA STEEL, RECLTD)
6 Month K + 1	(VEDL, TITAN, LICHSGFIN)
9 Month K − 1	(BAJAJFINANCE, ONGC, BOSCH)
9 Month K	(BAJAJFINANCE, RECLTD, TECHMAHINDRA, UPL)
9 Month K + 1	(BAJAJFINANCE, LT, TECHMAHINDRA, UPL, PFC)

For finding optimal number of clusters (k) elbow method is used and in the current experiment, clustering has been performed with k − 1, k and k + 1 cluster choices. Where K − 1 is 1 portfolio is ignored.

(B)   **Analysis of the Portfolio**

After clustering we have selected 7 individual portfolios consisting of various stocks with different time frames (3 months, 6 months, 9 months) according to performance and similarity, for more accuracy to build an optimum portfolio we have calculated average monthly return of stocks along with sensex. As seen from the plots that 9-month (K + 1) portfolio gives a suitable return, which can create an effective portfolio and help an investor in taking a suitable investment decision (Table 2 and Fig. 1).

Table 2. Portfolio Return

Portfolio	1 Month	3 Month	Current month
3 Month K	0.03	−0.15	−0.06
3 Month K + 1	0	−0.07	−0.03
6 Month K	−0.02	−0.21	−0.2
6 Month K + 1	0	−0.04	−0.04
9 Month K − 1	−0.02	−0.06	−0.02
9 Month K	0.04	0.01	0.03
9 Month K + 1	0.07	0.06	0.1

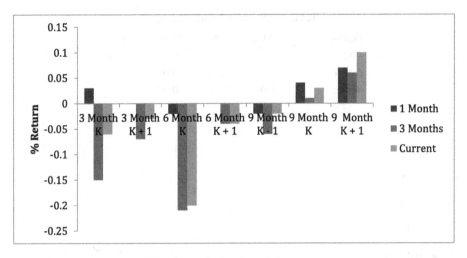

Fig. 1. Analysis of portfolio return

(C) Comparison with Sensex

In this experiment monthly return is shown and compared with sensex. The return of portfolio 3 is very near to sensex (Tables 3, 4, 5 and Figs. 2, 3, 4)

Table 3. Portfolio 1 with Sensex

Portfolio	1 Month	3 Month	Current month
3 Month K	0.03	−0.15	−0.06
3 Month K + 1	0	−0.07	−0.03
Sensex	0.06	−0.03	0.04

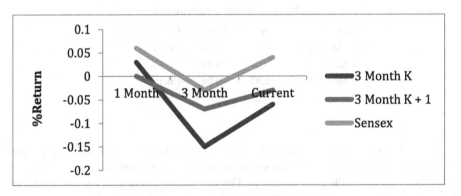

Fig. 2. 3-month portfolio returns with respect to sensex

Table 4. Portfolio 2 with Sensex

Portfolio	1 Month	3 Month	Current month
6 Month K	−0.02	−0.21	−0.2
6 Month K + 1	0	−0.04	−0.04
Sensex	0.06	−0.03	0.04

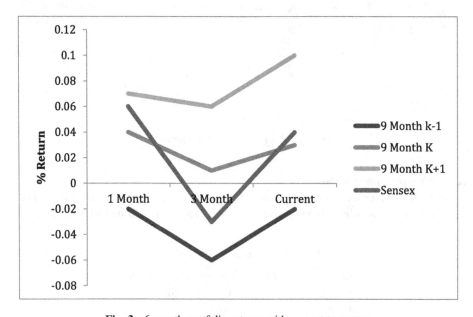

Fig. 3. 6 month portfolio returns with respect to sensex

Table 5. Portfolio 3 with Sensex

Portfolio	1 Month	3 Month	Current month
9 Month k − 1	−0.02	−0.06	−0.02
9 Month K	0.04	**0.01**	0.03
9 Month K + 1	**0.07**	**0.06**	**0.1**
Sensex	0.06	−0.03	0.04

It is observed that large clustering over a relatively larger tine period produces better result for optimum portfolio selection, in this experiment we have obtained 7 portfolios based on different parameters. Out of these 9 month k + 1 portfolio shows better performance for with 1month return of 7%, 3 month return of 6%, and year to date return of 10%, which is superior than the return of sensex.

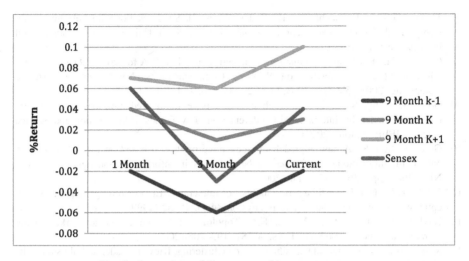

Fig. 4. 9 month portfolio returns with respect to sensex.

6   Conclusion

A portfolio needs to be optimally diversified to minimize the risk. For a retail investor to enumerate all possible combination of stocks for constructing a diversified portfolio is not possible. In this paper, a simple correlation based time series clustering technique has been used to design such a portfolio. Right now an equal investment strategy has been adopted, which can be further improved. The longer term time series behavior gives better diversification and return as observed from the empirical study. The portfolio built using 9 months data is shown to outperform benchmark index like sensex, in terms of current return, 1 month return and 3 month return.

References

1. Zolhavarieh, S., Aghabozorgi, S., Teh, Y.W.: A Review of Subsequence Time Series Clustering (2014)
2. Banerjee, D.: Forecasting of Indian stock market-using time-series ARIMA model. In: 2014 2nd International Conference on Business and Information Management (ICBIM), 9 Jan 2014, pp. 131–135. IEEE (2014)
3. Bini, B.S, Mathew, T.: Clustering and regression technoques for stock prediction. In: International Conference on Emerging Trends in Engineering Science and Technology (ICETEST), pp. 1248–1255 (2015)
4. Chevalier, J., Ellison, G.: Risk taking by mutual funds as a response to incentives. J. Polit. Econ. **105**(6), 1167–1200 (1997)
5. Kenett, D.Y., Tumminello, M., Maid, A., Gur-Gershgoren, G., Mantegna, R.N.: Dominating clasp of the financial sector revealed by partial correlation analysis of the stock market. PLoSONE **5**(12), e15032 (2010). https://doi.org/10.1371/journal.pone.0015032
6. Dorr, D.H., Denton, A.M.: Establishing relationships among patterns in stock market data. Data Knowl. Eng. **68**(3), 318–337 (2009)

7. Thakur, G.S.M., Bhattacharyya, R., Sarkar (Mondal), S.: Stock Portfolio Selection using Dempster-Shafer evidence theory. Journal of King Saud University – Computer and Information Science (2016)

8. Guo, C., Jia, H., Zhang, N.: Time series clustering based on ICA for stock data analysis. In: 4th International Conference on Wireless Communications, Networking and Mobile Computing, 2008, WiCOM 2008. Oct 12 2008, pp. 1–4. IEEE (2008)

9. Gong, J., Song, S.: A new approch of stock price trend prediction based on logistic regression model. In: International Conference on New Trends in Information and Service Science. IEEE, Xplore (2009)

10. Gong, J., Sun, S.: A new approach of stock price prediction based on logistic regression model. In: International conference on New Trends in Information and Service Science, NISS 2009, pp. 1366–1371, June 2009

11. Lehnertz, K.: Non-linear time series analysis of intracranial EEG recordings in patients with epilepsy—an overview. Int. J. Psychophysiol. **34**(1), 45–52 (1999)

12. Naylor, M.J., Rose, L.C., Moyle, B.J.: Topology of foreign exchange markets using hierarchical structure methods. Phys. A **382**, 199–208 (2007)

13. Mirkin, B.G.: Mathematical Classification and Clustering. Kluwer Academic Publishing The Netherland, Dordrecht (1996)

14. Nanda, S.R., Mahanty, B., Tiwari, M.K.: Clustering Indian stock market data for portfolio management. Expert Syst. Appl. **37**(12), 8793–8798 (2010)

15. Mantegna, R.N.: Hierarchical structure in finance market. Eur. Phys. J. B **11**, 193–197 (1999)

16. Goswami, S., Mitra, A., Chakroborty, B., Jalan, A., Chakroborti, A.: A time series clustering technique to analyze the stock market movement after the budget announcement. In: International Conference on Time Series ITISE 2017, Granada, Spain, 18–20 September 2017

17. Jung, S.S., Chang, W.: Clustering stocks using partial correlation coefficients. Phys. A **462**, 410–420 (2016)

18. Aghabozorgi, S., Shirkhorshidin, A.S., Teh,Y.W.: Time series clustering – A decade review (2015)

19. Li, X., Qiu, T., Chen, G., Zhong, L.X., Wu, X.R.: Market impact and structure dynamic of the chinese stock market based on partial correlation analysis. Phys. A **471**, 106–113 (2017)

An Approach Towards Development of a Stem Borer Population Prediction Model Using R Programming

Sudipta Paul[1](✉), Sourav Banerjee[2], and Utpal Biswas[1]

[1] Department of Computer Science and Engineering, University of Kalyani,
Kalyani 741235, India
sudiptap48@gmail.com, utpal01in@yahoo.com
[2] Department of Computer Science and Engineering,
Kalyani Government Engineering College, Kalyani 741235, India
contact200683@gmail.com

Abstract. The rice is a major crop of India. It is the staple food of the eastern and southern parts of this country. The total yield of rice can be in a massive loss if it is affected by pests. The stem borer pest creates a lot of trouble. It affects the production of rice. As the control procedure with pesticide is not much effective on this pest, therefore, a forecasting model can play a major role in taking preventive measure. The objective of this research is to forecast the population occurrence of stem borer pest in the paddy. This paper highlights the improvement of the performance of backpropagation artificial neural network (BP-ANN) model using principal component analysis (PCA) to develop a prediction model by minimizing the error. The Convolution of data is proposed here instead of PCA to enhance the reduction of the dimensions of data which eventually results in less error in prediction.

Keyword: Backpropagation artificial neural network (BP-ANN) ·
Principal component analysis (PCA) · Stem borer · Convolution

1 Introduction

The stem borer (*Scirpophaga Incertulas*) is widespread in all world, especially in Asia. The stem borer is a major pest of paddy in India. This pest is endemic and is distributed in most parts of India. Insecticides are not a good option to control this kind of pest because of its monophagous nature and peculiar boring habit. Therefore, a forecast is highly needed to take early measure to prevent the appearance of this pest. Here we did not get any Indian statistics data regarding the appearance of this pest through a period of definite times of years. This is why we are using here the database from the work Yang et al. [1], in 2009. At first, we implemented according to their work. After that, we enhanced it slightly to get a better result in prediction with less error rate using convolution in place of principal component analysis. Our proposed work results better than the existing works with respect to the error rate and dimension reducing of raw, uncleaned data for prediction of the population occurrence of stem borer in paddy. Artificial Neural Network (ANN) [15] is used in many fields of science because of its

© Springer Nature Singapore Pte Ltd. 2019
J. K. Mandal et al. (Eds.): CICBA 2018, CCIS 1031, pp. 145–154, 2019.
https://doi.org/10.1007/978-981-13-8581-0_12

different characteristics which are very special in its own way, such as parallel calculations in a large-scale, storage of information which is distributed in nature,
adaptability with its own capability, organization in its own capability and high fault-
tolerant properties, and also for nonlinear relations it has a very good simulation of
fitness. Thus ANN has its widespread use in such areas as pattern recognition, handling
of knowledge, nonlinear transformation, the technology regarding remote sensing,
research on the robot, and projects on biomedicine according to the work of Yang et al.
[1]. Among a lot of various Artificial Neural Network algorithm, the Back Propagation
(BP) network is used mostly. Generally, the transmission functions used here are
nonlinear in nature. The common transfer functions are the logarithm S type (logsig)
function and the hyperbolic tangent S type (tansig) function. In a BP network, the
linking between neurons works in a front feedback neural network manner and the
learning method works in a supervision study manner. A Convolutional Neural Network (CNN) [8] has recently been popularised for its success in classification in several
kinds of problems (e.g. image recognition [13] or time series classification [14]). This
network consists of a sequence of convolution layers. The output in the layers is passed
only to local regions of theinput. This is achieved by doing the dot product between the
input and the filter sliding at each data-point. This whole process of calculation is called
convolution. This convolution process allowsthe CNN filters to know and acknowl-
edgea specific pattern in the given data-sets.

According to [8], the convolution of two one-dimensional signals f and g, which is
discrete in nature, is written as $f * g$ and defined as:

$$(f * g)(i) = \sum_{j=-\infty}^{\infty} f(j)g(i - j) \tag{1}$$

Here, definition of the convolution states that, the nonexistent data-samples in the
input may have values of zero, it is often described as zero padding. Therefore it is
evident that the computing of the products take place only at the data-points where
samples exist in both filter and data set. A point is to be noted here that the process of
convolution is commutative, i.e. $(f * g) = (g * f)$. If the data-pointsare finite, the infinite
convolution is permitted to be truncated. In other words, suppose f = [f(0), ..., f(N −
1)] and g = [g(0), ..., g(M − 1)], the convolution is,

$$(f * g)(i) = \sum_{j=0}^{m-1} f(j)g(i - j) \tag{2}$$

The current models for the forecasting of population dynamics of stem borer
inpaddy have three major shortcomings with some benefits [1, 10]: the ability of data-
fitting is insufficient, the generality of the whole model is weak and the error rate
between reality and the predicted result is too large. This paper develops a new model
of prediction using BP ANN with Convolution of data matrix using a suitable filter, to
find a non-linear relation between the population of stem borer and the main meteorological factors, then using ANN build a prediction model for the population occurrence of paddy stem borer.

2   Related Works/Literature Review

After a thorough background work some of the valuable works on the field are the following:

In 2009, Yang et al. [1] has published "A prediction model for population occurrence of paddy stem borer (Scirpophaga Incertulas), based on Back Propagation Artificial Neural Network and Principal Components Analysis". In this paper they have done a survey at the Plant Protection Station of JianShui County, Yunnan and associated meteorological data were obtained from the JianShui County Meteorologic Observatory in China. In this paper, they have applied PCA and BP-ANN methods to analyze the aforesaid obtained data on population occurrence to find out a non-linear relation between the stem borer population and the meteorological factors to build a prediction model which have a good accuracy level of prediction. We took it as the base prediction model and then enhanced this model on the basis of their database in our project. Rad et al. [2] in 2014, also have made another prediction model using Artificial Neural Network. The estimation of the non-linear relation between the data-point in the data set can be very helpful for calculating the amount of variance of a particular data-point with the comparison to other data-point in a dataset. This paper aimed to calculate the variance of different agronomic and phenologic factors on the total mass of melon fruit produced. Sun et al. [3] in 2015 have also compared some existing prediction models in their paper regarding rice strip virus by using three different models: stepwise regression, back propagation neural network, and support vector machines. Günther and Fritsch [4] have described the way the package "neuralnet" work, its pros and cons in their paper regarding its use in R statistics software. In 2009, Smith et al. [5], has coined an ANN based model for year around temperature prediction. They have explored various applications of ANNs for the prediction of temperature during the entire year. Their ANNs were developed using detailed data collected by the Georgia Automated Environmental Monitoring Network (AEMN). The ANNs were able to give predictions with a mean absolute error (MAE) which was less during the winter months than the MAE of the previously developed winter-specific models. In 2015, Sengar and Kalpana [6] has shed some light regarding the climate or atmospheric conditions changing effects on paddyyielding. Atmospheric conditions are significant factors in the distribution, yielding, and security of food. This book discusses in global detail, with special reference to India about the recommendations for achieving climate-smart agriculture. Javad et al. [7], in 2016, shed some light on the determination of a model on a prediction of soil cation exchange capacity. This project shed some light on the comparison of multiple linear regression, multiple non-linear regression, adaptive neuro-fuzzy inference system and artificial neural network including feed-forward back propagation (FFBP) model to calculate the soil cation exchange capacity in Guilan province, northern Iran. In 2017, Borovykh et al. [9] present a method for conditional time series forecasting based on the CNN architecture. The proposed model contains stacks of convolutions between filters and the datasets which allow an access of a broad range of data-points when predicting; multiple filters are applied here in parallel to separate time series datasets and allow the fast processing of data and the utilization of the correlation structure between the multivariate time series.

3 Proposed Work

Here, we are using the database used by Yang et al. [1], in 2009. According to their survey, the factors that are influential for the population occurrence of stem borer are sixand stated in Tables 1 and 2. Therefore, the six factors from Table 1 and another batch of six factors from Table 2 give all total 12 influencing factors for the proposed model.

Table 1. The population occurrence of paddy stem borer in the 1st generation and its relative meteorological factors' data in March from 2000 to 2008

Year	March						The population occurrence in 1st generation
	Average temperature (c)	Maximum temperature (c)	Minimum temperature (c)	Rainfall (mm)	Potential evaporation (mm)	Relative humidity (%)	
2000	17.3	28.7	6.5	39.2	203.6	64	92
2001	18.5	29.7	10.3	25.7	222.2	63	132
2002	18.9	30.3	6	26.8	267	58	30
2003	17.9	28.2	7.8	32.5	250.9	61	16
2004	19.6	31.6	6	0.2	250.9	57	207
2005	16.6	30	2.5	44.5	201.8	64	201
2006	19.5	30.3	6.2	1.3	226.7	53	128
2007	20.1	31.6	7.8	0.5	272.8	48	191
2008	17.2	28.9	3.4	28.5	161.8	64	60

Table 2. The population occurrence of paddy stem borer in the 2nd generation and its relative meteorological factors' data in April from 2000 to 2008

Year	April						The population occurrence in 2nd generation
	Average temperature (c)	Maximum temperature (c)	Minimum temperature (c)	Rainfall (mm)	Potential evaporation (mm)	Relative humidity (%)	
2000	21.7	31	11.7	16.6	259.8	62	92
2001	23.1	32.2	12.7	18.4	321.8	50	132
2002	22.2	31.7	11.3	39.1	308.5	56	30
2003	22.9	32.5	13.1	7	326.3	53	16
2004	20.1	31.1	11.4	104	213.7	67	207
2005	21.6	32.8	8.8	37.9	258	60	201
2006	22.3	30.3	12.4	85.7	241.2	54	128
2007	19.2	30.9	9.2	108.6	179.1	66	191
2008	22	33	12.4	38.6	251.9	59	60

Table 3. The proposed steps

Steps	Description
Model type	A three-layer BP network because of its ability to approximate any function
Transfer function	$\frac{1}{1+e^{-x}}$
Number of neurons in the hidden layer	10 neurons
Input layer	Considering the convoluted data set that influence the paddy stem borer population occurrence, take m elements as the input which have the least value in its columns. Therefore there are m neurons in the input layer of BP ANN
Output layer	One Neuron. This Neuron will state the occurrence of the population of the stem borer

Step 1: Normalizing the dimension of the datasets using convolution of data matrix
As there are all total 12 parameters, to draw a neural network with this much parameters is a chaotic work. Therefore it has been taken account the process of convolution of data matrix which will eventually use its power per parameter per input (PPPPI) to extract features by taking advantage of the structural information of the datasets. Also it will reduce the dimension of the datasets too. In the process of taking convolution at first the dataset is padding with extra "zeros" in the borders of the dataset. Therefore 2 extra rows and 2 extra columns of data is introduced here. It will help not to lose any essential data variation from the original dataset. After that a kernel matrix of dimension 3×3 is taken where all the diagonal values are 1. Taking a kernel matrix is a tricky work, because there is no hard and fast rule. A lot of kernels have been tried and only after the trial and error method the aforesaid kernel gave the best result.

As the main aim is to reduce the dimension of the datamatrix efficiently the convolution Quantile() function of the imagine package in the R statistical software is used here. Here the quantile function will divide each of the data set of values with a variance, which further divide a frequency distribution of equal groups, each contained the same fraction of the total frequency of the data sets.

Step 2: Backpropagation Neural Network with the convoluted data matrix as input neuron
From [1] (Chen et al. [11], Yang et al. [1]) it is known that the three-layer ANN model has the ability to simulate any nonlinear system of equations. Thus, any continuous time series or map type data sets can be easily modelled by a three-layer ANN. The proposed steps to build a BP ANN model for predicting the population occurrence of stem borer in paddy is stated in the following Table.

4 Experimental Results and Comparisons

According to the proposed model in Sect. 3 at first we normalize the dimension of the datamatrix with the given method of convolution, then we simply follow the steps of the back propagation Neural Network to implement the model. Following are the discussion of the results of the proposed work.

4.1 Result of the Proposed Method

Step 1: Normalize the dimension of the datasets using convolution of data matrix

Table 4. Normalized datasets using convolution of data matrix with less dimension

	E1	E2	E3	E4	E5	E6	E7	E8	E9	E10	E11	E12
Y1	NA	NA	NA	NA	NA	NA	NA	NA	NA	NA	NA	NA
Y2	NA	NA	NA	NA	NA	NA	NA	NA	NA	NA	NA	NA
Y3	NA	NA	6.0	10.3	25.7	22.9	22.2	13.1	7.0	12.7	18.4	16
Y4	NA	NA	0.2	6.0	26.8	20.1	22.9	11.4	13.1	7.0	39.1	53
Y5	NA	NA	6.0	0.2	32.5	21.6	20.1	8.8	11.4	13.1	7.0	67
Y6	NA	NA	1.3	6.0	0.2	22.3	21.6	12.4	8.8	11.4	54.0	60
Y7	NA	NA	0.5	1.3	44.5	19.2	22.3	9.2	12.4	8.8	37.9	54
Y8	NA	NA	7.8	0.5	1.3	22.0	19.2	12.4	9.2	12.4	59.0	60
Y9	NA	NA	NA	NA	NA	NA	NA	NA	NA	NA	NA	NA

Here, it is being seen that the dataset has been reduced quite an amount in its dimension. Here the rows and columns of "NA" indicates the extra padded zeros which have been introduced here to help not to lose any data variation. Also it is now easier to handle them as inputs in the backpropagation neural network because of its less dimension. Here E1 to E12 are the columns of data elements from which the columns with least range of variation will be taken as input in the ANN. Also Y1 to Y9 indicate the effective factors in the dataset (Table 4).

Here the kernel matrix is following (Table 5):

The quantile function in R programming language which gave the Table 3 is following:

TestCase1 < - convolutionQuantile(Proposed_Matrix, kernel, x = 0.7)

Table 5. Kernel matrix with diagonal value all 1

1	0	0
0	1	0
0	0	1

Here kernel is the aforesaid matrix, x is numeric vector of probabilities with values in [0,1] which will help the function convolutionQuantile to find the position of quintile 'x' in each cell of the data matrix.

Step 2: **Backpropagation Neural Network with the convoluted data matrix as input neuron**

The description of the experiment using the proposed model of BP ANN is in the following table (Table 6):

Table 6. The experiment description using the proposed steps in tabular form of the BP ANN model

Steps	Description
Model type	As told earlier we are taking a 3-layer backpropagation neural network
Transfer function	$\frac{1}{1+e^{-x}}$
Number of neurons in the hidden layer	10 neurons
Input layer	Here we are taking dataelement3 (E3 as de3), dataelement4 (E4 as de4), dataelement5 (E5 as de5), dataelement9 (E9 as de9) as the input neuron as they have the least range of data variation in their columns
Output layer	One Neuron. This Neuron will state the occurrence of the population of the stem borer

The obtained Neural Network according to the aforesaid proposed method is the following (Fig. 1):

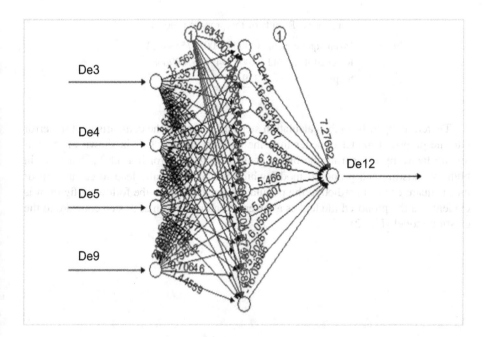

Fig. 1 Obtained Neural Network of the proposed method.

In the proposed method it has been used 50% of the convoluted data as the training set to train the neural network and 50% of the data to test the output of the neural network.

4.2   Comparison with the Existing Model

ANN is an excellent choice to use in prediction. In the time of applying ANN to predict the population occurrence of stem borer, here ANN system tried to imitate the thinking process of humanbeings, such as observing, learning and concluding. Then a model environment is set up to learn and gather information based on appropriate data structures. The existing model depicts these in the following way:

Step 1: Normalize the influencing factors
Step 2: Principal Components Analysis to reduce the dimensions of dataset
Step 3: Backpropagation ANN training with the principal components from the previous steps.

After implementing the existing model the result is in the following table (Table 7):

Table 7. Results of the existing model

Mean square error	0.001148403589
Reached threshold	0.009284247547
Steps	33

In the proposed model the result is in the following table (Table 8):

Table 8. Results of the proposed model

Mean square error	0.000000001675894812
Reached threshold	0.005154583570896686
Steps	229

Therefore, apart from the calculation steps according to the comparison of the error rate the proposed model is better than the existing model. This is shown in the following figure by comparing the intercept of propagated error in each hidden layer in both the existing and proposed model which would eventually lead to calculation of mean square error in predicting the population occurrence. In the following figure it is evident that the proposed model has a lower spread in error in each step compare to the existing model (Fig. 2).

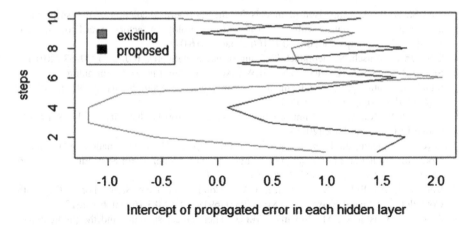

Fig. 2 Comparison of intercept of propagated error in each hidden layer with each interception step in the existing and proposed model

5   Conclusions and Future Work

Anything one can do with a Convolution Neural Network (CNN), one can also do it with a fully connected architecture just as well. But as it has a lot of PPPPI. It is more convenient for use. That means when one has a lot of features (like an image does), using a CNN, one can get comparable learning potential with far fewer parameters. As a result, one can train faster and use less data. Convolutional networks work so well because they exploit an assumption about weight sharing. This is why they only work with data where that assumption holds. As shown in the result analysis portion the size of the database becomes very less compare to the already existed model by using the CNN with compare to Principal Component Analysis. According to Yang et al. [1, 12], on the basis of experience, experiment, and statistical method, there are three main ways to forecast pest occurrences. Anything that is modeled by ANN and has a time series data flow one can also depict it as a CNN. This is why the next approach is to make the prediction model more improved by using the other steps of the CNN along with the BP-ANN network to enhance the performance of the model by utilizing advanced statistical data analytics.

References

1. Yang, L.N., Peng, L., Zhang, L.M., Li-lian, Z., Yang, S.S., et al.: A prediction model for population occurrence of paddy stem borer (Scirpophaga incertulas), based on back propagation artificial neural network and principal components analysis. Comput. Electron. Agric. **68**(2009), 200–206 (2009). https://doi.org/10.1016/j.compag.2009.06.003
2. Rad, M.R.N., Koohkan, S., Fanaei, H.R., Rad, M.R.P.: Application of Artificial Neural Networks to predict the final fruit weight and random forest to select important variables in native population of melon (Cucumis melo. Pahlavan). Sci. Hortic. **181**, 108–112 (2015). https://doi.org/10.1016/j.scienta.2014.10.025

3. Sun, S., et al.: A comparison of models for the short-term prediction of rice stripe virus disease and its association with biological and meteorological factors. Acta Ecol. Sin. **36**, 166–171 (2016). https://doi.org/10.1016/j.chnaes.2016.04.002
4. Günther, F., Fritsch, S.: neuralnet: Training of neural networks. R J. **2**(1), 30–38 (2010)
5. Smith, B.A., Gerrit, H., McClendon, R.W.: Artificial neural networks for automated year-round temperature prediction. Comput. Electron. Agric. **68**(2009), 52–61 (2009). https://doi.org/10.1016/j.compag.2009.04.003
6. Sengar, R.S., Kalpana, S.: Climate Change Effect on Crop Productivity. Taylor & Francis Group LLC, Milton Park (2015)
7. Seyedmohammadi, J., Esmaeelnejad, L., Ramezanpour, H.: Determination of a suitable model for prediction of soil cation exchange capacity. Model. Earth Syst. Environ. **2**, 156 (2016). https://doi.org/10.1007/s40808-016-0217-4
8. Borovykh, A., Bohte, S., Oosterlee, C.W.: Conditional Time Series Forecasting with Convolutional Neural Networks. arXiv:1703.04691v3[stat.ML] 16 October 2017
9. Aaron, C., Cristopher, M., Newman, M.E.J.: Hierarchical structure and the prediction of missing links in networks. Nature **453**, 98–101 (2008)
10. Cai, Z.X., Xu, G.Y.: Artificial Intelligence (AI) and Its Application. Tsinghua University Press, Beijing (1996)
11. Chen, X.J., Wang, C.N., Chen, S.T.: The Principle and Application of Neural Network, pp. 1–3. National Defense and Industry Press, Beijing (1995)
12. Maria, J.D.: Artificial neural networks as an alternative tool in pine bark volume estimation. Comput. Electron. Agric. **48**(3), 235–244 (2005)
13. Krizhevsky, A., Sutskever, I., Hinton, G.E.: ImageNet classification with deep convolutional neural networks. Adv. Neural. Inf. Process. Syst. **25**(2012), 1097–1105 (2012)
14. Wang, Z., Yan, W., Oates, T.: Time Series Classification from Scratch with Deep Neural Networks: A Strong Baseline. CoRR, abs/1611.06455 (2016)
15. Hagan, M.T., Demuth, H.B., Beale, M.H., De Jesus, O.: Neural Network Design (2 edn, ebook). hagan.okstate.edu/nnd.html

Evaluation Criteria of Project Risk and Decision Making Through Beta Analysis and TOPSIS Towards Achieving Organizational Effectiveness

Biswanath Chakraborty$^{(\boxtimes)}$ ⓘ and Santanu Das ⓘ

Department of Mechanical Engineering, Kalyani Government Engineering
College, Kalyani, Nadia 741235, West Bengal, India
bchakraborti85@gmail.com, sdas.me@gmail.com

Abstract. Value of a project of an organization is primarily determined by two major factors – risk and return. The most important aspect of a business analysis, therefore, lies with the analysis of the risks and their associated returns. The basic objective of an organization is to increase the productivity to grab more market share. But the problem is that market risk is inherent in all projects and, by nature, it is stochastic. It can hardly be avoided but can be mitigated at most through diversification. Through Capital Asset Pricing Model (CAPM), the systematic or un-diversifiable risks can be described and measured by beta, β. In order to mitigate the risk, investments are to be made on a combination of different projects or portfolio of projects rather than a single project. Through β-hedging, a proper hedging strategy can be developed to reduce the systematic risk. But it has also been observed that the concept of CAPM has been plagued by the stochastic nature of the economy. Therefore, in the first part of this work, the systematic risk has been evaluated through time-varying β analysis. According to the results of the hedge performance of individual projects of the portfolio, it will be possible to select/rank the projects according to their risk-return trade-off capacity and in the second part, the Technique for Order Preference using Similarity to Ideal Solution (TOPSIS), one of the most important MCDM techniques, has been merged with CAPM in order to provide a more justified selection procedure of projects considering four more attributes, other than risk, which may confirm a more realistic basis of creating the portfolio for increasing organizational effectiveness.

Keywords: Project risk and return · Portfolio project · β analysis · β-hedging · CAPM · TOPSIS · MCDM

1 Introduction

Selecting a proper portfolio of products that may yield an optimal return is one of the most critical decisions that are to be taken by an entrepreneur, nowadays. Optimal portfolio selection is one of the most critical decisions to be taken by an investor or an organization in today's global economic scenario. The product may be related to financial assets, like mutual funds, stocks of other companies, bonds, etc. It may also be

© Springer Nature Singapore Pte Ltd. 2019
J. K. Mandal et al. (Eds.): CICBA 2018, CCIS 1031, pp. 155–164, 2019.
https://doi.org/10.1007/978-981-13-8581-0_13

related to different brands or models manufactured by a particular production house. Any production house, instead of producing one particular product/brand, produces a bundle of products or brands, or rather, a portfolio of products. Each manufactured product, in this case, is treated as individual cost centres so that the yield can be reviewed for each and every product at a time interval. Every product that is to be produced is related to its corresponding projects. So, for an entrepreneur, it is an important task to select the project which will yield the maximum return so they can improve the organizational effectiveness.

Here, risks refer to the dispersion of a probability distribution and it implies how much the outcomes deviate from the expected value. On the other hand, return from an asset or a project is the realizable cash in-flow earned by the entrepreneur during a given period of time. By risks, it is understood, the market risks which are also known as systematic risks or un-diversifiable risk and they are inherent to the entire market. The degree of volatility or instability of the market is a measure of this systematic risk. The more unstable the market or economy, the more chance will be there to face a movement of return on either direction. Systematic risk is difficult to avoid. It can be mitigated through hedging. Investors are required to hedge one investment of a project by making another. **Beta** (β) is a measure of the volatility of systematic risk of a portfolio measured against the market as a whole. In other words, Beta is not necessarily a performance measure, it is a volatility measure. Through β-hedging, the overall systematic risk of the portfolio can be minimized. This can be done through investments in projects with offsetting βs or investing in projects having negative correlation.

Risk management is an operational process that comprises of uncertainty in the estimation of the consequences of the uncertain events. Risk is involved in the generation of response strategies of an expected outcome. Throughout the life cycle of a project, risk prevails [1]. Considerable empirical research works were conducted to establish the relationship between the financial and accounting variables and market based measures of risk. Robert G. Bowman conducted a research and the result of his research indicated that some financial and accounting variables are highly correlated with a market based measures of risk (beta, β) and they are useful in the forecasting of future risk [2]. Hamada [3, 4] conducted a research on the relationship between portfolio analysis and corporate finance. Markowitz introduced Mean-Variance Portfolio Model [5, 6]. Sharpe [7], Lintner [8] and Mossin [9] subsequently referenced the model proposed by Markowitz and developed the Capital Asset Pricing Model (CAPM) to establish the fact that the expected return on a security is influenced by risk-free rate, expected market return and beta of the security.

CAPM has gained the ability to predict expected stock return by establishing a link with risk and thus, it has been helping the investors or entrepreneurs to take their decisions for investments [5]. In 2013, Avinash Samvedi and others quantified risks in Supply Chain through integration of Fuzzy AHP and fuzzy TOPSIS [10], while Jolanta Tamosaitiene conducted Multi-Criteria risk assessment of a construction project [1]. Zamani et al. reported the work on portfolio selection using Data Envelopment Analysis (DEA) in 2014 [11], when Hsu, in the same year, conducted a study on hybrid multiple criteria decision-making model for investment decision making [12]. Monjazeb et al. in 2015 carried out performance Evaluation and Optimal Portfolio Selection among Industries and investment funds [13]. In 2016, Haghshenas reportedly took up

Dam Construction Projects and the associated risk assessment using fuzzy TOPSIS [14]. In 2017, Subya et al. made a risk assessment of Highway Construction Projects using fuzzy logic and multiple regression analysis [15].

So far, research works were conducted for evaluating the portfolios on the basis of systematic risk only. But risk is not the only attribute of evaluation for selecting a project and it is observed that there has been little initiation at evaluation of the projects or a portfolio considering a group of attributes that are prevailing in the economy. Therefore, the objective of the present work is evaluation and ranking the projects of a portfolio. This will be done not only on the basis of risk analysis but also by considering the other major attributes of the economy, like Rate of Return, Marketability, Tax shelter and Convenience using Technique for Order Preference using Similarity to Ideal Solution (TOPSIS). To be more precise, the objective of this work is to minimize the collective risk of the set of projects known as Portfolio through a method known as diversification. In the present work, first, the associated risk of a portfolio of projects has been ascertained through β analysis. After ascertainment of risks associated with each and every project of a portfolio, the projects are to be ranked with the help of TOPSIS. Utilizing this method introduced, this ranking would have to be reviewed periodically by an organization for improving organizational effectiveness either by dropping the most unprofitable project or by allocating more resource to the most profit yielding project.

2   Risk and Methodology of Analyzing Risk

Finding out the inherent risk against the expected return and to analyze the risk are the prime concerns of the present work. The following methodology has been adopted in this work.

For any outcome of a project, if the entrepreneurs are assured to get a fixed tangible benefit then the question of chance of not happening the outcome or the corresponding probability of not occurring the benefit will not arise. But in reality, the situation seems to be other way round. In most of the cases, the entrepreneurs have to face the game of chance and they have to be aware of the probabilistic return of the outcome. So, the entrepreneur should keep an eye of the probabilistic nature of the distribution of the return on the basis of which the decision whether the project should be taken in to action, is taken.

In this backdrop, a random variable, X, can be considered for any project, be it a construction or a manufacturing process and on the basis of this random variable, decisions are to be taken. Corresponding to this random variable, the average or mean of the outcome or the expected value denoted by E(X) can be obtained. With this obtained average return, the corresponding cost that is involved in the outcome can be obtained. This cost or the uncertainty regarding the outcome is known as risk [16].

Risk is generally denoted by variance given by:

$$\sigma^2 = E[X - E(X)]^2 \tag{1}$$

Where $E(X) = \mu$ = Mean. If X becomes a discrete variable then

$$E[X] = \sum_{\forall i} x_i f(x_i) \tag{2}$$

$$V[x] = \sum_{\forall i} (x_i - E[x])^2 f(x_i) \tag{3}$$

If X becomes continuous then

$$E[x] = \int_{-\infty}^{+\infty} xf(x)dx \tag{4}$$

$$V[x] = \int_{-\infty}^{+\infty} (x - E[x])^2 f(x)dx \tag{5}$$

Thus, Return is the expected value and risk is the variance or the standard deviation.

3 Methodology of Risk Analysis in a Portfolio

For minimizing the risk of investment, diversification is required. Portfolio manage-ment is probably the best option for this diversification. As a result, risk analysis of a portfolio is required to be carried out. The following methodology has been adopted for analyzing the risk of the portfolio in this current work.

Portfolio is basically a conglomeration of eclectic combination of financial assets or projects in order to optimize profit or to improve organizational effectiveness.

According to Markowitz's theory [5], risks can be characterized by variance. This variance, along with covariance determines the return from the portfolio (a set of different projects).

In case of consolidation of projects in to a portfolio, the question that arises is whether the entrepreneur combines the projects in equal proportion or the projects will be combined in different combinations so as to optimize the overall yield. This is also known as portfolio optimization.

A hypothetical case may be considered where there is 'n' number of projects denoted by i = 1, 2, ..., n. if the overall risk is considered for the portfolio projects, it could be expressed as:

$$\sum_{i=1}^{n} \sum_{j=1}^{n} w_i w_j \sigma_{ij} \tag{6}$$

where w_i and w_j are the weights which are being assigned in the corresponding project i & j and σ_{ij} is the covariance structure which is existing between projects i and j varies from 1...n. Plotting these values to an n × n matrix, it can be observed that along the principal diagonal the covariance of any particular project with itself [i.e. (1, 1), (2, 2) ...., (n, n)] will basically be the variance of each project. Symbolically it can be denoted as $\rho_{ii}\sigma_i\sigma_i = \sigma_i^2$ [since, $\rho_{ii} = 1$ which indicates a strong positive relationship]. So, all the elements (projects) along the principal diagonal are variances and off-diagonal elements (projects) are covariances because ρ_{ij} will all be zero where $i \neq j$ (for the sake of generalization, it is considered that every project is not correlated to every other project).

On the other hand, return is calculated by $\sum_{\forall i} w_i \bar{r}_i$ where $\bar{r}_i$ is the average return. 'r', the return, is the same like Internal Rate of Return (IRR) or Rate of Return of the Banks.

Return of a project will basically be the mean (m) i.e.

$$\bar{r}_p = \frac{1}{n} \sum_{i=1}^{n} r_i = \bar{r} = m \tag{7}$$

By using the probabilities, the variance of the overall set of portfolio will be derived as:

$$\sigma_p^2 = \frac{1}{n^2} \sum_{i=1}^{n} \sigma^2 \Rightarrow \frac{n\sigma^2}{n^2} \Rightarrow \frac{\sigma^2}{n} \tag{8}$$

i.e. as 'n' increases, σ^2 or variance or the risk will be decreasing, where projects are non-correlated.

4 Capital Asset Pricing Model (CAPM)

In the economy, there is a so-called theoretical concept of portfolio of the projects which is known as market and from here each of the projects is undertaken by different players in the market. So, market is basically a theoretical or hypothetical concept which considers the portfolio of projects that can be taken up by any individual at any point of time. For example, for financial market, there are Bombay Stock Exchange (BSE), National Stock Exchange (NSE), etc. This is the generalized concept of CAPM [17].

The risk of a portfolio can be measured in various ways. The two most commonly used measures of risk are: Variability and Beta (β). In this current work, β has been considered as the measure of risk. To calculate β of a portfolio, it is required to regress the rate of return of the portfolio on the rate of return of a market index. The slope of this regression line is the portfolio beta, which represents the un-diversifiable or systematic risk of the portfolio [18]. Therefore, risk can be denoted by β_i ($i = 1, 2, 3, \ldots$, n) for any particular i^{th} project such that:

$$r_i - r_f = \beta_i(r_m - r_f) + \varepsilon_i \tag{9}$$

where

$r_i \Rightarrow$ Return from the ith project
$r_f \Rightarrow$ Risk free rate of return
$r_m \Rightarrow$ Rate of return on the market index
$\varepsilon_i \Rightarrow$ Error term for the ith project.

Here, r_i and r_m are stochastic, and hence, ε_i is also stochastic. Taking expected value on both the sides, r_f being risk free rate of return, the value remain same. ε_i

generally follows Normal Distribution with Mean 0 and Standard Deviation = 1 i.e. $\varepsilon_i \sim N(0, 1)$. Therefore, expected value of Left Hand Side of Eq. (9) will be $\overline{r_i} - r_f$ ($\because r_f$ is constant) and the Right Hand Side will be $\beta_i(\overline{r_m} - r_f)$.

Assuming Normal Distribution for the returns and also considering $\varepsilon_i \sim N(0, 1)$, the expected value will be:

$$\overline{r_i} - r_f = \beta_i(\overline{r_m} - r_f) \tag{10}$$

If $\beta = 1 \Rightarrow$ Average Risk in Investment
If $\beta > 1 \Rightarrow$ Above Average Risk in Investment
If $\beta < 1 \Rightarrow$ Below Average Risk in Investment
If $\beta = 0 \Rightarrow$ Riskless Investment.

CAPM can also be used as a pricing model of a portfolio through the following relation:

$$\frac{\overline{P_t} - P_0}{P_0} = r_f + \beta(\overline{r_m} - r_f) \tag{11}$$

Thus,

$$P_0 = \frac{\overline{P_t}}{1 + r_f + \beta(\overline{r_m} - r_f)} \tag{12}$$

where

$\overline{P_t} \Rightarrow$ actual Expected Value of the portfolio of project at a certain time 't' after the investment process has been started.
$P_0 \Rightarrow$ Initial Investment, which is known.
$\frac{\overline{P_t} - P_0}{P_0} \Rightarrow$ Rate of Return of the Investment in the project which is equal to $\overline{r_i}$.
$r_f \Rightarrow$ Risk-free interest rate.

From Eq. (11), it follows:

$$\overline{r_i} - r_f = \beta(\overline{r_m} - r_f) \tag{13}$$

This is exactly like Eq. (10) which was considered in deterministic sense.

5 Linearity of Pricing

Portfolio is basically a conglomeration of multiple projects. Therefore, for finding out the overall prices of the portfolio, the summation of individual prices is to find out [19]. Linearity of Pricing has been used for this purpose, because the prices of two projects are the linear sum of the prices of the individual two projects. Thus, from Eq. (12), it is evident that:

$$P_{0_A} = \frac{\overline{P_{t_A}}}{1 + r_f + \beta_A(\overline{r_m} - r_f)} \tag{14}$$

and

$$P_{0_B} = \frac{\overline{P_{t_B}}}{1 + r_f + \beta_B(\overline{r_m} - r_f)} \tag{15}$$

Where P_{0_A} and P_{0_B} are the return or the prices as of now of Project A and Project B respectively.

From Eqs. (14) and (15), it is evident that:

$$P_{0_A} + P_{0_B} = \frac{\overline{P_{t_A}} + \overline{P_{t_B}}}{1 + r_f + \beta_{A+B}(\overline{r_m} - r_f)} \tag{16}$$

Where $\beta_A + \beta_B = \beta_{A+B}$ and $P_{0_A} + P_{0_B}$ is overall return or the price of these conglomeration of the projects at time $t = 0$.

The denominator of Eq. (16) is the discounted risk factor of the overall portfolio.

The objective, at this point, is to find out β. Given a project, with initial investment P_0 (known) and final return P_t (unknown), β can be derived through:

$$\beta = \frac{\text{Cov}\left[\left\{\left(\frac{P_t}{P_0}\right) - 1\right\}, r_m\right]}{\sigma_m^2} \tag{17}$$

where $\sigma_m^2 \Rightarrow$ market risk.

Numerator of relation (17) is the covariance that exists between the rate of return of project A or B, etc. w.r.t. the market.

Substituting the value of β in Eq. (12) it is found:

$$P_0 = \frac{\overline{P_t}}{1 + r_f + \frac{\text{Cov}\left[\left\{\left(\frac{P_t}{P_0}\right) - 1\right\}, r_m\right]}{\sigma_m^2}(\overline{r_m} - r_f)}$$

$$\Rightarrow P_0 = \frac{1}{1 + r_f}\left[\overline{P_t} - \frac{\text{Cov}(\overline{P_t} - r_m)(\overline{r_m} - r_f)}{\sigma_m^2}\right] \tag{18}$$

The interpretation of Eq. (18) is that it is a ratio between one of the particular investments out of a project in the market divided by the overall risk of the market.

The term in the bracket is known as the certainty equivalent. Certainty equivalent is the amount which provides a guaranteed return of a risky project to an individual.

Adding the RHS of Eq. (18) with negative P_0 (Initial Outlay), Net Present Value (NPV) can be derived as follows:

$$P_0 = -P_0 + \frac{1}{1+r_f} \cdot \left[\overline{P_t} - \frac{Cov\left(\overline{P_t} - r_m\right)\left(\overline{r_m} - r_f\right)}{\sigma_m^2} \right] \tag{19}$$

Where NPV is the expected value of the overall project, as of now. If NPV is positive, the portfolio will be worthy to invest. So, there is a set of 'n' number of projects in a portfolio and these projects are required to be ranked according to their respective NPV in descending order.

But as stated earlier, risk analysis is one of the few attributes for selecting a project where the entrepreneur can invest. The other attributes are Rate of Return, Marketability, Tax Shelter, Convenience, etc.

Therefore, ranking of the projects of a portfolio only on the basis of risk analysis will be a partial work. For getting a holistic approach, therefore, TOPSIS has been adopted as a multi-criteria decision making technique. However, for space constraint, only the basic outline of TOPSIS has been mentioned. Detailed procedure and steps of TOPSIS can be found in [20].

Assuming that there are 4 projects (Alternatives) in the Portfolio namely A_1, A_2, A_3, A_4 and the Criteria are Rate of Return (X_1), Risk (X_2), Marketability (X_3), Tax shelter (X_4) and Convenience (X_5). The Decision Matrix will, therefore, be as follows (Table 1):

Table 1. Decision matrix

	X_1	X_2	X_3	X_4	X_5
A_1	R_{11}	B_{12}	Average	T_{14}	Very high
A_2	R_{21}	B_{22}	Low	T_{24}	Average
A_3	R_{31}	B_{32}	High	T_{34}	High
A_4	R_{41}	B_{42}	Average	T_{44}	Average

Out of these 5 criteria, 4 criteria are of similar type in a sense that higher the values in these criteria, better will be the project. But in case of 2nd criterion, X_2, which is related to risk, lesser the value of this criterion, better will be the project.

After using the numerical scale for tangibles, the Revised Decision Matrix may be as follows:

Table 2. Revised decision matrix

	X_1	X_2	X_3	X_4	X_5
A_1	R_{11}	B_{12}	M_{13}	T_{14}	C_{15}
A_2	R_{21}	B_{22}	M_{23}	T_{24}	C_{25}
A_3	R_{31}	B_{32}	M_{33}	T_{34}	C_{35}
A_4	R_{41}	B_{42}	M_{43}	T_{44}	C_{45}

But the numerals in Table 2 are all in incommensurate units. So, Normalization will be required. Obtaining Normalized Decision Matrix R through the following formula:

$$r_{ij} = \frac{x_{ij}}{\sqrt{\sum_{i=1}^{n} x_{ij}^2}} \tag{20}$$

The Weighted Decision Matrix V is to be obtained by multiplying each column of R by the corresponding weight. The Weighted decision Matrix embodies the preferences of the decision maker on various criteria. The largest values of each column are the desirable one excepting the 2nd column – the risk column where lower the risk, better is the project.

The Ideal Solutions (A^*) and the negative ideal (A^-) solutions from the Weighted Decision Matrix V is to be obtained.

Computation of Separation measures from the Ideal S_i^* and the Negative Ideal S_i^- solutions for all alternatives are to be derived where i = 1, 2, 3, …, n.

Computation of Relative Closeness to the Ideal Solution for each alternative is to be found out. Finally, on the basis of Relative Closeness values, the projects can finally be ranked. Higher the rank, better will be the Project.

6 Conclusion

This research work provides a theoretical basis for establishing the relationship of risk analysis associated with every project under a portfolio. β analysis has been conducted to mitigate the systematic risks of a portfolio. But apart from risk analysis, which is certainly one of the most important attributes of any investment decision, total five attributes have been considered in this work to generate the final ranking of all the projects under a portfolio. It is recommended to rebalance the projects of the portfolio through this method in due course of time for optimizing the total gain. In this way, the total risk and uncertainties imposed through the economy can be mitigated and thus, it can have a positive impact on the overall improvement of the organization.

References

1. Jolanta, T., Edmundas, K.Z., Zenonas, T.: Multi-criteria risk assessment of a construction project. Procedia Comput. Sci. **17**, 129–133 (2013). https://doi.org/10.1016/j.procs.2013.05.018

2. Bowman, R.G.: The theoretical relationship between systematic risk and financial (accounting) variables. J. Finan. **34**(3), 617–630 (1979). https://doi.org/10.2307/2327430

3. Hamada, R.: Portfolio analysis, market equilibrium and corporation finance. J. Finan. **24**(1), 13–31 (1969). https://doi.org/10.1111/j.1540-6261.1969.tb00339.x

4. Hamada, R.: The effect of the firm's capital structure on the systematic risk of common stocks. J. Finan. **27**(2), 435–452 (1972). https://doi.org/10.2307/2978486

5. Markowitz, H.: Portfolio selection. J. Finan. **7**(1), 77–91 (1952). https://doi.org/10.1111/j.1540-6261.1952.tb01525.x

6. Jerry, H.W.R., Tsai, C.L., Tzeng, G.H., Fang, S.K.: Combined DEMATEL technique with a novel MCDM model for exploring portfolio selection based on CAPM. Expert Syst. Appl. **38**, 16–25 (2011). https://doi.org/10.1016/j.eswa.2010.05.058

7. Sharpe, W.F.: Capital asset prices: a theory of market equilibrium under conditions of risk. J. Finan. **19**(3), 425–442 (1964). https://doi.org/10.2307/2977928

8. Lintner, J.: The valuation of risk assets and the selection of risky investments in stock portfolios and capital budgets. Rev. Econ. Stat. **47**(1), 13–37 (1965). https://doi.org/10.2307/1924119

9. Mossin, J.: Equilibrium in a capital asset market. Econometrica **34**(4), 768–783 (1966). https://doi.org/10.2307/1910098

10. Samvedi, A., Jain, V., Chan, F.T.S.: Quantifying risks in a supply chain through integration of fuzzy AHP and fuzzy TOPSIS. Int. J. Prod. Res. **51**(8), 2433–2442 (2013). https://doi.org/10.1080/00207543.2012.741330

11. Zamani, L., Beegam, R., Borzoian, S.: Portfolio selection using data envelopment analysis (DEA): a case of select Indian investment companies. Int. J. Curr. Res. Acad. Rev. **2**(4), 50–55 (2014)

12. Hsu, L.C.: A hybrid multiple criteria decision making model for investment decision making. J. Bus. Econ. Manag. **15**(3), 509–529 (2014). https://doi.org/10.3846/16111699.2012.722563

13. Monjazeb, M., Habibi, M., Sharifi, A.: Performance evaluation and optimal portfolio selection among industries and investment funds. MAGNT Res. Rep. **3**(5), 41–46 (2015). 14.9831/1444-8939.2015/3-5/magnt.6

14. Haghshenas, S.S., Neshaei, M.A.L., Pourkazem, P., Haghshenas, S.S.: The risk assessment of dam construction projects using fuzzy TOPSIS (case study: Alavian Earth Dam). Civil Eng. J. **2**(4), 158–167 (2016)

15. Subya, R., Manoj, M.: Risk assessment of highway construction projects using fuzzy logic and multiple regression analysis. Int. Res. J. Eng. Technol. (IRJET) **4**(4), 2344–2349 (2017)

16. Gifford, S.: Risk and uncertainty. In: Acs, Z., Audretsch, D. (eds.) Handbook of Entrepreneurship Research, vol. 5, pp. 303–318. Springer, New York (2010). https://doi.org/10.1007/978-1-4419-1191-9_12

17. Rosenberg, B.: The capital asset pricing model and the market model. J. Portfolio Manag. **7**(2), 5–16 (1981)

18. Chandra, P.: The Investment Game – How to Win, 6th edn. Tata McGraw-Hill Publishing Company Limited, New Delhi (1995)

19. Connor, G.: A unified beta pricing theory. J. Econ. Theory **34**(1), 13–31 (1984). https://doi.org/10.1016/0022-0531(84)90159-5

20. Jahanshahloo, G.R., Lzadikhah, M.: An algorithmic method to extend TOPSIS for decision-making problems with interval data. Appl. Math. Comput. **175**(2), 1375–1384 (2006). https://doi.org/10.1016/j.amc.2005.08.048

Intelligent Data Mining and Data Warehousing

An Approach Towards Classification of Fruits and Vegetables Using Fractal Analysis

Susovan Jana[1]([✉]), Ranjan Parekh[2], and Bijan Sarkar[1]

[1] Department of Production Engineering, Jadavpur University, Kolkata, India
jana.susovan2@gmail.com,
bijan.sarkar@jadavpuruniversity.in
[2] School of Education Technology, Jadavpur University, Kolkata, India
rparekh@school.jdvu.ac.in

Abstract. Agriculture-related works include harvesting, sorting, and packaging etc. Those works require lots of time and a huge number of expert resources for manual execution. Automation may be the solution to this problem. There are lots of challenges for the automation of those works with the help of image processing. One of the major challenges is the identification of fruit and vegetable class accurately from various viewing positions. In this paper, a viewpoint independent solution is proposed for fruit and vegetable classification. Firstly, input RGB color image is converted to a grayscale image. Multiple threshold values are calculated from the grayscale image using multi-level thresholding technique. Then a set of the binary images is generated using those threshold values. In the next step, the border image is extracted from each of the binary images. Finally, the fractal dimension is computed from the border image and used to classify the fruit and vegetable. The proposed method was tested on a dataset of 1080 images, which contains 15 classes of fruits and vegetables. Complete 360° viewing positions are considered for experimentation. The range of overall system accuracy is 97.78% to 100% using k-NN classifier.

Keywords: Viewpoint independent · Multi-level thresholding · Fractal dimension · Classification

1 Introduction

Computer vision is one of the superior technologies for automating the process in various industries. Agriculture is one of the major application areas of this technology. Automation is necessary for every aspect of planting, treatment, pest control, harvesting, sorting and packing. The reason behind this automation is not only to make the process faster but also reducing the human effort in repetitive works. Among the agricultural products, fruits and vegetables are necessary for everyday life. In recent days there is a trend of buying fresh fruit and vegetables from a supermarket in India as well as in other developing countries. There are challenges to identify a fruit and vegetable class in supermarkets. Barcode or Catalogue based approach partially solves the problem, but barcode-based tracking is not possible when the number of fruit and vegetable is large. Searching preferred item from the large catalog is time-consuming.

© Springer Nature Singapore Pte Ltd. 2019
J. K. Mandal et al. (Eds.): CICBA 2018, CCIS 1031, pp. 167–180, 2019.
https://doi.org/10.1007/978-981-13-8581-0_14

The image-based solution may be effective to address that problem. In this universe, there are lots of species of fruit and vegetable [1]. All the species are not consumable. Among the consumable fruits and vegetables though there are variations of taste but lots of similarity in outlook. Categorizing based on an image feature is very challenging. There are many existing works for automating this task based on image analysis. Fruit and vegetable color, shape, size and texture [2] features were used to recognize the object. Fruit and vegetable image may be captured from various positions in real life scenario. This makes the classification task more critical. The motivation of this work is to propose a system framework, which will be able to classify specific fruit and vegetable though the image is captured from various positions.

In Sect. 2, a literature review is done on image-based fruit and vegetable classification. Section 3 illustrates the proposed method in details with equations and diagrams. Section 4 brings the experimentations and results of this work. A comparative analysis is introduced in Sect. 5 followed by the conclusion and future scope of this research in Sect. 6.

2   Previous Works

It is needed to classify the class of fruit and vegetable accurately for every aspect of agricultural works. There are some previous works of classification among different fruit classes based on visual features like color, texture, shape, and size. A fruit and vegetable classification method was proposed using CENTRIST and color feature [3]. Census transformed histogram and hue, saturation color histogram were extracted and used as a classification feature after normalization. Rachmawati et al. also proposed a RGB color histogram quantization [4] technique to classify 32 classes of fruit. In a texture based approach [5], Improved Sum and Difference Histogram (ISADH) feature was used for recognition of fruit from a color image. Multiple region-based features were used for classification of fruits in a shape based approach [6]. This approach is geometrical transformation invariant. A combined features based approach [7] was proposed for fruit classification using color and shape features. Color means for each of RGB component, area, perimeter, and roundness of the object were combined in the feature vector. A nearly similar mixed approach was proposed combining color, shape, and texture based features [8]. Zawbaa et al. [9] proposed two sets of classification features to classify 3 fruit class. The first set combined color (variance, mean, kurtosis, and skewness) and shape (eccentricity, centroid, and Euler number) features. The second set used only SIFT feature. In a work [10], 64 color feature, 7 texture feature and 8 shape features were extracted from fruit image. Then PCA was used to reduce the dimension of the feature vector. The classification of the subtypes of particular fruit and vegetable class is also a tough job. Various shape features were adopted to predict subtypes [11] using Naïve Bayes classification algorithm.

It is observed that most of the previous work was tested on less number of fruit and vegetable classes. All the approaches considered only one viewing position but result degrades when multiple viewing positions are introduced. This is one of the most difficult obstacles to recognize fruit and vegetable properly from an image. In this paper, a new classification approach is proposed to address the problem of viewing position change.

3   Proposed Method

This approach adopted few steps to normalize the effect of viewpoint in classification as well as selects a feature which is able to discriminate among multiple classes of fruit and vegetables irrespective of the viewing positions.

3.1   System Overview

Figure 1 shows the flow of the different process in the proposed system. Input image (I) is converted to grayscale image (I_g). Multilevel Otsu thresholding is applied on I_g to get a set (T), which contains number of threshold values same as the number of threshold level (N_t). The graysacle image is binarized (I_{bw}) using the threshold values. The border image (I_b) is extracted from the binary images (I_{bw}). The fractal dimension (D) is computed from every border image and stored as feature vector (FV) in database. Finally, the class label (i) prediction has been done by the trained classifier using FV.

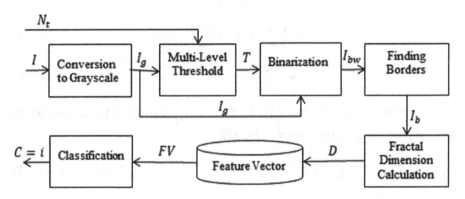

Fig. 1. Process flow diagram of the proposed system

3.2   Conversion to Grayscale

RGB input image (I) is split into three components i.e. IR, IG, IB. A grayscale image (I_g) is generated using those components and Eq. (1).

$$I_g = 0.2989 \times IR + 0.5870 \times IG + 0.1140 \times IB \tag{1}$$

3.3   Multi-level Threshold

Multilevel Otsu thresholding technique [12] is applied on the grayscale image. It's a very fast algorithm in terms of processing speed and requires low storage space. Assuming, the grayscale image (I_g) contains M number of pixels with gray level from 1 to L. Total count of the pixel for gray level i is denoted by f_i. The probability of gray level i in the image is p_i. Refer to Eq. (2).

$$p_i = \frac{f_i}{M} \tag{2}$$

The number of threshold level (N_t) is an input to the system. Output is a set T of N_t threshold values $\{T_1, T_2, T_3, \ldots, T_{N_t}\}$, based on the gray level histogram distribution. It divides the image into $K = (N_t + 1)$ number of classes. The ω_k in Eq. (3) represents cumulative probability of kth class and μ_k in Eq. (4) depicts mean intensity of kth class. Therefore, the mean intensity of the whole image is μ_T and between class variance is σ_B^2. Refer to Eqs. (5) and (6).

$$\omega_k = \sum_{i \in C_k} p_i \tag{3}$$

$$\mu_k = \sum_{i \in C_k} \frac{i \cdot p_i}{\omega_k} \tag{4}$$

$$\mu_T = \sum_{i=1}^{L} i \cdot p_i = \sum_{k=1}^{K} \mu_k \omega_k \tag{5}$$

$$\sigma_B^2 = \sum_{k=1}^{K} \omega_k (\mu_k - \mu_T)^2 \tag{6}$$

The optimal threshold values $\{T_1^*, T_2^*, T_3^*, \ldots, T_{N_t}^*\}$ are chosen by maximizing the between class variance (σ_B^2). Refer to Eq. (7).

$$\{T_1^*, T_2^*, T_3^*, \ldots, T_{N_t}^*\} = ArgMax\{\sigma_B^2(T_1, T_2, T_3, \ldots, T_{N_t})\}, 1 \leq T_1 < \ldots < T_{N_t} < L \tag{7}$$

3.4   Binarization

The grayscale image is binarized using Eq. (8) for each threshold value of set T. It gives the same number of binary image as number of threshold level. Figure 2 shows the sample images after binarization with a fixed threshold value for pineapple fruit where number of threshold level is 4.

$$I_{bw}(x, y) = \begin{cases} 1 & if\ I_g(x, y) > T \\ 0, & otherwise \end{cases} \tag{8}$$

Fig. 2. Sample binary images using Eq. (8) and $N_t = 4$

Again, the grayscale image is binarized using Eq. (9) for each range of the threshold values from lower threshold (T_l) to higher threshold (T_h). If the number of threshold level is N_t then the number of threshold range will be ($N_t - 1$). This process produces same number of binary image as the number of threshold range. Figure 3 shows the sample images after binarization with range of threshold values for pineapple fruit where the number of threshold level is 4.

$$I_{bw}(x,y) = \begin{cases} 1 & if\ I_g(x,y) > T_l\ and\ I_g(x,y) < T_h \\ 0, & otherwise \end{cases} \tag{9}$$

Fig. 3. Sample binary images using Eq. (9) and $N_t = 4$

Total numbers of binary images after the complete binarization process are N_{bw}. It can be calculated using Eq. (10). Each of the binary images represents detailing of fruit and vegetable surface for the particular threshold value or range.

$$N_{bw} = 2(N_t) - 1 \tag{10}$$

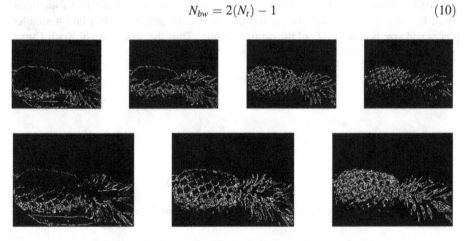

Fig. 4. Border images of Figs. 2 and 3 using Eq. (11)

3.5   Finding Borders

Next task is to find border pixels from the binary image. In the binary image, if a pixel $I_{bw}(x,y)$ has the value 1 and any of its 8-connected neighboring pixels $N_8[(x,y)]$ have the value 0 then the pixel is selected as border pixel. Rests of the pixels in I_{bw} are the non-border pixel. Border pixels are set as 1 and rests are set as 0 for the each of the image in the set of binary image. Border image (I_b) for each of the binary image (I_{bw}) are processed using Eq. (11). Figure 4 shows the (Row1) border image of Fig. 2 and (Row2) border image of Fig. 3 processed using this technique. The border pixels of each fruit and vegetable image contain a specific pattern. Multiple border images are assisting to identify the pattern more accurately.

$$I_b(x, y) = \begin{cases} 1 & if\ I_{bw}(x, y) = 1\ and\ I_{bw}(x', y') = 0 \\ & where\,(x', y') \in N_8[(x, y)] \\ 0, & otherwise \end{cases} \tag{11}$$

3.6   Fractal Dimension Calculation

Mandelbrot discovered the fractals dimension [13], which is a never-ending pattern. Fractal dimension (D) can be computed using Eq. (12), where N is the number of broken pieces from the larger one and F is the scale factor to which smaller pieces is compared to larger one.

$$D = \frac{\log N}{\log(1/F)} \tag{12}$$

Koch Snowflake [15] can be taken as an example to demonstrate fractal dimension calculation. Figure 5 shows four versions of Koch Snowflake for the first four iterations. In each step every side of the triangle or Koch Curve is broken into 4 smaller pieces and size is exactly 1/3 of the original length. Thus the dimension of Koch Curve is 1.231, which is a fraction, not an integer.

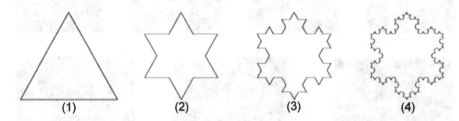

Fig. 5.   First four iterations of Koch Snowflake [18]

Hausdorff's box-counting method [14] is used here to calculate fractal dimension from the border image. Assuming that size of the border image (I_b) is ($H \times W$). Initial value of the box size (S) is computed using Eq. (13).

$$S = 2^{\lceil \log_2(\max(H, W)) \rceil} \tag{13}$$

The border image is resized to $S \times S$ by padding $(S - H)$ number of row and $(S - W)$ number of column with $I_b[H \times W]$. Then $I_b[S \times S]$ is divided into a grid made with a number of squares of size $\in \times \in$, where initial value of $\in$ is S. Then it counts the number of box $(\overline{N}(\in))$ which has at least one pixel of object in the $\in \times \in$ sized box. After that size of the square block is reduced to half of the previous size $(\in /2)$ in each direction. Again it will count the number of box $(\overline{N}(\in))$ which has at least one pixel of object. This iteration continues until $\in \ > 1$. In each iteration it computes the point set $\{x, y\}$ with the $\log(1/ \in)$ as x value and the $\log N(\in)$ as y value. Then least square method is used to fit the set of points into a straight line. The slope of this line is the desired fractal dimension (D) of the border image (I_b). Equation (14) depicts this calculation formula.

$$D = \frac{\Delta\{\log N(\in)\}}{\Delta\{\log(1/ \in)\}} \tag{14}$$

3.7 Feature Vector

Feature vector plays a vital role in pattern recognition and supervised machine learning problems. It is an n-dimensional vector of numerical values which represents some object. Figure 6 shows sample feature plot of 7 classes where the number of the threshold level is 7. The horizontal axis represents training file index and the vertical axis represents fractal dimension. Each color represents a class mentioned in the legend. First two plots in Fig. 6 show the variation of fractal dimension among the classes binarized using Eq. (8) for two higher threshold values. The third plot in Fig. 6 shows the variation of fractal dimension among classes, binarized using Eq. (9) for the range of those two higher threshold values. Twelve samples from each class have 30° viewing angle variation still the fractal dimension is able to discriminate among the fruit and vegetable classes. It proves the discrimination power of fractal dimension. Fractal dimension for each of the border image is computed. All the fractal dimensions are combined in the final feature vector. Final feature vector FV contains $2(N_t) - 1$ number of fractal dimension. Refer to Eq. (15).

$$FV = \{D_1, D_2, D_3, \ldots\ldots\ldots\ldots\ldots\ldots\ldots\ldots, D_{2N_t-1}\} \tag{15}$$

3.8 Classification

Classification based on few feature values some time became a tedious job. In broader prospect, the perfect classification for all samples is not always possible. The reason behind that is the variability of intra-class features and noise. The performance of classification mainly depends on two things, i.e. features set and classifier. Selection of good classification feature is very important. Also, the choice of the classifier for particular features and decision rule is needed to make a good decision boundary for classification. Each class is identified by its feature values T_i during the training phase, where there are i number of fruit classes. A sample fruit image SP is belongs to a

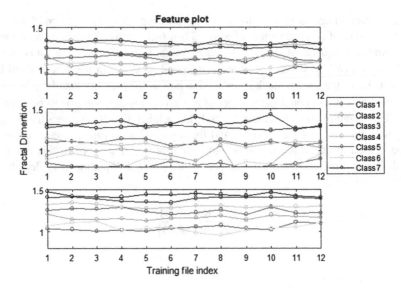

Fig. 6. Fractal dimension variations across 7 classes of fruit and vegetable where $N_t = 7$

specific class among i number of fruit classes. Decision rule will decide the class of fruit for *SP* image is i, if the matching probability of the feature values of *SP* is high with i^{th} class.

This decision rule differs based on the classification algorithm. In this paper, k-NN algorithm for classification is proposed. k-NN is a non-parametric and lazy learning algorithm. It does not build a model based on training data like the other supervised learning algorithms. The decision for class prediction is performed by calculating the distance between the features of the unknown test sample and all training features. The class of training sample, which has minimum distance from the unknown test sample, is labeled to the unknown test sample. Prediction is done based on the vote of k number of nearest neighbor when $k > 1$. The k-NN algorithm has two drawbacks - (1) space overhead and (2) slowness due to computation overhead. Space overhead is not a serious issue in today's world but the technique to deal with computation overhead is mentioned in the next section.

4   Experimentations and Results

The experimentations are done with 15 classes of fruit and vegetable to validate the proposed method. Dataset is collected from Amsterdam Library of Object Images (ALOI) [16]. In total, 72 viewing directions are introduced with 5° variations to cover 360° viewing angle. There are 72 images for each fruit and vegetable class and 1080 images in the complete dataset used for experimentation. Among 72 of each class, 12 images used to train the system and the viewing angles of the images are $0°, 30°, 60°, 90°, 120°, 150°, 180°, 210°, 240°, 270°, 300°$ *and* $330°$. Figure 7 shows the training images for pineapple. The 60 images from the remaining directions are used for testing purpose. The ratio of number of training and testing image is 1: 5 i.e. Dataset Version-1. The number and the viewing angle of training and testing images are taken randomly there are no such restriction of choosing training and testing sample. The system is implemented using MATLAB R2017a version. The entire experimentations are performed in windows 7 operating system with Intel Core i5 3.00 GHz Processor and 4 GB RAM.

Fig. 7. Variation of viewing angle for a specific class [16]

Table 1 shows that classification accuracy using four classifiers and different number of threshold level on Dataset Version-1. Classification accuracy on same test dataset is varying from 68.67% to 97.78%. Since k-NN is not restricted to a model and prediction is done based on all training data. The k-NN classifier gives maximum accuracy but the major issue with k-NN is slowness. It is tackled here using very less amount of data for training purpose. Among the other classifiers, Discriminant Analysis classifier and Naïve Bayes are also showing a satisfactory result.

Table 1. [Dataset Version-1] overall classification accuracy using different classifiers and different number of threshold level (N_t)

Type of classifier	Accuracy % ($N_t = 4$)	Accuracy % ($N_t = 5$)	Accuracy % ($N_t = 6$)	Accuracy % ($N_t = 7$)
k-Nearest Neighbor (k-NN)	94.22	96.22	96	97.78
Discriminant Analysis (DA)	89.44	93.44	95	95.78
Naïve Bayes (NB)	85.78	90.22	92	95
Support Vector Machine (SVM)	68.67	73.78	76.11	83.44

The ratio of the number of training and the testing image was 1:5 for Dataset Version-1. To test the robustness of the proposed algorithm training and testing dataset are swapped. After swapping the dataset, this ratio becomes 5:1 i.e. Dataset Version-2. Table 2 shows the result of the different classifier with a different number of threshold level after swapping the training and testing dataset. Here also, the k-NN classifier with 7 threshold level giving the best accuracy.

Table 2. [Dataset Version-2] overall classification accuracy using different classifiers and different number of threshold level (N_t)

Type of classifier	Accuracy % ($N_t = 4$)	Accuracy % ($N_t = 5$)	Accuracy % ($N_t = 6$)	Accuracy % ($N_t = 7$)
k-Nearest Neighbor (k-NN)	97.78	98.33	99.44	100
Discriminant Analysis (DA)	91.67	92.78	93.89	96.67
Naïve Bayes (NB)	88.33	90.56	92.78	96.11
Support Vector Machine (SVM)	77.22	81.67	85.56	96.67

Also measured the average time required to classify a test sample when the system tested with the proposed approach. The average classification time is around 1 s for a fruit or vegetable sample, which is acceptable for automatic classification of fruits and vegetables. It has been noticed that classification time required per sample increases with the increment of number of threshold level. The increment of number of threshold level causes more binary image and more computations which causes an increment in the processing time.

5   Analysis

It is observed that there is a fractal pattern for a class of fruit and vegetable surface. This pattern is different from other class of fruit and vegetable. This is the reason behind choosing the fractal dimension to address the viewpoint problem of fruit and vegetable classification. It becomes more accurate when it is calculated for multiple binary version of an image. These are generated from one single grayscale image using multiple threshold values. Experimentation results demonstrate that increment in the dimension of feature vector causes improvement in accuracy up to a certain limit. Figure 8 shows the improvement of classification accuracy using k-NN classifier for both versions of the dataset with the increment of the number of threshold level. This figure also shows that after certain number of threshold level accuracy degrades for both the versions of the dataset. The reason is over decomposition of a grayscale image. There is no fruit and vegetable object for some images when the input image is thresholded with the lower range of threshold values. In this work, the classification accuracy degrades when $N_t \geq 8$.

Table 3 depicts that comparison of some previous and popular approach with the proposed approach. Shape, Color, Texture as well as mixed previous approaches are experimented here and compared with the proposed approach. Approach (1) [11] is a complete shape-based approach to classify three types of mangoes. But the shape of most of the fruit completely changes when 360° viewing position considered. This is the reason for the poor accuracy of approach (1). Approach (2) is a mixed approach of texture, color, and shape. This approach [8] is also not suitable for this problem because of the feature descriptors, which were used by them, are not enough to classify a large

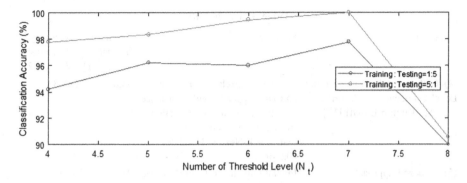

Fig. 8. Classification accuracy using k-NN classifier vs. number of threshold level (N_t)

number of classes. Shape descriptor like Area, Perimeter varies by fruit size or shape. Approach (3) is a complete histogram [3] based approach. In this approach, both gray & color histogram was used. The overall accuracy is good with this approach but the length of feature vector is 60 times larger than that of the proposed approach. This performs badly for the classes, where the fruit is a mixture of too many colors or the color changes when the image captured from another viewing angle. Approach (4) is a very popular approach of image classification based on texture analysis. Some statistical features are measured with a distance of 1 pixel and in four directions from GLCM [17]. Overall system accuracy using approach (4) is better than some other approaches but low in comparison with the proposed approach. This is the motivation for texture analysis to address the viewpoint problem of fruit and vegetable classification. Another good thing is that proposed approach requires very less number of images for training, which is a major advantage of this technique.

Table 3. Overall accuracy comparison of proposed approach with previous approaches

Approach	Strategy	Accuracy % [Dataset Version-1]	Accuracy % [Dataset Version-2]
(1) Roomi et al. (Shape Based) [11]	Eccentricity, Major Axis/Minor Axis, and Circulatory Ratio of fruit object + Naive Bayes Classifier	58.11	57.22
(2) Ninawe et al. (Mixed Feature Based) [8]	Entropy of grayscale image, Mean value of the 3 channel of RGB color image and Roundness, Area, Perimeter of fruit object + k-Nearest Neighbor Classifier	69.22	78.89
(3) Cornejo et al. (Color Based) [3]	Normalized histogram of Census transformed gray image and hue, saturation channel of HSV color image + Support Vector Machine Classifier	97	96.11

(continued)

Table 3. (*continued*)

Approach	Strategy	Accuracy % [Dataset Version-1]	Accuracy % [Dataset Version-2]
(4) Texture Analysis using Gray Level Co-occurrence Matrix-GLCM (Texture-Based) [17]	Contrast, Correlation, Energy, and Homogeneity with a distance of 1 pixel and in four directions from gray-level co-occurrence matrix + k-Nearest Neighbor Classifier	93.67	98.33
(5) Proposed approach	Fractal Dimension from Bordered Binary Image + k-Nearest Neighbor Classifier	97.78	100

Figures 9 and 10 shows the accuracy variation on 15 fruit and vegetable classes using different classifier for two versions of the dataset respectively. The red line in both Figs. 9 and 10 depicts that accuracy is consistently good for most of the classes when k-NN Classifier was used. Figures 11 and 12 shows the class wise accuracy variation using different approaches for two versions of dataset respectively. The red line in Figs. 11 and 12 indicates that proposed approach is performing better than other approaches for most of the classes.

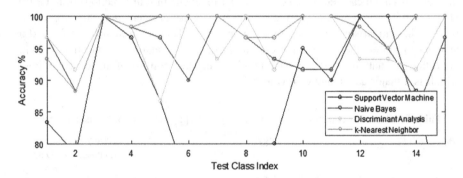

Fig. 9. Accuracy variations of 15 classes of fruits and vegetables using different classifiers when $N_t = 7$ (Dataset Version-1) (Color figure online)

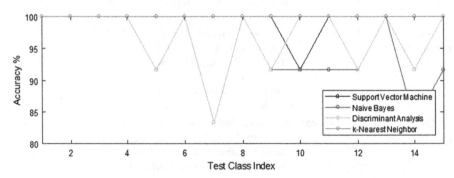

Fig. 10. Accuracy variations of 15 classes of fruits and vegetables using different classifiers when $N_t = 7$ (Dataset Version-2) (Color figure online)

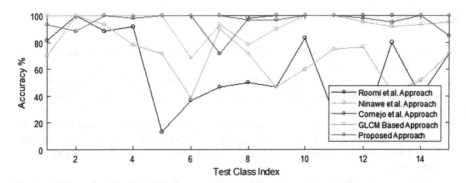

Fig. 11. Class wise accuracy variation using different approaches [3, 8, 11, 17] (Dataset Version-1) (Color figure online)

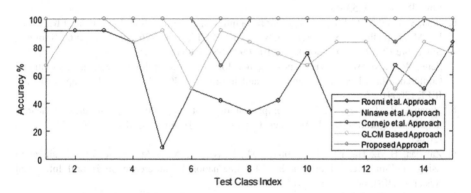

Fig. 12. Class wise accuracy variation using different approaches [3, 8, 11, 17] (Dataset Version-2) (Color figure online)

6 Conclusion and Future Scope

In this work, a fruit and vegetable classification system is proposed. A grayscale image is decomposed into multiple binary images using multiple threshold values. Then keeping the border pixel remaining all the pixels are discarded from each of the binary images. Fractal dimension is computed for each of the border image using box-counting technique and these dimension values are used as the classification features. k-NN Classifier gives the best accuracy (97.78% to 100%) among the four classifiers, which was tested. Performance of Discriminant Analysis Classifier and Naïve Bayes Classifier is also satisfactory. The main contribution of this paper is that the different types of fruits and vegetables will be classifiable irrespective of the viewing angle. There are few other factors i.e. occlusion, illumination condition etc., which affects the classification result of fruit and vegetable. Those problems may be the motivation of future research.

References

1. Pennington, J.A., Fisher, R.A.: Classification of fruits and vegetables. J. Food Compos. Anal. **22**, S23–S31 (2009)
2. Meruliya, T., Dhameliya, P., Patel, J., Panchal, D., Kadam, P., Naik, S.: Image processing for fruit shape and texture feature extraction-review. Int. J. Comput. Appl. **129**(8), 30–33 (2015)
3. Cornejo, J.Y.R., Pedrini, H.: Automatic fruit and vegetable recognition based on CENTRIST and color representation. In: Beltrán-Castañón, C., Nyström, I., Famili, F. (eds.) CIARP 2016. LNCS, vol. 10125, pp. 76–83. Springer, Cham (2017). https://doi.org/10.1007/978-3-319-52277-7_10
4. Rachmawati, E., Khodra, M.L., Supriana, I.: Histogram based color pattern identification of multiclass fruit using feature selection. In: International Conference on Electrical Engineering and Informatics (ICEEI), pp. 43–48. IEEE (2015)
5. Dubey, S.R., Jalal, A.S.: Robust approach for fruit and vegetable classification. Procedia Eng. **38**, 3449–3453 (2012)
6. Jana, S., Parekh, R.: Shape-based fruit recognition and classification. In: Mandal, J.K., Dutta, P., Mukhopadhyay, S. (eds.) CICBA 2017. CCIS, vol. 776, pp. 184–196. Springer, Singapore (2017). https://doi.org/10.1007/978-981-10-6430-2_15
7. Seng, W.C., Mirisaee, S.H.: A new method for fruits recognition system. In: International Conference on Electrical Engineering and Informatics, ICEEI 2009, vol. 1, pp. 130–134. IEEE (2009)
8. Ninawe, P., Pandey, M.S.: A completion on fruit recognition system using k-nearest neighbors algorithm. Int. J. Adv. Res. Comput. Eng. Technol. (IJARCET) **3**(7), 2352–2356 (2014)
9. Zawbaa, H.M., Hazman, M., Abbass, M., Hassanien, A.E.: Automatic fruit classification using random forest algorithm. In: 14th International Conference on Hybrid Intelligent Systems (HIS), pp. 164–168. IEEE (2014)
10. Zhang, Y., Wu, L.: Classification of fruits using computer vision and a multiclass support vector machine. Sensors **12**(9), 12489–12505 (2012)
11. Roomi, S.M.M., Priya, R.J., Bhumesh, S., Monisha, P.: Classification of mangoes by object features and contour modeling. In: International Conference on Machine Vision and Image Processing (MVIP), pp. 165–168. IEEE (2012)
12. Liao, P.S., Chen, T.S., Chung, P.C.: A fast algorithm for multilevel thresholding. J. Inf. Sci. Eng. **17**(5), 713–727 (2001)
13. Mandelbrot, B.: How long is the coast of Britain? Statistical self-similarity and fractional dimension. Science **156**(3775), 636–638 (1967)
14. Costa, A.F., Humpire-Mamani, G., Traina, A.J.M.: An efficient algorithm for fractal analysis of textures. In: 25th SIBGRAPI Conference on Graphics, Patterns and Images (SIBGRAPI), pp. 39–46. IEEE (2012)
15. Von Koch, H.: Sur une courbe continue sans tangente obtenue par une construction géométrique élémentaire. Norstedt & soner (1904)
16. Geusebroek, J.M., Burghouts, G.J., Smeulders, A.W.: The Amsterdam library of object images. Int. J. Comput. Vis. **61**(1), 103–112 (2005)
17. Haralick, R.M., Shanmugam, K.: Textural features for image classification. IEEE Trans. Syst. Man Cybern. **3**(6), 610–621 (1973)
18. Francis, M.: Galileo's Pendulam - Fractals for Fun. https://galileospendulum.org/2012/01/31/fractals-for-fun/. Accessed June 2018

Categorization of Bangla Medical Text Documents Based on Hybrid Internal Feature

Ankita Dhar[1(✉)], Niladri Sekhar Dash[2], and Kaushik Roy[1]

[1] Department of Computer Science, West Bengal State University, Kolkata,
West Bengal, India
ankita.ankie@gmail.com, kaushik.mrg@gmail.com
[2] Linguistic Research Unit, Indian Statistical Institute, Kolkata, India
ns_dash@yahoo.com

Abstract. This paper aims to develop an automatic text categorization system that classifies Bangla medical and non-medical text documents based on two primary features, that is, word length and the presence of English equivalent words in the text documents. To start with, it has been shown that based on the word length and the number of English equivalent words present in a particular text, Bangla medical text documents can be identified among other text documents of any domain. SGD (Stochastic Gradient Descent) classification algorithm is used and an accuracy of 97.75% has been achieved. Comparisons have also been done with other commonly used classifiers to test the system from which it has been observed that SGD performs better than those classifiers.

Keywords: Bangla text categorization · Medical text · Word length ·
English equivalent terms · SGD

1 Introduction

The amount of information in digital form available with us is increasing rapidly day-to-day. The available information would be useful if we are able to access the relevant information efficiently. When the amount of information is not in huge amount, people can read the text documents and categorize them manually but when the information is in large quantity, for example, in terms of thousands text documents, categorizing the text documents manually is quite time consuming, hectic, error prone and tedious task. Thus to do it efficiently, we need a tool which can assign the text documents to their predefined category or domain by using some supervised or unsupervised learning task. Text classification or text categorization is one of the most challenging tasks in natural language processing which is basically the task of assigning the text documents to their respective categories or classes.

Very few bits and pieces of researches has been done for Bangla in the area of text classification with respect to other languages like English, Arabic, Chinese and others; due to the problems faced such as: non-availability of standard databases, its rich and complex morphology, scarcity of resources and tools and others. So there is a pressing need for developing an automatic text classification system that can classify Bangla text documents into their respective categories.

J. K. Mandal et al. (Eds.): CICBA 2018, CCIS 1031, pp. 181–192, 2019.
https://doi.org/10.1007/978-981-13-8581-0_15

Here, an attempt is made to build a system that can classify Bangla text documents into their respective domains (medical or non-medical) based on the word length of the tokens appear in the text documents as well as the number of English equivalent tokens present in the documents. So, both these criteria have been used as the feature extraction approaches for extracting features to train the model and classifying the Bangla medical text documents using SGD classifier. The motivation behind choosing this classification algorithm is due to its promising performance in terms of accuracy in text classification for various languages [8]. News corpus from various Bangla websites is employed to evaluate the capabilities of these methods in categorization of high dimensional, sparse and relatively noisy document features.

In the remaining sections of the paper, related work is discussed in Sect. 2 followed by the proposed work in Sect. 3; Sect. 4 cast's light on result and discussion. Finally, the conclusion and future work is described in Sect. 5.

2   Existing Work

English and Arabic have gained great attention by the researchers followed by Chinese, Persian but very few researches have been performed on Indian languages. For English language, a clustering-based approach has been proposed by DeySarkar *et al.* [1] using 13 datasets based on Naive Bayes classification algorithm. Guru and Suhil [2] used Term_Class relevance as the feature selection method on the 20 Newsgroup dataset using SVM and K-NN classifiers. Jin *et al.* [3] implemented a bag-of-embeddings model on Reuters 21578 and 20 Newsgroups, using Support Vector Machine (SVM) classifier for classification task. Wang *et al.* [4] worked based on term frequency and t-test feature selection methods on Reuters21578 and 20Newsgroups datasets and classification are done using various commonly used classifiers.

In case of Arabic text classification, associative rule-based classifiers have been used by Al-Radaideh and Al-Khateeb [17] for classifying Arabic medical text documents. Light stemming and rootification methods along with TF-IDF and dependency grammar properties have been proposed on Kalimat corpus by Haralambous *et al.* [18]. Gupta and Gupta [5] implemented hybrid approach by combining Naive Bayes and Ontological Based classifiers for classifying Punjabi text documents. ArunaDevi and Saveeth [13] extracted compound features from CIIL and Mozhi corpus and used as feature for classification task. Vector Space Model and TF-IDF weighting scheme based on Zipf's law have been used by Swamy and Thappa [14] for classifying 100 text documents each for Kannada, Tamil, and Telugu and applied Decision Tree (J48), Naive Bayes (NB) and K-NN as classifiers. Patil and Bogiri [15] implemented LINGO clustering algorithm for classifying 200 Marathi news text documents. Dictionary based classification approach is adopted by Bolaj and Govilkar [16] for computing the feature vector and classifying Marathi text documents using several classification algorithms.

In case of Bangla text classification, N-Gram based technique has been implemented by Mansur *et al.* [6] to categorize Bangla newspaper text corpus obtained from a single newspaper (i.e., Pratham Alo) including just one-year data. Mandal and Sen [7] shows the comparison of four supervised learning techniques for classifying 1000 labeled news web documents into five categories with total number of tokens being 22,218. Accuracy achieved for four classifiers as follows; SVM, NB, DT (C4.5) and K-NN are 89.14%, 85.22%, 80.65% and 74.24% respectively. Kabir *et al.* [8] used Stochastic Gradient Descent (SGD) classifier for classifying Bangla text documents from 9 different categories by achieving accuracy of 93.85%. A comparative study of different types of methods of classifying Bangla text document is provided in the work of Islam *et al.* [9]. In another work of Islam *et al.* [10], TF-IDF has been applied as feature selection method and SVM as classifier and an accuracy of 92.57% have been achieved for classifying Bangla text documents covering twelve text categories. Dhar *et al.* [11] used Cosine Similarity and Euclidean Distance as the similarity measures based on TF-IDF weighting scheme on 1000 web text documents from five domains namely Business, State, Medical, Sports, and Science and achieved accuracy of 95.80% for Cosine Similarity and 95.20% for Euclidean Distance. In another work [12], they opt for a reduction technique by considering top 40% tokens from the set of tokens being extracted using TF-IDF method. They carried out the experiment on 1960 documents from five domains and achieved encouraging results using LIBLINEAR classifier.

3   Proposed Model

The following block diagram (Fig. 1) illustrates the overall process adopted in this experiment for developing an automatic Bangla text categorization or text classification system. Before extracting and selecting the feature values and accomplishing the classification process, it is necessary to perform pre-processing of texts which includes tokenization - the segmentation of sentences into tokens and stopwords removal - where the tokens with less weightage in terms of relevancy to domain-specific information are removed. At the stopwords removal stage, elimination of tokens treated as stopwords such as punctuations, postpositions, conjunctions, interjections, articles, some adverbs, some adjectives and English and Bangla numerals which are frequently used in a Bangla text documents has been done. Then, extraction and selection of proper feature sets are required to train the model for achieving an encouraging result for text document classification. Here, in this experiment, two internal characteristics frequently observed in Bangla medical text documents have been proposed as feature extraction methods to train the Stochastic Gradient Descent (SGD) classifier for allocating any random Bangla text document to its category (medical and non-medical) respectively. A detailed description of the model is provided below.

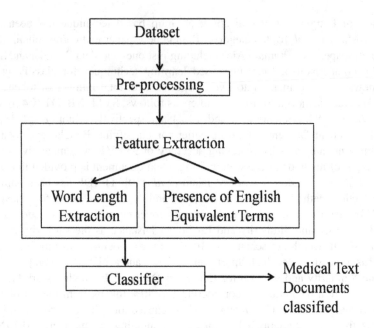

Fig. 1. Block diagram of the proposed method.

3.1 Data Collection

Collection of proper data is one of the most important stages in carrying out a research. Since there is no standard dataset available for Bangla with adequate amount of medical data, therefore the first thing we need to do is to build our own dataset consisting of Bangla text documents of medical and non-medical domains. Data collection needs thorough planning, hard work, patience and perseverance. Here, total 2000 text documents, 1000 documents each for medical and non-medical domains have been considered for the experiment. The dataset is collected from various on-line Bangla news text corpus produced by Bangla daily newspapers and also from on-line magazines and various web pages:

(a) AnandabazarPatrika:: http://www.anandabazar.com
(b) Bartaman::http://allbanglanewspapers.com/bartaman
(c) Ebelatabloid::http://www.ebela.in
(d) Bangla Recipe::https://deshirecipe.wordpress.com,
    http://www.ebanglarecipe.com, http://recipebangla.com
(e) Bangla Adda::http://www.banglaadda.com
(f) AmaderChuti::http://amaderchhuti.com
(g) Bangla Travel::https://www.ebanglatravel.com

In total there are 5,37,236 words before normalization and 5,29,784 words after removal of stopwords that includes punctuation marks, postpositions, conjunctions, interjections, some adjectives, some adverbs, articles, pronouns and English and Bangla numerals. Several domains such as Business, Food, State, Legal, National,

International, Travel, Nature, Science, Sports and Entertainment have been taken into consideration for non-medical text documents so that the contents of the dataset covers maximum variations. Text documents have been collected from news corpus to incorporate maximum realness among the data.

3.2 Feature Extraction

3.2.1 Word Length

Word length for each token of the text documents have been considered as the feature for the experiment. Extraction of word length is done based on the number of characters present in a token. The steps that have been used for word length measurement technique are as follows:

Step_01: Removal of stopwords like (tāke), (tomrā), (ebang) etc. from each sentence of a particular text domain.

Step_02: Task of tokenization carried out over the sentences to get individual tokens.

Step_03: Algorithm is invoked to measure word length at the character level.

Step_04: Maximum word length is counted from words of all text documents depending on the threshold been taken into consideration.

Here, the threshold is considered as 11. The total number of words, which has character strength equal to or greater than 11 is taken into consideration for all the documents. Value 11 is considered as threshold as it has been seen from Table 1 that the highest word length for medical domain is 19 or more, therefore, it is reasonable to consider 55% of the character length as a threshold mark so that the differences in the number of tokens of the considered length for medical as well as non-medical can be seen clearly and classification can be done accordingly.

3.2.1.1 Constraints

In this experiment, few constraints that have been taken care of are as follows whose oversight may cause change in the results:

[1] Diacratic markers such as , ্র(ra-phalā), ্য(ya-phalā), ং(anusvar), ঃ(bisarga), ঁ(candrabindu), ্(hasanta), etc. and vowel allographs like া(ā-kār),ি (ī-kār), ী (Ī-kār), ু(ū-kār), ূ(Ū-kār), are considered as single characters.

[2] Two-letter clusters for instance, the cluster ন্ত(nt) is a combination of three characters, namely, ন(n) +্(hasant) + ত(t). Similarly, the cluster ন্দ্র(ndr) is combined with five characters, namely, ন(n) +্(hasant) + দ(d) +্(hasant) + র(r).

[3] The use of hyphen between two words [e.g., বেরি-বেরি (beri-beri)] is also treated as a single character.

3.2.1.2 Observations

From the experiment of word length extraction, results of the five text domains have been considered for comparison. Among all the categories considered for non-medical text documents in this experiment, four domains have been selected based on their maximum word length. It is noted that, in average, the word length of medical text is comparatively larger than the words of other text domains. Some examples of this claim are furnished in Table 1.

Table 1. Maximum length of words of five different text domains

Domains	Bangla word	Roman	Character Length
Sports	অস্ট্রেলিয়ানদের	astreliyander	15
Business	নির্মাণকর্মীদের	nirmankarmider	15
Medical	স্বাস্হ্যকেন্দ্রগুলিতে	svasthyakendragulite	19
Politics	বিক্ষোভকারীদের	biksobhkarider	15
Legal	আত্মনিয়ন্ত্রণহীনতা	atmaniyantranhinata	18

Table 1 given above shows word with maximum length from five categories. It shows that while words with maximum length 15 belongs to sports, business and politics domains, words with maximum length 18 belong to legal text domain and words with highest length (19 characters) belongs to medical text domain. This observation, however, requires more intensive study on larger amount of texts.

3.2.2 Presence of English Equivalent Words

Another feature considered here for the experiment is the number of English equivalent terms present in the text documents of both medical and non-medical domain. Normally, we can observe that the presence of English equivalent terms is more in case of medical text documents followed by science and legal text documents. So, this internal feature can be proved to be one of the major features required to classify the Bangla text documents among medical and non-medical text documents. Here, in the experiment, the number of occurrences of the English equivalent terms in each file of these two domains has been calculated and used as the feature values along with the total number of tokens present in the text documents.

3.2.2.1 Observations

From the experiment of extracting the count of occurrences of English equivalent terms in a text document it can be noted that, the number of presence of English equivalent terms in medical text is comparatively larger compare to other text domains. The accuracy obtained for medical and non-medical domains is presented in the following Fig. 2.

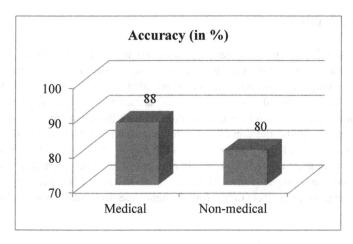

Fig. 2. Presence of English equivalent words in both domains

3.3   Classifier

For this experiment Stochastic Gradient Descent classification algorithm [8] is used as a model classifier. The motivation behind choosing this classifier is its promising performance as compared to others. Stochastic Gradient Descent (SGD) is a simple yet efficient method for discriminating learning of linear classifiers under convex loss functions. Even though it is being used in the machine learning field for a long time, but recently it has gained considerable amount of attention in the field of natural language processing. It can be applied successfully to large-scale and sparse machine learning dataset often experienced in text classification and natural language processing. Stochastic gradient descent is an optimization approach for unconstrained optimization problems. In compare to normal gradient descent, SGD approximates the true gradient of E(w, b) by taking into account a single training example at a time. The SGD classifier executes a first-order SGD learning routine and iterates over the training data and for each data the model gets updated according to the rule used by the following Eq. 1.

$$w \leftarrow w - \eta(\alpha \frac{\partial R(w)}{\partial w} + \frac{\partial L(w^T x_i + b, y_i)}{\partial w}) \qquad (1)$$

where η is the learning rate for controlling the step-size in the parameter space which can be constant or reduce gradually. The intercept b has similar update without regularization. For classification, the default learning rate is calculated by using the following Eq. 2 where t is the time step, t_0. is estimated based on a heuristic so that the initial updates are comparable with the anticipated size of the weights.

$$\eta^{(t)} = \frac{1}{\alpha(t_0 + t)} \qquad (2)$$

4 Result Analysis

We have used 5-fold cross validation scheme on the dataset of 2000 Bangla text documents for medical and non-medical domains. Weka tool have been used for classification purpose [19]. An average recognition accuracy of 97.75% for SGD classifier is achieved for this experiment. The accuracies obtained for word length, English equivalent words and the combination of both these features are presented in the following Fig. 3 and the domain-wise accuracy achieved by using SGD classifier on the hybrid internal feature is provided in the Fig. 4 below. From Fig. 3, it can be observed that compare to the feature extraction approaches being separately applied on the text documents, the combined feature extraction approaches performs better in achieving encouraging accuracy for Bangla medical and non-medical text classification.

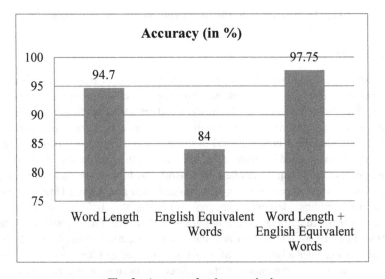

Fig. 3. Accuracy for three methods

Several other commonly used machine learning classifiers such as Naive Bayes Multinomial (NBM), MultiLayer Perceptron (MLP), Naive Bayes (NB), Random Tree (RT), Decision Tree (J48), BayesNet (BN), and Simple Logistic (SL) have been used to test the performance of SGD classifier based on the combination of both the features extraction method on the dataset. The accuracies in terms of precision, recall and F1 measure achieved for all the classifiers being applied are provided in the following Table 2 below. From this comparison among classifiers it can be observed that SGD outperforms other classification algorithms on these dataset for classifying Bangla text documents.

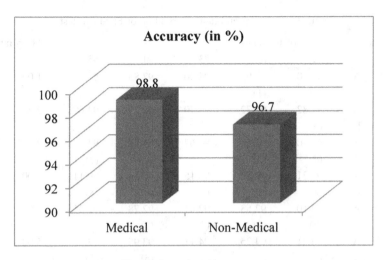

Fig. 4. Domain-wise accuracy

Table 2. Precision, recall and F1 measure for various classifiers

Classifier	Precision	Recall	F1 measure
SGD	0.978	0.978	0.978
NBM	0.942	0.941	0.941
MLP	0.946	0.946	0.946
NB	0.900	0.891	0.890
RT	0.922	0.922	0.922
J48	0.939	0.939	0.939
BN	0.928	0.928	0.928
SL	0.945	0.945	0.945

4.1 Statistical Significance Test

Statistical significance test has been done using the Friedman test [1] to compare various classifiers for machine learning problems like Naive Bayes Multinomial (NBM), MultiLayer Perceptron (MLP), Naive Bayes (NB), Random Tree (RT), Decision Tree (J48), BayesNet (BN), and Simple Logistic (SL). The test was performed on the dataset by dividing it into 5 parts. The numbers of datasets (N) and classifiers (k) have been fixed to 5 and 8 respectively. The accuracy (A) and rank (R) distribution for the above mentioned setup is shown in Table 3. The Friedman statistic (χ_F^2). was calculated using Eq. 3. The critical value for (χ_F^2) and degree of freedom (df) at a significance levels of 0.05 were 33.800 and 7 respectively.

$$\chi_F^2 = \frac{12N}{k(k+1)} \left[\sum_j R_j^2 - \frac{k(k+1)^2}{4} \right] \tag{3}$$

Table 3. Accuracy and rank distribution of Friedman test

Classifiers		Parts of the dataset					Mean rank
		#1	#2	#3	#4	#5	
SGD	A	98.20	97.99	98.00	97.85	97.92	1.00
	R	(1)	(1)	(1)	(1)	(1)	
NBM	A	94.82	94.72	94.70	94.79	94.60	2.60
	R	(3)	(2)	(2)	(3)	(3)	
MLP	A	94.30	94.51	94.67	94.88	94.64	2.80
	R	(4)	(3)	(3)	(2)	(2)	
NB	A	90.21	89.89	90.15	90.34	90.11	8.00
	R	(8)	(8)	(8)	(8)	(8)	
RT	A	92.10	92.53	92.41	92.78	92.32	7.00
	R	(7)	(7)	(7)	(7)	(7)	
J48	A	94.21	94.25	94.11	93.95	93.97	5.00
	R	(5)	(5)	(5)	(5)	(5)	
BN	A	93.13	93.42	92.98	92.84	92.78	6.00
	R	(6)	(6)	(6)	(6)	(6)	
SL	A	94.85	94.34	94.51	94.66	94.52	3.60
	R	(2)	(4)	(4)	(4)	(4)	

5 Conclusion

The most tentative inference of this experiment is that 'character level word length', and 'presence of English equivalent words in texts' may be considered as two important parameters in automated classification of Bangla prose text documents. In future, this observation may be further substantiated with more text data obtained from other subject areas to inspect whether this study can be generalized across all text domains in Bangla. Further, some other standard feature extraction and selection methods can also be applied to build an automatic system that can classify or categorize Bangla text documents of different domains. Also, hybrid approaches which can be the combination of different feature selection approaches may be adopted in the future work. Since there are limited numbers of works done for Bangla web texts, the development of a robust tool of this kind can help the language to move little far towards the state of digitalization. The availability of such automatic text classification system that the present work desires to develop will certainly solve many challenging problems of the language as well as the urgent needs of the Bangla text users eagerly waiting for a reliable system for retrieving useful information from the language can also be addressed.

Acknowledgement. One of the authors would like to thank Department of Science and Technology (DST) for support in the form of INSPIRE fellowship.

References

1. DeySarkar, S., Goswami, S., Agarwal, A., Akhtar, J.: A novel feature selection technique for text classification using Naive Bayes. Int. Sch. Res. Not. **2014**, 10 (2014)
2. Guru, D.S., Suhil, M.: A novel term_class relevance measure for text categorization. In: Proceedings of International Conference on Advanced Computing Technologies and Applications, pp. 13–22 (2015)
3. Jin, P., Zhang, Y., Chen, X., Xia, Y.: Bag-of-embeddings for text classification. In: Proceedings of International Joint Conference on Artificial Intelligence, pp. 2824–2830 (2016)
4. Wang, D., Zhang, H., Liu, R., Lv, W.: Feature selection based on term frequency and T-test for text categorization. In: Proceedings of ACM International Conference on Information and Knowledge Management, pp. 1482–1486 (2012)
5. Gupta, N., Gupta, V.: Punjabi text classification using naive bayes, centroid and hybrid approach. In: Proceedings of Workshop on South and South East Asian Natural Language Processing, pp. 109–122 (2012)
6. Mansur, M., UzZaman, N., Khan, M.: analysis of n-gram based text categorization for bangla in a newspaper corpus. In: Proceedings of International Conference on Computer and Information Technology, pp. 08 (2006)
7. Mandal, A.K., Sen, R.: Supervised learning methods for Bangla web document categorization. Int. J. Artif. Intell. Appl. **05**, 93–105 (2014)
8. Kabir, F., Siddique, S., Kotwal, M.R.A., Huda, M.N.: Bangla text document categorization using stochastic gradient descent (SGD) classifier. In: Proceedings of International Conference on Cognitive Computing and Information Processing, pp. 1–4 (2015)
9. Islam, Md.S., Jubayer, F.E.Md., Ahmed, S.I.: A comparative study on different types of approaches to bengali document categorization. In: Proceedings of International Conference on Engineering Research, Innovation and Education, p. 06 (2017)
10. Islam, Md.S., Jubayer, F.E.Md., Ahmed, S.I.: A support vector machine mixed with TF-IDF algorithm to categorize bengali document. In: Proceedings of International Conference on Electrical, Computer and Communication Engineering, pp. 191–196 (2017)
11. Dhar, A., Dash, N.S., Roy, K.: Classification of text documents through distance measurement: an experiment with multi-domain Bangla text documents. In: Proceedings of International Conference on Advances in Computing, Communication and Automation, pp. 1–6 (2017)
12. Dhar, A., Dash, N.S., Roy, K.: Application of TF-IDF feature for categorizing documents of online Bangla web text corpus. In: Proceedings of International Conference on Frontiers of Intelligent Computing: Theory and Applications, pp. 51–59 (2017)
13. ArunaDevi, K., Saveetha, R.: A novel approach on tamil text classification using C-Feature. Int. J. Sci. Res. Dev. **02**, 343–345 (2014)
14. Swamy, M.N., Thappa, M.H.: Indian Language text representation and categorization using supervised learning algorithm. Int. J. Data Min. Tech. Appl. **02**, 251–257 (2013)
15. Patil, J.J., Bogiri, N.: Automatic text categorization Marathi documents. Int. J. Adv. Res. Comput. Sci. Manag. Stud. **03**, 280–287 (2015)
16. Bolaj, P., Govilkar, S.: Text classification for Marathi documents using supervised learning methods. Int. J. Comput. Appl. **155**, 6–10 (2016)
17. Al-Radaideh, Q.A., Al-Khateeb, S.S.: An associative rule-based classifier for Arabic medical text. Int. J. Knowl. Eng. Data Min. **03**, 255–273 (2015)

18. Haralambous, Y., Elidrissi, Y., Lenca, P.: Arabic language text classification using dependency syntax-based feature selection. In: Proceedings of International Conference on Arabic language Processing, p. 10 (2014)
19. Hall, M., Frank, E., Holmes, G., Pfahringer, B., Reutemann, P., Witten, I.H.: The WEKA data mining software: an update. SIGKDD Explor. **11**, 10–18 (2009)

A Critical Survey of Mathematical Search Engines

Sourish Dhar[1]([✉]), Sudipta Roy[1], and Sujit Kumar Das[2]

[1] Department of Computer Science and Engineering, Assam University,
Silchar, Assam, India
dsourish80@gmail.com, sudipta.it@gmail.com
[2] Department of Computer Science and Engineering,
National Institute of Technology, Silchar, Assam, India
dassujit88@gmail.com

Abstract. Traditional text retrieval systems cannot effectively search for mathematical expressions because it may contain formulae ranging from simple symbols to complex structures. In the area of math retrieval system, index data structure and document representation play a vital role in ranking and relevancy of results. The paper investigates the current math aware search engines to provide a critical overview of their relative strengths and limitations and to explore the current challenges related to the field.

Keywords: Math information retrieval · Unification ·
Canonicalization · Indexing schemes

1 Introduction

The conventional text retrieval system and math retrieval system can be distinguished based on the fact that text retrieval system has the ability to find documents based on terms and keywords [1]. On the other hand, math retrieval system emphasizes mathematical expressions and formulae ranging from simple symbols to complex structures. As a result, text retrieval systems cannot effectively search for mathematical expressions because they are not suitable for text with complex structures [2]. Mathematical formulae are extensive means for dissemination and imparting of scientific information [3]. Apart from numerical calculations, it can be used for clarifying definitions or disambiguate explanations that are written in natural language. In order to make the process effective, mathematical expressions and their structure should be also encoded along with their symbolic content. The remainder of the paper is organized as follows: in Sect. 2 we have discussed various operations required for designing mathematical search engine (MSE). Section 3 addresses related works already accomplished in this domain. The comparison table of existing mathematical search engines is presented in Sect. 4. Finally results and discussions and subsequently concluding remarks on possible research directions are covered in Sects. 5 and 6 respectively.

© Springer Nature Singapore Pte Ltd. 2019
J. K. Mandal et al. (Eds.): CICBA 2018, CCIS 1031, pp. 193–207, 2019.
https://doi.org/10.1007/978-981-13-8581-0_16

2   Operations Required for Designing MSE System

Designing any retrieval system requires certain operations. Mathematical Information Retrieval (MIR) system is also not an exception. These steps may vary with respect to different MIR systems. In this section, we briefly outline these operations, which are as follows:

2.1   Preprocessing

This step in MSE includes basic tasks like defining format of the document i.e. how the document will be represented and tokenization which decides the important terms and keywords, and play a very vital role in any information retrieval system and natural language tasks. It also eliminates insignificant elements. Mathematical expressions are pre-analyzed in several steps to facilitate searches not only for exact formulae, but also its sub-formula or sub-expression . Identifying encoding scheme for mathematical expressions like MathML [4], TEX/LATEX [5], OpenMath [6] and OMDoc [7] is another concern of this operation.

2.2   Canonicalization

Mathematical expressions although represent differently but their semantic meanings may be similar. Canonicalization is a process to reduce this mismatch among the expressions which are semantically similar in nature [8]. For example, enumeration of variables in operator trees allows variables to be matched without concern for their specific symbol identities [9]. More illustratively, for query

$$\int_0^1 sin(x)$$

canonicalization gives the facility to retrieve relevant documents where the integral's domain is specified using an interval and encoded as

$$\int_{(0,1)} sin(x).$$

Canonicalization also helps to reduce index size, which results in less space requirement and faster retrieval.

2.3   Indexing in MSE

Indexing is a technique where terms are stored using appropriate data structures (generally stored in memory) for faster retrieval. A retrieved result of any information retrieval system greatly depends on its indexing scheme.

In case of the mathematical retrieval system, various indexing schemes have been incorporated to give efficient retrieval results. The methods used in this step are variable ordering, term unification, and normalization of constants. The same methods may also be used for query processing and query refinement as well to get efficient results. One of the frequently used indexing techniques in numerous math search engines is a tree or substitution tree indexing [10].

2.4   Query Language and Interface

It deals with the ability provided to the user to generate the queries for their retrieval task. It also addresses that how queries may be formulated and how queries may be refined for the retrieval system. The most important goal for any query language is to be simple and user-friendly as possible but with no limits to its expressiveness.

In designing a query language for mathematical formulae, the designer must be aware of the fact that it must satisfy different conflicting constraints and clarity must be maintained. The query language should be content-oriented and recognizable, but it should not be specialized for a given content representation format [9].

3   Related Work

A number of contributions have already been made in designing mathematical search engines using different techniques by the researchers in the last decade. However, nine search engines are considered here based on their efficiency, current status, and acceptability at the user level. These are MathDex [11], Ego-Math [12,13] LaTeXSearch [14], MathWebsearch [3], LeActiveMath [15], MIaS [16], SearchOnMath [17] , Eu-DML [18,19] and WikiMirs [20,21].

3.1   MathDex

MathDex (formerly MathFind) is the oldest mathematical aware full text search engine based on Apache Lucene search engine. It went public at the beginning of 2007. The key features are :

- support for semantically poor documents
- accepting different types of mathematical encoding for semantically poor documents
- allows searching on both mathematical notation and text
- attempts to match user text search expectations rather than strictly following the query

It was designed by National Science Foundation through the National Science Digital Library program headed by Robert Miner of Design Science . It is composed of a MathFind processing layer implemented on top of a typical text-based search engine layer. This layer was responsible for analyzing MathML which is an XML representation for mathematical notations. It encodes mathematics as text tokens and uses Apache Lucene framework [22] as if searching for text. Using similarity with search terms ranked results are produced by the search algorithm while matching n-grams of presentation MathML [23]. Again using n-gram ranking technique, it could not take several kinds of elementary mathematical equivalence in its account and put undue weights on variables names.

3.2   EgoMath

A full-text search engine designed by Jozef Misutka as an extended version of Egothor by Leo Galambos, MFF UK Prague. Later on upgraded version, Egomath2 was released to make enable mathematics to access from worlds most common digital library- Wikipedia. As mathematical notations are in TEX fragments so it does not contain any semantic information. The designers have considered retrieval of equal formula as a key issue for similarity search of mathematical expressions. To deal with this the designers considered the same mathematical formulae with different textual annotation into one unit. Like

$$x^2$$

will be represented in simple text consisting of three terms
$x, \char`^, 2$. The augmentation algorithm [12] which was responsible for representation of mathematical formula stored in postfix notation to eliminate parenthesis and ordering algorithm which was responsible for canonicalization process.The previous version was modified so that Egomath2 is able to work towards full-text search in cooperation with Wikipedia. The designers have made the augmentation process more extensible and configurable by using XML configuration files.

3.3   LaTeXSearch

It is a free service provided by Springer for researchers to get LaTeX code within scientific publications. LaTeXsearch actually helps the researchers to locate and view over 1 million LaTeX equations . It also enables to view equations containing LaTeX code that is similar to another LaTeXstring belonging to a specific digital object identifier (DOI) and article for a specific user query. LaTeXSearch's unique "similarity" algorithm normalizes and compares LaTeX strings so that if similar equations are written slightly differently, the outputs are normalized and matched, granting user with the broadest possible results set, that makes researcher to discover equations those are very similar to their own. Currently it works on the content available from Springer's corpus of literature [14, 23, 24].

3.4   MathWebSearch

MathWebSearch (MWS) system is a content-based search which could index MathML formulae by automated theorem proving term indexing technique. MathWebSearch [25] is optimized for fast query responses anSd interactive applications. Any corpus whose formulae can reference by URIs and converted to Content MathML can be indexed by MWS . MWS was developed by the KWARC

Fig. 1. ZBLSearch query interface (http://search.mathweb.org/zbl/)

group at Jacobs University. It uses a substitution tree [10] for indexing which makes it different than other search engines. Recently it has been combined with other web based front-ends like

- TeMaSearch - combined text and Math search for Zentralblatt Math
- ZBLSearch - a content-oriented search engine for the formulae in the 3.3 million reviews and abstracts in the Zentralblatt Math data base. Queries in LaTeX extended with search variables as illustrated in the Fig. 1.
- XLSearch - a search engine for spreadsheet formulae. Queries in Excel + variables
- FlatSearch - a search engine for formal
- SentidoSearch - a multi-format input front-end for search queries based on the Sentido system. It includes a generic panel-based content formula editor.

3.5   LeActiveMath

Language-Enhanced, User Adaptive, Interactive eLearning for Mathematics has been designed and developed as part of Active-Math EU project started in the year of 2004, which aims to build and offer the mathematical community a platform for peer-reviewed open access journals using open source software [26]. LeActiveMath used Lucene framework for indexing string tokens from OMDoc(Open Mathematical Documents) with an OpenMath semantic notation [15, 27, 28]. OMDoc is a semantic markup format for mathematical documents. It allows writing down the meaning of texts about mathematics. OMDoc can be used for e-learning application, data exchange and document preparation where documents about mathematics can be prepared in OMDoc and later exported to a presentation-oriented like LaTeX or MathML format.

3.6   MIaS

It is developed by Petr Sojka and Martin Liska. It can process the document which is on MathML notation. Mathematical Indexer and Searcher (MIaS) enable the user to search mathematical formulae along with textual content of documents [23] as shown in Fig. 2. Another advantage is that searching single words and phrases (sub-formulae casted down to single variables, symbols, constants, etc.). It actually considers the textual and mathematical part of a document separately and uses various pre-processing tasks before indexing them using Apache Lucene.

Fig. 2. WebMIaS query interface (https://mir.fi.muni.cz/webmias-demo/)

Textual parts of the document indexed in conventional way. Secondly for mathematical part, formulae are pre-analyzed in various steps for exact match as well as sub-formula matching along with formula modification [16,23]. These involve creating several representation of each input formula which all are indexed. Each index term is given a weight based on the modification done (more the modification less the weight given).

When all formulae converted from their XML node to a string format is handled by indexer. Initial and final XML tags are replaced by the tag name and followed by arguments within these tags. The under mentioned process helps to make an unambiguous representation of each XML node. It is illustrated the process more practically and the MathML code for mathematical expression $x^2 - y^2$ will be:

```
<math>
<mrow>
<msup>
<mi>x</mi>
```

```
<mn>2</mn>
</msup>
<mo> − </mo>
<msup>
<mi>y</mi>
<mn>2</mn>
</msup>
</mrow>
</math>
```

This MathML code for the expression x^2-y^2 will be converted to following string:

$$math(mrow(msup(mi(x)mn(2)))mo(-)msup(mi(y)mn(2))))$$

Subsequently this string is indexed by Lucene while using the following procedures [16] as shown in Fig. 3:

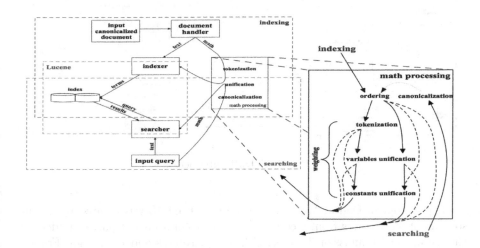

Fig. 3. MIaS workflow for math processing

Ordering. To match the mathematical expression X+10 with query term 10+X, a simple ordering of operands have been used for commutative addition and multiplication operations. This helps to order arguments of an operation in an alphabetical manner. The XML node denoting variable X is named mi and the node denoting number 3 is named mn. By giving priority to mn(mi < mn) makes the mathematical expression and the query term similar.

Tokenization and Unification. It is done to get sub-formula or sub-expression and to remove insignificant data. During variable unification, all variables in the expressions are replaced by unified symbols (ids) in both indexing and searching phase so those expressions with same semantic meaning but with different variables would match. For example after variable unification expression like $x + y^a$ and $a + b^x$ will be $id_1 + id_2^{id3}$. Moreover, like variable unification constants are also replaced by a unified symbol.

3.7 EuDML

Fig. 4. EuDML interface

The European Digital Mathematics Library EuDML was created by a consortium of 15 partners from 9 countries in frames of a project partly funded by the European Commission in the EC Competitiveness and Innovation Framework Programme, Information and Communication Technology Policy Support Programme, in the period from 1 February 2010 to 31 January 2013.

The EuDML provides a free access to a large volume of scholarly mathematical literature including the content of the Czech Digital Mathematics Library DML-CZ. Scientific journals and articles are included in Eu-DML as shown in Fig. 4. Currently 260413 documents across 14 collections are searchable. Of those, 223,723 full-texts are indexed and 13,269 were made accessible to print disabled users [14, 18, 29].

3.8 SearchOnMath

The first version of SearchOnMath was released in 2013. Later on, it had become a start-up by the end of 2015 and consequently a part of Microsoft BizSpark

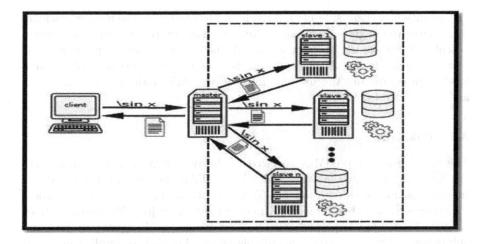

Fig. 5. SearchOnMath architecture

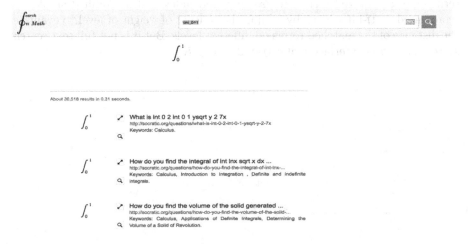

Fig. 6. SearchOnMath interface

program. It considered four math contained datasets namely English version of Wikipedia, Wolfram Math Word, DLMF and planet Math for indexing and retrieval task till 2016. During 2016, as SearchOnMath began preparations for expansion by adding Socratic (1063754 formulas) with previous four and a final database was constructed as the union of all five . The resulting database contains 1905358 indexed formulas.

A distributed system was developed and tested on Microsoft Azure with the goal of assessing of 38 possible configurations. This investigation was based on a set of 120 pre-selected formulas that were to be worked on by SearchOnMath within a domain of almost 2 million formulas and aimed at discovering which of the candidate configurations was capable of delivering the best response time.

For operation, a client submits a formula to be searched to the master machine, which runs the engines front-end. After reception by the master, the formula is sent to the slave machines, which do all the necessary processing to find out which formulas in the database are similar to the query formula [17]. A high level architecture and the user interface of SearchOnMath is shown in Figs. 5 and 6 respectively.

3.9   WikiMirs

The first version of WikiMirs surfaced in the year of 2013 and WikiMirs 3.0, the latest version, in the year 2015. While WikiMirs 2.0 only takes formula information into consideration but WikiMirs 3.0 also added a context index. The basic system is based on LATEX markups extracted from Wikipedia dataset [20,21]. Then input is preprocessed and represented as Presentation Tree and subsequently parsed two different templates based explicit or implicit operands notion of LATEX/ markup. It uses term normalization process to generate original terms and generalized terms. It uses inverted index and a modified similarity score based on tf-idf scheme by adding the concept of weight of level to evaluate the distance of the matched terms on different levels. But it is not full text search system .The user interface is illustrated in Fig. 7.

Fig. 7. WikiMirs interface (http://59.108.48.32:8080)

4   Comparison

The mathematical search engines discussed in Sect. 3 are compared in Table 1 considering following parameters:

Table 1. Comparison of different math search engines

System	Input Document	Internal Representation	Approach	α Equivalence	Query Language	Queries	Indexing Core	Index Data Size
MathDex	Html TeX/LaTeX Word,Pdf	Presentation MathML	Syntactic	x	?	Text, Math Mixed	Apache Lucene	25000 Documents From The Arxiv, 12000 Pages Containing Mathematics From Wikipedia,1300 Pages From Connexions Portal, 1000pages Of Wolfram Mathworld.
Egomath	Presentation MathML Content MathML Pdf	Presentation MathML Trees	Mixed	✓	LaTeX	Text, Math, Mixed	Egothor	30 Gb of Wikipedia article. https://en.wikipedia.org/wiki/Wikipedia:Database_download
LatexSearch	LaTeX	LaTeX	Syntactic	x	LaTeX	Title, Math Digital Object Identifier(doi)	?	Enable Search Through Over 8,223,138 LaTeXCode Snippets.
MathWebSearch	Presentation MathML Content MathML OpenMath	Substitution Tree	Syntactic	✓	Qmath, LaTeX Mathematica, Maxima, Maple, Yac As Styles	Text, Math Mixed	Apache Lucene (For Text Only)	100 000 Articles From arriv.Org (New Version) NTCIR-Math Pilot Task
LeActive Search	OmDoc OpenMath	OpenMath (As String)	Syntactic	x	?	Text, Math Mixed	Apache Lucene	?
MIaS	Any MathML	Canonical Presentation (MathML)	Tree Similarity and Normalization	✓	LaTeX or MathML	Text, Math Mixed	Apache Lucene	MREC (Mathematical REtrieval Corpus) with 439,423 scientific documents was used . https://mir.fi.muni.cz/MREC/
SearchOnMath	Html TeX or LaTeX, Word,Pdf	LaTeX(as per Query Interface)	?	✓	LaTeX	Text, Math Mixed	?	1963858 Mathematical Formulas From Wikipedia, Wolfram MathWorld, DLMF, PlanetMath And Socratic Databases
Eu-DML	Html TeX or LaTeX, Word,Pdf	Canonical Presentation (MathML)	Hybrid	✓	LaTeX and Plain Text	Text, Math Mixed	Uses WebMIaS as back-end engine	269413 documents across 14 collections are searchable. Of those, 223,723 full-texts are indexed and 13,269 were made accessible to print disabled users.
WikiMirs	LaTeX	Presentation Tree	Syntactic	✓	LaTeX and Plain Text	Text, Math Mixed	Uses inverted index and a modified similarity score based on tf-idf scheme	WikiMirs used Wikipedia dataset. The version being used is the 2012-10-01 dump with a size of approximately 30 GB uncompressed. This dataset contains approximately 13 millions web pages and 495,958 mathematical formulae.

- **Input documents:** The collection of documents containing plain text and mathematical expressions which will be indexed.
- **Internal Representation:** It is the encoding scheme to represent a mathematical expression.
- **Approach:** It tells us whether, structural representation (syntactic) along with semantic meaning of mathematical expressions have been consider or not.
- **α-equivalence:** It tells that two mathematical expressions having different variable names are equivalent as long as expressions used in same manner.
- **Query Language:**   The language to write queries to retrieve documents from the collection.
- **Query :** The type of information we can get from the mathematical information retrieval system.
- **Indexing Scheme:**   Describes the indexing scheme that has been used to generate term indices.
- **Indexed data size:** The details of the data set containing mathematical expressions that has been used for indexing.

5   Results and Discussion

The designers introduced a new graphical user interface for EgoMath2, but we have not been able to access the resource (http://egomath.projekty.ms.mmf.cuni.cz). Likewise, the official site (http://www.leactivemath.org/) of the FP6-project "LeActive" is currently under construction. Many important parameters for all MIR systems again are not clearly explained by all; for example indexed data size for LeActiveSearch and indexing technique used in SearchOnMath . In fact Springer's LaTeXSearch interface was also not available although it was illustrated and reported in [14].

Study on existing Mathematical Information Retrieval (MIR) systems makes us understand that MIR systems can further be optimized or designed to handle all the challenges faced in retrieving documents containing mathematical expressions. There are several factors which govern these decisions which are summarized below:

- Mathematical encoding schemes like LaTeX, MathML and OMDoc etc. are quite different from each other and vast in nature. Many Mathematical Information Retrieval systems cannot effectively handle all the facets of these encoding schemes yet.
- Equivalence of mathematical expression is another challenging area, where all these MIR systems are susceptible to erroneousness. As same formula/expression can be written in several ways although they are semantically similar.
- Indexing schemes plays major role in any information retrieval system which again is a good area for exploring possibilities of further research.
- Lastly, query interface and language still needs a lot attention in terms of simplicity and expressivity for an amateur user as most of the search engines are having an user interface where a query can be issued using LaTeX strings.

We have not discussed different ranking schemes thereby, their precision and recall value of the whole system in this study. Also we have not included the search engines like Tangent [30] discussed in NII Testbeds and Community for Information access Research Project (NTCIR-11: Math-2 Wikipedia subtask) in this study Exploring meta-data of mathematical expressions can also play a good direction for further research efforts. For e.g., MIaS although tried to cover all challenges faced by previous systems, but weighting scheme for mathematical expressions used in MIaS sometimes give more recall value (irrelevant results) when the expression to be indexed become large, containing more symbols.

6 Conclusion

A lot of work was devoted towards developing MIR systems in the last decade but only a handful of systems are available. This area of research is still evolving and is gradually gaining attention from the researchers and organizations like NTCIR etc. Various mathematical search engines are discussed here in this study along with their design and working principle. Semantically same formulae can be represented in various formats in various mathematical notations and pooling them into one unified platform is a huge task.

Again most of the search engines are designed for specific mathematical annotation and their internal representation of documents based on their specific task. Also, not all of the search engines discussed in this survey have the ability to provide partial results.

For indexing, most of the search engines take mathematical expressions as a string token and uses Lucene or related framework based on the requirements except for EgoMath2 which uses its own indexing tools.

MIR systems still need enormous improvements to be a mature information retrieval system; which can handle all the challenges of annotations and ambiguities associated with mathematical or scientific data.

References

1. Sojka, P.: Exploiting semantic annotations in math information retrieval. In: Proceedings of the Fifth Workshop on Exploiting Semantic Annotations in Information Retrieval. ESAIR 2012, pp. 15–16. ACM, New York (2012)
2. Pathak, A., Pakray, P., Sarkar, S., Das, D., Gelbukh, A.: MathIRs: retrieval system for scientific documents. Computación y Sistemas **21**(2), 253–265 (2017). http://www.redalyc.org/articulo.oa?id=61551628007
3. Kohlhase, M., Sucan, I.: A search engine for mathematical formulae. In: Calmet, J., Ida, T., Wang, D. (eds.) AISC 2006. LNCS (LNAI), vol. 4120, pp. 241–253. Springer, Heidelberg (2006). https://doi.org/10.1007/11856290_21
4. W3C: Mathematical Markup Language. https://www.w3.org/TR/WD-math-980106/. Accessed 12 Feb 2018
5. Latex A Document Preparation System. https://www.latex-project.org. Accessed 12 Feb 2018
6. Openmath. http://www.openmath.org/. Accessed 12 Feb 2018

7. Omdoc. http://www.omdoc.org/. Accessed 12 Feb 2018
8. Archambault, D., Moço, V.: Canonical MathML to Simplify Conversion of MathML to Braille Mathematical Notations. In: Miesenberger, K., Klaus, J., Zagler, W.L., Karshmer, A.I. (eds.) ICCHP 2006. LNCS, vol. 4061, pp. 1191–1198. Springer, Heidelberg (2006). https://doi.org/10.1007/11788713_172
9. Zanibbi, R., Blostein, D.: Recognition and retrieval of mathematical expressions. Int. J. Doc. Anal. Recogn. 15(4), 331–357 (2012). https://doi.org/10.1007/s10032-011-0174-4
10. Graf, P.: Substitution tree indexing. In: Hsiang, J. (ed.) Rewriting Techniques and Applications, pp. 117–131. Springer, Heidelberg (1995). https://doi.org/10.1007/3-540-59200-8_52
11. Miner, R., Munavalli, R.: An approach to mathematical search through query formulation and data normalization. In: Kauers, M., Kerber, M., Miner, R., Windsteiger, W. (eds.) Calculemus/MKM -2007. LNCS (LNAI), vol. 4573, pp. 342–355. Springer, Heidelberg (2007). https://doi.org/10.1007/978-3-540-73086-6_27
12. Mišutka, J., Galamboš, L.: Extending full text search engine for mathematical content. In: Proceedings of the DML 2008, Towards Digital Mathematics Library, Birmingham, UK, 27th July 2008, pp. 55–67. Masaryk University, Brno (2008). Zbl 1170.68488)
13. Mišutka, J., Galamboš, L.: System description: EgoMath2 as a tool for mathematical searching on wikipedia.org. In: Davenport, J.H., Farmer, W.M., Urban, J., Rabe, F. (eds.) CICM 2011. LNCS (LNAI), vol. 6824, pp. 307–309. Springer, Heidelberg (2011). https://doi.org/10.1007/978-3-642-22673-1_30
14. Pineau, D.C.: Math-Aware Search Engines: Physics Applications and Overview, CoRR, vol. abs/1609.03457 (2016). (http://arxiv.org/abs/1609.03457)
15. Libbrecht, P., Melis, E.: Methods to access and retrieve mathematical content in ACTIVEMATH. In: Iglesias, A., Takayama, N. (eds.) ICMS 2006. LNCS, vol. 4151, pp. 331–342. Springer, Heidelberg (2006). https://doi.org/10.1007/11832225_33
16. Sojka, P., Líška, M.: The art of mathematics retrieval. In: Proceedings of the ACM Conference on Document Engineering, DocEng 2011, pp. 57–60. Association of Computing Machinery, Mountain View, CA September 2011. https://doi.org/10.1145/2034691.2034703
17. Oliveira, R.M., Gonzaga, F.B., Barbosa, V.C. Xexéo, G.B.: A distributed system for SearchOnMath based on the Microsoft BizSpark program, CoRR, vol. abs/1711.04189 (2017). http://arxiv.org/abs/1711.04189
18. Borbinha, J., Bouche, T., Nowiński, A., Sojka, P.: Project EuDML – a first year demonstration. In: Davenport, J.H., Farmer, W.M., Urban, J., Rabe, F. (eds.) CICM 2011. LNCS (LNAI), vol. 6824, pp. 281–284. Springer, Heidelberg (2011). https://doi.org/10.1007/978-3-642-22673-1_21
19. Eu-DML. https://eudml.org/. Accessed 12 Feb 2018
20. Hu, X., Gao, L., Lin, X., Tang, Z., Lin, X., Baker, J.B.: WikiMirs: a mathematical information retrieval system for wikipedia. In: 2013 Proceedings of the 13th ACM/IEEE-CS Joint Conference on Digital libraries (JCDL) (2013)
21. Wang, Y., Gao, L., Wang, S., Tang, Z., Liu, X., Yuan, F.: WikiMirs 3.0: a hybrid MIR system based on the context, structure and importance of formulae in a document. In: JCDL (2015)
22. Apache Lucene Core. https://lucene.apache.org/core/. Accessed 17 Feb 2018
23. Sojka, P., Líška, M.: Indexing and searching mathematics in digital libraries. In: Davenport, J.H., Farmer, W.M., Urban, J., Rabe, F. (eds.) CICM 2011. LNCS (LNAI), vol. 6824, pp. 228–243. Springer, Heidelberg (2011). https://doi.org/10.1007/978-3-642-22673-1_16

24. Springer Innovations: LaTexSearch.com. https://www.springer.com/in/partners/
    society-zone-issues/springer-innovations-latexsearch-com/4516. Accessed 17 Feb
    2018
25. Kohlhase, M., Matican, B.A., Prodescu, C.-C.: MathWebSearch 0.5: scaling an
    open formula search engine. In: Jeuring, J., et al. (eds.) CICM 2012. LNCS (LNAI),
    vol. 7362, pp. 342–357. Springer, Heidelberg (2012). https://doi.org/10.1007/978-
    3-642-31374-5_23
26. Anca, S.: Natural Language and Mathematics Processing for Applicable Theorem
    Search. Master's Thesis, Jacobs University (2009)
27. Grigore, M., Wolska, M., Kohlhase, M.: Towards context-based disambiguation of
    mathematical expressions. In: The Joint Conference of ASCM, pp. 262–271 (2009)
28. Libbrecht, P., Melis, E.: Semantic search in LeActiveMath. In: First WebALT Con-
    ference and Exhibition, pp. 97–110, Technical University of Eindhoven, Nether-
    lands (2006)
29. Sylwestrzak, W., Borbinha, J., Bouche, T., Nowiski, A.W., Sojka, P.: EuDML
    towards the european digital mathematics library architecture and design, pp. 11–
    26, Masaryk University Press (2010)
30. Stalnaker, D., Zanibbi, R.: Math expression retrieval using an inverted index over
    symbol pairs. In: Document Recognition and Retrieval XXII, San Francisco, Cali-
    fornia, USA, 11–12 February 2015

Removing Irrelevant Features
Using Feature Information Map
for Unsupervised Learning

Sagarika Saroj Kundu$^{(\boxtimes)}$, Pritika Sarkar, and Amit Kumar Das

Institute of Engineering and Management, Salt Lake, Kolkata, India
tiakundu3@gmail.com, pritikasarkar987@gmail.com, amitkumar.das@iemcal.com

Abstract. In this paper, an information contribution based graph-theoretic approach is used to remove the irrelevant features from the feature set for unsupervised learning. The graph-based mapping of information contribution and the process of selecting a subset of the features has been named Feature Information Map based Feature Selection for Unsupervised Learning (FIMFSUL). This approach is based on three main parameters - entropy of the features, inter-feature correlation and subset derivation using minimal vertex cover algorithm. Features are subsequently passed through three stages, wherein we decide the relevancy of each of the features. The efficacy of this approach has been proved by conducting experiments with publicly available data sets.

Keywords: Feature information · Feature redundancy ·
Graph-based visualization · Feature selection

1 Introduction

Unsupervised learning deals with data sets having no labels or classification [1]. The outcome of unsupervised learning is not a prediction. Instead it produces clusters or groups the data instances based on similarity or dissimilarity, on the basis of the pattern it observes in the data.

Feature selection is widely used for supervised learning as it increases the accuracy of the prediction. For supervised learning we are given labels. So selecting an optimal set of features which contribute towards the prediction will increase efficacy of the algorithm. However, in case of unsupervised learning the data set is unlabelled and determining which features are relevant is difficult. The motivation which still drives us to select an optimal set of features for unsupervised learning is that not all the features are relevant and some features deviate the clustering results [2,3]. Reducing the dimensionality also decreases the space and time complexity as well as solves the problem where unsupervised algorithms fail because of high-dimensional data [4–6].

Different approaches have been used for feature selection which includes filter approach, wrapper approach, embedded approach and hybrid approach. In filter

© Springer Nature Singapore Pte Ltd. 2019
J. K. Mandal et al. (Eds.): CICBA 2018, CCIS 1031, pp. 208–218, 2019.
https://doi.org/10.1007/978-981-13-8581-0_17

approach, learning algorithms are not used to determine the effectiveness of the feature subset. This method is faster and is used for high-dimensional data set. Wrapper approach uses learning algorithm and determines the optimal feature subset based on the predictive accuracy. This method has higher time complexity but gives better accuracy. Embedded approach selects optimal feature subset at the time of training the data set. Hybrid approach exploits both wrapper and filter approach. The graph theoretic approach graphically represents the features as the vertices of the graph and edges are shown as a similarity measure or association between two features [7,8].

The method proposed in this paper, uses graph theoretic approach to visualize the data and the association between the features. The approach rejects features based on the entropy of that feature, determines the associated features using Pearson's correlation coefficient and finds the optimal subset of features by 2-approximation algorithm of minimal vertex cover.

2 Related Work

Graph-based feature selection uses the principles of graph theory for deriving subsets of features from the full feature set. But before that, in general, most of the works in this area have modelled the features as the vertices of a graph. The relationship between features have also been modelled based on different aspects like inter-feature similarity, relative information contribution by the feature, etc.

In a related work on graph-based feature selection [9], an approach of representing the feature set as a feature graph is proposed, where each node represents a feature and edges between two vertices are drawn based on the similarity of the features representing the vertices. Then a vertex cover and independent set based sub-graph derivation approach is followed to get a subset of the feature set.

In another similar work [11], the feature set as an undirected graph is proposed, where each node represents a feature and the weight of the edge between two vertices is based on the dissimilarity of the features representing the vertices. The densest sub-graph is identified as the final feature subset which ensures minimum correlation.

Another work [12] proposed an approach to map the feature set into a graph with the vertices of the graph as features and the weight of the edges based on inter-feature mutual information. In the first stage proposed, the densest sub-graph is obtained to ensure minimum redundancy. In the second stage, reduced feature set is obtained by feature clustering around the non-redundant features.

A weighted feature graph is formed with the weights based on the similarity of the features in yet another related work [13]. Community detection algorithm is used to cluster the features and select the reduced feature subset. An iterative search process checks for the features from the clusters having influential value more than a threshold value, until no feature with influential value more than the threshold value exists.

3   Basic Underlying Concepts

In this section, the concepts required for FIMFSUL have been outlined. The base of FIMFSUL is filter approach. In the proposed approach we have three stages wherein either the most relevant features are added to the selected features list, or the features are directly excluded from the list or, the features are passed to the further stages of relevancy checking by the well known and established, algorithms and threshold values.

3.1   Entropy

The average information content can be determined by its entropy, which measures the unpredictability of the state. The lower the probability, the higher is the information content. According to Shannon, entropy H is defined as,

$$H(X) = \sum_{i=1}^{n} P(x_i)\, I(x_i) = -\sum_{i=1}^{n} P(x_i) \log_b P(x_i)$$

where b = base of logarithm used. Entropy is an important factor in determining the redundancy on a feature on the basis of the average information contributed by that feature.

3.2   Association Between Features

Pearson's correlation coefficient is one of the most established methods which can indicate how similar or dissimilar the features in the feature set are. If the correlation between two features f_1 and f_2 is high, that implies that these two features are similar. Hence, if both f_1 and f_2 are kept in the feature set while clustering, then the results obtained will be similar to the result obtained when either of these features is used. Association thus can infer clearly the redundancy between two features f_1 and f_2, which can help us in eliminating the similar features.

Correlation coefficient can have values in the range of −1 and +1. + 1 indicates maximum linear correlation, −1 indicates minimum linear correlation and 0 indicates no correlation at all. Values between 0.68 to 0.9 indicate high correlation and values between 0.9 to 1.00 can be considered as very high correlation [14].

4   Proposed Approach

In the proposed approach, each feature in the data set is represented as a vertex of a graph. The mapping has three stages wherein after passing through each stage, the features are either added to the list of relevant features or passed further to other stages of relevancy checking or are directly eliminated from the list of relevant features.

- Stage 1 : Highlight the least informative (or irrelevant) features
  Entropy is a measure of the average information that a feature can contribute. Features having high entropy are determined to have a high information contribution to the clustering of the data. Hence these features are essential and need to be considered for further evaluation. The entropy of all the features is calculated, which determines how relevant or irrelevant a feature is towards the overall performance of the algorithm. The relevance threshold β is accepted as user parameter to the algorithm. Only the top β portion contributing features having high entropy are coloured "green" which will be evaluated further. The rest of the $(1 - \beta)$ portion of the features are coloured "red" and are eliminated due to low entropy (or average information contribution). This stage highlights the irrelevant features in "red".
  Refer to "Stage-1" of Figs. 1 and 2 for the visualization that will be achieved at the end of stage 1.
- Stage 2: Highlight similar (or potentially redundant) features
  In this stage, the features marked "green" are evaluated for potential similarity between them. A similarity matrix is generated by calculating inter-feature correlation. Each cell in the similarity matrix holds the correlation value between the features represented by the respective row and column for that cell. The threshold value of correlation α is used which indicates a high correlation among the features. Features having correlation lesser than α are considered to be dissimilar. α may be varied according to the extent of correlation is to be detected.
  An adjacency matrix is made using the similarity matrix and the threshold value of α. The cells having correlation value greater than α are made 1, and lesser than that are made 0. The auto correlation of each feature is reflected in the leading diagonal of the similarity matrix indicating a value of 1, which is hence made 0. The adjacency matrix finally denotes the similar features as vertices coloured in "blue". These features have high information contribution but potential redundancy. The remaining vertices which were initially "green" and have no similarity with the other features, are the relevant features which have high information contribution as well as no redundancy. They are directly included in the feature subset. These features are hence kept coloured as "green". By the end of stage 2, we have a graph indicating similar features coloured in "blue".
  Refer to "Stage-2" of Figs. 1 and 2 for the visualization that will be achieved at the end of stage 2.
- Stage 3 : Highlight the redundant features to be rejected
  From the connected features marked in "blue", a subset is selected as representative of the whole set. This is done by the concept of minimal vertex cover algorithm. This algorithm determines a subset of vertices from the whole set of vertices of a graph, whose edges are incident to at least one the vertices selected in the subset. Since this algorithm is a minimizing algorithm, the number of features in the subset will be minimum possible by a 2-approximation algorithm. Hence with minimum vertices we can have the representation of all the associated features which would indicate a simi-

lar result of classification as that when all these features would have been included.

Finally, the vertices selected by the vertex cover algorithm are changed to "green" as they are going to be a part of the feature subset, and the remaining "blue" vertices are marked "red" as they will be rejected.

Refer to "Stage-3" of Figs. 1 and 2 for the visualization that will be achieved at the end of stage 3.

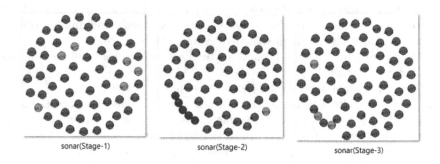

sonar(Stage-1)   sonar(Stage-2)   sonar(Stage-3)

Fig. 1. Illustration for "sonar" data set

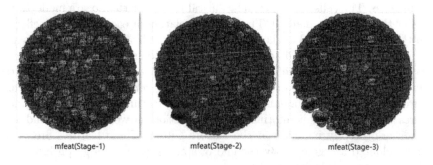

mfeat(Stage-1)   mfeat(Stage-2)   mfeat(Stage-3)

Fig. 2. Illustration for "mfeat" data set

At the end of Stage 3, the FIMFSUL corresponding to the data set is ready. The features representing the "red" coloured vertices in the FIMFSUL are the ones to be excluded and the features representing the "green" coloured vertices are included in the final feature subset. All three stages of FIMFSUL contribute important information regarding the features in the data set.

Algorithm. Feature Information Map Feature Selection for Unsupervised Learning (FIMFSUL)
Input:
N-dimensional data set D_N
Relevance threshold (β)
Output: Optimal feature subset F_{opt}.

Begin
//Stage 1: Entropy of the features is calculated and only top contributing features are coloured green.
1: For i = 1 to N
2:      E_i = ENTROPY(f_i)
3: Next
4: SORT(E)
5: For i = 1 to (β%)N
6:      color(f_i) = "green"
7: Next
8: For i = 1 to (1-β%)N
9:      color(f_i) = "red"
10: Next
11: g_1 = generateFIMFSUL(F)
//Stage 2: The associated features among the possible optimal feature set(which were marked "green" in the previous stage) will be coloured "blue" in this stage.
12: F' = {x: x $\subseteq$ F and color(x) = "green"}
13: C_{mat} = absolute-correlation(D_N[F'])
14: For i = 1 to $|F'|$
15:      For j = 1 to $|F'|$
16:           If($C_{mat} \geq \alpha$) then
17:                add-edge(F_i, F_j, g_1)
18:                color(F_i) = "blue"
19:                color(F_j) = "blue"
20:           End If
21:      Next
22: Next
//Stage 3: Minimal vertex cover algorithm selects the minimal set of optimal features from features marked "blue". These are coloured "green" and are the optimal feature subset selected by FIMFSUL.
23: F" = {x: x $\subseteq$ F and color(x) = "blue"}
24: V = Minimal-vertex-cover(F")
25: color(V) = "green"
26: color(F" - V) = "red"
27: F_{opt} = {x: x $\subseteq$ F and color(x) = "green"}
End

5   Experiments and Outcome

Benchmark data sets from UCI Machine Learning Repository [10] are used to apply the proposed approach. Graphs have been generated using 'igraph' library of R. Table 1 depicts the summary of the characteristics of the data sets used in the experiment. The threshold value for similarity α i.e. Pearson's correlation coefficient is assumed to be 0.67 as it represents a good amount of correlation between features [14]. The value of relevance threshold, β, selected in this experiment is 10%. The results of FIMFSUL have been compared with three benchmark unsupervised feature selection algorithms - UFAM [9], Laplacian [15], Principal Feature Analysis (PFA) [16] and a dense subgraph based algorithm (DSUB) [11].

Table 1. UCI data sets used in experiment

Data set	# of Features	# of Instances
apndcts	7	106
btissue	9	106
cleave	13	297
Ecoli	7	336
glass	9	214
ILPD	10	579
mfeat	649	2000
pima	8	768
sonar	60	208
Vehicle	18	846
wbdc	30	569
wine	13	178
wiscon	9	682

The three stages of FIMFSUL in which features as vertices are coloured either "red", "green" or "blue" are as follows.

- Stage-1: The features having lowest information contribution (or entropy) are coloured "red" and the rest are coloured "green" and evaluated further.
- Stage-2: The subset of features among the "green" coloured vertices in Stage-1 are coloured "blue" if they have high similarity with other features. An adjacency graph is hence drawn. An edge between two vertices indicates a high correlation between these two features.
- Stage-3: Final selection of features is done in this stage. From the "blue" vertices, a subset of vertices as representatives is chosen and marked "green". The features representing these vertices are the final set of accepted features. The remaining vertices are marked "red".

5.1   Summary of Outcome

In Table 2, a summary of the features selected for each of the data sets used in experiment is presented. Features with high relevance and low redundancy have been selected. It is to be noted that the number of features selected is based on the user input value for relevance threshold β. If the value of β is changed, the number of features selected will also change.

Table 2. Features with high relevance and low redundancy

Data set	Number of features	Number of features selected	Selected features
apndcts	7	1	"At6"
btissue	9	1	"HFS"
cleave	13	1	"Chol"
Ecoli	7	1	"aac"
glass	9	1	"Si"
ILPD	10	1	"TB"
mfeat	649	45	"fac1", "fac10", "fac12", "fac15", "fac24", "fac25", "fac35", "fac36", "fac60", "fac61", "fac7", "fac19", "fac26", "fac38", "fac50", "fac56", "fac27", "fac31", "fac39", "fac51", "fac55", "fac63", "fac9", "fac14", "fac16", "fac21", "fac28", "fac40", "fac45", "fac52", "fac17", "fac30", "fac54", "fac23", "fac29", "fac41", "fac53", "fac42", "fac32", "fac33", "fac57", "fac58", "fac49", "fac59", "fac64"
pima	8	1	"Plasmaglucose"
sonar	60	3	"att6", "att2", "att4"
Vehicle	18	1	"Length_rectangular"
wbdc	30	2	"ATT2", "ATT3"
wine	13	1	"Hue"
wiscon	9	1	"Clump_Thickness"

Tables 3, 4 and Fig. 3 presents a summary of results of the experiments:

- As per Table 4, the proposed FIMFSUL algorithm demonstrates the best mean rank compared to all the competing algorithms as well as all features. The mean rank of FIMFSUL is 1.92 compared to the closest value of 2.77 of the UFAM algorithm.
- The proposed algorithm shows the most number of wins/ties. None of the other algorithms show closely match with the results of FIMFSUL.
- FIMFSUL also shows a significant proportion of feature reduction as shown in Fig. 3.

– In case of both the data sets mfeat and sonar, which have higher number of features than the other data sets, the silhouette width value of FIMFSUL algorithm is less than the value with all features. However, the point to be noted is in both the both the cases the feature reduction is very high - 93% for mfeat and 90% for sonar.

Table 3. Comparison of Silhouette width value

Dataset	FIMFSUL	UFAM	ALL	LAPLACIAN	PFA	DSUB
apndcts	0.66	0.6	0.46	0.44	0.48	0.43
btissue	0.66	0.62	0.58	0.56	0.53	0.58
cleave	0.57	0.31	0.27	0.57	0.58	0.27
Ecoli	0.55	0.54	0.44	0.56	0.47	0.44
glass	0.59	0.61	0.52	0.54	0.53	0.52
ILPD	0.87	0.71	0.49	0.72	0.72	0.49
mfeat	0.22	0.2	0.24	0.18	0.14	0.19
pima	0.56	0.27	0.51	0.27	0.27	0.24
sonar	0.38	0.17	0.47	0.19	0.12	0.39
Vehicle	0.62	0.52	0.32	0.43	0.38	0.47
wbdc	0.45	0.44	0.65	0.49	0.29	0.4
wine	0.58	0.4	0.002	0.35	0.31	0.32
wiscon	0.64	0.69	0.19	0.66	0.65	0.65

Table 4. Summary of performance (Silhouette width)

Algorithm	Mean rank	Number of Win/Tie
FIMFSUL	1.92	6
UFAM	2.77	2
ALL	3.92	3
LAPLACIAN	3.23	1
PFA	4.15	1
DSUB	4.31	0

Some more observations related to Tables 3, 4 and Fig. 3 are summarized below:

• The ratio of the optimal feature subset selected by FIMFSUL to all the features in the data set has a maximum value of 14.28%. This indicates that all the data sets have high number of irrelevant or associated data.

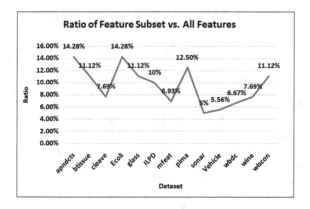

Fig. 3. Comparison of data sets - All features vs. Optimal features

- In most of the data sets, the features having high entropy are not associative or similar. However, data sets like 'mfeat', 'sonar' and 'wbdc' have correlated features among the highly informative features.
- 'sonar' is a unique data set with highly correlated features among the highly informative features. It has shown a 5% ratio in Fig. 3 which is the lowest of all the ratios indicating a 5% of correlated features among the 10% of features having high entropy.

6 Conclusion

In this paper, the proposed approach justifies the results of selecting highly informative features among all the features which are further verified for any correlation among them. The 2-approximation minimal vertex cover algorithm has further narrowed down the number of features without any compromise on the amount of information contributed by the features.

The proposed approach provides the graphical view of all the features in all the three stages which ensures a better understanding of the features and their association. For most of the data sets FIMFSUL gives better results than the other benchmark algorithm thus proving its efficacy.

References

1. Elisseeff, A., Guyon, I.: An introduction to variable and feature selection. J. Mach. Learn. Res. **3**, 1157–1182 (2003)
2. Mitra, P., Murthy, C.A., Pal, S.K.: Unsupervised feature selection using feature similarity. IEEE Trans. Pattern Anal. Mach. Intell. **24**(3), 301–312 (2002)
3. John, G.H., Kohavi, R., Pfleger, K.: Irrelevant features and the subset selection problem. In: ICML (1994)
4. Dougherty, E.R., Hua, J., Tembe, W.: Performance of feature-selection methods in the classification of high-dimension data. Pattern Recogn. **42**, 409–424 (2009)

5. Dash, M., Liu, H.: Feature selection for classifications. Intell. Data Anal.: Int. J. **1**, 131–156 (1997)
6. Liu, H., Yu, L., Feature selection for high-dimensional data: a fast correlation-based filter solution. In: International Conference on Machine Learning (2003)
7. Das, Amit Kumar, Goswami, Saptarsi, Chakraborty, Basabi, Chakrabarti, Amlan: A graph-theoretic approach for visualization of data set feature association. In: Chaki, Rituparna, Saeed, Khalid, Cortesi, Agostino, Chaki, Nabendu (eds.) Advanced Computing and Systems for Security. AISC, vol. 568, pp. 109–124. Springer, Singapore (2017). https://doi.org/10.1007/978-981-10-3391-9_7
8. Goswami, S., et al.: An approach of feature selection using graph-theoretic heuristic and hill climbing. Pattern Anal. Appl. **22**, 615–631 (2017)
9. Das, A.K., Goswami, S., Chakrabarti, A., Chakraborty, B.: A new hybrid feature selection approach using feature association map for supervised and unsupervised classification. Expert Syst. Appl. **88**, 81–94 (2017)
10. Bache, K., Lichman, M.: UCI machine learning repository. University of California, Irvine (2013). School of Information and Computer Sciences
11. Mandal, Monalisa, Mukhopadhyay, Anirban: Unsupervised non-redundant feature selection: a graph-theoretic approach. In: Satapathy, Suresh Chandra, Udgata, Siba K., Biswal, Bhabendra Narayan (eds.) Proceedings of the International Conference on Frontiers of Intelligent Computing: Theory and Applications (FICTA). AISC, vol. 199, pp. 373–380. Springer, Heidelberg (2013). https://doi.org/10.1007/978-3-642-35314-7_43
12. Bandyopadhyay, S., Bhadra, T., Mitra, P., Maulik, U.: Integration of dense subgraph finding with feature clustering for unsupervised feature selection. Pattern Recogn. Lett. **40**, 104–112 (2014)
13. Moradi, P., Rostami, M.: A graph theoretic approach for unsupervised feature selection. Eng. Appl. AI **44**, 33–45 (2015)
14. Taylor, R.: Interpretation of the correlation coefficient: a basic review. J. Diagn. Med. Sonogr. **6**(1), 35–39 (1990)
15. He, X., Cai, D., and Niyogi, P. Laplacian score for feature selection. In: NIPS (2005)
16. Lu, Y., Cohen, I., Zhou, X.S., Tian, Q.: Feature selection using principal feature analysis. In: ACM Multimedia (2007)

Target Protein Function Prediction by Identification of Essential Proteins in Protein-Protein Interaction Network

Soukhindra Nath Basak[1], Ankur Kumar Biswas[1], Sovan Saha[1(✉)], Piyali Chatterjee[2], Subhadip Basu[3], and Mita Nasipuri[3]

[1] Department of Computer Science and Engineering,
Dr. Sudhir Chandra Sur Degree Engineering College,
Dum Dum, Kolkata 700 074, India
soukhindranathbasak@gmail.com, ankurbsws@gmail.com,
sovansaha12@gmail.com
[2] Department of Computer Science and Engineering,
Netaji Subhash Engineering College, Garia, Kolkata 700152, India
chatterjee_piyali@yahoo.com
[3] Department of Computer Science and Engineering, Jadavpur University,
Kolkata 700032, India
subhadip.basu@jadavpuruniversity.in,
mitanasipuri@yahoo.com

Abstract. Protein is one of the most essential components of a living cell. Any living organism requires a modest amount of protein to function well. With the advancement in science and technology, researchers have identified numerous protein sequences, while the functions of most of them still remains unannotated. So a considerable amount of research works is being carried out to study and observe the behavior and the functions of the unannotated proteins. One of the most common approaches that is being followed since old times is to predict the functions of these target proteins from their corresponding neighbors. But the neighborhood approach based predictions involve the presence of false positives in a certain amount. So, in the proposed computational model, a two-step pruning has been executed initially with the aim of identifying the denser sub-network, within the entire protein interaction network. Now each protein in this pruned, denser sub-graph is considered as target protein, the function of which has been evaluated by betweenness centrality which formed the basis for the function prediction. The proposed methodology achieves an overall precision, recall and F-Score of 0.58, 0.67 and 0.62 respectively which highlights the fact that this work is far more efficient than most of the existing state-of-arts.

Keywords: PPIN (Protein-protein interaction Network) ·
Common neighbor score · Degree score · Betweenness centrality ·
Protein function · Function prediction

© Springer Nature Singapore Pte Ltd. 2019
J. K. Mandal et al. (Eds.): CICBA 2018, CCIS 1031, pp. 219–231, 2019.
https://doi.org/10.1007/978-981-13-8581-0_18

1 Introduction

In a protein-protein interaction network (PPIN), a node represents a protein while an edge between the two provides knowledge about their interaction. It is believed that the target protein performs almost similar functions as that of its neighborhood. But functional assignment to the target proteins from their corresponding neighbors is really a challenging task since all of the neighborhood proteins do not hold similar importance. Hence, selection of essential proteins is a prime step before function prediction such that a higher accuracy can be achieved. This is where the concept of densely and loosely connected network slides in. Densely connected networks are considered to be those networks where interconnectivity between the proteins is maximum while the loosely connected networks are considered to be those networks where interconnectivity is minimum. Introduction of a proper model thus becomes indispensable which can detect essential proteins in the neighborhood and hence can transmit appropriate functional groups from them to the target protein. This dual concept of detection along with the prediction of the target protein functions has been followed in this current work. But before proceeding into the detailed implementation of the proposed methodology, few of the relevant existing works have been discussed in the upcoming section to have a clear idea about the working procedures of neighborhood based prediction approaches.

The golden era of function prediction starts with a simple and effective methodology proposed by Schwikowski et al. [1]. A list has been prepared where the functions of all the immediate neighbors of the target protein are placed in decreasing order of their occurrences. The algorithm includes the first three or fewer entries of the most frequent functions, while the rest are simply discarded. Due to such elimination of functions without proper reasoning or logic, this methodology could yield an accuracy rate of only 12.2%. Hishigaki et al. [2], tried to improvise on this approach by assigning a value to each of the function of the neighboring proteins based on which function prediction has been done. This methodology comparatively yields better result giving an accuracy of 52.7%. The work by Chen et al. [3] is a bit unique from the above two mentioned methods as in this, a heuristic network motif labeling algorithm called LaMoFinder has been employed instead of looking for functional similarities in the neighboring proteins. This algorithm tries to exploit topologically similar proteins for function prediction. Similarly, works by Vazquez et al. [4], Karaoz et al. [5], Nabieva et al. [6] are also based on the topology of the protein network but with different approaches. Vazquez et al. [4] employed a simulated annealing optimizing method to focus on maximum connectivity among the unclassified proteins. Here the interactions among unannotated or unclassified proteins have also been considered for function prediction. Karaoz et al. [5], attempted to interpret gene functions by combining the data obtained from PPIN and gene-expression with that of functional-linkage networks. Nabieva et al. [6] performed function prediction on basis of a functional score which keeps track of the number of times a particular function reaches the target protein from different annotated source proteins. This methodology also includes the concept of distance effect. A yet another unique and an interesting approach is observed in the work by Deng et al. [7] in which an interpretation of domain-domain interactions has been done from a PPIN. This interpretation has notable contributions towards the understanding of the nature and behavior of biological interactions. The works by Pruzli *et al.* [8], King *et al.* [9], Xiong *et al.* [10], Haque *et al.* [11] are also worth mentioning in which Restricted Neighborhood Search Clustering Algorithm, probabilistic model, a combination of PPIN information and protein sequence information, common neighbor score has been respectively used for identification of protein complexes. Identification of protein complexes has crucial roles to play in the invention of important drugs that can cure or prevent difficult diseases. Many recent works in the field of function prediction have also come up as an improvisation of older methods. It can be seen in the work of Xiaoxiao *et al.* [12], where an iterative approach of function prediction yields a better result than the various existing non-iterative approaches. Similarly, Qingyao *et al.* [13] used a Markov chain based collective classification (CC) algorithm to tackle the label deficiency problem that exists in earlier CC based approaches. So far, among the existing inductive approaches of function prediction, only the local ones gained a limelight. Rahamani *et al.* [14] focused on a global protein description mechanism which improved the F-measure values up to 9%. The other recent works by Moosavi *et al.* [15], Saha *et al.* [16, 17], Zhang *et al.* [18], Prasad *et al.* [19] also highlights very interesting and unique approaches towards function predictions.

The observations of the advantages as well as corresponding disadvantages and limitations of the above mentioned works have revealed the fact that there is a scope of improvement in certain fields, some of which are explored while the others are still unexplored. This actually motivates us to analyze this field of study and lift protein function prediction a step forward. The proposed work can be disintegrated in two phases: In the first phase, a two way or double filtering of the original PPIN of *Saccharomyces cerevisiae* has been performed to identify the essential proteins in the network based on three thresholds: High, Medium and low estimated on the basis of degree score of each protein by the application of k-sigma [18]. In the second phase, each protein under the three thresholds is considered as target protein and their corresponding annotated neighborhood graph is formed. Then selected functional groups from the neighborhood graph are assigned to the target protein based on betweenness centrality score and other neighborhood features.

2   Related Terminologies

PPIN [16, 20] plays a significant role in the proposed work which comprises of proteins (nodes) as well as interaction between them (edges). PPIN related terminologies like level-1 neighbors [16], level-2 neighbor [16], common neighbor [11], common neighbor score [11], k-sigma [18] and Betweenness Centrality [21] convey the same meaning. Beside these, several other relevant network terminologies like Degree Score, Common Neighbor and Common Neighbor Score have been used which have been discussed below:

2.1   Degree Score

Degree score of a protein i is a unique value, which is calculated as the sum of the degree of protein i and the average of all the degrees of its immediate nodes. Mathematically it can be defined as:

$$Degree\ Score(i) = degree(i) + \frac{\sum(degrees\ of\ immediate\ nodes\ of\ i)}{number\ of\ nodes} \tag{1}$$

2.2   Common Neighbor

A protein P_k is said to be a common neighbor of two proteins P_i and P_j, if P_k is a neighbour of both P_i and P_j. Mathematically, it is defined as:

$$CN(P_i, P_j) = \{P_1, P_2, \ldots, P_k\} \tag{2}$$

where both P_i and P_j have edge between each of $P_1, P_2, \ldots, P_k$.

2.3   Common Neighbour Score

Common Neighbor Score is defined as the total number of common neighbors between two proteins P_i and P_j. Mathematically, it is defined as:

$$CN_{Score}^{P_i, P_j} = |CN(P_i, P_j)| \tag{3}$$

3   Dataset

The dataset of yeast from the Munich Information Center for Protein Sequences (ftp:// ftpmips.helmholtz-muenchen.de/fungi/Saccharomycetes/CYGD/PPI/) database [16, 22] has been considered in the proposed work. The PPIN data of *Saccharomyces cerevisiae* in MIPS dataset includes 4554 unique proteins in 13528 protein-protein interactions (PPIs) after the elimination of self-replicating and self-interacting protein pairs. The overall generated network has been highlighted in Fig. 1 where each node represents a protein and is marked in green.

4   Methodology

There are basically two phases of the proposed work: (1) Double Filtering/Pruning and (2) Function Prediction of the target protein. The first phase can be categorized into first and second level pruning. The first level pruning attempts to identify a densely connected sub-graph of proteins using common neighborhood score. The second level pruning aims at further filtration of the sub-graph obtained from the first level of pruning based on degree score. The second phase or the final phase predicts the

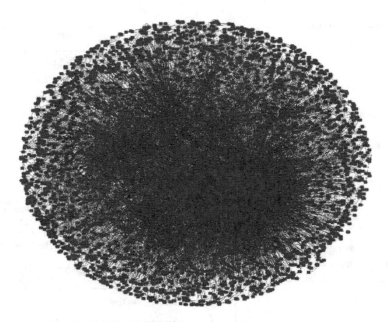

Fig. 1. The overall PPIN of yeast used in the proposed work

function of target proteins using betweenness centrality of the essential proteins. The entire methodology of the proposed method is discussed below:

4.1 First Level Pruning

A sample PPIN has been highlighted in Fig. 2, where there are three levels of proteins. The level-0 protein is YMR263w. The level-1 proteins are YHR128w, YAL001c, YLR085c, and YER077c. The level-2 proteins are YDL011c and YBR164c. At first, pruning is performed on the original network based on common neighbors score (CN_{score}). Then essential proteins are identified from the resulting densely connected protein groups using neighbourhood score as depicted in Fig. 2.

After the first level of pruning, YLRO85c, YMR263w and YAL001c have been identified as the essential proteins (marked in green). The initial pruned network comprising of the essential proteins along with their neighboring proteins (marked in blue) has been also shown in the Fig. 2.

4.2 Second Level Pruning

Now, the initial pruned network generated from the first level of pruning is taken as an input for a second level pruning based on degree score. In Fig. 3 the initial pruned network of YMR263w has been shown with YAL001c, YER077c, YHR128w and YLR085c as level-1 proteins. Initially degree score has been calculated as highlighted in Table 5 in Fig. 3. Once it is calculated, threshold has been set with the implementation of k-sigma where k = 1, 2, 3 represents low, medium and high threshold

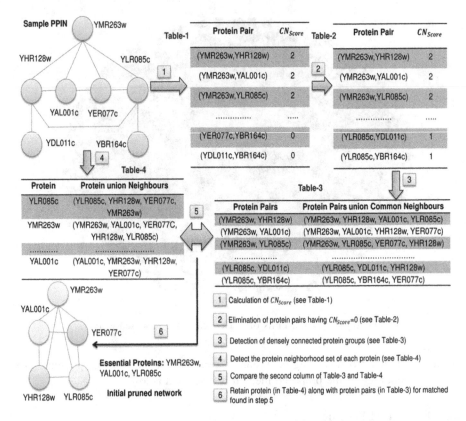

Fig. 2. Stepwise detailed implementation of first level pruning

respectively. Based on these thresholds, protein interactions having lower degree score than the threshold value have been discarded. It should be noted here that if the lower degree score nodes have any connection with a node having higher degree that connection is retained throughout.

Thus all the non-essential proteins in the PPIN have been eliminated thereby reducing the chance of increasing false positives in the function prediction accuracy. While the first level of pruning ensures the selection of densely connected sub-graphs, the second level of pruning eliminates the possibility of existence of loose interconnections among the child nodes of a query protein in the selected denser sub-graphs from first level of pruning.

4.3   Function Prediction of Target Proteins

Each protein obtained after second level of pruning is considered to be the target protein and its corresponding annotated neighbourhood sub-graph has been constructed up to level-3. Hence, few selected functions from the neighborhood, based on betweenness centrality, have been assigned to the target protein the detailed implementation of which have been highlighted in the below mentioned algorithm.

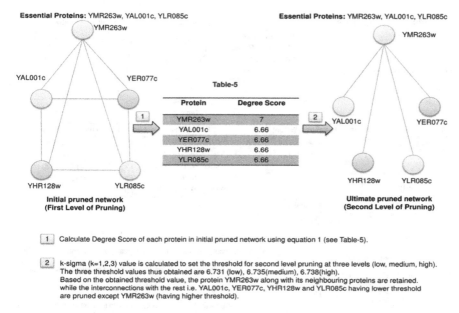

Fig. 3. Stepwise detailed implementation of second level pruned network based on degree score

A sample PPIN of target protein YMR263w has been considered in Fig. 4 with YAL001c, YHR28w, YLR085c and YER077c as level-1 proteins. At first, betweenness centrality of each protein from the final pruned network is calculated (see Table 7 in Fig. 4). A weight has been assigned to the functions of each protein pair. The weight is calculated as the mean of the betweenness centrality of each protein from the protein pair (see Table 8 in Fig. 4). Following this, for functions occurring more than once, their respective weight values are added and then all the redundancies are removed (see Table 9 in Fig. 4). Finally, k-sigma (k = 1,2,3) threshold value is calculated at three levels (low, medium, high) from the function-weight list. The threshold value so obtained filters the list of functions that are selected to be assigned to the target protein YMR263w (see Table 10 in Fig. 4).

5   Results and Discussions

The proposed work thus aims at finding target proteins based on the interactions of the respective proteins as well as their neighboring proteins. Predicting the function of such a densely connected protein just by looking at its immediate neighbors leads to inefficiency as well as wrong outcomes. The above-mentioned algorithms thus look into the greater depth of connections to avoid false assumptions. This has been possible through calculations of the common neighbor score, degree score and betweenness centrality score of proteins at different phases. Calculation of k-sigma (k = 1,2,3) sets a threshold value at three levels (low, medium, high) for pruning of less significant interactions and false function predictions. The three levels of threshold values focus on

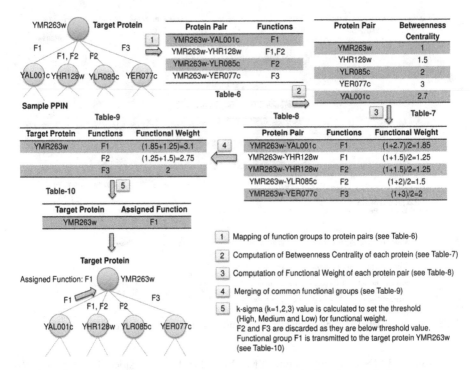

Fig. 4. Detailed implementation of target protein function prediction

different sets of target proteins and yield different performance score for each set (see Table 1).

Table 1. Different number of target proteins obtained for different threshold values based on degree scores

Threshold type	No. of target proteins
High	39
Medium	42
Low	101

It has been observed that a high threshold value results in 21% (39) target proteins. Similarly, medium and low threshold values resulted in 23% (42) and 56% (101) target proteins respectively (see Figs. 5 and 6). Even though the target proteins for high threshold value showed low values for true positive, the false positives were low as well, giving a fairly accurate outcome. On the other hand, target proteins for low threshold value showed an increase in both true as well as false positives.

The performance score for function prediction of three different sets of target proteins has been evaluated in terms of precision (P), recall (R) and f-score (F) as has been shown below:

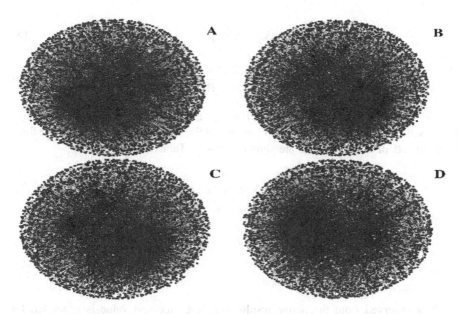

Fig. 5. A: Overall PPIN used in the proposed work, B: PPIN showing annotated and target proteins at high threshold, C: PPIN showing annotated and target proteins at medium threshold, D: PPIN showing annotated and target proteins at low threshold. (Here the target proteins are the yellow colored nodes and the threshold is calculated based on the degree score.)

Degree Score Threshold
vs
No. of Target Proteins

■ High Threshold   ■ Medium Threshold   ■ Low Threshold

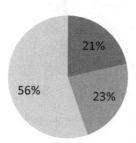

Fig. 6. Variation of number of target proteins with thresholds (high, medium and low)

$$P = \frac{TP}{TP + FP} \tag{4}$$

$$R = \frac{TP}{TP + FN} \tag{5}$$

$$F = \frac{2^*P^*R}{P + R} \tag{6}$$

Here TP represents True Positives, FP represents False Positives and FN represents False Negatives. Precision, recall and f-score obtained by the proposed work for three different sets of target proteins are shown below in Table 2:

Table 2. Performance scores of the proposed methodology

Threshold type	Precision	Recall	F-score
High	0.58	0.67	0.62
Medium	0.60	0.66	0.63
Low	0.49	0.68	0.57

It is observed from the above results that best Precision value is generated for medium threshold value whereas best Recall and best F-Score are generated for low and medium threshold values respectively. A detailed graphical view of the same is represented in Fig. 7.

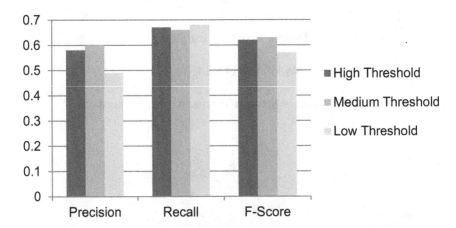

Fig. 7. Precision, recall and F-score obtained for the proposed methodology at three levels of threshold (low, medium, high)

A relative performance study was carried out between the proposed methodology and the already established methodologies on the same target set of the proposed methodology. The graph generated out of this study has been shown in Fig. 8.

Figure 8 clearly indicates improved output of the proposed methodology over the others. The major limitation of Funpred 1.1 [16] was a relatively low recall value which

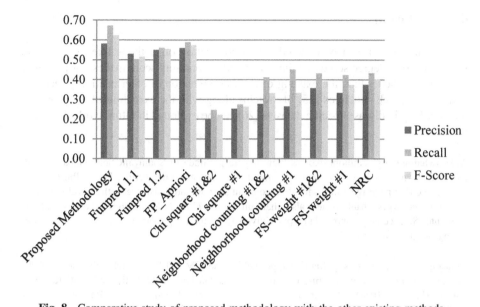

Fig. 8. Comparative study of proposed methodology with the other existing methods

suggested an inefficiency of obtaining the required outcomes. This observation was improved to a certain extent in the proposed work which had its own limitations as well. The proposed methodology was observed to be best fit for medium threshold target proteins. This was due to the similarity in the behavior of true positives and false positives, which showed an equal increase in low threshold target proteins as well as an equal reduction in high threshold target proteins. Some of the methods used in the proposed work can be traced back to those used in the existing ones. The common neighbor counting method of Haque et al. [11] and similarly the neighborhood counting method of Schwikowski et al. [1], Saha et al. [16] were extended. The function prediction work by A. Prasad et al. [19] used closeness centrality score which had motivated us to research and study the protein sets with other centrality scores. The betweenness centrality score was chosen as the basis for function prediction in the proposed work, as it does not require a fully connected graph which is essentially required for closeness centrality score. The works by Hishigaki et al. [2], Moosavi et al. [15] are also worth mentioning as they gave us the inspiration to proceed with our work and their limitations motivated us to indulge in more research works and discussions with the aim of overcoming them in the proposed work. It was observed that chi-square methods (Chi-square #1 and Chi-square #1&2) were inefficient in delivering right outcomes as its methods were designed for densely connected networks and mostly failed in regions of loose interactions. This limitation was surpassed in the proposed method. Another feature of the proposed work which makes it better is the consideration of three levels of interactions whereas most of the existing works like those by Hishigaki et al. [2], Schwikowski et al. [1], Moosavi et al. [15] focuses either on level-1 neighbors only or till level-2 neighbors only.

6   Conclusion

So, in a nutshell, it can be concluded that application of methods like the common neighbor score, degree score and the betweenness centrality score makes our proposed methodology better than the existing ones. A combination of other centrality features, domains [23, 24], structures [25] of proteins along with the execution of the proposed methodology in disease specific datasets [26] can be exploited in future works for better predictions.

Acknowledgement. Authors express their sincere gratitude to Soumyajit Seal, Nabanil Chatterjee and Urmila Nair, Department of Computer Science and Engineering, Dr. Sudhir Chandra Sur Degree Engineering College, for their constant support and assistance in the development of the proposed work. Authors are also thankful to the CMATER research laboratory of the Computer Science Department, Jadavpur University, India, for providing infrastructure facilities during progress of the work.

Funding. This project is partially supported by the CMATER research laboratory of the Computer Science and Engineering Department, Jadavpur University, India, and UGC Research Award (F.30-31/2016(SA-II)) from UGC, Government of India, and DBT project (No. BT/PR16356/BID/7/596/2016), Ministry of Science and Technology, Government of India.

References

1. Schwikowski, B., Uetz, P., Fields, S.: A network of protein-protein interactions in yeast. Nat. Biotechnol. **18**, 1257–1261 (2000)
2. Hishigaki, H., Nakai, K., Ono, T., Tanigami, A., Takagi, T.: Assessment of prediction accuracy of protein function from protein–protein interaction data. Yeast **18**, 523–531 (2001)
3. Chen, J., Hsu, W., Lee, M.L., Ng, S.K.: Labeling network motifs in protein interactomes for protein function prediction. In: Proceedings of the International Conference Data Engineering, pp. 546–555 (2007)
4. Vazquez, A., Flammini, A., Maritan, A., Vespignani, A.: Global protein function prediction from protein-protein interaction networks. Nat. Biotechnol. **21**, 697–700 (2003)
5. Karaoz, U., et al.: Whole-genome annotation by using evidence integration in functional-linkage networks. Proc. Natl. Acad. Sci. **101**, 2888–2893 (2004)
6. Nabieva, E., Jim, K., Agarwal, A., Chazelle, B., Singh, M.: Whole-proteome prediction of protein function via graph-theoretic analysis of interaction maps. Bioinformatics **21**, 302–310 (2005)
7. Deng, M., Mehta, S., Sun, F., Chen, T.: Inferring domain–domain interactions from protein–protein interactions. Genome Res. **12**(10), 1540–1548 (2002)
8. King, A.D., Pržulj, N., Jurisica, I.: Protein complex prediction via cost-based clustering. Bioinformatics **20**, 3013–3020 (2004)
9. Asthana, S., King, O.D., Gibbons, F.D., Roth, F.P.: Predicting protein complex membership using probabilistic network reliability. Genome Res. **14**, 1170–1175 (2004)
10. Xiong, W., Liu, H., Guan, J., Zhou, S.: Protein function prediction by collective classification with explicit and implicit edges in protein-protein interaction networks. BMC Bioinform. **14**, S4 (2013)

11. Haque, M., Sarmah, R., Bhattacharyya, D.K.: A common neighbor based technique to detect protein complexes in PPI networks. J. Genet. Eng. Biotechnol. **16**(1), 227–238 (2017)
12. Chi, X., Hou, J.: An iterative approach of protein function prediction. BMC Bioinform. **12** (1), 437 (2011)
13. Wu, Q., Ye, Y., Ng, M.K., Ho, S.-S., Shi, R.: Collective prediction of protein functions from protein-protein interaction networks. BMC Bioinform. **15**, S9 (2014)
14. Rahmani, H., Blockeel, H., Bender, A.: Predicting the functions of proteins in Protein-Protein Interaction networks from global information. Syst. Biol. (Stevenage) **8**, 82–97 (2009)
15. Moosavi, S., Rahgozar, M., Rahimi, A.: Protein function prediction using neighbor relativity in protein–protein interaction network. Comput. Biol. Chem. **43**, 11–16 (2013)
16. Saha, S., Chatterjee, P., Basu, S., Kundu, M., Nasipuri, M.: FunPred-1: protein function prediction from a protein interaction network using neighborhood analysis. Cell. Mol. Biol. Lett. **19**, 675–691 (2014)
17. Saha, S., Chatterjee, P., Basu, S., Nasipuri, M.: Gene ontology based function prediction of human protein using protein sequence and neighborhood property of ppi network. In: Satapathy, S.C., Bhateja, V., Udgata, Siba K., Pattnaik, P.K. (eds.) Proceedings of the 5th International Conference on Frontiers in Intelligent Computing: Theory and Applications. AISC, vol. 516, pp. 109–118. Springer, Singapore (2017). https://doi.org/10.1007/978-981-10-3156-4_11
18. Zhang, Y., Lin, H., Yang, Z., Wang, J., Liu, Y., Sang, S.: A method for predicting protein complex in dynamic PPI networks. BMC Bioinform. **17**(7), 229 (2016)
19. Prasad, A., Saha, S., Chatterjee, P., Basu, S., Nasipuri, M.: Protein function prediction from protein interaction network using bottom-up L2L apriori algorithm. In: Mandal, J.K., Dutta, P., Mukhopadhyay, S. (eds.) CICBA 2017. CCIS, vol. 776, pp. 3–16. Springer, Singapore (2017). https://doi.org/10.1007/978-981-10-6430-2_1
20. Saha, S., Chatterjee, P., Basu, S., Kundu, M., Nasipuri, M.: Improving prediction of protein function from protein interaction network using intelligent neighborhood approach. In: Proceedings of the 2012 International Conference on Communications, Devices and Intelligent Systems. CODIS 2012. pp. 584–587. IEEE (2012)
21. Freeman, L.C.: A set of measures of centrality based on betweenness. Sociometry **40**, 35 (1977)
22. Saha, S., Chatterjee, P., Basu, S., Nasipuri, M.: Functional group prediction of un-annotated protein by exploiting its neighborhood analysis in saccharomyces cerevisiae protein interaction network. In: Chaki, R., Saeed, K., Cortesi, A., Chaki, N. (eds.) Advanced Computing and Systems for Security. AISC, vol. 568, pp. 165–177. Springer, Singapore (2017). https://doi.org/10.1007/978-981-10-3391-9_11
23. Chatterjee, P., Basu, S., Zubek, J., Kundu, M., Nasipuri, M., Plewczynski, D.: PDP-CON: prediction of domain/linker residues in protein sequences using a consensus approach. J. Mol. Model. **22**, 72 (2016)
24. Chatterjee, P., Basu, S., Kundu, M., Nasipuri, M., Plewczynski, D.: PPI_SVM: prediction of protein-protein interactions using machine learning, domain-domain affinities and frequency tables. Cell. Mol. Biol. Lett. **16**, 264–278 (2011)
25. Chatterjee, P., Basu, S., Kundu, M., Nasipuri, M., Plewczynski, D.: PSP_MCSVM: brainstorming consensus prediction of protein secondary structures using two-stage multiclass support vector machines. J. Mol. Model. **17**, 2191–2201 (2011)
26. Saha, S., Sengupta, K., Chatterjee, P., Basu, S., Nasipuri, M.: Analysis of protein targets in pathogen–host interaction in infectious diseases: a case study on Plasmodium falciparum and homo sapiens interaction network. Brief. Funct. Genomics **17**(6), 441–450 (2017)

Mutual Information –The Biomarker of Essential Gene Predictions in Gene-Gene-Interaction of Lung Cancer

Anjan Kumar Payra[1(✉)] and Anupam Ghosh[2]

[1] Department of Computer Science and Engineering,
Sudhir Ch. Sur Degree Engineering College, Dumdum 700074, Kolkata, India
anjan.payra@gmail.com
[2] Department of Computer Science and Engineering,
Netaji Subhash Engineering College, Garia 700152, Kolkata, India
anupam.ghosh@rediffmail.com

Abstract. Lung cancer is a biggest epidemic in current decade. Recent statistical results clearly accounted that higher percentage of male and female had been under its trap. Researchers are engaged by themselves to reduce its percentage periodically. It is observed that macromolecules acted as an essential role in this improvement. One of the important macromolecules of life is gene and its complex. Genes in interaction participates in more number of functional activities as compared to individuals. Normally, similar set i.e. functionally similar set of genes stay in same network. Initially the proposed work starts with gene expression microarray dataset which consists of sets of both normal as well as disease gene samples. A total collection of 7129 genes are involved in the dataset out of which 3556 variant set of genes have been filtered out by applying two-tailed T-test. Hence Mutual information and K -means clustering algorithms are executed on these variant set of genes to obtain most similar set of genes. Interactions of these filtered genes have been studied using String DB and Gene Mania from where the most reliable genes have been retained using node and edge weight. 109 most reliable genes are finally identified as diver nodes or controller genes which can play an essential role in lung cancer. Our methodology achieves an overall accuracy of 88%.

Keywords: Controllability · Mutual information · Centrality · Edge weight · Node weight etc.

1 Introduction

The nature of a system in real time depends on input. Desire output means next state of a gene interaction network which depends on the suitable sets of input and set of states or macromolecules. Approach of study of interactions can be observed in form of hierarchical or closed graphical mapping of genes [1, 2]. Network of macromolecules is still complex in layout of statistical mechanics. Studies of the network monitoring or controlling are governed with several basic principles [3–5]. A study of the network means to include the principals which are based on miscellaneous graphical topologies

© Springer Nature Singapore Pte Ltd. 2019
J. K. Mandal et al. (Eds.): CICBA 2018, CCIS 1031, pp. 232–244, 2019.
https://doi.org/10.1007/978-981-13-8581-0_19

and measures of statistical centralities. The goal of set of principals is used to predict controller genes to control the network [6, 7].

The study of the expression profiles, sequences or networks are mainly aimed with the prediction of similarity of genes, and function prediction of genes. Recent trends of experiments are also extended towards prediction of essential genes or controllability of networks. Function prediction, similarity measure, essential gene prediction are the most relevance branches of study. Liu et al. [8] introduces maximum matching approach in a directed network. While the concept of minimum dominating set (MDSets) to control of undirected network is proposed by Nacher and Akutsu [9]. Jeong et al. [10], Yu et al. [11] suggest the concept of denser (highly connected) network [12, 13], such as hub, mesh etc. and their importance in their complex involvement [14] (centrality-lethality). Correlation between degree and essentiality has been also highlighted in their work. While similar properties like degree centrality for counting for direct neighbours and betweenness centrality [13] for counting the shortest path in a network has been also taken under consideration in certain works [15–17] for controllability analysis. The objective is to predict the set of controller genes in a specific disease gene expression profile. GeneMANIA [18], Weka [19], R [20], FuncAssociate [21] etc. tools are used to predict controller genes for controllability of gene-gene interaction network.

The term "controller gene" has been introduced in this work for observing of the controllability of complex networks [22]. Nodes that must control other nodes in its associated network are called as driver nodes or controller. A set of genes (driver nodes or controller genes) which participate more frequently in an interacting dense network have obviously higher degree values in respect to the other sets of participated genes. So, genes in same network should be strictly dependent on that set of controller genes for different functionality. Controllability concerns the ability to change of the states from initial to any other required final state [11, 23]. In other word it can be said that the controllability of a network means control functionality, which is essential to restrict, the disease. So, strong control on controller genes will lead to the control of the other genes in the network too. In a nutshell the controller genes must be observed and controlled to persuade any deadlier impact resulting from them.

2 Proposed Methodologies

2.1 Selection Variant Set of Genes

A coupled set of sample values, in the context of Gene expression dataset, can be represented by an ordinary differential Eq. (1). It can be also regarded as a deterministic model which relates the instantaneous change in mRNA concentration of a gene with respect to that of the other genes in the system [24].

$$X_i' = f_i(X_1, \ldots \ldots, X_N) \tag{1}$$

Where, X_i denotes the vector of mRNA concentrations of the i th gene (of N) at times $\{t_1, \ldots, t_M\}$, with time-derivative (X_i'). The variant set genes (g_i) are selected using two-tailed T-test of X_i vectors. The output also has the ability to predict whether the mean values of the selected set of genes are significantly differing from rest of the genes of gene expression dataset or not. The selected (g_i) genes expression values are used in Sect. 2.2.

2.2   Grouping and Index Validation

Data processing [25] of GED of variant set of genes are also one of the factors to consider to obtain functionally [26] similar groups of genes. Thus different types of clustering principles (like Hierarchical, Simple K-means and DBSCAN etc.) are used to obtain similar set of genes as given in Fig. 1 [27]. The DB-Index and Dunn-index are used for the validation of obtained clusters. Both indices are described below in brief. Simple K-means algorithm produces better outcome compare to others as discuss in analysis of result section. Thus results of Simple K-means are used in later Sect. 2.3. Grouping and Index validation details are given in Fig. 1.

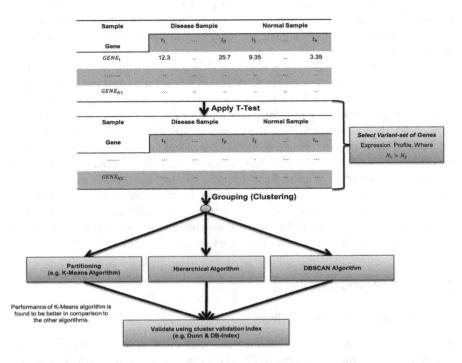

Fig. 1. Select of variant-set of genes using two tailed T-test algorithm on gene expression profile. Grouping similar set of genes using clustering algorithms and validate result for selection of best clustering algorithm.

The DB-index criterion is calculated based on a ratio of within-cluster and between-cluster distances (intra and inter cluster distance). The Davies-Bouldin [28] index is defined as in Eqs. (2–3) and Fig. 1.

$$DB = \frac{1}{k} \sum_{i=1}^{k} max_{j \neq i} \{D_{i,j}\} \tag{2}$$

k is the number of clusters. $D_{i,j}$ is the within-to-between cluster distance ratio for the ith and jth clusters. In mathematical terms,

$$D_{i,j} = \frac{\left(d_i' + d_j'\right)}{d_{i,j}}$$
$$d_i' = avg\{euclidean(d_{p_i}, c^i)\} \tag{3}$$
$$d_{i,j} = \{euclidean(c^i, c^j)\}$$

The corresponding Eq. (3) represent both intra and inter cluster distance and their ratio. Where, d_i' is the average distance between each point (d_{p_i}) in the ith cluster and the centroid (c^i) of the ith cluster. d_j' is the average distance between each point in the jth cluster and the centroid of the jth cluster. $d_{i,j}$ is the Euclidean distance between the centroids of the ith and jth clusters.

Dunn Index [29] is selected to minimize the intra-cluster distance while maximizing the inter-cluster distance. The Dunn index for k clusters is defined by Eq. (4) and Fig. 1.

$$DU_k = min_{i=1.,k} \left\{ min_{j=1+1,...,k} \left(\frac{diss(c_i, c_j)}{max_{m=1,...,k} diam(c_m)} \right) \right\} \tag{4}$$

Where, k is the number of clusters in dataset or maximum number of observation. $diss(c_i, c_j)$ is the dissimilarity between both i and j clusters. $diam(c_m)$ is the intra-cluster function (or diameter) of the cluster. If Dunn index is large, it means that compact and well separated clusters exist.

2.3 Information Sharing

The validated cluster results are initially normalized and then calculate sharing information (e.g. Entropy, Mutual information) between two genes. The normalized value of e_i for expression values E in the ith row is calculated as (5).

$$Normalized(e_i) = \frac{e_i - E_{min}}{E_{max} - E_{min}} \tag{5}$$

Where, E_{min} = the minimum value in ith row, Emax = the maximum value in ith row

If E_{max} is equal to E_{min} then *Normalized* (e$_i$) is set to 0.5. Expected calculated values are converted to either 0 or 1 depending on the range of threshold value [30]. It is highlighted in Fig. 2.

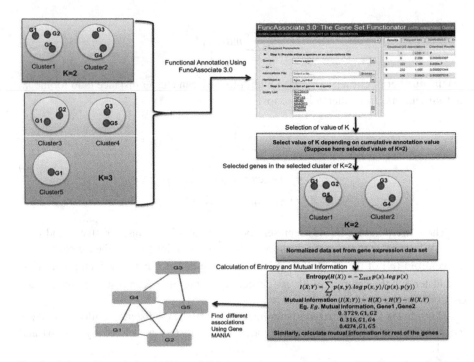

Fig. 2. Select of cumulative addition of GO-annotation to assign value of K. Grouping the most similar set of genes in the group using entropy and mutual information. Assemble physical associations are present in the most similar set of genes.

Entropy (H) is defined as the measure of average uncertainty in a random variable [31]. Entropy of a random variable X with probability mass function p(x) is defined by Eq. (6).

$$H(X) = -\sum_{x \in X} p(x) . \log p(x) \tag{6}$$

Mutual information(MI) is the quantitative measure of the amount of information that can be deduced about one random variable by observing another one [32]. Ad hoc time delay has been proposed in the past to overcome the issue of directional information which is not present in MI. The joint entropy is calculated using Eq. (7). The gene system is assumed to be event driven, i.e. all the regulations are performed step by step and in each step all regulations happen only once as given in Fig. 2. MI is defined in Eqs. (7–8).

$$I(X; Y) = \sum_{x,y} p(x, y) . \log p(x, y) / (p(x) . p(y)) \tag{7}$$

MI can also be defined in terms of entropies as

$$I(X;Y) = H(X) + H(Y) - H(X,Y) \tag{8}$$

Select largest set of similar genes with respect to obtain values of mutual information. Considered set is used for construction of gene-gene interactions network in Sect. 2.4.

2.4   Controller Gene Prediction

The genes are used to find all possible intra-inter physical associations using String DB, Gene Mania repositories. Network weighting properties (e.g. Edge weight, Node weight) are calculated to predict essential or controller set of genes as given in Fig. 3. Properties are described below in brief.

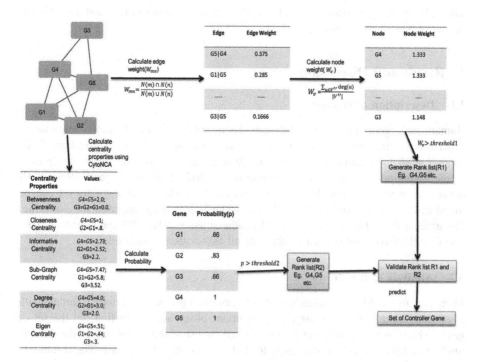

Fig. 3. Calculation of edge weight and node weight to predict controller of the network. Validate our prediction using different centrality measures.

In the proposed work, the edge weight (W_{mn}) is represented by Eq. (9). The similarity of a network is measured using Jaccard's co-efficient [33] where common neighbours of two nodes in all distinct neighbour of the nodes are important.

$$W_{mn} = \frac{N(m) \cap N(n)}{N(m) \cup N(n)} \tag{9}$$

Where, $N(m)$ and $N(n)$ are neighbors of u and v respectively. $N(m) \cap N(n)$ represents all common neighbors of u and v, and $N(m) \cup N(n)$ represents all distinct neighbors of u and v. The node weight (W_v) [33] of node $v \in V$ in a network is the average degree of all nodes in G'_v. It is represented by Eq. (10). In an interaction network (G_v), there are some nodes with degree 1 that only have connections with v are often considered to be less essential nodes according to topological reliability measures. So nodes with degree 1 and corresponding edges are removed from the network. The remaining sub graph of the network is marked as G'_v.

$$W_v = \frac{\sum_{u \in V''} \deg(u)}{|V''|} \tag{10}$$

where, V'' is the set of nodes in G'_v. $|V''|$ is the number of nodes in G'_v. And deg(u) is the degree of a node $u \in V''$ in W_v.

3 Result and Discussion

3.1 Description of Dataset

Human lung gene expression data has been obtained by Affymetrix microarray experiments with tumors and normal lung samples. In this data set, there are 7129 genes for 86 lung tumor and 10 normal lung samples. The gene expression profile represent 86 primary lung adenocarcinomas, including 67 state I and 19 state III tumors, as well as 10 neoplastic lung samples. More details on this data set can be found in Beer et al. (2002) [34]. Weka.jar, weka 3.6.12 and R are used for clustering. The generated clusters are analyzed and validated using index [20] and FuncAssociate. The GeneMANIA tool is used to generate all association or network.

3.2 Analysis of Result

There are $(n_1 = 86)$ time variant sample of tumor and $(n_2 = 10)$ of normal sample with 7129 gene entries in the dataset. The important observation is to find out the set of genes which change significantly as compared to rest of the genes stay in the dataset. Student distribution or T-test is used to find the variant set of genes. The results are given in below in Table 1.

Table 1. The result of T-test, where P: probability value.

Degree of freedom = 86 + 10 -2 = 94	Gene (P = .05)	Gene (P = .01)	Gene (P = .001)	Two tailed
Count	2471	1862	1337	3556

Almost 50% genes are selected as variant set of genes using two tailed T-test approach. The filtered set of genes is used to calculate similarity measures using clustering methodologies. DBSCAN, K-mean and Hierarchical clustering etc. algorithms are applied on dataset. Both DBSCAN and Hierarchical approaches have not given positive result for our dataset. The result of DBSCAN is given in Table 2. The largest cluster contain 170 instances with *epsilon* > .1 and *minpoint* > 2 where other clusters contains <20 instances. The un-clustered point's increases rapidly with min point values. So, DBSCAN and hierarchical clustering algorithms are not selected to extend the work.

Table 2. The result of DBSCAN algorithm

Epsilon	Min point	No. of clusters	Unclustered instances
0.9	1	3142	0
	2	211	2932
	3	26	3302
	4	6	3362
	5	3	3374
	6	1	3384
	7	1	3384
0.5	7	1	3385
0.1	7	1	3398
1.1	7	1	170
1.5	7	1	11
2	7	1	4

Different clustering index i.e. DB-Index and Dunn index are calculated to obtain best clustering algorithm. The results are given in Table 3. So, the results of K-mean algorithm are selected with respect to rest two clustering methodologies. But, there is a challenge to select the value of K in K-mean algorithm. The validity index and within cluster sum of square (%) values are highlighted in Table 3. It is clearly shown that within cluster sum of square (%) is 81.9%. which is significantly higher due to $K = 12$. So, it is best to select $K = 12$ in K-mean clustering. FuncAssociate tool is used to functionally annotate genes of a cluster. The disease is a functional impact of a gene. The objective is to control disease by controlling the deadliest functionality of macromolecules of the network. The functional annotations of the genes are crucial to calculate of a cluster. Similar set of genes is lies in a cluster and consider the probability (p) value is the threshold parameter.

FuncAssociate 2.1 to estimate and select most suitable set of cluster with threshold parameter (p) value initially set to 5×10^{-6}. Consider, If $K := m$, where $2 \leq m \leq n$ and clusters are $c_1, c_2, c_3, \ldots\ldots, c_m$ with and select C_{select} by evaluating max value of C^{total}.

Table 3. Results of cluster validity index, Betweenness and within cluster sum of square (%).

K	DB-Index	Dunn Index	Betweenness	Within cluster sum of square (%)
2	.7076726	.06418438	639443235721	57.5%
3	.974422	.01665936	771000403894	69.3%
4	1.150246	.02053786	833651531760	74.9%
5	1.350844	.01239572	859085590712	77.2%
6	1.58838	.009013059	872033206894	78.3%
7	1.390051	.009013059	878166630719	78.9%
8	1.554123	.006175468	885553473106	79.6%
9	1.574713	.005762412	901540501393	81.0%
10	1.644092	.005762412	901604166744	81.0%
11	1.729012	.006321075	9.06351e+11	81.4%
12	1.931203	.005446997	911496062959	81.9%
13	2.116782	.004956644	9.10089e+11	81.8%

$$c_1^{count}, c_2^{count}, \ldots\ldots, c_m^{count} \text{ values} \geq p$$
$$C_m^{total} = \sum_{i=1}^{m} c_i^{count} \qquad (11)$$
$$C_{select} = Max\left(C_K^{total}\right), \text{where} K = 1, 2, .., n$$

Few samples of the results are given below in Table 4. The cumulative sum due to $K = 11$ are 213 using Eq (11). So, depending on the functional annotation select $K = 11$ of K-mean clustering.

Table 4. Results of FuncAssociate. Where CLi: cluster with index no i.

CL 11	CL 10	CL 9	CL 8	CL 7	CL 6	CL 5	CL 4	CL 3	CL 2	CL 1	CL 0	Total	Avg
			42	2	7	9	–	99	15	16	11	201	22.33
		19	47	2	7	—	10	76	5	1	33	200	20
	7	6	31	2	19	—	6	89	3	9	41	213	19.36
–	7	4	46	8	13	—	11	58	4	6	37	194	17.63

In the result of functional annotation, it is observed that the annotation of CL_4, CL_5, CL_5 genes is not possible due to value of $K = 9$, 10 and 11 . So, it can be said that the set of genes are less important in our selected set of significance genes. The set is: LGALS4, CTSE, TFF3, CEACAM5, TM4SF3, TFF1, GPX2, SPINK1, HSAPO-MUCN etc. The mutual information (MI) is a measure to quantify the non-linear dependency between two random variables. The most popular strategies for estimating mutual information values are based on a discretized model for continuous data [35]. Entropy and mutual information both are frequently used in information theory. Both properties are robustly used in the similarity of the genes. The gene expression dataset are normalized using Eq. (5) and joint entropy is estimated to obtain mutual information using Eqs. (6–8). There are total 457 entries against the gene NULL in the considered human lung cancer dataset. One of the significance outcomes of mutual information is that similarity mapping is possible with respect to a threshold value. The results predict that the NULL is mapped in between RAB9P40, UREB1 and SLC6A14. These prediction helps to increase the accuracy in prediction of controller of a network. After mutual information calculation, the obtained sets of genes are considered as most similar set of genes. Details of result are given in Mutual-info. Different categories of network association are collected from GeneMANIA and edge weight, node weights are calculated using Eqs. (9–10) to generate rank list of the genes present in same network. Rank list is studied to predict controller set of the network. Different centrality measures of genes in the network are also calculated. The set of the controller are predicted depending on the probability cutoff value. The details of our predicted results are given in Predicted _result. Our prediction is validated with the result of controller genes set using centrality. The CytoNCA [36] tool is used to get different category of centrality. Details of results of CytoNCA are given below in Result_cytoNCA. The sample result of validation is given below in Table 5 and Fig. 4. Details of results are given in Contl_validate.

Table 5. Validate the predicted results.

Cluster	Unique Gene	Controller predicted using CytoNCA	Controller predicted using our approach	Identical Genes	Odd Genes	Newly predicted genes
C8	55	31	35	22	9	12
C3	61	37	42	28	8	13
C2	23	10	14	9	1	5
C0	29	12	18	12	0	6

Result set of predicted genes are also validated with NCBI literature survey. Details of validation are given in Validate_NCBI. In our predicted approach, the precision value is 88.07% with F score value .881as stated in Table 6.

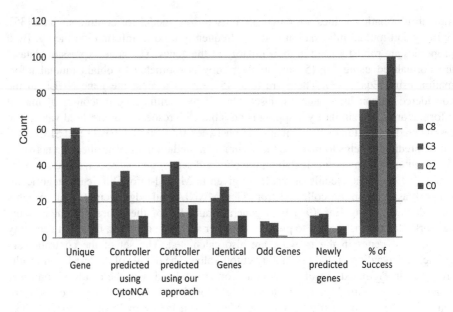

Fig. 4. Result of validation of sample clusters

Table 6. Accuracy statistics of our methodology

Generated statistics of our methodology	Scores/Values
Total genes count rank list	**109**
Responsible genes count in NCBI	**109**
Common genes	**96**
Precision	**88.07%**
Recall	**88.07%**
F score	**0.881**

4 Conclusion

Lung cancer is an alarming threat to normal living traits. The deadliest threat can only be restricted through the prediction of essential macromolecules. In our work, 7129 genes are involved in the dataset out of which 3556 variant set of genes have been extracted using two-tailed T-test. Then both mutual information and clustering algorithms are used to predict most similar set of genes. Interactions of those similar set genes have been studied using String DB and Gene Mania from where the most reliable genes have been retained using node and edge weight. 109 most reliable genes are finally identified as diver nodes or controller genes which can play an essential role in lung cancer.

Our proposed methodology achieves an overall accuracy of 88% which can be further improved through various other statistical approaches in our future work.

References

1. Blackhall, L., Hill, D.J.: On the structural controllability of networks of linear systems. IFAC Proc. Vol. (IFAC-PapersOnline) **43** 245–250 (2010)
2. Liu, Y.Y., Slotine, J.J., Barabasi, A.L.: Control centrality and hierarchical structure in complex networks. PLoS One **7**, e44459 (2012)
3. Müller, F.-J., Schuppert, A.: Few inputs can reprogram biological networks. Nature **478**, E4 (2011)
4. Wang, W.X., Ni, X., Lai, Y.C., Grebogi, C.: Optimizing controllability of complex networks by minimum structural perturbations. Phys. Rev. E Stat. Nonlinear, Soft Matter Phys. **85**, 026115 (2012)
5. Mesbahi, M., Egerstedt, M.: Graph theoretic methods in multiagent networks (2010)
6. Nepusz, T., Vicsek, T.: Controlling edge dynamics in complex networks. Nat. Phys. **8**, 568–573 (2012)
7. Cowan, N.J., Chastain, E.J., Vilhena, D.A., Freudenberg, J.S., Bergstrom, C.T.: Nodal dynamics, not degree distributions, determine the structural controllability of complex networks. PLoS One **7**, e38398 (2012)
8. Liu, X., Pan, L.: Identifying driver nodes in the human signaling network using structural controllability analysis. IEEE/ACM Trans. Comput. Biol. Bioinform. **12**, 467–472 (2015)
9. Nacher, J.C., Akutsu, T.: Analysis on controlling complex networks based on dominating sets. J. Phys. Conf. Ser. **410**, 12104 (2013)
10. Jeong, H., Mason, S.P., Barabási, a L., Oltvai, Z.N.: Lethality and centrality in protein networks. Nature **411**, 41–42 (2001)
11. Liu, Y.-Y., Slotine, J.-J., Barabási, A.-L.: Controllability of complex networks. Nature **473**, 167–173 (2011)
12. Wuchty, S.: Controllability in protein interaction networks. Proc. Nat. Acad. Sci. U.S.A **111**, 7156–7160 (2014)
13. Zhang, X.F., Ou-Yang, L., Zhu, Y., Wu, M.Y., Dai, D.Q.: Determining minimum set of driver nodes in protein-protein interaction networks. BMC Bioinform. **16**, 146 (2015)
14. Barabasi, A.-L., Oltvai, Z.N.Z.N., Barabási, A.-L.: Network biology: understanding the cell's functional organization. Nat. Rev. Genet. **5**, 101–113 (2004)
15. Yu, H., et al.: High-quality binary protein interaction map of the yeast interactome network. Science **322**, 104–110 (2008)
16. Freeman, L.C.: A Set of Measures of Centrality Based on Betweenness (1977). http://www.jstor.org/stable/3033543?origin=crossref
17. Vinayagam, A., et al.: Controllability analysis of the directed human protein interaction network identifies disease genes and drug targets. Proc. Nat. Acad. Sci. U.S.A. **113**(18), 4979–4981 (2016). 1603992113
18. Warde-Farley, D., et al.: The GeneMANIA prediction server: biological network integration for gene prioritization and predicting gene function. Nucleic Acids Res. **38**, W214–W220 (2010)
19. Holmes, G., Donkin, A., Witten, I.H.: WEKA: a machine learning workbench. In: Proceedings of ANZIIS 1994 - Australian New Zealnd Intelligent Information Systems Conference, pp. 357–361 (1994)
20. Venables, W.N., Smith, D.M.: R core team: an introduction to R. User Man. **2**, 99 (2015)
21. Berriz, G.F., King, O.D., Bryant, B., Sander, C., Roth, F.P.: Characterizing gene sets with FuncAssociate. Bioinformatics **19**, 2502–2504 (2003)
22. Liu, Y.-Y., Slotine, J.-J., Barabási, A.-L.: Observability of complex systems. Proc. Nat. Acad. Sci. U.S.A. **110**, 2460–2465 (2013)

23. Basler, G., Nikoloski, Z., Larhlimi, A., Barabási, A.L., Liu, Y.Y.: Control of fluxes in metabolic networks. Genome Res. **26**, 956–968 (2016)
24. Bansal, M., Belcastro, V., Ambesi-Impiombato, A., di Bernardo, D.: How to infer gene networks from expression profiles. Mol. Syst. Biol. **3**, 78 (2007)
25. Pandey, G., Kumar, V., Steinbach, M.: Computational approaches for protein function prediction a survey. Pediatrics **108**, 197–205 (2006)
26. Zur, H., Tuller, T.: New universal rules of eukaryotic translation initiation fidelity. PLoS Comput. Biol. **9**, e1003136 (2013)
27. Walther, C., Lüdeke, M., Janssen, P.: Cluster analysis to understand socio-ecological systems: a guideline. PIK Rep. 2–90 (2012)
28. Davies, D.L., Bouldin, D.W.: A cluster separation measure. IEEE Trans. Pattern Anal. Mach. Intell. **1**, 224–227 (1979)
29. Dunn, J.C.: Well-separated clusters and optimal fuzzy partitions. J. Cybern. **4**, 95–104 (1974)
30. Gola, D., Mahachie John, J.M., Van Steen, K., König, I.R.: A roadmap to multifactor dimensionality reduction methods. Brief. Bioinform. **17**, 293–308 (2016)
31. Gray, R.M.: Entropy and information theory (2011)
32. Casini, H., Huerta, M., Myers, R.C., Yale, A.: Mutual information and the F-theorem. J. High Energy Phys. **2015**(10), 3 (2015)
33. Wang, S., Wu, F.: Detecting overlapping protein complexes in PPI networks based on robustness. Proteome Sci. **11**, S18 (2013)
34. Beer, D.G., et al.: Gene-expression profiles predict survival of patients with lung adenocarcinoma. Nat. Med. **8**, 816–824 (2002)
35. de Matos Simoes, R., Emmert-Streib, F.: Influence of statistical estimators of mutual information and data heterogeneity on the inference of gene regulatory networks. PLoS One **6**(12), e29279 (2011)
36. Tang, Y., Li, M., Wang, J., Pan, Y., Wu, F.X.: CytoNCA: a cytoscape plugin for centrality analysis and evaluation of protein interaction networks. BioSystems **127**, 67–72 (2015)

Biometric Template Generation Framework Using Retinal Vascular Structure

Nilanjana Dutta Roy[1(✉)], Sushmita Goswami[1], Suchismita Goswami[1], and Arindam Biswas[2]

[1] Department of Computer Science and Engineering,
Institute of Engineering and Management, Kolkata, India
nilanjanaduttaroy@gmail.com, sushmita.g24@gmail.com,
suchismita.g24@gmail.com
[2] Department of Information Technology,
Indian Institute of Engineering Science and Technology, Shibpur, India
barindam@gmail.com

Abstract. Biometric identification devices depend on some characteristics of human body such as face, fingerprint, hand palm, eye etc. Among all these features, vascular structure based retinal biometry provides the most secure person identification system. In this paper, we propose biometric authentication framework with some existing and unique features present on human retinal vascular structure. The approach begins with segmentation from colored fundus images, followed by selecting unique features like center of optic disc (OD), macula, the distance between OD and macula, bifurcation points and their angles. A 96 bytes digital template is prepared then against each image by concatenating every selected features and finally, every template is compared with each other for finding dissimilarity. The study shows around 92% accuracy in template preparation and matching on all the images of DRIVE database.

Keywords: Biometric authentication · Image registration ·
Image verification · Retinal template

1 Introduction

Study of recognizing individuals by their unique existing biological features is biometry. It is conquering the world by overcoming the difficulties in traditional authentication system. Reliable biological parts like face, voice, hand palm, fingerprint, iris, retina etc., are normally used as biometric features. Retinal vascular structure is unique for every individual and remains intact throughout the life span of a human being [3] except any surgical abnormalities. It is not easy to tamper without user's cooperation because it is anatomically situated under the layer of conjunctiva of human eye. Moreover, vessels structure can not

© Springer Nature Singapore Pte Ltd. 2019
J. K. Mandal et al. (Eds.): CICBA 2018, CCIS 1031, pp. 245–256, 2019.
https://doi.org/10.1007/978-981-13-8581-0_20

be changed through plastic surgery [11]. Also, as per the version of [12], retinal structures are the most secure features as it can not be imitated. And this
is employed in high security environment like nuclear research centres, weapon
factories and areas where extreme security measures are needed [3].

Biometric authentication work has gained it's velocity with the invention of
new techniques by many scientists in last few years. An automated personal
identification system was developed in 2011 which was able to remove retinal
degeneration in an image. It was able to handle the rotation, scaling and translation factors also [3]. In some of the retina recognition work, segmentation and
vessel detection played major roles [13] to [18]. Bifurcation and crossover points
are also considered as landmarks for retinal registration in [19]. In this paper,
we propose biometric authentication framework with some existing and unique
features present on human retinal vascular structure. 96 bytes digital templates
are the final outcome of this work against each image by concatenating every
detected features. Finally, every template is compared with each other for finding
dissimilarities between them. The study shows around 92% accuracy in template
preparation and matching on all the images of DRIVE database [10].

This paper is organized as follows. Section 1 is the introduction and Sect. 2
describes the total framework which includes feature selection, template generation and matching. Results are shown in Sect. 3 and Sect. 4 draws the final
conclusion and future work.

2   Proposed Method for Biometric Template Generation Framework

Following five major phases, preprocessing, segmentation, feature selection, template creation and template matching, the digital retinal templates are created
against every image from DRIVE database [10] (Fig. 1).

2.1   Image Preprocessing and Segmentation

The fundus images from DRIVE [10] database are captured by Canon CR5
non-mydriatic 3 CCD cameras with a 45 degree FOV for medical imaging. The
images have to pass through few image enhancement and preprocessing operations. Grayscale conversion of the original RGB images is applied at the initial
stage of preprocessing. Image sharpening using CLAHE is the next step, followed by Otsu thresholding [1] to transform the image into a good shape. Then
2-D median filtering is used for de-noising and finally, a smooth textured binary
image is presented. Figure 2 illustrates the stages for segmentation.

2.2   Feature Selection

Localization of OD Center. Optic disc (OD) center localization is used as
a significant feature here in retinal biometric template formation. The distance
between OD center (within the white bright region of fundus images) and macula

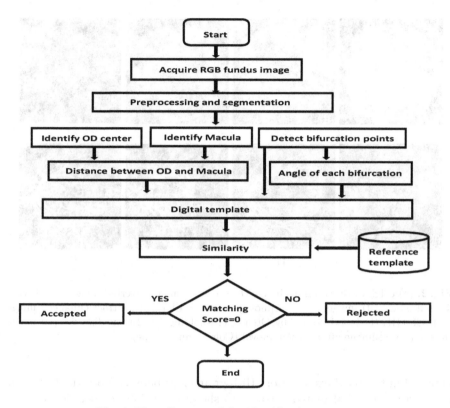

Fig. 1. Flow diagram of the identification system

is a measurable feature in retinal template. This robust method will successfully work with low resolution images, in presence of pathological regions and even in the images with cotton wool spots and exudates. The complete process has been described in Fig. 3. It is seen in binary images, that major blood vessels near optic disc often bifurcate and cross each other which further form few closed polygonal structures, called 'rings'. We are considering these rings as a trademark to locate the optic disc in this method. Sometimes, tiny dendrites also form such rings which carry redundant information. So it is required to remove dendrites to keep the rings near OD intact.

A morphological thinning operation [2] is applied on the segmented fundus image to get a thinned, skeleton view of it, shown in Fig. 3(b). To remove the tiny vessels, width [4] of all the existing vessels are measured. Any vessel, having width less than 5 pixels (threshold used in this method), is a dendrite and it is removed from the original segmented image, see Fig. 3(c). Removing vessels from terminal points would end up at any closed polygonal rings. A white pixel whose seven neighbors are black in a 3 × 3 scanning window, is assumed as terminal point in this method. Terminal points are removed from the thinned image by making them 0 and it is being compared with the histogram of thinned image

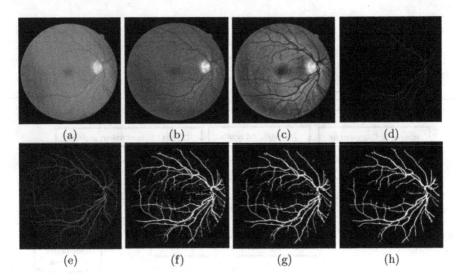

Fig. 2. (a) original RGB fundus image (b) green channel converted image (c) CLAHE filtered image (d) image after morphological bottom hat (e) contrast enhanced image with CLAHE (f) blood vessels by Otsu's thresholding (g) 2-D median filtered image (h) segmented image after noise removal (Color figure online)

obtained in the previous iteration. Histogram error between both the images at every iteration is calculated. Error zero shows the similarity between images, whereas some error indicates scope for further removal. This process continues till no end points are left and the rings are found on images.

Formation of Convex Hull from Junction Points Near OD. The image with only rings is filled up then by a region filling algorithm [5], see Fig. 3(f). A 3 × 3 scanning window moves around horizontal direction to determine a polygon with maximum number of single lines or neighbors connected with it. The single lines, attached with the region are now removed. Finally, the junction points [6] within the bounded region are found. We now try to convert those scattered junction points into a convex hull [7] or minimal convex polygonal (MCP) shape to locate the centroid of the hull.

Centroid of MCP as Center of OD. For the centroid of convex hull with N vertices and $N - 1$ line segments, the area is calculated by the formula 1 where (x_i, y_i) to (x_N, y_N) are the line segments and $i = 0$ to $N - 1$.

$$A = \frac{1}{2} \sum_{i=1}^{N-1} (x_i y_{i+1} - x_{i+1} y_i) \tag{1}$$

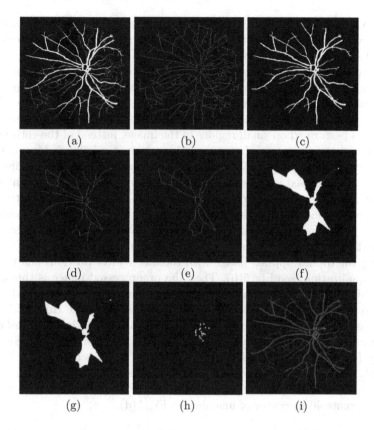

Fig. 3. (a) Segmented fundus image (b) Thinned image obtained after applying morphological function (c) Image after removing the dendrites (d) Image after a few iteration (e) After extracting the loops in the image (f) After applying area fill function to bridge the holes (g) Further removal of lines connecting the loops (h) All junction points detected (i) Optic disc located

Area further helps to calculate the centroid of the bounded region where (x_N, y_N) is assumed to be same as (x_0, y_0).

$$C_x = \frac{1}{6A} \sum_{i=1}^{N-1} (x_i + x_{i+1})(x_i y_{i+1} - x_{i+1} y_i) \tag{2}$$

and

$$C_y = \frac{1}{6A} \sum_{i=1}^{N-1} (y_i + y_{i+1})(x_i y_{i+1} - x_{i+1} y_i) \tag{3}$$

The point (C_x, C_y) is finally considered as the center of OD in the proposed method.

Macula Center Detection. The macula in human eye is a dark avascular area near the center of the retina which is responsible for central and high-resolution color vision in enough light [8]. It is also a significant feature in this research because we have considered the distance between macula and OD as a parameter in forming retinal template. Macula detection starts by converting the image into green channelled image (Fig. 4(a)). To redistribute the non-uniform intensity on the image for image enhancement, CLAHE is used (Fig. 4(b)). The enhancement operation is performed on small regions of the image, instead of the entire image at a time and thus contrast of every smaller region is enhanced. Morphological tophat operation, which is a morphological opening operation using a disc of 50 pixels in radius, is used later to show the difference between an input image and its opening. As a result of this operation (Fig. 5(a)), bright retinal structures like optic disc, possible presence of exudates and reflection artifacts are removed and the darker structures like blood vessels, macula, fovea and haemorrhages remain same. At this stage, the contrast of the image is enhanced again using CLAHE by adding the tophat applied image with the image after previous adaptive histogram equalization, see Fig. 5(b). Then the preprocessed image is thresholded with OTSU's thresholding by keeping the information intact below the threshold value and giving the rest of the image the same value as the threshold. Thus, cluster based algorithm is used to perform clustering based image thresholding and the preprocessed gray scale image is reduced into binary image, shown in Fig. 5(c). From the detected OD center, the binary image is then traced horizontally with a 50×50 window to find a cluster of maximum concentration of black pixels. Again, forming a convex hull out of these points, defined earlier, helps in finding its centroid as center of macula, see Fig. 5(d).

Distance Between Macula and OD. The distance between macula and optic disc is considered as a feature in this research. So, distance calculation is done by

$$De = \sqrt{(x-s)^2 + (y-t)^2} \tag{4}$$

where (x, y) and (s, t) are the center of OD and center of macula respectively.

Distinct Bifurcation Point Extraction. In a segmented and thinned binary image, distinct bifurcation calculation method is able to identify all possible bifurcation points. Within a 3×3 scanning window, in a clockwise trip, objects are identified by connected component labeling [2]. Non vascular regions are labeled by their region numbers and within the scanning window, any structure with exactly three regions are considered. During this boundary wise trip for exactly three regions, no repetition of the same region numbers except source and destination, is concluded as distinct bifurcation point [6]. Figure 6(a) is the original RGB image and Fig. 6(b) shows distinct bifurcation points detected in the fundus image.

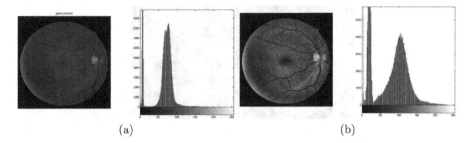

(a)   (b)

Fig. 4. (a) green channeled image and its histogram (b) CLAHE enhanced image and its histogram

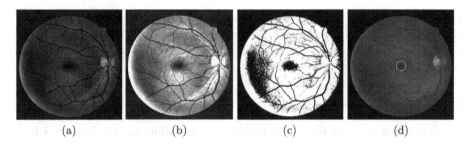

(a)   (b)   (c)   (d)

Fig. 5. (a) image after tophat operation (b) contrast enhanced image (c) binarized image (d) final detection of macula

Bifurcation Angle Calculation. Any vessel bifurcates into two more child vessels and three consecutive angles are formed around each bifurcation point. The angular difference between two child vessels is an acute angle in a total 360^0 angular span [9]. To find the angles between parent and child vessels, a 3×3 scanning window is set upon each bifurcation point to mark three consecutive end points. A white pixel in the centerlined image is marked as a current end point (x_i, y_i) $(1 \leq i \leq 3)$ from the bifurcation point (x, y) within a 3×3 scanning window clockwise and a straight line is drawn between them. The process continues for all three vessels upto an empirically tested value of 18 pixel distance from the bifurcation point. Then, three tangents were drawn between bifurcation point and other three end points on each vessel by following the Eq. 5.

$$m = \tan = \frac{(y_2 - y_1)}{(x_2 - x_1)} \tag{5}$$

where (x_1, y_1) is the bifurcation point and (x_2, y_2) is one of the three points found on other vessels.

Finally, the angle between two consecutive vessels is found by the Eq. 6.

$$\theta = \tan^{-1} \frac{m_1 - m_2}{1 + (m_1 * m_2)} \tag{6}$$

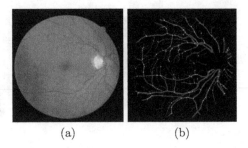

(a)   (b)

Fig. 6. (a) original image (b) distinct bifurcation points detected

where θ is the angle between two tangents and m_1 and m_2 are the gradients of two tangents respectively. An acute angle is found here, θ_1 which is less than the addition of other two angles, θ_2 and θ_3. Now, minimum of these three angles is considered as the bifurcation angle in this research.

2.3 Template Generation

To accomplish the goal for digital template preparation, unique features which bear significance in it, are identified. Features are appended one after another to get the 96 bytes template. The significance of 96 bytes template could raise a probability of uniqueness among 2^{96} people which is commendable. An illustrated example is shown here for template generation with imaginary values. Considering OD-macula relative distance as 10, total 2 bifurcation points and their angles as $(100, 200), 80°$ and $(300, 400), 45°$, the generated template is 101002008030040045. For any image, due to more number of bifurcation points, the extra information are truncated if the template exceeds 96 bytes. Also, 0 padding at the right side till limit is allowed in case of deficiency of information.

2.4 Template Matching

When a user registers his retina for a secured system, a digital retinal template is created against him and stored in system's database for future reference. To use the system further, digital retinal template is created for the user following the same method and matched with the registered one. Matching score $0(+5)$ indicates the authenticity of the user whereas some positive scores other than the value prove the user as imposter.

3 Results and Discussion

Some of the detected results on OD-macula distance is shown in Table 1. Detected bifurcation points and their accuracy measures [6] are shown in Table 2. The experimental results are comparable to some of the other existing methods. Using vessel topological structure, 95% of accuracy has been achieved in [20] and

Table 1. Distance between OD and macula (in pixels)

Image	OD center	Macula center	Distance
2	(250,488)	(294,272)	220
3	(289,82)	(293,291)	209
5	(268,80)	(293,282)	203

Table 2. Performance evaluation of detected bifurcation points on few images of DRIVE

	Image 12	Image 26	Image 19	Image 3
Actual bifurcations present	73	64	42	84
Detected bifurcation points	75	63	42	83
Correctly detected points	73	63	41	83
Bifurcation points not detected	0	1	1	1
Incorrect	2	0	0	0
Sensitivity	1	1	.976	.988
Specificity	0	0	0	0
Accuracy	97.33%	98.41%	97.6%	98.8%

based on bifurcation point calculation, a novel approach to generate biometric template [21] has achieved 100% recognition rates for the DRIVE database.

Table 3 shows some of the digital retinal templates for the images from DRIVE database, generated by following the above mentioned method.

Table 3. Digital retinal template generation

Image	Retinal template
1	82247205642984988264849940487100247108101248841032405910420477104241151052449010938911711522675
11	632542214820876541899554200108572005566378506817127701732974396297539759784032180156278115572844
22	471284190543204910332982128384881374916313910093155379721563809616821569169206101170385621722309
30	4692631858036060853659586264479831670101298511023051091042184610931068109442861121954616041669 17
37	510282225733515990141699042163912799212019090121189921223588912617088127351701291907134313371463

After a comparison between all the images of the databases, no two images are found to be identical, a glimpse of that is shown in Table 4. Hence, the

Table 4. Similarity measurement between images

	Image1	Image11	Image22	Image30	Image37
Image1	0	74	74	67	73
Image11	74	0	75	79	77
Image22	74	75	0	69	71
Image30	67	79	69	0	73
Image37	73	77	71	73	0

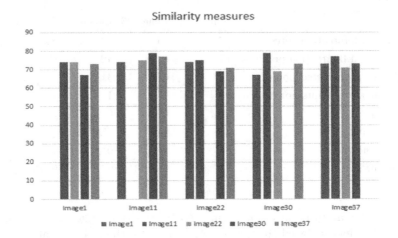

Fig. 7. Graph shows no similarity found between images except same image

extracted features are claimed as reliable and thus the method is also proved as a robust one (Fig. 7).

4   Conclusion and Future Work

To provide best possible security in less time is a challenging task against vulnerable threats. Biometric authentication using retinal vascular structure thoughtfully does this work. Identification of reliable and unique retinal features is an essential task in making digital retinal template. In this research, few features which are unique and prominent, like center of OD, center of macula, their distance, bifurcation points and their angles have been identified as parameters for preparing retinal template. The detected geometric locations and values are added together respectively to form digital template. As each of the detected features is a unique identifier, adding all of them together strengthens the final template. String matching algorithm using Levenstein's edit distance calculation [22] finally checks every generated template from the DRIVE database. Experimental results, showing no 0 match value found after the calculation, are indicative to the uniqueness of all the images from DRIVE database. In future, we will only focuses on the ring network made by the major blood vessels in a retina. Tiny, disconnected dendrites will be removed at the beginning to avoid redundant information and chances of false detection. Finding bifurcation points and their angles in only ring network will reduce the searching time and complexity as well.

References

1. Otsu, N.: A threshold selection method from gray-level histograms. IEEE Trans. Syst. Man Cybern. **9**(1), 6266 (1979)
2. Gonzalez, R.C., Woods, R.E., Eddins, S.L.: Digital Image Processing using Matlab, 3rd edn. Prentice-Hall, Upper Saddle River (2006)
3. Kose, C., Ikibas, C.: A personal identification system using retinal vasculature in retinal fundus images. Expert Syst. Appl. **38**(11), 13670–13681 (2011)
4. Goswami, S., Goswami, S., De, S.: Automatic measurement and analysis of vessel width in retinal fundus image. In: Mandal, J., Satapathy, S., Sanyal, M., Bhateja, V. (eds.) Proceedings of the First International Conference on Intelligent Computing and Communication. Advances in Intelligent Systems and Computing, vol. 458, pp. 451–458. Springer, Singapore (2017). https://doi.org/10.1007/978-981-10-2035-3_46
5. Hearn, D., Baker, M.P.: Computer Graphics, 3rd edn, Paperback publishers (2003)
6. Dutta Roy, N., Goswami, S., Goswami, S., De, S., Biswas, A.: Extraction of distinct bifurcation points from retinal fundus images. In: Mandal, J., Satapathy, S., Sanyal, M., Bhateja, V. (eds.) Proceedings of the First International Conference on Intelligent Computing and Communication. AISC, vol. 458, pp. 443–450. Springer, Singapore (2016). https://doi.org/10.1007/978-981-10-2035-3_45
7. Graham, R.L.: An efficient algorithm for determining the convex hull of a finite planar set. Inf. Process. Lett. **1**, 132–133 (1972)
8. Lu, S., Lim, J.H.: Automatic macula detection from retinal images by a line operator. In: IEEE ICIP. pp. 4073–4076 (2010)
9. Roy, N.D., , Biswas, A.: Detection of bifurcation angles in a retinal fundus image, In: 8th International Conference on Advances in Pattern Recognition (ICAPR), ISI, Kolkata, India (2015)
10. The DRIVE database, ìImage sciences institute, university medical center utrecht, î The Netherlands (2007). https://www.isi.uu.nl/Research/Databases/DRIVE/index.html
11. Jafariani, H., Abhishami, H., Moein, M.: A new approach for human identification based on retina image. In: proceedings of the 11th Conference of Iran Biomedical Engineering, Amir Kabir University of Technology (2003)
12. Nanni, L., Lumini, A.: A supervised method to discriminate between impostors and genuine in biometry. Expert Syst. Appl. **36**(7), 10401–10407 (2009)
13. Staal, J., Abramoff, M.D., Niemeijer, M., Viergever, M.A., Ginneken, V.B.: Ridge-based vessel segmentation in color images of the retina. IEEE Trans. Med. Imag. **23**(4), 501–509 (2004)
14. Soares, J.V.B., Leandro, J.J.G., Cesar, R.M., Jelinek, H.F., Cree, M.J.: Retinal vessel segmentation using the 2-D gabor wavelet and supervised classification. IEEE Trans. Med. Imaging **2**(9), 1214–1222 (2006)
15. Yen, G.G., Leong, W.F.: A sorting system for hierarchical grading of diabetic fundus images, a preliminary study. IEEE Trans. Inf. Technol. Biomed. **12**(1), 118–130 (2008)

16. Chaudhuri, S., Chatterjee, S., Katz, N., Nelson, M., Goldbaum, M.: Detection of blood vessels in retinal images using two-dimensional matched filters. IEEE Trans. Med. Imag. **8**(3), 263–269 (1989)
17. Marn, D., Aquino, A., Emilio, G.A.M., Bravo, J.M.: A new supervised method for blood vessel segmentation in retinal images by using gray-level and moment invariants-based features. IEEE Trans. Med. Imaging **30**(1), 146–158 (2011)
18. Hoover, A., Kouznetsova, V., Goldbaum, M.: Locating blood vessels in retinal images by piecewise threshold probing of a matched filter response. IEEE Trans. Med. Imag. **19**(3), 203–210 (2000)
19. Ortega, M., Penedo, M.G., Rouco, J., Barreira, N., Carreira, M.J.: Retinal verification using a feature points-based biometric pattern. EURASIP J. Adv. Sig. Process. **2009**, 1–13 (2009). https://doi.org/10.1155/2009/235746. Article ID 235746
20. Yavuz, Z., Köse, C.: A retinal image identification method using blood vessel topological information. In: Medical Technologies National Congress (TIPTEKNO). IEEE (2017)
21. Pabitha, M., Latha, L.: Efficient approach for retinal biometric template security and person authentication using noninvertible constructions. Int. J. Comput. Appl. **69**(4), 28–34 (2013)
22. Fiscus, J.G., Ajot, J., Radde, N., Laprun, C.: Multiple dimension Levenshtein edit distance calculations for evaluating automatic speech recognition systems during simultaneous speech. In: Proceedings of the LREC (2006)

Graph Theoretical Characterization of Retinal Vascular Network–Finding Minimum Cost Spanning Tree

Nilanjana Dutta Roy[1(✉)] and Arindam Biswas[2]

[1] Department of Computer Science and Engineering,
Institute of Engineering and Management, Kolkata, India
nilanjanaduttaroy@gmail.com
[2] Department of Information Technology,
Indian Institute of Engineering Science and Technology, Shibpur, Howrah, India
barindam@gmail.com

Abstract. Representing a retinal vascular network into a graph is a compulsive and yet challenging task. Analysis on graph representation of human retina helps in person identification and detection of ocular diseases also. In this paper, the authors tried to find similarities between a retinal vascular network and a graph and later the minimum cost spanning tree (MCST) has been generated from the plotted graph of retinal vascular network. For simplicity in plotting the graph, the images are passed through several stages of thin and tiny vessel removal process after segmentation. Then, its terminal points and distinct bifurcation points have been calculated to mark them as nodes of the graph. Distance between each consecutive bifurcation point reveals the path cost or weight of the adjacent nodes or edges of the undirected graph. Finally, by applying Prim's algorithm, minimum cost spanning tree has been formulated for the desired result out of the retinal graph. Experiments are done on a publicly available database, DRIVE and experimental results are appreciable and comparable to other standard methods available in literature.

Keywords: Graph · Minimum cost spanning tree ·
Retinal vascular network · Edges · Nodes · Characterization

1 Introduction

Human retina shares a distinct vascular network pattern. Contemplating retinal vascular structure with a graph is a challenging task and analyzing this can exhibit many directions of person identification and ocular disease detection. In this work, considering vascular structure as a connected graph, we try to reveal a minimum cost spanning tree (MCST) which will cover every node in less cost. This will be effective in faster image matching and helpful for the ophthalmologists to detect ocular diseases within a small section of the retina.

© Springer Nature Singapore Pte Ltd. 2019
J. K. Mandal et al. (Eds.): CICBA 2018, CCIS 1031, pp. 257–266, 2019.
https://doi.org/10.1007/978-981-13-8581-0_21

In this method, our primary focus is on searching few existing features of the retinal vessel tree which resembles a graph. Based on this assumption that there are few similar characteristics between a graph and a retinal vascular network, we have accomplished the experiments successfully on a publicly available database called DRIVE [1]. The terminal points of the vessels in a retinal vascular network and its bifurcation points are considered as the nodes of the graph.

The three principal phases of the approach are graph generation, graph analysis and finding minimum cost spanning tree from the generated graph. The method has been initiated by extracting a graph from the retinal vascular network, and then it decides the type of each junction which are labelled as nodes of the generated graph. Weight or cost of each adjacent nodes has been calculated and finally, based on the calculated cost, a minimum cost spanning tree has been drawn out of the entire vessel network. The detailed phases of the proposed method are described below.

2   Methodology

2.1   Graph Generation

In this method, a graph has been defined as a representation of the vascular network, where each node is denoted by bifurcation points and the end points of the vascular tree and each edge corresponds to a vessel distance (in pixel) between two bifurcation points. For generating the graph, few corresponding steps of the algorithm have been followed. A segmented image have been considered as an input of this algorithm. A rigid width calculation is performed to decide for a cut off threshold [12] to eliminate the tiny, thin and below threshold vessels. Next, a centerline calculation is accomplished upon the vascular network with existing major and thick vessels. Primary focus was given on finding the vessel's end points and on various bifurcations. Finally, the graph has been generated from the thinned image by making all the bifurcations and end points as its nodes and their distances as edges, and some modifications are further applied to the graph.

Segmentation of Blood Vessels. Image segmentation is the fundamental, indispensable and yet challenging issue in digital image processing [4]. For extraction of various graph features, segmented result plays an important role. For segmentation of retinal vessels, the method proposed by [5] was used in this paper. There are three phases in the pixel processing-based method which has been used here. The initial phase is the pre-processing one, where the normalization of intensity is done by image background subtraction. In the next phase, using information provided by a set of four directional difference of Offset Gaussian filters, centerline pixels are detected. Vessel segmentation is the third phase where enhancement of the vessels are done to make binary maps by few morphological operations. Reconstruction is the phase to be completed later on. By adding centerlined images iteratively with reconstructed images, the final image is obtained [5]. The method shows an accuracy of 94.66% for DRIVE [1] database. The average sensitivity of the approach is 0.75 and specificity is 0.98 from DRIVE images [6].

End Point Selection. End points are also considered as a vital parameters for any graph analysis process. This is the end of any vessel in the vascular structure. End point selection is a very simple process for 8-connectivity for a single vessel. But for many cases, defined in Fig. 1, we have followed a separate mechanism. Connected component labelling [7] for object separation, followed by finding number of transitions in a circular trip throughout the outer boundary finishes the task of detecting end points in any vessel. Connected component labelling method makes our task more simpler in identifying an object in an image. We then apply a 3×3 mask which moves throughout the whole image and enhances the probability of finding potential end points. Any pixel is kept at the center of the masking window and filters this pixel as an end point if it follows certain pixel formation within the eight neighborhood connectivity. While scanning a single object with this mask along its boundary pixels in clockwise direction, if it finds a single transition of black-white-black (refer Fig. 2), it proceeds for a further check. A specific white point in the single object, around which almost 7 neighbor pixels are black, is therefore established as an end point of the vessel. For case 1 of Fig. 1, there is a single object identified by connected component labeling method and during a round trip of clockwise direction along the boundary, a single black-white-black transition is found. Then a neighborhood checking for each white pixel of the object is accomplished to determine the end point. But for cases 2, 3 and 4, there is a single object identified with more than one transitions. Hence, no end points could be established. For cases 5 and 6, there are two distinct

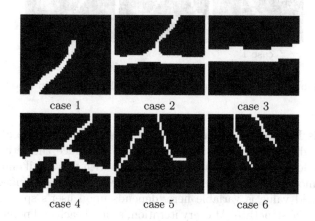

Fig. 1. Showing various occurrences of end points

Table 1. Showing transition based end point selection within a small window

Case	Objects	No. of transitions	No. of end points
Case 1	1	1	1
Case 2	1	3	0
Case 3	1	3	0
Case 4	1	4	0
Case 5	2	2	2
Case 6	2	2	2

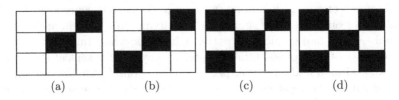

(a)   (b)   (c)   (d)

Fig. 2. Showing different phases of transactions (a) Single White-Black-White transition (b) two transitions (c) three transitions (d) four transitions

objects found and after accomplishing the above mentioned method, their end points are also specified (Table 1). Figure 3 exhibits the detected end points in few cropped samples and Fig. 4 shows detected outputs in retinal blood vessels.

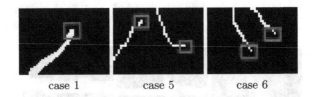

case 1   case 5   case 6

Fig. 3. Showing various occurrences of detected end points in blood vessels

Tiny Vessels Removal. To make the image ready for the proposal, they need to pass through few more preprocessing steps. To reduce the retinal vascular structure into least possible network, we continue with this small and thin vessel (dendrite) removal process. Here, the vessels with less than a specified threshold value (threshold value is variable here, depends upon user's specification) are removed from the structure. At every iteration, around each end point, width [12] of it is calculated to decide the major vessels. Width, having less value than a specified threshold, is decided as thin one and has been removed from that end point by making them same as background. Otherwise, the vessels remain intact and no further endpoint detection and removal of the vessel is carried out. These

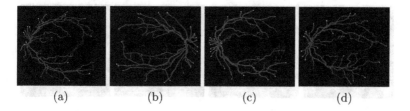

Fig. 4. Showing detected end points in retinal vascular network

iterations continue until no endpoint is found at which the vessels are holding less than the above mentioned threshold value. The wide vessels around the optic disc are thus identified as major vessels, ignoring the thin and tiny ones as they carry lesser amount of information. The process continues with eliminating all the small and tiny vessels from the whole image, leaving it as a ultimate image with least possible network. Figure 6 shows the images with major and wide vessels without small and tiny ones.

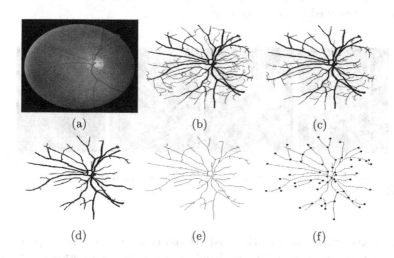

Fig. 5. Graph generation (a) Original image (b) Segmented image (c) Thin vessels removed (d) More thin and tiny vessels removal (e) Thinned image (f) Extracted graph

Centerlined Image. A thinning algorithm, described in [11] is used here to get the centerlined image on segmented result based on an iterative method. The algorithm works by removing outer pixels iteratively till the object reduces to a single threaded pixel. The centerlined image from the segmented result of Fig. 5(b) is shown in Fig. 5(e).

Distinct Bifurcation Point Selection. Next, the graph nodes are extracted from the centerlined image by finding its distinct bifurcation points, ignoring

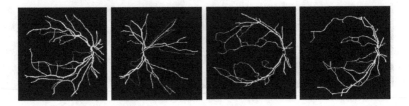

Fig. 6. Showing least possible fundus image structure with no dendrites

the crossovers. Here, a clockwise trip has been performed around the border of a masking window (around 15×15). Within the window boundary, different regions are identified using region growing algorithm [7]. During scanning, if there are exactly three regions found with no repetition of the same region except the source, it is then fixed as a bifurcation point [13]. On the other hand, four regions with no repetition of the same region during circular trip is concluded as crossing point. Here, to maintain the clarity of the method, any point with degree 3 has been considered. Figure 7 depicts the identified bifurcation points on dendrite removed vascular structure.

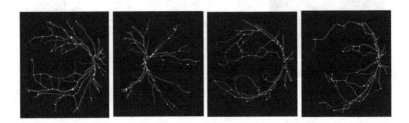

Fig. 7. Showing distinct bifurcation points on dendrite removed least possible vascular network

Graph Extraction and Path Cost Measurement. As the purpose of this work is to represent a weighted graph out of retinal vascular network, it is essential to measure the path length between two adjacent nodes (vessel segments). To accomplish this work, all the detected distinct bifurcation points are removed from the thinned result. Finally, we get an image with many separate components which are the segments of the vessels [3]. Next, each vessel part is traced by following its white background path and the process terminates with the black background to represent it as a connection between two nodes. Figure 5(f) shows the generated graph from the centerlined image of Fig. 5(e). The graph has several adjacent nodes, and at each node, several edges are connected and their path costs can also be measured. On the other hand, any two nodes can be connected by a given link. The number of adjacent nodes decide the degree of a node. If two nodes are connected by one link in a graph, they are called adjacent nodes then.

For better understanding of the concept, a portion from the original result has been taken out and its equivalent graph has been plotted. Please refer Fig. 8 for the plotted graph. As the graph comes as separate components after removal of all the bifurcation points, it becomes easier to trace it till the next node.

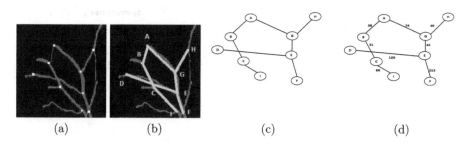

(a)   (b)   (c)   (d)

Fig. 8. Graph extraction (a) a small section of bifurcation detected retinal structure (b) adjacent nodes and edges pointed out (c) equivalent graph of the image (d) equivalent minimum cost spanning tree with source vertex A

Path cost has been measured depending on the difference between distinct bifurcation points on a specific vessel. Distance, in terms of number of pixels between two adjacent bifurcations, has been calculated by following the formula.

$$dist = \sqrt{((y_2 - y_1)^2) + ((x_2 - x_1)^2)}$$

2.2   Formation of Minimun Cost Spanning Tree

Spanning tree of a undirected graph $G = (V, E)$ is defined as a subgraph T if it is a tree and contains every vertex of G. A Minimum Cost Spanning Tree is a minimum weight or cost (among all spanning trees) [9] undirected connected weighted graph. And an weighted graph is the one where each edge has its weight (in terms of some real number). Figure 9 shows the other possible types of spanning trees with their total cost, among which the spanning tree with least cost (Fig. 9(d)) has been chosen as minimum cost spanning tree of the given retinal graph.

3   Results and Discussion

The experiments are performed on the DRIVE database in a Intel Core2 Duo 2.67 GHz with 2 GB RAM machine. The RGB images of DRIVE are captured

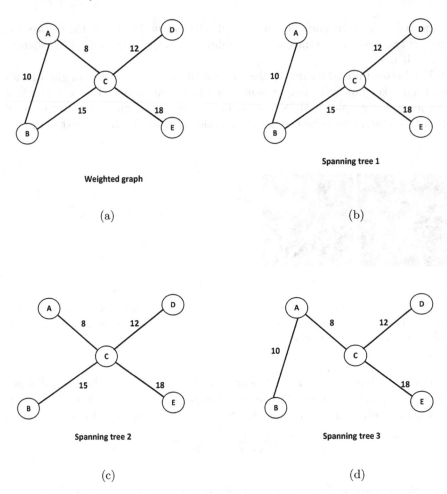

(a)

Weighted graph

(b)

Spanning tree 1

(c)

Spanning tree 2

(d)

Spanning tree 3

Fig. 9. Another example of minimum cost spanning tree generation (a) An weighted undirected graph (b) Spanning tree1 with path cost 55 (c) Spanning tree 2 with path cost 53 (d) Spanning tree 3 with path cost 48

Table 2. Performance measurement

Sensitivity	$(TN)/(TN+TP)$
Specificity	$(TP)/(TP+TN)$
Accuracy	$(TP+TN)/(TP+FP+TN+FN)$

through a fundus camera with a 45 degree FOV for medical imaging. The accuracy, sensitivity and specificity decide the performance of any algorithm. Sensitivity is the true positive rate which calculates the percentage of correctness satisfying the desired condition. Specificity is true negative rate which measures

Table 3. Results of Databases

Database	No. of images	Accuracy	Sensitivity	Specificity
DRIVE	40	0.86	0.90	0.82

the proportion of negative results that are correctly identified as not satisfying the desired condition (Table 2). We observe that the proposed work accomplished its goal with an average accuracy of 86% (Table 3).

4 Conclusion

Defining a MCST from retinal vasculature is essentially an important task for faster image registration/verification and ocular disease detection. By matching the nodes and weights of generated MCST from the images, verification process becomes faster compare to every junction point wise verification. Also, tracking the vascular structure becomes easy for the ophthalmologists as it comes as a spanning tree with major vessel sections. The experimental results show that the task has been accomplished with an average accuracy of 86% and sensitivity and specificity as 0.90 and 0.82 respectively on all the images of DRIVE database.

References

1. The DRIVE database, Image sciences institute, university medical center utrecht, The Netherlands. https://www.isi.uu.nl/Research/Databases/DRIVE/index.html. Accessed July 2007
2. Staal, J., Abramoff, M.D., Niemeijer, M., Viergever, M.A., Ginneken, B.: Ridge based vessel segmentation in color images of the retina. IEEE Trans. Med. Imaging **23**(4), 501–509 (2004)
3. Dashtbozorg, B., Mendoçna, A.M., Campilho, A.: An automatic graph-based approach for artery/vein classification in retinal images. IEEE Trans. Image Process. **23**(3), 1073–1083 (2014)
4. Forsyth, D., Ponce, J.: Computer Vision: A modern approach, 2nd edn. Pearson publication, London (2011)
5. Mendonca, A., Campilho, A.: Segmentation of retinal blood vessels by combining the detection of centerlines and morphological reconstruction. IEEE Trans. Med. Imag **25**(9), 1200–1213 (2006)
6. Divya, K.S., Anita Sofia Liz, D.R.: Classification of artery/vein in retinal images using graph-based approach. Int. J. Adv. Res. Trends Eng. Technol. **1**(2), 86–91 (2014)
7. Gonzalez, R.C.: Richard Eugene Woods, Digital Image Processing Book, 3rd edn. Paperback publishers (2008)
8. Campilho, A., Dashtbozorg, B., Maria Mendonça, A.: Segmentation of the vascular network of the retina, image analysis and modelling in ophthalmology, Chap. 5, p. 26. Taylor & Francis (2014)
9. Cormen, T.H., Leiserson, C.E., Rivest, R., Stein, C.: Introduction to Algorithms, 3rd edn. MIT Press, Cambridge (2009)

10. Feynman, R., Vernon Jr., F.: The theory of a general quantum system interacting with a linear dissipative system. Ann. Phys. **24**, 118–173 (1963)
11. Guo, Z., Hall, R.W.: Parallel thinning with two-sub iteration algorithms. Image Process. Comput. Vis. **32**(3), 359–373 (1989)
12. Goswami, S., Goswami, S., De, S.: Automatic measurement and analysis of vessel width in retinal fundus image. In: Proceedings of the First International Conference on Intelligent Computing and Communication, pp. 451–458 (2016)
13. Roy, N.D., Goswami, S., Goswami, S., De, S., Biswas, A.: Extraction of distinct bifurcation points from retinal fundus images. In: Proceedings of the First International Conference on Intelligent Computing and Communication, pp. 443–450 (2016)

Empirical Analysis of Programmable ETL Tools

Neepa Biswas[✉], Anamitra Sarkar, and Kartick Chandra Mondal[✉]

Department of Information Technology, Jadavpur University, Kolkata, India
biswas.neepa@gmail.com, anamitra1992@gmail.com, kartickjgec@gmail.com

Abstract. ETL (Extract Transform Load) is the widely used standard process for creating and maintaining a Data Warehouse (DW). ETL is the most resource, cost and time demanding process in DW implementation and maintenance . Now a days, many Graphical User Interfaces (GUI) based solutions are available to facilitate the ETL processes. In spite of the high popularity of GUI based tool, there is still some downside of such approach. This paper focuses on alternative ETL developmental approach taken by hand coding. In some context, it is appropriate to custom develop an ETL code which can be cheaper, faster and maintainable. Some well-known code based open source ETL tool (Pygrametl, Petl, Scriptella, R_etl) developed by the academic world has been studied in this article. Their architecture and implementation details are addressed here. The aim of this paper is to present a comparative evaluation of these code based ETL tools. Not to acclaim that code based ETL is superior to GUI based approach. It depends on the particular requirement, data strategy and infrastructure of any organization to choose the path between Code based and GUI based approach.

Keywords: Data warehouse · Code based ETL · Empirical analysis · ETL tools · Pygrametl · Petl · Scriptella

1 Introduction

Now a days data analysis has become an integral part of any organization to achieve optimized performance. Data Warehouse (DW) [18] is a wide storage of data which is mainly used for analytical reporting. To construct a DW, data is generally collected from heterogeneous data sources, clean and restructure as per the required standard and finally loaded into the DW. This is a well known process called ETL (Extract Transform Load). ETL [31] is one of the important components in DW environment. It is observed that the ETL process consumes most time, cost and complexity overhead of any DW project [17].

ETL tools come as a solution providing a user friendly graphical user interface (GUI) to map data items between the source and target system in a fast hassle free manner. In spite of developing and maintaining a custom hand-coded ETL systems, it is easier and faster to select and use any ETL tool. The User needs

© Springer Nature Singapore Pte Ltd. 2019
J. K. Mandal et al. (Eds.): CICBA 2018, CCIS 1031, pp. 267–277, 2019.
https://doi.org/10.1007/978-981-13-8581-0_22

to configure the tool as per their requirement. Many open-source (e.g.Pentaho Kettle, Talend) [7,8] and commercial (e.g. Informatica, SAS, ODI, IBM) ETL tools [9–11] comes with nice GUI which is easy to use for non-programmers. Using this type of tool, developers design the visual flow of data throughout the ETL process. One disadvantage of this kind visual approach is, sometimes it is difficult to design a specific ETL scenario with the limited item available in the graphical tool.

Writing a few lines of code can be a better way for this type of problems. Because it is tricky to drag icons, draw flow lines, setting properties for a complex case design with respect to writing own customizable ETL codes. Here, one of the main consideration should be the productivity of any system. Using any GUI based tool cannot assure more productivity compared to code based approach. Generally, ETL development is done by skilled technical people. So it is justified to go for a code based ETL option rather than GUI based option. We agree that graphical program is effective for self documentation and standardized features. But still, there is some aspect where code based approach can give an effective solution.

Some review article [22,25,27] over ETL tools is done so far. However, they are typically done over commercial ETL tools available in the market. Only high-level view is included by those works without covering any technical details. But no such work is noticed so far regarding the code based ETL tool developed by academic peoples. The focus of this paper is to give an integrated analysis report in the research domain of programmable ETL system.

The contribution of this paper is to highlight a new area by programmable ETL development technique. For this purpose, four prominent work on code based ETL framework is selected namely Pygrametl, Petl, Scriptella and etl. An in-depth experimental evaluation is done on each tool. Subsequently feature-wise and performance wise analysis report is provided.

Rest of the paper is organized in the following manner. Section 2 outlines the research development related to this area. Each of the evaluated ETL tools is discussed with their unique features in Sect. 3. Section 4 states the experimental detail and result following with a comparative performance analysis report. Finally, Sect. 5 summarizes the overall contribution of this article with the future direction.

2   Related Work

A number of commercial and open source data integration tools are available in the market. Besides, some renowned DBMS vendors are integrating ETL functionalities with it. Every year Gartner Inc. publishes a market research reports [1] on these tools where Informatica, IBM, SAS, SAP, Oracle, Microsoft are suggested as leading commercial tools and Talend, Pentaho are the open source challengers in the market. All those tools offer GUI based ETL process design.

Thomsen and Pedersen [30] have done a survey on open source business intelligence tools. It includes some ETL tool outline also. An overview of ETL tools characteristics is discussed there without any performance comparison.

A detailed survey is done by Vassiliadis [31] which mainly addresses research work in each stage of the ETL process with some academic ETL tools (Ajax, Arktos, Potter's Wheel, HumMer - Fusion). These tools mainly offer data cleaning or work-flow designing task. Following that work, Vassiliadis et al. addressed three commercial ETL tools (SQL SSIS, OWB, DataStage) and made a taxonomy of distinct ETL characteristics in article [32]. A detailed discussion on macro-level ETL flow generation process is studied in this article.

ETLator [26] is a scripting language based ETL framework. It is implemented in python language and provides support for both slowly changing dimensions and parallel task execution. Parallelism is achieved by file as well as directory naming and nesting protocol. It facilitates with logging and documentation enable to produces data flow images.

Liu et al. has extended *Pygrametl* [28] framework by using a Map-Reduce based approach in ETLMR [20]. It supports basic DW features like star as well as snowflake schema and slowly changing dimension (SCD). Use of Map-Reduce results in much scalability and fault tolerance for managing parallel ETL processing and data synchronization. A performance comparison with popular ETL tool Pentaho Data Integration (PDI) proves the efficiency of this approach [21].

SETL [23,24] is a new proposal in python code based ETL framework which will construct a semantic warehouse. Data integration is achieved by utilizing semantic web technology. SETL performs well to handle both relational data and RDF data. A use case proves more productivity and better quality compared to traditional ETL solutions.

Another tool Bubble is evaluated but could not be included in this paper as this module is not properly maintained now. Bubbles [2,13] is an open-source Python based framework for the purpose of data processing and data analysis. Data processing pipeline [3] are used to depict any ETL task in the form of directed graphs. Metadata is used for expressing pipelines. It does not provide SCDs or parallelism facility. Till now it is a prototype and has limited transformation and source variety support.

The focus of this article is programmable ETL tools. Some survey was conducted regarding comparative study on popular GUI based ETL tools which are available in market [19,22,25]. But, no such survey covering experimental analysis work is found in this area from where features and performance based overview of code based ETL tool can be evaluated. For this purpose, we have selected three code based ETL tools that are well accepted by the academic world. Two python based tool *Pygrametl* and *Petl*, one java based tool *Scriptella* and one R tool *etl* is evaluated. The architectural and characteristic overview of these tools are discussed in next section.

3   ETL Tools Overview

The availability of less degree of customization facility for modeling and integrating extension environment in GUI-based ETL tools has led many organizations to go for programmable solutions for ETL process. In this paper, we have selected some code based ETL tools. All these tools are open source and no graphical user interface is offered.

3.1 Pygrametl

Most remarkably, Pygrametl [28,29] is an open source python based ETL framework first released in 2009. This software is licensed under BSD. Till now continuous up-gradation is done on this tool.

Without drawing any ETL process using GUI based tool, Pygrametl [12] suggest performing ETL tasks by writing python codes. It offers some commonly used ETL functionality to populate data in DW. The data flow can be achieved into three stages, namely extraction, cleaning and insert into DW. Data is represented using python dictionary having key and value pair. PostgreSQL, MySQL, Oracle are the supported databases. Seamless integration of any new kind of data source can be done using merge-join, hash-join, union-source functions. Both the batch or bulk load can be performed as per the requirement.

It is easy to populate fact and dimension tables from the source data through one iteration. It offers to insert data into star dimension or snowflake dimension which span into several tables. Besides, it provides advancement on dimension support applying SCD type 1 and 2.

3.2 Petl

Most notably, Petl [4] is a general purpose Python package which is able to perform conventional tasks of ETL. This package is supported under MIT License. Petl provides support both object-oriented and functional programming style. A well explained documentation is available to implement general ETL tasks. Petl can handle a wide range of data sources with structured file like CSV, Text and semi-structured file like XML, JSON etc. PyMySQL, PostgreSQL, SQLite are three compatible databases with this package.

Petl support maximum transformation patterns required in any ETL process. Besides timing, materialized view, lookup etc. utility function provided extra benefit to the developer. Addition of any third party package can be easily done within it. Efficient use of memory is implemented by the use of lazy evaluation and iterator. ETL data flow are synchronized using ETL pipelines. However, it does not have SCD or parallelism handling mechanism.

3.3 Scriptella

Scriptella [5,6] is another script based ETL tool written in Java. It is licensed under Apache Version 2.0. Plain SQL queries are executed using JDBC bridge in this scripting language. In case of non-JDBC provider can be added using mixed SQL script. For describing various ETL task, XML script is used. SQL or other scripting language can be used for transformation purpose.

The main application is focused on executing script those are written in SQL, JEXL, Javascript and velocity for the purpose of ETL operations to/from various databases as well as file format like text, CSV, XML, LDAP etc. A thin wrapper created by XML script can give extra facility to make dynamic SQL script.

Multiple data sources can be added to an ETL program with additional support to some JDBC features like batching, escaping etc. No installation is required for deploying the tool or it can be worked as *Ant* task. Only JDK or JRE with version above 5.0 is required. Execution of this tool is also very simple. It is compatible with many popular databases having JDBC/ODBC compliant driver. For non-JDBC data sources a Service Provider Interface (SPI) is developed. It's integration provision cover Java EE, JMX, Spring framework, java mail, JNDI for easy scripting with enterprise standards.

Basic ETL task can be executed but with limited transformation support. Both batch load and bulk load can be implemented through this tool. It does not provides any support for parallelism as well as warehouse specific facility like SCD. Scriptella does not provide any GUI facility.

3.4   R_etl

Now a days, R is a promising language which is gaining popularity in the field of Data Science. A newly developed package for R [16] named *etl* is selected for this piece of work. It is licensed under CC0 with version 0.3.7 and available in CRAN [14,15]. It provides a pipeable framework to execute core ETL operations. It is suitable for working with medium size data.

This *etl* package can work as a basis for extending its dependent packages for managing any particular data sets. Seven open source and cross-platform dependent packages are available to easily access and analyze publicly accessible medium data sets (PAMDAS). This *etl* package can be extended to perform ETL operation for any data which is stored in an R package.

RPostgreSQL, RPostgreSQL, RSQLite are the DBI drivers for R is compatible with this package. It is suitable to handle data which can reside either in the local or remote database. Database creation or management can be done without having any expertise in SQL. Some utility functions like dbRunScript, smart_download, smart_upload, src_mysql_cnf etc. can provide some additional benefits to the developers. Very few lines of code are required to implement this tool. But only some basic ETL functionalities are enabled here. It does not meet the requirements of current ETL technologies.

After deploying each tool on-premise different features have been identified. On the basis of these characteristics, a comparison table is done. The comparison matrix is given in Table 1 represents a feature wise brief overview of these tools. These are the general characteristics which can be taken as criteria when evaluating any ETL tool.

Table 1. Feature comparison matrix on selected code-based ETL tools

Specifications	Pygrametl	Petl	Scriptella	R_etl
Easy usability	N	Y	Y	Y
Data centric approach	Y	Y	Y	Y
SOA-enabled	N	N	N	N
Reusable functionality	Y	Y	N	Y
Single installation	Y	N	N	N
Big data handle	N	Y	Y	N
Data segregation	Y	Y	Y	N
Real-time triggers	N	N	N	N
Unstructured data support	N	Y	Y	N
Multiple source join	Y	Y	Y	N
Complex transformation	N	Y	N	N
Data validations	N	Y	N	Y
SCD support	Y	N	N	N
Parallelism support	Y	N	N	N
Bulk load	Y	N	Y	N
Data pipeline	N	Y	N	Y
Easy data mapping	Y	Y	Y	Y
Lookup support	N	N	Y	N
Code re-usability	Y	Y	N	Y
Exception handling	Y	Y	Y	N
Documentation available	Y	Y	N	Y
Third-party dependency	N	Y	Y	Y
Version control	Y	Y	Y	Y
Deploy in cloud	N	N	N	N
Licensed	Y	Y	Y	Y
Community based forum	Y	Y	Y	Y

4   Experimental Analysis

The availability of different functionality about these tools makes it difficult to create a ranking. Because all of them has some special type of features. So, respective aspect is the main point to choose any tool for use. General specification of these tools is discussed in the previous section. This section will discuss about performance evaluation of each tool based on their characteristics.

4.1   Performance Analysis of Code-Based ETL Tools

For evaluation purpose, all the selected ETL tools have been deployed in the
local machine. After that, the performance analysis is evaluated on each tool.
The hardware specifications of the machine and software description are given
below.

Hardware Specifications: The hardware configuration is as follows:

 - Processor: Intel(R) Core(TM) i5-6500 CPU @3.20 Ghz 3.20 Ghz
 - Installed Memory(RAM): 4.00 GB
 - System Type: 64-bit Operating System, X64 based processor
 - Operating System: Windows 8.1

Software Specifications: Above mentioned ETL tools have been installed in
the machine with following specifications.

 - *Pygrametl* Version 2.6 has been installed with database PostgreSQL and
   MySQLdb for deploying purpose. Python 3.6 version is employed in IDE
   Spyder.
 - *Petl* Version 1.1.1 is used. It does not have any installation dependencies.
   SQLAlchemy and PostgreSQL databased has been used. Here also Python
   3.6 is used in Spyder.
 - *Scriptella* Version 1.1 has been installed along with HSQLDB database.
 - *etl* package version 0.3.7 and PostgreSQL is installed along with DBI RPost-
   greSQL. For IDE RStudio is utilized along with R version 3.4.4.

Before starting the assessment of these tools, some criteria should be selected.
We have evaluated the performance of four code based ETL tools on the basis of
four criteria. They are execution time, transformation support, throughput, and
code length. Each of the cases has been evaluated on these tools. After evaluating,
the results have been graphically represented to justify the performance analysis.

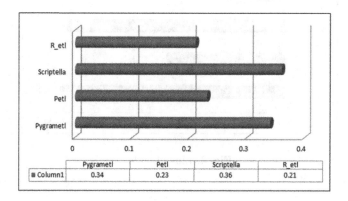

	Pygrametl	Petl	Scriptella	R_etl
■ Column1	0.34	0.23	0.36	0.21

Fig. 1. Execution timing

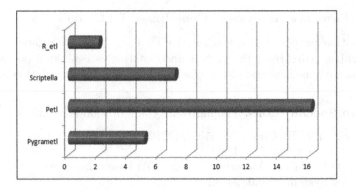

Fig. 2. Transformation support

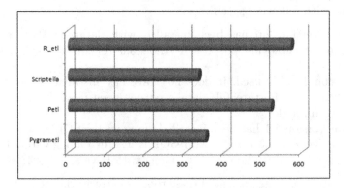

Fig. 3. Throughput rate

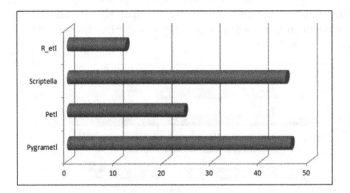

Fig. 4. Line of code

Execution Timing. Quantifying the amount of time taken to execute any ETL process is the most important case to analyses any tool. For this purpose, each of the tools is executed on premise. The execution time taken for each tool are collected and plotted in a graph in Fig. 1. Among the two sources input file, one file contains 120 row elements and another file contains 8 row elements which need to move in DW. The execution time is calculated in number of seconds. It is observed that R_etl is much efficient than other three options with respect to execution timing taken.

Transformation Support. Performing required transformation is the most important task in ETL process. The key process is to selecting proper source data and apply required transformation rules. Generation of correct data depends upon the successful completion of the transformation process. So it is a key aspect for any data integration tool is to provide a good range of data transformation support. In this study, a list of transformation supported by each tool has been identified. Based on the range of transformation support provided by each tool a comparative graph has been drawn in Fig. 2. It is observed that Petl is the highest number od transformation variety provider.

Throughput. To evaluate any system efficiency, throughput is one of the important metrics. Here throughput of each ETL tool is measured after deploying each four system on premise. The graphical Fig. 3 presents the throughput performance of them. Here the throughput is measured with respect to the number of rows processed per second. Performance of R_etl is better compared to other ones.

Line of Code. It is a measure of how many lines of code is required for accomplishing the total ETL process. A comparative graph is presented in Fig. 4 will show the line of code required for each tool to establish the task. A approximate value is considered for this case. Less line of code means how easily and in less time a code for implementing ETL can be written. From the graph, it is visible that *etl* using R takes less number of code than the others.

5   Conclusion

At present, the requirement of the continuous and increasing amount of data handling within more complex environment is a great challenge in the research domain. It demands standardized ETL process which has a great business impact on the BI industry. Most of the organization opt for taking any vendor made GUI based product for their ETL solution. But still in some of the cases custom coded ETL can be the best option in respect of performance.

This paper has chosen the second option for ETL solution. Some notable academic contribution in this program based ETL solution is studied. Among those four promising code based ETL tool Pygrametl, Petl, Scriptella and etl has been chosen in this paper. Their overall characteristics have been estimated as well as deployed. Both performance and feature based analysis are presented over these tool.

This paper summarizes as well as evaluated recent work in the domain of programmable ETL development approach in a novel way. The main objective does not point out on which ETL tool is good or bad. It totally depends on particular requirement and competence of any organization like scalability, costing, infrastructure support and more. Hope that this piece of work will help to grow a deep perspective in the research field of ETL.

The future work aims to design a unified code based ETL framework supporting relational and NoSQL database with rich transformation library.

References

1. 2017 Gartner Magic Quadrant for Data Integration Tools. https://www.informatica.com/in/data-integration-magic-quadrant.html. Accessed 06 Dec 2017
2. Bubbles — Data Brewery. http://bubbles.databrewery.org/. Accessed 06 Dec 2017
3. Data Pipeline. https://www.northconcepts.com/. Accessed 06 Dec 2017
4. Petl - Extract, Transform and Load (Tables of Data). http://petl.readthedocs.io/en/latest/. Accessed 06 Dec 2017
5. Scriptella/scriptella-etl. https://github.com/scriptella/scriptella-etl/wiki. Accessed 06 Dec 2017
6. Welcome to Scriptella ETL Project. http://scriptella.org/. Accessed 06 Dec 2017
7. Data Integration. http://www.pentaho.com/product/data-integration. Accessed 06 Feb 2018
8. Data Integration: Talend Enterprise Data Integration Services. http://www.talend.com/products/data-integration. Accessed 06 Feb 2018
9. Data Integration Tools and Software Solutions — Informatica India. https://www.informatica.com/in/products/data-integration.html. Accessed 06 Feb 2018
10. IBM, InfoSphere Information Server. http://www-03.ibm.com/software/products/en/infosphere-information-server/. Accessed 06 Feb 2018
11. Oracle Data Integrator. http://www.oracle.com/technetwork/middleware/data-integrator/overview/index.html. Accessed 06 Feb 2018
12. Pygrametl, ETL programming in Python. http://www.pygrametl.org/. Accessed 25 Feb 2018
13. Stiivi/bubbles. https://github.com/stiivi/bubbles. Accessed 25 Feb 2018
14. ETL. https://cran.r-project.org/web/packages/etl/README.html. Accessed 10 Mar 2018
15. Baumer, B.: etl: Extract-Transform-Load Framework for Medium Data (2017). R package version 0.3.7. http://github.com/beanumber/etl
16. Baumer, B.: A grammar for reproducible and painless extract-transform-load operations on medium data. arXiv preprint arXiv:1708.07073 (2017)
17. Eckerson, W., White, C.: Evaluating ETL and data integration platforms. Report of the Data Warehousing Institute 184 (2003)
18. Inmon, W.: Building the Data Warehouse. Wiley, Hoboken (2005)
19. Kabiri, A., Chiadmi, D.: Survey on ETL processes. J. Theor. Appl. Inf. Technol. **54**(2), 219–229 (2013)
20. Liu, X., Thomsen, C., Pedersen, T.: Mapreduce-based dimensional ETL made easy. Proc. VLDB Endow. **5**(12), 1882–1885 (2012)
21. Liu, X., Thomsen, C., Pedersen, T.B.: ETLMR: a highly scalable dimensional ETL framework based on MapReduce. In: Cuzzocrea, A., Dayal, U. (eds.) DaWaK 2011. LNCS, vol. 6862, pp. 96–111. Springer, Heidelberg (2011). https://doi.org/10.1007/978-3-642-23544-3_8

22. Majchrzak, T.A., Jansen, T., Kuchen, H.: Efficiency evaluation of open source ETL tools. In: Proceedings of the 2011 ACM Symposium on Applied Computing, pp. 287–294. ACM (2011)
23. Nath, R., Hose, K., Pedersen, T.: Towards a programmable semantic extract-transform-load framework for semantic data warehouses. In: Proceedings of the ACM Eighteenth International Workshop on Data Warehousing and OLAP, pp. 15–24. ACM (2015)
24. Nath, R., Hose, K., Pedersen, T., Romero, O.: SETL: a programmable semantic extract-transform-load framework for semantic data warehouses. Inf. Syst. **68**, 17–43 (2017)
25. Pall, A.S., Khaira, J.S.: A comparative review of extraction, transformation and loading tools. Database Syst. J. BOARD **4**(2), 42–51 (2013)
26. Radonić, M., Mekterović, I.: ETLator-a scripting ETL framework. In: 2017 40th International Convention on Information and Communication Technology, Electronics and Microelectronics (MIPRO), pp. 1349–1354. IEEE (2017)
27. Schmidt, N., Rosa, M., Garcia, R., Molina, E., Reyna, R., Gonzalez, J.: ETL tool evaluation-a criteria framework, pp. 1–12 (2011)
28. Thomsen, C., Pedersen, T.: Pygrametl: a powerful programming framework for extract-transform-load programmers. In: Proceedings of the ACM Twelfth International Workshop on Data Warehousing and OLAP, pp. 49–56. ACM (2009)
29. Thomsen, C., Pedersen, T.: Easy and effective parallel programmable ETL. In: Proceedings of the ACM 14th International Workshop on Data Warehousing and OLAP, pp. 37–44. ACM (2011)
30. Thomsen, C., Pedersen, T.B.: A survey of open source tools for business intelligence. In: Tjoa, A.M., Trujillo, J. (eds.) DaWaK 2005. LNCS, vol. 3589, pp. 74–84. Springer, Heidelberg (2005). https://doi.org/10.1007/11546849_8
31. Vassiliadis, P.: A survey of extract - transform - load technology. Int. J. Data Warehouse. Min. **5**(3), 1–27 (2009)
32. Vassiliadis, P., Simitsis, A., Baikousi, E.: A taxonomy of ETL activities. In: Proceedings of the ACM Twelfth International Workshop on Data Warehousing and OLAP, pp. 25–32. ACM (2009)

Design and Implementation
of an Improved Data Warehouse
on Clinical Data

Nilkantha Garain[1], Samiran Chattopadhyay[1], Gautam Mahapatra[2],
Santanu Chatterjee[2], and Kartick Chandra Mondal[1](✉)

[1] Department of Information Technology, Jadavpur University, Kolkata, India
nilkantha.garain.cse@gmail.com, samirancju@gmail.com,
kartickjgec@gmail.com
[2] Research Centre Imarat, DRDO, Ministry of Defence, Govt of India,
Hyderabad, India
{gautam,santanu}@rcilab.in

Abstract. Data Warehouse is a repository to store huge detailed and summaries data for historical data analysis. In a decision support system which stores data from remote, complex and heterogeneous operational data sources . A clinical data warehouse contains complex, heterogeneous data from different data sources. In literature, there are different data warehouse architectures are present with there own design issues, which are relevant to different application areas. In this paper, we proposed a conceptual and logical view of data warehouse architecture along with physical implementation of the data warehouse. Our main focus in this paper is to efficiently handle the complex heterogeneous medical data stored into the warehouse and improve the performance of data warehouse for data analysis. Here, we proposed a partitioning concept of the dimension tables and fact tables for optimizing the response time, minimizing the disk IO, along with reducing the joining cost of the data warehouse. To show the effectiveness of our system, we, compare with different joining techniques of the dimension and fact tables of fact-consolidated data warehouse schema. A mathematical cost model of disk IO optimization is being calculated. SQL window partitioning techniques are being used for data analysis of the proposed data warehouse. After storing complex heterogeneous data in well organized and efficient way in a data warehouse, efficient searching techniques need to be incorporated. Here, bitmap indexing technique is used for the purpose.

Keywords: Data warehouse architecture · Performance analysis · Query processing · Performance optimization

1 Introduction

Data warehouse [1,2] is a repository which integrated different operational complex, remote and heterogeneous data [3,4] from different sources for historical

© Springer Nature Singapore Pte Ltd. 2019
J. K. Mandal et al. (Eds.): CICBA 2018, CCIS 1031, pp. 278–290, 2019.
https://doi.org/10.1007/978-981-13-8581-0_23

data analysis [5], decision support system. This will allow better decision analysis, as data analyst [6,7] do not need to access different data sources that will save their amount of time, which wasted for accessing different data sources.

Data warehouse [1] is a subject area which has the characteristics of Subject Oriented, Time Variant, Non-Volatile, and Integrated properties. We survey different data warehouse architectures and pointed out there different methodologies, schema, and the success of any architecture in different application area. Primarily, there are six different data warehouse architecture, commonly available are

1. Base Architecture.
2. Centralized Architecture.
3. Hub and Spock Architecture, known as Inmon Corporate information factory architecture.
4. Independent data mart architecture, known as kimball architecture.
5. Distributed data warehouse architecture.
6. Federated data warehouse architecture.

Data warehouse stores large amount of data from gigabyte to petabyte as a central repository. Data are being collected from different operational data sources, as complex, heterogeneous, unstructured data format; and make it structure through ETL (Extract, Transform, Load), and store into a data warehouse. Each data warehouse can have many data marts based on different subject areas. Each data mart is then represented by different schemas, like more denormalized version as star schema or normalized snowflake schema. In snowflakes type of warehouses, data analyst need less number of join as compare to star schema. In star schema, a large fact table and multiple small dimension tables are used to represent data. When more than one fact tables are use, instead of a single big fact table then it is called fact-consolidated schema. For our experiment, we have used clinical data, and our clinical data warehouse model has used more than one fact table in data warehouse schema implementation.

Storing all the complex pieces of information in a single fact table would make it large and complex. Business Intelligence on this data may dramatically be enhanced the response time of a simple query. Although in storing complex data in a single table is good for doing Business Intelligence. Query operation will take less join but as the number of entries in the fact table increases it will increase the size of the fact table. This makes a longer responses time for the simple query due to it linear search on the entries.

Quick access to information needs a structured repository which reduces the search cost and improves the performance for BI. Here, we mainly focused on different data warehouses architecture along with there application areas. In this paper, we have concentrated on the conceptual and logical view of our data warehouse architecture and the physical implementation of it. Also, show the application of our data warehouse on clinical data. Performance of our clinical data warehouse has improved as complex heterogeneous data are stored in dimension tables and some measurement in fact tables. Bitmap indexing is being used to reduce the response time of star schema, and TPC-H benchmarking has been used for searching query from the data warehouse and updating efficiently into the repository. The proposed model is being designed using python language on PostgreSQL database.

1.1 Contribution

Data has structure, semistructured and unstructured formate along with huge data are stored in different remote, complex homogeneous and heterogeneous operational sources. For a decision support system to analyzed those data need a repository, which effectively accesses those data for data analysis in Business Intelligence.

To access the data-warehouse data in decision support, minimizing the response time, optimization of disk IO cost, and reduce the joining cost of fact and dimension tables are needed.

In the proposed model partitioning of fact and dimension tables are being used along with a mathematical cost model for disk IO optimization has been proposed. Different indexing techniques are being used to minimize the response time, optimized disk IO cost, and reduce joining cost.

This paper is organized as follows: Sect. 2 present a brief study on architecture and application of data warehouse. Section 3 used to describe our proposed model. Experimental result and analysis on performance has been discussed Sect. 4. Finally, in Sect. 5 conclusion and future work is presented.

2   Related Work

In this section, we have explained different data warehouse architecture and classified those architectures on the basis of there application area. Data warehouse architecture design is a crucial work. Architecture design process can be decomposed into three phases, such as conceptual design, logical design and physical implementation. Most stable methodologies are kimball and inmon for data warehouse architecture design [1,2]. An important factor in designing a data warehouse is to decide the normalized vs de-normalized approach to store the data in a data warehouse. According to Kimball [1], data warehouse model is a dimensional model (star schema or snowflake schema). On the other hand, Bill Inmon [2] states that data warehouse should be modelled using E-R model or Normalized model. In [8], a hybrid model based on Inmon and Kimball consist of third normal form and star schema. This hybrid model is known as the data vault. It is a graph-based model but doesn't include complex heterogeneous data analysis.

Authors in [4] combine a large amount of dimensional tables data in a single fact table which increases the size and number of row entries into the fact table. This degrades the performance of data warehouse in terms of memory and IO operation. No methodology on disk IO optimization techniques has considered in the literature. In [9], describe the multicolumn partitioning on column store data but they did not give any physical implementation and there is no indexing techniques to access the particular complex, aggregated query analysis. In [10], authors consider column partitioning for the optimized response time of an ad-hoc complex query having aggregations, multi-way join but the methodology to do an index on each column partition is not given.

Authors in [4,11,12] have discuss different joining on dimension tables with single fact table and not considered multiple fact tables in these works. In [13–15], researchers have proposed the materialized view for data warehouse data scanning. Using materialized view, it dramatically reduces the response time of query analysis but it has refreshing and integrity constraints checking problem. Each time if some modification needs to be done on data warehouse then we have to refresh the materialized view. This refreshing process adds extra overhead in the performance of materialized view.

Most of the queries for business intelligence are complex, ad-hoc and itera-tive in nature. So, to improve the performance of a data warehouse needs good column indexing methodology. In papers [16,17], considered different indexing methodology but they fail in complex heterogeneous clinical health data. Their algorithms are efficient on simple data like e-commerce sector but performance dramatically degrades for complex, heterogeneous clinical health data. The pro-posed approached, considered all these issues and partition dimension tables and fact tables such a way that data loads are balanced and minimized the execution time of queries in terms of response time, disk IO, space and CPU utilization. In Table 1, we have mentioned some advantages and disadvantages of some of the existing indexing techniques.

Table 1. Summary of evaluation of existing indexing techniques

Indexing techniques	Advantages	Disadvantages
B-Tree index	Efficient for low cardinality dataset	Use more space, Fetches the key value in order of row id, More page fault occurs
Pure Bitmap index	Efficiently handle high cardinality data	Sparsity problem required more space and processing time
Encoded Bitmap index	Improves the space utilization and solves sparsity problems	Degraded with complex queries
Bitmap join index	Support star queries	Order of indexed column is important
Projection index	Speed-up the performance when some columns in the table are retrieved	It can be used to retrieve raw data

3   Scenario and Propose Model

3.1   Example Scenario

Ours propose is to design fact-consolidated star schema, which is given below in Fig. 1. Here we have considered more than one fact table as the measurement unit instead of one as used in [4].

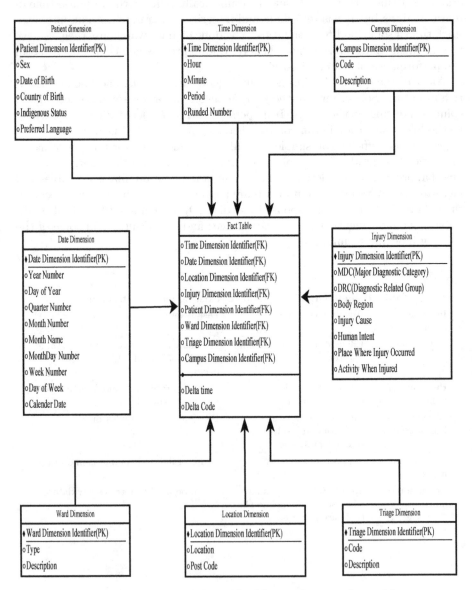

Fig. 1. Star schema of clinical health-care data warehouse [4].

Figure 1 is the logical schema of a data warehouse architecture known as star schema used as an example scenario in this paper. We used this tables as standards of a Victoria State Government health-care data collection format as an example. It has one fact table and consist of eight dimension tables which are Patient Dimension, Time Dimension, Campus Dimension, Date Dimension, Injury Dimension, Ward Dimension, Location Dimension and Triage Dimension. This example has been collected from [4] where complex medical data are being loaded first into the dimension tables from different heterogeneous data sources. Every dimension table has a unique primary key by which we can distinctly identify every entry of the data from the dimension table. Fact table of the star schema has all the properties of dimension tables linked via foreign keys along with some pre-calculated measurement values. That pre-calculated measurement improves the performance of data analysis for an analyst.

3.2   Proposed Model

We have proposed a conceptual view and logical design of our data warehouse architecture and physical implementation of the proposed model. In the proposed model, fact-consolidated star schema has been adopted considering data quality issues for clinical health-care data analysis. We have considered the partition of column data of the dimension tables for constructing the fact tables. For performing business intelligence on a data warehouse data, star query required

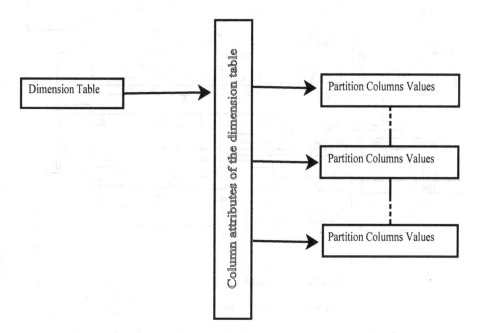

Fig. 2. Dimension table partitioning used in the proposed model

to scan the entire a fact table rows to retrieve the required result. If the number entries of the fact table are large, it will take more time to give required results for analysis. Instead of using single fact table, here we consider more numbers of fact table to optimize response time for ad-hoc TPC-H star query analysis. These multiple fact tables reduce the response time due to less scan on the data to fetch the relevant information.

The example design of our data warehouse for vertical and horizontal partition of dimension table has been shown in Fig. 2 For our experiment, we have used PostgreSQL which generally follows shared memory architecture [18]. Using this partitioning concept we can improve the scalability of the data in data

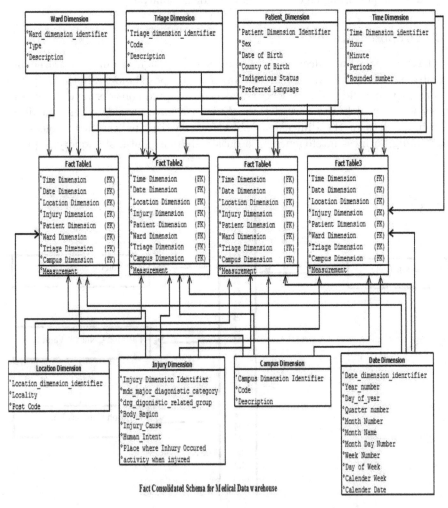

Fact Consolidated Schema for Medical Data warehouse

Fig. 3. Proposed fact-consolidated schema using multiple fact tables

warehousing design without using share nothing architecture. We have studied the logical modelling techniques of the data warehouse implementation for the purpose of fact-consolidation schema to handle heterogeneous complex medical data for analysis. The example of the fact-consolidated date warehouse as per the above scenario is shown in Fig. 3.

4 Experiment and Result Discussion

4.1 Experimental Setup

For this clinical data warehouse implementation, we have used PostgreSQL as database and developed using python language. We have used our data set from [19] as used in [4]. The hardware specifications and software description used during physical deployment of the proposed data warehouse are given below.

- Processor: Intel(R) Core(TM) i5-2500 CPU @3.30 Ghz.
- Installed Memory(RAM): 4.00 GB
- System Type: 64-bit Operating System, X64 based processor
- Operating System: Windows 7

4.2 Matrix Consider for Performance

For performance analysis of the proposed architecture, following key matrix have been used for analysis.

- IO Time is the main causes for data warehouse performance. IO configuration should be the key configuration of data load balance, index builds and for the business analysis materialized view.
- The mathematical cost model for IO in the proposed data warehouse.
- CPU Time is the sum of compilation time and query execution time.
- Memory and Response Time: Memory required to perform a task and quick response time of an OLAP query are also critical issues.

IO Time. In our model, join between fact Table 1 with dimension table ward dimension have 15 and 10 numbers of entries respectively. Size of tuples in ward dimension and fact table are 1 and 10 respectively. We achieve processing cost 91% compared to previous star schema as shown in Fig. 4.

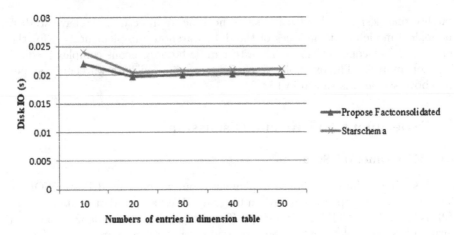

Fig. 4. Disk IO time vs number of entries in dimension table

4.3   Cost Model of Join Algorithms

Table 2. Cost model notation symbol

Factors	Meanings
n_{d_i}	Number of records in dimensions table
n_{f_i}	Number of records in facts table
s_{d_i}	Size of records in dimension table
s_{f_i}	Size of recordes in facts table
b	Size of disk block
r_{sel}	Selectivity
r_{parti}	Participating rate in join
k	Number of disk blocks to used

Total Cost = Eq. 1 + Eq. 2 + Eq. 3 + Eq. 4 where Eq. 1 is the cost for bitmap index, Eq. 2 is the cost of processing the predicate from the dimension table and store in a temporary table, Eq. 3 is the cost of shorting of the data using k merge sort, and Eq. 4 is the cost to retrieve data from the fact table. Explanations of notations used in these equations are presented in Table 2.

$$\lceil((r_{sel}) \times (r_{parti}) \times (n_{d_i}))\rceil \times \lceil \frac{(n_{f_i})}{8 \times b} \rceil \tag{1}$$

$$\lceil \frac{(s_d) \times ((n_{d_i}) \times (r_{sel}))}{b} \rceil \tag{2}$$

$$2\lceil \frac{(s_d) \times ((n_{d_i}) \times (r_{sel}))}{b} \rceil \times \log_K \lceil (s_{d_i}) \times (n_{f_i} \times (r_{sel}))\rceil \tag{3}$$

$$((n_{d_i}) \times (r_{sel})) \tag{4}$$

4.4   Performance Analysis

Query Performance During Measurement Creation. We need to collect data from dimension table for inputting the value in the measurement field of each fact table. These measurement values are collected using different joining operation. Here, we have shown the performance of our proposed warehouse against different joining operations for collecting values of measurement field. Primarily, we have taken values of hash join, partition join, and bitmap indexing. Data collected from our experiment are given in Table 3 and the graph has been shown in Fig. 5.

Table 3. Performance analysis of joining during measurement value creation

Performance	Response time	CPU time	IO time
Hash	0.045	8.1	33.04
Partition	.4350	2.8	33.07
Bitmap Index	.003	24.9	32.22

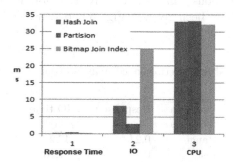

Fig. 5. Response time, IO time and CPU time of joining during measurement value creation

Comparison on Different Querying Techniques. For this experiment, we have used three different queries and run to our proposed data warehouse to get the required result. These three queries use four types of function inside them, viz., window, range, list and hash functions. Query 1 below is the example of a query using window function, Query 2 uses range function and Query 3 uses list functions. At first, these queries have been transformed using other three functions and then used for the experiments. We have shown response time and IO cost consumed by three queries using four different SQL functions for analyzing the performance of our system.

Query 1: select t.hour, d.day_of_week, count(1) over (partition by d.day_of_week) from fact1 f, time_dimension t, date_dimension d, patient_dimension p where f.time_dimension_identifier = t.time_dimension_identifier and f.date_dimension _identifier = d.date_dimension_identifier and f.patient_dimension_identifier = p.patient_dimension_identifier and (p.indigenous_state = '2' or p.indigenous_state = '7') group by d.day_of_week, t.hour

Query 2: select count(*) from fact1 f ,time_dimension t, date_dimension d, patient_dimension p where f.time_dimension_identifier = t.time_dimension_ identifier and f.date_dimension_identifier = d.date_dimension_identifier and f.pati ent _dimension_identifier = p.patient_dimension_identifier and (p.indigenous_ state ='2' or p.indigenous_state ='7') group by d.day_of_week,t.hour

Query 3: select i.injury_cause from fact1 f,time_dimension t, patient_dimension p, injury_dimension i where f.time_dimension_identifier = t.time_dimension_ identifier and f.patient_dimension_identifier = p.patient_dimension_identifier and f.injury _dimension_identifier = i.injury_dimension_identifier and p.indigenous_ state IN('2','7')

Performance of query 1, query 2 and query 3 using four different functions have been given in Tables 4, 5 and 6, respectively. Also, the comparison of response time and disk IO time for three queries using four different functions have been given in Figs. 6 and 7, respectively.

Table 4. Performance analysis of query 1

Partition techniques	Response time	IO time
Range	0.24	47.25
List	0.22	57.76
Hash	0.167	57.80
Window functions	.003	33.04

Table 5. Performance analysis of query 2

Partition techniques	Response time	IO time
Range	0.033	72.30
List	0.035	48.01
Hash	.008	47.95
Window functions	0.007	48.00

Table 6. Performance analysis of query 3

Partition techniques	Response time	IO time
Range	0.109	47.92
List	0.172	47.83
Hash	0.007	47.90
Window functions	0.007	48.00

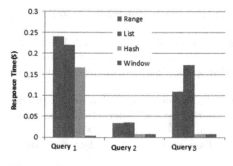

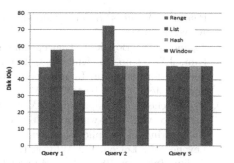

Fig. 6. Comparison of response time for different functions used in each queries.

Fig. 7. Comparison of disk IO time for different functions used in each queries.

5   Conclusion and Future Scope

Data Warehouse architecture design goes through different phases, namely, conceptual design, logical schema design and physical implementation. In this paper, we proposed a model based on partition indexing technique to design physical implementation of the data warehouse using logical fact-consolidated schema. In our proposed model, dimension tables and fact tables data are store column-wise. Then we partition each column data and used encrypted bitmap indexing technique on column data. Finally, we have used hash indexing to access the data for OLAP analysis. Proposed model experimented on small size clinical data and analyzed the performance of the proposed model. For real-time performance analysis, one may need much bigger sample size on real-time medical historical data. Future work on this proposal is to compare performance on handling the large volume of real-time medical data on the proposed data warehouse architecture. Also, we can use other indexing, and be joining techniques to optimize the performance of a decision support system.

References

1. Kimball, R., Ross, M.: The Data Warehouse Toolkit: The Complete Guide to Dimensional Modeling. Wiley, New York (2011)
2. Inmon, W.H.: Building the Data Warehouse. Wiley, USA (2005)
3. Ado, A., Aliyu, A., Bello, S.A., Garba, A.U.: Building a diabetes data warehouse to support decision making in healthcare industry. Int. Organ. Sci. Res. J. Comput. Eng. (IOSR-JCE) **16**(2), 138–143 (2014)
4. Nealon, J., Rahayu, W., Pardede, E.: Improving clinical data warehouse performance via a windowing data structure architecture. In: International Conference on Computational Science and Its Applications (ICCSA 2009), pp. 243–253. IEEE (2009)
5. Chaudhuri, S., Dayal, U., Narasayya, V.: An overview of business intelligence technology. Commun. ACM **54**(8), 88–98 (2011)
6. Ni, Z., Guo, J., Wang, L., Gao, Y.: An efficient method for improving query efficiency in data warehouse. JSW **6**(5), 857–865 (2011)

7. Pentaho Analysis Service: Mondrian Project. http://mondrian.pentaho.org/. Accessed 29 Dec 2017
8. Jovanovic, V., Bojicic, I.: Conceptual data vault model. Proc. SAIS **23**, 1–6 (2012)
9. Kim, J.W., Cho, S., Kim, I.: Column partitioning to improve data warehouse queryperformance. In: International Workshop on Ubiquitous Science and Engineering, Jeju, South Korea (2015)
10. Bellatreche, L., Karlapalem, K., Mohania, M., Schneider, M.: What can partitioning do for your data warehouses and data marts? In: 2000 International Database Engineering and Applications Symposium, pp. 437–445. IEEE (2000)
11. Levene, M., Loizou, G.: Why is the snowflake schema a good data warehouse design? Inf. Syst. **28**(3), 225–240 (2003)
12. Chmiel, J., Morzy, T., Wrembel, R.: Multiversion join index for multiversion data warehouse. Inf. Softw. Technol. **51**(1), 98–108 (2009)
13. Ross, K.A., Srivastava, D., Sudarshan, S.: Materialized view maintenance and integrity constraint checking: trading space for time. ACM SIGMOD Rec. **25**, 447–458 (1996)
14. Zhang, C., Yao, X., Yang, J.: An evolutionary approach to materialized views selection in a data warehouse environment. IEEE Trans. Syst. Man Cybern. Part C Appl. Rev. **31**(3), 282–294 (2001)
15. Rizzi, S., Saltarelli, E.: View materialization vs. indexing: balancing space constraints in data warehouse design. In: Eder, J., Missikoff, M. (eds.) CAiSE 2003. LNCS, vol. 2681, pp. 502–519. Springer, Heidelberg (2003). https://doi.org/10.1007/3-540-45017-3_34
16. Wu, M.C., Buchmann, A.P.: Encoded bitmap indexing for data warehouses. In: 1998 Proceedings of the 14th International Conference on Data Engineering, pp. 220–230. IEEE (1998)
17. Koudas, N.: Space efficient bitmap indexing. In: Proceedings of the 9th International Conference on Information and Knowledge Management, pp. 194–201. ACM (2000)
18. DeWitt, D.J., Madden, S., Stonebraker, M.: How to build a high-performance data warehouse (2005). http://db.lcs.mit.edu/madden/high_perf.pdf. Accessed June 2011
19. V. G. H. Information, Information about Health Data Standards and Systems (HDSS) used in Victoria's Hospital (2008). http://www.health.vic.gov.au/hdss/index.html. Accessed 23 Dec 2017

Dynamic FP Tree Based Rare Pattern Mining Using Multiple Item Supports Constraints

Sudarsan Biswas[1](✉) and Kartick Chandra Mondal[2](✉)

[1] Department of Information Technology, RCC Institute of Information Technology, Kolkata, India
biswas.sudarsan@gmail.com
[2] Department of Information Technology, Jadavpur University, Kolkata, India
kartickjgec@gmail.com

Abstract. Data mining is a fundamental ingredient for making association rules among the largest variety of itemsets. Rare pattern mining is extremely useful judgment to generate the unknown, hidden, unusual pattern, using predefined minimum support confidence constraint from transactional datasets. Rare association rule is related to rare items that represent useful knowledge. Mining rare patterns from those database is more interesting rather than frequent pattern mining. In this paper, we presents the taxonomy of different support constraint model for rare pattern mining. Also we have performed a comprehensive literature review on existing tree based rare pattern mining algorithms. Finally, we have proposed a multiple item support constraint based dynamic rare pattern tree approaches that only generates rare itemset without considering frequent itemsets generation.

Keywords: Dynamic FP tree · Dynamic FP growth · Rare itemset · Multiple support constraint · MCDRP tree

1 Introduction

Rare association rule mining (RARM) is a novel aspect of growing research in association rule mining (ARM) with several application areas. ARM technique proposed by Agrawal et al. [3] has a significant contribution in data mining knowledge discovery database (KDD). It has been played a most imperative role in finding unknown hidden correlations and interesting pattern between items in transactional datasets. Association rule is expressed as, $(A \rightarrow B)$ where $A \subseteq T$, $B \subseteq T$ and $(A \cap B) = \phi$. A Rule defines relationship presence between the itemset like Bread, Butter, Milk. It represents whenever itemset Bread, Butter was present in a given transaction, item Milk was also present. However, frequent rules is defined as regular tendency to buy $\{Bread, Butter\}$ or $\{Bread, Milk\}$ that has high support and high confidence association among a set of itemsets. RARM determine all rules that persuade the prerequisite of minimum support

© Springer Nature Singapore Pte Ltd. 2019
J. K. Mandal et al. (Eds.): CICBA 2018, CCIS 1031, pp. 291–305, 2019.
https://doi.org/10.1007/978-981-13-8581-0_24

and confidence framework also some measurement that describes their strength and quality of the rules.

$$\{Sugar, Diabieties\} \rightarrow Pressure$$
$$Support = 2\%$$
$$Confidence = 94\%$$

Support value means this specific pair of three items represents 2% of the transactions that were tested. Confidence value represents 94% of the time that itemset $\{Sugar, Diabieties\}$ were found together, the item $\{Pressure\}$ was also found. So the analysis of rare patter represented knowledge about purchasing patterns. A rare association rule mining is a counterpart of the ARM. Occasionally known as non-frequent, unusual patterns, abnormal sporadic patterns [22]. Rare rule represents an unpredictable or unknown association between items. It reflect the relationship between items which occurs uncommonly in a transactional database. Mostly ARM finds out frequent rules but sometimes it is very useful when some items occurrence with low support and high confidence is known as a rarely purchased pattern. So it is more interesting than frequent patterns [40].

A rare item set(patterns) is an itemset that consist of all rare items [21]. It may be measured in term of interesting rare association or uninteresting rare association. An interesting rare association has defined low support with the high confidence association whereas uninteresting rare association has described low support with the low confidence association between itemsets. Objective of RARM is to find out meaningful rare items or low-rank item sets and those type of interesting rare association is not generated by traditional ARM algorithms.

To beat the drawbacks of Apriori associated algorithms [4], FP Growth algorithm is proposed by Han et al. [16] by extending prefix tree structure. That mines complete set of frequent as well as rare item sets without using candidate generation process. This approach has afforded immense impact than other techniques [39]. FP growth mining involves two steps process. Firstly FP tree construction with every branch represents frequent itemsets. Next itemset generation from FP tree that extracts the frequent itemsets directly from FP tree using header table. However, it has created conditional pattern base from an initial suffix pattern and then constructing its conditional FP-tree recursively in the same order of magnitude as the numbers of frequent patterns. The narrative contributions of this paper includes:

- Taxonomy is presented on different support constraint model for rare pattern mining. That will helps to understand the researchers how single support constraint convey rare item set problem [27]. How itemset can be generated by the different constraint model to exact rare patterns efficiently without involving the frequent itemset (FIs), maximal frequent itemset (mFIs) and minimal rare itemset (mRI).
- A comprehensive literature review is performed on existing tree based rare pattern mining algorithms. Also we have presented a comparison of all those rare pattern generation algorithms with major theoretical issue like type of

database used, database layouts (HIL, HIV, VTL, VTV), no of database scan required, types of data structure used, type of approaches used, and lastly what are the support constraint are using those rare pattern mining algorithms.

- Finally, a tree based rare itemset mining algorithm is proposed using maximum constraint dynamic rare pattern (MCDRP) tree. This approach is based on the interestingness, support constraints at the different levels of abstraction that prunes uninteresting (Non rare) pattern among frequent patterns from the database where item support changes extensively.

The rest of paper is structured as follows. At first rare pattern generation's motivation and issues are discussed in Sect. 2. The problem specification is formulated in Sect. 3. Section 4 briefly presents a literature review on this domain. Some basic terminologies and measures of rules interestingness are given in Sect. 5. An existing work on rare pattern generation is exercised in Sect. 6. A new algorithm named MCDRP tree is proposed and discussed with an example in Sect. 7. Finally Sect. 8 discuss about overall contribution of this paper with some concluding remarks.

2   Rare Pattern Generation: Issues and Motivation

A Rare pattern is an event that occurs very infrequently in a database. The presence of those items support values may typically vary within 0.1% to less than 10%. Some previous works have suggested the fact that, when those pattern are present in the database, their consequences can be dramatic and quite often in a negative sense. However, a major important issue related to rare pattern generation is that with a single minimum support constraint may always not be possible to generate all set of rare patterns. But, the choice of minimum support is set too high, that may omit frequent pattern including rare patterns because rare pattern fails to satisfy high minimum support. Analysis of those type patterns conveys different information about the database. Here each category of patterns demonstrates the data analysis for a specific kind of knowledge extraction [6].

Following are some key issues regarding rare pattern mining research area.

- User-defined minimum support confidence has a great impact in traditional rule mining process. These parameters mostly depends on database.
- Selection of minimum support constraint is very difficult without prior domain knowledge.
- Single minimum support confidence framework may ignore some interesting rare rules.
- Using pattern growth based approach design a compact memory efficient, scalable rare pattern mining technique that only generates rare rules without investing time to frequent pattern mining form a large database is a very difficult task.
- Design and analysis of static as well as dynamic database using single minimum support confidence approach is also difficult task for rare rule generation.

3   Problem Specification

In RARM, an assignment of support constraint is a fundamental task of usual or unusual pattern generation because support distributions are often skewed. We have often assumed that all items present in the datasets are similar types of patterns and occurrence of all patterns with the same frequency. But in practice, all data sets are not equal in nature.

So it is very much important aspect specifying appropriate support threshold. Mining those rare and low ranked patterns with very low support but high confidence cannot be exposed easily using traditional patterns mining algorithms. This type of pattern generation is a difficult task in rule mining. Generally, to capture these patterns using traditional approaches like [4], minimum support is defined very low. As a result, it will generate a massive amount of redundant patterns. However, a single minimum "support confidence constraint framework" like Apriori [4] or FP Growth [16] based pattern mining is not enough capable to generates rare pattern efficiently. Therefore rare pattern generation using "single minimum support constraint" approach conveyed rare item itemsets problem phenomena [27] is defined in below.

- When single minimum support has a very higher threshold, it is always not possible to mine those pattern that consists of interesting rare items. So there are many chances to miss some interesting patterns.
- When single minimum support has very lower threshold, it produces combination of large frequent and rare pattern which are not always meaningful and also it computationally expensive.

To solve this issue many authors has proposed different itemsets generation approach towards rare pattern using minimum constraint model [40], maximum constraint model [21] and weighted constraint models [6, 24] etc. In a minimum constraint, model approaches has pruned effectively uninteresting rules that have low support with only frequent items but low support with highly frequent and rare items not be pruned by this approach. Generation of a rare pattern using multiple minimum support constraint still suffers from the same problem and also dropped some of the important rare patterns. Another issue of rare pattern generation is a large number of minimal rare pattern generation among rare item itemsets.

Many research literature has suggested mining rare patterns using single minimum support constraint like Apriori [4], FP growth [16] pattern mining algorithms are not suitable to mine rare patterns efficiently. Because of its high computational time complexity to generates frequent pattern rather than rare patterns. However, we have classified how rare patterns are mined using different support constraints models is shown in Figs. 1, 2 and 3.

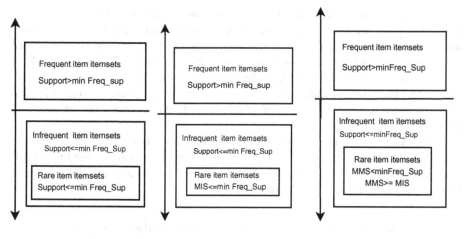

Fig. 1. Single   **Fig. 2.** Minimum.   **Fig. 3.** Maximum.

4   Related Work

From its introduction, ARM has significant contribution in different domains including market basket analysis [3], telecommunication network [9], risk analysis in business environments, advertisement [11], bio informatics [32], epidemiology, disease prediction [35], gene expression [8], fluid dynamics, fraud detection and crime prevention [31], network attacks detection [23], sports, weather prediction [30], web [36] and counter terrorism, web recommendation system [26], social networking, opportunities identification [20], preterm births analysis [12], molecular biology [7], statistical disclosure risk assessment from census data [28], cross marketing, e-commerce [41], catalog design, e-learning [29], etc. Apriori is the most well exercised algorithm [4] for generating the frequent patterns. This method has suffered a huge number of candidates generation [27]. For avoiding too much candidates generation process suggested FP growth approach by frequent pattern tree to represent the database [16].

Abdullah et al. [1] suggested critical relative support (CRS) to generates the criticality or significant level of least association rules and able to reduce the number of unwanted rules compared to the single minimum support constraint. They have considered CRS value between 0 and 1 using Jaccard similarity coefficient or multiplying the highest value either supports of the antecedent divide by consequence. Koh et al. [22] presented Apriori-Inverse generates sporadic rules based on multiple minimum support threshold using one minimum support value and one maximum support value. It can generate the sporadic itemsets known as perfectly sporadic rules much more quickly than apriori. But it is not enough to generate all the rare item itemsets. Needless to say, this approach can generate rules beyond the maximum support threshold.

Ding et al. [10] suggested Transactional co-occurrence matrix (TCOM) that extract rare items. However, the design and generation of itemsets using this algorithm is high cost. Tsang et al. presented a Rare Pattern tree (RP tree)

[40] approach to find out rare rules generated from rare item itemsets. It keeps only rare items or both consist of frequent items and rare items. The most advantage of RP tree is, it only generates a specific type of rare rules without investing time find out non interesting rare item itemsets. RP Tree is a FP-growth based pattern mining algorithm that efficiently works on long patterns. It escapes the time consuming candidates generation and pruning steps. Finally, authors also did some modification of RP tree algorithm based on information gain components.

A general observation has been presented in Table 1 between a list of pattern growth based rare association rule generation algorithms with some important parameters. Also we have reported shown in Fig. 4 that represents the year wise research exploration in the area of RARM.

Table 1. Overview of tree based RARM generation algorithms

Algorithms	Database	Database type	Scan	Data structure/Approach	Support constraint
RP-Tree [40]	HIL	Synthetic, Real	Two	FP tree, IG	minRare, minfreq
DynTARM [24]	HIL	Synthetic	Two	Dynamic Min-Max Tree	Window
RPDD [19]	HIL	Stream	Single	M-measure, PCD, DST, FSFW	Multiple
MIFPOD [17]	HIL	Synthetic, Real	Single	TWF, MIFPOF	MIPDF
Talky-G [37]	VTL	Census, Sparse, Real	Two	IT tree, ICT	minsup
IWI Miner [6]	HIL	Synthetic, Weighted	Two	Projection, Cond. FP tree	IWI sup
MIWI Miner [6]	HIL	Synthetic, Weighted	Two	Projection, Recursive pruning	IWI min, IWI max
TCOM [10]	HIL, VTL	Synthetic	Two	Random access, TCOM	Multiple
DLAR [2]	HIL	Real	Two	LP Tree, LP Growth	Definite factors
Walky-G [38]	VTL	Census, Sparse, Real	Two	Hash structure	minsup
IFP min [13]	HIL	Dense	Two	Projected tree, Residual Trees	Multiple
LP Miner [34]	HIL	Synthetic	Two	TP, PP, NP	Length decreasing
MCCFP [21]	HIL	Binary	Single	Prefix path, Cond. FP tree	Multiple
MCRP [5]	HIL	Binary	Single	RP tree, Conditional FP	minfreq, minraresup
IIMMDS [33]	HIL	Sampled	Single	Pyramidal Tree, DWM	Entropy
SRP-Tree [18]	HIL	Synthetic	Single	Bottom up	Multiple
TRARM-RS [25]	HIL	Synthetic	Two	Ordered Min-Max tree	minRelsup, Multiple

There are various pattern growth based techniques to compute rare patterns which is useful in different constraint model. For example, minimum constraint model [40], maximum constraint model [21] and weighted constraint models [6,24]. In the other word different frameworks is being developed in order to efficiently rare pattern mining.

5   Basic Terminologies and Interesting Measures

In this section, we presents the overview of some basic definition related to rare pattern mining with single support and multiple item supports constraints.

Here we have taken a simulation market basket transactional database D (5×10) are in a lexicographical order shown in Table 2. Rare association rule mining find out set of rare relationship between item sets. We have

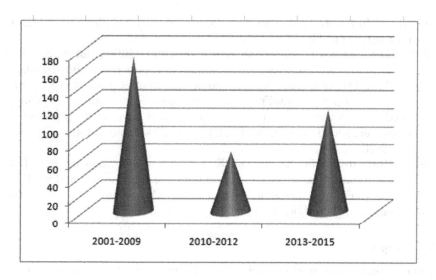

Fig. 4. Year wise research impact of RARM algorithms

Table 2. An example database

TID	Items
1	$\{B, D\}$
2	$\{A, C, D\}$
3	$\{C, D\}$
4	$\{C\}$
5	$\{A, C, D\}$
6	$\{B, C, D\}$
7	$\{D, E\}$
8	$\{B, D, E\}$
9	$\{A, B, C, D\}$
10	$\{A, B, C, D, E\}$

assumed $I = \{i_1, i_2, i_3 \ldots i_n\}$ are set of distinct items in transactional database D, $T = \{t_1, t_2, t_3, \ldots t_n\}$. Where each transaction is defined as a set of items $I \subseteq T$ a transaction T contains A if $A \subseteq T$.

5.1 Itemsets

Itemset (patterns) is defined as a set of items A such that itemset A is subset of I. An itemset A with k distinct items is called as k-itemset [3]. For example $\{laptop, Pendrive, Compactdisk\}$.

- **Frequent itemset:** An itemset X whose support $(X) \geq \beta$ where $\beta =$ minimum support constraint [3].
- **Infrequent itemset:** An itemset X is known to be infrequent itemset if an only if Support $(X) \leq \alpha$. Where $\alpha =$ minimum support constraint [10,39].
- **Rare itemset:** An itemset X is said to be rare itemset if its sup $(X) \geq$ min-Raresup and sup(X) < minFreqSup. Hence not all interesting rare itemsets satisfied these properties. If $\{C\}$ is a rare itemset then all its supersets are also rare item set. If an itemsets $\{A, B\}$ is rare, its superset $\{A, B, C\}$ is also rare as well.
- **Rare item itemsets:** An itemset X is known as rare item itemset (RIIs) if its rare itemset and $\forall$ x $\subset$ X with sup(x) *geq* minRaresup and sup(x) < minFreqSup. For example, itemsets that has a only rare items or itemset that combination of those both rare and frequent items [40].

5.2 Support

An item support is defined by probability of observing a transaction in D that containing both item A and B. Computed as support $(A \rightarrow B) = \frac{\eta(A \cup B)}{T}$, Where $\eta =$ support count, T = Number of transactions shown in Table 2.

5.3 Confidence

Predictive accuracy or Confidence of a rule is the ratio that measures degree of correlation between itemsets, while the support of a rule measures significance of correlation between itemsets. Confidence is the conditional probability of B in transactions with item A. Confidence $(A \rightarrow B) = \frac{\eta(A \cup B)}{supp(A)}$.

5.4 Define Rare Pattern with Single Minimum Support Constraint

Considered transactional database D in Table 2 with set of items I having user given support threshold is minsup. A set of rare pattern in Table 2 are selected that support is bellow user-defined minimum support constraint. For example let TID 2, 3 shown in Table 2 with two itemsets $K_1 = \{A, C, D\}$ and $K_2 = \{C, D\}$ has actual support 40% and 60% respectively & minimum support is set 45%. From the above assumption, we have selected K_1 is an interesting pattern where support 40% bellow the single minimum support constraint.

5.5 Define Rare Pattern with Multiple Minimum Support Constraint

Let I $= \{i_1, i_2, i_3 \ldots i_n\}$ are set of distinct items. Itemset $K_1 = \{A, C, D\}$, the minimum itemsup is defined $MIS(K_1) = \min\{min(i_1), min(i_2), min(i_3)\}$. For example with TID 2 shown in Table 2 itemset $K_1 = \{A, C, D\}$ has the actual support 40% and individual support is sup(A) = 40%, sup(C) = 70% and sup(D) = 90%. Let the MIS of item K_1 are chosen as min $\{40\%, 70\%, 90\%\} = 40\%$. So itemset K_1 is infrequent with support = 40%, which is bellow MIS of $K_1 = 50\%$.

6   Rare Pattern Generation Algorithm

Rare pattern tree (RP Tree) proposed by Tsang et al. [40], a FP growth based rules generation approach for mining subset of interesting rare association rules using FP tree structure. They have used entropy based information gained component to remove frequent itemset which are poor predictors of rare items. For RP Tree construction, it only select rare transactions and remove all non rare transactions. Because those node may not shown interestingness in itemset generation. So FP tree initially contain all rare item node with all nodes that have a lower support than a rare item are themselves rare items. Transactions that having more than one rare item are renewed into many transactions during the information gain calculation so that each transaction having only one rare item.

Example of RP Tree. Assumed minRaresup = 3 and minFreqSup = 6. Rare patterns is chosen if an item has support > minRaresup and support < minFreqsup. Now selected rare transactions that has at least one rare item in database D is shown in Table 4. Using RP tree approach we have chosen rare item itemset $\{A, B\}$ having item support 4 and 5 respectively from Table 3. Here, Table 3 is used for representing the occurrence of items present in the transactional database D. Table 4 contains the rare transactions after discarding non rare items.

<table>
<tr><td colspan="2">Table 3. Support count</td><td colspan="2">Table 4. Discarded non rare items</td></tr>
</table>

Item	Support
D	9
C	7
B	5
A	4
E	3

TID	Items
1	$\{B, D\}$
2	$\{A, C, D\}$
5	$\{A, C, D\}$
6	$\{B, C, D\}$
8	$\{B, D, E\}$
9	$\{A, B, C, D\}$
10	$\{A, B, C, D, E\}$

To constructed RP tree all non rare items are removed bellow min rare support and above min frequency support. Finally constructed RP tree using selected transaction from Table 4 is displayed in Fig. 5.

7   Proposed Maximum Constraint Dynamic Rare Pattern Tree (MCDRP)

In this section, we have presented a tree based rare pattern mining using multiple items support framework in Dynamic FP tree [14] approach. MCDRP Tree algorithm is a non-recursive Dynamic FP-tree based item sets mining approach

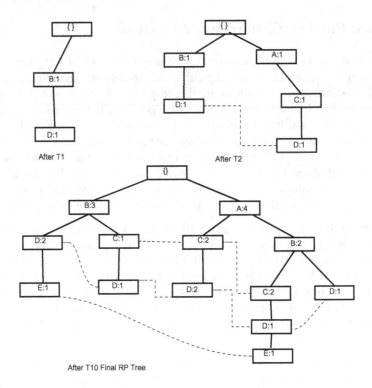

Fig. 5. Final rare pattern tree

that used a dynamic data structure called Dynamic FP-growth [14,15]. However, for item set generation first used dynamic prune search to reduced storage and partially store into a shared buffer. All items are stored in a node structure with counter, data and two pointers called down pointer and next pointer. Where every down pointer is used to represented the next item in the same transaction and next pointer store item at the same level of another transactions. Here each rare transaction is read and straightforward to stored into MCDRP tree.

Proposed work formulated in Algorithm 1 shows a step by step procedure. It will extract the maximum constraint dynamic rare pattern tree ending with all rare itemset. Later, the presented algorithm is explain with a suitable example.

7.1   Construction of MCDRP Tree

We have assumed transactional dataset shown in Table 2 and their original frequency support and calculated new MIS values are defined shown in Table 5.

$$|NewMIS| = \begin{cases} Support - X & \text{if } support \geq minRaresup \\ minRaresup & \text{otherwise} \end{cases}$$

$X = \eta(1 - \beta)$ Where $\beta =$ Scaling factor of database belongs to 0 to 1, $\eta =$ original support of items in Table 2.

Algorithm 1. Rare Rules Generation Using Dynamic Rare Pattern Tree (MCDRP Tree)

Input: Transactional Dataset D with minFreqsup, minRaresup, Support Difference (SD), Database scaling factor β.

Output: M⟵Rare item itemset, Rare Association Rules.

1 Method: Call Dyn-FP Growth(MCDRP tree, $NULL$). The MCDRP Tree is in the following steps:

2 Set minFreqsup, minRaresup support and calculate Support Difference(SD).

3 Read dataset, D first time.

4 Assign (p) ⟵{All unique items of D}

5 MIS⟵Support count (p)

6 Define New frequency support of itemsets

$$|NewMIS| = \begin{cases} Support - X & \text{if } support \geq minRaresup \\ minRaresup & \text{otherwise} \end{cases}$$

Where X =$\eta(1\text{-}\beta)$

7 rare items ⟵ {|j ϵ p|(j.New MIS$\geq$minRaresup $\cap$ j.NewMIS$\leq$minFreqsup $\cap$ New MIS$\geq$ SD and New MIS < min freqsup)}

8 rare transaction ⟵ {tϵ D|Discarded non rare items transactions of D }

9 α ⟵ Create MCDRP tree (rare transaction)

10 Mining (Second scan of D): Call Dyn-FP Growth (MCDRP tree, α)

11 Create root node and marked as root T.

12 Assume the selected rare transaction Trans be:$[x|X,T]$

13 To insert the node (N) into the tree performed as followed insert tree (Trans).

14 **if** *T has a child node (N)* **then**

15 ⎸ Such that **if** *N.ItemName = x.ItemName* **then** Increment the counter of N by one

16 ⎿

17 **else** Create a new node N and set count as one

18

19 **if** *X! = NULL* **then**

20 ⎿ *Inserttree(X, N)*.

21 **for** *node N in tree do* **do**

22 ⎸ **if** *x ⟵ T* **then**

23 ⎸ ⎸ Construct x's conditional pattern base then make x's conditional MCDRP Tree

24 ⎸ ⎿ $M \longleftarrow M \cup FPGrowth(T)$

25 **for** *all Conditional MCDRP Tree* **do**

26 ⎿ Construct Rare Association Rules(M), RAR

27 **return** RAR

Let minRaresup $= 3$, minFreqSup $= 6$ and $\beta = 0.75$ is chosen, so rare itemsets is considered New MIS $\geq$ SD and New MIS < minFreqsup. Where SD $= \{minFreqsup - minRaresup\}$. So rare itemsets are selected MCDRP

Table 5. Support count & calculate new MIS

Items	Support	New MIS
D	9	7
C	7	6
B	5	3
A	4	3
E	3	3

Table 6. Selected rare transactions

TID	Items
1	$\{B\}$
2	$\{A\}$
5	$\{A\}$
6	$\{B\}$
8	$\{B, E\}$
9	$\{B\}$
10	$\{A, B, E\}$

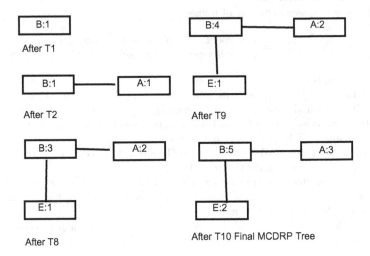

Fig. 6. Final MCDRP tree

Tree: $\{A, B, E\}$. During MCDRP tree designed selected only rare transactions from Table 2 shown in Table 6 and ignore all non rare items. During MCDRP tree construction all the rare transactions are straight forward to read and stored using Dynamic FP tree. Finally, mine rare association rules using non recursive data structure known Dynamic FP-growth. The main advantage of this approach all single itemset is not been considered to be interesting like Apriori [4] or FP Growth [16] approaches.

- **Rare itemsets selection:** Initially select set of items those support belongs to New $MIS \geq SD$ and New $MIS < minFreqsup$.
- **Rare rules generation:** Next projection of all high confidence rules with low support itemset is selected from initial step.

Final construction of MCDRP tree is exhibited in Fig. 6. After evaluation both the MCDRP tree and RP tree, this new proposed approach shows more memory and cost efficient. It produce interesting rules without wasting time to identify uninteresting non rare item sets. Also MCDRP tree minimizes the cost of storage and do not traverse huge number of conditional pattern base respect to the RP tree approach.

8 Conclusion and Future Work

Conventional single support confidence framework with traditional rule mining algorithms are not suitable enough for dealing such complex problems. Construction complexity mining only rare pattern is highly depends on specific database. This paper we presents a comprehensive literature review on existing tree based rare pattern mining algorithms. A dynamic FP tree based compact memory efficient, scalable MCDRP tree algorithm is proposed for mining rare association rules without investing time to generate frequent item set that looks only rare itemsets. MCDRP tree is typically smaller in size because all non rare transactions removes more effectively using dynamic prune search. Reduce search cost, MCDRP tree don't traversal huge number of conditional pattern base. During tree construction keeps track of the support counts changes efficiently.

As a part of future work, there is a plan to research additional applications for this algorithm. We will be able to take benefit of the distributed computation using our approach and examined a suitable methodology for conveying support confidence values in a dynamic manner to produce rare patterns at a different site.

References

1. Abdullah, Z., Herawan, T., Ahmad, N., Deris, M.: Mining significant association rules from educational data using critical relative support approach. Procedia-Soc. Behav. Sci. **28**, 97–101 (2011)
2. Abdullah, Z., Herawan, T., Noraziah, A., Deris, M.: Mining least association rules of degree level programs selected by students. Int. J. Multimedia Ubiquitous Eng. **9**(1), 241–254 (2014)
3. Agrawal, R., Imielinski, T., Swami, A.: Mining association rules between sets of items in large databases. In: ACM SIGMOD Record, vol. 22, pp. 207–216. ACM (1993)
4. Agrawal, R., Srikant, R.: Fast algorithms for mining association rules. In: Proceeding of 20th International Conference Very Large Data Bases, VLDB, vol. 1215, pp. 487–499 (1994)
5. Bhatt, U., Patel, P.: A novel approach for finding rare items based on multiple minimum support framework. Procedia Comput. Sci. **57**, 1088–1095 (2015)
6. Cagliero, L., Garza, P.: Lnfrequent weighted itemset mining using frequent pattern growth. IEEE Trans. Knowl. Data Eng. **26**(4), 903–915 (2014)
7. Cong, G., Tung, A.K., Xu, X., Pan, F., Yang, J.: Farmer: finding interesting rule groups in microarray datasets. In: Proceedings of the 2004 ACM SIGMOD International Conference on Management of Data, pp. 143–154. ACM (2004)
8. Creighton, C., Hanash, S.: Mining gene expression databases for association rules. Bioinformatics **19**(1), 79–86 (2003)
9. Deng, X., Jin, C., Higuchi, Y., Han, C.: An efficient association rule mining method for personalized recommendation in mobile e-commerce, December 2010

10. Ding, J., Yau, S.S.: TCOM, an innovative data structure for mining association rules among infrequent items. Comput. Math. Appl. **57**(2), 290–301 (2009)
11. Giuffrida, G., Cantone, V., Tribulato, G.: An apriori based approach to improve on-line advertising performance. Appl. Data Min. e-Bus. Finan. **177**, 51 (2008)
12. Grzymala-Busse, J.W., Goodwin, L.K., Grzymala-Busse, W.J., Zheng, X.: An approach to imbalanced data sets based on changing rule strength. In: Pal, S.K., Polkowski, L., Skowron, A. (eds.) Rough-Neural Computing, pp. 543–553. Springer, Heidelberg (2004). https://doi.org/10.1007/978-3-642-18859-6_21
13. Gupta, A., Mittal, A., Bhattacharya, A.: Minimally infrequent itemset mining using pattern-growth paradigm and residual trees. In: Proceedings of the 17th International Conference on Management of Data, p. 13. Computer Society of India (2011)
14. Gyorodi, C., Gyorodi, R., Cofeey, T., Holban, S.: Mining association rules using dynamic FP-trees. In: Proceedings of Irish Signals and Systems Conference, pp. 76–81 (2003)
15. Gyorodi, C., Gyorodi, R., Holban, S.: A comparative study of association rules mining algorithms. In: Hungarian Joint Symposium on Applied Computational Intelligence, Oradea (2004)
16. Han, J., Pei, J., Yin, Y.: Mining frequent patterns without candidate generation. In: ACM SIGMOD Record, vol. 29, pp. 1–12. ACM (2000)
17. Hemalatha, C.S., Vaidehi, V., Lakshmi, R.: Minimal infrequent pattern based approach for mining outliers in data streams. Expert Syst. Appl. **42**(4), 1998–2012 (2015)
18. Huang, D., Koh, Y.S., Dobbie, G.: Rare pattern mining on data streams. In: Cuzzocrea, A., Dayal, U. (eds.) DaWaK 2012. LNCS, vol. 7448, pp. 303–314. Springer, Heidelberg (2012). https://doi.org/10.1007/978-3-642-32584-7_25
19. Huang, D.T.J., Koh, Y.S., Dobbie, G., Pears, R.: Detecting changes in rare patterns from data streams. In: Tseng, V.S., Ho, T.B., Zhou, Z.-H., Chen, A.L.P., Kao, H.-Y. (eds.) PAKDD 2014. LNCS (LNAI), vol. 8444, pp. 437–448. Springer, Cham (2014). https://doi.org/10.1007/978-3-319-06605-9_36
20. Karimi-Majd, A., Mahootchi, M.: A new data mining methodology for generating new service ideas. Inf. Syst. e-Bus. Manag. **13**(3), 421–443 (2015)
21. Kiran, R.U., Krishna Reddy, P.: An efficient approach to mine rare association rules using maximum items' support constraints. In: MacKinnon, L.M. (ed.) BNCOD 2010. LNCS, vol. 6121, pp. 84–95. Springer, Heidelberg (2012). https://doi.org/10.1007/978-3-642-25704-9_9
22. Koh, Y.S., Rountree, N.: Finding sporadic rules using apriori-inverse. In: Ho, T.B., Cheung, D., Liu, H. (eds.) PAKDD 2005. LNCS (LNAI), vol. 3518, pp. 97–106. Springer, Heidelberg (2005). https://doi.org/10.1007/11430919_13
23. Kong, H., Jong, C., Ryang, U.: Rare association rule mining for network intrusion detection. arXiv preprint arXiv:1610.04306 (2016)
24. Lavergne, J., Benton, R., Raghavan, V., Hafez, A.: DynTARM: an in-memory data structure for targeted strong and rare association rule mining over time-varying domains. In: Proceedings of the 2013 IEEE/WIC/ACM International Joint Conferences on Web Intelligence (WI) and Intelligent Agent Technologies (IAT), vol. 01, pp. 298–306. IEEE Computer Society (2013)
25. Lavergne, J., Benton, R., Raghavan, V.V.: TRARM-RelSup: targeted rare association rule mining using itemset trees and the relative support measure. In: Chen, L., Felfernig, A., Liu, J., Raś, Z.W. (eds.) ISMIS 2012. LNCS (LNAI), vol. 7661, pp. 61–70. Springer, Heidelberg (2012). https://doi.org/10.1007/978-3-642-34624-8_7

26. Lin, W., Alvarez, S.A., Ruiz, C.: Collaborative recommendation via adaptive association rule mining. Data Min. Knowl. Discov. **6**, 83–105 (2000)
27. Liu, B., Hsu, W., Ma, Y.: Mining association rules with multiple minimum supports. In: Proceedings of the Fifth ACM SIGKDD International Conference on Knowledge Discovery and Data Mining, pp. 337–341. ACM (1999)
28. Manning, A.M., Haglin, D.J., Keane, J.A.: A recursive search algorithm for statistical disclosure assessment. Data Min. Knowl. Discov. **16**(2), 165–196 (2008)
29. Merceron, A., Yacef, K.: Interestingness measures for association rules in educational data. In: Educational Data Mining 2008 (2008)
30. Mishra, N., Soni, H., Sharma, S., Upadhyay, A.: A comprehensive survey of data mining techniques on time series data for rainfall prediction. J. ICT Res. Appl. **11**(2), 168–184 (2017)
31. Phua, C., Lee, V., Smith, K., Gayler, R.: A comprehensive survey of data mining-based fraud detection research. arXiv preprint arXiv:1009.6119 (2010)
32. Raza, K.: Application of data mining in bioinformatics. arXiv preprint arXiv:1205.1125 (2012)
33. Saha, B., Lazarescu, M., Venkatesh, S.: Infrequent item mining in multiple data streams. In: Seventh IEEE International Conference on Data Mining Workshops, 2007. ICDM Workshops 2007, pp. 569–574. IEEE (2007)
34. Seno, M., Karypis, G.: LPMiner: an algorithm for finding frequent itemsets using length-decreasing support constraint. In: Proceedings 2001 IEEE International Conference on Data Mining ICDM 2001, pp. 505–512. IEEE (2001)
35. Sharma, N., Om, H.: Extracting significant patterns for oral cancer detection using apriori algorithm. Intell. Inf. Manag. **6**(02), 30 (2014)
36. Srivastava, J., Cooley, R., Deshpande, M., Tan, P.: Web usage mining: discovery and applications of usage patterns from web data. ACM SIGKDD Explor. Newsl. **1**(2), 12–23 (2000)
37. Szathmary, L., Valtchev, P., Napoli, A., Godin, R.: Efficient vertical mining of frequent closures and generators. In: Adams, N.M., Robardet, C., Siebes, A., Boulicaut, J.-F. (eds.) IDA 2009. LNCS, vol. 5772, pp. 393–404. Springer, Heidelberg (2009). https://doi.org/10.1007/978-3-642-03915-7_34
38. Szathmary, L., Valtchev, P., Napoli, A., Godin, R.: Finding minimal rare itemsets in a depth-first manner. In: Analysis for Artificial Intelligence (FCA4AI), p. 73 (2012)
39. Troiano, L., Scibelli, G., Birtolo, C.: A fast algorithm for mining rare itemsets. In: Ninth International Conference on Intelligent Systems Design and Applications, ISDA 2009, pp. 1149–1155. IEEE (2009)
40. Tsang, S., Koh, Y.S., Dobbie, G.: Finding interesting rare association rules using rare pattern tree. In: Hameurlain, A., Küng, J., Wagner, R., Cuzzocrea, A., Dayal, U. (eds.) Transactions on Large-Scale Data- and Knowledge-Centered Systems VIII. LNCS, vol. 7790, pp. 157–173. Springer, Heidelberg (2013). https://doi.org/10.1007/978-3-642-37574-3_7
41. Woon, Y., Ng, W., Das, A.: Fast online dynamic association rule mining. In: Proceedings of the Second International Conference on Web Information Systems Engineering, vol. 1, pp. 278–287. IEEE (2001)

A Meetei Mayek Basic Characters Recognizer Using Deep Features

Neeta Devi Chingakham[1(✉)], Debaprasad Das[2], and Mamata Devi Haobam[3]

[1] Computer Science and Engineering Department,
National Institute of Technology Manipur, Imphal 795004, Manipur, India
`neeta.chingakham@gmail.com`
[2] Electronics and Communication Engineering Department, Assam University,
Silchar 788011, Assam, India
`dasdebaprasad75@gmail.com`
[3] Computer Science Department, Manipur University,
Imphal 795003, Manipur, India
`mamata_dh@rediffmail.com`

Abstract. This paper presents a Meetei Mayek Isolated Handwritten Basic Character Recognition System (MMIHBCRS) which is a part of an undergoing development of a full-fledged Optical Character Recognition (OCR) system for Meetei Mayek script. In this work, we have developed a standard Meetei Mayek Isolated Handwritten Basic Character Database consisting of 8000 plus characters. The proposed work has used the concept of Transfer Learning where a pretrained Convolutional Neural Network (CNN) has been used for Deep Convolutional Features extraction. The performance of two classifiers K-Nearest Neighbour (K-NN) and Support Vector Machine (SVM) are compared using the extracted Deep Features. Using the Deep Features, the classifiers have achieved very high recognition accuracies for a dataset of 8000 characters where SVM has shown better recognition accuracy compared to K-NN giving an accuracy of 97.55% compared to K-NN's 96.63%.

Keywords: Meetei Mayek · Database · CNN · K-NN · SVM

1 Introduction

Optical Character Recognition (OCR) has been a very popular area of research. The research on this area has become exhaustive for languages like English. An accurate OCR is required for any language for carrying out language processing tasks like Transliteration, Machine Translation, and Text to Speech Conversion etc. In addition to that, in today's world, volumes of data need to be stored in digital format. Therefore, development of an accurate OCR has become indispensable for any language. It is even more important for developing languages like Manipuri for which a full-fledged handwritten OCR has not been developed yet. Manipuri is a language which is the mother tongue of Meiteis and is mainly spoken by them in Manipur - a state in India and across the world.

© Springer Nature Singapore Pte Ltd. 2019
J. K. Mandal et al. (Eds.): CICBA 2018, CCIS 1031, pp. 306–315, 2019.
https://doi.org/10.1007/978-981-13-8581-0_25

Today's technology has reached to a height where OCRs have been developed for many languages worldwide. For popular languages like English, Chinese etc., many works [1–3] on Handwritten Digits and Character Recognition are found in literature. For Indian languages, works have been reported in literature for offline handwritten recognition [4–6]. Character Recognition still remains a challenge for many Indian Languages which are less popular and developed. One such language is Manipuri language which has two scripts – Meetei (also known as Meitei) Mayek and Bangla. The Bangla script was borrowed from Bengali Language and already efficient OCRs have been reported in literature [6,7] for it. A lot of work can be done in Optical Character Recognition of Meetei Mayek Script since only few works have been reported till today.

This paper presents a Meetei Mayek Isolated Handwritten Basic Character Recognition System (MMIHBCRS). The adopted processes of the proposed Basic Character Recognition System MMIHBCRS are shown in Fig. 1. The proposed work is the initial product of the development of a complete Meetei Mayek Recognition System. The proposed work consists of Data Acquisition, Preprocessing, Data Extraction from forms, Deep Feature Extraction using Alexnet Convolutional Neural Network (CNN). Comparison of two classifiers K-NN and SVM, are done using the extracted Deep Features.

The paper is divided into in five sections where Sect. 1 gives a brief introduction emphasising on why an OCR system is a must for Manipuri Meetei Mayek script. Section 2 presents brief review of works that have been carried out before. In Sect. 3, a brief introduction of Meetei Mayek Basic Characters and Data Collection till feature extraction is explained. Section 4 explains the different classifiers used for experimental purpose using the deep features to find out the best classifier among them in term of accuracy. Section 5 shows the experimental results obtained for the proposed system. Section 6 concludes the paper by summarising the results obtained and explaining further scope of work for development of complete Handwritten OCR for Meetei Mayek.

Fig. 1. Proposed Meetei Mayek basic characters recognizer.

2 Related Works

Various works have been reported in literature for some famous Indian Languages. Precedent works in Meetei Mayek Character recognition have been found in limited number in literature.

A Handwritten Digit Recognizer [1] has been proposed using well known databases CENPARMI, CEDAR and MNIST. For feature extraction, they have used directional features which includes Chaincode, Gradient Features with Sobel and Kirsh operators and peripheral direction contributivity. The authors have employed eight classifiers namely nearest neighbours (K-NN), Multilayer Perceptron (MLP), Neural Network using Radial Basis Function (RBF), quadratic PC, Learning Vector Quantization (LVQ), Discriminative Learning Quadratic Discriminant Function (DLQDF), Support Vector Classifier with polynomial kernel (SVC-poly) and Support Vector Classifier with Radial Basis Function (SVC-rbf).

Ujjwal and Bidyut [6] have presented an isolated handwritten numeral recognition system for three Indian scripts viz. Devanagari, Bangla and English. The authors have implemented Daubechies Wavelet filter based multi-resolution analysis using Multilayer Perceptron (MLP) in a cascaded way. For feature extraction, they have used Chain Code Histogram features for three resolutions of the numeral images. Multistage classification has been carried out using a cascade of MLP classifiers. Their classification starts at a lowest resolution level. The test sample is classified or rejected according to a precision index. The authors have achieved high accuracies for mixed and unmixed numerals.

Research in Optical Character Recognition of Manipuri script has not been widely introduced and found in literature till date. A research work on isolated handwritten and printed Meetei Mayek digits has been reported in [8]. They have carried out binarisation using Otsu's global thresholding method. Segmentation of isolated digits has been done in explicit manner. After that they have thinned the segmented digit and dilated so that the digits have uniform stroke. For feature extraction, they have used Gabor Filter and classification for both printed and handwritten have been done using SVM. They have carried out the experiments for images of size 14 × 10 and achieved optimal accuracy by extracting Gabor Filters with 5 spatial frequencies. The set of different spatial frequencies has been obtained for 8 distinct orientations. The authors have achieved recognition accuracy rate for handwritten digit as 89.58% and printed digits as 98.45%.

An OCR system for handwritten Meetei Mayek script has been developed by Thokchom et al. [9]. Their work incorporates binarisation using Otsu's method. Character segmentation has been done using Sobel Edge Detection, dilation and filling processes. For feature extraction they have used a total of 79 features that include 31 probabilistic and 48 fuzzy features. Using the extracted features, Neural Network using Back-Propagation algorithm is trained and recognition is done. This work was the first recognition system of handwritten Manipuri Meetei Mayek script reported in literature achieving an accuracy of 90.3%.

3   Meetei Mayek Basic Characters Data Collection, Data Extraction and Feature Description

This section describes the proposed MMIHBCRS's data acquisition using forms, data extraction from the forms, creation of database and feature extraction and description using Alexnet in details. The proposed system forms a part of development of a full-fledged Meetei Mayek Recognizer.

3.1   Meetei Mayek Basic Characters Data Collection

Meetei Mayek is the script of Manipuri language of Manipur. Manipuri language is spoken by Meiteis mainly in India, Myanmar, Bangladesh and all over the world. It has two scripts—Bangla and Meetei Mayek. Bangla script was used for Manipuri Language from 18th century but Meetei Mayek has been revived recently, therefore, a lot of work needs to be done for Meetei Mayek. Meetei Mayek Basic Character consists of total of 27 letters.

In a Character Recognition System, the creation of a database plays an important part. The database can be created only after the collection of data. In order to collect the data, a form is being designed, first two pages of the form are shown in Fig. 2. The forms have been distributed to 100 persons in order to get varied handwriting styles. The data have been collected from different persons ranging from children of age 9 years to elders who are 70 years of age.

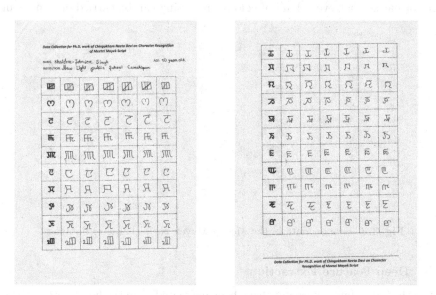

Fig. 2. Sample form pages for data collection

3.2   Preprocessing

The handwritten character forms are scanned at 300 dpi. Before noise removal, the forms are cropped to consist of the handwritten part only. The cropped images are preprocessed using bilateral filter [10] and skew detection and correction is done. The cleaned images are used for extraction of the handwritten basic characters from the forms.

3.3 Data (Basic Characters) Extraction

From the preprocessed images, as the characters are isolated, connected components are detected. Large connected components are filtered to remove the lines used to separate the characters. As such, other components detected other than the basic characters are filtered giving only the characters as shown in Fig. 3 from the processed forms.

3.4 Database Creation

The most crucial part of development of an OCR is the creation of the database. The data that have been extracted in the previous step is used for creation of Meetei Mayek Basic Characters database. The database created is the first standard Basic Character database of Meetei Mayek. There are around 8000 characters in total in the database. The characters images are stored in colour .tiff format so that every kind of colour processing can be carried out on them.

Fig. 3. Character data in the Meetei Mayek basic character database.

3.5 Deep Feature Extraction

After the individuals characters have been extracted from the handwritten forms, feature extraction is to be done. Deep (Convolutional) Features are extracted using already pretrained Alexnet [11] which represents one of the milestone architecture of Convolutional Neural Networks (CNNs). Using Pretrained CNNs as generic feature descriptors are becoming popular nowadays, because training a CNN from scratch takes very long time. As the CNNs have already been trained on very large datasets, the CNNs have acquired much knowledge.

Alexnet CNN [11] has been trained on a fraction of Imagenet Dataset which contains more than 15 million images which are labelled to near 22000 categories. Alexnet have used 1.2 million images of 1000 categories from Imagenet. Alexnet uses Rectified Linear Units (ReLUs) as they result in faster training time. ReLUs are neurons whose output are given by

$$f(x) = max(0, x) \tag{1}$$

with non-saturating nonlinearity which gives faster training time compared with saturating nonlinearities:

$$f(x) = tanh(x) \tag{2}$$

Local Response Normalisation is also carried out in Alexnet. Inspired by real lateral inhibition found in neurons, this is done to create a competing environment among the neurons. The normalisation makes it easier to find high frequency features having large responses. Pooling layers are used in overlapping manner. Pooling layers are used to represent the output of previous stage of the CNN. This techniques has been adopted as this makes the model avoid overfitting.

Alexnet has eight layers-convolutional layers make up the first five layers and fully connected layers in the last three. The seventh layer's activations are extracted which represents the deep features. This activations represent the features of each character and acts as a feature descriptor. This features can be used for training classifiers like SVM which is now a very popular concept popularly known as Transfer Learning.

4   Classification

Basic Characters have been extracted from preprocessed cleaned images and deep features have been extracted for the characters in the database. The task of use of classifiers comes into picture. Two well performing classifiers have been chosen for the basic character classification task.

4.1   K-Nearest Neighbour Classification

Nearest Neighbour is a learning algorithm that can be used for both classification and regression problems. K-Nearest Neighbour (K-NN) is a non-parametric classification algorithm that finds K training examples closest to an unknown instance. The unknown instance x is classified to a particular category based on these K training examples identified according to a similarity measure. The similarity measure is a distance metric given by Euclidean Distance given below:

$$d(x, y) = \sqrt{\sum_{i=1}^{n} \{x^i - y^i\}^2} \tag{3}$$

Here n is the number of training samples. The unknown instance x is classified as the most frequently occurring class among the nearest K training samples identified using Euclidean Distance.

4.2   Support Vector Machine

SVM is a binary linear classifier which finds a hyperplane which separates feature points into two classes in the feature plane. Given a training set X, the equation of the hyperplane that separates the two classes in the feature space is

$$H(x) = \mathbf{w}^T x^i + w_0 \tag{4}$$

For linear problem, SVM finds the optimal value of $\mathbf{w}$ and w_0 such that the margin from the hyperplane to the nearest training samples i.e. Support Vectors, on either side of it, is maximised. In order to maximize the margin, the following objective function is minimised:

$$J(w) = \frac{1}{2}||\mathbf{w}||^2$$
(5)

For problems which are not linearly separable, the following objective function is minimised:

$$J(w, \delta) = \frac{1}{2}||\mathbf{w}||^2 + C\sum_{i=1}^{n}\delta_i$$
(6)

where C is the trade-off controlling factor between generalisation and training errors and δ is the slack variable representing the error tolerance but which has to be minimised.

Kernel functions of SVM are used to reduce computational complexity. The Linear Kernel function of SVM is given by the formula below:

$$K(\mathbf{x}_i, \mathbf{x}_j) = \mathbf{x}_i^T \mathbf{x}_j$$
(7)

In the proposed work, as Character Recognition is a multiclass problem, we use One-against-One strategy for creating a multiclass SVM classifier.

5 Experimental Results

This section describes the experimental results of the proposed MMIHBCRS. After extracting character from the forms, the database for Meetei Mayek basic characters has been created. After feature extraction using Pretrained CNN-Alexnet, two classifiers K-NN and SVM have been employed for classification and a comparison is done between them in terms of Recognition Accuracy.

For carrying out the experiments, using the characters in the database four different datasets have been used of sizes 2000, 4000, 6000 and 8000. For each set, 70% of the data is used as training data and 30% as testing data. Deep features have been extracted for each dataset. Pretrained Alexnet has been chosen as it marked a milestone in the field of CNN and has given very good results and takes lesser time compared to other CNN with more layers. The length of deep feature vector is 4096 which represents the activations of the seventh layer of Alexnet. Classification using K-NN has been done by setting the value of $K = 5$ since this value has given the optimal recognition accuracy. For SVM classification, linear kernel has been used which has given very high accuracy. To implement Multiclass SVM classification, One-against-One strategy has been used. A SVM classifier is constructed for each two classes, resulting in constructing C(C-1)/2 SVMs, where C = 27 represents the number of classes. An unknown instance get classified to the class getting the maximum votes from the combined classifiers used for multiclass classification. The recognition accuracies obtained for both K-NN and SVM have been plotted and the graph is shown in Fig. 4.

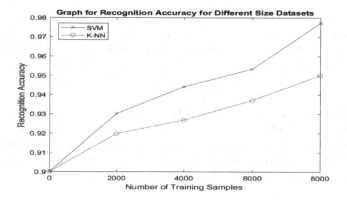

Fig. 4. Comparison of K-NN and SVM for datasets of size 2000, 4000, 6000 and 8000.

Table 1. Recognition accuracy of each Meetei Mayei basic character for a dataset of 8000 characters

Meetei Mayek Letters		Recognition Accuracy Achieved		Meetei Mayek Letters		Recognition Accuracy Achieved	
No.	Letters	K-NN	SVM	No.	Letters	K-NN	SVM
1.	☒	1	1	15.	ᯒ	1	.99
2.	ᯃ	1	1	16.	ᯓ	.98	.99
3.	ᯄ	.93	.95	17.	ᯔ	.90	.89
4.	ᯅ	.96	.97	18.	ᯕ	.89	.97
5.	ᯆ	.95	.96	19.	ᯖ	.99	.98
6.	ᯇ	.92	.89	20.	ᯗ	.98	.99
7.	ᯈ	1	1	21.	ᯘ	1	1
8.	ᯉ	.96	.98	22.	ᯙ	1	.96
9.	ᯊ	.95	.97	23.	ᯚ	.98	1
10.	ᯋ	.97	.99	24.	ᯛ	.94	.94
11.	ᯌ	.95	1	25.	ᯜ	.99	1
12.	ᯍ	.99	.98	26.	ᯝ	.94	.95
13.	ᯎ	1	1	27.	ᯞ	1	1
14.	ᯏ	.98	.99				

The graph shows the comparison of the accuracies for the two classifier for different datasets. As can be seen from the graph, SVM gives better recognition accuracy than K-NN. The Recognition Accuracies for each Meetei Mayek basic character is shown for a dataset of 8000 characters in Table 1 for the two classifiers K-NN and SVM. The results shows that 100% accuracy is achieved for 9 characters by SVM and 8 by K-NN.

From the table, the classification performance of each classifier can be understood for the dataset of size 8000 where 70% of the data has been used for training and 30% for testing purposes. The average Recognition Accuracy for the experimental dataset consisting of total of 8000 characters have been found to be 97.55% and 96.63% for SVM and K-NN respectively.

6   Conclusion and Future Works

The paper has presented a Meetei Mayek Isolated Handwritten Basic Character Recognition System (MMIHBCRS) using Transfer Learning. This work is a part of development of a complete Character Recognition System for Meetei Mayek. A Color Handwritten Basic Character Database has been developed which comprises of more than 8000 characters. For feature extraction, a pretrained CNN-Alexnet has been used for extracting Deep Features of the characters. A comparison of classifiers K-NN and SVM has been done where SVM has shown superior average recognition accuracy of 97.55% compared to K-NN's 96.63% for a dataset comprising of 8000 characters. In future, a full-fledged Character Recognition System for Meetei Mayek will be developed where different Deep CNNs feature descriptor will be compared after feature reduction using classifiers. CNNs can also be used for classification tasks for the developing Meetei Mayek Recognition System.

References

1. Cheng-Lin, L., Kazuki, N., Hiroshi, S., Hiromichi, F.: Handwritten digit recognition: benchmarking of state-of-art techniques. Pattern Recogn. **36**, 2271–2285 (2003)
2. Leung, K.C., Leung, C.H.: Recognition of handwritten Chinese characters by critical region analysis. Pattern Recogn. **43**, 949–961 (2010)
3. Mohammad, T.P., Sabri, A.M.: Arabic handwriting recognition using structural and syntactic pattern attributes. Pattern Recogn. **46**, 141–154 (2013)
4. Javad, S., Mohammad, R.Y., Javad, S.: A novel comprehensive database for offline persian handwriting recognition. Pattern Recogn. **6**, 378–393 (2016)
5. Apurva, A.D.: Gujarati handwritten numeral optical character reorganization through neural network. Pattern Recogn. **43**, 2582–2589 (2010)
6. Ujjwal, B., Bidyut, B.C.: Handwritten numeral databases of Indian scripts and multistage recognition of mixed numerals. IEEE Trans. Pattern Anal. Mach. Intell. **31**, 444–457 (2009)
7. Nibaran, D., Ram, S., Subhadip, B., Punam, K.S., Mahantapas, K., Mita, N.: Handwritten Bangla character recognition using a soft computing paradigm embedded in two pass approach. Pattern Recogn. **48**(6), 2054–2071 (2015)

8. Kansham, A.M., Renu, D.: Recognition of cheising Iyek/Eeyek – Manipuri digits using support vector machine. Int. J. Comput. Sci. Inf. Technol. **1**, 1–6 (2014)
9. Tangkeshwar, T., Bansal, P.K., Renu, V., Seema, B.: Recognition of handwritten character of Manipuri script. J. Comput. **5**, 1570–1574 (2010)
10. Tomasi, C., Manduchi, R.: Bilateral filtering for gray and color images. In: International Conference on Computer Vision, pp. 839–846 (1998)
11. Alex, K., Ilya, S., Geoffrey, E.H.: Imagenet classification with deep convolutional neural networks. In: Advances in Neural Information Processing Systems 25, pp. 1106–1114 (2012)

Face Image Retrieval Using Discriminative Ternary Census Transform and Spatial Pyramid Matching

Abul Hasnat[1(✉)], Santanu Halder[2], Debotosh Bhattacharjee[3], and Mita Nasipuri[3]

[1] Government College of Engineering and Textile Technology, Berhampore, West Bengal, India
email.abulhasnat@gmail.com
[2] Government College of Engineering and Leather Technology, Kolkata, India
sant.halder@gmail.com
[3] Jadavpur University, Kolkata, West Bengal, India
debotosh@ieee.org, mitanasipuri@gmail.com

Abstract. Face image retrieval is a process to efficiently select one or more faces from face databases which are similar to the query face image. This study proposes a new face image retrieval method where images are indexed using Discriminative Ternary Census Transform Histogram (DTCTH) which captures the discriminative structural properties of an image by avoiding unwanted background information. It encodes local micro structures of an image such as line, edge, corners etc. and uses a dynamic threshold during image transformation thus makes it more stable against intensity fluctuation. Global structure of the Discriminative Transformed image is captured using Spatial Pyramid representation during histogram index computation. The computed histogram index is used as face image descriptor. The computed histogram index along with the face image is stored in the database. In this way face image database is built. In the retrieval phase, when a query image is given, the histogram index is computed using the same process and then distance between the feature vectors of query images and feature vectors of the database images are computed. Images with less distance are registered as output. The proposed solutions are experimentally evaluated on the standard constrained FRAV2D, JAFFE and FERET face image databases. Experimental result shows that the face retrieval method is very effective on databases containing face images with facial expression and intensity variations.

Keywords: Face image retrieval · Discriminative ternary census histogram · Histogram index · Spatial pyramid matching · Local binary pattern · Chi-square distance

J. K. Mandal et al. (Eds.): CICBA 2018, CCIS 1031, pp. 316–330, 2019.
https://doi.org/10.1007/978-981-13-8581-0_26

1 Introduction

Face image retrieval is a process to search face images which are similar to a given query image from large scale face database [1–13]. Content-based face image retrieval process requires building a large face database where each image along with its feature descriptor is stored. An image is indexed by an n dimensional feature vector/descriptor. Given a query image, it is indexed into its feature descriptor and in next step; system compares the feature vector of the input/query image with each of the stored feature vectors of the stored images. Images with less distance are selected as results. Face retrieval algorithms reported in the literature achieve impressive result in controlled conditions [1].

Although many face image retrieval techniques [1–12] reported in the literature still it is challenging to refine face search outputs based on subtle shape attributes that are easy to see in human eyes but hard to describe in text. Current face image retrieval methods (using geometric face attributes) give unsatisfactory result [2]. To address this problem, Smith et al. [2] proposed a face search method that uses shape manipulation which is complementary to contemporary search techniques. They concluded that face alignment requires further improvement to enhance the system performance in terms of query accuracy and construction of the indexed database [2]. Most of the face image retrieval techniques exploit low-level features to represent face [3] but many times low-level features fails to capture semantic meanings of face images. Therefore such techniques results are not satisfactory [3]. To address this problem, Wu et al. [4] used identity based quantization and Chen et al. [5] proposed identity based sparse coding technique. But they concluded that their methods may require clean training data and huge human annotations [3]. In 2013, another method [3] on content based face image retrieval was introduced where they used high-level human attributes for face image representation and index structure. They stated face images of different people may be very close in the low-level feature space but high-level human attributes may distinguish them. Therefore low-level features and high-level human attributes are combined to get better feature representations for better retrieval results. Face retrieval techniques face more challenges when face images have different poses, various expressions and captured in different illumination conditions. State-of-the-art scalable image retrieval methods use bag-of-visual-words representation model [4] but such techniques when applied on face images, performs unsatisfactorily because geometric features of a face image are not taken into account.

Objective of this article is to address this challenging issue–content-based face image retrieval in large-scale database. Present study proposes a face image retrieval technique where Discriminative Ternary Census Transform (DTCTH) [14] captures local micro structure and Spatial Pyramid Matching (SPM) [15–18] is used to capture global structure for effective face image indexing.

The contributions of this study include: (a) Development of a feature descriptor which combines local structure of face image (using Discriminative Ternary Census Transform) and global structure of face image (captured using SPM). It balances global geometric properties and local microstructure of face image to improve content-based face image retrieval. (b) Use of dynamic threshold in DTCTH that normalizes the intensity variations of the face image and (c) Extensive application of the proposed method on constrained and unconstrained public datasets which gives real time response.

This scheme of the article is as follows: Sect. 2 explains the Discriminative Ternary Census Transform. Section 3 depicts the method of image indexing for image retrieval and Sect. 4 shows the experimental results. Finally Sect. 5 concludes about some of the points analyzed in this paper.

2 Discriminative Ternary Census Transform

Image representation using Discriminative Ternary Census Transform (DTCT) [14] captures most of the key properties of an image. DTCT encodes micro-structures of an image such as line, edge, corners etc. It uses dynamic threshold to produce local feature that is intensity invariant. In other words, DTCT is stable against intensity variation and monotonic illumination [14]. Also, DTCT effectively separates foreground and background of an image. The DTCT catches the highly discriminative features while ignoring the fine details. It is a ternary code that enhances the discrimination ability. DTCTH features are more robust to noise compared to CENTRIST [14, 15] and Local Binary Pattern [16–24] which fail [14] to assemble the same code in case of intensity variation. The ternary coding approach namely Discriminative Ternary Census Transform (DTCT) [14] is expressed using Eq. 1.

$$DTCT_{n,r}(x_c, y_c) = \sum_{i=0}^{n-1} q(p_i - p_c) \times 3^i \tag{1}$$

Where $q(d) = \begin{cases} +1, & if\ d \geq T_d \\ -1, & if\ d \leq T_d \\ 0, & otherwise \end{cases}$

Here, T_d is a dynamic threshold, n is the total number of neighbors and r is the radius of the neighboring pixels and the center pixel coordinate is (x_c, y_c). p_c is the intensity of the center pixel (x_c, y_c) and p_i is intensity of ith neighboring pixel. The ternary pattern is divided into two census transformed images namely upper (UP_DTCT) and lower (LP_DTCT) pattern. The upper and lower pattern is calculated using Eqs. 2 and 3 respectively.

$$UP\_DTCT_{n,r}(x_c, y_c) = \sum_{i=0}^{n-1} q(p_i - p_c) \times 2^i \tag{2}$$

Where $q(d) = \begin{cases} 1, & if\ d \geq T_d \\ 0, & otherwise \end{cases}$

$$LP\_DTCT_{n,r}(x_c, y_c) = \sum_{i=0}^{n-1} q(p_i - p_c) \times 2^i \tag{3}$$

Where $q(d) = \begin{cases} 1, & if\ d \le -T_d \\ 0, & otherwise \end{cases}$

Then two separate histograms, HI_UP_DTCT and HI_LP_DTCT of these two binary patterns are computed using Eqs. 4 and 5 respectively. The final feature vector is obtained by concatenation of these two histograms.

$$HI\_UP\_DTCT^k = \sum_{i=1}^{h} \sum_{j=1}^{w} \delta^k_{UP\_DTCT_{n,r}(i,j)} \tag{4}$$

Where $\delta^k_p = \begin{cases} 1, & if\ p = k \\ 0, & otherwise \end{cases}$

$$HI\_LP\_DTCT^k = \sum_{i=1}^{h} \sum_{j=1}^{w} \delta^k_{LP\_DTCT_{n,r}(i,j)} \tag{5}$$

Where $\delta^k_p = \begin{cases} 1, & if\ p = k \\ 0, & otherwise \end{cases}$

Here, $UP\_DTCT_{n,r}(x_c, y_c)$ and $LP\_DTCT_{n,r}(x_c, y_c)$ are the upper and lower DTCT of coordinate (i, j). k is the kth bin of the histogram. Height and width of the face image are h and w respectively.

After exhaustive experimental analysis on 10^9 cases, Rahman et al. [14] reported that considering the square root of the intensity of the center pixel as the value of T_d gives in optimized result in terms of discriminative accuracy and computational cost. In this work also, T_d is taken as the square root f the intensity of the center pixel. Figure 1 shows sample output of Discriminative Ternary Census Transformed images.

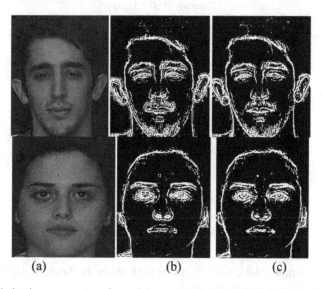

Fig. 1. Discriminative census transformed images (a) original image (b) lower DCT image (c) upper DCT image.

3 Proposed Method

In the present work, all images are stored in the database along with their feature descriptor. At first, the proposed method captures local micro structure of the input image and then Spatial Pyramid Representation (SPM) [15–18] is used to capture the global structure for DTCT face image. Objective is to represent the image using global descriptor by collecting the statistics of local features over fixed sub-regions. SPM subdivides the image repeatedly and computes histograms of local features at increasingly fine resolutions. In this study, level 0, level 1 and level 2 histogram are computed on both lower DTCT and upper DTCT images. After that, these two histograms of different levels are concatenated to form the image descriptor. These two image descriptors (one for upper DTCT image and one for lower DTCT image) are combined to form the final face image descriptor. The block diagram of the image indexing process is shown in Fig. 2.

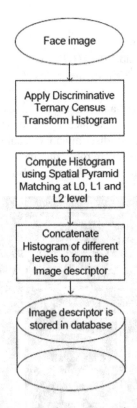

Fig. 2. Face descriptor computation process

The final descriptor along with the image is stored in the database. Histogram index computation process is shown in Fig. 3.

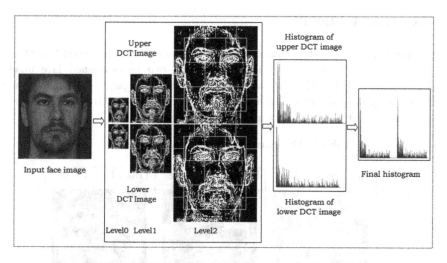

Fig. 3. DCT histogram index computation of a face image

Figure 3 shows the DTCT histogram index computation of a face image. Here, initially upper DTCT and Lower DTCT is applied on the input image and then the histogram index is computed for DTCT image using Spatial Pyramid representation. Level 0 computes histogram for entire DTCT image, Level 1 computes Histogram index of four $(2^1 \times 2^1)$ blocks and one inner block and finally Level 2 computes histogram of sixteen $(2^2 \times 2^2)$ sub-regions and nine $((2^2 - 1) \times (2^2 - 1))$ inner blocks. Histogram index is computed for 1 to 254 bins excluding 0 and 255 [14]. Thus for upper DTCT image concatenated feature vector is of dimension $(1 + 4 + 1 + 16 + 9) \times 254 = 31 \times 254$ dimension. In the same way, feature vector of lower DTCT image is of 31×254 dimension also. The final feature vector contains the concatenation of histogram of upper and lower DTCT image. Hence final histogram index is of length $(31 + 31) \times 254 = 15748$.

In this way, all the images along with its feature vectors are stored in the database. When a query image is given to the system, feature vector of the query image is computed in the same way as discussed above. Now the distance between feature vector of the query image and the features vectors of stored faces are computed. Here, Chi-square [21] distance metric is used to measure the distance between query image and stored image. The minimum distance between two feature sets gives the maximum similarity between them [21]. Hence, the image having the minimum distance with the query image is shown as the output image. Chi-square distance is defined using Eq. 6.

$$X^2_{x,\,y} = \sum_{i,j} \frac{(x_{i,j} - y_{i,j})^2}{x_{i,j} + y_{i,j}} \tag{6}$$

4   Experimental Result

The proposed face retrieval technique has been applied on two constrained face image databases namely FRAV2D [25], JAFFE [26] and two unconstrained face image databases namely FERET [27, 28] and PubFig [29, 30]. In this paper, the mean average precision (MAP) and the precision at K (P@K) [3, 31] are used as the performance metric. Sample DTCT face images are shown in Table 1.

Table 1. Discriminative census transformed images

SL	Face image	Upper DCT image	Lower DCT image
1			
2			

For testing purpose, a random image is selected from the database as the query image and the selected image is excluded from the database during search time. Top five selections are shown in Table 2. The experimental results of the proposed methodology on four different databases are discussed below.

(A) FRAV2D [25] Database: This dataset contains 3058 face images of 109 people. This is a constrained database that contains multiple horizontally rotated face images for a single subject. Also, the database contains images with a different facial expression of a single subject. The database is queried hundred times; each time taking a different query image. A sample result is shown in Table 2; where 2nd column shows the query image and 3rd, 4th, 5th, 6th and 7th column show the 1st selection, 2nd selection, 3rd selection, 4th selection and 5th selection respectively when applied on FRAV2D database.

The proposed methodology retrieved nearly 75–80% correct set of face images of FRAV2D in the top five selections.

(B) The JAFFF [26] database: It has 213 images of 7 facial expressions- 6 basic facial expressions and one neutral pose by 10 Japanese females. Original images are used for the experiment. The query is repeated thirty times; each time taking a different query image. Top five images are selected as result. A sample result is shown in

Table 3; where 2nd column shows the query image and 3rd, 4th, 5th, 6th and 7th column show the 1st selection, 2nd selection, 3rd selection, 4th selection and 5th selection respectively when applied on JAFFE [26] database.

Table 2. Sample result images of the proposed face retrieval technique on FRAV2D database

SL	Face image	1st Selection	2nd Selection	3rd Selection	4th Selection	5th Selection
1						
2						
3						
4						
5						
6						
7						

The present face retrieval method has been applied on JAFFE database to test performance on images of different facial expression. The proposed method retrieves 70–75% right set of images in top five selections from JAFFE database.

(C) FERET [27, 28] database: This database contains 4432 images. During experiment, 4432 number of images are used to construct the database. The database has multiple images of the same person with different poses and different lighting condition. Some of the images are cropped to use only facial part by excluding lower part of images. The query is repeated hundred times each time taking a different query image. Again the query image is randomly selected, and the query image is excluded from search space. Top five images are selected as result. A sample result is shown in Table 4 where 2nd column shows the query image and 3rd, 4th, 5th, 6th and 7th column show the 1st selection, 2nd selection, 3rd selection, 4th selection and 5th selection respectively when applied on FERET database. The proposed method retrieves 55–60% right set of images in top five selections on FERET dataset.

Table 3. Sample result images of the proposed face retrieval technique on JAFFE database

(D) PubFig [29, 30] database: The PubFig database is a large, real-world face dataset consisting of 58,797 images of 200 people collected from the internet. These images are captured in completely uncontrolled situations with non-cooperative subjects. Therefore, there is large variation in pose, lighting, expression, scene, camera, imaging conditions and parameters [29, 30]. The database has multiple images of the single person with different poses and different lighting condition. Four thousand images of 77 people, only facial part are cropped to exclude lower part and background for face image retrieval, and these cropped images are used here for an experiment in this study. The database is queried many times by taking a different query image each time. The query image is randomly selected, and the selected image is excluded from search space. A sample result is shown in Table 5; where 2nd column shows the query image and 3rd, 4th, 5th, 6th and 7th column show the 1st selection, 2nd selection, 3rd selection, 4th selection and 5th selection respectively when applied on PubFig database.

The proposed method retrieves nearly 50–55% correct face images in the top five selections on the PubFig dataset. The images in this database are captured in different lighting condition, in the varying background (unconstrained database). Also, the images are of different resolution and captured using different cameras. Therefore it becomes more challenging to normalize the images in face retrieval process resulting in lower accuracy.

Table 4. Sample result images of the proposed face retrieval technique on FERET database

SL	Query image	1st Selection	2nd Selection	3rd Selection	4th Selection	5th Selection
1						
2						
3						
4						
5						

The performance of the proposed face retrieval method on FRAV2D, JAFFE, FERET and PubFig dataset is summarized in Table 6. The experimental result shows that the proposed method is robust against expression variation and intensity variation.

The proposed face retrieval method uses a face image indexing technique, DTCTH. DTCTH captures the low-level discriminative structural properties of a face image. Experiments are conducted on four different standard face image databases (two constrained and two unconstrained database). This approach exploits local level features using DTCTH and global features using Spatial Pyramid Representation for face image characterization. The combination of local and global features plays a very effective role to achieve higher accuracy in face image retrieval. This method is stable in the presence of noise and different lighting conditions while capturing the face images.

This face retrieval method works well on a database containing faces of a person having 0–10% angle rotation horizontally of the queried face image. Suppose a database contains face images of a side view of a person and the queried face image is a frontal one, in this case, the proposed retrieval algorithm gives a dissatisfactory result because the algorithms characterize a face image using local texture(with dynamic

Table 5. Sample result images of the proposed face retrieval technique on PubFig database

SL	Query image	1st Selection	2nd Selection	3rd Selection	4th Selection	5th Selection

Table 6. Result of the proposed face retrieval technique on standard databases

	FRAV2D	JAFFE	FERET*	PubFig*
Database size	3060	213	4432	4000
Number of people	109	10	507	77
Number of queries	100	30	100	100
Precision at five (P@5)	0.80	0.71	0.58	0.52

*Images are cropped to consider only facial part where lower part of the image was excluded

threshold) features and spatial layout of those features. With the increase in angle of rotation of the face, local texture features and its spatial layout tends to change gradually. Therefore when the query face image and stored face images are captured from a significantly different angle, their respective local texture features and their spatial layout also changes significantly.

The method performs better if the used images considered are of higher resolution. A human face image contains local features which are very important attributes for human face characterization. If we use face images with higher resolution, then local level features become prominent in the image. As in the proposed method, DTCTH captures these local micro features effectively and these entire local features collectively used in Spatial Pyramid Matching to form the global vector (structure) of the face image. Therefore more effectively we capture local features; global features become more robust features descriptor. Thus if we use face images of higher resolution in the proposed face retrieval method, the chance of selection of a right set of faces from the database increases. That is why we get better face image retrieval accuracy in case of FRAV2D database (this database contains images of higher resolution) compared to other database used in the study.

The proposed methodology has been compared with three state-of-the art works which are- (1) LBP: 59-dimension uniform LBP features computed from 175 local patches and concatenated; (2) ATTR: 73-dimensional human attributes; (3) SC: the sparse representation calculated from LBP features. In the literature, datasets like PubFig is a widely used for face image retrieval. It is also observed from experimental result that the retrieval of the resultant images is highly dependent on the selection of query images. Some of the query images can achieve more than 90% average precision (AP) [31], some other query images can only achieve less than 5% AP. Table 7 shows the statistics and the performance of three different baseline methods and the proposed method on PubFig database. It is compared with LBP (one of the state-of-the-art low-level features), human attributes alone (ATTR), and the conventional sparse coding method. The setting in LBP (175 grids * 59 dimensions) reaches the best performance. ATTR obtains low P@10 in dataset because it only has 73 dimensions and has very limited discriminability [3]. Also, ATTR obtains a slightly higher MAP (15.1%) compared to SC-based approach (14.7%) and proposed method (14.4%). However, the proposed method has superior P@5 (51.8%) compared to ATTR (39.7%) because DTCTH preserves the distinctive face traits of a specific person that helps to retrieve the faces with similar visual appearances. The performance of proposed method cannot be directly compared to the performance of those methods [3, 31] that incorporate high-level human attributes like- gender, race, skin color, etc. Methods that incorporates high level human attributes are (a) ASC-D: attribute-enhanced sparse representation with dictionary selection [3], (b) ASC-W: attribute-enhanced sparse representation [3] with attribute weights, (c) AEI: attribute-embedded inverted indexing, (d) Suchitra et al. [31] method etc. Future work may be directed to incorporate DTCTH feature with high-level human attributes to improve the face image retrieval performance.

Table 7. Comparison result of performance of different face retrieval techniques

Database	PubFig	
# of people	43	
Database size	4300	
# of queries	430	
Performance	MAP	P@10
LBP	11.6%	47.4%
ATTR	15.1%	39.7%
SC	14.7%	49.0%
Proposed method	14.4%	51.8%

5 Conclusion

This study proposes a new face image retrieval method where images are indexed using Discriminative Ternary Census Transform Histogram. DTCTH captures the discriminative structural properties of an image by suppressing unwanted background information. It encodes local micro structures of an image such as line, edge, corners etc. and uses a dynamic threshold during image transformation thus makes it more stable against intensity fluctuation. Global structure of the Discriminative Transformed image is captured using Spatial Pyramid representation during histogram index computation. The computed histogram index is used as face image descriptor. The computed histogram index along with the face image is stored in the database. In this way face image database is built. In the retrieval phase, when a query image is given, the histogram index is computed using the same process. Images with less distance are selected as result. The proposed solutions are experimentally evaluated on the standard constrained FRAV2D, JAFFE and FERET face image databases. Experimental result shows that the proposed face retrieval method is stable in the presence of noise and different lighting conditions. Future work may be incorporation of geometric features along and high level human attributes with DTCTH to achieve higher face retrieval accuracy.

References

1. Sedmidubsky, J., Mic, V., Zezula, P.: Face image retrieval revisited. In: Amato, G., Connor, R., Falchi, F., Gennaro, C. (eds.) SISAP 2015. LNCS, vol. 9371, pp. 204–216. Springer, Cham (2015). https://doi.org/10.1007/978-3-319-25087-8_19
2. Smith, B.M., Zhu, S., Zhang, L.: Face image retrieval by shape manipulation. In: IEEE Computer Society Conference on Computer Vision and Pattern Recognition (CVPR), pp. 769–776, June 2011
3. Chen, B.C., Chen, Y.Y., Kuo, Y.H., Hsu, W.H.: Scalable face image retrieval using attribute-enhanced sparse codewords. IEEE Trans. Multimedia 15(5), 1163–1173 (2013)
4. Wu, Z., Ke, Q., Sun, J., Shum, H.Y.: Scalable face image retrieval with identity-based quantization and multireference re-ranking. In: IEEE International Conference on Computer Vision and Pattern Recognition (CVPR 2010), pp. 3469–3476 (2010)
5. Chen, B.C., Kuo, Y.H., Chen, Y.Y., Chu, K.Y. Hsu, W.: Semisupervised face image retrieval using sparse coding with identity constraint. In: Proceedings of 19th ACM International Conference on Multimedia, pp. 1369–1372 (2011)
6. Douze, M., Ramisa, A., Schmid, C.: Combining attributes and fisher vectors for efficient image retrieval. In: IEEE Conference on Computer Vision and Pattern Recognition (2011)
7. Kumar, N., Berg, A., Belhumeur, P.N., Nayar, S.: Describable visual attributes for face verification and image search. IEEE Trans. Pattern Anal. Mach. Intell. 33(10), 1962–1977 (2011)
8. Siddiquie, B., Feris, R.S., Davis, L.S.: Image ranking and retrieval based on multi-attribute queries. In: IEEE Conference on Computer Vision and Pattern Recognition (2011)
9. Halder, S., Hasnat, A., Bhattacharjee, D., Nasipuri M.: A novel approach for searching of a color facial image based on the similarity of complexion. In: 3rd International Conference on Computational Intelligence and Information Technology, CIIT 2013, India (2013). https://doi.org/10.1049/cp.2013.2581

10. Ewald, M.: Content-based image indexing and retrieval in an image database for technical domains. Trans. MLDM **2**(1), 3–22 (2009). ISSN 1865-6781
11. Nister, D., Stewenius, H.: Scalable recognition with a vocabulary tree. In: CVPR 2006 (2006)
12. Philbin, J., Chum, O., Isard, M., Sivic, J., Zisserman, A.: Object retrieval with large vocabularies and fast spatial matching. In: CVPR (2007)
13. Roy, H., Bhattacharjee, D.: Local-gravity-face (LG-face) for illumination-invariant and heterogeneous face recognition. IEEE Trans. Inf. Forensics Secur. **11**(7), 1412–1423 (2016)
14. Rahman, M., Rahman, S., Rahman, R., Hossain, B.M.M., Shoyaib, M.: DTCTH: a discriminative local pattern descriptor for image classification. EURASIP J. Image Video Process. **2017**(1), 30 (2017)
15. Wu, J., Rehg, J.M.: CENTRIST a visual descriptor for scene. IEEE Trans. Pattern Anal. Mach. Intell. **33**(8), 1489–1501 (2011)
16. Lazebnik, S., Schmid, C., Ponce, J.: Beyond bags of features: spatial pyramid matching for recognizing natural scene categories. In: IEEE Computer Society Conference on Computer Vision and Pattern Recognition (2006). https://doi.org/10.1109/cvpr.2006.68
17. Shahiduzzaman, M., Zhang, D., Lu, G.: Improved spatial pyramid matching for image classification. In: Kimmel, R., Klette, R., Sugimoto, A. (eds.) ACCV 2010. LNCS, vol. 6495, pp. 449–459. Springer, Heidelberg (2011). https://doi.org/10.1007/978-3-642-19282-1_36
18. Yang, J., Yu, K., Gong, Y.: Linear spatial pyramid matching using sparse coding for image classification. In: IEEE Conference on Computer Vision and Pattern Recognition, USA (2009). https://doi.org/10.1109/cvpr.2009.5206757
19. Chen, C., Dantcheva, A., Ross, A.: An ensemble of patch-based subspaces for makeup-robust face recognition. Inf. Fusion **32**, 80–92 (2016)
20. Girish, G.N., Naika, C.L.S., Das, P.K.: Face recognition using MB-LBP and PCA: a comparative study. In: International Conference on Computer Communication and Informatics (ICCCI 2014), India (2014). https://doi.org/10.1109/iccci.2014.6921773
21. Neeru, N., Kaur, L.: Face recognition based on LBP and CS-LBP technique under different emotions. In: IEEE International Conference on Computational Intelligence and Computing Research (2015). https://doi.org/10.1109/iccic.2015.7435803
22. Meena, K., Suruliandi, A.: Local binary patterns and its variants for face recognition. In: IEEE-International Conference on Recent Trends in Information Technology, pp. 782–786 (2011)
23. Shan, C., Gong, S., McOwan, P.: Facial expression recognition based on local binary patterns: a comprehensive study. Image Vis. Comput. **27**, 803–816 (2009)
24. Huang, D., Shan, C., Ardabilian, M., Wang, Y., Chen, L.: Local binary patterns and its application to facial image analysis: a survey. IEEE Trans. Syst. Man Cybern. Part C (Appl. Rev.) **41**(6), 765–781 (2011)
25. FRAV2D Database (2004). http://www.frav.es/databases/frav2d/
26. Lyons, M.J., Akemastu, S., Kamachi, M., Gyoba, J.: Coding facial expressions with gabor wavelets. In: 3rd IEEE International Conference on Automatic Face and Gesture Recognition, pp. 200–205 (1998)
27. Phillips, P.J., Wechsler, H., Huang, J., Rauss, P.: The FERET database and evaluation procedure for face recognition algorithms. Image Vis. Comput. J. **16**(5), 295–306 (1998)
28. Phillips, P.J., Moon, H., Rizvi, S.A., Rauss, P.J.: The FERET evaluation methodology for face recognition algorithms. IEEE Trans. Pattern Anal. Mac. Intell. **22**, 1090–1104 (2000)
29. Pinto, N., Stone, Z., Zickler, T., Cox, D.D.: Scaling up biologically-inspired computer vision: a case study in unconstrained face recognition on Facebook. In: Proceedings of Workshop on Biologically Consistent Vision (in conjunction with CVPR) (2011)

30. Kumar, N., Berg, A.C., Belhumeur, P.N., Nayar, S.K.: Attribute and simile classifiers for face verification. In: International Conference on Computer Vision (ICCV) (2009)
31. Suchitra, S.: Face image retrieval of efficient sparse code words and multiple attribute in binning image. Braz. Arch. Biol. Technol. **60**, 1–15 (2017). https://doi.org/10.1590/1678-4324-2017160480

Cloud ERP Adoption Pitfalls and Challenges – A Fishikawa Analysis in the Context of the Global Enterprises

Sajal Bhadra$^{(\boxtimes)}$, Manas Kumar Sanyal$^{(\boxtimes)}$, and Biswajit Biswas$^{(\boxtimes)}$

Department of Business Administration, University of Kalyani, Kalyani,
West Bengal, India
sajal.bhadra@gmail.com, manassanyal123@gmail.com,
biswajit.biswas0012@gmail.com

Abstract. Enterprise Resource Planning (ERP) systems are leveraged by Enterprises for improving and streamlining their internal processes linked to various resources like customers, suppliers, human capitals, machineries etc. for almost last few decades. ERP strengthens and enhances the overall business performance to survive in the volatile business environment along with the strong global challenges. ERP provides competitive edges for an organization over its competitors by integrating all the various wings of an organization within quick response time and with low operating cost. In the era of fourth Industry revolution, where Enterprises are driven by current technology trends like Cognitive Computing, Internet of Things, Cloud Computing etc., Cloud ERP Systems are getting popularity among the Enterprises due to its low implementation time and costs. But the implementations of Cloud ERP Systems involve various complexities and it may end up with total failure causing loss of efforts and investments. The authors have explored and identified the critical factors for the implementation of Cloud Resolutions for any Enterprises. The Fishbone (Ishikawa) analysis technique is used to identify the critical factors to be addressed for the successful implementation of the Cloud ERP solutions for any organizations. The outcomes focus on the certain factors, like ensuring system and data security, managing customizations to unique internal processes, agility to ever changing business environment etc., play the significant role on the successful implementation of Cloud ERP Systems.

Keywords: Cloud ERP solutions · Ishikawa diagram ·
Fourth industrial revolution

1 Introduction

An ERP system is, an information system, designed to synchronize and optimize all the business processes available in an enterprise by integrating multiple business units having various functional areas like supply chain, operations and logistics, accounting and financial, human resources, sales and marketing etc. [1]. It ensembles all the business entities exist in an enterprise, along with the transactional data, to ensure competitive advantages than their competitors [2].

© Springer Nature Singapore Pte Ltd. 2019
J. K. Mandal et al. (Eds.): CICBA 2018, CCIS 1031, pp. 331–342, 2019.
https://doi.org/10.1007/978-981-13-8581-0_27

ERP Systems have a long history to be matured and popular among the enterprises. Information Systems were introduced back in 1960s for Inventory Control to take care inventory of Organizations. In 1970's it was MRP Systems (Material Requirement Planning) which were designed for better planning for raw material and their procurement. After MPR, MRP-II came in the market in 1980's which was an extension of MRP additionally to take care shop floor and distribution management activities along with optimizing the entire plant production process. But during late 1980's, MRP-II was further extended to include areas like Finance, Human Resource, Marketing, Planning, Engineering, Project Management etc. [3]. With further improvement of MRP-II, ERP came into market, which covered the cross-functional coordination and integration in support of the production process. In 2000's the ERP system got more refined and matured in nature which is regarded as Extended ERP systems or ERP II, considering complex and integrated global business scenarios [4]. ERP II had extended access of outside stakeholders like Suppliers for Organizations to automate the refilling of their inventories to add more value to the business. With the evolvement of the Cloud Technology, new type of ERP solutions, termed as Cloud ERP, are getting popularity among the enterprises. Though it's came in market in late 2000s, but it has gained momentum in past few years (Fig. 1).

Period	EPR Evolution
2010-	Cloud ERP
2000s	Extended ERP Systems (ERP II)
1990s	Enterprise Resource Planning(ERP)
1980s	Manufacturing Resources Planning (MRP II)
1970s	Manufacturing Resources Planning(MRP)
1960s	Inventory Control Packages

Fig. 1. ERP system evolution

Enterprises are witnessing the revolution of Industry, Industrial revolution 4.0, in recent years with upcoming technology packs like Cloud Computing, Artificial Intelligence, Cognitive Computing, Big Data, Internet of Thinking and many more. Enterprises are getting more and more agile by adopting these technology packs to get competitive advantages. These technology packs are working as value enhancer for an organization to sustain in the market as well to emerge as brand value in their own market place [5].

Cloud computing enables new distributed computing capability that share IT resources through the Internet. Organizations can get the services from a huge pool of virtualized IT infrastructures, facilitating an on-demand, subscription based billing model. Cloud ERP Solutions are nothing but IT Solutions provided by cloud vendor by harnessing the power of cloud computing environment [2].

Cloud ERP vendors or providers have 3 service models for its' customers. Software as a Service (SaaS) is a software service model where the ERP applications are hosted by Cloud vendors and made available to customers on subscription basis over the

Internet [7]. Infrastructure as a Service (IaaS) is another service model where an organization outsources the infrastructure required for supporting its operations, including hardware, servers, storage, networking components etc. The Cloud vendors is sole responsible for running, commissioning, decommissioning and maintaining them [7]. Platform as a Service (PaaS) is another service model where its' provisioning to rent operating systems, hardware, servers, storage and network capacity over the Internet [7]. The EPR market players i.e. SAP, Oracle, Microsoft are also in business to provide Cloud EPR solutions. Figure 2 shows the current market shares in the context of Cloud ERP solution [8].

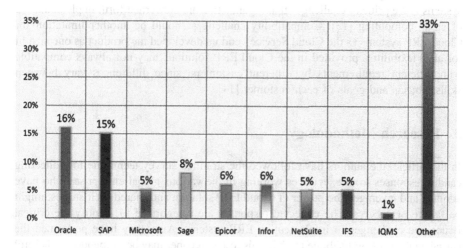

Fig. 2. Cloud ERP vendors market shares

In this research paper, the authors have highlighted the critical factors and the challenges using Fishikawa diagram that should be considered during each steps of cloud ERP Implementation.

2 Literature Review

The Cloud ERP solutions are getting popularities in recent years due to its reduced costs and efforts during implementations. Organizations are moving their majority of the IT systems due to the budget cut in IT system spending. Recent study by Computer Economics (2016) shows that the IT systems moved to cloud environment helped organizations to reduce their annual IT spending by an average 15%. Moreover, the cloud ERP systems require minimal attention as it is the responsibility of cloud vendors for continual business support [9]. Cloud ERP systems require very minimum internal resources like computer system and internet. There is no need to invest money for procuring IT hardware, Servers, Storage etc. causing it more and more popular among medium and small sized organizations [10].

There are many challenges that are encountered during implementation of Cloud ERP systems. Organizations moving their IT solution to cloud can expected to face various challenges like Data Security, controls to the system, performance instability as these have the sole ownership to Cloud vendors [11]. Any Organizations should have some unique business processes which help it to survive amidst their competitors. These unique processes are required to be customized in the EPR systems to map them with the standard processes available in the EPR systems. Cloud ERP systems generally allows very minimal customizations. Thus, sometimes its' difficult to map these unique processes in Cloud ERP [12].

Security Aspects i.e. data security, data confidentiality, privacy etc. in Cloud ERP systems is the primary challenges that organization are concerned forth implementation of cloud computing [13]. Compatibility challenges should be another limitation for Cloud ERP systems as the Cloud Service vendors developed the product as one size fit for all. Flexibilities provided in the Cloud ERP solutions may not always compatible with different requirements by different customers; since differences vary between skills, objects and goals of each customer [14].

3   Research Methodology

In this article, the authors have followed the stratified survey technique for collecting candid responses from executives working in the various global enterprises who have adopted and leveraged the power of Cloud ERP solution and shared their stories, might be failure or success. The collected responses are categorized to identify the critical issues and challenges in implementing ERP systems. Also, they have performed the causal analysis using fishbone model. This research paper may be tremendously helpful for any enterprises to plan their strategies prior to implementation of Cloud ERP systems to make it successful stories and can leverage the power of the same for the competitive advantages among its competitors. Thus, there are two activities organized by authors in this article – (1) Collecting Data & (2) Developed the Fishbone Diagram based on the collected response.

3.1   Collecting Data

The aim of this research is to find out the critical gaps and challenges which are certain to happen during implementation of Cloud ERP systems for any Enterprises. Because of these inevitable challenges, most of the Enterprising are ending up with failure causing wastage of time, efforts and costs. Authors have tried to analyse all these critical significant factors minutely to know how they are contributing to an unsuccessful end along with the probable mitigation plans to remove or bypass those gaps for achieving success in adopting the Cloud ERP Systems for these organizations.

The stratified survey technique was applied to gather responses from wide range of enterprises, operating business in various part of the globe and in various business domains like Financial, Banking and Insurance, Retail Industries, Telecom Industries, Manufacturing Industries, and Utilities etc. The survey was performed for both the public and private sector business bodies ranging from large organizations to median and small scaled organizations across the globe. Any organization is categorized as large scaled, medium scaled & small scaled based on the staffing head counts. The organization is categorized as small scaled if the staffing head count is within 50 and medium scaled organization should have staffing headcount between 50 and 250, whereas large scaled industries should have more than 250 employees. A total number of 148 responses were collected from both large enterprises and SMIs, out of which 55 responses were from large enterprises and 93 responses were from medium and small scaled enterprises as shown in Fig. 3.

Industry Segments	Number of Enterprises	Large Scaled Enterprises	SMIs
Banking and Insurance	9	9	0
Retail Industries	16	7	9
Manufacturing Industries	74	12	62
Telecom Industries	4	4	0
Utilities	7	2	5
Information Technology	14	14	0
Government Organizations	24	7	17

Fig. 3. Enterprises across various industry segments

The responses were taken from the enterprises having various phases of cloud ERP systems like early, progressive or last stages of Implementation or implemented few years back as shown in Fig. 4. Around 43% responses are taken from those who have already adopted the Cloud ERP systems and enjoying the power of it whereas 57% responses are taken from those who are in the process of implementing the same in their enterprises. The authors have taken responses from people having various roles like System Manager, Product Owner, Business Users, and Implementation Teammates. Also, they have taken feedback from the top management from Cloud ERP vendors to know their focus of the product based on geography and domain of the business.

Implementation Phases	Number of Enterprises	Overall %
In Early stage of Implementation	19	14.2
In Progress stage of Implementation	43	32.1
In Last Stage of Implementation	14	10.4
Implemented within last 1 Year	27	20.1
Implemented between 1 Year & 3 Years	14	10.4
Implemented before 3 Years	17	12.7

Fig. 4. Cloud ERP implementation stages

The authors had prepared well formatted questionnaires based on the inputs they gathered as part of literatures before they start the survey activity on October last year i.e. 2017. The initial questionnaires were used for few enterprises initially. The questionnaires were modified further based on their feedback. Thus, the latest questionnaires were evolved after little iteration. The survey process continued for six months and completed in April 2018.

3.2   Fishikawa Analysis

Fishikawa Analysis (popularly called as Fishbone Analysis, sometimes called as Ishikawa diagrams based on its' creator Kaoru Ishikawa (1960)) presents a comprehensive pictorial view of various causes for a particular event. The authors have drawn Fishikawa diagram based on the identified critical factors contributing towards the pitfalls or failures in implementing Cloud ERP systems for the organizations.

4   Results and Findings

Based on the survey activities performed for six months considering 134 organizations, operating business across the globe, the authors have found the seven critical causes which are responsible the delay or failure of any Cloud EPR solutions.

- Security Aspects
- Adaptability with Change
- System Migration to Cloud
- System Performances
- Vendor Selection
- Costs incurred for whole Product Cycle
- User Satisfactions

All the organizations have common processes based on the business domain along with the unique and niche practices for their own survivals amidst number of its competitors. Generally large scaled Organizations aimed to invest for IT solutions like ERP system to extract value and strategic decisions and interested in sustainable solution for scaling up their business. On the other hand, medium and small scaled organization is opted for adroit solution for increasing its efficiency over core processes. Thus, the factors played different roles for different Organizations based on their size, business domain and its own business styles. For example, the large scaled organizations are always critical to the Security Aspects like Data Security, Data Confidentiality. There are 39 Organizations out of 41 large scaled Organizations raised their concerns on security aspects for adopting Cloud ERP solutions. On the other hand, there are 46 organizations out of 93 medium and small scaled organizations raised their concerns on the security aspects. Figure 5 shows the responses authors received for each of the critical factors during the survey.

It's clear that the two factors Adaptability with Change and Cloud Vendor selection are the main dominating factors contributing 40% for any successful implementation of

Critical Factors	Large Scaled Enterprises (41)	SMIs (93)	Total
Security Aspects	39	46	85
Adaptability with Change	31	71	102
System Migration to Cloud	38	29	67
System Performances	34	12	46
Cloud Vendor Selection	39	81	120
User Satisfaction	32	43	75
Costs incurred for whole Product Cycle	27	31	58

Fig. 5. Critical factors reported by industries

Cloud ERP systems. Figure 6. Shows how the critical factors contribute for ensuring the successful implementation of Cloud ERP solutions.

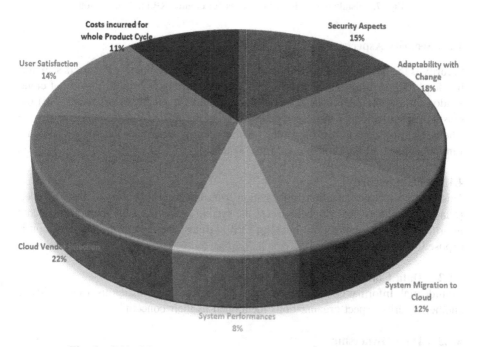

Fig. 6. Critical factors contribution for successful cloud ERP adoption

Figure 7 demonstrates the Fishbone model or Fishikawa analysis based on the identified critical factors. The critical factors or major causes are placed across the ribs along with the sub-factors across the sub-branches.

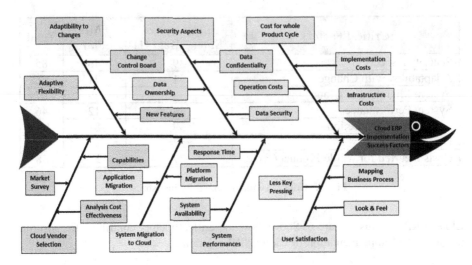

Fig. 7. Fishikawa analysis for successful cloud ERP implementation

4.1   Security Aspects

Security is the backbone of any Information Systems organizations or its users seek for. In Cloud ERP systems, as the system and infrastructure is within the custody of cloud vendors, it's a genuine concern for an organization for mainly two reasons – (i) the sensitive information of the organization is available to the cloud vendor & (ii) the whole security aspects are only rely on the security measures taken by the cloud vendors against all the probable security breaches.

4.1.1   Data Security
This is to protect organizations information from unauthorized users or Data Invader. Data Masking, user credentials to access the system are some of the methods to secure information for an application. In cloud EPR systems, the organization information is exposed to cloud vendors.

4.1.2   Data Confidentiality
Confidential Information should be kept secret from the malicious users. This is another security aspect organizations mentioned as their concern.

4.1.3   Data Ownership
Data ownership is nothing but the legal right or control of the data. In cloud EPR solutions the organization information is stored and maintained at cloud vendor premises, its' always a concern for the organization to finalize the term and conditions in the context of Data Ownership.

4.2 Adaptability to Changes

Organizations are opted for the IT solutions which are agile enough to respond to changes due to various factors like immediate business process changes to survive in the market, new statutory requirements, government rule changes etc. The Cloud ERP systems deployed as Seas model has developed as standardized product based on the global industry practices. It's not flexible enough to take care customization based on the particular organization needs.

4.2.1 Change Control Board

Each Organization's IT Support team should have change control board to manage deployment of the changes or enhancements of a product. For Cloud ERP applications, the cloud vendors are sole authority to deploy any changes to application, its' beyond the scope of change control board of the organization.

4.2.2 New Features

It's very difficult to add new features to the Cloud ERP solutions as the cloud vendors have the sole responsibility to add new features in the product. First, the cloud vendors do not encourage the extra features to be added for the organization. Also, the cloud vendors ask for separate charges for the new features to be added to the product.

4.2.3 Adaptive Flexibility

The cloud ERP solutions are not fully flexible to the customization. This is truly a big challenge reported by the organizations during the survey.

4.3 System Migration to Cloud

System migration from non-cloud system to cloud system is another challenge mentioned by many respondents during survey. Expert knowledge is required from Cloud Vendors or Implementation partners for successful migration to cloud environment.

4.3.1 Application Migration

In case of adopting Cloud ERP SaaS model, the challenges are faced by team and reported during survey.

4.3.2 Platform Migration

There are many migration complexities reported by Cloud vendors and Implementation Partners during deploying PaaS model.

4.4 System Performance

The cloud vendors are responsible for taking regular backups, maintain storage of the Cloud ERP systems. They should have fallback policy in case of any disasters. Service Level Agreement (SLA) should have all the details in the context of system performance and system availability.

4.4.1   Response Time

Response Time is measure of System Performance i.e. how quick the request is executed in the cloud environment. Sometime due to network issue or Cloud infrastructure shortage, the application becomes slow and non-workable. This was reported during survey process.

4.4.2   System Availability

Cloud ERP system may become unavailable rarely due to many number of reasons like system down due to hardware or software issue, network down, system outage etc.

4.5   Cloud Vendor Selection

The cloud vendor selection and implementation partner selection is another critical factor for the successful Cloud ERP implementation. The flexibility of the cloud product & in-depth knowledge of the implementation team on the business domain and cloud product lead to a success story.

4.5.1   Market Survey

Organization should do minute analysis on the internal business need & market survey for the suitable cloud product. Otherwise it may lead to a failure story.

4.5.2   Implementation Team Capabilities

In-depth knowledge of the implementation team on the business domain and cloud product is must for the successful adoption of cloud ERP systems.

4.5.3   Analyze Cost Effectiveness

Organization should analyze the cost for the all the available cloud EPR product and finalize the best one based on cost and flexibility factor.

4.6   Costs for Whole Product Cycle

As per the product life cycle, it starts with implementation, followed by support, enhancement, maturity and retirement at the end. The Cloud ERP systems are getting popularity due to significant reduction of implementation costs for organizations. This is always true for adopting Cloud ERP systems in SaaS model where the organizations are pays for the services as requested. But in case hybrid model where both public cloud from cloud vendors and private cloud owned by the organization are in place together, cost is another concern for them. This concern is reported mainly from large scaled organizations

4.6.1   Implementation Costs

Cloud ERP implementation cost and effort is always less than non-cloud ERP solutions. Non-Cloud ERP systems generally takes 6–12 months to implement based on the organization size and needs. Whereas it takes 2–3 months to implement cloud ERP system for an organization.

4.6.2   Operation Costs

Operating cost may increase based on cloud vendors discretion after regular intervals. Considering the life cycle of a software product as 10 years, it is quite possible to have increased operating cost due to increase of the charges from cloud vendors.

4.6.3   Infrastructure Costs

This is applicable for the cases where the organizations are opted for private cloud or hybrid cloud solutions. It may increase exponentially due to improper planning & contracts with the cloud vendors.

4.7   User Satisfactions

User Experience or User Satisfaction is the main criteria for a software product to be successful or popular. It's measured by user opinion based on the screen layout, screen color, fonts, navigation style, and number of key press for an activity for a software product. The cloud ERP system provides less flexibilities to its' users to change the screen layout, color, font etc.

4.7.1   Mapping Business Process

Any cloud ERP solution is developed on standardized processes followed by global organizations. Mapping of the existing process of an organization to the available processes in the ERP package is one of most critical challenges reported during survey. Customizations are required to bridge the gaps between the organization process and the cloud ERP packages.

4.7.2   Look and Feel

Look and Feel of IT software depends on the screen layout, font, color, key navigations etc. The cloud ERP solutions provide less flexibility to change these looks and feel factors.

4.7.3   Less Key Process

Any user always wants to perform an activity with as much as less number of key press or navigation possible. This is value added features of any IT Solutions.

All the above-mentioned factors or sub-factors are reported during the survey as the critical factors for any successful cloud ERP adoptions. Any organizations, planning for adopting cloud EPR system or in the process of adopting the same should pay attention to these critical factors to make it success story.

5   Conclusion

The findings mentioned just above are based on the survey conducted over six months across the globe. The causal analysis using Fishikawa model has clearly depicts the critical factors and sub-factors lead to successful cloud EPR implementation. This research paper may act as useful tool for an organization to know the various challenges that may come up during Cloud ERP adoption. The top managers of any organizations, opt for Cloud ERP implementation, can identify the key pitfalls and can plan accordingly to mitigate the challenges and make it a success story.

With the fourth Industrial revolution, its' urgently required for an organization to stay tuned with the current technology trends. Cloud ERP solutions are only IT Systems that any organizations should adapt to sustain in the global competitive market. A well-configured and cohesively integrated cloud ERP system enables organization agility with relatively low costs and increased efficiency.

References

1. Moon, Y.B.: Enterprise resource planning (ERP): a review. Int. J. Manag. Enterp. Dev. **4**(3), 235–264 (2007)
2. https://www.cisco.com/c/en/us/solutions/collateral/service-provider/global-cloud-index-gci/white-paper-c11-738085.html
3. Correll, J.G.: Reengineering the MRP II environment: the key is successfully implementing change. IIE Solut. Norcross **27**(7), 24–27 (1995)
4. Jaiswal, M.P.: Enhancing business value through ERP enabled e-business transformation. J. E-Bus. **2**(2), 1–9 (2002)
5. Kessler, J.: MRP II: in the midst of a continuing evolution. Ind. Eng. Norcross **23**(3), 38–40 (1991)
6. Continelli, A.: Managing resources: ERP industry trends that impact bottom line. Business. com/Technology. Accessed 22 Feb 2017
7. Makkar, G.D., Meenakshi, B.: EAAS - ERP as a service. J. Inf. Oper. Manag. **3**(1), 141–145 (2012)
8. ERP Reports Panorama 2018. https://www.panorama-consulting.com/resource-center/erp-industry-reports/panoramas-2018-erp-report/
9. George, B.: Top 5 Reasons to Adopt Cloud-Based ERP Solutions (2016)
10. Catteddu, D.: Cloud computing: benefits, risks and recommendations for information security. In: Serrão, C., Aguilera Díaz, V., Cerullo, F. (eds.) IBWAS 2009. CCIS, vol. 72, p. 17. Springer, Heidelberg (2010). https://doi.org/10.1007/978-3-642-16120-9_9
11. Hofmann, P.: Cloud computing: the limits of public clouds for business applications. IEEE Internet Comput. **14**(6), 90–93 (2010)
12. Mijač, M., Picek, R., Stapić, Z.: Cloud ERP System Customization Challenges, September 2013
13. Takabi, H., Joshi, J.B., Ahn, G.-J.: Security and privacy challenges in cloud computing environments. IEEE Secur. Priv. **8**(6), 24–31 (2010)
14. Jonathan, G.: To cloud or not to cloud: that is the question for ERP. MHD Supply Chain. Solut. **42**(1), 36 (2012)

Computational Forensics (Privacy and Security)

An Interactive Practical Approach for Traditional Cryptanalysis of Vigenere Cipher

Rikhi Ram Jagat[1(✉)], Shefalika Ghosh Samaddar[1],
and Aurunima Samaddar[2]

[1] Department of Computer Science and Engineering,
National Institute of Technology Sikkim, Ravangla, Sikkim, India
rikhiramjagat@gmail.com, shefalika99@yahoo.com
[2] Department of Electronics and Communication,
National Institute of Technology Sikkim, Ravangla, Sikkim, India
aurunima94@gmail.com

Abstract. Vigenere cipher is a polyalphabetic cipher with a very large key space capable of generating streaming cipher text. The difficulty level of cryptanalysis somewhat depends on the size of the key space. However, there are methods of pattern analysis and statistical analysis that can overrule the difficulties of cryptanalysis due to the large key space. Cryptanalysis of Vigenere cipher is one such method of testing code breaking even if the key domain is very large. The proposed algorithm of cryptanalysis works best when the size of the key string is less than the size of the dataset.

Cryptanalysis is a way to break the cipher text by either brute force method or some analytical techniques. The paper describes a traditional method of deciphering encrypted message of Vigenere cipher cryptosystems irrespective of whether the message is long or short using Kasiski test and Friedman test or Kappa test. The ready algorithm and the program execution lead to success of key finding with high probability. The paper also surveys the other methods applied for cryptanalysis of Vigenere Cipher, such as cryptanalysis using Particle Swarm Optimization with Markov chain random walk and Genetic algorithm with Elitism. The existence of a cryptanalysis library for cracking polyalphabetic cipher such as Vigenere Cipher is analysed.

Keywords: Vigenere cipher · Cryptanalysis · Kasiski test · Freidman test ·
Kappa test · Index of coincidence · Mutual index of coincidence ·
Polyalphabetic cipher · Ciphertext

1 Introduction

The study of cryptography and cryptology have found its place in the books of history. In fact, the ancient book of history by Herodotus contains a number of methods of cryptography [1].

Cryptography was used by ancient Egyptians for military and diplomatic communications from ancient time onward. Cryptography has been used traditionally for war

© Springer Nature Singapore Pte Ltd. 2019
J. K. Mandal et al. (Eds.): CICBA 2018, CCIS 1031, pp. 345–359, 2019.
https://doi.org/10.1007/978-981-13-8581-0_28

operation and espionage [2]. With the introduction of modern age computers and other peripherals, the classical method of cryptography proved inadequate and require special protection in the name of security, privacy, confidentiality, integrity and authentication.

Shannon in his landmark paper in 1949 provides the formal definition of a cryptosystem [4]. According to him, a cryptosystem is a five-tuple (P, K, C, E, D) where P is a finite set of plaintext, K is a finite set of keys, C is a finite set of cipher texts, and for each $k \in K$, there is an encryption rule $E_k \in E$ and its inverse (decryption) rule $D_k = E_k^{-1}. \in D$.

Any plaintext message after an application of key gets converted into a cipher text message. The cipher text message is irreversible if the key is not known. The decryption is only possible once the key is known to receiver. Otherwise cipher text conveys no meaning to the recipient. The rule of decryption is second part of the algorithm of cryptographic adventure to get back the original plain text. A model of cryptosystem is provided in Fig. 1.

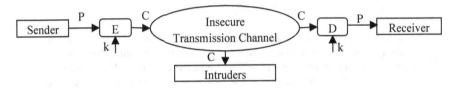

Fig. 1. Simple model of a traditional cryptosystem

The development of cryptosystem are divided into two distinct part traditional and classical cryptography, which is based on number theory and linear algebra and modern cryptosystems including public key cryptography. The proposed study has been under taken in the realm of traditional symmetric key ciphers. Modern cryptography works are also based on number theory but massive computational infrastructure is necessary for such system.

Vigenere cipher is one of such classical or traditional cryptographic algorithm, which is symmetric in nature. When encryption and decryption use the same key, the algorithm is said to be symmetric in nature. Any symmetric key cryptosystem suffers from the problems of key security. Key distribution become a hazard and distribution technique are yet to take-up the pace so that symmetric key cipher are considered to be fully protected.

The present paper studies the cryptanalysis of Vigenere cipher and its representation over leakage of a key in the process. It was a 16th century cipher in the category of polyalphabetic substitution cipher. The paper developed interactive computer program for cryptanalysis of Vigenere cipher using Kasiski test and computation of Index of Coincidence and Mutual Index of Coincidence, these two indexes of coincidence are necessary for finding the key.

Section 2 is covering the works of others authors related to cryptanalysis of Vigenere cipher which happens to be an age-old process. Section 3 describes Vigenere cipher in details as presented in any textbook of cryptography and network security. Section 4 is devoted to the cryptanalysis algorithm developed and the test result obtained from the program. Section 5 deals with the experimental result and its significance. Section 6 concludes the paper in order to provide an insight for future researchers for breaking ciphers.

2 Related Work

A Vignenere cipher can be methodically broken using the various ways to determine the key length. The Kasiski test, naned after Major F W Kasiski, [14] a German cryptologist, is based on unicity distance or distance between identical strings of length of three characters or more. The other test is Friedman test, named after William Frederick Friedman, is based on finding the index of coincidence. The test is also referred to as Kappa test. It may be recalled, given the average of length n, the following definition holds good

$$\text{Index of Coincidence } I = \frac{\sum_{i=1}^{26} n_i(n_i - 1)}{n(n-1)} \tag{1}$$

n_i = number of occurrences of the ith letter index of any language source can be calculated if the probabilities of occurrence of each of the letters are known if P_a is the probability of occurrence of the letter, then

$$I_{Source} = p_a p_a + p_b p_b + \ldots + p_z p_z = \sum_{i=a}^{z} p_i^2 \tag{2}$$

$$I_{English} \cong 0.065$$

And the source is randomized with English letters then

$$I_{Random} \cong 0.038$$

This is obtained by considering $p_a = \frac{1}{26}$

Important metadata can be collected by using calculation of indexes, such as whether the enciphered message is a transposition or mono alphabetic cipher based on the result of $I_{message}$. If $I_{message} \cong I_{English}$ then the above is true. If the $I_{message}$ has a reduced value, then there is a high probability that it is a polyalphabetic cipher. Typically, polyalphabetic cipher randomizes the occurrence of the letter.

Let the length of the ciphertext be n and the length of keyword be k. obviously $n \gg k$. The position corresponding to the same letter of the keyword, the behavior in the ciphertext will be that of a mono alphabetic cipher in those selected position. Therefore, if index of those same positional letters are determined, it must be around 0.065. Conversely, if index is calculated for the pairs from different letters of the keyword, the behavior is typically polyalphabetic. The index in that case will be much lover as near to 0.038 as the keyword letters were randomly chosen. We are required to calculate the expected number X of pairs of equal letters by picking up any of the n letters of the ciphertext.

Then if the total text is covered by repetitive k there will be $\left(\frac{n}{k}-1\right)$ remaining letters after selecting one letter that have been used as the same latter of the keyword. So the number of pairs will be

$$\frac{n\left(\frac{n}{k}-1\right)}{2}=\frac{n^2-kn}{2k}=\frac{n(n-k)}{2k} \tag{3}$$

Again, there are $\left(n-\frac{n}{k}\right)$ remaining letters that have used a different keyword letter. So the number of pairs can be calculated

$$\frac{n\left(n-\frac{n}{k}\right)}{2}=\frac{n^2k-n^2}{2k}=\frac{n^2(k-1)}{2k}$$

$$\therefore X=\frac{n(n-k)}{2k}\times 0.065+\frac{n^2(k-1)}{2k}\times 0.038$$

$$\therefore I_{ciphertext}=\frac{X}{\left[\begin{array}{c}n\\2\end{array}\right]}$$

$$=\frac{\frac{n(n-k)}{2k}\times 0.065+\frac{n^2(k-1)}{2k}\times 0.038}{(n-2)!2!}$$

$$=\frac{X}{\frac{n(n-1)}{2}}=\frac{2X}{n(n-1)}=\frac{n-k}{k(n-1)}\times 0.065+\frac{n(k-1)}{k(n-1)}\times 0.038$$

$$I_{ciphertext}=\frac{1}{k(n-1)}(0.027n+k(0.038n-0.065)) \tag{4}$$

Therefore, keyword length k can be determined easily in the traditional method.

The earlier approach has been followed in order to find the keyword used in the ciphertext.

There are experimentation cryptanalysis of Vigenere cipher using particle swarm optimization (PSO) with Markov Chain Random work [11]. The efficiency of PSO algorithm has been enhanced by replacing some of the worst particles with new better random particles. In order to implement fitness function, the frequency of each character of ciphertext is determined and the Eq. (4) is suitably used for the design of the fitness. The prospered algorithm goes through the initialization of PSO search algorithm parameters followed by initialization of discrete birds or population. The fitness function value is determined to update velocity and position of the particles. Next the worst particles are discarded using Markov Chain Random walk and this happens to be a crucial step before termination. Experimental results justifies the proposed approach.

Bhateja and Kumar further substantiated the approach by using genetic algorithm with elitism in 2014 [12]. The fitness function remained the same as has been used in the last paper. But the component of Genetic Algorithm are described such as elitism, selection, cross over, mutation etc. Maximum number of iteration for generation of progeny was uninitialized. After taking the input of ciphertext, maximum iteration and key length, a population of 20 chromosomes each of size k randomly chosen. Decryption is performed by each of the 20 chromosomes and fitness value is found. The best 2 chromosomes are chosen from the population and are reserved for new population. If the size of the new population is 20 then one iteration is considered to be completed and value of iteration is increased by 1. If it reaches maximum iteration then the output is considered as best solution. If the size of the new population is less than 20, then parent chromosome from population are selected using Roulette Wheel and then cross over and mutation are applied. Again, decryption of ciphertext by offspring is performed and new fitness value is found. The two best chromosome among the present population are selected and the process continues until the size of new population become 20. The proposed algorithm is supported by experimental result and a comparison of Genetic Algorithm with elitism and without elitism has been made where the former one provides better result. From time complexity analysis it was concluded that the elitism increases efficiency and performance of algorithms because it can avoid loss of best chromosomes that ultimately forms the actual key. Thus, key finding is guaranteed to some extent with elitism.

The other approaches of cryptanalysis of Vigenere cipher are hybrid in nature. In fact, some optimization techniques of a number of cryptanalytic schemes provide better results. Based on such assumption, a cryptanalytic library has been suggested [13]. The analysis of the classical ciphers has been made including frequency analysis and it various uses on mono alphabetic cipher. Its limited application on polyalphabetic cipher makes it usable in Kasiski test, Friedman test or Kappa test used in Vigenere cipher. A number of other test or attacks are considered to consider these cryptanalytic techniques in the workflow. A new instance of workspace has been created when the program start (Fig. 2).

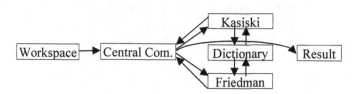

Fig. 2. A simplified modular view

The workspace is capable of sending parameter about the current cracking session to the Central Command. The Central Command is having its own secondary workflow. It is up to Central Command to use various tests in combination. If the key is generated, it is reported to the Central Command, and in case of failure the best possible key length is determined. An implementation has been shown and result are evaluated in a real time environments. Different length of ciphertext have been used in evaluation. Success rate are determined and hybrid approach ultimately give better result than a single test mechanism. The implementation is useful in case of polyalphabetic cipher.

The section provide a clear view of the cryptanalysis of Vigenere cipher starting from a classical one to modern techniques such as PSO and Genetic Algorithm and various hybrid approaches. The strength of the paper lies in the thought that ever an age-old technique can generate interest with the application of the modern tools if the classical or traditional method is well understood.

3   Cryptanalysis of the Vigenere Cipher

Cryptanalysis is the method of finding the key without the application of brute force method. Brute force method tries each and every key in the key domain in order to find the correct key. The larger the key space the difficult is the method of application of brute force attack. Any method of cryptanalysis avoids such long route and prepare short cuts to find the key by statistical inference or analytical methods. The Arabs were the first to make advancement in cryptanalysis. Frequency analysis was first applied in 8th century Arabic world. An Arabic author Qalqashandi discovered a technique for solving ciphers, which was published in 1990 in English translated from Arabic, and still frequency analysis happens to be one of the techniques of cryptanalysis. The technique can be applied in an English language text. In the Vigenere cipher, it is required to write down all the cipher text letter from A to Z and count the frequency of each symbol in the cipher text. The frequency of each letter is then matched with corresponding frequency of plaintext letter. The matching frequency indicates the substitution that has been made in case of mono alphabetic substitution cipher. The method of frequency analysis has drawback and not enough yielding in case of polyalphabetic substitution cipher such as Vigenere cipher (Table 1).

Table 1.   Vigenere cipher table or Tabula Recta

	A	B	C	D	E	F	.	.	.	T	U	V	W	X	Y	Z
A	A	B	C	D	E	F	.	.	.	T	U	V	W	X	Y	Z
B	B	C	D	E	F	G	.	.	.	U	V	W	X	Y	Z	A
.	.	.	.	.	.	.	.	.	.	.	.	.	.	.	.	.
.	.	.	.	.	.	.	.	.	.	.	.	.	.	.	.	.
.	.	.	.	.	.	.	.	.	.	.	.	.	.	.	.	.
Y	Y	Z	A	B	C	D	.	.	.	R	S	T	U	V	W	X
Z	Z	A	B	C	D	E	.	.	.	S	T	U	V	W	X	Y

Vigenere cipher uses a table of English alphabets representing plaintext and letters of polyalphabetic substitution cipher key. The table is known as tabula recta, which is a 26×26 matrix including alphabetic letters. The algorithm was discovered by Blaise de Vigenere of France in 16th century; to be precise in 1586. The algorithm could not be solved for cryptanalysis until 1970 when Friedman and Kasiski found out analysis method for cryptanalysis. The paper presents the same text and method for analytical purpose and any computation can be performed for generalized Vigenere cipher.

Mathematically, the procedure of encryption and decryption Vigenere Cipher can be seen in the following equation:

$$Ci = E\,(Pi + Ki)\,mod\,26. \tag{5}$$

$$Pi = D\,(Ci - Ki)\,mod\,26. \tag{6}$$

Where C is the ciphertext, P is the plaintext, K is the Key, E is Encryption than D is Decryption. The encryption process of vigenere cipher used tabula recta where every plaintext alphabets is intersected by table with the alphabet of the key and intersection give the corresponding ciphertext which is again an alphabet. If the key string is smaller in size then the plaintext, the key will be repeated again and again until it equals to the length of the plaintext.

For example, supposing that the plaintext "THIS IS MY PROJECT WORK" with the keyword "CRYPTO", then, based on the tabula recta, illustration encryption can be computed as follows:

Plaintext: THISISMYPROJECTWORK
Keyword: CRYPTOCRYPTOCRYPTOC
Ciphertext: VYGHBGOPNGHXGTRLHFM

For decryption process, the same tabula recta is used. The intersection of the cipher text and the key after applying mod 26 operation gives out the plaintext or in other words, resulting plaintext is obtained from the alphabet matching to the key and the cipher text by picking up by corresponding alphabets.

Ciphertext: VYGHBGOPNGHXGTRLHFM
Keyword: CRYPTOCRYPTOCRYPTOC
Plaintext: THISISMYPROJECTWORK

Thus, Vigenere cipher uses k shift cipher where each k_i decides which of the n (26) mono alphabetic substitution for a particular language (English) to be used. The structure of the plaintext cannot be fully hidden by the usage of Vigenere cipher the key size is always smaller than the plaintext. There is some repetition of the key for the same letters if the key string is repeated.

These patterns may reveal the letters behind cipher text to some extent. Vigenere cipher makes a plaintext letter to be denoted by up to k different cipher text letters where k is the number of symbols used in the plaintext and cipher text.

We consider the following cipher text that we believe that it was encrypted using a Vigenere cipher.

LIOMWGFEGGDVWGHHCQUCRHRWAGWIOWQLKGZETGZLKQKMU-
BRATSIITFHHVCDWEOHWCFFMRVHVKHLWCBDHFWWMXSFMRVH-
VYWWLVVHOGMVIVHRXJFHIGOFLEVDVCQWIT WQXJSSPCWQXGLWMU
GKMHHHHVVUIGQKETOFXGFVXQQUICHHXJSFMRVHVVSAX

English letter frequency has been presented in Fig. 3 and ciphertext letter frequency has been presented in Fig. 4.

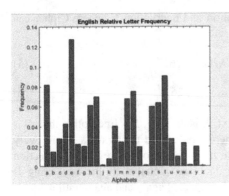

Fig. 3. English letter frequency   **Fig. 4.** Cipher text letter frequency

3.1   Determining the Cipher Period, m

The determining cipher period m for the given example has been carried out by Kasiski test and the Index of Coincidence test. It determines the size of the key m. Kasiski test is best on the observation of the pattern if two matching pattern of length two or more appear in cipher text their corresponding plaintext are same. Also, the distance between the occurrences has to be a multiple of the key size m [14] (Table 2) .

In the example, the segment FMR appears three times start at position 67, 87 and 175.

Table 2. Kasiski test difference factors

String	First index	Second index	Difference	Factor of distance
'HHV'	55	147	92	2 4 23 46 92
'FMR'	67	87	20	2 4 5 10 20
'FMR'	67	175	108	2 3 4 6 9 12 18 27 36 54 108
'RVH'	69	177	108	2 3 4 6 9 12 18 27 36 54 108
'VHV'	70	178	108	2 3 4 6 9 12 18 27 36 54 108
'SFM'	86	174	88	2 4 8 11 22 44 88
'XJS'	128	172	44	2 4 8 11 22 44

Common factors 2 and 4 are the key length candidates to be further tested by the Index of Coincidence (IC) defined below.

Definition Let $x = \{x_1, x_2, ..., x_n\}$ be a string of n alphabetic characters. The index of coincidence of x, $IC(x)$, is the probability that randomly chosen two alphabets of string x are the same [4, 5]. If the frequencies of A, B,..., Z in x are denoted by the $f_0, f_1, ..., f_{25}$ [14].

$$IC(x) = \frac{\sum \binom{f_2^i}{2}}{\binom{n}{2}} = \frac{\sum f_i(f_i - 1)}{n(n-1)} = \sum \left(\frac{f_i}{n}\right)^2 = \sum p_i^2 \qquad (7)$$

When used a natural language, the index of coincidence is the standard distribution. Therefore, the use of IC can be done to determine whether the ciphertext substring frequency distribution is similar to the standard distribution of source language. The match will not be correct for a small length sample, but a closed one is generally acceptable. We have got this test named IC Test for determining of unicity distance between repetitive patterns of letters of alphabet.

Using the m value of the Kasiski test, we arrange the given alphabetic string $y = y_1$, $y_2, ..., y_n$ into m substrings [14].

$$Y_1 = y_1 y_{m+1} y_{2m+1} \cdots$$
$$Y_2 = y_2 y_{m+2} y_{2m+2} \cdots$$
$$\cdots$$
$$Y_m = y_m y_{2m} y_{3m} \cdots$$

In the example, using Kasiski test m different values are obtained. To try $m = 4$ we divide the ciphertext into 4 substrings so that each substring is encrypted by the same key letter i.e., $S_1 = \{c_1, c_5, c_9, ...\}$, $S_2 = \{c_2, c_6, c_{10}, ...\}$, ..., $S_4 = \{c_4, c_8, c_{12}, ...\}$. If the assumption about m is correct, then the IC value of each of these substrings will be close to source language IC, for example English language. In our test we get the following IC values for different substring, $IC(S_1) = 0.0628$, $IC(S_2) = 0.0731$, $IC(S_3) = 0.0780$ and $IC(S_4) = 0.0796$. Considering, the IC of standard English language is around 0.068, $m = 4$ is correct with very high probability. If our assumption is not correct, then the substrings will be more like random strings with much smaller IC values. For example, if we have used $m = 6$ that is $S_1 = \{c_1, c_7, c_{13}, ...\}$, $S_2 = \{c_2, c_8, c_{14}, ...\}$, ..., $S_6 = \{c_6, c_{12}, c_{18}, ...\}$. Then we would obtain $IC(S_1) = 0.0470$, $IC(S_2) = 0.0360$, $IC(S_3) = 0.0404$, $IC(S_4) = 0.0389$, $IC(S_5) = 0.0548$ and $IC(S_6) = 0.0288$. (Figures 5, 6, 7, 8, 9 and 10 shown the execution result).

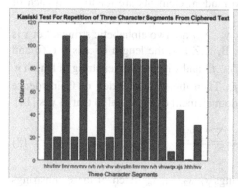

Fig. 5. Kasiski test distance graph

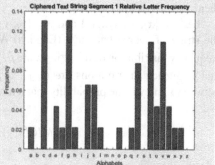

Fig. 6. Cipher segment 1 IC frequency

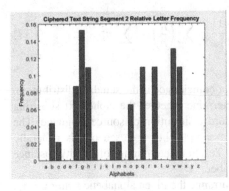

Fig. 7. Cipher segment 2 IC frequency

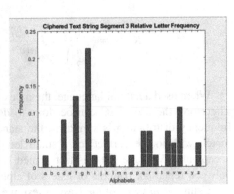

Fig. 8. Cipher segment 3 IC frequency

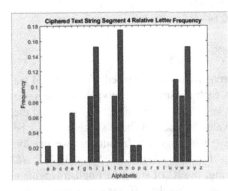

Fig. 9. Cipher segment 4 IC frequency

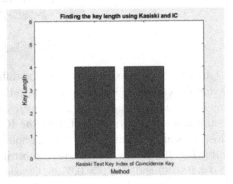

Fig. 10. Kasiski test and IC test results

3.2   Determining the Keyword

We use mutual index of coincidence (MIC) for determination of key string. The technique is suggested by Dan Vellman [6]. The mutual index of coincidence of x and y, shows as MIC(x, s), it is likely that two random elements are identical in each of them.

Let $x = \{x_1, x_2, x_3...x_n\}$ and $y = \{y_1, y_2, y_3...y_n\}$ are two alphabetic strings. Let x is the string of source language (English) A, B, ...Z and the length of x is n (26) and frequency distribution of the string x are $f_0, f_1, ...f_n$. and y is the another string of length n' and frequency distributions are $f'_0, f'_1, ...f'_n$. Then the Mutual Index of Coincidence between x and y is the probability that a random element of x is equal to that of y is [14].

$$MIC(x,y) = \frac{\sum_{i=0}^{n} f_i f'_i}{nn'}$$

(8)

Suppose s is the ciphertext of m substrings s_1, s_2, ..., s_m. Each of these substrings are obtained by shift cipher encryption of the unknown plaintext. However, the plaintext is unknown, its probability distribution and its IC is known. Consider, substring s_j ($1 \leq j \geq m$) is encrypted by unknown key k_j. Suppose we shift s_j by b ($1 \leq b \leq n$) and obtain n different s_j^b each of which corresponds to a decryption with a different key value. If s_j has frequency distribution f_1'', f_2'', ..., f_n'' and length l'' [14], then

$$MIC\left(x, s_j^b\right) \cong \frac{\sum_{i=1}^{n} f_i f_{i-b}''}{l''} \qquad (9)$$

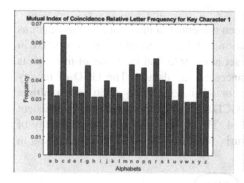

Fig. 11. MIC relative frequency of key character 1

Fig. 12. MIC relative frequency of key character 2

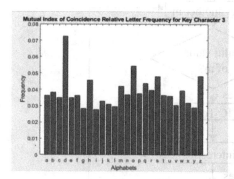
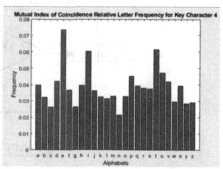

Fig. 13. MIC relative frequency of key character 3

Fig. 14. MIC relative frequency of key character 4

It is expected that $MIC\left(x, s_j^b\right) \cong IC$ (English language) if b is the additive inverse of the correct key modulo n, otherwise we got a very smaller MIC value. For example, cipher text our prediction is $m = 4$ that we get from the Kasiski test. Therefore, we divide the ciphertext into 4 substrings, and compute the MIC values shown in Figs. 11, 12, 13 and 14. By selecting the maximum MIC value for each substring, we get a potential keyword, in the example this is CODE. To see whether the keyword we have obtained is correct we decrypt the cipher text and got a passage [14].

JULIUSCAESARUSEDACRYPTOSYSTEMINHISWARSWHICHISNOW-
REFERREDTOASCAESARCIPHERITISANADDITIVECIPHERWITHTHEKE
YSETTOTHREEEACHCHARACTERINTHEPLAINTEXTISSHIFTEDTHREE
CHARACTERSTOCREATETHECIPHERTEXT

4   Cryptanalysis Algorithm

The proposed cryptanalysis algorithm has been presented in the form of a flow chart as well as pseudo code (Fig. 15) after initialization and the corresponding data structure in place Kasiski test is performed on the data set in order to find the value of m which is equivalent to the GCD of all unicity distances on the dataset. The GCD of unicity distances will be having several multiples for other occurrences if no such multiple occurrences have found that indicates the GCD of all unicity distance is nonexistent once value of m is decided IC test is applied. The IC test indicates the possibility of presenting the dataset in a row column matrix there may be some incompleteness in

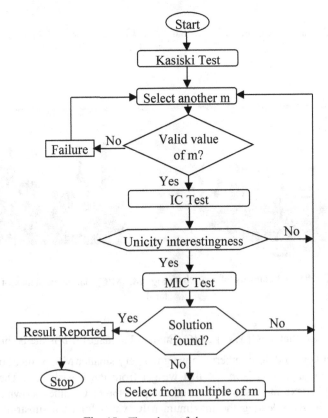

Fig. 15. Flowchart of the program

rows and columns as it may not be a perfect $m \times m$ matrix from the time being null values for those letters which are equivalents to blank spaces indication of promising results obtained from IC values of substring that are close to the IC of standard plaintext distribution if such result is not obtained then we consider another multiple of m and formulate the matrix of similar manner otherwise the algorithm continues the Mutual Index of Coincidence test (MIC) for processing further.

The next step is consider to be a solution when one gets a key string after MIC test if the key is correct and valid then the solution is obtained and the proposed crypt-analysis program is considered to provide the valid key. If the plaintext is not mean-ingful then it is considered that the key is not correct then another value of m (another multiples of m) is considered for IC and MIC test the process is run again and again with all possible value of m till all multiple value of m are exhausted for measured unicity distance.

The proposed algorithm does not guarantee the existence of a solution in case the size of the data set and the key string are same. If n is the length of data string are same unicity distance is difficult to determine and GCD happens to be a single value. There is no repetition of pattern and in such cases; proposed algorithm may report a failure. However, if the key string is smaller in size then data set the trails may lead to perfect run after a number of trials.

5 Experimental Results

To test our cryptanalysis program, we used the following procedure. We prepared twelve plaintext files of length 25, 50, 100, 150, 200, 250, 300, 400, 500, 600, 800, 1000. We allowed up to 5% deviation on the size of the plaintext files. Then, each plaintext file is encrypted with four different keys. Key lengths vary from 2 to 13 characters. Thus, we have forty-eight different ciphertext files are processed. Then, we used the ciphertext files for the test without any plaintext files or key information. Next, the cryptanalysis program run and test each of the ciphertext files. While the ones running on larger ciphertexts almost always ended in perfect runs, the smallest ciphertext files were difficult to break.

Table 3. The Kasiski test result

Correctness of result	Incorrectness of result
30	18
62.50%	37.50%

As shown in Table 3, individual test for the same data set in Kasiski test success rate is only 62.50%.

Table 4. The IC test result

Correctness of result	Incorrectness of result
27	21
56.25%	43.75%

As shown in Table 4, individual test for the same data set in IC test success rate in only 56.25%.

Table 5. Overall test result for the program

Correctness of result	Incorrectness of result
34	14
70.83%	29.17%

The overall results of tests given in Table 5 show that 70.83% of the test gives the correct result and 29.17% of the test gives the incorrect result. We observe that we get the incorrect result because of the small sized ciphertext files where there were no repeated patterns in the ciphertext and therefore unicity distance could not be determined.

6 Conclusions

In this paper reported a program for Vigenere cipher cryptanalysis that has been successfully implemented in an interactive mode. The implementation has been captured through video and uploaded in the youtube.com which may be seen at the link https://youtu.be/1c0x0_UhOew. It is evident from the program execution that the created tool makes better result for lengthy English text. Some other classic cryptanalysis techniques such as Kasiski test, Index of Coincidence test and Mutual Index of Coincidence, it has been evaluated that the performance of the individual test of Kasiski test and Index of Coincidence test and proposed cryptanalysis program. The combination of Kasiski test and Index of Coincidence test and new use of IC test that is Mutual Index of Coincidence proved to be the exceptionally good success rate of 70. 83%. This approach may also use in other languages under the different number of enciphering alphabets.

Using all the facts observe that (i) multiple round encryption techniques increase the strength of a cipher, and (ii) a ciphertext running key is very difficult to perform cryptanalysis.

References

1. Johnson, N.F., Jajodia, S.: Exploring steganography: seeing the unseen. IEEE Comput. **31**(2), 26–34 (1998)
2. Kahn, D.: The Codebreakers: The Story of Secret Writing. Macmillan, NewYork (1967). Abridged edition. New American Library, NewYork (1974)
3. Van Tilborg, H.C.: An Introduction to Cryptology. Kluwer Academic Publishers, Dordrech (1988)
4. Shannon, C.: Communication theory and secrecy systems. Bell Syst. Tech. J. **28**, 656–715 (1949)
5. Menezes, A., van Oorschot, P., Vanstone, S.: Handbook of Applied Cryptography. CRC Press, Boca Raton (1997)
6. Stinson, D.R.: Cryptography: Theory and Practice. CRC Press, Boca Raton (1995)
7. Ariyus, D.: Introduction to Cryptography, Theory, Analysis and Implementation. Andi Publisher, Yogyakarta (2008)
8. Agrawal, S., Tripathi, R.: Comparative study of symmetric and asymmetric cryptography techniques. Int. J. Adv. Found. Res. Comput. (IJAFRC) **1**(6), 68–76 (2014)
9. Cover, T.M., Thomas, J.A.: Elements of Information Theory, 2nd edn. Wiley, Hoboken (2006)
10. Bulu, E., Buyuksaracoglu, F., Sakalli, M.T.: Cryptography Education for Students. IEEE (2004). 0-7803-8596-9/04
11. Bhateja, A., Kumar, S., Bhateja, A.K.: Cryptanalysis of Vigenere cipher using particle swarm optimization with Markov chain random walk. Int. J. Comput. Sci. Eng. (IJCSE) **5**, 422 (2013)
12. Bhateja, A., Kumar, S.: Genetic algorithm with elitism for cryptanalysis of Vigenere cipher. IEEE (2014). 978-14799-2900-9/14
13. Ilie, V., Gheorghe, L., Popeea, T.: A hybrid approach to a cryptanalysis library. IEEE (2013). https://doi.org/10.1109/roedunet.2013.6714186
14. Forouzan, B.A., Debdeep, M.: Cryptography and Network Security, 3rd edn., pp. 70–80. Mc Graw Hill (2016)

A Secure Anonymous Mobile Handover Authentication Protocol for Content Centric Network

Sharmistha Adhikari[(✉)] and Sangram Ray

Department of Computer Science and Engineering, National Institute
of Technology Sikkim, Ravangla 737139, Sikkim, India
sharmistha.adhikari@gmail.com, sangram.ism@gmail.com

Abstract. In current technological era, content centric network (CCN) is envisaged as a clean-slate future Internet architecture to meet the growing demand of information exchange as well as to ease smooth distribution of content. Recently, with the popularity of mobile devices, wireless mobile network (WMN) has become an integral part of our daily life. Through WMN mobile users can access information/content from Internet anytime even in roaming from one cellular network to another. However, due to limitation of coverage of an access point (AP) in WMN, mobile handover occurs frequently between the AP and mobile device. During handover process, privacy and security of a mobile consumer becomes a serious challenge since mobile user's anonymity and non-traceability have to be maintained. However, mobility of consumer and content producer in CCN is a major concern which needs to be addressed along with its security aspect. In this paper, a lightweight anonymous handover authentication protocol for mobile users in CCN is proposed. The proposed scheme is designed to provide secure and seamless roaming service to mobile users. To overcome the limitations of resource constrained mobile devices, identity based cryptography (IBC) is used to design an anonymous mobile handover authentication and session key negotiation protocol in CCN. The security analysis of the proposed protocol is done to show its resilience against relevant cryptographic attacks.

Keywords: Content centric network (CCN) · Wireless mobile network (WMN) · Mobile handover authentication · Identity based cryptography (IBC)

1 Introduction

In 2009, CCN was proposed as a new network paradigm to leverage scalable content distribution with Interest based content retrieval, name based routing, in-network caching and Interest packet aggregation as salient features [1–7]. Generally, CCN has four types of network entities namely consumer, content provider, publisher and CCN routers where publisher works as the interface of content providers. CCN uses two types of packets namely Interest packet, generated by consumer for sending content request and Content packet, generated by publisher for sending the content. Later on, another type of CCN packet, called manifest packet was introduced to communicate

© Springer Nature Singapore Pte Ltd. 2019
J. K. Mandal et al. (Eds.): CICBA 2018, CCIS 1031, pp. 360–373, 2019.
https://doi.org/10.1007/978-981-13-8581-0_29

access control information [3]. The CCN routers manage two tables namely, forwarding information base (FIB) and pending Interest table (PIT). The content naming scheme for CCN is organized as the human readable and hierarchical structure as depicted in the following Fig. 1 [2]. CCN can use conventional routing algorithms and uses name based routing using longest prefix match mechanism instead of IP based routing.

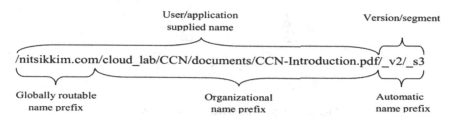

Fig. 1. CCN content naming structure

Since efficient and smooth content delivery is the prime concern of CCN, it is important to provide frequent access and transmission of content from Internet to the mobile users anytime and anywhere [8–14]. Due to the use of conventional WMN architecture for mobility, it is important to address mobile handover scheme in CCN.

1.1 Mobile Handover Process

Mobile device operates through WMN which is a combination of wired and wireless technology. The WMN has three basic entities namely authentication server (AS), access point (AP) and mobile node (MN). Initially, both AP and MN register with the AS before entering the network. AS is connected with several APs through wired connections to provide coverage of the mobile network, and MN connects to the AP through wireless mode. An AP is responsible for providing mobile service to an MN which is in the AP's range. Due to the mobility of MNs and limited geographical coverage of the APs, handover between MN and AP occurs frequently to provide seamless network connectivity in WMN [8–14]. For example, i^{th} mobile node MN_I connects to AP_H for mobile service. When MN_I moves out from the transmission range of AP_H and enters into the range of another AP called AP_F, a handover authentication is needed between the AP_F and the MN_I to ensure security, user anonymity and non-traceability. Moreover, considering the resource constrained mobile devices and need of uninterrupted service, the handover authentication protocol should be lightweight [8–14]. A typical scenario of handover in WMN is shown in Fig. 2.

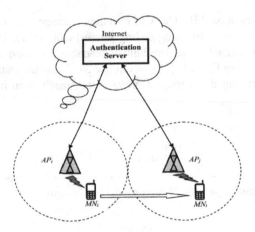

Fig. 2. A typical handover scenario in WMN

1.2   Our Contribution

In this paper, our main objective is to design a lightweight anonymous handover authentication protocol for mobile device in CCN to ensure security and privacy of the mobile users and provide uninterrupted roaming service. Considering the resource constrained mobile device, a lightweight mutual authentication and session key negotiation scheme using IBC is proposed.

1.3   Organization of the Paper

The remaining paper is organized as follows. Section 2 provides a brief literature review on CCN and mobile handover authentication scheme. The proposed handover authentication protocol and its security analysis are presented in Sects. 3 and 4, respectively. The performance analysis is given in Sect. 5 and finally, Sect. 6 concludes the paper.

2   Literature Review

The existing research in CCN mainly focuses on content naming [4], content caching [5, 6], content routing [6] and content security [7]. However, to be widely adopted by the Internet community, the mobility management in CCN is considered as one of the important research aspects to be taken care of. Lee et al. [15] have discussed the challenges of content source mobility and as a solution used tunneling approach similar to Mobile IPv6 but they have not discussed the security aspects. In this paper, our aim is to incorporate mobility management in CCN through the conventional WMN architecture. In addition, our major concern is to take care of the overall security in a cost-effective manner. Now, to understand the state-of-the-art mobile handover security and develop an efficient and secure mobility management solution for CCN, we have studied several papers which are briefly discussed here.

To ensure seamless handover between the MN_I and the AP_F and to protect the privacy and security of the mobile consumers, lots of researches have been done so far. In 2012, He et al. [11] proposed an anonymous handover authentication protocol for WMN. He et al. [11] first time used identity based public key cryptography, built on the security strength of bilinear pairing. However, in the same year, He et al. [12] pointed out that [11] suffers from a serious security vulnerability where any adversary can extract the private key of the MN_I from the intercepted messages. He et al. [12] also proposed an improved scheme to address the problem of [11] but still it has some security weaknesses like compromised key problem [13]. In 2013, Liao et al. [16] proposed an anonymous mobile user authentication protocol using self-certified public key cryptography but in 2014, Hsieh et al. [17] reported few drawbacks such as non-traceability in their scheme [16]. Later, Wang et al. [18] and He et al. [19] also pointed out that He et al's [12] scheme suffers from compromised key problem and both of them presented improved schemes to overcome this weakness. In the timeline, few researchers [14, 20–22] have proposed Elliptic Curve Cryptography (ECC) based handover authentication protocol in mobile environment. Li et al. [20] have designed an ECC based handover authentication protocol but Chaudhry et al. [14] and Xie et al. [21] found some vulnerabilities such as impersonation attack in Li et al.'s [20] scheme. Very recently, in 2018, Zeng et al. [22] also proposed an attribute based anonymous handover authentication protocol. Thus, we find that an efficient and secure handover authentication protocol in mobile environment is a relevant research domain. Therefore, considering the resource constrained mobile devices, our objective is to design a lightweight mobile handover authentication protocol compatible to CCN using IBC [23–26].

3 Proposed Scheme

In this section, we keep the provision for mobility management in CCN. The mobility of a device in CCN is categorized in two cases – (1) mobility of consumer and (2) mobility of content provider, which are discussed below in following two cases.

3.1 Case 1

The receiver driven architecture of CCN supports consumer's mobility during the handover of device from one AP to another. However, during hand over in CCN, resource consumption and network service latency time is increased due to the repeated transmission of Interest packets by the consumer for not received content.

3.2 Case 2

The mobility management of content provider in CCN has enormous challenges and demands attention of the research community. When a mobile content provider (MCP) moves to a new location, it intimates the nearest router for updating the FIB. Accordingly, the nearest router announces the FIB update for the respective MCP and all routers update their FIB as well as PIT for successful reception of the ongoing/future content requests. In addition, Interest packets stored in the routers of the previous location, have to be forwarded to the routers of the new location. Hence, the mobility of a MCP results in frequent routing table (FIB and PIT) updates and long service disruption.

Since both cases are based on the mobility of a device and *case 1* is compatible in CCN with increased resource consumption and network service latency, our main aim is to handle *case 2* in an efficient and secure way. In our scheme, we consider that all MCPs use conventional WMN framework and WMN access points act as CCN content routers. Thus, when a MCP/MN_I initiates content transmission, the nearest access point of that location is called home domain access point (AP_H) and other access points where MCP/MN_I may move is called foreign domain access point (AP_F). In the proposed scheme, we use Manifest packet to exchange the access control specification such as algorithms, hash function, cryptographic parameters, acknowledgement etc. among the mobile node (MN_I), the foreign access point (AP_F) and the authentication server (AS). Here, Manifest is used to send registration request ($Manifest_R$), login request ($Manifest_L$), prefix update ($Manifest_{PU}$) and acknowledgement ($Manifest_{Ack}$). However, Manifest packets are never cached by the CCN routers. Now a brief workflow of the proposed MCP/MN_I handover scheme is discussed here.

Step 1. Each AP periodically broadcasts a beacon message containing its identity ID_{AP}. Upon receiving a new AP's (AP_F) beacon message, the MN_I identifies a network change.

Step 2. After identifying a network change, MN_I prepares for handover by running a secure handover authentication protocol with the AP_F. The proposed handover authentication protocol is briefly described in Subsect. 3.3.

Step 3. After successful handover to the AP_F, the MN_I sends a $Manifest_{PU}$ to its AP_H. $Manifest_{PU}$ contains MN_I's name prefix along with current AP_F's name prefix.

Step 4. After receiving $Manifest_{PU}$, AP_H updates respective MCP's entry in the FIB and PIT by adding new AP_F's prefix before the original Interest prefix. As a result, the Interest of the old location will be redirected to the new location. The PIT structure is shown in Fig. 3. Each Interest name prefix which is redirected to a new location gets a new value in *'redirected name prefix'* column in PIT. The example of prefix update procedure for Interest packet redirection is shown in Fig. 4(a).

Interest name prefix	Incoming face	Outgoing face	Redirected name prefix	...
.	.	.	.	.
.	.	.	.	.

Fig. 3. Routing table/PIT structure

Step 5. The AP_H then redirects all the receiving Interests for the respective MN_I to AP_F according to the redirected name prefix of PIT.

Step 6. After receiving the Interest packets through AP_F, the MN_I transmits Content packets via AP_F using redirected name prefix. The example of prefix update procedure for Content packet redirection is shown in Fig. 4(b).

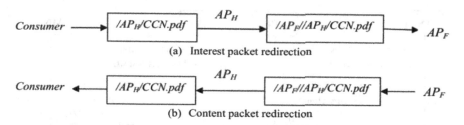

(a) Interest packet redirection

(b) Content packet redirection

Fig. 4. Name prefix update procedure for interest and content packet redirection

Step 7. After receiving the content, AP_H replaces the prefix of the content received with the original prefix of the received Interest from its PIT and sends to the consumer using reverse Interest path.

As mentioned in *step 2*, a detailed mobile handover authentication protocol for CCN is described below. The proposed authentication protocol is applicable for both the mobile consumer and content provider.

3.3 Anonymous Handover Authentication Protocol

In this section, handover authentication protocol between the MN_I and the AP_F is described. Initially both the MN_I and AP_F have to register to the AS. This registration procedure is done through a secure channel. A high speed wired connection connects AP_F with AS and MN_I is connected with AP_F through wireless connectivity. Due to the openness of the wireless connection, the handover authentication is performed over an insecure channel. Now, (1) the system initialization and registration phase between MN_I/AP_F and AS and (2) handover authentication phase between MN_I and AP_F are described in the following subsections.

System Initialization and Registration Phase: AS selects two groups G_1 and G_2 with the same prime order p, a generator G of G_1, a bilinear pairing function *Pair: G_1 X $G_1 \rightarrow G_2$* and two secure one way hash function h and h_1 where $h_1: \{0, 1\}^* \rightarrow \mathbb{Z}_p^*$. AS also selects a random number $s \in \mathbb{Z}_p^*$ and calculates its public key as: $s.G$. Finally, AS publishes the system parameters as: $\{G_1, G_2, p, G, h, h_1, s.G\}$.

Any MN_I and AP_F need to register to AS for accessing WMN service. To get registered, AP_F sends its identity ID_A $_p$in a secure channel and AS supplies AP_F's secret private key as: $s.h_1(ID_{AP})$. Similarly, MN_I sends its identity ID_M in a secure channel and gets its private key as: $s.h_1(ID_M)$. The registration procedure is depicted in Fig. 5.

Handover Authentication Phase: The detailed handover authentication procedure is depicted in Fig. 6 and stepwise described below where $X \rightarrow Y : M$ means sender X sends message M to receiver Y.

Step 1. $MN_I \rightarrow AP_F$: $\{Auth_M, PID_M, R_M, Manifest_L\}$

Initially, the MN_I selects a random number $r_i \in \mathbb{Z}_p^*$ and calculates $R_M = r_i.G$. Then, the MN_I uses the bilinear pairing function along with AP_F's identity ID_{AP} and AS's

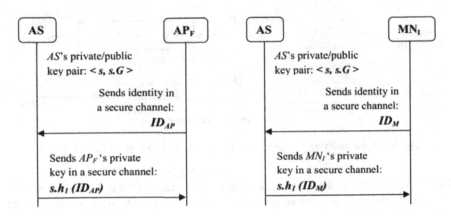

Fig. 5. Registration of MN_I and AP_F to AS

public key to calculate $K_M = Pair(r_i.h_1(ID_{AP}), s.G)$. MN_I uses XOR operation to calculate $PID_M = ID_M \oplus K_M$ and uses concatenation operation to calculate $Auth_M = h(ID_M||K_M||R_M)$. Finally, the MN_I sends $Auth_M$, PID_M and R_M along with a $Manifest_L$ packet as a handover authentication request to the AP_F.

Step 2. $AP_F \rightarrow MN_I$: $\{Manifest_{Ack}, Auth_{AP}, R_{AP}\}$

After receiving the handover authentication request from the MN_I, the AP_F initially checks whether R_M is previously received? If yes, AP_F drops the authentication request. Else, the AP_F uses pairing function along with its own private key and received R_M and calculates $K_M^* = Pair(s.h_1(ID_{AP}), R_M)$. Then, the AP_F calculates $ID_M^* = PID_M \oplus K_M^*$ and $Auth_M^* = h(ID_M^*||K_M^*||R_M)$. Now it checks $Auth_M^* = Auth_M$?. If yes, the MN_I is authenticated; otherwise AP_F drops the session. After the successful authentication of MN_I, AP_F selects a random number $r_j \in \mathbb{Z}_p^*$ and calculates $K_{AP} = Pair(r_j.h_1(ID_M^*), s.G)$. AP_F also calculates its session key part $R_{AP} = r_j.G$, contributory session key $SK = r_j.R_M.h_1(ID_M^*)$ and $Auth_{AP} = h(ID_M^*||K_{AP}||SK||R_{AP})$. Finally, the AP_F sends its authentication request $Auth_{AP}$ and session key part R_{AP} to the respective MN_I along with a $Manifest_{Ack}$, containing the acknowledgement of the authentication of MN_I.

After receiving the message in *step 2*, the MN_I calculates $K_{AP}^* = Pair(s.h_1(ID_M), R_{AP})$, contributory session key $SK = r_i.R_{AP}.h_1(ID_M)$ and $Auth_{AP}^* = h(ID_M||K_{AP}^*||SK||R_{AP})$. Then, the MN_I checks whether $Auth_{AP}^* = Auth_{AP}$? If yes, the AP_F is authenticated and a secure session between the MN_I and AP_F is initiated with the session key SK. Otherwise, the session is aborted.

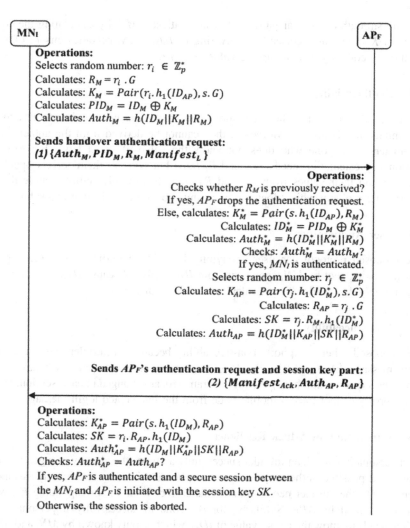

Fig. 6. Anonymous handover authentication protocol between MN_I and AP_F

4   Security Analysis

An in-depth security analysis of the proposed handover authentication protocol is given in this section where the mutual authentication between MN_I and AP_F as well as user anonymity are ensured and a number of relevant cryptographic attacks are considered.

4.1   Mutual Authentication

Mutual authentication means that the parties communicating become sure of the identity of each other. This property is ensured in the proposed protocol based on the security strength of bilinear pairing. AP_F authenticates MN_I by calculating the correct value of K_M* and also correctly uncovering $h_1(ID_M)$. MN_I becomes ensure of AP_F's identity by correctly calculating the value of K_{AP}*.

4.2 Confidentiality

The proposed scheme maintains confidentiality property as none of the secrets and user credentials travels openly. Moreover, they cannot be derived from the authentication parameters by anyone who does not know the value of secret keys. For example, session key calculation needs r_i/r_j and $h_1(ID_M)$ but none of them travels openly. In order to find their values from R_M and R_{AP}, one has to solve elliptic curve discrete logarithmic problem which does not have any sub exponential time algorithm.

4.3 User Anonymity

The proposed protocol has user anonymity because an intruder capturing a packet which is being sent by MN_I cannot find out ID_M. This is because ID_M is XORed with K_M and only MN_I and AP_F can calculate the value of K_M.

4.4 Non-traceability

The proposed scheme supports non-traceability because an intruder can intercept the login message $\{Auth_M, PID_M, R_M, Manifest_L\}$ but cannot trace MN_I's behaviour. As MN_I uses a random number r_i, the login parameters are changed in each session. Hence, an adversary cannot trace a mobile node from the intercepted login message.

4.5 Impersonation Attack Resilience

In impersonation attack an intruder successfully assumes the identity of a genuine user. This is not possible in the proposed protocol, because in order to correctly assume the identity ID_M the intruder needs to know the correct value of corresponding K_M which will be verified by AP_F. Similarly, for someone to successfully impersonate AP_F, he/she needs to know the actual value of ID_M, which is only known by MN_I and AP_F as already discussed.

4.6 Replay Attack Resilience

In replay attack, an intruder replays genuine data captured at an earlier time. One of the most well know ways to prevent replay attack is to use timestamps. However, use of timestamps introduces the problem of time synchronization between two parties. The proposed protocol prevents replay attack without using timestamp. This is because MN_I chooses a new and random value of r_i to calculate R_M in every session. As R_M is included in $h()$ and sent with authentication request, any repeated value will be detected by AP_F. Similarly, AP_F uses an unique and random value of r_j to calculate R_{AP} in every session and also includes R_{AP} in $h()$ to send authentication request. Thus, if AP_F's message is replayed it will be detected by MN_I.

4.7   Man-in-the-Middle Attack Resilience

In man-in-the-middle attack an intruder seats in the middle of the communication line between two genuine parties and captures and modify their communication without them being aware of his presence. Although, all the communication between MN_I and AP_F takes place through an insecure channel, the intruder cannot gather any secret data as explained in confidentiality section. Moreover, the intruder cannot impersonate or replay the message of MN_I or AP_F, as explained in replay attack resilience section. Thus man-in-the-middle attack is successfully prevented in the proposed protocol.

4.8   Perfect Forward Secrecy

Perfect forward secrecy means even if the long term keys become known at a point of time, the sessions before that time are secure. The proposed protocol uses unique values of r_i and r_j to calculate the session key for each session. Thus, even if the long term secret keys of MN_I and AP_F (which are $s.h_1(ID_M)$ and $s.h_1(ID_{AP})$ respectively) become known nobody will be able to compute the SKs before that time.

4.9   Known Session Key Attack Resilience

A protocol is vulnerable to known session key attack if the knowledge of the session key in one session reveals the session keys of other sessions. This is not possible in the proposed protocol because none of the session keys' value depend on the previous session's key. The session keys are calculated by using r_i and r_j whose values change in every session.

4.10   Brute Force Attack Resilience

The proposed scheme is resistant to brute force attack because the intruder cannot guess the secret session key SK. The session key SK is calculated as: $SK = r_j.R_M.h_1(ID_M) = r_i.R_{AP}.h_1(ID_M)$. As SK is dependent on two secret random values from $\mathbb{Z}_p^*$ and anonymous identity of MN_I (ID_M), our session key is strong. Moreover, as SK is a point on the elliptic curve, based on the security strength of elliptic curve discrete logarithmic problem, it is impossible for an intruder to guess SK in polynomial time.

5   Performance Analysis

In this section, a brief performance analysis is presented to show that the proposed scheme is efficient in terms of low computational overhead and high security.

As the proposed scheme uses ECC based scalar point multiplication operation, it incurs lower computational overhead than other schemes which use RSA based modular exponentiation operation. Further, ECC (160 bits) provides same level of security with smaller key comparing to RSA (1024 bits). In addition, the proposed scheme uses identity based private keys and hence, eliminates the extra overhead of managing public key certificates. Computational cost of the proposed scheme is analyzed and compared with other related schemes [16, 17] where approximately esti-

Table 1. List of estimated running time of different operations [27]

Notation	Definition	Running time (ms)
T_{BP}	Running time of bilinear paring operation	32.713
T_{h1}	Running time of map to point hash function	33.582
T_{SPM}	Running time of scalar point multiplication	13.405
T_{PA}	Running time of point addition operation	0.081
T_{EXP}	Running time of exponentiation operation	2.249
T_{MUL}	Running time of multiplication operation	0.008
T_h	Running time of general hash function	0.056

mated running times (in milliseconds) of certain operations are used. We have taken the list of estimated running times from He et al. [27] and presented in Table 1. Further, the computational cost analysis of the proposed scheme with other related schemes [16, 17] is shown in Table 2 where we have considered computational overhead of the resource

Table 2. Comparative cost analysis of MN_I with other related schemes [16, 17]

Schemes	Computational overhead (in ms)
Liao et al. [16]	$T_{h1} + 7T_{SPM} + T_{PA} + 5T_h \approx 127.77$
Hsieh et al. [17]	$T_{h1} + 7T_{SPM} + T_{PA} + 8T_h \approx 127.94$
Proposed Scheme	$2T_{BP} + T_{h1} + 3T_{SPM} + 2T_h \approx 111.02$

constrained mobile node only and it shows that our scheme has less computational overheads comparing to other existing schemes.

Moreover, the security strength of the proposed scheme is dependent on the Elliptic Curve Discrete Logarithmic Problem (ECDLP) and it is already established that there is no polynomial time algorithm to solve ECDLP.

Therefore, in terms of low computational overhead and high security, the proposed scheme is efficient enough to deal with the requirements of resource constrained mobile environment. Finally, a comparative study of overall security analysis is presented in the Table 3.

Table 3. Comparative security analysis with other related schemes [16–19]

Security parameters	Liao et al. [16]	Hsieh et al. [17]	Wang et al. [18]	He et al. [19]	Proposed scheme
Mutual authentication	Yes	Yes	Yes	Yes	**Yes**
Confidentiality	Yes	Yes	Yes	Yes	**Yes**
User anonymity	No	No	Yes	Yes	**Yes**
Non-traceability	No	No	No	No	**Yes**
Session key generation	Yes	Yes	Yes	Yes	**Yes**
Perfect forward secrecy	Yes	Yes	No	No	**Yes**
Brute force attack resilience	Yes	Yes	Yes	Yes	**Yes**

6 Conclusion

Mobility management in CCN environment and its security aspect is proposed in this paper. The solution for consumer mobility and content source mobility is briefly outlined in the given scheme. As any mobile user of CCN avails the conventional WMN architecture, we have presented a mobility management scheme in CCN scenario. Considering the frequent need for handover in WMN architecture, we have designed a handover authentication and session key negotiation protocol using IBC. Due to the use of light weight IBC and ECC point multiplication, the proposed protocol is free from the overhead of public key certificate management and incurs low computation and communication overheads that support frequent handover of a resource constrained mobile device efficiently. Moreover, the user anonymity property is preserved to maintain mobile user's privacy. Finally, the security analysis and performance analysis of the proposed protocol shows that our scheme is well protected against the existing relevant cryptographic attacks as well as efficient enough to work in a resource constrained CCN based mobile environment.

Acknowledgement. This research work is financially supported by Visvesvaraya PhD Scheme, Ministry of Electronics and Information Technology, Government of India.

References

1. Jacobson, V., Smetters, D.K., Thornton, J.D., Plass, M.F., Briggs, N.H., Braynard, R.L.: Networking named content. In: Proceedings of the 5th International Conference on Emerging Networking Experiments and Technologies, pp. 1–12. ACM (2009)
2. Mahadevan, P.: CCNx 1.0 Tutorial. PARC, Technical report (2014)
3. Kurihara, J., Uzun, E., Wood, C. A.: An encryption-based access control framework for content-centric networking. In: IFIP Networking Conference (IFIP Networking), pp. 1–9 (2015)

4. Ghodsi, A., Koponen, T., Rajahalme, J., Sarolahti, P., Shenker, S.: Naming in content-oriented architectures. In: Proceedings of the ACM SIGCOMM Workshop on Information-Centric Networking, pp. 1–6 (2011)

5. Zhang, G., Li, Y., Lin, T.: Caching in information centric networking: a survey. Comput. Netw. **57**(16), 3128–3141 (2013)

6. Bari, M.F., Chowdhury, S., Ahmed, R.: A survey of naming and routing in information-centric networks. IEEE Commun. Mag. **50**(12), 44–53 (2012)

7. Zhang, X., Chang, K., Xiong, H.: Towards name-based trust and security for content-centric network. In: Proceedings of 19th IEEE International Conference on Network Protocols (ICNP), pp. 1–6 (2011)

8. Sun, H.M., Chang, S.Y., Lin, Y.H., Chiou, S.Y.: Efficient authentication schemes for handover in mobile WiMAX. In: Eighth International Conference on Intelligent Systems Design and Applications, ISDA 2008, vol. 3, pp. 235–240 (2008)

9. Yang, X., Huang, X., Liu, J.K.: Efficient handover authentication with user anonymity and untraceability for mobile cloud computing. Futur. Gener. Comput. Syst. **62**, 190–195 (2016)

10. Cao, J., Ma, M., Li, H.: An uniform handover authentication between E-UTRAN and non-3GPP access networks. IEEE Trans. Wirel. Commun. **11**(10), 3644–3650 (2012)

11. He, D., Chen, C., Chan, S., Bu, J.: Secure and efficient handover authentication based on bilinear pairing functions. IEEE Trans. Wirel. Commun. **11**(1), 48–53 (2012)

12. He, D., Chen, C., Chan, S., Bu, J.: Analysis and improvement of a secure and efficient handover authentication for wireless networks. IEEE Commun. Lett. **16**(8), 1270–1273 (2012)

13. Tsai, J.L., Lo, N.W., Wu, T.C.: Secure handover authentication protocol based on bilinear pairings. Wirel. Pers. Commun. **73**(3), 1037–1047 (2013)

14. Chaudhry, S.A., Farash, M.S., Naqvi, H., Islam, S.H., Shon, T.: A robust and efficient privacy aware handover authentication scheme for wireless networks. Wirel. Pers. Commun. **93**(2), 311–335 (2017)

15. Lee, J., Cho, S., Kim, D.: Device mobility management in content-centric networking. IEEE Commun. Mag. **50**(12), 28–34 (2012)

16. Liao, Y.P., Hsiao, C.M.: A novel multi-server remote user authentication scheme using self-certified public keys for mobile clients. Future Gener. Comput. Syst. **29**(3), 886–900 (2013)

17. Hsieh, W.B., Leu, J.S.: An anonymous mobile user authentication protocol using self-certified public keys based on multi-server architectures. J. Supercomput. **70**(1), 133–148 (2014)

18. Wang, W., Hu, L.: A secure and efficient handover authentication protocol for wireless networks. Sensors **14**(7), 11379–11394 (2014)

19. He, D., Khan, M.K., Kumar, N.: A new handover authentication protocol based on bilinear pairing functions for wireless networks. Int. J. Ad Hoc Ubiquitous Comput. **18**(1–2), 67–74 (2015)

20. Li, G., Jiang, Q., Wei, F., Ma, C.: A new privacy-aware handover authentication scheme for wireless networks. Wirel. Pers. Commun. **80**(2), 581–589 (2015)

21. Xie, Y., Wu, L., Kumar, N., Shen, J.: Analysis and improvement of a privacy-aware handover authentication scheme for wireless network. Wirel. Pers. Commun. **93**(2), 523–541 (2017)

22. Zeng, Y., Guang, H., Li, G.: Attribute-Based Anonymous Handover Authentication Protocol for Wireless Networks. Security and Communication Networks (2018)

23. Joye, M., Neven, G. (eds.): Identity-Based Cryptography, vol. 2. IOS Press, Amsterdam (2009)

24. Smart, N.P.: Identity-based authenticated key agreement protocol based on weil pairing. Electron. Lett. **38**(13), 630–632 (2002)

25. Hankerson, D., Menezes, A.J., Vanstone, S.: Guide to Elliptic Curve Cryptography. Springer, Heidelberg (2006). https://doi.org/10.1007/b97644
26. Lauter, K.: The advantages of elliptic curve cryptography for wireless security. IEEE Wirel. Commun. 11(1), 62–67 (2004)
27. He, D., Zeadally, S., Kumar, N., Wu, W.: Efficient and anonymous mobile user authentication protocol using self-certified public key cryptography for multi-server architectures. IEEE Trans. Inf. Forensics Secur. 11(9), 2052–2064 (2016)

ECC Based Remote Mutual Authentication Scheme for Resource Constrained Client in Cloud

Sayantan Chatterjee[✉] and Shefalika Ghosh Samaddar

National Institute of Technology Sikkim, Ravangla 737139, South Sikkim, India
sayanc2011@gmail.com, shefalika99@yahoo.com

Abstract. Cloud computing is a state-of-the-art technology using which a resource starved client can access various services from a remote cloud server. Accessing such remote services requires that the client and server authenticate each other and come to agree on a common session key in secure manner. Most of the recent mutual authentication and key agreement protocols use two and three factor smart card and biometric based techniques. However, due to the consequent increase in cost of resources and added operational complexity, one factor authentication schemes are still popular. In this paper a lightweight Elliptic Curve Cryptography based one factor three way mutual authentication and key negotiation scheme between a lightweight client and server is proposed with proven safety.

Keywords: Cloud computing · Mutual authentication · Key negotiation · Elliptic curve cryptography (ECC) · AVISPA

1 Introduction

Cloud computing is one of the major innovations in the field of Information Technology in recent times. Cloud computing can be defined as the technology of making IT resources available as internet based services to the client elastically. The client can demand as much resource (in terms of software, platform or infrastructure) as is needed from the cloud service without being aware of how the demand is satisfied. In turn, the client is billed according to his resource consumption. This frees the client from a potentially huge investment in IT resources that may go underutilized in the future.

Advances in circuit miniaturization and processing power has led to large scale adoption of lightweight devices in all major technological areas. Due to limited processing power and battery life, the support of cloud infrastructure is very suitable for these devices. In fact, many lightweight devices have limited resources such as hard disk space, internal memory, etc. so that it is best to offload non-essential tasks to the cloud. The devices can act as a thin client concerned with only the specialized tasks it is meant for while all other supporting tasks are taken care of by the cloud.

Taking advantage of the cloud in this way is not, however, simple in terms of computation. One of the major concerns for the devices connected to the cloud is security. According to a recent survey, security issues over cloud services is the third

© Springer Nature Singapore Pte Ltd. 2019
J. K. Mandal et al. (Eds.): CICBA 2018, CCIS 1031, pp. 374–387, 2019.
https://doi.org/10.1007/978-981-13-8581-0_30

most prevalent cause of concern in the industry [1].When a device connects with the cloud, the device must have assurance that the cloud is authentic. Similarly, the cloud must also be assured of the device's authenticity. Moreover, data exchanged between the device and cloud should remain confidential. In addition, there are plethora of other security requirements such as message integrity, forward security, etc. to be taken care of.

Although these issues are present in all areas where two devices connect remotely in order to communicate, lightweight devices have limited processing power and storage and hence cannot use resource intensive security algorithms.

In this paper, a novel mutual authentication and session key negotiation scheme is outlined between a device/cloud client and cloud server using Elliptic Curve Diffie-Hellman Key Exchange (ECDH) protocol. Elliptic curve cryptography (ECC) is a state-of-the-art lightweight cryptosystem which has smaller key-size and uses less processing power compared to other public-key cryptosystem such as RSA. In recent years, ECC has been adopted by the mobile computing community because of its low memory requirements and faster processing [2]. The proposed protocol aims to leverage this advantage of ECC where it is most needed in order to develop a robust and secure mutual authentication and key negotiation protocol.

1.1   Background Study

In this section, a brief overview of current works related to security of cloud computing is discussed. In addition, a brief overview of ECC is also given.

Cloud Security. The cloud computing framework has undergone widespread industry adoption during recent years [1]. Gartner has predicted that the worldwide public cloud services market will grow by 18% in 2017 [3]. However, security is still one of the major concerns for potential cloud adoptees [1]. A list of the most prevalent security threats for cloud was published by Cloud Security Alliance (CSA) [4]. Subhashini et al. [5] has classified cloud security problems into four categories: data storage security, data transmission security, application security and security related to third party resources. Khalil et al. [6] has given a comprehensive survey of cloud security. They have identified 28 security issues which they have categorised into five classes like Security Standards, Network, Access Control, Cloud Infrastructure and Data Security. Halabi et al. [7] have given four aspects of cloud security viz. Cloud Confidentiality, Cloud Integrity, Cloud Availability and Cloud Accountability, and Compliance. They have also categorized cloud computing security services into 12 types such as Authentication, Authorization and Access Control, Web Application Security, Network Security, Data and Storage Security, Virtualization Security, Physical Security, Data and Computing Integrity, Data Availability, Service Availability, Security Auditing and Testing and Compliance with Regulatory and Industrial Standards. The same paper has presented some quantitative metrics to measure security performance of cloud.

Kalra et al. [8] has given Elliptic Curve Diffie–Hellman (ECDH) based mutual authentication scheme between IoT/Embedded devices and cloud server. Their work, however, assumes existence of secure channel in order to share pre-secret key between the device and server. Kumari et al. [9] has also used ECDH and biometric password to perform authenticated user registration with cloud server. Their scheme also requires presence of secure connection during registration phase. Qi et al. [10] has given a three way authentication protocol between client and server in mobile environment using ECC. Chandrakar et al. [12] has given a three factor (password, biometric and smart card) authentication technique between device, server and registration centre using a trustworthy medium during server registration phase.

A lot of current work on authentication use biometric, smart card, etc. based techniques to improve security of the protocols. However, using a biometric reader or smart card brings on extra complexity including cost of the implementing the protocol. Keeping in mind the wide prevalence of mobile and thin clients, the protocol presented in this paper does not use any such techniques.

Elliptic Curve Cryptography. Elliptic Curve Cryptography (ECC) [13, 14] was independently invented by Victor Miller [15] and Neal Koblitz [16]. ECC is a very efficient public key cryptosystem requiring relatively small sized key compared to other cryptosystems such as RSA. An ECC scheme with 160-bit key gives security comparable to 1024-bit key size RSA scheme. In practice, elliptic curve key size of 256-bit is commonly used. Moreover, doubling the effort of an attacker for a given ECC system requires an increase in ECC parameter by 2-bits whereas for RSA it requires 20 to 30-bit increase in length [14].

Let Zp be the set $\{1, 2, ..., p - 1\}$ where p is a prime number. The elliptic curve over Zp, $p > 3$, is the set of all pairs $(x, y) \in Zp$ which satisfy the following equation:

$$y^2 \equiv x^3 + a.x + b \ mod \ p \tag{1}$$

Here $a, b \in Z_p$ and the condition is satisfied:

$$4.a^3 + 27.b^2 \neq 0 \ mod \ p \tag{2}$$

The points of an elliptic curve satisfying the above conditions form a group for the following operations:

Point Addition. This operation (denoted by '+') over two elliptic curve points P and Q is defined as the third point R which is constructed by taking the mirror image over x-axis of the point of intersection of the line joining P and Q and the elliptic curve. The operation of point addition can be extended to other operations as follows:

Point Doubling. This operation is point addition when $P = Q$ (i.e. $R = P + P$) and gives the point R which is the mirror image over x-axis of the point of intersection of the tangent through point P with the elliptic curve.

Point Subtraction. The point of infinity O is an imaginary point which can be visualized as a point that is located at plus infinity towards positive y-axis or at minus infinity towards negative y-axis. It is the identity element of the group, i.e. $P + O = P$. Point subtraction operation for the point P involves finding the inverse of P, $-P$ such that $P + (-P) = O$.

Scalar Point Multiplication. For an integer k the scalar point multiplication of elliptic curve point P is defined as $P + P + \ldots$ upto k times $= k \cdot P$. If P is a primitive element (also called generator) then all the elements of the elliptic curve group can be generated by doing scalar point multiplication of P with different values of k.

The security of ECC depends on the hardness of Elliptic Curve Discrete Logarithmic problem (ECDLP). Given and elliptic curve E, its primitive element P and another point of the curve T, the ECDLP is to find another integer d such that $P + P + \ldots$ upto d time $= d \cdot P = T$. Although it has not been theoretically proven that ECDLP is an intractable problem, still after years of research no sub-exponential time algorithm has been found for solving ECDLP [14].

There are many security protocols that use Elliptic Curves. The given scheme has used ECC in negotiating session key between the client and the server using Elliptic Curve Diffie–Hellman key exchange (ECDHKE) protocol.

In plain ECDHKE protocol, two clients Alice and Bob securely exchange a common key. It is assumed that Elliptic curve E along with its public parameters like a, b, E's order p and generator G are known to both parties. Alice first chooses a secret parameter $\alpha \in Z_P$ and sends $\alpha.G$ to Bob. Bob in his turn chooses another secret $\beta \in Z_P$ and sends $\beta.G$ to Alice. Here the multiplication operation (.) is actually scalar point multiplication. Now both Alice and Bob can compute their common secret key as $\alpha.\beta.G$. The security of ECDHKE is ensured by the hardness of ECDLP [14].

2   Proposed Scheme

This section presents the proposed mutual authentication and session key generation scheme between the cloud client and the cloud server. This scheme uses ECDHKE protocol to generate the session key. It is assumed that the medium of communication between the client and the cloud server is insecure, i.e. an intruder can observe, capture and modify any data travelling through the medium. Hence, no confidential information can travel openly through this medium. The scheme is divided into two phases, viz. registration phase and login, and session key generation phase. Once a registered client logs in, a session key is generated which is used as a symmetric key for encrypting (and decrypting) all subsequent communication between the client and the server in that session. Every session has a new key so that even if a session key becomes known the subsequent and previous session data is still secret.

Figure 1 shows the graphical representation of the scheme. In the figure and the subsequent explanation the following notations have been used:

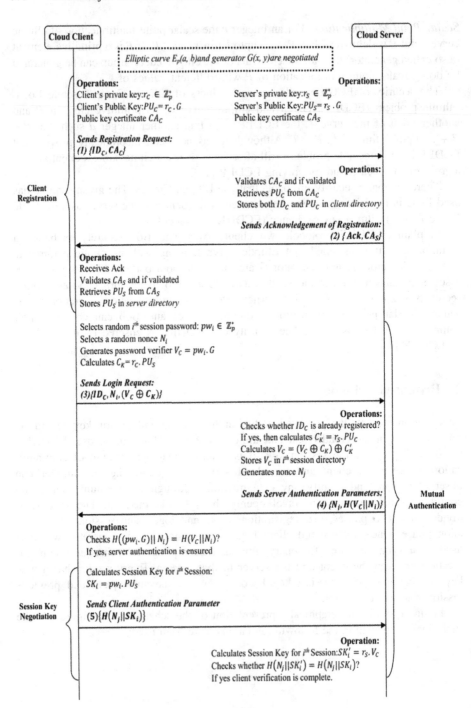

Fig. 1. Authentication and session key negotiation protocol between cloud client and cloud server

Table 1. List of special symbols used

$H()$	A secure one-way hash function
$\oplus$	XOR operator
r_s, r_c	Cloud server's and client's respective private keys
PU_S, PU_C	Cloud server's and client's respective public keys
CA_S, CA_C	Cloud server's and client's respective public key certificates
G	The primitive element/generator of ECC used in the scheme
ID_C	Identity of the client
Ack	Server acknowledgement sent to the client during client registration phase
N_i, N_j	Random nonce
pw_i	Random password chosen by the client for the ith session
V_C	Password verifier
C_K, C_K'	Authentication parameters
SK_i, SK_i'	Session key for the ith session

2.1 Registration Phase

The ECC curve E along with all the parameters like ECC generator G are pre-determined as part of the protocol. The client first chooses a cloud server whose services it wants to use in the future and registers itself to the server by sending its public key certificate CA_C along with its identity ID_C. The server, after verifying the validity of CA_C, extracts the public key PU_C of the client and stores it along with ID_C in its database. It then sends an acknowledgement Ack along with its own public key certificate CA_S to the client. The client in its turn validates CA_S and then extracts and stores the public key PU_S of the server.

2.2 Login and Key Generation Phase

In this phase the client tries to log in and authenticate itself with the server. The server, in its turn authenticates itself to the client, after which both the client and the server generate the session key separately.

The client first selects a random number $pw_i \in Z_p$. It also calculates a verifier $V_C = pw_i.G$ and the authentication parameter $C_K = r_c.PU_S$, where r_c is the private key of the client. It then sends the packet containing $\{ID_C, N_i, (V_C \oplus C_K)\}$, where N_i is a random cryptographic nonce, to the server. A nonce is a random value which is used only once.

The server first checks for the presence of ID_C in its database. The server then calculates $C_K' = r_s.PU_C$, where r_s is the server's private key. It may be noted that, $C_K' = r_s.PU_C = r_s.(r_C.G) = r_C.(r_s.G) = r_C.PU_S = C_K$ and, C_K and C_K' can only be calculated by the client or the server respectively.

Now the server computes $V_C = (V_C \oplus C_K) \oplus C_K'$ and stores it to be used in the future to construct the session key. It generates a nonce N_j, another unique random number, and sends the packet containing data $\{N_j, H(V_C||N_i)\}$ to the client.

The client on receiving the packet, checks whether $H((pw_i.G)||N_i) = H(V_C||N_i)$. This proves that the server has correctly computed the value of V_C, and hence is authentic. Also the presence of N_i within the hash function prevents any replay attack.

Now the client calculates the session key $SK_i = pw_i.PU_S$ and concatenates the nonce N_j with SK_i and sends its hashed value to the server. The server generates the same session key $SK_i' = r_S.V_C$ and checks whether $H(N_j||SK_i') = H(N_j||SK_i)$. If both values are equal then the server becomes sure of the authenticity of the client. It may be noted that $SK_i = pw_i.PU_S = pw_i.(r_S.G) = r_S.(pw_i.G) = r_S.V_C = SK_i'$.

3   Security Analysis

In analyzing the security properties of the given scheme it is assumed that the adversary has full control of the medium of communication between the client and the server. Thus the adversary can observe, modify and impersonate all the messages sent between the client and the server. Below, an informal analysis of the security properties of the given scheme is discussed.

3.1   Mutual Authentication

During the login phase the client calculates and sends the value $C_K = r_c.PU_S$ by xoring it to V_C. The server in its turn calculates $C_K' = r_S.PU_C$. Clearly C_K can only be calculated by the client or the server as it requires knowledge of private keys r_C or r_S.

Using C_K' the server in its turn finds the value of V_C, includes it inside a hash function with the random nonce N_i and sends it to the client. Once the client verifies that the server has been able to correctly calculate V_C it knows the server is authentic because the server would need to know C_K' and hence its private key r_S to find V_C. Similarly, the client sends the hashed value of the nonce generated by the server, N_j, concatenated with the session key SK_i to the server. When the server calculates its own SK_i' and checks equality of the value sent by the client then it knows that the client is authentic as it has successfully calculated the session key.

3.2   Confidentiality

As the medium of communication is insecure, the intruder has access to all data passing between the client and the server. However, in this scheme, no confidential data travels openly. For example the value C_K and V_C, which the client sends during login, are xored together. No sensitive data like private keys of the client or the server, pw_i, etc. ever travels openly through the medium. Hence, confidentiality of the data is preserved in this scheme.

3.3   Resistance Against Man-in-the-Middle Attack

Man-in-the-middle attack is a type of attack in which an intruder captures and possibly modifies the data travelling between two parties while the parties believe that they are communicating between themselves. In the given scheme, the intruder may observe the data passing between the client and the server but cannot come to know of any secret information as explained above.

Moreover, if the intruder replaces the data $V_C \oplus C_K$, sent by the client during login phase, with its own data, the server will calculate the wrong V'_C. The value of session key SK_i, calculated by the intruder will not match with that calculated by the server. Similarly if the intruder changes the data sent by server, viz. $H(V_C||N_i)$ the client can detect the change and can decide to stop the protocol.

3.4 Resistance Against Replay Attack

In replay attack the adversary captures packets of data and resends them at a later time. Generally, timestamp or nonce can be used to prevent this form of attack. However, using timestamp is a problem because time must be synchronized between the client and the server. Hence, the given scheme has used nonce to stop replay attack.

During login phase the client generates a nonce N_i and sends it to the server. The server includes the nonce in a hash function and resends it to the client. If an intruder captures this packet and sends it to the client at a later time, the client verification will fail due to the fact that value of N_i cannot be repeated. Similarly, the client hashes the nonce N_j, generated by the server, with the session key and sends it to the server. As new session key is generated every session, this value cannot be replayed at a later time by the intruder.

3.5 Perfect Forward Secrecy

Perfect forward secrecy means that even if the long term key becomes known at some point of time, the sessions before that point of time are still undecipherable [17]. This is the case in the given scheme, as even if the client's or the server's private keys, viz. r_C or r_S becomes known by the adversary at some point of time, the session keys for sessions before that point of time depend on those sessions' pw_i and V_C and hence remain hidden from the adversary.

3.6 Resistance Against Known Session Key Attack

A protocol is vulnerable to known session key attack if knowing the session key for a session reveals the session keys of other sessions. Given protocol is full proof against known session key attack as session keys in different sessions have no relation to each other.

4 Formal Verification of the Protocol Using AVISPA Tools

Automated Validation of Internet Security Protocols and Applications (AVISPA) is a security protocol analysis tool. Using AVISPA, the security goals (for example secrecy and mutual authentication) of a protocol can be specified and the satisfaction of those goals can also be verified.

A protocol in AVISPA is generally specified using High Level Protocol Specification Language (HLPSL). The HLPSL code is then converted to Intermediate Format (IF) using HLPSL2IF tool. This is done automatically by AVISPA. AVISPA contains a bunch of other tools like On-the-fly Model Checker (OFMC), CL-Based Attack Searcher (CL-AtSE), SAT-based Model Checker (SATMC) and Tree Automata-based Protocol Analyser (TA4SP), which are used to further analyze the specified protocol and check for any weaknesses and attacks [18].

The given protocol has been analysed using both OFMC and CL-AtSE. The OFMC analyses a protocol using lazy data types and a demand driven intruder modelling technique [19, 20]. The CL-AtSE tools takes as input a protocol specified in IF language and finds any attacks on the protocol if they exist [21]. Both OFMC and CL-AtSE uses the *Dolev-Yao* (DY) intruder modelling. In this model the intruder is given full control of the medium of communication and can capture, modify and send any type of data [22].

In the given HLPSL code, the roles *role_C* and *role_S* (Figs. 2. and 3.) represent the client and the server respectively. The role *session* (Fig. 4) instantiates the two roles *role_C* and *role_S* with concrete arguments. The role *environment* (Fig. 5) starts up multiple sessions, viz. two parallel sessions between client and server, to check for replay attacks, one session between the client and an intruder and one session between an intruder and the server. The *goal* section defines the security goals of the protocol, which are that V_C should remain a secret known only to the client and the server and the client and the server should authenticate each other based on the values of N_i and N_j.

The result of executing the protocol using *OFMC* and *CL-AtSE* are shown in Fig. 6. As shown, AVISPA has declared the protocol to be safe as far as the stated goals are

```
role role_C(C:agent,S:agent,H:function,Ck:symmetric_key,Sk:symmetric_key,SND,RCV:channel(dy))
played_by C
def=
        local
                State:nat,Ni,Nj,Vc:text
        init
                State := 0
        transition
                1. State=0 ∧ RCV(start) =|>
                        State':=2 ∧ Ni'=new() ∧ Vc':=new()
                                ∧ SND(C.Ni'.{Vc'}_Ck)
                                ∧ secret(Vc', vc, {C,S})

                2. State=2 ∧ RCV(S.Nj'.H(Vc.Ni)) =|>
                        State':=4 ∧ request(C, S, auth_ni, Ni)
                                ∧ SND(C.{Nj'}_Sk)
                                ∧ witness(C, S, auth_nj, Nj')
end role
```

Fig. 2. Role cloud client

```
role role_S(S:agent,C:agent,H:function,Ck:symmetric_key,Sk:symmetric_key,SND,RCV:channel(dy))
played_by S
def=
        local
                State:nat,Ni,Nj,Vc:text
        init
                State := 1
        transition
                1. State=1 ∧ RCV(C.Ni'.{Vc'}_Ck) =|>
                State':=3 ∧ Nj':=new()
                        ∧ SND(S.Nj'.H(Vc'.Ni'))
                        ∧ witness(S, C, auth_ni, Ni')

                2. State=3 ∧ RCV(C.{Nj}_Sk) =|>
                State':=5 ∧ request(S, C, auth_nj, Nj)
end role
```

Fig. 3. Role cloud server

```
role session(C:agent,S:agent,H:function,Ck:symmetric_key, Sk:symmetric_key)
def=
        local
                SND1,RCV1,SND2,RCV2:channel(dy)
        composition
                role_C(C,S,H,Ck,Sk,SND1,RCV1) ∧ role_S(S,C,H,Ck,Sk,SND2,RCV2)
end role
```

Fig. 4. Role session

```
role environment()
def=
        const
                client,server:agent,
                h:function,
                ck,sk,ci,si:symmetric_key,
                vc,auth_ni,auth_nj:protocol_id
        intruder_knowledge={client,server,h}
        composition
                session(client,server,h,ck,sk)
                ∧ session(client,server,h,ck,sk)
                ∧ session(client,i,h,ci,si)
                ∧ session(i,server,h,ci,si)
end role

goal
        secrecy_of vc
        authentication_on auth_ni
        authentication_on auth_nj
end goal

environment()
```

Fig. 5. Role environment

```
% OFMC
% Version of 2006/02/13
SUMMARY
 SAFE
DETAILS
 BOUNDED_NUMBER_OF_SESSIONS
PROTOCOL
 /home/span/span/testsuite/results/cloud.if
GOAL
 as_specified
BACKEND
 OFMC
COMMENTS
STATISTICS
 parseTime: 0.00s
 searchTime: 0.01s
 visitedNodes: 5 nodes
 depth: 4 plies
```

```
SUMMARY
 SAFE
DETAILS
 BOUNDED_NUMBER_OF_SESSIONS
 TYPED_MODEL
PROTOCOL
 /home/span/span/testsuite/results/cloud.if
GOAL
 As Specified
BACKEND
 CL-AtSe
STATISTICS
 Analysed  : 9 states
 Reachable : 5 states
 Translation: 0.00 seconds
 Computation: 0.00 seconds
```

Fig. 6. Result using OFMC-safe and CL-AtSe-safe

concerned. Figure 7 is a screenshot of the protocol execution as shown in SPAN. SPAN or *Security Protocol Animator* is a software which uses AVISPA tools to visually simulate protocols and show the interactions between the concerned parties as well as intruder.

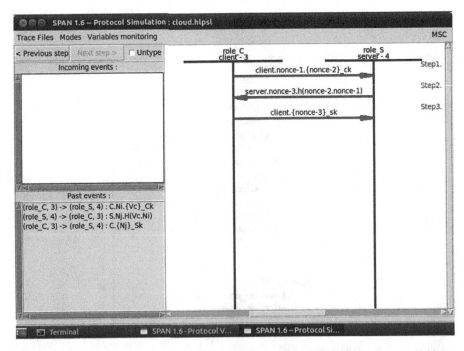

Fig. 7. Protocol simulation snapshot using SPAN + AVISPA simulator (Video available at: https://www.youtube.com/watch?v=seS_-oa3upg&feature=youtu.be)

5   Computation Cost Analysis

This section gives the approximate computation cost of the proposed protocol. For relevance, the computational cost of the protocol is also compared to three other recent authentication protocols proposed by Karla et al. [8], Qi et al. [10] and Chen et al. [11].

The given protocol uses lightweight ECC with maximum key size of 256 bits. No timestamp is used as using timestamps lead to the additional complexity of time synchronization between the client and the server. Nonces are used for authentication and prevention of replay attack.

Let T_H, T_{EM} and T_{ME} be the cost of doing one hash computation, one ECC point multiplication operation and one modular exponentiation operation respectively. The cost of doing xor operation is negligible. Then, $T_{ME} > T_{EM} > T_H$.

Wander et al. [23] have shown that doing ECC based operations require 1/12th of as much energy as required to do RSA based exponentiation operation.

Table 1 gives a comparison of the security features of the given scheme with other recent protocols on mutual authentication. The approximate cost of the proposed scheme along with the cost of the same protocols is given in Table 2. As can be seen from the table below, the given scheme has substantial cost reduction compared to other related schemes (Table 3).

Table 2. Comparison of features of the given scheme with other protocols

Security attributes	Schemes			
	Karla et al. [8]	Qi et al. [10]	Chen et al. [11]	Proposed scheme
Mutual authentication and key agreement	Yes	Yes	Yes	Yes
Session key negotiation	No	Yes	Yes	Yes
Session key security	Yes	Yes	Yes	Yes
Forward secrecy	Yes	Yes	No	Yes
Clock synchronization problem resistance	Yes	Yes	No	Yes
Replay attack resistance	Yes	Yes	Yes	Yes
Man-in-the-middle attack resistance	Yes	Yes	Yes	Yes
Fully operates in insecure channel	No	No	No	Yes

Table 3. Comparative analysis of approximate costs of the selected schemes including proposed scheme

Schemes	Registration phase		Authentication phase	
	Client	Server	Client	Server
Karla et al. [8]	–	$T_{EM} + 3T_H$	$4T_{EM} + 4T_H$	$4T_{EM} + 5T_H$
Qi et al. [10]	–	$3T_H$	$3T_{EM} + 5T_H$	$3T_{EM} + 5T_H$
Chen et al. [11]	–	$T_{ME} + T_H$	$2T_{ME} + 2T_{EM} + 3T_H$	$T_{ME} + T_{EM} + 2T_H$
Proposed Scheme	–	–	$3T_{EM} + 2T_H$	$2T_{EM} + 2T_H$

6   Conclusion

The protocol presented in this paper is a lightweight security solution for the problem of remote user authentication and session key generation suitable for a wide range of devices including resource constrained thin-client communicating with a cloud server. The given protocol uses ECC, which is a lightweight public key cryptosystem which provides same level of security as RSA with smaller key size. The security strength of the given protocol depends on the hardness of ECDLP, which does not have any polynomial time algorithm. The protocol does not use any time-stamps to avoid time synchronization complexity. It does not use any smart card or other physical devices and hence has enhanced general applicability. Moreover, by not depending on such devices the loss of security due to theft or loss of such device does not arise.

One shortcoming of this protocol is that it does not address denial-of-service (DoS) attack. However, normally DoS attacks are prevented by packet control analyses and network flow analyses and are taken care of by firewalls and other intrusion-detection software.

References

1. CASB. "Cloud Report." Skyhigh. www.skyhighnetworks.com/cloud-report/. Accessed 10 Apr 2018
2. Gura, N., Patel, A., Wander, A., Eberle, H., Shantz, S.C.: Comparing elliptic curve cryptography and RSA on 8-bit CPUs. In: Joye, M., Quisquater, J.-J. (eds.) CHES 2004. LNCS, vol. 3156, pp. 119–132. Springer, Heidelberg (2004). https://doi.org/10.1007/978-3-540-28632-5_9
3. Roundup of Cloud Computing Forecasts. https://www.forbes.com/sites/louiscolumbus/2017/04/29/roundup-of-cloud-computing-forecasts-2017/#70ee0b9a31e8. Accessed 10 Apr 2018
4. The Notorious Nine Cloud Computing Top Threats in 2013. https://cloudsecurityalliance.org/download/the-notorious-nine-cloud-computing-top-threats-in-2013/. Accessed 10 Apr 2018
5. Subashini, S., Kavitha, V.: A survey on security issues in service delivery models of cloud computing. J. Netw. Comput. Appl. **34**(1), 1 (2011)
6. Khalil, I.M., Khreishah, A., Azeem, M.: Cloud computing security: a survey. Computers **3**(1), 1–35 (2014)
7. Halabi, T., Bellaiche, M.: Towards quantification and evaluation of security of cloud service providers. J. Inf. Secur. Appl. **33**, 55–65 (2017)
8. Kalra, S., Sood, S.K.: Secure authentication scheme for IoT and cloud servers. Pervasive Mob. Comput. **24**, 210–223 (2015)
9. Kumari, S., Li, X., Wu, F., Das, A.K., Choo, K.K.R., Shen, J.: Design of a provably secure biometrics-based multi-cloud-server authentication scheme. Future Gener. Comput. Syst. **68**, 320–330 (2017)
10. Qi, M., Chen, J.: An efficient two party authentication key exchange protocol for mobile environment. Int. J. Commun Syst **30**(16), e3341 (2017)
11. Chen, B.L., Kuo, W.C., Wuu, L.C.: Robust smart-card-based remote user password authentication scheme. Int. J. Commun Syst **27**(2), 377–389 (2014)

12. Chandrakar, P., Om, H.: A secure and robust anonymous three-factor remote user authentication scheme for multi-server environment using ECC. Math. Comput. **110**, 26–34 (2017)
13. Paar, C., Pelzl, J.: Understanding Cryptography: A Textbook for Students and Practitioners. Springer, Heidelberg (2009). https://doi.org/10.1007/978-3-642-04101-3
14. Hankerson, D., Menezes, A.J., Vanstone, S.: Guide to Elliptic Curve Cryptography. Springer, Heidelberg (2006). https://doi.org/10.1007/b97644
15. Miller, V.S.: Use of elliptic curves in cryptography. In: Williams, H.C. (ed.) CRYPTO 1985. LNCS, vol. 218, pp. 417–426. Springer, Heidelberg (1986). https://doi.org/10.1007/3-540-39799-X_31
16. Koblitz, N.: Elliptic curve cryptosystems. Math. Comput. **48**(177), 203–209 (1987)
17. Diffie, W., Van Oorschot, P.C., Wiener, M.J.: Authentication and authenticated key exchanges. Des. Codes Cryptogr. **2**(2), 107–125 (1992)
18. von Oheimb, D.: The high-level protocol specification language HLPSL developed in the EU project AVISPA. In: Proceedings of APPSEM 2005 workshop, pp. 1–17, September 2005
19. Lafourcade, P., Terrade, V., Vigier, S.: Comparison of cryptographic verification tools dealing with algebraic properties. In: Degano, P., Guttman, J.D. (eds.) FAST 2009. LNCS, vol. 5983, pp. 173–185. Springer, Heidelberg (2010). https://doi.org/10.1007/978-3-642-12459-4_13
20. Basin, D., Mödersheim, S., Vigano, L.: OFMC: a symbolic model checker for security protocols. Int. J. Inf. Secur. **4**(3), 181–208 (2005)
21. Turuani, M.: The CL-Atse protocol analyser. In: Pfenning, F. (ed.) RTA 2006. LNCS, vol. 4098, pp. 277–286. Springer, Heidelberg (2006). https://doi.org/10.1007/11805618_21
22. Dolev, D., Yao, A.: On the security of public key protocols. IEEE Trans. Inf. Theory **29**(2), 198–208 (1983)
23. Wander, A.S., Gura, N., Eberle, H., Gupta, V. Shantz, S.C.: Energy analysis of public-key cryptography for wireless sensor networks. In: Third IEEE International Conference on Pervasive Computing and Communications, PerCom 2005, pp. 324–328. IEEE (2005)

An Approach Towards Design and Analysis of a Non Contiguous Block Cipher Based Cryptographic System Using Modular Arithmetic Technique (NCBMAT)

Debajyoti Guha[1(✉)] and Rajdeep Chakraborty[2]

[1] Department of CSE,
Siliguri Institute of Technology, Siliguri, West Bengal, India
debajyoti.aec@gmail.com
[2] Department of CSE, Netaji Subhash Engineering College,
Kolkata, West Bengal, India
rajdeep_chak@rediffmail.com

Abstract. In this article a new Cryptographic System based on Modular Arithmetic using block ciphers has been considered. The original data which is a stream of bits, is assumed to be divided into a number of blocks & each block contains m bits, where m is anyone of (3, 9, 27, 81, 243). The technique is based on the concept of data redundancy. A Number of redundant zeros will be appended at the MSB of bit stream to make total number of bits odd in each block. The binary addition has been made between first and the ultimate block taking modulus of addition as 2^m. The sum replaces the content of ultimate block, first block remains unaltered to get the cipher text. In the next step the binary addition has been made between the ultimate block and the second block and the result replaces the second block. The technique proposed here involves operations on non-contiguous blocks (unless only two blocks are left which are adjacent to one another). In any two consecutive operations, one block is common, which makes the encryption unpredictable and thereby enhances security. The carry generated (if any) out of the MSB is discarded. The technique is applied on blocks with varying sizes from 3 to 3^n. The modulo subtraction technique is adopted for decryption to get back the plain text.

Keywords: Cryptographic system · Encryption · Decryption · Plain text · Cipher text · Non contiguous block cipher · Modular arithmetic

1 Introduction

We are living in an age of information and hence the information needs to be protected from all sorts of attacks. Information needs to be hidden from unauthorized access to maintain its integrity and should only be delivered to the authorized recipient. There is a list of security attacks like spoofing, traffic analysis, modification, masquerade, replay, repudiation, denial of service that often breaks the goals of security policy [8–10]. Proper technique should be incorporated to get rid of such attacks and maintain

© Springer Nature Singapore Pte Ltd. 2019
J. K. Mandal et al. (Eds.): CICBA 2018, CCIS 1031, pp. 388–401, 2019.
https://doi.org/10.1007/978-981-13-8581-0_31

a full proof system of security so as to confirm the confidentiality and integrity and information.

In this article efforts have been to design a cryptographic system using symmetric key cryptography [3] by involving block cipher technique. The technique is unique in its implementation because of the following threefold characteristics.

(i) The algorithm discussed in this article is applicable on odd number of bits. It can also be extended to apply on even number of bits without changing the algorithm.

(ii) The inclusion of a common block in any two consecutive operations makes the encryption unique.

(iii) The key generated in each round will be unpredictable and therefore strengthen the security of the proposed algorithm.

In Sect. 2 of this article we deal with the proposed scheme. A flow diagram of implementation and validation is given in Sect. 3. Comparative study of results is described in Sect. 4. Section 5 deals with conclusions and references are given in below Sect. 5.

2 The Modular Encryption and Decryption Technique (NCBMAT)

To implement the proposed work, the stream size of 729 bits has been taken. The scheme may be implemented for bigger stream sizes too. The input stream, Z, is initially segregated into a number of blocks (T_1, T_2..., T_X). Starting from LSB each block containing m bits (m = 3^P, p = 1, 2, 3...) so that Z = T_1, T_2, T_3, .., T_x where x = 729/m. Starting from the MSB, the Non adjacent blocks are paired as (T_1, T_X), (T_X, T_2), (T_2, T_{x-1}), (T_{x-1}, T_3), ...($T_{x/2}$, $T_{x/2+1}$). The Modulo Arithmetic Addition operation is applied to each pair of blocks for obtaining the cipher text [4–6]. The process is repetitive with increasing block size till k = 243. To get back the original plain text message, Modular subtraction technique have been adopted. Mathematically operation between blocks can be done as:

(i) $Z^` = \sum_{i=1}^{n/2} \left( \sum_{j=n, k=i+1}^{\frac{n}{2}+1} T_{ij} + T_{jk} \right)$, where i < j and j ≠ k and $Z^`$ is the encrypted data stream.

(ii) $Z^{``} = \sum_{i=n/2}^{1} \left( \sum_{j=\frac{n}{2}+1, k=i+1}^{n} T_{kj} + T_{ij} \right)$, where i < j and j ≠ k and $Z^{``}$ is the decrypted data stream.

If Z==$Z^{``}$, algorithm will be accepted.

2.1 The Proposed Algorithm

The input stream has been segregated into blocks. Each block contains 3 bits and block pairing is done as explained in Sect. 2. The below steps are involved starting from the most significant side:

Round 1: For every non-adjacent block pair, the 1st block is added with the last block with modulus of addition as 2^m for block size m. The last block then added with the 2nd block. For 3-bit blocks, the addition modulus will be 8.

This round is repetitive for finite number of times and the number of iterations will form a part of the session key.

Round 2: Similar operation as described in Round1 is performed with block size 9. The rounds will be continued between non-adjacent blocks (except the last pair of blocks which are adjacent to one another) till no blocks are left. The process is repeated, each time increasing the block size till m = 243.

Thus several rounds are completed till we reach **Round 5** where the block size is 243 and we get the encrypted bit-stream. Here a new content of T_X is obtained from addition of content from T_1 and previous content from T_X. Therefore T_X now will be added to T_2 and changes will be made in T_2. Thus in every two subsequent operations, one block is common which increases the complexity of the algorithm resulting in the enhancement of security.

During decryption, the opposite method i.e. modulo subtraction is performed, between the adjacent block pairs starting from LSB decreasing the block size from 243 to 3.

2.2   The Modulo Addition

The proposed technique is to thrown away the carry from Most Significant Bit (if any) after addition for getting the outcome e.g. if 110 and 111 are added we get 1101 (13 in decimal). Due to modulus addition is 1000 (in decimal 8 or 2^3), therefore the result of addition will be 101(1101 − 1000 = 101). Removal of the carry from 1101 is equivalent to subtracting 1000 (i.e. 8 in decimal). That is why the result is 101 or 5 in decimal. This policy is applicable to all blocks irrespective of their sizes.

2.3   Example of the Scheme

The scheme under consideration is applicable to 729-bit input stream. Let us consider a bit-stream of 16 bits, 1100100111100111. To ensure odd number of bits in each block we have to add extra zeros in the given bit stream.

The Encryption Scheme

Considering $Z=$ 001100100111100111(Inclusion of two redundant zeros in the beginning)

Round 1: Block Size = 3, No. of Blocks = 6.

INPUT:

001	100	100	111	100	111
T_1	T_2	T_3	T_4	T_5	T_6

ITERATION 1:

001	100	100	111	100	**000**
T1	T2	T3	T4	T5	**T6**

(T1, T6) mod8, Alter T6.

ITERATION 2:

001	**100**	100	111	100	000
T1	**T2**	T3	T4	T5	T6

(T6, T2) mod8, Alter T2.

ITERATION 3:

001	100	100	111	**000**	000
T1	T2	T3	T4	**T5**	T6

(T2, T5) mod8, Alter T5.

ITERATION 4:

001	100	**100**	111	000	000
T1	T2	**T3**	T4	T5	T6

(T5, T3) mod8, Alter T3.

ITERATION 5:

001	100	100	**011**	000	000
T1	T2	T3	**T4**	T5	T6

(T3, T4) mod8,Alter T4.

Round 2: Block Size = 9, No. of Blocks = 2.

INPUT:

001100100	011000000
T_1	T_2

ITERATION1:

001100100	011000000
T_1	**T_2**

(T1, T2) mod 512 Alter T2

Thereby, we obtain the encrypted bit stream as Z` =001100100011000000.

The Decryption Scheme

For decryption 2's complement arithmetic has been followed to retrieve the plain text message in Z (in term of bits).

Round 1: Block Size = 9, No. of Blocks = 2.

INPUT:

001100100	011000000
T_1	T_2

ITERATION1:

001100100	**011000000**
T_1	**T_2**

(T1, T2) mod 512 Alter T2

Round 2: Block Size = 3, No. of Blocks = 6.

INPUT:

001	100	100	011	000	000
T1	T2	T3	T4	T5	T6

ITERATION1:

001	100	100	**111**	000	000
T1	T2	T3	**T4**	T5	T6

(T3, T4) mod8, Alter T4

ITERATION2:

001	100	**100**	111	000	000
T1	T2	**T3**	T4	T5	T6

(T5, T3) mod8, Alter T3

ITERATION3:

001	100	100	111	**100**	000
T1	T2	T3	T4	**T5**	T6

(T2, T5) mod8, Alter T5

ITERATION4:

001	**100**	100	111	100	000
T1	**T2**	T3	T4	T5	T6

(T6, T2) mod8, Alter T2

ITERATION5:

001	100	100	111	100	**111**
T1	T2	T3	T4	T5	**T6**

(T1, T6) mod8, Alter T6

The Decrypted bit stream has been received as Z`` = 001100100111100111. After discarding the redundant zeros from MSB we obtain 1100100111100111 which is identical with Input bit stream.

Therefore whatever shown in the above example considering six blocks can be mathematically expressed in the following manner.

Encryption:

$$\sum_{i=1}^{n/2} \left(\sum_{j=n,k=i+1}^{\frac{n}{2}+1} T_{ij} + T_{jk} \right), \text{where } i < j \text{ and } j \neq k$$

in which

(i)   When i = 1, j = 6 then k = 2 and block pair operation is: $T_1T_6 + T_6T_2$.
(ii) When i = 1, j = 6 then k = 3 and block pair operation is: $T_2T_5 + T_5T_3$.
(iii) When i = 1, j = 6 then k = 4 and block pair operation is: T_3T_4. (Since operation is between adjacent block pair and no blocks are left)

Decryption:

$$\sum_{i=n/2}^{1} \left(\sum_{j=\frac{n}{2}+1,\, k=i+1}^{n} T_{kj} + T_{ij} \right), \text{where } i < j \text{ and } j \neq k$$

in which

When i = 3, j = 4 then k = 4 and block pairing is done as: T3T4. (Since operation is between adjacent block pair).

When i = 2, j = 5 then k = 3 and block pairing is done as: $T_3T_5 + T_2T_5$.

When i = 1, j = 6 then k = 2 and block pairing is done as: $T_2T_6 + T_1T_6$.

3 Flow Diagram of the Technique

The workflow [1] of the proposed system is depicted in Fig. 1. Data bytes are fed into this cryptographic system and subsequently encryption and decryption are done simultaneously to check its performance. Finally testing is carried out to establish its feasibility which has been furnished in Sect. 4.

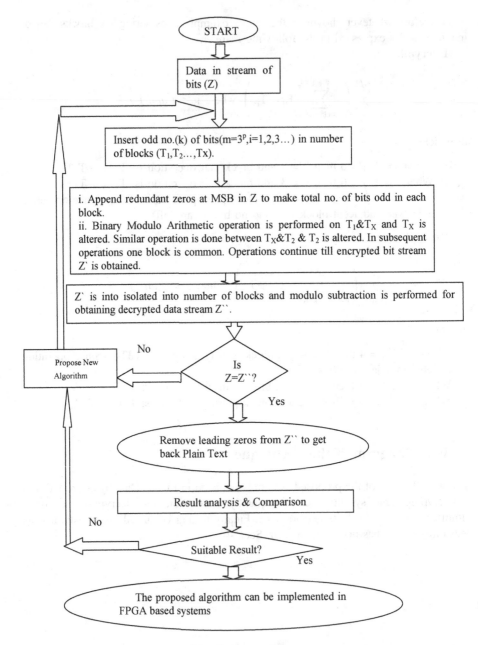

Fig. 1. Our workflow

4   Results and Comparisons

The evenly distribution of character frequency of all 256 ASCII characters, over the 0–255 [7] region for encrypted file of different algorithms are compared for validation and testing of NCBMAT.

We have checked the usefulness of NCBMAT and RSA on 10 different files (exe, txt, doc, png, jpg) to get plaintext and cipher text messages. For this article one of the 10 files have been chosen for result analysis [4, 5]. Figures 2 and 3 demonstrates the frequency occurrence of all 256 ASCII characters in the source file, encrypted file with NCBMAT & RSA and it is clear that the characters in encrypted file using NCBMAT are moderately well distributed throughout the character space [6]. Hence NCBMAT may be equivalent to RSA.

NCBMAT ensures better security against the source file and it also shows heterogeneity between the two files. The frequency distribution graph is drawn according to the percentage of occurrence of a particular character, not the total number of occurrence.

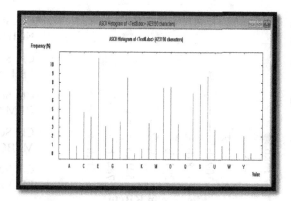

Fig. 2. Frequency diagram of source file

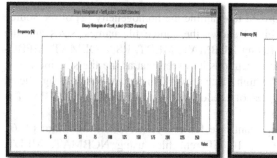
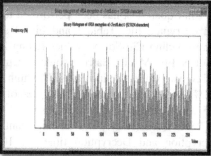

Fig. 3. Frequency diagram of RSA encrypted file and NCBMAT encrypted file

Table 1. Indicates ChiSquare value for MEDT algorithm and RSA algorithm

File size	Chi square value					
	NCBMAT	MEDT	OEMAT	MFBOMAT	FBOMAT	RSA
15 kb	46758.678	50865.846	41334	41142	36237	22861.966
21 kb	43453.897	50649.971	546547	515344	521449	22861.966
51 kb	49657.987	49783.842	564367	57468	48582	81858.947
102 kb	22576.926	25862.820	322342	3563897	2951266	23852.709
138 kb	27682.879	33215.645	137349	125321	113132	23852.709
201 kb	50867.453	63309.245	206543	237842	194253	22861.966
301 kb	42356.584	56233.193	1023567	135915	145367	22861.966
501 kb	37685.132	35776.117	5734845	5634921	593456	39723.202
744 kb	35567.654	45461.436	4865334	4732583	4678392	23852.709
1 Mb	24567.874	22861.966	2787592	2456781	2574849	22861.966

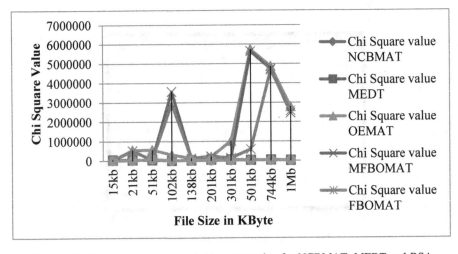

Fig. 4. Graphical representation of chi-square value for NCBMAT, MEDT and RSA

Chi-Square test has been performed to examine the homogeneity [2] of the source and encrypted file. Table 1 and Fig. 4 shows the source file names, sizes and the corresponding Chi-Square values (using NCBMAT, MEDT, RSA, OEMAT, MFBO-MAT & FBOMAT). Barring some exceptions it is seen that as the file size increases, Chi-Square value also increases. The high value proves Chi-Square is highly significant at 1% level of significance. The degree of freedom (shown in Table 2) of NCBMAT is 255 which is quite higher than RSA.

Time Complexity plays an important role for every encryption algorithm [2, 6]. Encryption and Decryption time for 10 different files using NCBMAT, MEDT,

Table 2. Degree of freedom of NCBMAT, MEDT, RSA, OEMAT & MFBOMAT

File size	Degree of freedom				
	NCBMAT	MEDT	MFBOMAT	FBOMAT	RSA
15 kb	255	255	255	251	255
21 kb	255	255	241	249	255
51 kb	255	255	201	197	195
102 kb	255	255	235	212	133
138 kb	255	255	178	167	133
201 kb	255	255	241	255	255
301 kb	255	255	255	249	255
501 kb	255	255	197	201	141
744 kb	255	255	242	231	255
1 Mb	255	255	231	254	255

Table 3. Encryption time of NCBMET, MED, RSA, FBOMAT & MFBOMAT

File size	NCBMAT	MEDT	RSA	FBOMAT	MFBOMAT
15 kb	.030	0.032 s	0.006 s	0.050	.040
21 kb	.020	0.028 s	0.010 s	0.050	.040
51 kb	.032	0.054 s	0.022 s	.122	.124
102 kb	.087	0.113 s	0.044 s	.029	.280
138 kb	.156	0.161 s	0.059 s	.038	.370
201 kb	.098	0.113 s	0.086 s	.049	.046
301 kb	.235	0.240 s	0.137 s	.247	.239
501 kb	.316	0.350 s	0.219 s	.378	.389
744 kb	.786	0.927 s	0.326 s	.453	.985
1 Mb	.876	1.320 s	0.444 s	.956	.943

Table 4. Decryption time of NCBMET, MEDT, FBOMAT, MFBOMAT and RSA

File Size	NCBMAT	MEDT	FBOMAT	MFBOMAT	RSA
15 kb	0.0176	0.199 s	0.000	0.000	0.088 s
21 kb	0.126	0.123 s	0.000	0.000	0.141 s
51 kb	0.0226	0.220 s	0.101	0.040	0.315 s
102 kb	0.567	0.401 s	0.170	0.180	0.635 s
138 kb	0.435	0.468 s	.0230	0.220	0.858 s
201 kb	0.0678	0.693 s	0.440	0.450	1.225 s
301 kb	1.345	0.937 s	0.874	0.952	1.850 s
501 kb	1.865	1.503 s	1.635	1.876	3.075 s
744 kb	1.659	1.712 s	2.654	2.941	4.578 s
1 Mb	3.438	2.364 s	4.105	4.653	6.328 s

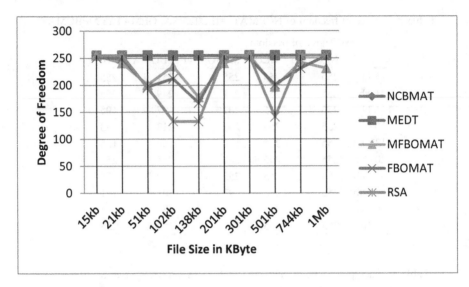

Fig. 5. Graphical representation of degree of freedom comparison between NCBMAT, MEDT, MFBOMAT, FBOMAT & RSA

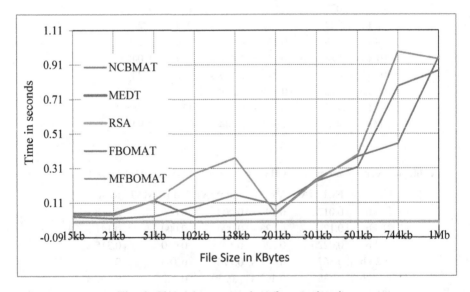

Fig. 6. Pictorial representation of encryption time

FBOMAT, MFBOMAT and RSA algorithms have been recorded and the corresponding graph has been plotted. Tables 3 and 4 give the recorded encryption time and decryption time for different files respectively. Figures 5 and 6 illustrate graphical

Table 5. Avalanche test of NCBMET, MEDT, FBOMAT, MFBOMAT and RSA

File size	Avalanche test				
	NCBMAT	MEDT	FBOMAT	MFBOMAT	RSA
15 kb	2.567402	2.654932	2.984299	2.984299	1.060675
21 kb	1.567232	1.456351	1.455033	1.567423	0.490015
51 kb	0.027532	0.034267	0.018504	0.240987	0.423044
102 kb	0.659532	0.453897	0.537936	0.537936	0.106013
138 kb	0.027563	0.056743	0.062475	0.002475	0.161049
201 kb	0.573633	0.785642	1.605645	0.224742	0.016164
301 kb	0.437684	0.432876	0.424502	0.546811	0.456071
501 kb	0.982243	1.732901	1.455033	1.455033	1.154788
744 kb	0.023473	0.048963	0.037288	0.037288	0.262948
1 Mb	0.495642	0.503842	0.512608	0.498027	0.137565

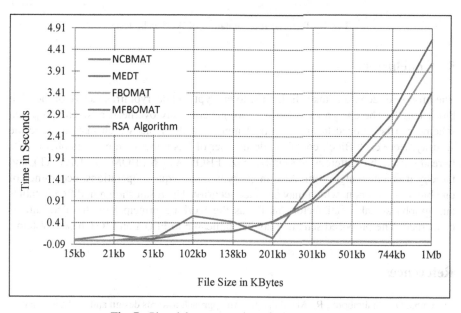

Fig. 7. Pictorial representation of decryption time

representation of the encryption and decryption time respectively. The time taken to decrypt a file using NCBMAT is very little compared to that using RSA. Table 5 gives the analysis of Avalanche test and Fig. 6 [1] distinguishes the significant changes among output cipher text files for the said algorithms. The graphical representation reflects that the result of NCBMAT is higher compared to RSA and other algorithms.

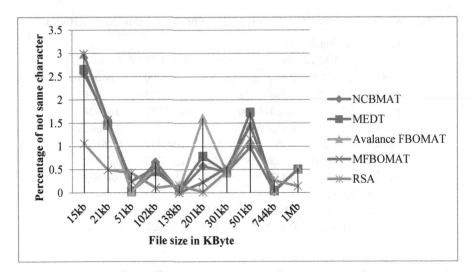

Fig. 8. Pictorial representation of Avalanche test

5   Conclusion

The proposed technique takes little time to encrypt and decrypt irrespective of the high block length. The encrypted string will not generate any overhead bits. The proposed scheme can be utilized to any length of input stream of bits which may enhance the security. Here each Block contains odd number of bits rather than even number of bits (already used by different algorithms viz. FBOMAT, MFBOMAT, OEMAT) and thereby it is a new algorithm. Also in every two subsequent operations, occurrence of one block is common, which may enhance security. The result shown in different tables and graphs are also satisfactory as far as the working principal of the algorithm is concerned. The proposed scheme may be applicable to FPGA and IOT based systems.

References

1. Guha, D., Chakraborty, R., Mandal, J.K.: An approach towards design and analysis of a new block cipher based cryptographic system using modular encryption and decryption technique (MEDT). Accepted and Presented in 52nd Annual convention of Computer Society of India (CSI 2017) as Indian National IT congress. Theme: "Social Transformation-Digital Way" Kolkata Chapter, 19–21 January 2018
2. Datta, A., Chakraborty, R., Mandal, J.K.: The CRYPSTER: a private key crypto system. Published in 2015 IEEE International Conference on Computer Graphics, Vision and Information Security (CGVIS), Bhubaneshwar, India, 2–3 November 2015. https://doi.org/10.1109/cgvis.2015.7449882
3. Chandra, S., Bhattacharya, S., Paira, S., Alam, S.S.: A study and analysis on symmetric cryptography. Published in 2014 IEEE International Conference on Science Engineering and Management Research (ICSEMR), Chenni, India, 27–29 November 2014. https://doi.org/10.1109/ICSEMR.2014.7043664

4. Guha, D., Basu, A.: An odd even block cipher based cryptosystem through modulo arithmetic technique (OEMAT). Publ. Int. J. Res. Eng. Technol. (IJRET) **2**(11), 138–146 (2013). e-ISSN 2319-1163, p-ISSN 2321-7308
5. Guha, D., Chakraborty, R., Sinha, A.: A block cipher based cryptosystem through modified forward backward overlapped modulo arithmetic technique (MFBOMAT). Int. Organ. Sci. Res. J. Comput. Eng. (IOSRJCE) **13**(1), 138–146 (2013). Article no. 22, e-ISSN 2278-0661, p-ISSN 2278-8727
6. Chakraborty, R., Guha, D., Mandal, J.K.: A block cipher based cryptosystem through forward backward overlapped modulo arithmetic technique (FBOMAT). Int. J. Eng. Sci. Res. J. (IJESR) **2**(5), 349–360 (2012). Article no. 7, ISSN 2277-2685
7. Mandal, J.K., Sinha, S., Chakraborty, R.: A microprocessor-based block cipher through overlapped modulo arithmetic technique (OMAT). In: Proceedings of 12th International Conference of IEEE on Advanced Computing and Communications ADCOM-2004, Ahmedabad, India, 15–18 December, pp. 276–280 (2004)
8. Stallings, W.: Cryptography and Network Security: Principles and Practices, 3rd edn. Prentice Hall, Upper Saddle River (2003)
9. Kahate, A.: Cryptography and Network Security, 2nd edn. TMH, India (2008)
10. Forouzan, B.: Cryptography and Network Security, 4th edn. TMH, India (2010)

A Security Framework for Service-Oriented Architecture Based on Kerberos

Ritika Yaduvanshi[1], Shivendu Mishra[2(✉)], Ashish Kumar Mishra[2],
and Avinash Gupta[3]

[1] Department of Computer Science and Engineering,
Institute of Engineering and Technology, Lucknow, India
ritikayaduvanshi22@gmail.com
[2] Department of Information Technology, Rajkiya Engineering College,
Ambedkar Nagar, Akbarpur, India
shivendu0584@gmail.com, akmishra.rec@gmail.com
[3] Department of Computer Science and Engineering,
Babu Banarasi Das Group of Educational Institutions, Lucknow, India
avinashg.mnnit@gmail.com

Abstract. Service-Oriented Architecture is a new paradigm in Software computing that focused on web-based Service-Oriented computing. This paradigm based on client services architecture and involves communication among three different entities: Service Provider, Service Consumer and Service Broker or Registry. These three entities are loosely coupled. Security is an important aspect for any application. In SOA, managing and organizing security is a challenging issue, because services are deployed in distributed environment. In SOA, security is defined in terms of services which are secure service registration and deregistration, secure service discovery, secure service delivery and availability of trustworthy services. This paper proposed a Kerberos based security framework that fulfills the security requirement needed for secure SOA. The implementation of the proposed security framework is also provided.

Keywords: SOA · Kerberos · SOA security requirements ·
SOA security standard · SOA security framework

1 Introduction

Service-oriented Architectures (SOA) [1] holds the promise of greater IT flexibility and agility due to the use of XML-based Web services. Service-Oriented Architecture is basically a collection of services [2]. These services are autonomous, platform independent and communicate with each other through standard interfaces and via standard message exchanging protocols (SOAP). The architecture of SOA [3] mainly consists of three entities: service provider, service consumer and service registry. The communication among service provider, consumer and registry is through standard SOAP messages over HTTP protocol.

Security is major concern for any system or application. In SOA, the service consumers have different ways to access the services and the services provider can set

© Springer Nature Singapore Pte Ltd. 2019
J. K. Mandal et al. (Eds.): CICBA 2018, CCIS 1031, pp. 402–410, 2019.
https://doi.org/10.1007/978-981-13-8581-0_32

wide-range of restrictions for gaining access to the services, due to that managing and organizing security aspect is a big task in Service-Oriented environment. SOA is basically based on secure searching and secure delivery, so there is a need of secure delivery process and a method to identify genuine users [4]. In traditional system, security requirements basically include authentication, authorization, confidentiality and integrity [5, 24]. In Service-Oriented Architecture, basic security requirements are secure service registration and deregistration, secure service discovery, secure service delivery and availability of trustworthy services. To deal with these security requirements, Service-Oriented Architecture uses a number of security standard that are WS-Security Framework, Extensible Access Control Markup Language (XACML), Extensible Rights Markup Language (XrML), XML Key Management (XKMS), Security Assertion Markup Language (SAML), .NET Passport, XML-Encryption and signature, Secure Sockets Layer (SSL), etc. [6, 7, 22, 23].

The main objective of this paper is to propose a security framework based on Kerberos and finally implement the proposed security framework that can fulfill the basic security requirement needed to secure Service-Oriented Architecture [6, 7]. For the same, we implement Kerberos protocol functionality as a service and use it in combination with the part of registry service to develop a security framework that meets the security requirements needed in SOA [6, 7]. Moreover our proposed framework is better than NASA's SOA security model [8].

The rest of this paper is organized as follows. In Sect. 2, the related work is described followed by security requirement needed for secure SOA, in Sect. 3. Related works motivate us to develop proposed security framework which is described with implementation details and security analysis, in Sect. 4. In Sect. 5 the comparative analysis with NASA's model [8] are given followed by conclusions and future work in Sect. 6.

2   Related Work

In order to deal with the problem of securing SOA, there has been much precious work done on SOA security and many companies have presented different models for secure service-oriented architecture. Among the more famous models are NASA security enhanced model for SOA [8], IBM service-oriented architecture security reference model [10], concurrent technologies corporation (CTC) SOA security model [11] or Catharina Candolin security framework [7]. In recent years some researches worked on service-oriented enterprise architecture like [15–18] and others are focusing on SOA based application framework like [19–21, 23, 24].

NASA model [8] upgrades the classic SOA model by splitting the service registry into public and private service registry. NASA model also uses proxy service to protect services from consumers so that all requests will have to go through the proxy service and the proxy gets authorization before forwarding any requests. The IBM SOA Security Reference Model [10] uses three main layers: Business Security Services, IT Security Services, and Security Policy Management to describe SOA security model. CTC [11] defines a conceptual model for SOA. CTC describes security as an inherent aspect of SOA functionality. The key objective is to minimize external attacks and to secure all interactions between the constituent stakeholders. The information assurance process is automated by using services like auditing which directs all required audits to a federated audit service, an alert service which automatically sends real-time alerts to relevant users. The processes like identification, authorization, alerting and federation are implemented by various supporting technologies. In Catharina Candolin security framework [7] security standards are placed in content layer. They provide means for authentication, access control, policy management, and key management. Confidentiality is ensured by encrypting the communication. Content based information security (CBIS) ensures protecting the data from its origin. Access control is handled through key management; only authorized users have the cryptographic keys necessary to access the non-encrypted content. In this framework, transport security relies on communication level of security such as SSL/TLS and SSH.

NASA's model focuses on a secure provider because everything between services is based on message exchange and therefore they give a sound model by taking into account the security of providers. Our proposed framework upgrade NASA's model by means of Kerberos [12, 13] and message level security [9].

3 Security Requirements in SOA

Security is an important issue in Service-Oriented application. To guarantee security in a Service-Oriented environment; several requirements must be met. These requirements are as follows [6, 7].

- **Secure Service Registration and Deregistration:** In Service-Oriented environment only authorized service providers should be permitted to register and deregister a service from the service registry. Replay attack is also consider during service registration/deregistration process as an attacker eavesdrop service registration message and later use it for own benefits.
- **Secure Service Discovery:** This requisite state that only authorized entities allowed to use the discovery protocol/and or access the service registry where the services are deployed. So that registry integrity is maintained and authentic services are registered by authentic service provider and service consumer discovered services will be trustworthy.
- **Secure Service Delivery:** After the secure discovery of services, the services must be delivered to service consumer securely. Through the mutual authentication, service provider can insure that the service is delivered to the intended consumer and consumer insures that service reply came from known service provider. Service confidentiality and integrity insure that the service delivered to the intended consumer is genuine and as deliberated by the service provider, without accidental or active modifications.
- **Availability of Services:** Availability of services insure that system always gives reply to any legitimate requests of authorized entities that is if any authorized user can request for a service then the user must get appropriate response if that service is available.

4 Proposed Security Framework

In this section, the Kerberos based our proposed security framework is described with implementation details and security analysis. Security analysis shows that the proposed framework fulfills the security requirements needed for a secure SOA [6, 7]. The proposed framework is described in following four steps:

1. The SP sends a SOAP request ($SOAP_1$) to register its services in the Registry. The SOAP request includes

$$SOAP_1 \rightarrow Service/timestamp/IDsp$$

   Here the service specifies Service name or Service ID, service descriptions, link of the service definition page, service-end-point etc., timestamp (time of registration, system time etc.) is used to remove the replay attack and IDsp is the ID of the Service Provider.
2. After checking the ID and other detail of SP, services are registered in registry service with the appropriate service ID and gives response ($SOAP_2$) to the SP.

$$SOAP_2 \rightarrow Service\ ID/timestamp_1/IDsp$$

3. If any consumer wants any service then, he/she sends a SOAP request $SOAP_3$ to the registry service.

$$SOAP_3 \rightarrow request/timestamp_2/IDsc$$

   Here request refer to the particular type of service which may includes Service ID or name, timestamp is unique time of request and IDsc is ID of service consumer.
4. When service registry gets requests from consumer, it searches the particular service in his registry and response ($SOAP_4$) as follows.

$$SOAP_4 \rightarrow Service\ ID\ list\ /SOAP_3$$

Here service ID list include list of service provider that provide the requested services. SOAP3 indicates that the response is came corresponds to SOAP3 request. After getting list of service ID the consumer chooses one of the Service ID and contacts to the corresponding service provider securely through Kerberos version 4 protocols [12, 13] and gets the service key. The service key will be used by service consumer to access services securely. Service provider acts as a server of Kerberos protocol where the required service is found and service consumer acts as client of Kerberos protocol (Fig. 1).

If any fraud service provider makes fraud then the consumer can detect it easily by seeing the information about that SP and service ID in the registry. The following block diagram Fig. 2 describes our complete proposed framework.

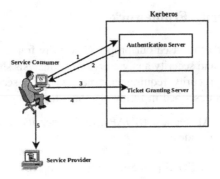

Fig. 1. Kerberos protocol

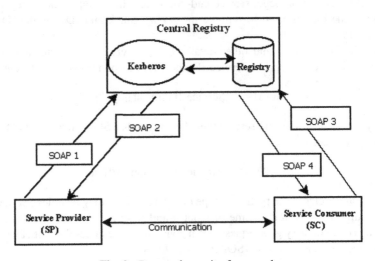

Fig. 2. Proposed security framework

4.1   Implementation

As per the proposed architecture, we have implemented the following scenario: we have implemented Kerberos 4.0 for secure delivery of service key. In the proposed framework secure login is maintained for each type of users (service provider, service requester and service broker) and only the authentic user can register Web services in the system. To obtain the service key, the service consumer must go through secure login phase and gets the key through Kerberos scheme. This service key is used by the service consumer to access the services securely.

The functions of the proposed framework are user registration, service registration, service listing and service searching and get service ticket as shown in Fig. 3. These functions are implemented through Web methods in a Web service. When a new user comes to the system, he/she can see the list of registered Web services with service details like service name, service providers name, service definition, service-end-point, etc.

The following operations are supported.

- **ClientRegister**
- **Login**
- **SearchService**
- **ServiceRegister**
- **getService**
- **getServiceTicket**
- **getTGT**

Fig. 3. Service list

The new user has to register into the system to register Web service or get the service key of any Web service. The system has a privilege to register any new service into the system. The user registration form is provided with necessary information to register service in the system. After user fills up the user registration form and submits details to the registry service, the user can login into the system with his credentials. Now the user can register any service and can access the service key of the any registered Web service. The service registration page is provided to user to submit details of the service to register into the system. Service name, service provider name, service descriptions, link of the service definition page, service-end-point, etc., are the some of the information user has to provide to the system while registering a service. After a service is registered into the system, the administrator of the register system verifies the service with different criteria such proper service description, valid link of service definition page, proper-end-point link, etc.

For getting the service key the consumer first authenticate through secure login and provides service URL to the Kerberos protocol and get TGT and then finally Service ticket (Fig. 4). Service ticket is used to access service (Fig. 5).

Home	Register User	Register Service	Access Service Search Service	
	Login to Access Service			
Service URL		http://mnnit.ac.in/websms.asmx?wsdl	*	
Get Ticket Granting Ticket		7777		
Ticket Granting Ticket		7777	*	
Get Service Ticket		6666		
Service Ticket		6666	*	
Get Service Link		http://mnnit.ac.in/websms.asmx		
		Logout		

Fig. 4. Get service ticket or key

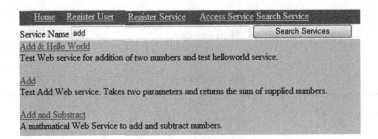

Fig. 5. Search service

The system has facility to search Web services. While registering a Web service many search keys are provided to the system. On the basis of these search keys, the search query returns number of Web services from the list of Web services. List of services with the service name, URL to the service definition page and service description is provides to the user that matches the search criteria.

Table 1. Proposed framework security analysis

Security requirements	Proposed framework
Secure registration	User name and password
Secure de-registration	Only perform by trusted registry
Secure discovery	By Kerberos
Secure delivery	By Kerberos
Availability of services	Provided
Authorization	SGT (service ticket)
Message level security	Xml security
SSL/TLS	Used

4.2   Analysis of Proposed Frame Work

The proposed framework fulfills the security requirements mention in [6, 7]. For secure registration, the framework uses user name and password. The password is stored in the database in encrypted form. Only authorized user can deregister services from the registry due to secure login. For Secure discovery, the framework uses Kerberos protocol. As only authentic user register the service, the service registered via the framework are genuine and trust worthy and Only the authorized user can get the service link so the framework provide secure discovery. For Secure delivery, the framework also uses Kerberos protocol. As only authentic and authorized user can get the service key or ticket via the Kerberos, so user access the services securely. For availability of services, the framework provides the search services which list all the available services in the system and for SOAP message security, the framework can use the standard like WS-Security, XML-Encryption and signature, Extensible Rights Markup Language (XrML), XML Key Management (XKMS). Thus the following Table 1 shows that our proposed framework fulfills the entire security requirement mention [6, 7].

5 Comparative Analysis with NASA's Model

The proposed framework upgrade NASA's [8] model by removing the need of two registries with single registry. And Kerberos service in the place of proxy service. Table 2 shows comparative analysis of NASA's model [8] with our proposed framework.

From Table 2 it is shown that the proposed model is better than NASA's model with respect to less number of registries, absence of proxy services, enhanced security using Kerberos and also cost effective.

Table 2. Comparative analysis: Nass's model vs proposed framework

Comparison points	NASA model [8]	Proposed framework
Registry	Public and private	One registry
Proxy service	Used	Not used
Kerberos	Not used	Used
Load balancing	At proxy service	Not needed
Cost	More	Less

6 Conclusion and Future Work

In this paper, we propose a SOA security framework based on Kerberos. The proposed framework uses Kerberos functionality for providing secure access of service key. The proposed framework upgrade NASA's [8] model by removing the need of two registries with single registry. And Kerberos service in the place of proxy service. Moreover we also provide implementation of our proposed framework and show that our proposed framework fulfills the entire security requirement needed in a secure SOA. The future work includes use of ID-Based Encrypion/Decryption [14] in place of PKI based Encryption/Decryption for XML security. The ID-Based Encryption/Decryption removes the needs of XKMS– XML Key Management Specification and provides efficient key management with low cost, adequate security.

Acknowledgements. This work is financially supported by Technical Education Quality Improvement Programme (TEQIP-III).

References

1. Jousttis, N.: SOA in Practice, the Art of Distributed System Design. O'Reilly Media Inc, Sebastopol (2007)
2. Wiebelhaus, S., et al.: Service orientation concepts and definitions. In: Workshop on Introducing Service-Oriented Computing, Tempe, September 2006
3. Earl, T.: Service-Oriented Architecture: Concepts, Technology & Design. Prentice Hall/Pearson PT, Upper Saddle River (2005)

4. Alagappan, D., et al.: Security in service-oriented architecture: a survey of techniques. In: Workshop on Introducing Service-Oriented Computing, Tempe, September 2006

5. Ponnusamy, R., et al.: Security issues in service-oriented architecture. In: Workshop on Introducing Service-Oriented Computing, Tempe, September 2006

6. Cotroneo, D., et al.: Security requirements in service-oriented architectures for ubiquitous computing. In: Middleware for Pervasive and Ad-hoc Computing. ACM (2004)

7. Catharina, C.: A security framework for service-oriented architectures. In: MILCOM 2007 (2007)

8. Pajevski, M.: A Security Model for Service-Oriented Architectures (2005). NASA Website. http://www.oasisopen.org/committees/download.php/17573/06-0400008.000.pdf

9. Buecker, A., et al.: Understanding SOA Security. IBM Publication, Indianapolis (2007)

10. Nagaratnam, N., et al.: SOA Security Reference Model. STSC Cross Talk (2007)

11. Youmans, J.: Methods of SOA Security Engineering and Certification. Concurrent Technologies Corporation Website (2009)

12. Menezes, J., et al.: Handbook of Applied Cryptography, 5th edn. CRC Press, Boca Raton (2001)

13. Cisco Systems. Kerberos Overview on Service for Open Network System. http://www.cisco.com/en/US/tech/tk59/technologieswhitepaper09186a00800941b2.shtml

14. Shamir, A.: Identity-based cryptosystems and signature schemes. In: Blakley, G.R., Chaum, D. (eds.) CRYPTO 1984. LNCS, vol. 196, pp. 47–53. Springer, Heidelberg (1985). https://doi.org/10.1007/3-540-39568-7_5

15. Sun, J., et al.: Intelligent enterprise information security architecture based on service oriented. In: International Seminar on Future IT and Management Engineering. IEEE (2008)

16. Menzel, M., et al.: Security requirements specification in service oriented business process management. In: International Conference on Availability, Reliability and Security (2009)

17. Tang, J., et al.: A classification of enterprise service-oriented architecture. In: Fifth IEEE International Symposium on Service Oriented System Engineering (2010)

18. Karimi, O.: Security model for service-oriented architecture. ACIJ 2(4), 48–58 (2011)

19. Huang, M., et al.: Research for E-commerce platform security framework based on SOA. In: Proceedings of the 4th International Conference on BMEI China, pp. 2171–2174, October 2011

20. Duggan, D., et al.: Service-oriented architecture. Enterprise Software Architecture and Design: Entities, Services, and Resources, pp. 207–358 (2012)

21. Ashish, L., et al.: Designing a logical security framework for e-commerce system based on SOA. Int. J. Soft Comput. (IJSC) 5(2), 1 (2014)

22. Shashwat, A., et al.: An end to end security framework for service oriented architecture. In: International Conference on Infocom Technologies and Unmanned Systems (ICTUS), Dubai, pp. 475–480 (2017)

23. McKee, D.W., et al.: n-Dimensional QoS framework for real-time service-oriented architectures. In: International Conference on Internet of Things and IEEE Green Computing and Communications (GreenCom) and IEEE Cyber, Physical and Social Computing (CPSCom) and IEEE Smart Data (SmartData), pp. 195–202 (2017)

24. Srinivasulu, P., et al.: Cloud service oriented architecture (CSoA) for agriculture through internet of things (IoT) and big data. In: International Conference on Electrical, Instrumentation and Communication Engineering (ICEICE), Karur, pp. 1–6 (2017)

Cryptanalysis of a Secure and Privacy Preserving Mobile Wallet Scheme with Outsourced Verification in Cloud Computing

Debarpan Tribedi, Dipanwita Sadhukhan$^{(\boxtimes)}$, and Sangram Ray

National Institute of Technology Sikkim, Ravangla 737139, Sikkim, India
tribedi.debarpan@gmail.com,
dipanwitasadhukhan2012@gmail.com,
sangram.ism@gmail.com

Abstract. Digital payment using mobile wallet is one of the easiest and frequent mode of payment methods in recent era. Payment through mobile wallet is becoming more widespread due to the rapid growth of smart device users as well as easy availability of Internet. However, it is very important to make the whole payment procedure of mobile wallet system safe and secure, otherwise it may be fatal for the users, as the users have to share their valuable credentials like real identity, secret key to make a successful payment. Also the service provider has to keep in mind that the resources available in a mobile device are not appropriate for carrying large computational overheads. To overcome these issues Qin et al. has proposed a secure and privacy preserving mobile wallet protocol integrating the digital signature and pseudo-identity technique using outsourced computing with the help of a cloud server. The cloud server performs the complex computation to reduce the computational overhead of mobile wallet. In this paper we have analyzed all possible security attacks that may occur in Qin et al. proposed scheme and also found that this scheme is vulnerable to various security attacks like known session specific temporary information attack, cloud server bypassing attack, untrusted cloud server and client colluding attack and impersonation attack. The aforesaid attacks are explained using mathematical model to show that this scheme is not enough secure.

Keywords: Mobile wallet · Certificate-less signature · Bilinear map ·
Securely outsourcing computation

1 Introduction

The growth rate of number of Internet connected mobile devices is reportedly surpassing the human population since past years [1, 2]. Mobile devices are playing a major role in latest business activities with new opportunities focusing on the ever-changing needs of the clients and the increasing utilization of mobile phones/devices in the commercial purposes [3]. One of them is mobile payment services that have been widely adopted by the merchants and the customers due to its effortless accessibility and ease of use. One of the current aspects of payment services through mobile devices

© Springer Nature Singapore Pte Ltd. 2019
J. K. Mandal et al. (Eds.): CICBA 2018, CCIS 1031, pp. 411–424, 2019.
https://doi.org/10.1007/978-981-13-8581-0_33

is mobile wallet which yields an expedient way to the customers to perform payment through personal mobile devices as required anytime and anywhere [4]. Although it has become extremely popular in a very short tenure due to its incredible benefit and efficiency, it also raised frightening security challenges of wireless communication. Mobile wallet would not be well accepted by the public if it does not ensure message authentication and privacy preservation of the client's vital credentials. Forged payment information as well as theft of client's vital credentials may become critical issues to the parties, the merchant and the clients [5]. So, it is the most essential to provide best security to preserve the privacy of the messages exchanged between the client and the merchant against any types of security breaches like impersonation, modification, eavesdropping, replaying or masquerading etc. [6–10]. Despite of security challenges related to the payment through mobile wallet some other issues like nature and size of the network, limited resources of the mobile devices etc. are also present and need to be handled carefully.

1.1 Literature Review

With the continual progress of mobile wallet services some novel research works have been done over the improvement of the security and efficiency of the mobile wallet. Unfortunately very limited attention has been paid in this field so far. Recently, in 2016 Qin et al. [11] proposed a privacy preserving mobile payment scheme that implements authenticity verification outsourced in cloud computing. The purpose of that paper is to identify the challenges of the mobile wallet services and propose a novel approach to preserve the privacy of the clients of the mobile wallet by outsourcing to the cloud server by integrating the digital signature [12] and pseudo identity techniques [13, 14]. According to Qin et al. [11], limited computation capability of the mobile devices can be conquered by utilizing the unlimited resource for computation and capability of taking heavy workload of the cloud service provider. Digital signature is used by them as it confirms authentication, confidentiality and non-repudiation of the information presented during the payment through mobile wallet. Yet, digital signature in conventional public key cryptography causes high overheads of maintaining certificate management. In this scenario, certificate-less signature [14, 15] has been incorporated by Qin et al. [11]. There are four main entities involved in this scheme [11] –a merchant, a customer, a service provider for payment (PSP), and an cloud server. At the time of purchase the consumer makes payment through the mobile wallet to the merchant. During payment the cloud server is used for reducing computational overheads of the resource constrained mobile devices. The basic goals of security i.e. integrity, availability, authentication, non-repudiation must be maintained during payment. Along with these security goals some other security features like user anonymity (the credentials of the consumer must not be disclosed), unforgeability (payment receipt of the consumer must not be copied), traceability (the real entities of the transaction must be maintained by the PSP), must be satisfied.

1.2   Our Contribution

Though Qin et al. scheme [11] is secure against various security attacks but not enough to preserve all the above mentioned security parameters. In this paper we have proved that Qin et al. scheme is vulnerable against known session specific temporary information attack, untrusted cloud server and consumer colluding attack [16] and impersonation attack.

1.3   Organization of the Paper

The rest of the paper is organized as follows: Sect. 2 illustrates the preliminary concepts required for understanding Qin et al. scheme, Sect. 3 includes the review of Qin et al. scheme in brief; the vulnerabilities of the Qin et al. scheme is presented in Sect. 4; and finally Sect. 5 concludes the paper.

2   Preliminaries

The fundamental concepts required for better understanding of Qin et al. scheme are given below.

2.1   Basic System Model

With the purpose of simplify the idea behind the Qin et al. [11] scheme the complex system model for mobile payment protocol with outsourced verification (MPP-OV) by cloud server is explained in the section. An insight of the prior works [1, 17, 18] of mobile payment system is followed by Qin et al. [11]. The idea of outsourcing certificate-less signature [17, 19, 20] is used for reducing large scale computing overheads of the mobile devices. The basic components and interaction among them are illustrated in Fig. 1.

- **Customer/Alice.** Customer is the entity who purchases commodities or services availed by the seller or merchant.
- **Merchant/Bob.** Merchant are the entity who sells commodities or provides services to the customer.
- **Payment Service Provider (PSP).** The trusted entity that ensures the confidentiality and privacy of the customer's credentials used for payment and responsible for maintaining the secrecy of payment receipt.
- **Cloud Server Verification Provider (CSVP).** The entity that is used for outsourcing the large scale computations to reduce the computational overheads of the resource constrained mobile devices.
- **Wallet Application.** An application runs on the mobile devices that allows users to execute any digital payment transaction.
- **Host Card Emulation API (HCE).** HCE is the software architecture that provides exact virtual representation of various electronic identity (access, transit and banking) using only software on Near Field Communication Point-of-Sale (NFC-POS) [11].

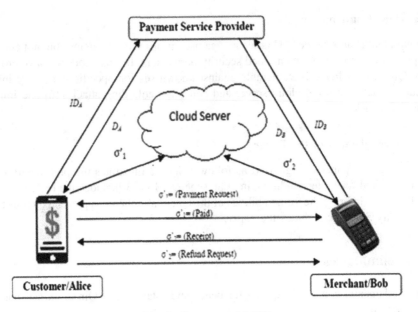

Fig. 1. System model [11]

- **Near Field Communication (NFC).** NFC indicates some communication protocols which facilitates two corresponding electronic devices, such as smart devices, to establish communication within a range of 4 cm [11, 21].
- **Secure Element (SE).** The SE refers to a tamper-resistant platform that is capable of hosting the customer's confidential information and provides a secure environment [11].

2.2 Bilinear Map

In this section, the basic concept of bilinear mapping or pairing is discussed. Let $\mathbb{G}_1$ and $\mathbb{G}_2$ be two additive cyclic group and multiplicative cyclic group of the prime order p respectively and p is the generator of $\mathbb{G}_1$, the admissible bilinear map $\hat{e} : \mathbb{G}_1 \times \mathbb{G}_1 \to \mathbb{G}_2$ [11, 17, 22, 23] if it satisfies the following properties:

- **Bilinear.** $\hat{e}(P + Q.R) = \hat{e}(P, R)\hat{e}(Q, R)$ and $\hat{e}(P, Q + R) = \hat{e}(P, Q)\hat{e}(P, R)$ for all $P, Q \in \mathbb{G}_1$.
- **Non-degenerate.** For all non-zero$P$ $P \in \mathbb{G}_1$ there exists $Q \in \mathbb{G}_1$, such that $\hat{e}(P, Q) \neq 1$ where 1 is the identity element of $\mathbb{G}_2$.
- **Computability.** There must exist an efficient algorithm that can compute $\hat{e}$ (P, Q) for all $P, Q \in \mathbb{G}_1$.

2.3 Discrete Logarithm Problem (DLP)

Given that $P, Q \in \mathbb{G}_1$ such that $Q = k.P$ and $k \in \mathbb{Z}_q^*$ where $\mathbb{G}_1$ is a cyclic group and P is the generator of that group. It is hard to find k from Q in polynomial time [12].

2.4 Computational Diffe-Helmen Problem (CDHP)

Computation of abP is difficult for any random instances $a,$ b and P where $(P, a.P, b.P) \in \mathbb{G}_1$ and $a, b \in \mathbb{Z}_q^*$ is hard [9, 12].

2.5 Design Goals

For the sake of maintaining security requirements of the mobile wallet the scheme must satisfy the following requirements.

- **Anonymity.** The real identity and the other valuable credentials of the user/customer must be preserved as secret [6, 7].
- **Traceability.** Any merchant or the customer cannot refuse the received and sent of any successful payment. Or else unique identifier will be applied to track the transaction [11, 17].
- **Unforgeability.** Illegal entity cannot impersonate himself as a legal user to make a fake payment [17].
- **Non-repudiation.** The merchant cannot disclaim the source and the accuracy of the payment transaction information as well as no customer can disagree with his/her established payment [9].
- **Low overhead.** As the scheme is meant for resource constrained mobile devices, low computation and communication overhead must be maintained.

3 Review of the Qin et al. [11] Scheme

This section describes Qin et al's [11] privacy- maintaining and secure scheme for mobile wallet payment services which is composed of three phases namely – (1) Set up and key generation phase, (2) Payment transmission phase and (3) Outsourced verification phase, where the symbols are used as given in Table 1.

Table 1. Notations for Qin et al.'s protocol

Notations	Descriptions	Notations	Descriptions
ID_A	Alice's real identity	ID_B	Bob's real identity
P_{ID_A}	Alice's pseudo identity	P_{ID_B}	Bob's pseudo identity
D_A	Alice's short term partial private key	D_B	Bob's short term partial private key
x_A	Alice's private key	x_B	Bob's private key
PP	Public parameters	P_{pub}	PSP's public master key
H_1, H_2	Two hash functions	$\hat{e}$	Bilinear pairing
T_{ID}	Transaction identity	$Amount \backslash R$	Amounts transferred/received
σ	Signature on message m	$\oplus$	Exclusive–OR operation (XOR)

3.1 Set Up Phase

The PSP takes input security parameters that composed of an additive cyclic group $\mathbb{G}_1$, a multiplicative cyclic group $\mathbb{G}_2$ of prime order p and a bilinear pairing $\hat{e} : \mathbb{G}_1 \times \mathbb{G}_1 \rightarrow \mathbb{G}_2$. Then the master key s is randomly selected such that $s \in \mathbb{Z}p*$ to compute public master key $P_{pub} = s.P$ where P is the generator of the group $\mathbb{G}_1$. It arbitrarily selects the hash functions such that $H_1 : \{0, 1\}* \rightarrow \mathbb{G}_1$ and $H_2 : \{0, 1\}* \rightarrow \mathbb{Z}p*$ and finally the system parameters are disclosed by the PSP as PP: $(\mathbb{G}_1, \mathbb{G}_2, \hat{e}, p, P, H_1, H_2, P_{pub})$.

3.2 Key Generation Phase

Step 1: Customer randomly selects her actual identity $ID_A \in \{0, 1\}*$ and transmits the credentials to PSP to store in a secure cloud storage.

Step2:
- Pseudo-identity generation: Alice's pseudo identity P_{ID_A} is composed of P_{ID_a} and P'_{ID_a} such that $P_{ID_A} = \left(P_{ID_a}, P'_{ID_a} \right)$. PSP randomly picks up $x \in R\, \mathbb{Z}p*$ and calculates $P_{ID_a} = x.P$ and $P'_{ID_a} = ID_A \oplus H_1\left(x.P_{pub}.\right)$
- Short-time partial private key generation: In this phase PSP calculates $Q_{P_{ID_a}} = H_1(P_{ID_a})$ and $DA = s. \; Q_{P_{ID_a}}$ where D_A is the short time private key of Customer/Alice. Then PSP forwards (D_A, P_{ID_A}) to Alice through a secure channel.

Step 3: *Full private and public key extraction:* Customer/Alice chooses her secret private key $x_A \in_R \mathbb{Z}_p^*$ to calculate her apparent public key as $PK_A = x_A.P$.

Step 4: Using the same procedure Bob registers himself to *PSP* and receives his pseudo identity P_{ID_B}, partial private key for short time D_B and public key $PK_B = x_B.$ P where x_B is the private key of Bob.

3.3 Payment Transaction Phase

This phase aims that the customer Alice cannot refuse that she has approved to pay for some commodities or services and the merchant Bob cannot disagree with that he has decided to trade commodities or services to Alice in the exchange of the payment. The stepwise description of the phase is illustrated below.

Step 1: Bob initiates the payment request to the customer Alice. The payment request contains a transaction identity T_{ID}, sum to be paid along with his pseudo identity P_{ID_A} as $payment = (T_{ID}||Amount_r||P_{ID_A})$.

Step 2: After acquiring the payment request Alice produces her signature σ by applying her short term partial private key D_A and private key x_A as $\sigma = D_A + H_2(Payment||P_{ID_A}||PK_A)x_A$ and sends it to Bob.

Step 3: With the received message containing a signature pair $(\sigma, payment)$, PK_A Alice can verify the legitimacy of the signature as mentioned below:

Checks if $\hat{e}(s, Payment) = \hat{e}(Q_{P_{IDA}}, P_{Pub}).\hat{e}(PK_A, H_2(Payment||P_{ID_A}||PK_A))$ holds. If yes, Alice is valid, otherwise message is rejected.

Step 4: After checking the integrity of the message containing payment data Bob signs the receipt utilizing his private key as given below:

- Generates the payment receipt as: $Receipt = (T_{ID}||Amount_R)$
- Sets his signature as $\sigma = D_B + H_2(Receipt|||P_{ID_B}||PK_A)x_B$

Step 5: Alice can also ensure the authority of the signature pair $(\sigma, Receipt)$.

3.4 Outsourced Verification Phase

In order to considerably reduce large scale of computation for the resource constrained mobile devices as well as ensuring the security of the payment procedure, cloud server verification provider (CSVP) is integrated to the scheme [11]. It is claimed that adaptation of the CSVP is important for significantly reduce the computation overheads. The interaction between CSVP and Bob is shown in Fig. 2 and described below.

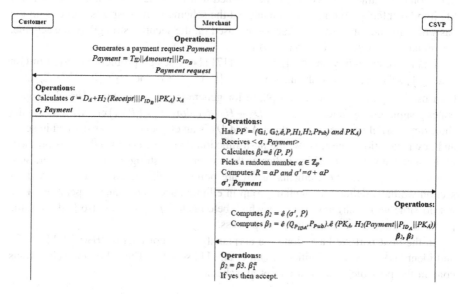

Fig. 2. Proposed outsourced verification phase by Qin et al. [11]

- Bob calculates $\beta_1 = \hat{e}(P,P)$ and chooses $\alpha \in_R \mathbb{Z}_p^*$ to compute $R = \alpha.P$ and $\sigma' = \sigma + \alpha P$. Finally sends the pair $(\sigma', payment)$ to CSVP.
- After receiving $(\sigma', payment)$ CSVP calculates $\beta_2 = \hat{e}(\sigma', P)$ and $\beta_3 = \hat{e}(Q_{P_{IDA}}, P_{Pub}).\hat{e}(PK_A, H_2(Payment||P_{ID_A}||PK_A)$ and sends them to Bob.
- Bob checks $\beta_2 = \beta_3. \beta_1^\alpha$ is true or not. If it is true, output is valid otherwise output is not valid.

4 Security Analysis of Qin et al. [11] Scheme

In the previous section we have reviewed the scheme proposed by of Qin et al. [11]. Although the Qin et al. scheme reduces the computational overhead of a mobile device by incorporating cloud server based verification procedure but we can still find security vulnerabilities of this scheme that indicates the scheme is not secure enough. A vulnerable mobile wallet payment scheme can be detrimental to both customer and the merchant because both of them share their valuable credentials like valid identity and secret data to make a successful payment. An insecure scheme can help adversary to pilfer or modify that valuable credentials. In this section we have prepared cryptanalysis of Qin et al. [11] scheme and mathematically proved that the scheme is vulnerable to attacks like known session specific temporary information attack, cloud server bypassing attack, untrusted cloud server and client colluding attack, and impersonation attack. Hence, it can be claimed that the scheme is not suitable for real life implementation. We have also analyzed the scheme in two aspects – one is on the basis of construction, and the other one is based on the security strength of the scheme. The detailed description is given below.

Firstly we are motivated by Liao et al. [17] about design problem occurred in Qin et al. [11] scheme. Two hash functions $H_1 : \{0, 1\}^* \rightarrow \mathbb{G}_1$ and $H_2 : \{0, 1\}^* \rightarrow \mathbb{Z}_p^*$ have been used in payment transaction phase for generating the signature. The client generates a signature by calculating $\sigma = D_A + H_2(Receipt|||P_{ID_B}||PK_A)x_A$, where D_A is the short time partial private key of client A and D_A is an element in $\mathbb{G}_1$ as defined in setup and key generation phase. Now, the hash function that have been used in this protocol H_2 is an element of $\mathbb{Z}p*$, which indicates that either it is a string of bits or number. So it is not a part of $\mathbb{G}_1$. The elements of $\mathbb{G}_1$ are points of elliptic curve. In the previous section we have defined an abelian group in elliptic curve thus binary operation '+' is not possible with a string or number which belongs to $\mathbb{Z}p^*$. We can also find the same problem during merchant's signature process.

In the next part we have done the cryptanalysis by considering $H_2 : \{0, 1\}^* \rightarrow \mathbb{G}_1$ and identified the vulnerabilities in Qin et al. [11] scheme. The following subsections contain the possible attacks in Qin et al. scheme.

4.1 Known Session Specific Temporary Information Attack

This attack is investigated by Canetti and Krawczyk [24] in 2001. Later on, the main reason of this attack is identified by Cheng et al. [25] and it is pointed out that the adversary $\breve{A}$ may gain the knowledge of the secret element that are being used by clients. The following conditions are the reason that the adversary $\breve{A}$ may get the secret elements.

- To generate a random element merchant and customer have to depend on a random number generator. The random number generator can be controlled by adversary $\breve{A}$. From there the adversary can easily get the secret element [26, 27].
- Generally the generated random number is stored in an insecure device. If the random number is not erased properly then the adversary may capture the computer and easily get the secret elements [26, 27].

Moreover, the verification is done by cloud server and the message is communicated through an insecure channel. There is no encryption procedure taking place during the communication. That indicates the adversary can easily monitor, steal or modify the communicating message. Finally, the acceptance of the payment by the merchant is only based on only one secret element α.

In Fig. 3, the known session specific temporary information attack occurring in the scheme is illustrated using a graphical representation. Let us consider that the adversary $\check{A}$ has gained the knowledge of secret element α as per the above mentioned discussion. Now, the adversary wants to purchase some goods or services from merchant and wants to pay less or even no money for the purchase to the merchant. To do that the adversary $\check{A}$ sends a false signature to merchant. In the merchant side there is no verification process undertaken by the merchant to check the incoming message is valid or not. The merchant performs further operations on false signature sent by the adversary. The procedure is shown in Fig. 3 and described below.

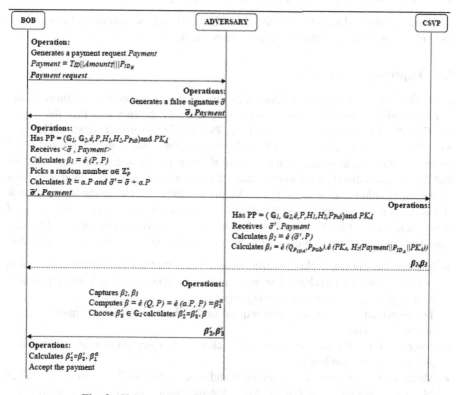

Fig. 3. Known session specific temporary information attack

- Initially adversary purchases from merchant and the merchant sends a payment request to adversary $\breve{A}$
- Adversary $\breve{A}$ generates a false signature $\overline{\sigma}$ for a fake transaction and sends it to merchant
- Merchant receives the false signature $\overline{\sigma}$ and accepts it without any verification. Then the merchant calculates $\beta_1 = \hat{e}(P, P)$, picks a random number $\alpha \in \mathbb{Z}p^*$, computes $\overline{\sigma}' = \overline{\sigma} + \alpha.P$ and sends $(\overline{\sigma}', Payment)$ to cloud server CSVP for outsource verification through an insecure channel.
- After receiving $(\overline{\sigma}', Payment)$ the untrusted CSVP calculates $\beta_2 = \hat{e}(\overline{\sigma}', P)$ and $\beta_3 = \hat{e}(Q_{P_{ID_a}}, P_{Pub}).\hat{e}(PK_A, H_2(Payment||P_{ID_A}||PK_A))$, and finally sends β_2, β_3 to merchant through an insecure channel.
- The adversary receives β_2, β_3 and calculates $\alpha.P$. Then adversary computes $\beta = \hat{e}(Q, P) = \hat{e}(\alpha.P, P) = \beta_1^\alpha$ where $Q = \alpha.P$. After that the adversary picks $\beta_3' \in \mathbb{G}_2$ and
- Computes $\beta_2' = \beta_3'.\beta$. Finally the adversary replaces β_2, β_3 with β_2', β_3' and sends to merchant.
- Merchant receives β_2', β_3' and computes $\beta_2' = \beta_3'.\beta_1^\alpha$.

From the above discussion we can claim that the Qin et al. scheme is vulnerable to known session specific temporary information attack.

4.2 Impersonation Attack

If an adversary successfully impersonates himself as an authorized customer to the merchant using some of the confidential information of the customer then the impersonation attack is successfully executed [28, 29]. The impersonation attack [28] is also possible in Qin et al. scheme [11] where the verification is done by the untrusted cloud server to reduce the computational overhead of the mobile device. Now let us consider that the untrusted cloud server impersonates itself as a client. Then the cloud server has all the information that is needed to make the payment. Moreover the verification is also done by the cloud server and the cloud server does not need to find out the value of secret element used by the merchant during outsourced verification phase. The step wise description of the possibility of this attack is shown in Fig. 4 and described below.

- Initially the untrusted cloud server impersonates itself as a customer and makes purchase from the merchant. The main aim of the cloud server is to make purchase with paying less or not even paying any money.
- The merchant sends the payment request to the cloud server who is impersonating himself as a client.
- After receiving the payment request the cloud server generates a false signature $\overline{\sigma}$ and sends it to merchant.
- Merchant receives the false signature $\overline{\sigma}$ and sends it to CSVP for verification. Then Merchant calculates $\beta_1 = \hat{e}(P, P)$. After that merchant picks a random number $\alpha \in \mathbb{Z}p^*$ and computes $\overline{\sigma}' = \overline{\sigma} + \alpha.P$ and sends $(\overline{\sigma}', Payment)$ to cloud server CSVP for outsource verification.
- The cloud server then calculates $Q = \overline{\sigma}' - \overline{\sigma} = \alpha.P$ and $\beta = \hat{e}(Q, P) = \hat{e}(\alpha.P, P) = \beta_1^\alpha$. After that it picks $\beta_3 \in \mathbb{G}_2$, computes $\beta_2 = \beta_3'.\beta$ and sends. β_1, β_2 to merchant.
- Merchant receives β_1, β_2; calculates $\beta_2 = \beta_3.\beta_1^\alpha$ and accepts the request.

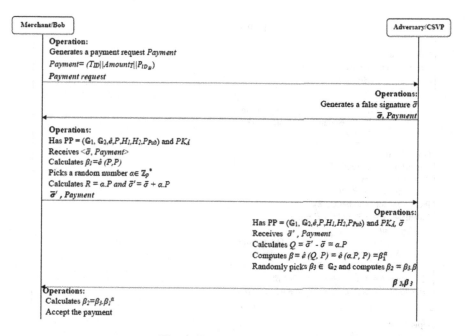

Fig. 4. Impersonation attack

4.3   Cloud Server Bypassing Attack

Cloud server is implemented in Qin et al. [11] scheme for the verification purpose. It may be possible that the adversary captures the sent message by the merchant and restrict it from reaching the message to the server. We call this attack as cloud server bypassing attack [7]. Due to lack of verification and encryption the message captured by the adversary can easily be modified according to its need. Without any knowledge of the cloud server the adversary does some easy calculations to get the original parameters and computes accordingly. Finally, when the message reaches to the merchant he cannot be able to identify the mismatch between the sent and received message. The detailed description is given below and the diagrammatic representation is shown in Fig. 5.

- Initially adversary purchases from merchant and the merchant sends a payment request to adversary $\check{A}$.
- Adversary $\check{A}$ generates a false signature $\overline{\sigma}$ for a fake transaction and sends it to merchant.

    Merchant receives the false signature $\overline{\sigma}$ and accepts it without any verification. Then the merchant calculates $\beta_1 = \hat{e}(P, P)$, picks a random number $\alpha \in \mathbb{Z}p^*$, computes $\overline{\sigma}' = \overline{\sigma} + \alpha.P$ and finally sends $(\overline{\sigma}, Payment)$ to CSVP for outsource verification through an insecure channel.

- The adversary $\check{A}$ hijacks the transmitted message from the insecure channel and performs $Q = \overline{\sigma}' - \overline{\sigma} = \alpha.P$, computes $\beta = \hat{e}(Q, P) = \hat{e}(\alpha.P, Q) = \beta_1^{\alpha}$, picks $\beta_3 \in \mathbb{G}_2$, computes $\beta_2 = \beta'_3.\beta$ and finally sends β_2, β_3 to merchant.
- Merchant receives β_2, β_3, calculates $\beta_2 = \beta_3. \beta_1^{\alpha}$ and accepts the receipt.

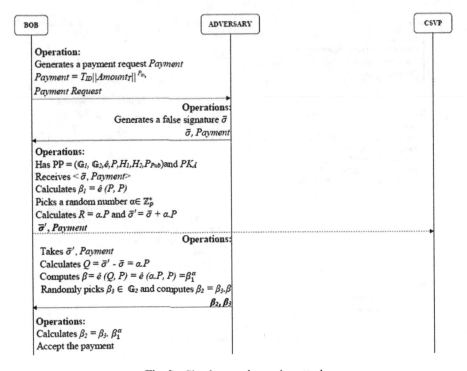

Fig. 5. Cloud server bypassing attack

4.4   Client and Untrusted Cloud Server Colluding Attack [16]

This attack is possible when the customer/client is colluding with the untrusted cloud server. The cloud server performs the outsourced verification and the merchant has to accept the value without any verification. The client can take the advantage of this by conspiring/colluding with the untrusted cloud server to make a false payment to merchant. The possibility of this attack is briefly described in the following steps:

- Initially the client makes a purchase from merchant. The merchant then sends a payment request to the client.
- Client generates a false signature $\overline{\sigma}'$ for a fake transaction and sends it to merchant.
- Merchant receives the false signature $\overline{\sigma}'$ and accept it without any verification. The merchant calculates $\beta_1 = \hat{e}(P, P)$, picks a random number $\alpha \in \mathbb{Z}p*$, computes $\overline{\sigma}' = \overline{\sigma} + \alpha.P$ and finally sends $(\overline{\sigma}', Payment)$ to the untrusted cloud server CSVP for outsource confirmation through an insecure channel.
- After receiving the $(\overline{\sigma}', Payment)$, the CSVP calculates $Q = \overline{\sigma}' - \overline{\sigma} = \alpha.P$ and $\beta = \hat{e}(Q, P) = \hat{e}(\alpha.P, P) = \beta_1^{\alpha}$. The CSVP also gets the value of $\overline{\sigma}$, picks $\beta_3 \in \mathbb{G}_2$, computes $\beta_2 = \beta_3.\beta_1^{\alpha}$ and finally sends β_2, β_3 to merchant.
- Merchant receives β_2, β_3, calculates $\beta_2 = \beta_3.\beta_1^{\alpha}$ and accepts the payment.

5   Conclusion

Qin et al. scheme utilizes certificate-less signature and bilinear pairing for a secure and privacy preserving mobile wallet payment service. This scheme also implements out-sourced verification to cloud server for large scale computations. Further, Qin et al. claimed that their scheme provides resistance against all cryptographic and security breaches. However, in this paper we have successfully shown that their scheme fails to be protected from known session specific temporary information attack, client imper-sonation attack, and cloud server bypassing attack, client and cloud server colluding attack. In future we will propose an efficient mobile wallet payment scheme with less overhead and well protected against all possible security attacks.

References

1. Yu, X., Kywe, S.M., Li, Y.: Security issues of in-store mobile payment. In: Handbook of Blockchain, Digital Finance, and Inclusion, vol. 2 (2017)
2. Smith, S.M., et al.: System and method of conducting transactions using a mobile wallet system. U.S. Patent Application (2010)
3. Sakalauskas, E., Muleravicius, J., Timofejeva, I.: Computational resources for mobile e-wallet system with observers. In: ELECTRONICS 2017, Palanga, pp. 1–5. IEEE (2017)
4. Kenneth, W.: Mobile payments, digital wallets and tunnel vision. In: Biometric Technology Today, pp. 8–9. Elsevier (2011)
5. Feifei, W.: Research on security of mobile payment model based on trusted third party. In: Second International Conference on Network Security Wireless Communication and Trusted Computing (NSWCTC), Wuhan, pp. 442–445. IEEE (2010)
6. Amin, R., Biswas, G.P.: A secure light weight scheme for user authentication and key agreement in multi-gateway based wireless sensor networks. Ad Hoc Netw. 36(1), 58–80 (2016)
7. Kalra, S., Sood, S.K.: Secure authentication scheme for IoT and cloud servers. Pervasive Mob. Comput. 24, 210–223 (2015)
8. Ray, S., Biswas, G.P.: An ECC based public key infrastructure usable for mobile applications. In: Second International Conference on Computational Science, Engineering and Information Technology, pp. 562–568. ACM (2012)
9. Ray, S., Biswas, G.P., Dasgupta, M.: Secure multi-purpose mobile-banking using elliptic curve cryptography. Wirel. Pers. Commun. 90(3), 1331–1354 (2016)
10. Turkanović, M., Brumen, B., Hölbl, M.: A novel user authentication and key agreement scheme for heterogeneous ad hoc wireless sensor networks, based on the internet of things notion. Ad Hoc Netw. 20, 96–1129 (2014)
11. Qin, Z., Sun, J., Wahaballa, A., Zheng, W., Xiong, H., Qin, Z.: A secure and privacy-preserving mobile wallet with outsourced verification in cloud computing. Comput. Stan. Interfaces 54, 55–60 (2017)
12. Stallings, W.: Cryptography and Network Security: Principles and Practices. Pearson Education India (2006)
13. Veeraraghavan, P.: Pseudo-identity based encryption and its application in mobile ad hoc networks. In: 2011 IEEE 10th Malaysia International Conference on Communications (MICC), Malaysia, pp. 49–52. IEEE (2011)

14. Islam, S.K., Biswas, G.P.: An improved pairing-free identity-based authenticated key agreement protocol based on ECC. Procedia Eng. **30**, 499–507 (2012)
15. Amin, R., Biswas, G.P., Giri, D., Khan, M.K., Kumar, N.: A more secure and privacy-aware anonymous user authentication scheme for distributed mobile cloud computing environments. Secur. Commun. Netw. **9**(17), 4650–4666 (2016)
16. Liao, Y., He, Y., Li, F., Zhou, S.: Analysis of a mobile payment protocol with outsourced verification in cloud server and the improvement. Comput. Stan. Interfaces **56**, 101–106 (2018)
17. Shin, D.: Towards an understanding of the consumer acceptance of mobile wallet. Comput. Hum. Behav. **25**(6), 1343–1354 (2009)
18. Amoroso, D.L., Watanabe, R.M.: Building a research model for mobile wallet consumer adoption: the case of mobile Suica in Japan. J. Theor. Appl. Electron. Commerce Res. **7**(1), 94–110 (2012)
19. Yu, Y., Mu, Y., Wang, G., Xia, Q., Yang, B.: Improved certificateless signature scheme provably secure in the standard model. IET Inf. Secur. **6**(2), 102–110 (2012)
20. Xiong, H.: Cost-effective scalable and anonymous certificateless remote authentication protocol. IEEE Trans. Inf. Forensics Secur. **9**(12), 2327–2339 (2014)
21. Coskun, V., Ozdenizci, B., Ok, K.: A survey on near field communication (NFC) technology. Wirel. Pers. Commun. **71**(3), 2259–2294 (2013)
22. Luo, Y., Fu, S., Huang, K., Wang, D., Xu, M.: Securely outsourcing of bilinear pairings with untrusted servers for cloud storage. In: Trustcom/BIGDATASE/ISPA, IEEE 2016, Tianjin, pp. 623–629. IEEE (2016)
23. Dutta, R., Barua, R., Sarkar, P.: Pairing-based cryptography: a survey. Cryptology ePrint Archive, Report 2004/064 (2004)
24. Canetti, R., Krawczyk, H.: Analysis of key-exchange protocols and their use for building secure channels. In: Pfitzmann, B. (ed.) EUROCRYPT 2001. LNCS, vol. 2045, pp. 453–474. Springer, Heidelberg (2001). https://doi.org/10.1007/3-540-44987-6_28
25. Chen, H.B., Chen, T.H., Lee, W.B., Chang, C.C.: Security enhancement for a three-party encrypted key exchange protocol against undetectable on-line password guessing attacks. Comput. Stan. Interfaces **30**(1–2), 95–99 (2008)
26. Islam, S.K.: Provably secure dynamic identity-based three-factor password authentication scheme using extended chaotic maps. Nonlinear Dyn. **78**(3), 2261–2276 (2014)
27. Islam, S.K., Khan, M.K., Obaidat, M.S., Muhaya, F.: Provably secure and anonymous password authentication protocol for roaming service in global mobility networks using extended chaotic maps. Wirel. Pers. Commun. **84**(3), 2013–2034 (2015)
28. Islam, S.K., Amin, R., Biswas, G.P., Farash, M.S., Li, X., Kumari, S.: An improved three party authenticated key exchange protocol using hash function and elliptic curve cryptography for mobile-commerce environments. J. King Saud Univ.-Comput. Inf. Sci. **29**(3), 311–324 (2017)
29. Sadhukhan, D., Ray, S.: Cryptanalysis of an elliptic curve cryptography based lightweight authentication scheme for smart grid communication. In: 2018 IEEE 4th International Conference on Recent Advances in Information Technology (RAIT), Dhanbad, pp. 1–6. IEEE (2018)

Secure Framework for Ambient Assisted Living System

K. Sowjanya$^{(\boxtimes)}$ and Mou Dasgupta

National Institute of Technology Raipur, Raipur, India
sowjanya.kandisa@gmail.com, elle.est.mou@gmail.com
http://www.nitrr.ac.in/

Abstract. The development in the field of miniature sensors and wireless communication enables the successful deployment of Internet of Things (IoT) in the healthcare sector. The healthcare data generated by the medical sensors is very sensitive and enough to qualify as an instance of big data. In this paper, a secure framework is designed to assist the diabetic patients. The sensors' data of each patient is used to generate context aware correlation rules by using map-reduce apriori algorithm. From these rules another labeled dataset is created to build a classifier for predicting the present state of the patient. After the successful deployment of this classifier on the service provider side, secure communication has been provided between the patient and the service provider using Key-Policy Attribute Based Encryption. Hence, providing an IoT based secure ambient assisted living system for diabetic patient may be helpful to the healthcare sector.

Keywords: Ambient assisted living · Map-reduce aprori · KPABE · Diabetes

1 Introduction

With the notion of the Internet of Things (IoT) the concept of Ambient Assisted Living (AAL) emerged to improve the healthcare quality. AAL is based on Ambient Intelligence (AI) and its primary objective is to enhance the living style of the patient such that they can live comfortably in their home by observing everyday activities and other related attributes [1]. Consequently, AAL brings challenges like security and privacy. Since the medical data in AAL system generally transmitted through wireless channels, therefore this sensitive medical data is vulnerable to various information attacks. In this paper, we have considered the chronic disease diabetes. In India and also all over the world, diabetes has become an epidemic [2,3]. Generally diabetes is categorized into four types, namely: Type 1, Type 2, Pre-diabetes and Gestational diabetes. Among these, Type 1 diabetes has an associated complication termed as Hypoglycemia (low blood glucose level), where a patient becomes unconscious and even this can lead to death. Besides, Hyperglycemia (high blood glucose levels) is an alert

© Springer Nature Singapore Pte Ltd. 2019
J. K. Mandal et al. (Eds.): CICBA 2018, CCIS 1031, pp. 425–440, 2019.
https://doi.org/10.1007/978-981-13-8581-0_34

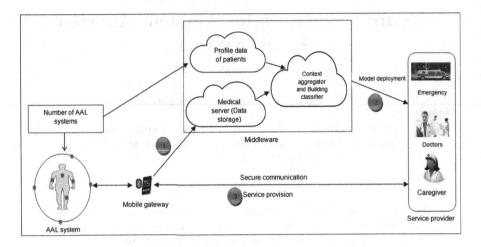

Fig. 1. Proposed framework

state for patients to supervise their regular activities and diet. Hence, by continuous monitoring of the vital signs (blood pressure, blood glucose level, heart rate etc.) of the diabetes patient may be helpful to control the alert and emergency situations. As the medical data is very sensitive in nature, so for this the US government has been created a federal law termed as the Health Insurance Portability and Accountability Act (HIPAA). Under this act, the rules are specified about who can have the right to access the medical data of the patient [4,5]. In this direction, we have designed a framework consists of IoT based secure AAL system for diabetes patients.

1.1   Architecture

The general architecture of the proposed framework is depicted in Fig. 1. Here, the live data of the patient is transmitted to the medical server, also to the service provider. The stored medical data is used to build a classification model which can predict the present state of the patient whether it is *normal, alert, warning* or *emergency*. Once the classification model has been built, it is deployed on the service provider side. After the successful deployment of the model, service provider can directly communicate with the patient through the mobile gateway. This communication is secured using Elliptic Curve Cryptography (ECC) based Key-Policy Attribute Based Encryption (KPABE). Thus, the live data of the patient is encrypted using proposed KPABE under some specified attributes and send to the service provider. At the service provider side, the decryption is done successfully if the attributes of the service provider satisfy the access policy defined by the system.

1.2 Related Work and State of the Art

The data generated by the AAL systems are very huge in nature and can be qualified as big data. This big data must be processed by some data mining algorithms. The conventional techniques used for data analytics are not sufficient to deal with this voluminous amount of data. In this context, the distributed data mining techniques are proven to be useful [6]. Lin [7] in 2014, have presented the distributed version of the apriori algorithm using map-reduce programming model on Hadoop platform. In 2015 Maitrey and Jha [8], have proposed the technique of handling big data using map-reduce. Their work presents the detailed step-by-step working of the map-reduce apriori algorithm. Forkan *et al.* [9] in 2014 have proposed a complete context aware environment for AAL. They further continued their work in [10] and [11] and have presented a big data based context aware monitoring and prediction of clinical events. But their scheme does not ensure the secure transmission of medical data over the cloud.

Recently, in 2018 [12] Rodrigues *et al.* illustrates the various techniques related to IoT for healthcare and AAL, consequently coined the term Internet of Health Things (IoHT). Their seminal work shows that the major issue in IoT based healthcare system is the security and without proper security mechanism the practical implementation of any AAL (or IoT based healthcare) system is not possible. In this context, Zhao [13] have proposed a lightweight anonymous authentication scheme for wireless body area networks using ECC. He and Zeadally [14] in 2015 have proposed an improved version of Zhao's authentication protocol for AAL. Recently, Attribute Based Encryption (ABE) is proved to be most effective security technique for the cloud based environment. ABE is a type of public key encryption and inherently supports the broadcasting data concept of IoT. KPABE is one type of ABE, where the message is encrypted under the set of attributes and the decryption key is associated with the access policy. Yao *et al.* in [15], have proposed a lightweight ECC based ABE scheme for IoT without bilinear pairing. In 2016, Hong and Sun [16], have proposed a high efficient key-insulated ABE algorithm without pairing but their scheme is secured under Computational Deffie-Hellman (CDH) assumption using random oracle model. In the same year, Karati *et al.* [17] have proposed a threshold based ABE scheme without bilinear pairing and without LSSS (Linear Secret Sharing Scheme).

In the view of above literature, we have designed a secure framework for AAL to assist diabetes patients. For this, we have observed the regular activities and vital sign values (collectively termed as context attributes) of three local diabetes patients under the concern of a domain expert (i.e., diabetologist). Based on the observation and considering the real factors, we have generated synthetic dataset for each patient. This dataset is used to build a classification model, which is deployed at the service provider side to predict the forthcoming state of the patient. As without proper security mechanism the practical implementation of any AAL system is worth nothing, so we have proposed an ECC based lightweight KPABE scheme to assure secure communication between the patient and service provider.

2   Concepts and Functionalities

This section presents the pre-requisite concepts and functionalities which are needed to understand the proposed framework. At first the description of the dataset considered in this paper is presented followed by the description of various cloud components used in the framework. Next the formal structure of KPABE is presented. Consequently, the access structure and Lagrange Interpolation are discussed.

2.1   Description of the Dataset

The schema of the dataset considered in the proposed framework is depicted in Table 1. In a typical AAL system the primary architecture involves the body sensors, ambient sensors and a software service to provide aid. In this paper, the dataset con-tains the values of the following domains: vital sign (GL, HR, SBP, DBP, BT) sensor readings, ambient sensors (room temperature (RT) and humidity (HD)) readings along with the daily activity logs representing the individuals' behavior (exercising, sleeping, eating, walking, resting, etc.) as shown in Table 1. These domains are collectively considered to define context for the corresponding patient. Here context refers to any situation where multiple attributes correlate with each other. A single vital sign value is not enough to make a conclusion i.e., an individual attribute has no meaning if it is not considered with some other attributes or situation. As an example consider an increment in HR value that looks like an abnormal situation if it is considered as a single context, but if the patient is doing some physical exercise then it can be normal condition. So using current and last activity, the present situation can be classified as normal or an abnormal one. Data related to vital signs, ambient conditions and activities can be collected through IoT based AAL system. We assume that the architecture for collecting this data is already present and only considered the data values generated by this IoT based AAL system.

2.2   Cloud Components

For the sake of explanation, we are considered the middleware of the proposed framework consists of various cloud components. The functionalities of these cloud components are briefly explained in this subsection.

- The *profile data cloud* stores the patients' related information like age, gender, weight, height etc. along with the identity of the patient. Initially this data is stored for each and every patient prior to the implementation of the system.
- The *medical server cloud* stores the sensor readings of the patient's consisting of all the domains. This sensor reading data is transmitted to the cloud through the mobile gateway.
- The *context aggregator and building classifier cloud* at first aggregates all the data (profile data and medical server data) related to a specific patient to create corresponding contexts for that patient. After the context aggregation

Table 1. Dataset schema

Domains	Name	Context attributes	Type or name	Range or values
D1	Vital signs	Glucose levels (GL)	Numeric	[30–200]
		Heart rate (HR)	Numeric	[30–140]
		Systolic BP (SBP)	Numeric	[50–230]
		Diastolic BP (DBP)	Numeric	[30–140]
		Body temp. (BT)	Numeric	[94–100]
		Sweating (S)	Boolean	0 or 1
D2	Ambient conditions	Room temperature	Normal	0
		Humidity	Hot	1
			Cold	2
			High	0
			Medium	1
			Low	2
D3, D4	Activities	D3: Current activity	Exercising	1
		D4: Last activity	Eating	2
			Sleeping	3
			Resting	4
			Walking	5
			Toileting	6
			Medication	7

phase, the distributed machine learning algorithms are employed in order to build a classification model to predict the present state of the patient.

2.3 Formal Structure of KPABE

The KPABE scheme generally consists of four algorithms, namely: Setup, Encryp-tion, Key generation and Decryption.

- **Setup:** This algorithm is run by an authority, generally known as Key-Authority (KA). Input to this algorithm is the implicit security level of the scheme. It outputs public parameters PPM (known to all) and master secret key MSK (kept secret under KA).
- **Encryption:** This algorithm is run by the data sender. Message M, PPM and set of attributes ω are taken as input to create a ciphertext CT.
- **Key generation:** This algorithm is run by the KA to generate the decryption key corresponding to an access structure/policy by taking master secret key (MSK), access structure Γ and the public parameters (PPM) as input.
- **Decryption:** This algorithm is run at the receiver side to reconstruct the encrypted message. It takes input: the decryption key for access structure Γ, the ciphertext CT encrypted under ω and PPM. This algorithm outputs the message M iff ω satisfy Γ.

2.4   Access Structure and Lagrange Interpolation

Access structure Γ defines the access control or access scope of the users' decryption key [15]. In ABE, the users' role is defined by the set of attributes. Therefore, the access structure contains attributes that are authorized to access the secret/decryption key. Access structure can be represented with the help of an access tree. Further knowledge on access structure and tree can be obtained from [15]. In this proposed mechanism, the secret key in decryption phase is reconstructed under the attribute set ω using *Lagrange Interpolation*. Here, if each attribute ω is associated with a unique random number in Z_q^* (a finite field of integers $\{1, 2, \ldots, q-1\}$). Then the Lagrange coefficient $\Delta_{i,\theta}$ is given by

$$\Delta_{i,\theta}(x) = \prod_{j \in \theta, j \neq i} \frac{x-j}{i-j} \tag{1}$$

where $i \in Z_q^*$ and θ is set of numbers corresponding to each attribute in the set ω.

3   Proposed Methodology

This section at first presents the primary contribution of this paper followed by the description of the proposed framework.

3.1   Our Contribution

The primary contributions of this paper are: 1. To find the association between various vital sign values and activities of the patient using map-reduce apriori algorithm. 2. To generate a labelled (*normal, alert, warning* and *emergency*) dataset using the rules generated in the previous step. 3. To analyze this labeled medical data and consequently building a classification model to predict the patients' present state. 4. To provide a secure communication between the patient and the service provider using proposed ECC based KPABE scheme.

In order to offer assisted living services based on IoT to diabetes patients, we have to first preprocess the sensors data so that map-reduce apriori algorithm can be employed on this data.

3.2   Data Preprocessing

The data collected from vital sign sensors are numeric (continuous) in nature. In order to generate association rules, this numeric data is discretized using the measures: *mean, standard deviation, min* and *max* values [10] and are given by:

First discrete interval: $[a_{imin}, a_{imean} - a_{istdev} - 1]$
Second discrete interval: $[a_{imean} - a_{istdev}, a_{imean} + a_{istdev}]$
Third discrete interval: $[a_{imean} + a_{istdev} + 1, a_{imax}]$

Thus, all the domains of the considered dataset are now having discrete values which make further analysis of the data easier.

3.3   Map-Reduce Apriori Algorithm

This section presents the map-reduce apriori algorithm for generating the association rules on the pre-processed data. For this, we have employed three map-reduce jobs. The first map-reduce job (MR1) takes the initial input dataset and generates the count of each and every item in the input dataset. The second map-reduce job (MR2) takes the output of the MR1 as input and generates the candidates (every possible subset of attributes) along with their counts. The final map-reduce job (MR3) generates the association rules by taking the output of the MR2 as input. The objectives/constraints considered in this paper to generate the association rules are *Confidence, Lift* and *Kulczynski with imbalance ratio*. Since, *Support* and *Confidence* alone are not sufficient at excluding uninteresting rules [18]. Therefore, to overcome this issue correlation measures: *Lift* and *Kulczynski with imbalance ratio* are used. This results in the generation of correlation rules rather than simply association rules [18]. For the rules i.e., $X \to Y$ (where X refers to the antecedent and Y refers to the consequent of the rule), the correlation measures are given by

$$Confidence = \frac{\sigma(X \cup Y)}{\sigma(X)} \tag{2}$$

Where σ is *Support* value. Equation 2 represents the measure *Confidence*, i.e., if X is present in the dataset then Y is also present. Next, the measure *Lift*, one of the fundamental correlation measures which represents the interdependence between X and Y and given by the Eq. 3.

$$Lift = \frac{Confidence(X \to Y)}{\sigma(Y)} \tag{3}$$

The third measure *Kulczynski* with *imbalance ratio* is given by the Eqs. 4 and 5. The detailed description of these measures can be obtained from [18].

$$Kulc(X,Y) = \frac{1}{2}\left[\frac{\sigma(X \cup Y)}{\sigma(Y)} + \frac{\sigma(X \cup Y)}{\sigma(X)}\right] \tag{4}$$

$$IR(X,Y) = \frac{|\,\sigma(X) - \sigma(Y)\,|}{\sigma(X) + \sigma(Y) - \sigma(X \cup Y)} \tag{5}$$

Hence, the MR3 considers these measures to generate the correlation rules. In order to obtain the interesting correlation rules, pre-defined user specific threshold values are to be set for each measure. The proposed map-reduce apriori algorithm is also represented in Algorithm 1.

This subsection finally outputs the interesting correlation rules by excluding the uninterested rules which does not satisfy the pre-specified threshold values.

3.4   Generation of Labeled Dataset

Once the correlation rules are generated (in the previous Subsect. 3.3), a new labeled dataset is synthetically created using the rules obtained and having the

---

Algorithm 1. Correlation Rule Mining

Input: Pre-processed dataset, Threshold values for considered measures
Output: Interesting correlation rules along with the measures.
procedure MR1
    Mapper(key ← row_id, value ← row)
        Assign *count* 1 for each and every word/item of the input dataset.
    Reducer(key ← word, value ← Iterable(count))
        Aggregate the *count* corresponding to each word.
end procedure

procedure MR2
    Mapper(key ← word, value ← count)
        Generate every possible combination of the words (candidate) and assign the corresponding *count* to 1.
    Reducer(key ← candidate, value ← Iterable(count))
        Aggregate the *count* corresponding to each candidate.
end procedure

procedure MR3
    Mapper(key ← candidate, value ← count)
        Generate rules using the candidates and maintain the *count* for each antecedent X and consequent Y part of the rule.
    Reducer(key ← rule, value ← list (count(X), count(Y))
        Compute the measures for each rule using the Equations 2 to 5.
    Output: (Rule, measures)
end procedure

---

labels: *normal, alert, warning* and *emergency* according to the Table 2. This table is created by taking the knowledge of domain expert (Diabetologist).

The primary reason for creating this new labeled dataset is to obtain an effective and accurate classification model for an individual or specific patient, instead of storing every rule for each and every context. Also, this step validates the generated correlation rules.

4 Simulation of the Proposed Framework

In order to evaluate the performance, the proposed framework is simulated using Java programming language. By using the Hadoop framework and map-reduce programming model, we have simulated map-reduce apriori algorithm using Java. Once the interesting correlation rules are obtained, another labeled dataset is generated to build a classification model. This section at first provides the description of the considered AAL example. Consequently, the analysis of the labeled dataset is presented. Based on this analysis the classification model is built to predict the present state/context of the patient. After the deployment of the classification model, the secure transmission between the patient and service provider is presented using ECC based KPABE.

Table 2. Class labels for context classification

Rule or context	Class label	Value
If all the vital signs are in their respective normal range	*normal*	0
If one of GL, HR, SBP, DBP or BT is not in the expected range according to given context	*alert*	1
If GL becomes greater than 150 mg/dl, medications not taken or more than two vital signs are not in the expected range according to the given context	*warning*	2
If GL becomes less than 60 and one or more vital signs are not in the expected range	*emergency*	3

4.1   Description of AAL Example

As per best of our knowledge, no real healthcare sensor data (diabetes perspective) are available publicly for a long period of time. Therefore, we have considered the regular activities of three local patients and observed their GL, BP and other symptoms. We have consulted a domain expert (i.e., diabetologist) and created one synthetic dataset by taking real factors and MIMIC II clinical database [19] into consideration. The data follows normal distribution if the vital sign ranges are restricted. Thus, the data is generated, which is normally distributed. Next, some specified values are randomly increased or decreased according to the current and past activities. For example, after meals the GL is bit high, but it is a normal situation when considering the current context. The range of vital signs and some specific symptoms vary from case to case. Therefore, establishing AAL system for each and every patient and analyzing this data in order to provide immediate and specific service is very substantive and helpful. Based on the health status of the considered three patients, synthetic data is generated for consecutive 500 days within a time interval of 15mins, i.e., 96 readings for a single day and 48000 records for a single patient. This data is operated upon proposed map-reduce apriori algorithm to generate correlation between various attributes in a context.

4.2   Analysis of the Labeled Dataset

Once the rules are obtained, the labeled dataset is generated using the MATLAB software/tool according to Table 2 to validate the generated rules. Now, this data is analyzed using WEKA data mining tool with *distributedWekaHadoop* package [20]. We have employed *K-Fold cross validation* technique for three machine learning algorithms namely, Decision Tree (DT), Naïve Bayes (NB) and Support Vector Machine (SVM), where the value of K is kept at $2, 4, 5$ and 10 respectively. The best results are observed at $K = 10$, where 90% of data is utilized to train the classification model and remaining 10% of the data is kept aside for testing. The accuracy of decision tree outperforms among the other two machine learning algorithms. The reason is intuitive that the data is generated using correlation rules. Therefore, decision tree classifier is used further to predict the unseen contexts or present state of the patient.

4.3 Secure Communication Between the Patient and Service Provider

Once the classification model is deployed at the service provider side, the patients' medical data is directly sent over the internet to the service provider. This classification model provides assistance to the service provider to offer fast help to the patient. But, the medical data of the patient is very sensitive in nature, sending without proper security mechanism may lead to serious consequences. Also, without proper security mechanism, the successful deployment of any IoT healthcare service is ineffective [12]. Hence, in this subsection, we have presented the secure communication between the patient and the service provider using ECC based KPABE. For implementation of secure AAL system, we have considered the universal attribute set: $U = hospitalA, hospitalB, diabetologist, nurse, emergency\_staff, admin\_staff, on\_duty$. For the sake of simplicity, only two hospitals and few departments are considered in the simulation. The access structure used in this simulation is depicted in Fig. 2. Now, if the patients' medical data, for example GL [30–90], HR [71–100], SBP [80–120], DBP [81–100], $BT99$, $S0$, $RT0$, $H1$, $CA4$, $LA2$ is supposed to be transmitted to the service provider using KPABE encryption under the attribute set $diabetologist, hospitalB, emergency\_staff, on\_duty$. Then the following phases of the considered KPABE is given as.

Setup Phase. In this phase, the KA defines the universal attribute set U and for each attribute $i \in U$, KA chooses a random number such that $a_i \in Z_q^*$. Consequently, the public key corresponding to each attribute i is given by $P_i = a_i.B$, where B is the base point of the elliptic curve E. Further KA defines one way hash function, which hashes the point on E to a sequence of $\{0,1\}$ of length m, where m is the length of the message being transmitted. This hash function is represented by $H : \{point\ on\ E\} \rightarrow \{0,1\}^m$. Finally, KA chooses its master secret key (MSK) as $s \in Z_q^*$, accordingly the master public key (MPK) is given by $P = s.B$. Hence, the systems' secret keys are: $\{a_i, s\}$ (kept secret with KA) and systems public parameters are given by P_i, P, H.

Encryption Phase. Now, say the medical data of the patient say $M =GL$ [30–90], HR [71–100], SBP [80–120], DBP [81–100], $BT99$, $S0$, $RT0$, $H1$, $CA4$, $LA2$ is encrypted under the attribute set $K = \{diabetologist, hospitalB, emergency\_staff, on\_duty\}$. Now, the data sender (patients' side) chooses a random number $r \in Z_q^*$ and computes the parameter $CT_1 = r.B$. Similarly for each attribute $i \in K$, data sender computes $CT_2 = r.P_i$. The third parameter computed by the data sender is $CT_3 = H(r.P) \oplus M$. Hence, the ciphertext created at sender side is given by $CT = \{CT_1, CT_2, CT_3\}$.

Key Generation Phase. In this phase, KA outputs the decryption key after receiving the request from the service provider for the key with his/her

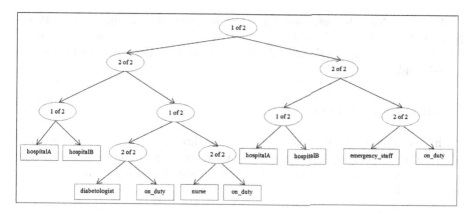

Fig. 2. An example of access structure

attributes. At first, KA checks whether the attributes associated with the data receiver (or service provider) satisfy the defined access structure or access tree or not. If not KA rejects the request, otherwise KA defines a polynomial $q_u(x)$ with degree $k_u - 1$, where k_u is the threshold value at node u. For the root node of the access tree, KA sets $q_R(0) = s$ (MSK). In order to define the polynomial of the root node uniquely, KA chooses $k_R - 1$ other points at random under Z_q^*. For all the other nodes u of the tree, KA defines $q_u(0) = q_{parent(u)}(index(u))$, here $index$ is the number given to each node u corresponding to the ordering of its children. The information regarding the notations and concepts of the access tree and structure can be obtained from [15]. Like $q_R(x)$, the polynomial $q_u(x)$ is defined uniquely by choosing $k_u - 1$ other points at random under Z_q^*. When the polynomial of the leaf node (or attributes in K) is defined, a share of the decryption key is associated with the leaf node (or attribute) as $D_u = q_u(0) + a_i$, where i represents the attribute associated with the leaf node (or attribute in K) u and a_i is the random number (corresponding to the attributes in K) chosen from Z_q^* in the Setup phase.

Decryption. This phase outputs the message M iff the attributes associated satisfy the defined access structure. This phase takes the input: ciphertext CT and the decryption key given by the KA i.e., D_u and computes the message using

$$M = H(decryptNode) \oplus CT_3 \tag{6}$$

where,

$$D_u.CT_1 - CT_2 = (q_u(0) + a_i).r.B - r.P_i$$
$$= q_u(0).r.B + a_i.r.B - r.P_i$$
$$= q_u(0).r.B + a_i.r.B - r.a_i.B$$
$$= q_u(0).r.B$$

Hence, for the root node R, the value of $(D_u.CT_1 - CT_2)$ is calculated using the *Lagrange coefficient* of Eq. 1 and given by $D_R.CT_1 - CT_2 = q_R(0).r.B =$

$s.r.B = r.P$. Now, by referring Eq. 6, the message M is computed as follows: $H(D_u.CT_1 - CT_2) \oplus CT_3 = H(r.P) \oplus H(r.P) \oplus M = M$. Hence, the message M consisting the patients' medical data is successfully decrypted at the service provider side (receiver).

5   Results and Discussion

We have evaluated the proposed approach on three patients suffering from diabetes with different specific symptoms. After applying the map-reduce apriori algorithm the number of correlation rules generated for each patient is depicted in the Fig. 3.

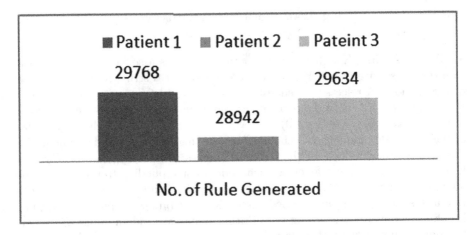

Fig. 3. Number of correlation rules generated for each patient

Some of the sample rules generated by the map-reduce apriori algorithm for patient 1 is depicted below:

GL[91-180] HR[71-100] SBP[80-120] DBP[81-100] = > CA1 LA2

GL[30-90] HR[101-140] SBP[80-120] =>CA7 S1

GL[91-90] HR[71-100] LA7 = > CA4 DBP[81-100] S0

GL[30-90] HR[101-140] SBP[80-120] =>LA7 S1 BT[94-95]

To test the map-reduce apriori algorithm over the cloud environment, we have used Amazon EMR [21]. The minimum execution time for generation of correlation rules is presented in Table 3. Intuitively, best results are obtained for the highest number of cores.

Further to validate the rules generated, the labeled dataset is analyzed using *K-Fold cross validation* technique by setting the value of $K = 2, 4, 5$ and 10. The best results are obtained at $K = 10$. The classification accuracy and the

Table 3. Execution time for map-reduce apriori algorithm

1 Core	2 Core	4 Core
80 min	51 min	38 min

Table 4. Performance measures of classification algorithms

Classifier	Average false positive rate			Classification accuracy (in percentage)		
Patient	P1	P2	P3	P1	P2	P3
DT	0.012	0.011	0.012	97.3	97.5	97.3
NB	0.015	0.016	0.014	96.4	96.2	96.41
SVM	0.021	0.022	0.019	95.5	95.3	95.9

average false positive rate (for $K = 10$) of the three classification algorithms are depicted in Table 4.

From Table 4, it can be observed that the classification accuracy of the DT for all the three patients is higher as compared to the other two algorithms. Further, the *average false positive rate* of the DT classifier is found to be better than the NB and SVM classifiers. Therefore, the DT classifier is further used to deploy as a classification model at service provider side, which can provide an aid to better classify the present state/context of the patient.

Now, by considering the running time of the various cryptographic operations provided in the work [17], we have calculated the minimum execution time of the proposed KPABE. The execution time also compared with the related schemes as shown in Table 5.

Table 5. Minimum execution time (milliseconds) taken by each phase ($n = 30$: no. of attributes in U and $k = 10$: no. of attributes in K)

Scheme	Setup	Encryption	Key generation	Decryption	Total time
[15]	68.51	22.1	47.1	91.3	229.01
[17]	270.80	165.05	106.20	115.91	657.96
[22]	41.28	409.8	136.6	620.3	1207.98
Our	68.51	29.56	17.99	29.14	145.20

Table 5 depicts that the total time taken by the schemes [17] and [22] is much higher as these schemes employ modular exponential and bilinear pairing operations respectively, which are more expensive than the elliptic curve operations. The *Setup* time of the scheme [15] and ours is equivalent. But the execution time of the phases: *Key generation* and *Decryption* of our scheme is significantly less as compared to [15]. Hence, the proposed KPABE provides a lightweight secure communication between the patient and the service provider.

Table 6. Comparison with related schemes

Scheme	Machine learning approach	Technique	Security mechanism
[23]	Yes	Rule based reasoning	No
[24]	No	-	Yes
[10]	Yes	Map-reduce apriori with *Support* and *Confidence* (accuracy: 95.2%)	No
Our	Yes	Map-reduce apriori with *Confidence, Lift* and *Kulczynski with imbalance ratio* (accuracy: 97%)	Yes

Further, the proposed framework is compared with other related schemes as depicted in Table 6. This shows that our framework is more effective by considering the security mechanism.

6   Conclusion

Today, diabetes has become an epidemic proportion in India as well as all over the globe. Hence, this paper provides an IoT based secure AAL framework for diabetes patients. Here, at first the medical data of the patient is stored at the medical cloud server. At medical cloud server, map-reduce apriori algorithm is applied on the patient' medical data with the objectives: *Confidence, Lift* and *Kulczynski with imbalance ratio*. Based on the generated correlation rules, one labeled dataset has been created to build a classification model which can predict the present context of the patient. The generated labeled dataset is analyzed using three machine learning algorithms, namely, Decision Tree, Naïve Bayes and Support Vector Machine. Among these decision tree outperforms and hence further used for deployment at the service provider side. Once the classification model has deployed, the medical data of the patient is directly sent to the service provider using the KPABE security mechanism. The proposed framework is compared with other related schemes and the results show that our framework is more effective. Thus, the proposed framework provides a secure IoT based AAL service to diabetes patients.

References

1. Rashidi, P., Mihailidis, A.: A survey on ambient-assisted living tools for older adults. IEEE J. Biomed. Health Inform. **17**(3), 579–590 (2013). https://doi.org/10.1109/JBHI.2012.2234129
2. Anjana, R.M., Deepa, M., Pradeepa, R., et al.: Prevalence of diabetes and pre-diabetes in 15 states of India: results from the ICMR-INDIAB population-based cross-sectional study. Lancet Diab. Endocrinol. **5**(8), 585–596 (2017). https://doi.org/10.1016/S2213-8587(17)30174-2

3. National Diabetes Statistics Report: 2017: Estimates of Diabetes and Its Burden in the United States. Accessed 8 Apr 2018
4. United States Department of Health and Human Services, Privacy, Security, and Electronic Health Records. https://www.hhs.gov/sites/default/files/ocr/privacy/hipaa/understanding/consumers/privacy-security-electronic-records.pdf. Accessed 19 Apr 2018
5. United States Department of Health and Human Services, Sharing Health Information with Family Members and Friends. https://www.hhs.gov/sites/default/files/ocr/privacy/hipaa/understanding/consumers/sharing-family-friends.pdf. Accessed 19 Apr 2018
6. Benjelloun, F.Z., Lahcen, A.A., Belfkih, S.: An overview of big data opportunities, applications and tools. In: IEEE Conference on Intelligent Systems and Computer Vision (ISCV), Fez, Morocco, pp. 1–6 (2015). https://doi.org/10.1109/ISACV.2015.7105553
7. Lin, X.: MR-Apriori: association rules algorithm based on MapReduce. In: IEEE 5th International Conference on Software Engineering and Service Science, Beijing, China, pp. 141–144 (2014). https://doi.org/10.1109/ICSESS.2014.6933531
8. Maitrey, S., Jha, C.K.: Handling big data efficiently by using map reduce technique. In: IEEE International Conference on Computational Intelligence and Communication Technology, Ghaziabad, India, pp. 703–708 (2015). https://doi.org/10.1109/CICT.2015.140
9. Forkan, A., Khalil, I., Tari, Z.: CoCaMAAL: a cloud-oriented context-aware middleware in ambient assisted living. Future Gener. Comput. Syst. 35, 114–127 (2014). https://doi.org/10.1016/j.future.2013.07.009
10. Forkan, A.R.M., Khalil, I., Ibaida, A., Tari, Z.: BDCaM: big data for context-aware monitoring-a personalized knowledge discovery framework for assisted healthcare. IEEE Trans. Cloud Comput. 5(4), 628–641 (2017). https://doi.org/10.1109/TCC.2015.2440269
11. Forkan, A.R.M., Khalil, I.: A probabilistic model for early prediction of abnormal clinical events using vital sign correlations in home-based monitoring. In: IEEE International Conference on Pervasive Computing and Communications (PerCom), Sydney, NSW, Australia, pp. 1–9 (2016). https://doi.org/10.1109/PERCOM.2016.7456519
12. Rodrigues, J.J.P.C., Segundo, D.B.D.R., Junqueira, H.A., et al.: Enabling technologies for the internet of health things. IEEE Access 6, 13129–13141 (2018). https://doi.org/10.1109/ACCESS.2017.2789329
13. Zhao, Z.: An efficient anonymous authentication scheme for wireless body area networks using elliptic curve cryptosystem. J. Med. Syst. 38(2), 1–7 (2014). https://doi.org/10.1007/s10916-014-0013-5
14. He, D., Zeadally, S.: Authentication protocol for an ambient assisted living system. IEEE Commun. Mag. 53(1), 71–77 (2015). https://doi.org/10.1109/MCOM.2015.7010518
15. Yao, X., Chen, Z., Tian, Y.: A lightweight attribute-based encryption scheme for the internet of things. Future Gener. Comput. Syst. 49(C), 104–112 (2015). https://doi.org/10.1016/j.future.2014.10.010
16. Hong, H., Sun, Z.: High efficient key-insulated attribute based encryption scheme without bilinear pairing operations. SpringerPlus: SpringerOpen J. 1–12 (2016). https://doi.org/10.1186/s40064-016-1765-9.
17. Karati, A., Amin, R., Biswas, G.P.: Provably secure threshold- based ABE scheme without bilinear map. Arab. J. Sci. Eng. 41(8), 3201–3213 (2016). https://doi.org/10.1007/s13369-016-2156-9

18. Pei, J., Han, J., Kamber, M. (eds.): Data Mining: Concepts and Techniques (English), 3rd edn. ElsevieR Publication, Amsterdam (2012)
19. https://physionet.org/works/MIMICIIClinicalDatabase/ . Accessed 20 Oct 2017
20. http://markahall.blogspot.in/2013/10/weka-and-hadoop-part-1.html . Accessed 15 Jan 2018
21. https://aws.amazon.com/emr/ . Accessed 11 Dec 2017
22. Singh, M., Rajan, M.A., Shivraj, V.L., Balamuralidhar, P.: Secure MQTT for internet of things (IoT). In: IEEE Fifth International Conference on Communication Systems and Network Technologies, Gwalior, India, pp. 746–751 (2015). https://doi.org/10.1109/CSNT.2015.16
23. Alsulami, M.H., Atkins, A.S., Campion, R.J., Alaboudi, A.A.: An enhanced conceptual model for using ambient assisted living to provide a home proactive monitoring system for elderly Saudi Arabians. In: IEEE/ACS 14th International Conference on Computer Systems and Applications (AICCSA), Hammamet, Tunisia, pp. 1443–1449 (2017). https://doi.org/10.1109/AICCSA.2017.214
24. Costa, S.E., et al.: Integration of wearable solutions in AAL environments with mobility support. J. Med. Syst. **39**(12), 1–8 (2015). https://doi.org/10.1007/s10916-015-0342-z

Shared Memory Implementation and Scalability Analysis of Recursive Positional Substitution Based on Prime-Non Prime Encryption Technique

Gaurav Gambhir[✉] and J. K. Mandal

University of Kalyani, Kalyani, West Bengal, India
gambhirgaurav9@gmail.com

Abstract. The paper reports shared memory implementation of Recursive Positional Substitution Based on Prime-Nonprime (RPSP) algorithm using OpenMP application programming interface. Recursive Positional Substitution Based on Prime-Nonprime (RPSP) is a secret-key cryptosystem that helps to protect electronic data, while transmitting over internet. Cryptography provides techniques for information authenticity, confidentiality and integrity, but at the same time implementing cryptographic algorithm involves challenges such as speed of execution, processor and memory requirements. Shared memory implementation of cryptographic algorithms exploiting the immense computational power provided by modern multicore architecture improves the performance of these algorithms. This paper proposes a parallel programming model of RPSP algorithm using OpenMP directives, runtime library routines and environment variables. Scalability analysis of the proposed parallel algorithm has been presented for encryption/decryption of different sizes of standard image eso1705a taken from the database provided online by European Southern Observatory(ESO). Results obtained confirm approximately linear scalability for both encryption/decryption phases of the parallelized algorithms.

Keywords: OpenMP · Encryption · Decryption ·
Parallel programming

1 Introduction

Data and information transmission through computer networks is increasing day by day at a very fast rate. Ecommerce, banking, financial and legal transactions are all happening over computer networks. Secure transmission of data and information over network is an uttermost requirement at moment. Symmetric and Asymmetric encryption algorithms used to meet the security requirements limit the speed of the transactions which is an upcoming challenge in this rising smart era. Parallelization of the one such cryptographic algorithm is explored and implemented as a solution to the problem.

© Springer Nature Singapore Pte Ltd. 2019
J. K. Mandal et al. (Eds.): CICBA 2018, CCIS 1031, pp. 441–449, 2019.
https://doi.org/10.1007/978-981-13-8581-0_35

Recursive Positional Substitution Based on Prime-Nonprime (RPSP) is a cryptographic algorithm that provide secure data transmission and hides sensitive data. This algorithm was first proposed by Dutta, S. et al. in their article which presents information Security using 252-Bit Integrated Encryption System (IES) using RPSP algorithm [1]. This symmetric block cipher algorithm provides high level security to electronic data [2]. The same RPSP technique was later used by Dasgupta et al. in image encryption [3], they proposed an algorithm that decomposes the original image into its binary bit-planes using bit-plane slicing. The bit-planes are encrypted by performing an XOR operation with a selected bit-plane of the key-image one by one. Scrambling method which uses RPSP is applied to all the resultant bitplanes and then invert the order of bit-planes. The encrypted image is obtained by combining all the bit planes.

In addition to security, the speed of a cryptographic algorithm plays an important role in real time application where we need faster encryption and decryption process. With the advent of multicore systems, parallel programming can facilitate the speed up of computationally complex cryptographic algorithms. [4–8] An overview of four high performance computing techniques, OpenMP, CUDA, MapReduce and MPI has been reported by Ansari et al. [9]. The goal of authors was to explore literature on the subject and provide a high level view of the features presented in the programming models to assist high performance users with a concise understanding of parallel programming concepts. Authors conclude that if the computing resources such as cores and memory are sufficient, OpenMP is a good choice.

In this paper we use software approach based on transformation of serial version of RPSP code in parallel using OpenMP. We divided the data into n number of units and created one thread per unit and assigned these threads to processors. This is called data parallelism. The proposed parallel algorithm has been tested for encryption/decryption of different sizes of standard image eso1705a taken from database provided online by European Southern Observatory (ESO) [10].

We measured speed up factor of serial and the parallel code. Parallelizing algorithms using OpenMP are gaining widespread importance as it is a simple and flexible interface for developing parallel applications on a wide range of platforms including Unix/Linux and Windows. Significant speed up in many benchmark computation problems has been obtained by using OpenMP directives. GNU GCC C/C++ FORTRAN compiler makes this implementations available to the general programmers [11–14].

The paper is organized as follows: Introduction to the problem have been discussed in Sect. 1. Section 2 gives the details of serial version of RPSP algorithm. Section 3 gives detail of parallelization of RPSP algorithm, Sect. 4 provides the details of implementation and analysis of results. Finally conclusions are drawn in Sect. 5.

2   RPSP Algorithm

Recursive Positional Substitution based on Prime-nonprime of cluster or RPSP, is a secret-key cryptosystem. The encryption and decryption process of the algorithm is as follows:

2.1   RPSP Encryption

In this technique, after decomposing the source stream of bits into a finite number of blocks of finite length, the positions of the bits of each of the blocks is re-oriented using a generating function. For a particular length of block, the block itself is regenerated after a finite number of such iterations. Any of the intermediate blocks during this cycle is considered to be the encrypted block. To decrypt the encrypted block from the cipher text, the same process is to be followed but the generating function may have to be applied different number of times.

RPSP encryption works by considering a block of data and by performing bit replacement operations as shown in the flowchart Fig. 1.

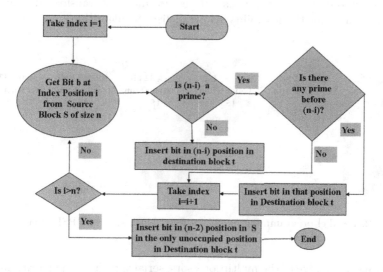

Fig. 1. Flow diagram of RPSP technique [1]

For a block of finite size n, a finite number of iterations are required to regenerate the source block. The number of iterations for encryption depend on the iterations required to generate the source block. If the block generated after the pth iteration in the cycle $(1 \leq p \leq (I - 1), I$ being the total number of iterations required to form the cycle) is considered to be the encrypted block, number of iterations required to decrypt the encrypted block is (I-p).

To achieve the security of a satisfactory level, it is proposed that different blocks or blocks should be of different sizes. Accordingly, for different blocks, number of iterations during the encryption and the number of iterations during the decryption also not necessarily should be fixed.

2.2 RPSP Decryption

The process of decryption is also a sub set of the entire set of work required to form the cycle for the block. The only difference is that one intermediate block of the cycle (the encrypted block) is considered to be the source block in the process of decryption.

3   Parallelization of RPSP

While parallelize an algorithm, the very important thing about algorithm to know is memory-boundness or computing-boundness. In short, a algorithm is memory-bound if it contains a few computational operations per 1 memory access. Otherwise, algorithm is called compute-bound. RPSP encryption algorithm is compute-bound and does not require memory transfers and synchronization. This gives the feasibility to parallelize the algorithm.

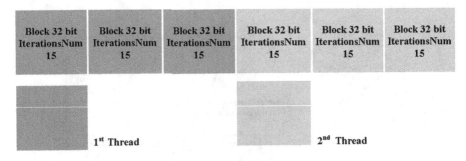

Fig. 2. Parallel programming model for fixed block sizes in RPSP encryption

To take advantage of the multiprocessors, serial version of an algorithm needs to be modified. The autonomous parts of the algorithms must be identified as mentioned in parallel computations paradigms [15], and then work is to be assigned to separate threads. Initially the RPSP algorithm is divided into parallelizable and un-parallelelizable parts. The two portions of the program are joined using the fork-join model.

Concurrency and parallelism are closely related terms but distinct concepts. Concurrency means multiple tasks are logically active at a time and parallelism means multiple tasks are actually executing at a time. OpenMP research is relevant for the parallel application in which by introducing parallelism, we can

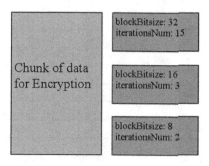

Fig. 3. Parallel programming model for variable block sizes in RPSP encryption

execute the programs faster. For that we need to find concurrency in programs which make the parallel execution of multiple tasks feasible. Concurrency in RPSP encryption algorithm has been found out in terms of splitting the data into chunks, dividing chunks into blocks and assigning chunks to threads. The resulting code is platform independent and the number of cores could be specified while executing the program.

Splitting of the blocks can be accomplished in two ways - (i) When all the block are of the same size Fig. 2 (ii) When the blocks are of different sizes Fig. 3. Comparative analysis of the execution time when the blocks are of different sizes with different number of threads has been presented. Although improvement in computational complexity with same and small size blocks is significant but it could lead to not very efficient security with RPSP. Different size blocks offer better security albeit enhancing computational complexity. Nevertheless, parallel programming with Open MP API improves performance for different sized blocks as evidenced in Tables 1, 2 and Figs. 4, 5.

4   Results

In the experimentation following system configuration is used - Intel$^{(R)}$ Core $^{(TM)}$ i7-3610QM CPU @ 2.30 GHz, processor with RAM of 8.00 GB (3.67 usable) (4-cores), 8 Logical Processor(s)in 64 bit Linux operating environment.

Significant speed up in parallelization of the RPSP algorithm is achieved by splitting the data into chunks and then the chunks into blocks which could be of same or different sizes. We have considered different size blocks in order to achieve high level of security. The chunks of data are then assigned to the threads. The basic operations/functions of bit replacements for every block is then performed by all the threads. Since this parallel programming model is a fork-join model, the encrypted data from all the thread is collected and combined at the end to make one encrypted file. This is achieved by using # pragma openmp directives. Here these are used with the static scheduler because otherwise manual optimization may degrade the performance. Standard image eso1705a from ESO(Euopropean Southern Observatory) image database with sizes: 443.1 KB,

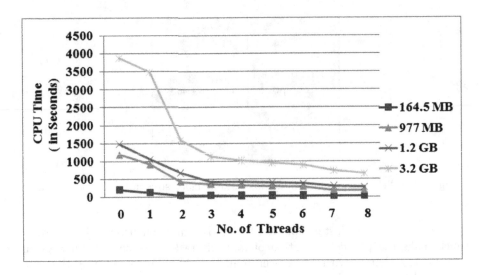

Fig. 4. Scalability analysis for RPSP encryption time of large size images using different no. of OpenMP threads. Here 0 refers to the serial execution time

4.3 MB, 48.3 MB, 164.5 MB, 977 MB, 1.2 GB and 3.2 GB have been considered as test images for computing the speed up in parallel RPSP encryption algorithm with 1 to 8 threads.

Figures 4 and 5 show the significant speed up while executing the parallel version of the code with threads starting from 1 to maximum 8 threads for encryption and decryption of standard image with image sizes ranging from 164.5 MB, 977 MB, 1.2 GB to 3.2 GB. Comparison of the execution times for encryption and decryption of 443.1 KB, 4.3 MB and 48.3 MB have not been shown for maintaining the clarity in the graph.

Table 1. Comparison of execution times of sequential and parallel code for encryption

File size	File type	Serial	1 Thread	2 Threads	3 Threads	4 Threads	5 Threads	6 Threads	7 Threads	8 Threads
443.1 KB	JPEG	0.569275	0.520471	0.261711	0.186148	0.17676	0.16536	0.16063	0.15543	0.14284
4.3 MB	JPEG	5.07477	4.70019	2.3224	1.5316	1.43397	1.40748	1.32931	1.31313	1.27041
48.3 MB	TIFF	58.6293	50.1674	13.7707	11.81201	9.55642	8.80214	7.3576	7.03584	6.64647
164.5 MB	TIFF	193.949	114.124	42.3367	36.9452	31.0045	29.8262	26.0889	24.7909	22.6062
977 MB	JPEG	1185.36	909.437	426.38	357.904	330.186	297.005	282.345	186.881	182.94
1.2 GB	TIFF	1469.28	1040.36	673.957	410.269	408.21	393.491	363.075	295.881	270.733
3.2 GB	TIFF	3874.32	3480.16	1577.89	1133.06	1017.103	94.432	883.07	722.696	650.106

Hence, the parallel programming model for RPSP allows the processing of even larger images in reasonable times. We have also shown that the new design is able to achieve greater efficiency and scalability. It is worth specifying that the execution of the parallel version of program with different number of the

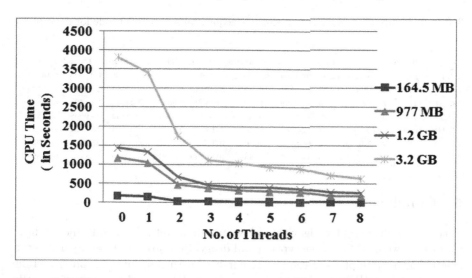

Fig. 5. Scalability analysis for RPSP decryption time of large size images using different no. of OpenMP threads. Here 0 refers to the serial execution time

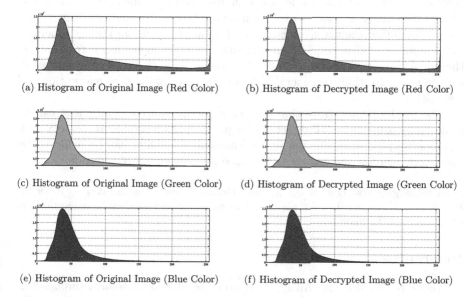

(a) Histogram of Original Image (Red Color)   (b) Histogram of Decrypted Image (Red Color)

(c) Histogram of Original Image (Green Color)   (d) Histogram of Decrypted Image (Green Color)

(e) Histogram of Original Image (Blue Color)   (f) Histogram of Decrypted Image (Blue Color)

Fig. 6. RGB image (eso1705a.jpg, size:4.3 Mb) histogram analysis of the original and the decrypted image (Color figure online)

threads were carried out in stand alone mode and the average CPU time without I/O, after 5 consecutive executions has been reported. Histogram analysis of the sample image in Fig. 6 validates the design of the parallelized algorithm.

Table 2. Comparison of execution times of sequential and parallel code for decryption

File size	File type	Serial	1 Thread	2 Threads	3 Threads	4 Threads	5 Threads	6 Threads	7 Threads	8 Threads
443.1 KB	JPEG	0.576628	0.521652	0.275549	0.185802	0.17869	0.16235	0.16564	0.15235	0.14452
4.3 MB	JPEG	5.43887	5.01895	2.18322	1.71823	1.44914	1.40337	1.32299	1.31521	1.28399
48.3 MB	TIFF	57.8966	42.8076	13.9528	11.9488	9.61169	8.5649	7.3324	7.0142	6.6641
164.5 MB	TIFF	180.514	166.029	43.899	36.3072	31.3716	29.4023	26.4152	24.0008	22.2897
977 MB	JPEG	1175.86	1049.22	474.84	388.673	332.787	297.534	281.264	187.631	184.697
1.2 GB	TIFF	1435.5	1337.32	682.969	470.937	403.806	403.092	364.981	279.904	265.058
3.2 GB	TIFF	3812.12	3414.25	1753.87	1118.67	1033.399	935.822	893.285	715.787	643.896

5 Conclusion

Speed of a cryptographic algorithm plays an important role in real time application where we need faster encryption and decryption process. This paper present shared memory implementation of Recursive Positional Substitution Based on Prime-Nonprime(RPSP) algorithm using OpenMP parallel programming API. OpenMP directives were used to parallelize the serial RPSP algorithm. The concept of OpenMP fork-join model was then used to merge the parts of code. The comparative analysis between execution times of sequential and parallelized programs shows that their is significant speed up after parallelization with increase in the number of threads. The implementation of the algorithm carried out on the multi core processor with multiple threads show that the applying parallelization in algorithms considerably boosts the time of the data encryption and decryption.

The results demonstrate that noticeable performance enhancement can be achieved by using OpenMP directives for parallelization on shared memory multiprocessing platforms. Further improvement in scalability can be achieved by using vectorization and hot spot analysis during execution of the code.

Acknowledgments. One of the authors Gaurav Gambhir is grateful to Emeritus Professor Pradosh K. Roy for his technical guidance and invaluable suggestions in preparation of the manuscript.

References

1. Dutta, S., Mandal, J.K.: An approach to ensure information security through 252-bit integrated encryption system (IES). IACR Cryptology ePrint Archive, p. 360 (2008)
2. Dutta, S.: An approach towards development of efficient encryption technique. Ph.D. thesis. University of North Bengal, India (2004)
3. Dasgupta, M., Mandal, J.K.: Bit-plane oriented image encryption through prime-nonprime based positional substitution (BPIEPNPS). Int. J. Comput. Sci. Eng. **4**(6), 65–70 (2016)
4. Sathawane, V., Diwan, T.: An optimized parallel computation of advanced encryption algorithm using open MP - a review. Int. J. Adv. Res. Comput. Commun. Eng. **5**(2), 384–386 (2016)

5. Nagendra, M., Sekhar, M.C.: Performance improvement of advanced encryption algorithm using parallel computation. Int. J. Softw. Eng. Appl. **8**(2), 287–296 (2014)
6. Kasahara, H., Narita, S.: Practical multiprocessor scheduling algorithms for efficient parallel processing. IEEE Trans. Comput. **33**(11), 1023–1029 (1984)
7. Harika, A.V., Saranya, T., Moorthi, M.N.: Performance analysis of encryption algorithm for network security on parallel computing environment. Int. J. Sci. Res. Dev. **7**(18), 9–9873 (2014)
8. Liu, B., Baas, B.M.: Parallel AES encryption engines for many-core processor arrays. IEEE Trans. Comput. **62**(3), 536–547 (2013)
9. Ansari, Z., Afzal, A., Muhiuddeen, M., Nayak, S.: Literature survey for the comparative study of various high performance computing techniques. Int. J. Comput. Trends Technol. (IJCTT) **27**(2), 80–86 (2015)
10. Source. http://www.eso.org/public/images/eso1705a/
11. Chandra, R.: Parallel Programming in OpenMP. Morgan Kaufmann, Burlington (2001)
12. Chapman, B., Jost, G., Van Der Pas, R.: Using OpenMP: Portable Shared Memory Parallel Programming. MIT Press, Cambridge (2008)
13. Mattson, T.G., Sanders, B., Massingill, B.: Patterns for Parallel Programming. Pearson Education, London (2004)
14. Kim, J., Yoo, T., Yeom, Y., Yi, O.: New entropy source for cryptographic modules using openMP in multicore CPUs. Int. J. Secur. Appl. **7**(4), 445–452 (2013)
15. Tudor, B. M., Teo, Y. M.: A practical approach for performance analysis of shared-memory programs. In: 2011 IEEE International Parallel & Distributed Processing Symposium (IPDPS), pp. 652–663 (2011)

An Approach to DNA Cryptography Using 10 × 10 Playfair Cipher

Swapnil Banerjee[1]([✉]), Rajarshi Roychowdhury[1], Moumita Sarkar[1],
Pradipta Roy[1,2], and Debashis De[2,3]

[1] Department of Computer Science and Engineering,
Swami Vivekananda Institute of Science and Technology, Dakshin Gobindapur,
P.S.: Sonarpur, Kolkata 700145, India
Swapnilbanerjee9@gmail.com, pradiptoroy@gmail.com
[2] Department of Computer Science and Engineering,
Maulana Abul Kalam Azad University of Technology, BF-142, Sector-1,
Salt Lake City 700064, Kolkata, India
[3] Department of Physics, University of Western Australia,
M013, 35 Stirling Highway, Crawley, Perth, WA 6009, Australia

Abstract. Nowadays, sensitive information is conveyed over public communication medium, where data security is an enormous problem and cryptography is the ideal mechanism to handle it. DNA cryptography is a modern cryptographic way to conceal data in terms of DNA. The rudimentary purpose of this cipher is to enhance the security features of classical playfair and making it more robust by applying DNA encoding. The duplets, in the original message are considered as a single unit and transformed into respective medialcipher text duplet. DNA encoding with interweaving step is applied on medialcipher text. Therefore, the terminalcipher text is a DNA sequence of data, which leaves a very thin relation between the original message and terminalcipher text, and makes this encryption technique more stochastic. Further, some performance analysis of the proposed cipher has been explained to get a clear view about the method.

Keywords: Cipher · Playfair · Duplets · Medialcipher · Interweaving ·
Terminalcipher · DNA cryptography

1 Introduction

Cryptography is a method to conceal original message for a secure communication in presence of adversaries. In 1900 BC it was started in Egypt with some hieroglyphs wordings. It has two main Components: Cryptographic process and Authentication and Integrity. Cryptographic process is the practice of concealing messages so that, they are unreadable other than the intended recipient. Authentication and Integrity ensures that users of the data are the persons they claim to be and the message has not been secretly altered. The cryptographic process consists of two procedure encryption and decryption. The algorithm which develops both encryption and decryption pair are called cipher, which is controlled by the algorithm and another secret component called key (Fig. 1).

© Springer Nature Singapore Pte Ltd. 2019
J. K. Mandal et al. (Eds.): CICBA 2018, CCIS 1031, pp. 450–461, 2019.
https://doi.org/10.1007/978-981-13-8581-0_36

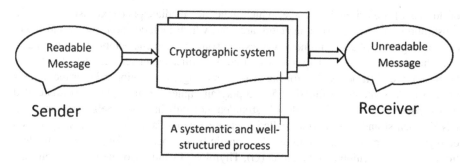

Fig. 1. Schematic view of cryptography.

The classical ciphers are of two types such as, substitution cipher which substitutes each character with different character to generate the cipher text, whereas in transposition cipher plaintext characters are shifted in some regular pattern to form cipher text [1].

Modern cryptography algorithms are classified into two parts: Symmetric key and Public key. Symmetric-key cryptography is the method in which both the sender and recipient share the one and the same key for encryption process as well as decryption process and potentiality of algorithm is determined by the size of the key. On contrast, in public-key cryptography mathematically related two different keys are used such as, a public key which can be distributed freely and a private key which is kept confidential to the sender [2].

Playfair cipher is a renowned symmetric substitution cipher which encrypts pairs of letters called duplet. This cipher uses a 5 × 5 substitution matrix that is created using a key and the ciphering process is performed out with some rules. Substitution matrix is able to accommodate only 25 letters keeping an option between I and J. Playfair cipher with these simple rules is still significantly hard to break. Although it holds a limit for the original message to be formed alphabets without numbers and punctuations [3]. In Recent days, some methods have been proposed in cryptography to enhance the security of the playfair cipher. An extended 8 × 8 playfair cipher method was proposed which was able to encrypt alphabets, some special characters and numbers. The symbols '|' and '^' are used to handle spaces and duplicate characters [4]. Another method appeared based on the ASCII values of characters. But in both the cases, 64 spots in the matrix were not enough to accommodate all the useful characters for the plain text [5]. Later, a generalized 8 × 16 playfair cipher was suggested, which considered the 128 ASCII characters [6]. Another 8 × 8 playfair cipher technique was proposed using codon substitution matrix, where the original message is grouped into codon triplets and the encryption is performed using the 8 × 8 substitution matrix [7]. Some others technique has been introduced which involves image encryption using DNA where a reference one DNA sequence is used for hiding data and another is used for embedding purpose [8]. Another image encryption technique was introduced using integer wavelet transform where spatial domain algorithm is applied to frequency domain [9]. Research is still going on to overcome the flaws in playfair cipher, and DNA cryptography is one of them. The proposed method initiates with an encryption of duplets of the original message, which generates medialcipher text, using 10×10 substitution matrix i.e., 100 characters are used which includes both upper and lower case of English alphabets, numeric values and some special characters including space. The character 'æ' (Latin: Dipthong) is used as a filler character between the double letter and in end (if necessary) for the original message. Encryption rule for the duplets of message is same as the classical 5×5 playfair cipher. Medialcipher text is encoded into a sequence of DNA. It is a double stranded molecule in double helix structure [10]. DNA's each strand is a polymer called nucleotide which is made up of a sugar called deoxyribose, a phosphate group and an organic base. There are four types of nucleotides, such as, Adenine (A), Guanine (G), Thymine (T) and Cytosine (C). Therefore, a sequence of DNA nucleotides pairs can be represented as a string made of these four characters i.e., ATGGCTGACTAAATCGTACCT. DNA is not only constrained to transfer and store data, it can be used performing computation [11]. The massive repository space, enormous parallelism can be utilized in methods of cryptography. The primitive convention behind DNA computing is DNA nucleotide base to binary conversion. Some rules are adopted according to Table 1 to convert DNA strings into binary values and vice versa.

For instance,

DNA sequence: ATGGCTGACTAAATCGTACCT

Binary Equivalent: 001110100111100001110000001101101100010111

Table 1. DNA codes.

Bases	A	C	G	T
Bits	00	01	10	11

Further an interweaving process is applied to scramble the DNA sequence. DNA sequence after the interweaving process is the terminalcipher text.

2 Motivation

In recent years, DNA cryptography has evolved as an optimistic approach in cryptography, which works on the concept of DNA computing that was introduced in the year 1994 by Leonard Adleman. DNA computing uses the properties of DNA such as faster computation, lower power dissipation and huge storage space for computing problems. Adopting these properties of DNA computing, DNA cryptography ensures a faster transmission of data over a secured network using less storage space. Researches are going on to overcome the flaws of traditional cryptography algorithms by using DNA cryptography. The proposed method overcomes the flaws of playfair cipher and forms a robust algorithm by using DNA cryptography.

3   Contribution

- The basic approach of the proposed method is to encrypt all types of commonly used characters including space in text files by reducing pre-processing for original message.
- The algorithm implements the properties of DNA computing in classical 5 × 5 playfair cipher. Therefore, the final encrypted message will be transferred in form of DNA which assures higher rate of data transmission in a lesser amount of time.
- The decryption operation ensures the return of exact original message.

4   Comparative Study

See Table 2.

Table 2. A comparative study between different playfair based ciphering methods.

Features	Method			
	Traditional & Existing Method			Proposed method
	Classical 5 × 5	Playfair Cipher by using 8 × 8 Matrix and Random Number Generation[4]	Playfair Cipher involving Intertwining, Interweaving and Iteration [6]	DNA Cryptography using 10 × 10 Playfair Cipher
Secret Message	English Alphabets (A–Z) keeping an option between I and J	Alphabets (A–Z), Numbers (0–9), Some special characters	128 ASCII characters	English Alphabets (A–Z, a–z), Numbers (0–9), all useful special characters including space
Plaintext pre-processing	Spaces are removed. 'X' is used to stuff between double letters and if necessary append in end	Spaces are replaced with |. Use ^ for stuffing double alphabets and if necessary append in end	Not specified	No pre-processing required for space. Diphthong (æ) is used as filler letter between double letters and if necessary append in end

(*continued*)

Table 2. (*continued*)

Key	25 characters i.e. English alphabets (A–Z)	64 characters i.e. English Alphabets (A–Z, a–z), Numerics and some special characters	128 ASCII characters	100 characters which includes all characters used for text
Form of Cipher Text	Textual without space, double letters, and special characters	Textual	Textual	DNA sequence
Length of Cipher Text	Same as plaintext	33% more than plaintext	25% more than plaintext	400% more than plaintext
Advantages	Simple and easy to use manually	Extended character set allowed, strong cipher and increased randomness using LFSR	Extended character set allowed. Strong due to interweaving, intertwining and iterations	Extended character set allowed, much less correlation between original message and ciphered text. Robust against cryptanalytic attack

5 Flowchart

The schematic diagram gives a synopsis of the proposed approach i.e., how the original message is encrypted using the proposed algorithm and decrypted back to the original message from terminalcipher text. Message is first encrypted into medialcipher text (intermediate cipher text) and then it is encrypted into terminalcipher text i.e., final encrypted form of the message (Fig. 2).

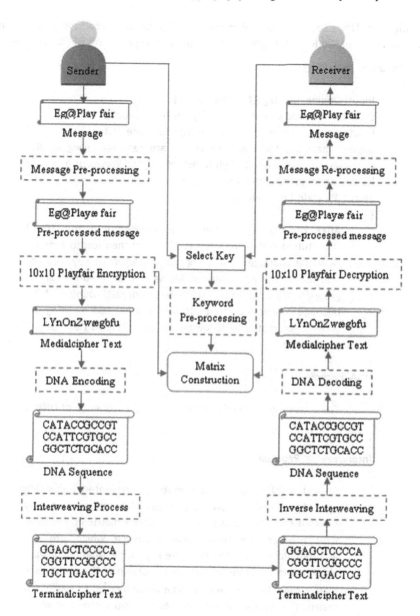

Fig. 2. Flowchart of the proposed method.

6 Proposed Algorithm

The proposed cipher is an approach in DNA cryptography, which remodels the classical 5 × 5 playfair cipher using DNA computing. The cipher initiates with a pre-processing step, where the message and the keyword are pre-processed. After that, the 10 × 10 substitution matrix is created using keyword and the message is encrypted into medialcipher text. Now, the medialcipher text is converted into a DNA sequence in the DNA encoding step. DNA sequence is further scrambled using an interweaving process by generating a stochastic terminalcipher text i.e., final encrypted form of the message.

dnacrypto_palyfair()
{

> **Input: Original message(M), Keyword(K)**
> Original message(M) and keyword(K) is taken as input.
> Input are pre-processed for removing duplicate letters. In case of original message, the duplicate letters are removed using a filler character 'æ' (Latin word: diphthong). In case of keyword, duplicate letters are removed without using keyword.
>
> **10×10_Playfair_Encryption()**
> {
>
>> After pre-processing keyword is inserted into the 10×10 substitution matrix from left to right and then top to bottom. Now the characters excluding the characters in keyword are inserted in the same manner. Message after pre-processing is grouped into a pair of two characters or duplets. Duplets of the message is now encrypted into medialcipher text by using the substitution matrix by following the same rule as classical 5×5 playfair cipher.
>
> }
>
> **DNA_Encoding()**
> {
>
>> The conversion of medialcipher text into a sequence of DNA is done.
>
> }
>
> **Interweaving_Process()**
> {
>
>> At first a interweave square matrix is generated depending upon the length of DNA sequence. DNA sequence is now inserted from the reverse into the square matrix in a column wise manner. Remaining DNA sequence which are not accommodated into the matrix are kept aside. Now, an upward circular rotation is performed on 1st column of the interweave matrix, then, left circular rotation is performed on 1st row of the matrix. These rotations are repeated till it is performed in all the rows and columns of the matrix. The interweave matrix is now represented in form of a sequence, and the remaining DNA sequence in reverse order is appended with the matrix generated sequence. Thus, the terminalcipher text is generated.
>
> }
>
> **Output()**
> {
>
>> Terminalcipher text is generated after the encryption procedure which is transferred to the receiver.
>
> }

6.1 Samples of the Proposed Method Steps and Output for Encryption Process

See Fig. 3.

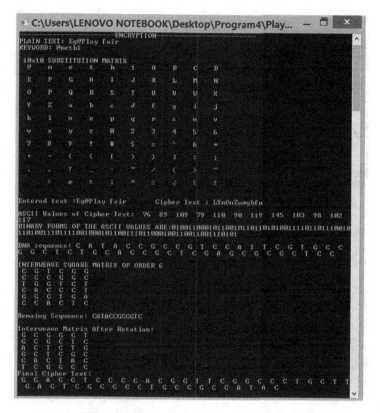

Fig. 3. Sample of steps of encryption implementations

6.2 Samples of the Proposed Method Steps and Output for Decryption Process

See Fig. 4.

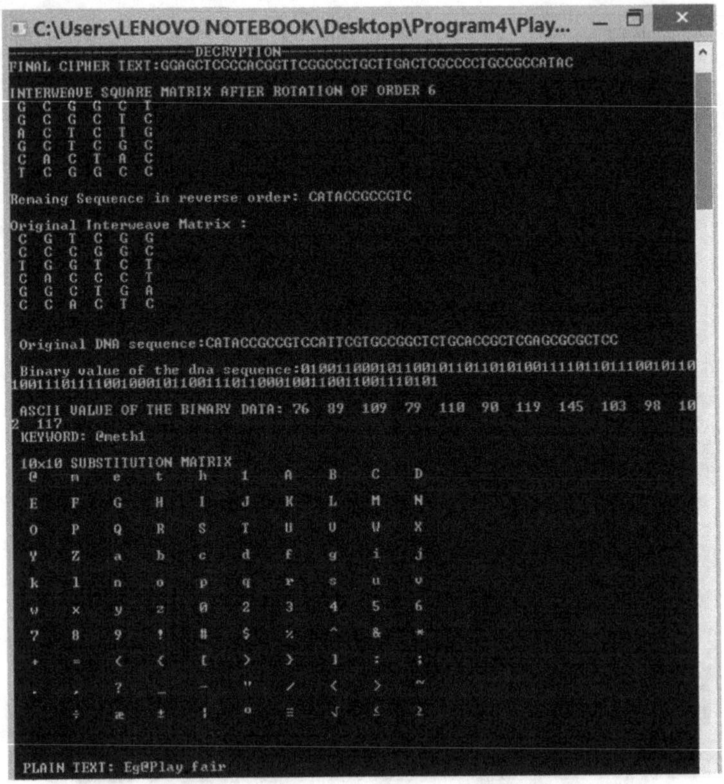

Fig. 4. Sample of steps of decryption implementations

7   Results and Analysis

Graphical analysis of the proposed method is represented based on sets of data which compares some of the specific parameters of the method. In Fig. 5, the graph compares the length of plain text with respect to the length of terminalcipher text. The length of the terminalcipher text increases with the increases in the size of plain text, therefore from the computational point of view it makes tougher for an attacker to decode the original message. The graph shown in Fig. 6 compares the execution time of the algorithm with the size of plain text for encryption. It is very obvious that the execution time will increase with the increasing characters in the plain text. But the lesser amount of preprocessing for the message in the beginning makes it faster compared to other techniques. In Fig. 7, the graph compares the execution time of the algorithm with the size of plain text for decryption. The execution time for decryption is comparatively faster than encryption. Therefore, these graphical analyses give a clear view about the performance of this algorithm based on various types of input.

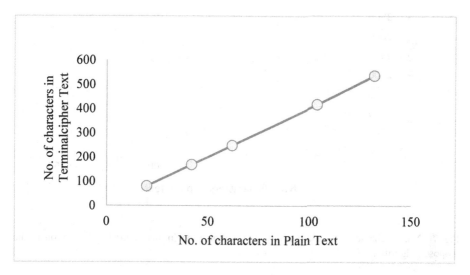

Fig. 5. No. of characters in Cipher Text vs Plain Text for the proposed algorithm

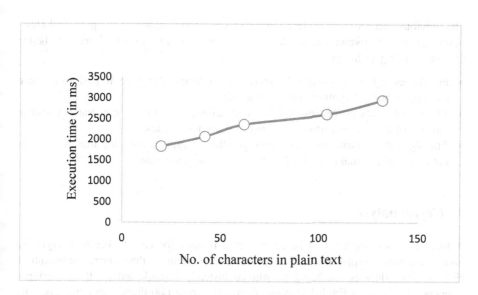

Fig. 6. No. of characters in plain text vs. Execution time (in millisecond) for encryption in the proposed algorithm

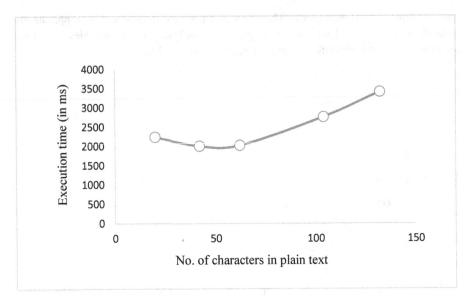

Fig. 7. No. of characters in plain text vs. Execution time (millisecond) for decryption in the proposed algorithm.

8 Performance of the System

The previous section gives a clear view about the performance of the proposed algorithm; the method overcomes the flaws of the other techniques which make it better than the existing techniques.

- Pre-processing of the original message is reduced; therefore it performs faster encryption and decryption compared to other.
- The system uses properties of DNA computing, for which it can transfer higher amount of data in less time compared to other techniques.
- The algorithm returns the exact message after decryption ensuring that there is no data loss, which makes easier for the receiver to understand.

9 Cryptanalysis

A technique is considered to be secure, if it is hard for an attacker to decrypt its implementation. Cryptanalysis of playfair cipher is difficult than normal substitution ciphers, since duplets are being substituted instead of single letters. If we perform frequency analysis on English duplets, there are almost 600 duplets in comparison to 26 single letter. So, the possibility of occurrence of any particular character in 5×5 Playfair is $1/26 = 0.0384$, although in 10×10 playfair matrix the chance of appearance of an element is $1/100 \approx 0.001$, making the frequency analysis a tougher job. Furthermore, the medialcipher text is encoded into DNA sequence. Another step, i.e., interweaving process scrambles the encrypted sequence at nucleotide level in the proposed cipher to strengthen it against any attacks.

10 Conclusion

The proposed cipher is an implementation of 10 × 10 playfair using DNA encoding. This modification is introduced to enhance the security of classical playfair. The proposed method does not require any pre-processing for space, and a DNA encoding step with interweaving process is used to strengthen the security of the method. Therefore, it is impossible for an attacker to perform frequency analysis as it leaves very few clues leading to playfair cipher.

Acknowledgements. The authors are grateful to The University Grants Commission, India, for the project under the UGC Major Project File No. 41-631/2012(SR).

References

1. David, K.: The Codebreakers – The Story of Secret Writing. Macmillan, New York (1967)
2. Whitfield, D., Martin, E.H.: Multiuser cryptographic techniques. In: Proceedings of the June 7–10, 1976, National Computer Conference and Exposition. ACM, New York (1976)
3. Stallings, W.: Cryptography and Network Security Principles and Practice, 4th edn. Pearson Education, Asia (2005)
4. Srivastava, S.S., Gupta, N., Jaiswal, R.: Modified version of playfair cipher by using 8 x 8 matrix and random number generation. In: IEEE 3rd International Conference on Computer Modeling and Simulation, Mumbai (2011)
5. Srivastava, S.S., Gupta, N.: A novel approach to security using extended playfair cipher. Int. Comput. Appl. **20**(6), 0975–8887 (2011)
6. Sastry, V.U.K., Shankar, N.R., Durga, S.B.: A generalized playfair cipher involving intertwining, interweaving and iteration. Int. J. Net. Mobile Technol. **1**(2) 45–53 (2010)
7. Hamad, S.: A novel implementation of an extended 8 x 8 playfair cipher using interweaving on DNA-encoded data. Int. J. Electr. Comput. Eng. **4**(1), 93 (2014)
8. Khalifa, A., Elhadad, A., Hamad, S.: Secure blind data hiding into pseudo DNA sequences using playfair ciphering and generic complementary substitution. Appl. Math. Inf. Sci **10**, 1483–1492 (2016)
9. Chakravarthy, S., Venkatesan, S.P., Anand, J.M., Ranjani, J.J.: Enhanced playfair cipher for image encryption using integer wavelet transform. Indian J. Sci. Technol. **9**(39), 1–12 (2016)
10. Watson, J.D., Crick, F.H.: The structure of DNA. In: Cold Spring Harbor Symposia on Quantitative Biology, vol. 18, pp. 123–131. Cold Spring Harbor Laboratory Press, January 1953
11. Adleman, L.M.: Computing with DNA. Sci. Am. **279**(2), 54–61 (1998)

Study of Information Diffusion and Content Popularity in Memes

Bani Maji, Indra Bhattacharya, Kaustav Nag$^{(\boxtimes)}$,
Ujjwal Prabhat Mishra, and Kousik Dasgupta

Department of CSE, Kalyani Government Engineering College, Kalyani, India
kaustav.nag24@gmail.com

Abstract. The tremendous use of internet, mobile platforms, online commerce sites, social media services, human behavior is very easily recorded in digital world. From these information various facts can be observed, like, in which discussion in online social network we participate, with whom we communicate the most, how we download or buy something from online e-commerce sites, are we influenced by certain classes of people etc. The major crux in all these activities are sharing of information and its diffusion. The study of the information diffusion has become a challenging proposition for the research fraternity. Some of these discussions sometimes becomes more popular and is called as meme. Modern research trends also show study of content popularity of these memes. The proposition becomes more challenging due to the fact that the information changes in real-time in the online social networks and the data generated is very huge or big data. In this paper a study is made to analyse how a piece of information spreads over the internet, and how some topics get very popular while others fade away. The approach in the paper begins with social network analysis (SNA) of the data to analyze and investigate underlying social structure. Then this information is used to detect most frequently used phrases and quotes or memes that becomes more popular across any communications over time. The results of the work are reported and compared with some recent study. The efficacy of the work is more evident as the approach is studied in not only standard data set but also in real time data.

Keywords: Information diffusion · Memes · Social network analysis (SNA) · Community detection · K-means

1 Introduction

With the extensive use of social network, huge amount of data is shared across social media (e.g., YouTube, Sina-Wibo and Twitter) every moment. These shared data become topic of discussion or a meme. Not all the topic or meme become popular. By detecting popular topics, it can be determined what people around the world are talking about, what may be the breaking news at a particular time etc. Off late researchers have become more interested to study this Big Data so that people can understand the spreading of information better, and then use this for optimizing business performance (marketing campaigns) and solving important issues such as natural hazards, terrorist attacks etc. [1]. Through this information we can observe not only individual behavioral patterns, but also interaction and communication among mass by investigating the Big Data.

© Springer Nature Singapore Pte Ltd. 2019
J. K. Mandal et al. (Eds.): CICBA 2018, CCIS 1031, pp. 462–478, 2019.
https://doi.org/10.1007/978-981-13-8581-0_37

Presently the information diffusion research domain is categorized into explanatory models and predictive models. Where the former, explanatory models thrive to retrace the spreading path of the information in Social Networks. Most of the research in this domain focuses on the measurement and analysis of the network structures [2–4] and the study of user interactions spreading characteristics using data mining [5, 6] and statistical modeling schemes [7, 8]. Other studies done by researchers is in exploring the predictive model. Where the model predicts how a specific information diffusion process would unfold in a given social network, based on the empirical results of the past process of the information spreading. Recognition of topics in the online scenario and social media have been studied extensively in [9–13]. Some of them include grouping of short and distinctive phrases by single-rooted directed acyclic graphs used as signatures for memes or topics [9, 10]. Feature extraction from content and metadata [11–13] as well as discovery of clusters in correlated keywords are also studied [11, 14].

In the era of digital communication, memes are very common now days. A meme can be a concept, an idea or a piece of information that is shared from one to another through social ties. The work in the papers aims to study how different stories compete for news and blog coverage each day and how certain stories persist and some simply fade away. The paper proposes use of SNA to analyze and investigate underlying social structure. Then detect most frequently used phrases and quotes that appear across internet over time. The results of the work have been on a dataset of Stanford Network Analysis Project [9].

1.1   Description of Dataset

The dataset contains information of articles like its article id, url, date of posting, quotes and phrases used in the article, url of link outs are present in the dataset. A snapshot of the data is as given below:

articles: 4,542,920 records, with the following fields:
article_id: a unique id for the article (int)
url: the URL of the article (text)
date: the date of the article (text), in the strptime format '%Y-%m-%d %H:%M:%S'

quotes: 7,956,125 records, with the following fields:
article_id: unique id for the article that this quote was found in (int)
phrase: the high-frequency phrase found in the article (text)

links: 16,727,125 records, with the following fields:
article_id: unique id for the article that this link was found in (int)
link_out: the URL of the link out (text)
link_out_id: unique id for the target article (int), if it exists; else NULL

The rest of the paper is organized as follows, Sect. 2 gives detailed description of use of SNA for investigation of underlying social structure in the data. The visualization results are depicted in the section. Section 3 details detection of memes using modified K-means algorithm. The trending topics are visualized using feature pivot method. Performance analysis and comparison of the proposed work is reported in Sect. 4. Finally, Sect. 5 concludes the paper with future scope.

2 Social Network Analysis (SNA) for Investigation of Underlying Social Structure in the Data

The first part of the proposed work investigates and analyzes structure of the social network generated from the dataset. The basic aim of any social network analysis (SNA) is to find the underlying social structure in the network. This social structure can be used to detect trending topics or popular memes from the network or the dataset. Because, if some pattern is found from the dataset (like communities), there is a good possibility that some topics can be extracted from the dataset and its popularity can be predicted in future. Such study of information diffusion in online social network consists of four critical components: actors, contents, underlying network structure and diffusion process.

The role of limited user attention plays a vital role in diffusion of online memes or topics. The wide adoption of online social media has increased the competition among ideas. It is very easily observed that people pays different attention among weak and strong ties. If one considers his/her Facebook network, they can observe they pay more attention on people with whom they are strongly connected or whom they know for a long time etc. From the studies of limited attention and weak tie hypothesis, it is known strong ties carry more information compared to weak ties, but weak ties act as bridges between distant communities and help propagate new information among groups.

Second component is content of the information. Here we try to detect topics in social media and how topical diversity affects content popularity. Information flows can be mapped in the topic space where each meme is represented as a node and community of memes forms a topic. So, one can learn topics by detecting communities in meme co-occurrence network. It is observed high topical diversity is good predictor of message popularity. It is also observed; people respond differently on a topic depending on whether it is a strong tie or a weak tie. A strong tie tends to respond a wider variety of topics while weak ties respond to only selective topics or popular topics. So, it can be concluded that popular topics are equally popular among strong and weak ties.

The future meme virality can be predicted by another hypothesis. We can say, a community of people, that is cluster of densely connected nodes are expected to trap information flow due to different reasons like structural trapping, homophil. A viral meme is less likely to be trapped from the early stage. The community detection in the dataset is explained in the section.

2.1 Community Detection

Detecting community structure in a meme co-occurrence network helps us understand which meme can get popular and which has chances of fading away. There are several algorithms used to detect communities for e.g. hierarchical clustering and betweenness clustering. Some other network properties are also studied which are used to analyze network structure like network diameter, page rank, graph density etc.

Further for the proposed community detection hypothesis and studies are done like influential user, dependence, herd behavior, information cascade, epidemic models etc.

The community detection is done by visualization of social network using a visualization tool Gephi [17]. Detailed analysis of the dataset was done to detect some patterns in the dataset. Some observations are:

1. Some quotes are common to many memes or articles. Two things can be concluded from here:
    (i) Memes using common quotes are related to each other
    (ii) A quote used in many memes is popular quotes that is used by many users. The results are given in form of visualization in Fig. 1
2. A community of memes or community of phrases represents a topic in the network. So, we have detected communities to identify different topics as visualized in Fig. 2.
3. From the description of dataset, it is also seen; many memes or articles used URLs that redirect the viewer to some web page that describes the content of that meme in detail. The web page may be some blog also. We hypothesized these two memes using a common link out are similar in terms of topic. We also detected which pages are referred by many memes while some pages are nearly isolated from the network and only referred by a small number of memes. The visualization is as given in Fig. 3.
4. By detecting communities of pages, we can similarly get an insight of the topic. Not only topic, we can also guess the trending topics. As detailed in Fig. 4.

Social network analysis of the dataset [9] has been represented as visualization in the next sections.

2.1.1 Visualization 1: Objective-Detecting Popular Phrases in a Meme vs. Phrase Network

Meme and Phrases network is visualized in Fig. 1 where blue nodes represent a phrase. Larger the node, more popular it is. Here popularity is represented by in-degree of a phrase. More the number of different memes use a particular Phrase, more its popularity. One reason to determine the most popular phrases in the network is phrases may also give us some insight about the topic. If it is a micro blogging meme, then it may only contain just a couple of phrases followed by a #hashtag and nothing else. In that case, the phrases solely represent the topic of that meme. Quotes table is used here for this visualization.

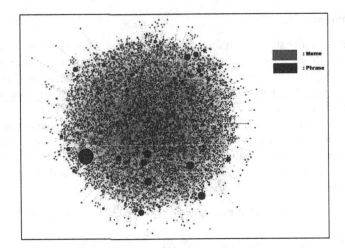

Fig. 1. Popular phrases in a meme network

2.1.2   Visualization 2: Objective-Detecting Community Structure in the Meme-Phrase Network

This result uses nearly 5700 quotes as given in Fig. 2. We used modularity for this purpose, each detectable community are numbered by some modularity class number. There were a large number of communities. Here only top giant communities (having maximum percentage of entities in it) are shown for better understanding the structure.

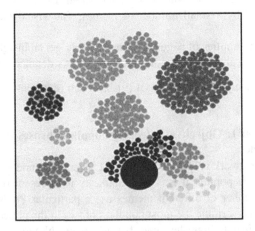

Fig. 2. Community structure in meme-phrase network. A community here is just a cluster of densely connected meme and phrases and it describes some topic or meme.

2.1.3 Visualization 3: Objective-Detecting Most Popular Web Pages in the Meme-Link Out Network

This shows network (as given in Fig. 3) of Meme-Link-out. Many meme uses some URLs that redirects to some web pages. Usually a meme gives URL of a related web page, clicking which the viewer can get a detail insight about the topic. Blue nodes represent web pages and red nodes represent Meme. It can be observed that some web pages are very popular compared to others. Popularity of a web page is represented by its in-degree. Though we didn't detect the community structure in here, still from the Fig. 3. some facts can be concluded is that there are many portions in the figure, where memes themselves are more concentrated together compared to with rest of the memes. The layout we used for visualization is FORCE ATLAS 2. It keeps related nodes together. Thus it can be seen that memes pointing out to common web pages are placed together. Those are nothing but a community of meme or a Topic. Because, a web page generally focuses on one or some particular points. So when a number of memes are pointing to a common web pages, it is a good indication that they describe similar topic.

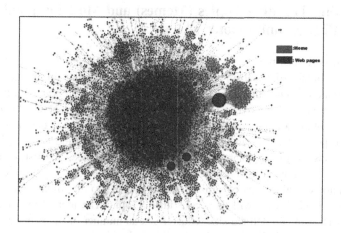

Fig. 3. Popular web pages in meme-web page network

2.1.4 Visualization 4: Objective-Detecting Community of Web Pages

Next we tried to detect underlying communities in the Meme-Web page network. It is shown in Fig. 4. Only giant communities are shown here. We detected ten (10) such community of web pages in the network.

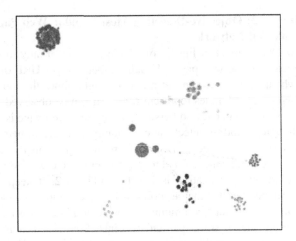

Fig. 4. Community structure in meme-web page network

3   Detecting Trending Topics (Memes) and Most Frequently Used Phrases and Quotes

This section describes the proposed approach used for detecting the trending topics. A group of similar articles form a topic. If size of a particular group exceeds a predefined threshold value, that topic is considered popular. Trending topics may be extracted in order to get an overview of what people are talking about. This may allow to show breaking news at the moment, major topic of discussion at the moment and so on. In short, people can get an idea of what is happening around the world.

As the dataset [9] is an unlabeled, items are not pre-labeled. So, first, items need to be labeled. It requires use of clustering algorithm. The goal is to split the items (Articles) into several groups of similar items. This group of similar items is nothing but a cluster. Each cluster will then constitute a topic. The idea is to detect clusters having at least some predefined size. Cluster size is number of items per cluster. As a cluster contains only similar items, larger cluster signifies most discussed topic. So, it can be concluded that those clusters contain popular topic. Once all the clusters are detected, each topic in the dataset can be labeled as either popular or not depending on in which cluster they belong.

For clustering, a modified version of K means algorithm is used. But before applying the algorithm, some data cleaning and related works need to be performed in order to increase the accuracy of clustering. The entire process of detection of trending topics is depicted below using a basic flow chart given in Fig. 5.

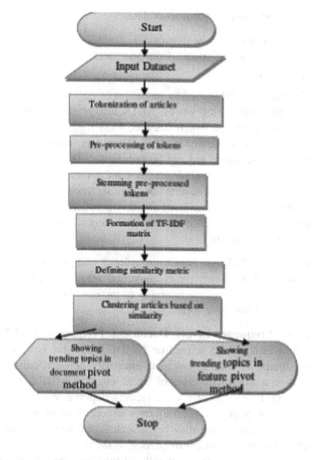

Fig. 5. Flowchart representation of trending topic detection process

The steps in the flow chart of Fig. 5 is explained as below:

Tokenization of Articles: Tokenization involves breaking down individual articles into collection of words and stored into a list. Tokenization is must because while comparing a pair of articles or simply a pair of sentences, its words are compared to calculate similarity between them in terms of meaning. Using Python, sentences can be simply broken down into words using built in method or TweetTokenizer, WordTokenizer etc. may be used.

Preprocessing of Tokenized Data: Text preprocessing is an important step in topic detection. In a sentence, many words are used that are common to most of the sentences and do not constitute the topic of the sentence. E.g., stop words (the, to, and, about etc.). Those words can be removed from any sentence without affecting the meaning of the sentence.

Three steps are performed to preprocess data:

- By removing stop words from sentences
- By removing certain parts of speech from sentences
- By using regular expressions

Python NLTK package [19] is used to get the list of stop words in a language or one may create his/her own list of stop words. NLTK also provide tagging facility to tag parts of speech of any sentence which is called POS tagging. Then certain parts of speech can be removed from sentences. Like pronouns, conjunctions etc. don not constitute meaning of a sentence and can be removed.

Then, it is seen, punctuation symbols (. , : ;), numbers and several URLs mentioned in a tweet also do not convey any meaning about the sentence and can be removed from a sentence. Regular expressions are used for this purpose. It looks for some given pattern (like http://....) in the sentence and removes them when finds them. @mentions are removed from tweets similarly.

Stemming Preprocessed Tokens: Stemming refers to the process of changing words into their root words. E.g. American is converted into America, Economically to economy and so on. Objective of stemming is to increase similarity between pairs of articles discussing about the same topic.

Calculating Term Frequency-Invert Document Frequency TF-IDF Values of Words: Converting articles into respective TF-IDF [18] value is very important. As cosine similarity metric is used to calculate similarity between pairs of articles, so articles need to be converted to vectors of equal length. TF-IDF is the vector representation of texts. TF-IDF value of a word reflects importance of the word to a document in a collection of corpus. Term frequency denotes how many times a particular word appears in a sentence. Result may be normalized by dividing it by length of the sentences (articles). Inverse document frequency, as the name suggests, assigns a lower weight to terms which appear very frequently in the entire corpus of documents and assigns higher weight to terms which appear very rarely in the corpus of documents. TF-IDF can be represented as given in Eqs. (1) and (2).

$$TF(term, article) = (No. \ of \ times \ a \ word \ appeared \ in \ the \ sent/(LEN(article)) \quad (1)$$

$$IDF(term, document) = \log|D|/1 + |\{d \in D : t \in d\}| \quad (2)$$

In Eq. (1), term represents a particular word in article and article represents a particular article. Whereas in Eq. (2), term represents a particular word and document represents the list of all articles. $|D|$ denotes size of document space. The term $|\{d \in D : t \in d\}|$ implies the total number of times in which term t appeared in our entire document d.

Thus TF-IDF value of a word is multiplication of these two values. So, $TF - IDF(Term) = TF(Term, Tweet) \times IDF(Term, Docuemnt)$. After we convert all articles into a list of $TF - IDF$ values corresponding to the terms used in that article and finally we get a $TF - IDF$ matrix.

Cosine similarity metric is used to measure similarity between pairs of articles as given in Eq. (3).

$$Similarity = Cos(\theta) = \frac{A.B}{||A||.||B||} = \frac{\sum_{i=1}^{n} A_i.B_i}{\sum_{i=1}^{n} A_i^2 . \sum_{i=1}^{n} B_i^2} \tag{3}$$

Where A and B are two vectors of same length representing two articles.

Clustering the Dataset Based on Similarity Measure: A modified version of K-means algorithm is used to group documents into clusters. It groups similar topic into same cluster. Unlike conventional K-Means algorithm, number of clusters is not pre-defined. Clusters are created dynamically whenever required. Throughout the process, each cluster is going to be represented by their centroids which are means of all the values belong to that cluster.

Algorithm of Modified K-Means Algorithm: A flow chart of modified version K-Means algorithm used for the purpose is shown in Fig. 6. It works as follows: Select an article from the dataset uniformly at random and make it a new cluster and add it to the list of cluster centroids.

Input to the algorithm are calculated TF-IDF values of collection of articles in the corpus, and list of cluster centroids (initially contains only a single cluster).

Algorithm:

- *Step 1*: Repeat step 2 to step 5 for all TF-IDF values in the list
- *Step 2*: Calculate Cosine similarity between TF-IDF value of the article and TF-IDF value of centroids of all the clusters in the list of cluster centroids.
- *Step 3:* Select maximum similarity among all the calculated similarities.
- *Step 4:* If maximum similarity is more than or equal to a predefined threshold value, then add the article to that cluster for which Cosine similarity between its centroid value and the article was maximum.
- *Step 5:* Else create a new cluster and make the article the centroid of that new cluster.
- *Step 6:* Update cluster centroids. New cluster centroids are the mean value of all the data points belonging to a cluster.
- *Step 7:* If no article changes its previous cluster, algorithm stops here. Else go to step 2.

This modified K-means algorithm outputs a list of clusters where each cluster contains similar articles thus forming a topic. As each cluster contains articles which are similar in terms of their meaning, it can be said each cluster forms a topic. Now a threshold value is set which indicates number of articles per cluster, exceeding which, a cluster is said to form a trending topic.

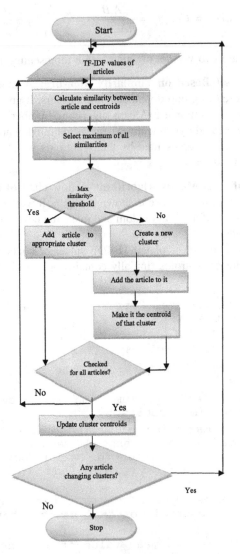

Fig. 6. Flow chart of modified K-Means algorithm

Showing Major Clusters Forming Trending Topics and the Respective Frequently Used Phrases in Document Pivot Method: In document pivot method, we extract frequently used phrases from trending topics. As stated, we get a cluster of documents where each cluster contains similar articles. So, if we get a large cluster, it is an indication that a particular topic has been discussed a lot and that can be a trending

Table 1. Trending topics and phrases.

Topic	Phrase
ten	gang of ten
daytona	daytona beach residents claim your economic stimulus payment
unto	do unto others
way	another way to die
azns	azns wit asses
extraordinarily	extraordinarily pleased and satisfied
kinder	kinder fr her f rdern
history	those who do not learn from history are doomed to repeat it
mac	i'm a mac i'm a pc
never	never retract never explain never apologize get things done and let them howl
dreams	dreams of my father
rudeness	rudeness and hate
rumors	rumors of mccain campaign's demise have been premature

topic. In document pivot method, frequently used phrases from each trending topic are printed as given in the Table 1.

Showing Trending Topics in a Feature Pivot Method: In Feature Pivot method [22], instead of showing frequently used phrases from each trending topic, we show most important words from that topic that sufficiently express meaning of the topic. It may be the #Hashtag used or may be some other words as given in Fig. 8. Three types of output are produced to identify the trending topics and the sample outputs are shown in Figs. 7, 8 and Table 2. Here Fig. 7 shows the frequency of trending topics in a portion of the dataset. The topic vs. frequency bar chart represents this. Whereas Fig. 8 shows the extracted trending topics in a feature pivot method. Feature pivot method attempts to extract a particular word sufficient to constitute the meaning of the topic. That particular word can be thought of as the name of the topic. Larger the topic name, more popular it is. Table 1 shows the trending topics in a document pivot method. Document pivot method extracts the topic along with the phrase posted by people under that topic.

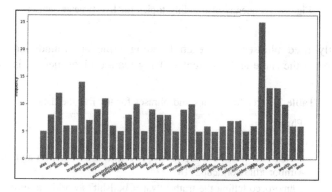

Fig. 7. Frequency of trending topics

Fig. 8. Trending topics using feature pivot method

4 Comparison and Performance Analysis of the Proposed Approach

The proposed model is applied on a live tweeter dataset. The dataset is about the Portugal vs Iran match of football world cup 2018. Frequency of trending topics found in a sample live tweeter dataset is shown in Fig. 9.

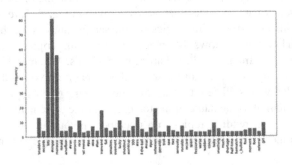

Fig. 9. Frequency of trending topics for live tweeter dataset

Frequently used phrases from each trending topic are found and reported in Table 2, whereas the same are represented using feature pivot method is Fig. 10.

Table 2. Trending topics and phrases for the live the dataset.

Topic	Phrase
#irnpor	: so true ! #irnpor #espmar
lots	: iran, you must be really proud. you won lots of respect and many hearts. #irnpor #fifaworldcup2018
#morocco	: #morocco telling the truth : "var = bullshit" #worldcup #irnpor

(continued)

Table 2. (*continued*)

Topic	Phrase
gentlemen	: group b ladies and gentlemen. not sure about you… but we're off for a lie down. #worldcup #espmar #irnpor
alireza beiranvand	: alireza beiranvand-iran goalkeeper - was a shepherd - worked at a pizza shop - used to wash suvs for money & clean the str …
ronaldo's	: #irnpor you saved ronaldo's penalty ! i repeat, you saved ronaldo's penalty ! ! ! cr7 who ?
lionel messi	: lionel messi misses penalty against 22nd ranked team, it's outraged for 10 days cristiano ronaldo misses penalty against …
penaldo	: today is the first game in the #worldcup 2018 after penaldo has failed to score a penalty. #irnpor #irapor
troll	: troll football deleted it for portugal fans so i'll tweet it again var is bullshit, morocco deserved a win and iran deserved …
ronaldo	: ronaldo missed a penalty. ronaldo missed a penalty. ronaldo missed a penalty. ronaldo missed a penalty. ronaldo missed a …

Fig. 10. Trending topics using feature pivot method for the live dataset

Performance evaluation of the proposed work can be done using Internal and external evaluation. In internal evaluation clustering results are evaluated based on the data that was clustered. Similarly, in external evaluation clustering results are evaluated based on data that was not used for clustering, such as known class labels. In this work as we don't have known class labels, we can't do external evaluation only internal evaluation has been reported.

Internal evaluation can be done using Davies–Bouldin index, Dunn index and Silhouette coefficient. Among these methods Silhouette coefficient works best for k-means clustering. It contrasts the average distance to elements in the same cluster with the average distance to elements in other clusters. Objects with a high silhouette value are considered well clustered, objects with a low value may be outliers.

For each data i, let $a(i)$ be the average distance between i and all other data within the same cluster and $b(i)$ be the lowest average distance of i to all points in any other cluster, of which i is not a member. A silhouette is then:

$$s(i) = \frac{b(i) - a(i)}{\max\{a(i), b(i)\}} \qquad (4)$$

The best value of $s(i)$ is 1 and the worst value is −1. Values near 0 indicate overlapping clusters. Negative values generally indicate that a sample has been assigned to the wrong cluster, as a different cluster is more similar. The Silhouette score is applied on the live twitter dataset and the results are shown in Fig. 11. In the figure Silhouette score of every cluster have been shown. There are total 216 clusters. The average Silhouette score or the Silhouette score of the whole dataset is shown by the red vertical line. The Silhouette score of the dataset comes out to be 0.766, which is a good measure.

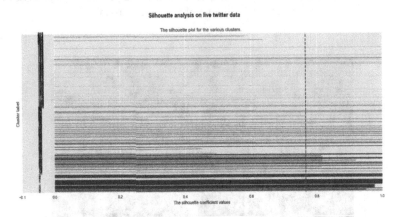

Fig. 11. Trending topics using feature pivot method for the live dataset

5   Conclusion and Future Scope

In social network analysis and study of social structure part, some communities were detected. It indicated that the dataset contains some pattern in it and further work can be proceeded. After detecting trending topics and phrases, a number of trending topics are found. One can relate these communities and trending topics so extracted. As cluster of similar articles forms a topic, it can be thought of as a community of articles similar in meaning. Hence both the results conform to each other.

One can find many applications of detection of trending topics. It is done in social networking sites like in Facebook to inform users what people around the world are saying about. It helps in producing real time breaking news directly from online spectrum. The future scope of the work is to predict future content popularity depending on present popularity of the content. The features extracted from a popular topic can be used on some other topic to predict whether it will become popular in future or not.

References

1. Guille, A., Hacid, H., Favre, C., Zighed, D.A.: Information diffusion in online social networks: a survey. SIGMOD Rec. **42**(2), 17–28 (2013)
2. Gomez-Rodriguez, M., Song, L., Daneshmand, N., Schölkpof, B.: Estimating diffusion network structures: recovery conditions, sample complexity and soft-thresholding algorithm. In: Proceedings of the International Conference on Machine Learning (ICML), pp. 1–9 (2014)
3. Yang, J., Leskovec, J.: Modeling information diffusion in implicit networks. In: Proceedings of the IEEE International Conference on Data Mining, pp. 599–608, December 2010
4. Saxena, A., Iyengar, S.R.S., Gupta, Y.: Understanding spreading patterns on social networks based on network topology. In: Proceedings of the IEEE/ACM International Conference on Advances in Social Networks Analysis and Mining (ASONAM), pp. 1616–1617, August 2015
5. Niu, G., Long, Y., Li, V.O.K.: Temporal behavior of social network users in information diffusion. In: Proceedings of the IEEE/WIC/ACM International Joint Conferences on Web Intelligence and Intelligent Agent Technologies (IAT/WI), vol. 2, pp. 150–157, August 2014
6. Kao, L.-J., Huang, Y.-P.: Mining inuential users in social network. In: Proceedings of the IEEE International Conference on Systems, Man, and Cybernetics (SMC), pp. 1209–1214, October 2015
7. Langa, J.A., Robinson, J.C., Rodriguez-Bernal, A., Suárez, A.: Permanence and asymptotically stable complete trajectories for nonautonomous Lotka-Volterra models with diffusion. SIAM J. Math. Anal. **40**(6), 2179–2216 (2012)
8. Choudhury, M.D., Lin, Y.R., Sundaram, H.: How does the data sampling strategy impact the discovery of information diffusion in social media? In: Proceedings of the ICWSM, pp. 34–41 (2010)
9. Leskovec, J., Backstrom, L., Kleinberg, J.: Meme-tracking and the dynamics of the news cycle. In: Proceedings of the ACM SIGKDD International Conference on Knowledge Discovery and Data Mining (KDD), pp. 497–506 (2009)
10. Xie, L., Natsev, A., Kender, J.R., Hill, M., Smith, J.R.: Visual memes in social media: tracking real-world news in Youtube videos. In: Proceedings of the ACM International Conference on Multimedia, pp. 53–62 (2011)
11. Simon, H.: Designing organizations for an information-rich world. In: Greenberger, M. (ed.) Computers, Communication, and the Public Interest, vol. 72, pp. 37–52 (1971)
12. Agarwal, M.K., Ramamritham, K., Bhide, M.: Real time discovery of dense clusters in highly dynamic graphs: identifying real world events in highly dynamic environments. Proc. VLDB Endow. **5**(10), 980–991 (2012)
13. Ferrara, E., JafariAsbagh, M., Varol, O., Qazvinian, V., Menczer, F., Flammini, A.: Clustering memes in social media. In: IEEE/ACM International Conference on Advances in Social Networks Analysis and Mining (ASONAM) (2013)
14. Tang, J., Sun, J., Wang, C., Yang, Z.: Social influence analysis in large-scale networks. In: Proceedings of the ACM SIGKDD International Conference on Knowledge Discovery and Data Mining (KDD), pp. 807–816 (2009)
15. Bastian, M., Heymann, S., Jacomy, M.: Gephi: an open source software for exploring and manipulating networks. In: International AAAI Conference on Weblogs and Social Media (2009)
16. Kanungo, T., Mount, D.M., Netanyahu, N.S., Piatko, C.D., Silverman, R., Wu, A.Y.: An efficient k-means clustering algorithm: analysis and implementation. IEEE Trans. Pattern Anal. Mach. Intell. **24**(7), 881–892 (2002)

17. Sanderson, M., Christopher, D., Manning, H.: Introduction to information retrieval. Nat. Lang. Eng. **16**(1), 100 (2010)
18. Perkins, J.: Python Text Processing with NLTK 2.0 Cookbook. Packt Publishing Ltd., Birmingham (2010)
19. Weng, L., et al.: The role of information diffusion in the evolution of social networks. In: Proceedings of the 19th ACM SIGKDD International Conference on Knowledge Discovery and Data Mining, pp. 356–364 (2013)
20. Zafarani, R., Abbasi, M.A., Liu, H.: Social Media Mining: An Introduction. Cambridge University Press, Cambridge (2014)
21. Argaiz, J.L.I., Egido, E.M.: The Dynamics of Viral Information Diffusion in Online Social Networks (2015)
22. Aiello, L.M., et al.: Sensing trending topics in Twitter. IEEE Trans. Multimedia **15**, 1268–1282 (2013)

Automatic Remote Car Locker Using Bluetooth Low Energy Wireless Communication

Syed Mohd Faraaz[1], B. Balaji Naik[1(✉)], and Dhananjay Singh[2]

[1] Department of Computer Science and Engineering,
National Institute of Technology Sikkim, Ravangla, Sikkim, India
faraazsyed4@gmail.com, balajinaik07@nitsikkim.ac.in
[2] Department of Electronics Engineering, Hankuk University of Foreign Studies,
Yongin, South Korea
dsingh@hufs.ac.kr

Abstract. The advancement in technology has enabled us to transform from manually controlled devices to automatically controlled devices and smartphones find extensive applications in such a transformed system. Smartphones have become an important part of our lives. The number of smartphone users have increased rapidly as nowadays smartphones not only provide the basic processes such as dialling and receiving calls or sending text messages but they also interact and control a variety of devices such as computers, televisions, locks, cars, etc. In this paper we design and implementation of a remote lock system using wireless Bluetooth communications. The remote lock system is controlled by a dedicated android application which interacts with the hardware installed in the car and locks/unlocks the car without providing any manual inputs through the android app.

Keywords: Automatic car lock system · Bluetooth low energy · Android · Microcontroller

1 Introduction

The increase in the number of mobile device users, especially smartphones has motivated developers to design various convenient applications which serve different purposes. Smartphones are not limited to make and receive phone calls or send text messages but they also communicate with other devices using wireless communications. The proposed system remotely controls a device through a dedicated android application. The hardware device is installed with the central lock system of the car and it locks or unlocks the car and provides a variety of other functions such as controlling the trunk, flashing the parking lights and sliding the glass. The users need not press any buttons in the app in order to lock or unlock their cars. As the user walks towards his car, Bluetooth gets auto connected and the car automatically unlocks. On the other hand when he walks

© Springer Nature Singapore Pte Ltd. 2019
J. K. Mandal et al. (Eds.): CICBA 2018, CCIS 1031, pp. 479–491, 2019.
https://doi.org/10.1007/978-981-13-8581-0_38

out of the range, Bluetooth gets disconnected and the car gets locked. Moreover the user may switch between auto lock mode and manual lock mode. With the auto lock mode turned off, the user will have to manually press the lock/unlock buttons in the app. Hence, the system serves both the purposes of automatic lock and manual lock. The lock and unlock ranges could be pre-defined by the user through the app. The ordinary metal locks [1] with key have been in use for the past 1500 years [2]. Locks with passwords have also been in use for a long time. However, these locking mechanisms have a few shortcomings such as people losing the key or forgetting their passwords. Our proposed remote lock system eliminates these problems and since this is a new remote lock technology, such products and patents can rarely be found. The application of this remote lock system is not only limited to cars but could be extensively used for remotely controlling locks for home doors, office, motor cycles, etc.

The remainder of this paper is organized in the following sections: Sect. 2 discusses a few related products and technology of our proposed remote lock system using Bluetooth wireless communications. Section 3 discusses the block diagram description of the proposed work. Section 4 describes implementation and results. Finally the conclusion and future work is described in Sect. 5.

2   Related Work and Technologies

In the fields of physical security and information security, access control (AC) is the selective restriction of access to a place or other resource. The act of accessing may mean consuming, entering, or using. Permission to access a resource is called authorization. A security system is designed to avoid intrusion or unauthorized entry into an accessible area. There are many security systems available nowadays and despite their ability to suite with the new technology, there is still scope for new systems which are more secure and have more advance features. Such systems are needed to eliminate the shortcomings of the existing systems and also to solve problems that may be encountered in future. The access control methods could be broadly classified into the following locking mechanisms: The mechanical lock method, password lock system, RFID (Radio Frequency Identification) lock system, biometric lock system, OTP lock system and cryptography based lock system [3]. The first lock method which came into existence was the mechanical lock method. This method uses a key and a lock and has a disadvantage of people losing their keys and carrying it around. Moreover they could be broken down easily by burglars using some tool. Electronic locks are preferred over mechanical locks to resolve the security issues. One of the most common forms of electronic lock system is the password lock system with a touchpad to enter a numeric code or password for authentication. Password lock system has the disadvantage that people must remember the password and the way it could be altered is limited. RFID (Radio Frequency Identification) lock system makes use of a remote key fob or an RFID card reader. In case of an RFID key fob, people must carry the key at all times and the risk of losing the key cannot be overlooked. The major constraint of the RFID lock system is the fact that these systems could easily be interrupted as they make use of electromagnetic spectrum. Battery drainage is a big problem in these systems along with security issues. Biometric authentication (or realistic authentication) is used in computer science as a form of identification and access control. The biometric lock system grants access to individuals by verifying their physiological or behavioural characteristics such as fingerprint, face recognition, DNA, palm print, hand geometry, iris recognition, retina, etc. The major drawback with the biometrics lock system is that with the current technology, the fingerprint could be duplicated by hackers and the iris scanner could also be hacked, thus making it vulnerable. OTP (One Time Password) is a dynamic password system. OTP gets generated by the server and sent to the system as well as the registered phone and the password is valid only for a short duration of time. This is an SMS based service and the messages are sent over air therefore it has its drawbacks such as unavailability of service, outside coverage area, etc. To eliminate these kind of problems, a previous publication [4] proposed technology using cryptographic locking method is proposed. The system has a keypad through which the password could be entered. If the entered password matches with the stored password in the EPROM of the microcontroller, the motor gets active and the door is opened. If a wrong password is entered a buzzer is switched ON and error is indicated on the LCD display. The user is required to enter the password again after some delay. This security method makes the system more secure compared to the other locking mechanisms however such a system has a few disadvantages. This is a password lock system and so the user will have to remember the password in order to access the system. Being a manual unlock system, the time consumption in this system is more compared to automated systems. In case a wrong password is entered, there will be a small delay before the user can re-enter the code again. Several objectives of our proposed system are taken into account to improve and solve the discussed problems as follows: First, the system will automatically unlock when the user is in the preset range of the hardware unit thereby reducing effort and time consumption and increasing convenience. Second, the android application acts as the graphical user interface through which the lock and unlock ranges could be pre-set by the user within 0 to 10 m radius.

2.1 Android

Android is a mobile operating system based on the Linux kernel and designed primarily for touchscreen mobile devices such as smartphones and tablets. Android's user interface is mainly based on direct manipulation using touch gestures that loosely correspond to real-world actions, such as swiping, tapping and pinching to manipulate on-screen objects, along with a virtual keypad for input. Android applications which extend the functionality of devices, are written using Android Software Development Kit (SDK) and often the Java programming language. Java may be combined with C/C++, together with a choice of non-default runtimes that allow better C++ support [5]. The SDK includes a comprehensive set of development tools, including a debugger, software libraries and a handset emulator. On top of the Linux kernel, there are middleware, libraries and API's written in C, and application software running on an application framework which includes Java-compatible libraries. So, basically Android system architecture is divided into five hierarchical categories: Applications, Application framework, Libraries, Android runtime and Linux kernel. Figure 1 shows android's architectural diagram.

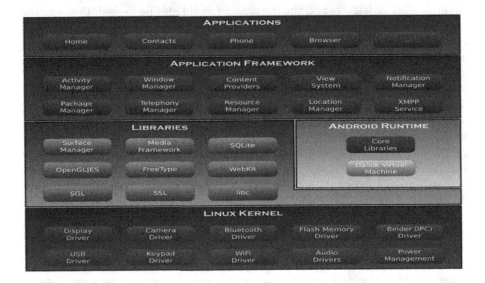

Fig. 1. Android system architecture.

2.2 Bluetooth Low Energy (BLE)

Bluetooth Low Energy (BLE) sometimes referred to as "Bluetooth smart" is a light-weight subset of classic Bluetooth and was introduced as a part of Bluetooth 4.0 core specification. While there is some overlap with classic Bluetooth, BLE has a completely different lineage and was started by Nokia as an in-house project called 'Wibree' before being adopted by the Bluetooth Special Interest Group (SIG). BLE is aimed at applications and products requiring low current consumption and low implementation complexity and having low production cost [6]. During the development of BLE and shortly after its introduction, it was predicted that the protocol would have a very wide application area. For example, in [7] the authors predicted that BLE-based devices would dominate the Wireless Sensor Network (WSN) application market by 2015. Bluetooth networks commonly referred to as piconets use a master/slave model to control when and where devices can send data. A pictorial representation of the piconet model is shown in Fig. 2. In this model, a single master device can be connected up to seven different slave devices. Any slave device in the piconet can only be connected to a single master. The master coordinates communication throughout the piconet. It can send data to any of its slaves and request data from them as well. Slaves are only allowed to transmit to and receive from their master. They cannot communicate with other slaves in the piconet. The block diagram of proposed stack architecture is shown in Fig. 3.

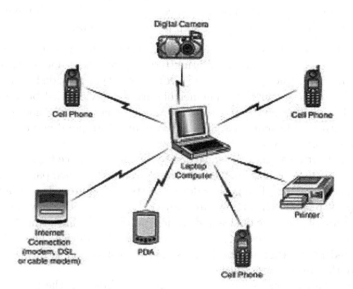

Fig. 2. Bluetooth piconet network

Similar to Bluetooth classic, a BLE transceiver consists of two major components: a Controller and a Host. The controller implements the lower layers. The upper layers which are implemented by the Host are Logical Link Control and Adaptation Protocol (L2CAP), Generic Attribute protocol (GATT), and Generic Access Profile (GAP). The security manager (SM) manages the pairing, authentication, bounding and encryption for BLE communication. Similar to classic Bluetooth (BT), BLE uses adaptive frequency hopping spread spectrum to access the shared channel. However, the number of hops is 43 and the channel width is 2 MHz. BLE device can operate either in master or slave role. A master can manage multiple simultaneous connections with a number of slave devices, but a slave can only be connected to a single master. Therefore, BLE uses star network topology. Differently from classic BT, discovery is done so that slave advertises on one or several of the three designated advertisement channels. Master scans these channels in order to discover slaves. After discovery, data transmission happens in the form of connection events in which the master and the slave wake up in synchrony to exchange frames. Both devices sleep the rest of time. The classic Bluetooth uses 79 1-MHz wide channels whereas

BLE uses 40 2-MHz wide channels. 37 of these 40 channels are used for transmitting data whereas the remaining 3 channels are used for advertising and network discovery and are called advertising channels. A Bluetooth connection is the periodical exchange of data at certain specific points in time (Connection Events) between the two peers involved in it. The Bluetooth connection procedure could be broadly classified into Inquiry procedure where the peer device is discovered and Paging procedure where the connection is established between the devices. According to the Bluetooth Baseband specification [8], Bluetooth point to point connection establishment is a three step process as follows:

- The first step of Bluetooth connection procedure is the enquiry of devices which is also called scanning. During Inquiry, initiating nodes (Master) discover and collect neighbourhood (Slave) information provided by nodes that are in an Inquiry Scan state. The neighbourhood device must be in proximity to the initializing device. A successful enquiry between two nodes results in the initiating node acquiring knowledge about the responding node's identity and Bluetooth clock value.
- After discovering a potential slave device the master device tries to establish a connection with the slave device and this procedure is called paging procedure or connection setup. The master device starts paging procedure as a response to inquiry response from the slave device. This is achieved by selecting the destination of the slave device and request pairing. The initiating device sends the passkey that has been entered to the responding device. The passkeys are compared and if they are both the same, a trusted pair is formed and thus Bluetooth pairing is established.
- Once the pairing has occurred, communication between the two devices has established and data can be exchanged between the two devices.

2.3   ATmega 328/P Microcontroller

This is the main component of the hardware device used which does all the work. When the program is loaded on the hardware unit, it is actually loaded to the memory of the microcontroller. ATmega 328 is a low cost, low power 8-bit CMOS microcontroller based on RISC architecture [9]. It combines 32 KB Flash memory with read-write capabilities, 1024 B EEPROM, 2 KB SRAM, 23 General purpose input/output lines, 32 general purpose working registers, three flexible timer/counters with compare modes, internal and external interrupts, serial programmable USART, a byte-oriented 2-wire serial interface, SPI serial port, a 6-channel 10-bit A/D converter (8-channels in TQFP and QFN/MLF packages), programmable watchdog timer with internal oscillator, and five software selectable power saving modes. The device operates between 1.8–5.5 volts. By executing powerful instructions in a single clock cycle, the device achieves throughputs approaching 1 MIPS per MHz, balancing power consumption and processing speed. The different parameters used in the ATmega 328 microcontroller along with the parameter values are shown in Table 1.

This service provides the authentication of the party at the other end of the line. In communication-oriented communication, it provides authentication of

Table 1. ATmega328 parameters and values

Parameter name	Value
Program memory type	Flash
Program memory (KB)	32
CPU speed (MIPS)	20
RAM bytes	2,084
Digital communication peripherals	1-UART, 2-SPI, 1-I2C
Capture/compare/PWM peripherals	1-input capture, 1-CCP, 6-PWM
Timers	2 X 8-bit, 1 X 16-bit
Comparators	1
Temperature range (oC)	−40 to 85
Operating voltage range (V)	1.8 to 5.5
Pin count	32
Low power	Yes

the sender or receiver during the connection establishment (peer entity authentication). In connectionless communication, it authenticates the source of the data (data origin authentication).

The Bluetooth Special Interest Group (SIG) is the body that oversees the development of Bluetooth standards and the licensing of the Bluetooth technologies and trademarks to manufacturers.

A piconet is a network that is created using a wireless Bluetooth connection and is formed when two or more devices discover each other and begin to communicate. A piconet can have up to seven devices, with one device acting as a master and the rest acting as slaves. The first device to initiate transmission becomes the master, although the specification provides for a master and slave unit to exchange roles.

A Reduced Instruction Set Cycle (RISC) is a processor design in which instruction set architecture (ISA) has a set of attributes that allow it to have lower cycles per instruction (CPI) than a Complex Instruction Set Computing (CISC). The general concept is that of a computer that has a small set of simple and general instructions, rather than a large set of complex and specialized instructions.

3   Proposed Work

Automatic remote car locker using Bluetooth low energy wire communication uses four major components – a Microcontroller, a Bluetooth low energy (BLE) module, 7805 voltage regulator and relay switches. In this circuit design we have used ATmega328/P microcontroller which is a low power CMOS 8-bit microcontroller. It is based on enhanced RISC architecture and combines a rich instruction

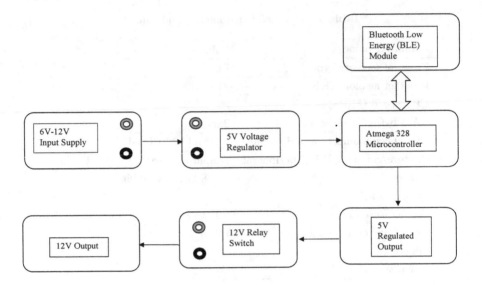

Fig. 3. Block diagram description

set with 32 general purpose working registers. All the 32 registers are directly connected to the Arithmetic Logic Unit (ALU), allowing two independent registers to be accessed in a single instruction executed in one clock cycle. The resulting architecture is more code efficient while achieving throughputs up to ten times faster than conventional CISC microcontrollers. This controller requires +5 V DC voltage. The regulated 5 V DC voltage is provided to the microcontroller using a 7805 power supply circuit. 7805 is a voltage regulated Integrated Circuit (IC). It is a member of 78xx series of fixed linear voltage regulator IC's. The voltage source in a circuit may have fluctuations and would not give the fixed voltage output. The 7805 IC maintains the output voltage at a constant value. The xx in 78xx indicates the fixed output voltage it is designed to provide. 7805 provides +5 V regulated power supply. The input voltage can vary from 5 V to 18 V but the output voltage is fixed at +5 V with a 0.2 V tolerance. The BLE module which is connected to the microcontroller gets powered on when the microcontroller is fed with the regulated voltage +5 V DC. Bluetooth Low Energy (BLE) also known as Bluetooth Smart is a wireless personal area network technology designed and marketed by Bluetooth special interest Group aimed at novel applications in the healthcare, fitness, beacons, security and home entertainment industries. Compared to classic Bluetooth, BLE is intended to provide considerably reduced power consumption and cost while maintaining a similar communication range. In this circuit design we have used HM-10 Bluetooth Low Energy module for wireless communication. HM-10 is a readily available Bluetooth 4.0 module based on Texas Instruments CC2540 Bluetooth Low Energy System on Chip (SoC) [7]. It is a low cost, low power Bluetooth module and is rated to operate at a supply voltage of 2.0 V to 3.7 V where its inputs and outputs are 3.3 V tolerant. The size of HM-10 Bluetooth module is 26.9 * 13 * 2.2 with 256 Kb flash memory.

3.1   I-Access Hardware Module

The i-access V1 module in Fig. 4 is (120×90) mm and mounted AVR Mega 328/P-AU printed circuit board (PCB) designed on Altium platform. The module is equipped with several electrical components such as capacitors, diodes, resistors, voltage regulator, Light Emitting Diodes (LED), reset switch, 16 MHz crystal oscillator, voltage suppressor, relay switches and Bluetooth Low Energy (BLE) module. This system is installed inside the car which controls the Bluetooth module and the relay module. Table 2 shows a total list of bill of materials used in the hardware module. This system takes 12 V as input voltage but the microcontroller requires +5 V DC voltage which is supplied to the microcontroller using 7805 voltage regulator. The pseudo code for proposed work is given in Fig. 5.

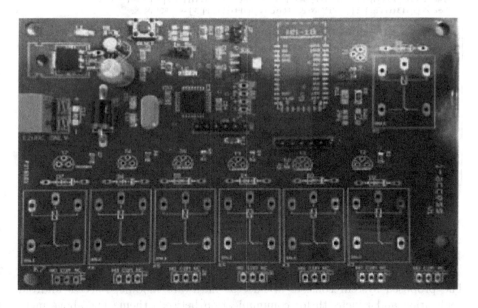

Fig. 4. Block diagram description

- Complex Instruction Set Computing (CISC) is a processor design where single instructions can execute several low-level operations (such as a load from memory, an arithmetic operation and a memory store) or are capable of multi-step operations or addressing modes within single instructions.
- A beacon is a hardware transmitter which is a class of BLE devices and broadcasts its identifier to nearby portable electronic devices. The technology enables smartphones, tablets and other devices to perform actions when in close proximity to the beacon.

Step 1 - Check if module is available.

Step 2 - Reset the BLE module.

Step 3 — Check if BLE is connected to the app.

Return 1 if connected

Step 4- IF (RecAppBuffer [0] =='4')

A. Keep Device in Auto mode: 4AUTO CS #

if (RecAppBuffer[1]=='A' && RecAppBuffer[2]=='U' && RecAppBuffer[3]=='T' && RecAppBuffer[4]=='O') digital Write(Relay1, LOW); // lock relay becomes OFF
B. Keep Device in Manual Lock mode: 4MLCK CS #

else if(RecAppBuffer[0]=='4' && RecAppBuffer[1]=='M' && RecAppBuffer[2]=='U' && RecAppBuffer[3]=='L' && RecAppBuffer[4]=='K')
C. Keep Device in Manual Unlock mode: 4MULK CS #

else if(RecAppBuffer[0]=='4' && RecAppBuffer[1]=='T' && RecAppBuffer[2]=='R' && RecAppBuffer[3]=='C' && RecAppBuffer[4]=='T')
D. Keep Device in TRUNK CONTROLLER mode: 4TRCT CS #

else if(RecAppBuffer[0]=='4' && RecAppBuffer[1]=='F' && RecAppBuffer[2]=='P' && RecAppBuffer[3]=='K' && RecAppBuffer[4]=='L')
E. Keep Device in flash Parking Light mode: 4FPKL CS #

else if(RecAppBuffer[0]=='4' && RecAppBuffer[1]=='W' && RecAppBuffer[2]=='G' && RecAppBuffer[3]=='S' && RecAppBuffer[4]=='U')
F. Keep Device in Window glass slider UP: 4WGSL CS #

else if(RecAppBuffer[0]=='4' && RecAppBuffer[1]=='W' && RecAppBuffer[2]=='G' && RecAppBuffer[3]=='S' && RecAppBuffer[4]=='D')
Step 5-End If

Step 6-Else

When no BLE is connected or (BLE_State == 1) or default state

Step 7-End Else

Fig. 5. Proposed algorithm

4   Implementation and Results

The proposed system consists of i-access hardware module, i-access android application and Bluetooth for communication between them. The above mentioned objectives are attained by the system by following these 6 steps:

- The proposed system consists of four major modules relay switches, main module, Bluetooth module and it communicates with an already paired android device via an android application. The i-access hardware module was programmed through the ISP pins on the module using Arduino platform. The ISP pins on the Arduino module could be connected to the ISP pins on the i-access hardware module and the program is burnt to the i-access hardware module using Arduino IDE. Even though the programming of the hardware module could be done directly by connecting it to the PC via a 6

Table 2. Bill of materials

Sr. no	Sr. no	Quantity component name	Value	Package
1	1	Reset switch	-	-
2	3	LED	-	1206
3	1	Voltage regulator	7805	DPACK
4	1	Capacitor	100 F/63 V	
5	6	Capacitor	Ceramic	C1206
6	1	Capacitor	10 F/50 V	-
7	2	Capacitor	22pF	C1206
8	2	Resistor	10 K	M1206
9	1	Resistor	10 K	R1206
10	1	Resistor	1 K	M1206
11	2	Resistor	1 K	R1206
12	1	Resistor	20 K	M1206
13	7	Resistor	2 K	R0805
14	1	Crystal oscillator	16 MHz	-
15	7	Diode	1000 V/1.0 A	1N4007
16	1	Diode	Vrms = 35 V, Vdc = 50 V	1N5400
17	7	Bipolar junction transistor	200 mA/40 V/625 mW	2N3904
18	1	Bluetooth module	BLE4.0	HM-10
19	1	Mega328		TQFP32-08
20	7	General purpose relay	12V DC	G5LE
21	1	Transient voltage suppressor	188 V	SMAJ188

pin bootloader, however we have used Arduino for programming because it expedites the process and is very simple.

- The application runs on an android device and communicates with the hardware using Bluetooth low energy. The user credentials such as user id, password and email are stored within the app itself using SQlite database. New users need to register first Fig. 6(a) and choose a username, a password, confirm password and entering email id. These credentials gets stored in the SQlite database and from here-on the user can login using these credentials
- Once the user logs in to the application Fig. 6(b), he needs to scan for the hardware module which is provided as a scanning option in the application itself. After finding the i-access hardware module, he needs to enter a pin for pairing which is stored in the hardware module and provided to the user. Once the devices are paired, they can exchange data between themselves.
- The auto-mode works as a Boolean function which could be switched between 0(OFF) and 1(ON). While the auto mode is in state 1, the user need not press any buttons in the application or even open the application to unlock/lock the system Fig. 6(c). As the user walks within a pre-defined range by the user, the

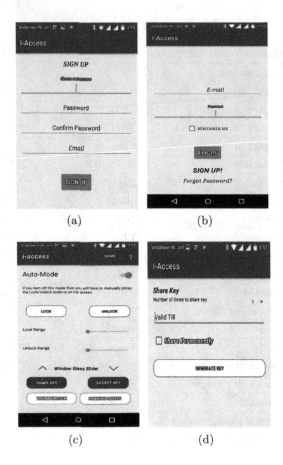

Fig. 6. (a) Sign up screen (b) sign in screen (c) share key screen (d) main screen

car will automatically unlock itself and as he walks out, it will automatically lock itself. The Bluetooth must be active at all times on the user's android device. The lock and unlock ranges could be selected by the user using the application.

- The auto-mode works as a Boolean function which could be switched between 0(OFF) and 1(ON). While the auto mode is in state 1, the user need not press any buttons in the application or even open the application to unlock/lock the system Fig. 6(c). As the user walks within a pre-defined range by the user, the car will automatically unlock itself and as he walks out, it will automatically lock itself. The Bluetooth must be active at all times on the user's android device. The lock and unlock ranges could be selected by the user using the application.

- While the auto-mode is in state 0, the car will not lock/unlock itself automatically. The user will have to manually press lock/unlock provided as inputs in the android application.

- Apart from lock/unlock option, the user can unlock the trunk using trunk unlock option in the application or can flash the parking lights of his car using flash parking lights option or press the window up or down options in the application itself Fig. 6(c)
- The user can even share his car with another person using the share key option in the application. The original user needs to press share key and the secondary user needs to press accept key in the application. A bar code will be generated which the secondary user must scan to get a temporary or permanent key Fig. 6(d)

5 Final Remarks

A new remote locking system is proposed in this paper which uses Bluetooth Low Energy wireless communication. The lock could be controlled remotely by a dedicated android application without providing any manual inputs by the user. Moreover this system could be used as both a manual and an automated system depending upon the preference of the user. The car is a very small subset of a very vast domain. The same system could be extended for controlling a variety of other access control systems such as home doors, office doors, etc.

References

1. Blaze, M.: Rights amplification in master-keyed mechanical locks. IEEE Secur. Priv. **99**(2), 24–32 (2003)
2. Çelik, S.S.: Lost treasures: locks. Int. J. Sci. Cult. Sport. (IntJSCS) **3**(1), 96–112 (2015)
3. Divya, R.S., Mathew, M.: Survey on various door lock access control mechanisms. In: 2017 International Conference on Circuit, Power and Computing Technologies (ICCPCT). IEEE (2017)
4. Jagdale, R., Koli, S., Kadam, S., Gurav, S.: Review on intelligent locker system based on cryptography, wireless and embedded technology. Int. J. Tech. Res. Appl. (Spec. issue 39), 75–77 (2016). e-ISSN 2320–8163
5. Kirthika, B., Prabhu, S., Visalakshi, S.: Android operating system: a review. Int. J. Trend Res. Dev. **2**(5), 260–264 (2015). ISSN 2394–9333
6. Gomez, C., Oller, J., Paradells, J.: Overview and evaluation of bluetooth low energy: an emerging low-power wireless technology. Sensors **12**(9), 11734–11753 (2012)
7. Mikhaylov, K., Plevritakis, N., Tervonen, J.: Performance analysis and comparison of bluetooth low energy with IEEE 802.15. 4 and SimpliciTI. J. Sens. Actuator Netw. **2**(3), 589–613 (2013)
8. Gehrmann, C., Nyberg, K.: Enhancements to Bluetooth baseband security. In: Proceedings of NordSec (2001)
9. Khadse, R., Gawai, N., Faruk, B.M.: Overview and comparative study of different microcontrollers. Int. J. Res. Appl. Sci. Eng. Technol. (IJRASET) **2**(XII), 311–315 (2014). ISSN 2321–9653

Author Index

Printed in the United States
By Bookmasters